D1918316

Get a FREE eBook

To register this book, scan the code or go to
www.manning.com/freebook/negro2

By registering you get

- **FREE eBook copy**
  download in PDF and ePub
- **FREE online access**
  to Manning's liveBook platform
- **FREE audio**
  read and listen online in liveBook
- **FREE AI Assistant**
  it knows the contents (and your exact location) when it answers
- **FREE in-book testing**
  fun tests to lock in your knowledge

In Manning's liveBook platform you can share discussions and comments with other readers, add your own bookmarks and highlights, insert personal notes anywhere on the page, see color versions of all the book's graphics, download source code and other resources, and more!
To register, scan the code or go to www.manning.com/freebook/negro2

MANNING

Knowledge Graphs and LLMs
in Action

Knowledge Graphs and LLMs in Action

ALESSANDRO NEGRO
GIUSEPPE FUTIA
VLASTIMIL KŮS
FABIO MONTAGNA

FOREWORDS BY MAXIME LABONNE
AND KHALIFEH ALJADDA

MANNING
SHELTER ISLAND

For online information and ordering of this and other Manning books, please visit www.manning.com. The publisher offers discounts on this book when ordered in quantity. For more information, please contact

Special Sales Department
Manning Publications Co.
20 Baldwin Road
PO Box 761
Shelter Island, NY 11964
Email: orders@manning.com

Manning Publications Co.
20 Baldwin Road
PO Box 761
Shelter Island, NY 11964

Development editor: Dustin Archibald
Technical editor: Dimitris Polychronopoulos
Review editor: Radmila Ercegovac
Production editor: Kathy Rossland
Copy editor: Tiffany Taylor
Development copy editor: Frances Buran
Proofreader: Olga Milanko
Technical proofreader: Sachin Panemangalore
Typesetter and Cover designer: Marija Tudor

ISBN 9781633439894
Printed in the United States of America

To Aurora, Filippo, and Flavia
– Alessandro

To my family—and especially my parents—for your unwavering love, support, and patience. To my friends and mentors, for walking with me, inspiring me, nudging me forward, and having the courage to be honest when it matters most.
– Vlastimil

To Debora—my constant since we collided on the cosmic graph of life—thank you for walking beside me through every node and edge of this journey. I'm deeply grateful to my parents, Marieta and Cosimo, for your unwavering support—and for only occasionally asking what on earth a knowledge graph is. And to my brother, Dante—your perfectly timed reality checks have kept me grounded (and reasonably sane).
– Giuseppe

To my wife Fiorella and my children Giulio, Azzurra, and Arianna, who patiently endured countless evenings of "I'm almost done writing."
– Fabio

brief contents

contents

The following appendices and references are available in the ePDF, ePUB, and liveBook versions of the book, as well as via download on the book product page at https://www.manning.com/books/knowledge-graphs-and-llms-in-action.

forewords

Working with graph neural networks and large language models over the years has taught me that each technology has profound strengths and equally profound limitations. Graph neural networks excel at understanding structured relationships but struggle with natural language interfaces. Large language models can engage in sophisticated conversations but frequently hallucinate facts and lack reliable grounding in structured knowledge.

Knowledge Graphs and LLMs in Action tackles an important challenge in AI: how do we combine these technologies to build systems that are both intelligent and trustworthy? Alessandro Negro, Giuseppe Futia, Vlastimil Kůs, and Fabio Montagna don't just theorize about this convergence; they provide practical recipes for making it work. Their approach bridges the gap between the precision of knowledge graphs and the accessibility of natural language, creating systems that can reason over complex data and explain their conclusions.

What impressed me most about this work is its rare emphasis on real-world implementation. The authors walk you through building knowledge graphs from messy, unstructured data and then show how to integrate them with language models for applications in healthcare, law enforcement, and beyond. The examples are concrete and the code is production-ready, making this both a learning resource and a practical guide.

The technical depth here is substantial, covering everything from graph construction to advanced retrieval systems, but the authors never lose sight of the practical goal: building AI systems that can serve as reliable advisors in critical decisions. This hybrid approach addresses the reliability and explainability challenges that have limited AI deployment in high-stakes environments.

If you're working on AI systems that need to be both powerful and trustworthy, *Knowledge Graphs and LLMs in Action* provides a clear framework for achieving it. The combination of knowledge graphs and language models represents a significant step toward AI that can handle complexity while maintaining the transparency and reliability that real-world applications demand.

—MAXIME LABONNE
HEAD OF POST-TRAINING, LIQUID AI

As a data science leader and passionate advocate for knowledge graphs, I'm thrilled to recommend *Knowledge Graphs and LLMs in Action.* We are witnessing a transformative moment in AI, shaped by the rise of generative AI and large language models (LLMs). Systems like Gemini and ChatGPT have opened the doors to natural language interaction at scale, offering a glimpse of intelligent machines. Yet we know these models are not without flaws. Hallucinations, outdated knowledge, limited transparency, and a lack of contextual grounding remain real challenges.

Addressing concerns like these is where knowledge graphs (KGs) shine, not just as a complement to LLMs, but as a necessary foundation for building accurate, explainable, and context-aware systems. This book demonstrates how the convergence of KGs and LLMs creates a powerful synergy, mitigating each other's weaknesses while unlocking their full potential.

The authors—Alessandro Negro, Vlastimil Kůs, Giuseppe Futia, and Fabio Montagna—bring years of hands-on experience and consulting expertise. Their work moves beyond theory to deliver actionable, production-ready insights grounded in real-world applications.

This book is more than a reference for knowledge graphs and LLMs. It's a practical toolkit for developing intelligent systems that enhance, not replace, human decision-making across domains like healthcare, finance, and law enforcement.

In an age where AI must be transparent, contextual, and trustworthy, this book is both timely and essential. It belongs on the shelf of every data scientist, engineer, architect, and knowledge-driven professional ready to build the next generation of intelligent systems.

Thank you, Alessandro, Vlastimil, Giuseppe, and Fabio, for this insightful and practical book!

—KHALIFEH ALJADDA
DIRECTOR OF DATA SCIENCE, GOOGLE CUSTOMER SOLUTIONS

preface

When I was nearing completion of my previous book, *Graph-Powered Machine Learning*, I reached out to my acquisitions editor, Mike Stephens, with a proposal for a natural continuation. That earlier work introduced knowledge graphs and demonstrated how they could be built using natural language processing, but many readers pointed out that graph neural networks were a significant missing piece. My proposed book would fill that gap while extending the knowledge graph story further, including detailed analysis and building techniques.

Mike accepted the proposal, and I embarked on a new adventure with the working title *Knowledge Graphs Applied*. Recognizing the scope of the challenge, I invited three colleagues from GraphAware—Fabio, Giuseppe, and Vlastimil—to join the effort, confident that their combined expertise would be invaluable. I naively thought that if one author could write a book in four years, four authors could complete a book in just a year. That assumption proved as flawed as expecting nine women to deliver a baby in one month.

Reality had other plans. Over the past years, significant changes swept through the technology landscape. Large language models (LLMs) and generative AI disrupted the field entirely, and knowledge graph practitioners suddenly found themselves with unprecedented opportunities to use this established technology in revolutionary ways. We initially planned to build on existing natural language processing (NLP) tools like BERT, but these were rapidly being superseded by LLM capabilities that opened new possibilities for building, querying, and analyzing knowledge graphs.

This was precisely where many practitioners, ourselves included, were struggling. Rather than resist this transformation, we decided, together with Mike and Dustin Archibald (our development editor), to embrace it. We adjusted our title to *Knowledge Graphs and LLMs in Action* and substantially revised the content to position LLMs as an integral component of our ultimate goal: intelligent advisor systems that empower humans in performing complex decision-making tasks. This pivot required extensive refactoring and a fundamental shift in our approach, but the result exceeded our expectations.

The book you are reading has evolved into a manifesto for the power of hybrid systems. It demonstrates how combining these technologies—knowledge graphs, which are well established, and LLMs, which are newly emerged—creates a flywheel effect that delivers remarkable long-term results. Knowledge graph practitioners will discover how to use LLM capabilities for greater impact, and LLM practitioners will learn techniques that address some of the major limitations of language models.

We invite you to join us on this journey toward more intelligent, more reliable, and more human-centered AI systems.

acknowledgments

This book took almost five years to complete, and during that time, many things changed around us, both professionally and personally. The technology landscape has transformed dramatically since we began writing: LLMs have fundamentally shaped our professions.

Writing a book requires dedication and countless hours, usually outside normal working hours, late at night, and on weekends and holidays. So first and foremost, we need to thank our families and all the people who somehow received a "no" or suffered a delay because of this book.

To my co-authors—Fabio, Giuseppe, and Vlastimil—thank you for embarking on this adventure with me. Each of you brought unique expertise and perspectives that made this book infinitely better than what I could have accomplished alone. Your dedication to excellence and willingness to adapt as the technology landscape shifted around us were nothing short of remarkable.

We owe an enormous debt of gratitude to the team at Manning Publications. In particular, Mike Stephens, Manning's associate publisher, not only accepted our book proposal but also provided invaluable guidance during the pivotal transformation from our original direction (*Knowledge Graphs Applied*) to what you are now reading (*Knowledge Graphs and LLMs in Action*). A special thank you to Dustin Archibald, our development editor, who followed us step by step with enormous patience and consistently provided excellent advice to make this a better book; your commitment to quality and your understanding during the extensive refactoring process made all the difference. We also want to thank the production and marketing teams at Manning—there are so many talented individuals that it's impossible to mention them all, but they are the reason Manning books are such high quality and so well presented.

Our sincere appreciation goes to Dimitris Polychronopoulos, our technical editor, whose meticulous attention to detail and expert feedback significantly improved the technical accuracy and clarity of this work. Dimitris is an R&D scientist and entrepreneur specializing in genomics and data-driven drug discovery. With roles across biotech and big pharma, he has led innovative work on applying knowledge graphs and AI to uncover novel targets in oncology and chronic liver diseases.

We also extend our gratitude to all the reviewers who provided valuable feedback throughout the development process, including those who shared comments and suggestions online: Alexey Ott, Angelo Simone Scotto, Ayush Tomar, Avinash Tiwari, Chalamayya Batchu, Charles Ivie, Chris Viner, Dan McCreary, David Cronkite, David Meza, Floris Bouchot, Gajendra Babu Thokala, Gourav Sengupta, Guillaume Alleon, James J Byleckie, Jeremy Chen, Kristof Leroux, Kumar Abhishek, Lawrence Nderu, Maria Ana, Nicolas Bievre, Or Golan, Ozan Evkaya, Pethuru Raj, R. P. Shrivastava, Richard Vaughan, Robert Wardenga, S. S. Narendran, Sachin Panemangalore, Samantha Berk, Shailja Gupta, Simeon Leyzerzon, Sophia Shvets, Sumit Pal, and Suvarsha Rai. Your insights and constructive criticism helped shape this book into its final form.

A special acknowledgment goes to Khalifeh and Maxime, who kindly agreed to write forewords for this book. They received an almost-final copy when the book was ready for production, requiring them to work under tight deadlines to provide the thoughtful forewords you'll find at the beginning—no small feat for professionals as busy as they are. Khalifeh and Maxime are among the most knowledgeable experts we know in their fields. Their endorsement carries particular weight because of their extensive experience in bringing these technologies to real-world applications, and their ongoing work continues to inspire us and the broader community.

We also want to acknowledge the companies that provided us with the knowledge, experience, and opportunities we needed to create this book. GraphAware, in particular, has been instrumental in shaping our understanding of real-world graph applications and the challenges organizations face when implementing these technologies at scale.

Finally, we extend our appreciation to the broader community of researchers, practitioners, and open source contributors whose work made many of our examples possible. The datasets, tools, and frameworks that power the demonstrations in this book represent countless hours of effort from dedicated individuals who chose to share their knowledge with the world.

This book exists because of all of you. Thank you for making this journey possible.

about this book

Knowledge Graphs and LLMs in Action is a comprehensive guide to building hybrid intelligent systems that combine the structured reasoning capabilities of knowledge graphs (KGs) with the natural language understanding of large language models (LLMs). This book demonstrates how these complementary technologies can work together to create more powerful, reliable, and explainable AI solutions that address real-world challenges across various domains.

Who should read this book

This book is designed for machine learning engineers, data scientists, graph experts, and AI engineers who want to harness the synergistic power of KGs and LLMs. Whether you're working with structured enterprise data, building recommendation systems, developing fraud detection algorithms, or creating question-answering applications, this book will show you how to use both technologies to achieve better results than either could deliver alone.

If you're a data scientist looking to enhance your models with structured knowledge, a machine learning engineer seeking to reduce hallucinations in LLM applications, or an AI practitioner interested in building explainable and verifiable systems, this book provides the practical guidance you need. Although some familiarity with machine learning concepts and graph databases is helpful, the book introduces all necessary concepts and builds complexity gradually.

How this book is organized: A roadmap

The book has 15 chapters organized into 5 parts, progressing from foundational concepts to advanced implementations.

Part 1 establishes the theoretical and practical foundations for hybrid intelligent systems:

- Chapter 1 introduces the powerful combination of KGs and LLMs, demonstrating their complementary nature through concrete examples and use cases.
- Chapter 2 explores fundamental concepts of intelligent systems, diving deep into knowledge representation and reasoning strategies, and illustrating how KGs and LLMs work together in practice.

Part 2 focuses on building KGs from structured data sources:

- Chapter 3 demonstrates KG construction through a healthcare example, showing how to help clinicians diagnose rare diseases using the Human Phenotype Ontology.
- Chapter 4 expands on these foundations with advanced analysis methodologies, including community detection algorithms and multisource integration across biomedical applications.

Part 3 tackles the challenging realm of extracting knowledge from unstructured text:

- Chapter 5 demonstrates the fundamental pipeline for converting text to KGs using both traditional natural language processing (NLP) and modern LLM-based methods through a case study at the Rockefeller Archive Center.
- Chapter 6 expands on document processing workflows, from OCR scanning to sophisticated graph analytics for identifying research networks and influence patterns.
- Chapter 7 explores named entity disambiguation in healthcare regulation, showing how to link entities to structured knowledge bases like the Unified Medical Language System (UMLS) and Systematized Nomenclature of Medicine (SNOMED).
- Chapter 8 introduces an innovative approach to disambiguation that combines open LLMs with domain ontologies for enhanced accuracy.

Part 4 explores machine learning applications on KGs:

- Chapter 9 introduces fundamental concepts for applying machine learning to KGs and establishes the theoretical foundation for learnable representations.
- Chapter 10 illustrates feature engineering approaches through practical examples in fraud detection and drug repurposing.
- Chapter 11 advances into graph neural networks, showing how these architectures automatically learn optimal representations from graph structures.
- Chapter 12 demonstrates real-world applications through anti-money laundering and movie recommendation systems.

Part 5 brings everything together in practical information retrieval systems:

- Chapter 13 explores integrating KGs with LLMs through retrieval augmented generation, demonstrating graph RAG systems.

- Chapter 14 shows how to build sophisticated question-answering systems that emulate domain expert reasoning through a law enforcement example.
- Chapter 15 provides a complete implementation using LangGraph and Streamlit, demonstrating how to build production-ready systems.

The book is designed to be read sequentially for comprehensive understanding, but experienced practitioners can focus on specific parts based on their immediate needs. Beginners should start with parts 1 and 2 to establish foundational knowledge before exploring specialized applications in later parts.

About the code

This book contains extensive source code examples demonstrating practical implementations of KG and LLM integration. Code appears both in numbered listings and in line with explanatory text, formatted in a `fixed-width font like this` to distinguish it from regular content. Sometimes code is also in **bold** to highlight relevant pieces.

In many cases, the original source code has been reformatted; we've added line breaks and reworked indentation to accommodate the available page space in the book. In rare cases, even this was not enough, and listings include line-continuation markers (➥). Additionally, comments in the source code have often been removed from the listings when the code is described in the text. Code annotations accompany many of the listings, highlighting important concepts.

All source code examples are available for download from the book's GitHub repository at https://github.com/alenegro81/knowledge-graphs-and-llms-in-action. The repository includes complete implementations for each chapter's examples, along with setup instructions and data files needed to run the code.

The examples require Python 3.8 or higher and various libraries, including Neo4j, NetworkX, transformers, LangChain, and Streamlit. Specific requirements and installation instructions are provided in each chapter and the repository's documentation. Some examples also require access to OpenAI APIs or other language model services, with instructions for setting up the necessary credentials.

You can get executable snippets of code from the liveBook (online) version of this book at https://livebook.manning.com/book/knowledge-graphs-and-llms-in-action. The complete code for the examples in the book is also available for download from the Manning website at https://www.manning.com/books/knowledge-graphs-and-llms-in-action.

liveBook discussion forum

Purchase of *Knowledge Graphs and LLMs in Action* includes free access to liveBook, Manning's online reading platform. Using liveBook's exclusive discussion features, you can attach comments to the book globally or to specific sections or paragraphs. It's a snap to make notes for yourself, ask and answer technical questions, and receive help from the authors and other users. To access the forum, go to https://livebook.manning.com/book/knowledge-graphs-and-llms-in-action/discussion.

Manning's commitment to our readers is to provide a venue where a meaningful dialogue among individual readers and between readers and the authors can take place. It is not a commitment to any specific amount of participation on the part of the authors, whose contribution to the forum remains voluntary (and unpaid). We suggest you try asking the authors some challenging questions lest their interest stray! The forum and the archives of previous discussions will be accessible from the publisher's website as long as the book is in print.

about the authors

Alessandro Negro is the chief scientist at GraphAware, where he supervises the science and technology area responsible for delivering Hume, a mission-critical analytics platform that uses knowledge graphs (KGs) at its core. He holds a Ph.D. in computer science and has successfully deployed machine learning systems combined with graphs for numerous organizations across various industries. Dr. Negro is the author of *Graph-Powered Machine Learning* (Manning, 2021). His recent work focuses on integrating LLMs with KGs to create more reliable and explainable AI systems at scale. Beyond his role at GraphAware, Alessandro actively mentors and advises startups, helping organizations in specialized domains create custom models tailored to their unique requirements.

Giuseppe Futia is a data scientist and research fellow with expertise in knowledge graphs, large language models, and graph neural networks. He holds a Ph.D. in computer engineering and bridges academia and industry through extensive experience in research and applied innovation. His work focuses on developing knowledge-driven intelligent systems that integrate symbolic and statistical AI to enable advanced decision-making across diverse domains.

VLASTIMIL KŮS is a lead AI engineer and data science leader specializing in knowledge graphs, Agentic AI, NLP, and unstructured data. With a background in subnuclear physics research and more than a decade of experience in advanced data science and machine learning, he combines deep technical expertise with a strong focus on delivering business impact.

FABIO MONTAGNA is a senior graph and AI engineer at GraphAware, with more than 15 years of experience in research-driven software engineering across neuroscience, operational oceanography, and natural language processing. As a pioneer in bridging scientific discovery and commercial application, he specializes in transforming complex research concepts into scalable production systems that deliver business value. His dual role as product strategist and technical expert enables him to translate theoretical breakthroughs into practical solutions across healthcare, earth sciences, and commercial applications. Beyond GraphAware, Fabio has been collaborating with neurologists in pharmaceutical research for Parkinson's disease treatment evaluation.

about the cover illustration

The image featured on the cover of this book is called "Mařaťanka" by Joža Uprka (1861–1940), a Czech painter renowned for his vivid portrayals of folk life in southern Moravia, a historic wine-growing region in the Czech Republic. The painting depicts a young woman from the village of Mařatice, whose name echoes the ancient designation "sons of Maria" for its inhabitants. Dressed in a traditional local costume, she carries a tray of grapes and fruit aloft, embodying the spirit of harvest, abundance, and the enduring rhythm of historical rural life. It is a celebration of shared European traditions rooted in the land, the seasons, and community rituals. Like wine itself, these themes transcend borders and bring people together, mirroring the Czecho-Italian nature of the co-authoring team.

Part 1

Foundations of hybrid intelligent systems

The convergence of knowledge graphs (KGs) and large language models (LLMs) marks a pivotal moment in the development of intelligent systems. This part of the book lays the foundation for understanding how these complementary technologies can work together to create more powerful and effective solutions.

The integration of these technologies addresses the key limitations of each approach while amplifying their strengths. KGs provide the explicit, verifiable, and updatable knowledge representation that LLMs often lack; and LLMs offer the natural language understanding and generation capabilities that make complex knowledge structures more accessible. This synergy enables the development of intelligent systems that can

- Handle both structured and unstructured data effectively
- Combine multiple types of reasoning strategies
- Provide explainable and verifiable results
- Continuously update their knowledge base
- Interact naturally with users while maintaining accuracy and reliability

Chapter 1 introduces the powerful combination of KGs and LLMs, establishing their complementary nature and illustrating how they can enhance each other's capabilities through concrete examples and use cases. It sets the stage for understanding the transformative potential of this hybrid approach.

Chapter 2 explores the fundamental concepts of intelligent systems, diving deep into different types of knowledge representation and reasoning strategies. It illustrates how KGs and LLMs can work together in practice, examining their roles in knowledge acquisition, representation, and various forms of reasoning.

The frameworks and concepts introduced in these chapters provide the foundation for the practical implementations and advanced applications discussed throughout the remainder of the book.

1 Knowledge graphs and LLMs: A killer combination

This chapter covers

- Introducing knowledge graphs
- Introducing large language models
- Building data-driven applications using knowledge graphs and large language models

Generative artificial intelligence (GenAI), powered by *large language models* (LLMs) like Google's Gemini and OpenAI's GPT, has transformed how we work and live, revolutionizing business after business. Despite this success, generative AI falls short in domains where specific domain knowledge, high accuracy, and explainability are essential. And it has other significant limitations, including hallucinations and a lack of context and relations. This is where *knowledge graphs* (KGs) come in, providing contextual information—such as experiences, environmental characteristics, cultural aspects, and social norms—needed to build the "third wave of AI" [1] for mission-critical applications.

KGs are sophisticated graph structures that represent real-world entities (people, places, diseases, proteins), define meaningful connections between them, and provide context. KGs provide structured, explainable knowledge representation but are challenging to build and query; LLMs offer natural language processing capabilities but suffer from hallucinations, stale information, and a lack of domain-specific grounding. Together, they are a "killer combination": LLMs can extract entities and relationships from unstructured text to build KGs more efficiently, providing more autonomous and powerful graph querying and analysis. Meanwhile, KGs provide reliable, up-to-date domain knowledge to ground LLM responses and prevent hallucinations.

Blending KGs and LLMs is a powerful approach to building sophisticated data-driven applications that can harmonize disparate data sources, provide natural language interfaces, and deliver contextually grounded intelligent responses. In this book, you'll learn to adopt business-focused approaches, model KG schemas, use LLMs for entity extraction, validate information integrity, and create conversational AI systems that can answer complex domain-specific questions using structured and unstructured data.

1.1 Knowledge graphs

KGs incorporate a structured representation of human knowledge into machines, enabling more intelligent behavior. This is achieved by creating a sophisticated graph structure with these elements:

- *Nodes* represent real-world entities (people, places, organizations, diseases, proteins, genes).
- *Relationships* define meaningful connections between these nodes (a person born in a place, a disease causing symptoms, a gene encoding a protein).
- *Properties* provide context (birth dates, geographic coordinates, organizational history, disease descriptions in multiple languages).

Figure 1.1 shows a healthcare KG in which entities (diseases, drugs, compounds, anatomical structures) are connected through meaningful relationships. This explicit representation enables machines to perform reasoning and inference on the structured knowledge, supporting complex intelligent systems for decision-making.

Despite their effectiveness and advantages in supporting the development of intelligent systems, KGs haven't been widely adopted for several reasons, including the following:

- They are expensive to build and maintain in terms of time, effort, and money.
- Intricate access patterns are required to navigate multiple hops.
- Their results scatter information across multiple nodes and relationships.

Building a KG requires recognizing and extracting relevant entities and connections from heterogeneous data sources, structured and unstructured. Dealing with structured data sources is vastly less complicated than working with unstructured data. In structured or semistructured data (from relational databases or files in CSV, XML, or JSON format), items are isolated, identified, and often typed. Such data must still be mapped from the original schemas to a common graph schema, but the process is controllable and predictable.

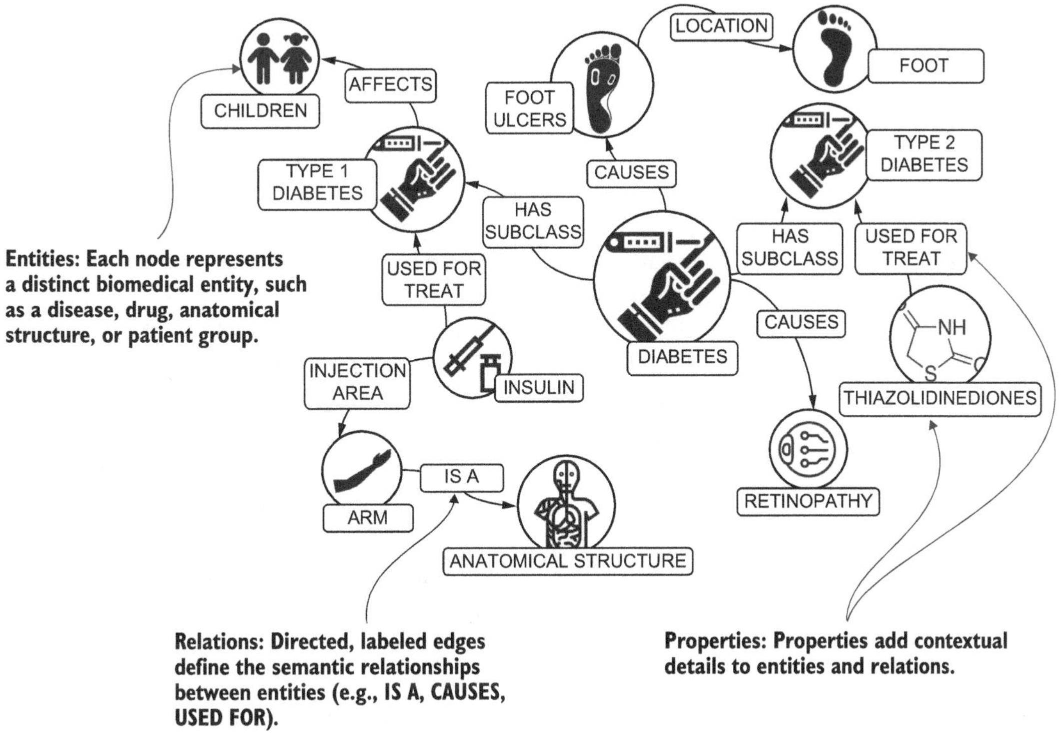

Figure 1.1 Example KG in the healthcare domain. Nodes (circles) represent entities, such as people, diseases, and anatomic parts. Edges (relationships) represent meaningful connections among entities. Nodes and edges have properties describing relevant details.

Unstructured data is another story. Extracting information from text has always been a complex task for the following reasons:

- *Multiple languages*—Each language has its own grammatical rules, vocabulary, idioms, and nuances. Processing text in multiple languages requires a system that understands and manages these differences. Additionally, languages can have unique writing systems (e.g., Latin, Cyrillic, Chinese), requiring support for various scripts and encodings.
- *Typos*—Human-written text often contains typographical errors, misspellings, and other mistakes requiring sophisticated algorithms to understand the intended meaning.
- *Pronouns*—Resolving what a pronoun refers to (*coreference resolution*) is vital for accurate comprehension. For example, in the sentence "John saw Bob and he waved," it is unclear whether "he" refers to John or Bob.
- *Different writing styles*—Authors use synonyms, varied sentence structures, and unique expressions, making it hard for systems to maintain consistency and accurately interpret different writing styles.

- *Domain-specific terminology and concepts*—Many specialized fields use unique vocabularies, technical jargon, and concepts that require domain expertise to understand and extract accurately.

Accurately extracting and interpreting information from human languages requires advanced techniques and robust systems. But building a KG is just the beginning. It holds vast, interconnected information (*knowledge*) that must be accessed correctly to obtain the right answers to questions and support intelligent systems. Flexibility in defining the schema for a KG helps with handling heterogeneous data sources and complex domain connections but complicates access by those who don't know how to query it properly. Predefined queries and analyses can help build specific intelligent systems but limit the types of users and the support these systems can provide. And results are often difficult to interpret by non-experts and across user interfaces.

Let's look at some examples. The best-known early adopter of KGs was Google, which used them to enhance user searches by providing "relevant" connected information. This approach emphasizes searching for things, not just strings, but it's limited to search applications.

Many analysts use KGs to answer complex investigative questions. But due to the complexity of the graph querying process and the need for specific interfaces, this use is confined to a smaller user base.

Imagine individuals posing questions to a KG using natural language, and the intelligent system finding the correct answers by querying the graph effectively and then transforming the results into simple summaries. We construct this scenario throughout this book.

1.2 Large language models

LLMs, which specialize in handling natural language, can eliminate barriers to the evolution of intelligent systems that use KGs as the core technology. These systems can help users accomplish tasks in complex domains.

The foundation of LLMs is *transfer learning*: the ability to reuse patterns learned in generic tasks (such as predicting masked tokens) for specific tasks (such as relation extraction) [2] (see figure 1.2). This breakthrough shifted the paradigm from training many small, task-specific models to training a few large models that are reusable across multiple tasks, significantly reducing the training data and computational resources required for supervised learning.

Pretrained language models (PLMs) trained with transformer architectures [3] on large-scale corpora demonstrated the capacity to perform *natural language processing* (NLP) tasks with a single big model. Enhancements in model scaling led to increased model capacities, and further investigations of scaling effects expanded the parameter scale. The term *large language model* refers to a PLM with significant scale—typically tens or hundreds of billions of parameters. The emergence of LLMs such as GPT-2 [5], which are trained on enormous volumes of textual data, transformed the field of AI. Their modern counterparts, including GPT-4 [5], Gopher [6], and PaLM [7],

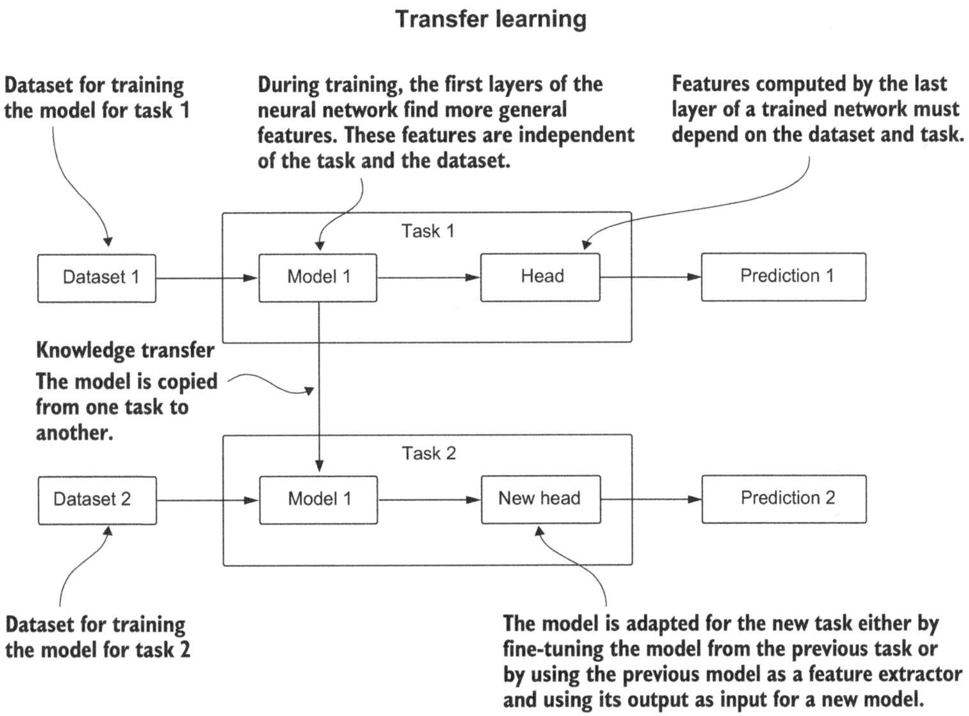

Figure 1.2 In transfer learning, a model (or part of it) trained on a specific task is used as part of the training and predictions for another task.

breathe new life into the phrase "unreasonable effectiveness of data" [8]. Their performance is deemed "unreasonable" for three interconnected reasons:

1. Model complexity (a.k.a. number of parameters)
2. Size—and, in the case of GPT, quality—of the training corpus
3. Their ability to reduce tasks requiring human intelligence to next token prediction

As shown in the paper "Scaling Laws for Neural Language Models" [9], larger neural models (i.e., those with more trainable parameters) require fewer data samples to reach the same performance in terms of the test-set loss. The same paper proves that the size of the training corpus is of paramount importance. Not surprisingly, the more data the model has to learn from, the better it gets. But data quality is equally crucial. Traditional machine learning typically followed a *model-centric* paradigm, focusing on identifying the best model architecture and fine-tuning hyperparameters. However, faulty data can lead to faulty predictions. A *data-centric* paradigm prioritizes data engineering to improve both the quality and quantity of data used for training high-complexity ML models. With these improvements, we can formulate tasks in natural language, and LLMs generate accurate answers with minimal model engineering required (see figure 1.3).

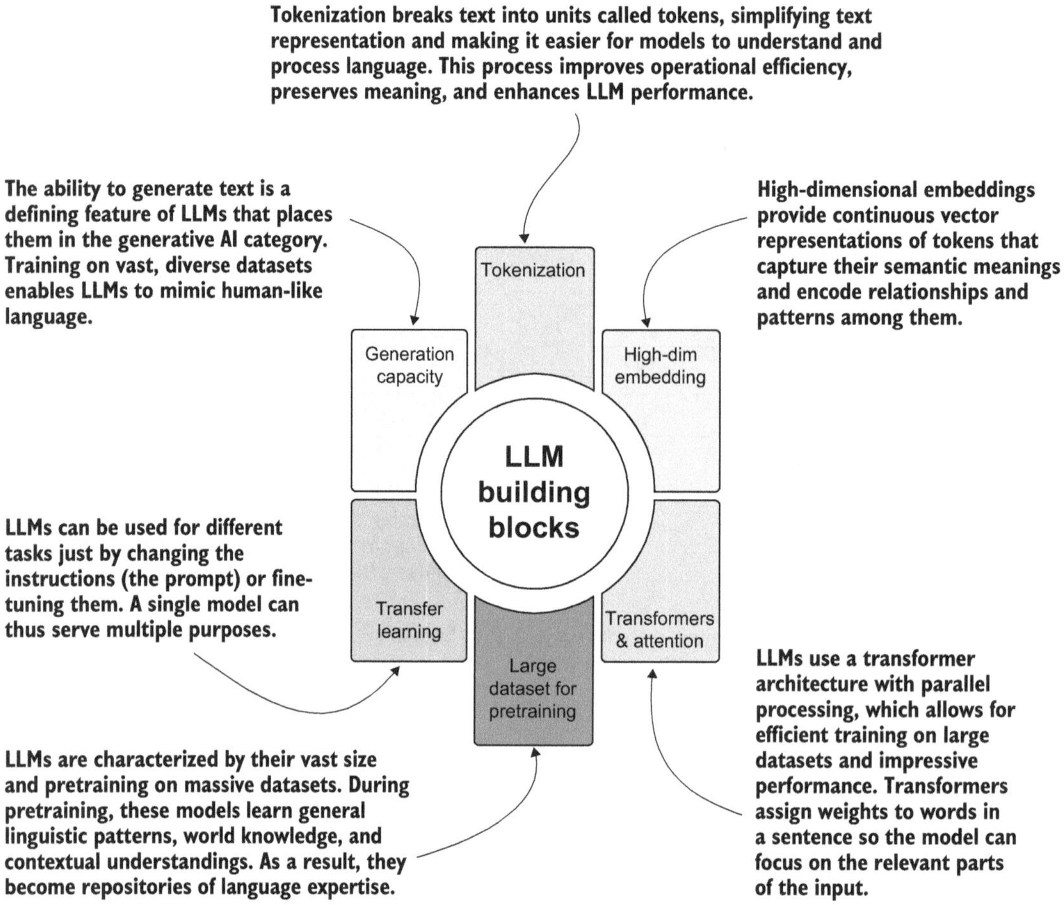

Figure 1.3 LLM building blocks and differentiating characteristics

1.3 KGs and LLMs: Stronger together

KGs and LLMs support each other in delivering better service, and together they can enhance the implementation of powerful, intelligent systems. We are particularly interested in these ways that LLMs can assist KG-based solutions:

- *Building KGs*—Specifically, extracting relevant concepts and connections from unstructured data. This task has traditionally required training custom NLP models for specific domains. LLMs have simplified this process by providing a model that can serve multiple purposes with minimal configuration (such as the prompt); see figure 1.4. We discuss building KGs in parts 2 and 3.

- *Querying KGs*—Extracting knowledge can involve multiple steps, or *hops*, from the starting concept to the destination. Such hops often require understanding the schema and query language. LLMs help by extracting relevant, precise information to support querying and search. We discuss this in part 5.
- *Summarizing*—Information extracted from KGs can be returned in text form rather than in a table, graph, chart, or other format.

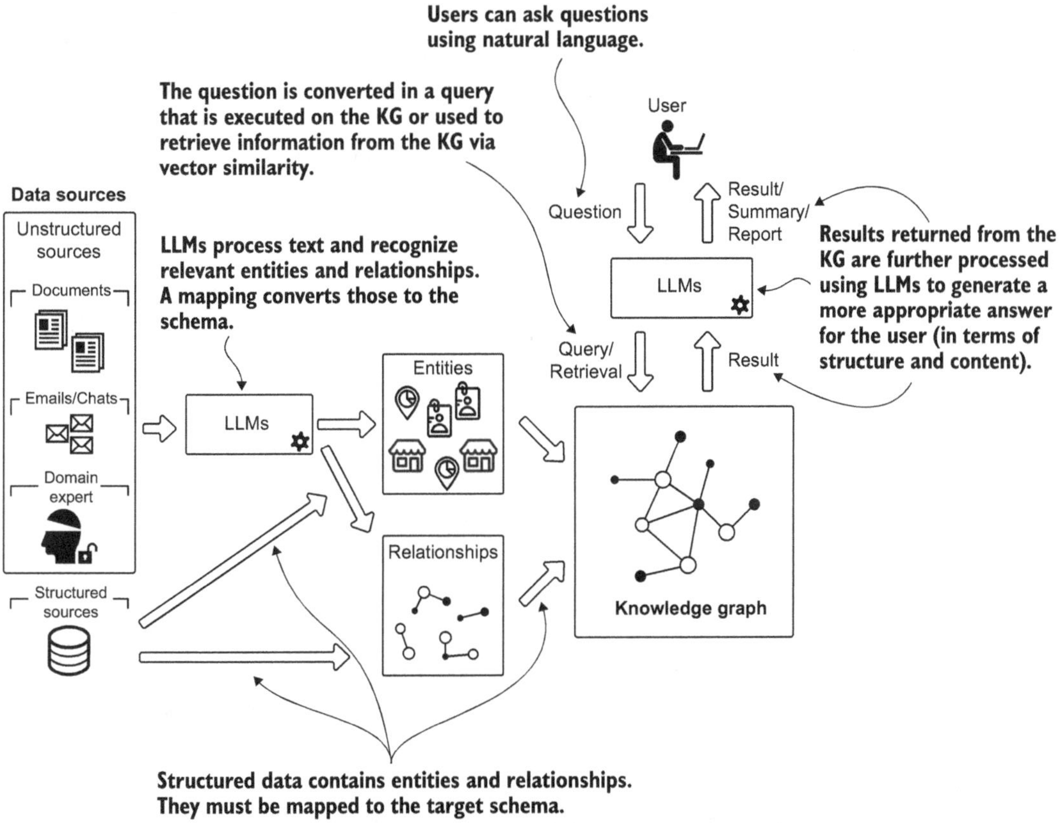

Figure 1.4 KGs building with and without LLMs and LLMs support for querying and retrieval

KGs can also help overcome LLM limitations related to domain-specific accuracy, transparency, and timeliness. Here are some drawbacks of LLMs that can be mitigated by integrating KGs [10]:

- *Hallucinations*—KGs provide structured, verified knowledge that acts as a factual foundation, significantly reducing LLMs' tendency to generate plausible but incorrect information. LLMs complement this by offering sophisticated query mechanisms, such as text-to-cypher translation, which enables natural language questions to be converted into precise graph queries that extract reliable information directly from the structured knowledge base.

- *Stale information*—KGs enable dynamic knowledge updates through advanced retrieval-augmented architectures. LLMs cannot be constantly retrained, but KGs can be continuously updated and accessed via techniques such as KG-based prompting and GraphRAG systems. GraphRAG organizes knowledge into meaningful clusters and community summaries, providing LLMs with the most current information available in constantly updated KGs.
- *Explainability*—KGs provide transparent information paths and structured reasoning that users can trace and validate, building trust through explainable AI processes. Combined with LLMs' natural language processing, this creates systems where knowledge extraction is understandable and repeatable, and findings can be summarized in an intelligible, human-readable format.

Figure 1.5 summarizes how these two technologies support and complement each other.

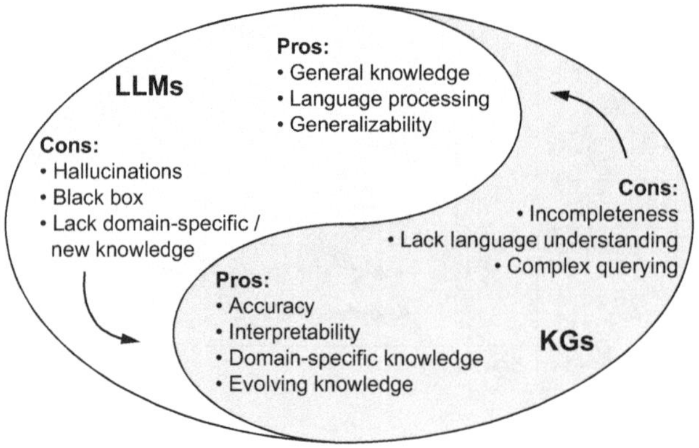

Figure 1.5 Summary of how LLMs and KGs can complement each other. Inspired by [11].

1.4 The paradigm shift in data-driven applications

Traditional paradigms build systems for specific purposes with structured, homogeneous databases. This approach works for tailored needs but is impractical for complex domains that need to adapt to user characteristics and integrate heterogeneous data. KGs capture connections, enabling relationship discovery through graph pattern matching and traversal. Both the Resource Description Framework (RDF) and Labeled Property Graphs (LPGs) provide machine-readable formats that humans can interpret. KGs emphasize rich, meaningful data representations usable by both humans and machines, enabling a paradigm shift where intelligent behavior is encoded in a unique source of truth.

According to McKinsey & Company [12], addressing data fragmentation can cut annual data spending by 5% to 15% in the short term. KGs overcome siloed data issues, creating knowledge sources while lowering barriers to data access and enhancing governance.

1.4.1 The four pillars of knowledge graphs

To encode this paradigm shift in a concrete implementation, we propose a new definition of a KG that includes all the features which affect the technical and business sides:

> **DEFINITION** A *knowledge graph* is an ever-evolving graph data structure composed of a set of typed entities, their attributes, and meaningful named relationships. Built for a specific domain, it integrates both structured and unstructured data to craft knowledge for humans and machines.

This definition provides the groundwork for the four pillars of KGs:

- *Evolution*—KGs allow us to continuously ingest, integrate, and unify information into a single source. The graph structure can be easily extended, evolving according to the needs of the analysis and our purposes. A KG can seamlessly incorporate new interactions or content without needing a complete overhaul of the existing structure.
- *Semantics*—A KG makes the meaning of the data—its *semantics*—explicit, modeling information in a knowledge infrastructure characterized by typed entities and meaningful relationships. New data is combined with existing data and is immediately available for analysis. Contextual knowledge emerges from this infrastructure and drives business activities and decisions. Such knowledge connects typed entities describing categorizations and supports, for instance, identity, transitive, or inverse relationships. This expressiveness in representing data opens the doors to *explainability* [13]. KGs provide a backbone for reasoning mechanisms ranging from consistency checking to causal inference.
- *Integration*—The KG serves as the central reference for all structured and unstructured data related to a domain. Because a KG represents information by focusing on the meaning of data, users can overcome challenges related to data types, formats, and provenance, connecting information from multiple data sources.
- *Learning*—A KG represents the core information and big picture of a domain. Humans can analyze, visualize, and query graph data to extract insights. Inference rules and machine learning algorithms are performed on top of the KG to infer new information not explicitly encoded within the KG. Analysts can use methods such as centrality and connectivity analysis to identify influential nodes, network analysis to detect the shortest path between nodes, and community analysis to recognize groups of similar nodes.

Figure 1.6 shows the four pillars that characterize a KG.

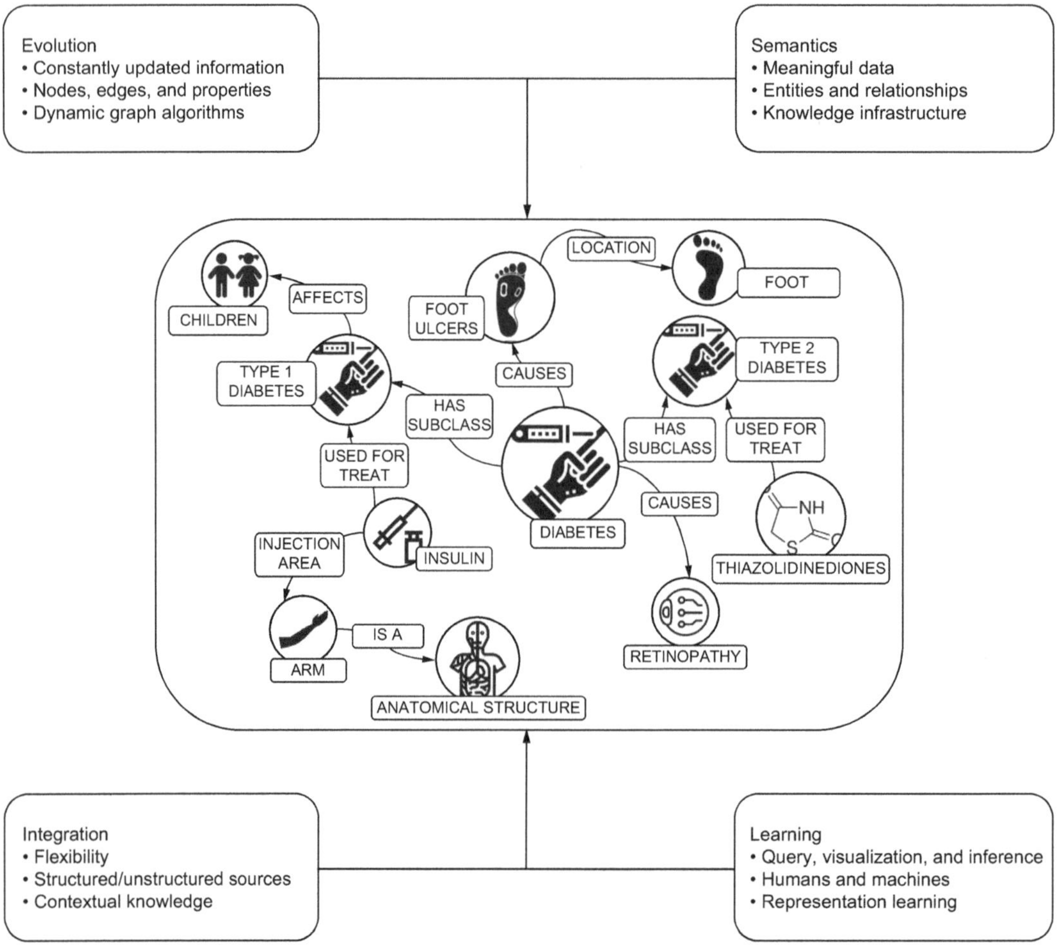

Figure 1.6 The four pillars of KGs: evolution, semantics, integration, and learning

1.5 Building data-driven applications using KGs and LLMs

In this section, we look at several examples of potential applications for KGs and LLMs in critical areas.

NOTE We frequently mention healthcare in this book because its characteristics, issues, and requirements can easily be applied to other domains. Healthcare also offers abundant publicly available data, so we can discuss real-world examples using datasets that are comparable to actual use cases.

1.5.1 Example use case: Drug discovery and development

Drug development integrates knowledge from numerous domains, from biology to chemistry, and bringing a new drug to market is costly and has a high chance of failure. Fast, practical approaches are essential to guide research in new drug development.

- *Challenge*—Integration of medical and pharmaceutical data must ensure data integrity, accuracy, and consistency while correctly contextualizing data points.
- *KG-based solution*—Models interactions between biological entities at different scales, connecting genes, diseases, and drugs using relationship types. Typed relationships with multiple rules better represent domain meaning, enabling transitive bonds and inference.
- *Role of LLMs*—Process unstructured data from scientific publications, clinical reports, and databases, ensuring consistency in integrated knowledge bases. LLMs expand KGs by analyzing literature and inferring potential relationships, as well as performing sophisticated text mining for chemical structures and experimental results.

Integrating LLMs enhances data integration, augments KGs, facilitates hypothesis generation, improves information retrieval, and enables advanced text mining. These capabilities ultimately accelerate the development of new therapeutics.

1.5.2 Example use case: Conversational AI for customer support

Personalized assistant systems must answer user queries and be able to ask follow-up questions. An effective tool needs to combine general expertise with specific user requests, managing vast amounts of information efficiently.

- *Challenge*—Despite advancements in natural language generation (NLG) techniques, answers from language models can be repetitive and uninformative (Zhang et al. [14]). For a conversational system to provide useful suggestions and information, it needs to extract relevant entities and relationships from the text while being supported by external and internal structured knowledge to ground the conversation.
- *KG-based solution*—Zhang et al. [14] claim that "conversations often develop around knowledge." In particular, natural conversations evolve around concepts that form this knowledge. KGs connect such concepts and establish meaningful relationships between them. KGs can ground conversations, integrate information, and support response generation: NLP technologies extract entities and relationships, and the graph-based background context of the dialogue drives the conversational flow.
- *Role of LLMs*—LLMs can handle a wide range of topics and provide coherent responses, making them valuable for building sophisticated conversational systems. However, without additional contextual grounding, their responses can become generic and lack depth.

By integrating LLMs with knowledge sources such as KGs, the conversational system can enhance its responses. LLMs can use structured information in KGs to provide more accurate and contextually relevant answers. This integration allows the system to navigate complex queries, offer precise information, and maintain a natural conversational flow.

1.5.3 Deciding whether to use a KG

Despite their diversity, the previous scenarios share common challenges. The following questions can help you understand whether a KG is the right solution to address your business and technical challenges.

Consider KGs if you answer *yes* to these questions:

- Do I need to harmonize disparate data silos into consistent overviews?
- Do I need to connect data meaningfully across structured and unstructured sources?
- Do I need flexible data representations where structure evolves?
- Do I need to track pipeline provenance and consistency?
- Do I need to equip advanced search and recommendation services?
- Do I need to visualize network structures, showing communities and interdependencies?
- Do I need to apply ML models that benefit from the relational nature of data?

Consider LLMs if you answer *yes* to these questions:

- Do I need to extract entities and relationships from unstructured data?
- Do I need to interpret complex user queries for accurate answers?
- Do I need to provide conversational interfaces?
- Do I need to summarize comprehensive results into text?

If you answer *yes* to even one of these, you need LLMs to empower your KG-based solution.

1.6 Knowledge graph technologies

In this book, we adopt a technologically agnostic approach and provide code examples that interchange two common paradigms in creating and querying KGs:

- RDF and the SPARQL query language, both defined by the World Wide Web Consortium (W3C). RDF is a data model that focuses on knowledge representation, where the graph is encoded as a collection of statements or triplets. It aims to standardize data publication and sharing on the web. The core of intelligent systems is based on reasoning performed on the semantic layer.
- The LPG approach and query languages such as openCypher (https://opencypher.org/) and Gremlin (https://tinkerpop.apache.org/gremlin.html). The LPG representation focuses on the structure (properties and relationships) of the graph. Nodes and edges have properties, emphasizing the features of the graph data.

RDF excels at data interoperability and consistency across systems through standardized statements, offering powerful hypergraph and federation features that enable linking different RDF graphs with rich contextual information. LPG implementations provide advantages in pathfinding queries and graph traversal operations. In LPG, each edge has a unique identity and properties, whereas in RDF, relationships are global predicates that can be reused across statements throughout the knowledge base.

RDF and LPG are distinct paradigms but can be complementary depending on the use case. RDF excels in scenarios requiring semantic consistency, web-scale interoperability, and the use of ontologies for knowledge inference, and LPG provides rich property-based representations and efficient graph traversals.

1.6.1 Taxonomies and ontologies

Modern implementations of KGs must use traditional features of graph data and, as defined by [15], the organizing principle enabled by semantics, turning the latent knowledge of a graph into a KG. Graph models can be instantiated from a collection of statements (RDF) or through the LPG model. But just incorporating this structural information does not fully capture the relationships within the data. We can inject these semantic features into KGs using taxonomies and ontologies:

- *Taxonomies* represent the hierarchical dimension of the data, organizing categories in broader–narrower relationships. For example, in a taxonomy, a "Vehicle" category might be broader than a "Car" category, which in turn is broader than a "Sedan" category. Complex KGs can integrate multiple taxonomies.
- *Ontologies* introduce more complex relationships beyond simple hierarchies. We can clarify identity, difference, and more intricate interconnections between entities. For instance, an ontology might specify that "Car" and "Automobile" are identical (synonyms), whereas "Car" and "Bicycle" are disjoint (cannot be the same). Ontologies support class definitions including union, complement, disjointness, and cardinality restrictions. They capture the domain's conceptual structure. Without an ontology, a vocabulary remains vague because it does not encode the intrinsic relationships between concepts.

Traditional approaches to defining taxonomies and ontologies are rigid and complex and make these systems less adaptable to evolving knowledge and diverse data sources. Modern KGs adopt a pragmatic approach characterized by "just enough semantics." This involves selecting a subset of ontology features that address current issues without being overly prescriptive. For example, in a healthcare KG, practitioners might focus on a specific medical domain—such as oncology or cardiology—while leaving room to expand into other specialties as needed.

Rather than enforcing rigid, complete taxonomies, modern KGs integrate partial ontologies that can be extended organically. This flexibility enables dynamic, scalable knowledge representation that adapts to real-world constraints and evolving business needs.

1.7 How do we teach KGs and LLMs?

This book will equip you with essential tools for creating and using KGs while demonstrating how to use LLMs for advanced intelligent applications. You will learn to do the following:

- Adopt a business-need mindset focusing on goals, then data, and then algorithms.
- Model KG schemas, considering future extensions, taxonomies, and ontologies.
- Import data from structured sources and map entities/relationships to schemas.
- Use LLMs to extract domain-relevant entities and relationships from text.
- Validate ingested information, ensuring integrity and accuracy.
- Perform analysis using the latest ML technologies, such as graph neural networks.
- Query and visualize graph portions, using LLMs for natural language questions.

We'll explain these concepts through concrete, practical examples drawn from our direct experience.

Summary

- KGs are ever-evolving graph data structures containing typed entities, attributes, and meaningful relationships. They are built for specific domains from structured and unstructured data to craft knowledge for humans and machines.
- KGs have four pillars: evolution, semantics, integration, and learning.
- KGs represent a core abstraction for incorporating human knowledge into machines, and LLMs provide natural language understanding. LLMs and KGs empower each other by overcoming their individual limitations.
- KG and LLM adoption represents a paradigm shift where intelligent behavior is encoded once in a unique source of trust. This empowers data representation for different applications and diverse tasks.
- Two key technologies represent KGs: the Resource Description Framework (RDF) and labeled property graphs (LPG).
- Taxonomies and ontologies play fundamental roles by incorporating semantic metadata that makes traditional graphs smarter.

2 Intelligent systems: A hybrid approach

This chapter covers

- Design concepts and architecture for intelligent advisor systems
- How hybrid systems use the complementary strengths of KGs and LLMs
- Combining KGs and LLMs in intelligent advisor systems

This chapter explores the foundational concepts behind intelligence and intelligent behavior. At the core of our discussion lies the application of knowledge graphs (KGs) and large language models (LLMs) to solve highly complex problems by combining existing knowledge and context with reasoning and natural language understanding capabilities to build intelligent systems.

To make informed decisions about the trustworthiness and safety of intelligent systems for critical applications, we must understand how these systems operate internally, avoiding attributing capacities they lack while using their genuine capabilities. By dissecting the functioning of these systems, we can better understand their limitations and take advantage of their potential.

2.1 What is intelligence?

What is intelligence? It is the ability to acquire and apply knowledge: to learn from experience, solve problems, and interact with the environment. This natural process, honed by evolution, gives humans a competitive edge over other species. Humans do this effortlessly and unconsciously, but to design an intelligent system and a detailed structure for each element, we must dissect these processes by breaking down the various tasks and components.

The first goal of an intelligent agent is to get examples, evidence, and rules from the world, memorize them, and use them to act or make decisions. From the outside, an intelligent system is a black box that accomplishes complex tasks. The first step in understanding it is to break it into simpler and smaller components based on their primary functions. We start by decomposing an intelligent agent into two components that accomplish the most relevant activities:

- *Knowledge representation* is the "language" that AI systems use to structure, encode, and communicate information about the domain they are modelling. AI systems need it to reason or predict, and we use it to interpret the results they produce. The choice of how to represent knowledge can significantly affect the capabilities and limitations of the AI system.
- *Reasoning* is the cognitive process of analyzing information, applying rules, and drawing conclusions based on evidence or premises. There are various types, such as deductive and inductive reasoning, each serving different purposes in problem-solving and decision-making. AI systems, particularly those combining KGs and LLMs, are increasingly adept at mimicking and even enhancing this fundamental cognitive skill.

Figure 2.1 depicts a high-level architecture of a generic intelligent system. This schema is the mental model for the chapter. It highlights how multiple instances of the two components can coexist in a single intelligent agent; they can interact in sequence and in parallel, and the same knowledge representation can be used for multiple reasoning engines or as a communication pattern among models. The output of one process can be the input for another, creating a cycle of knowledge refinement.

There's often a trade-off between how expressive a knowledge representation is and how efficiently it can be processed. Effective knowledge representation also often depends on the domain and task. Knowledge representation and reasoning are interconnected and influence each other.

One of our central arguments is that KGs serve as fundamental data structures for efficiently representing knowledge, deriving fresh insights, and laying the groundwork for precise and effective reasoning. When used in combination with LLMs, they

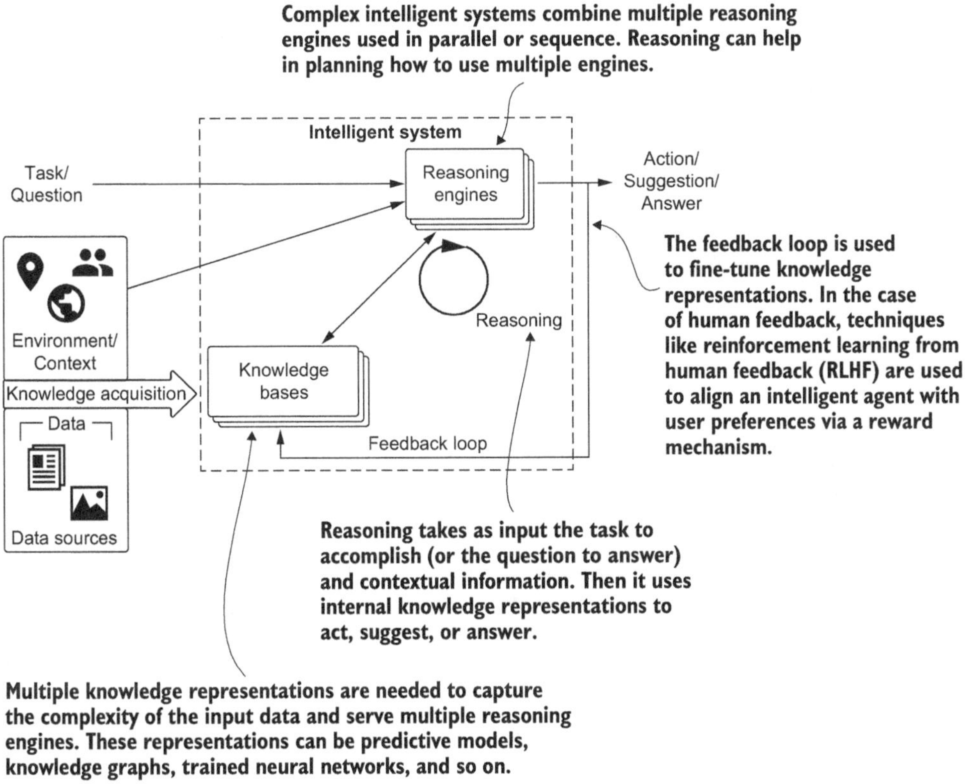

Figure 2.1 A high-level schema of an intelligent system. It is made of two component types: knowledge bases and reasoning engines. Each type can have multiple instances based on the system's tasks.

can improve how data sources are converted into knowledge and facilitate interpreting tasks and providing answers to users.

In this chapter, we will design a basic intelligent system that can do the following:

- Gather and effectively represent knowledge
- Autonomously reason using that knowledge
- Answer questions and support informed decisions

Many concepts discussed here apply broadly to generative AI, but our emphasis is on LLMs.

2.2 Designing an intelligent system

To define an intelligent system, we'll implement a high-level architecture and identify its most critical aspects. To do that, let's consider a concrete task. Suppose you have been tasked to create an autonomous medical diagnostic system that will support doctors in choosing a sequence of actions (e.g., queries, medical tests, therapies) to diagnose diseases and heal patients. We will use this complex scenario to understand the type of system we will build and its structure. Such a system combines global generic knowledge with contextualized information and provides more accurate and specific answers.

To unlock the power of machine learning (ML), we need to build a system of algorithms and tools in which the output of one algorithm is often used as the input of another, or the output of two algorithms is combined. We will examine how approaches that include KGs and LLMs enable practitioners to implement more efficient, explainable, and effective systems.

2.2.1 What is an intelligent system?

We prefer the definition of an intelligent system offered by Geoff Hulten [1]:

> **DEFINITION** *Intelligent systems* connect users to AI and ML to achieve meaningful objectives. An intelligent system is one in which intelligence evolves and improves over time, particularly when it improves by watching how users interact with the system.

This definition emphasizes the pivotal role of the user. The primary objective of the intelligent system is to support users in accomplishing complex tasks—not by replacing them, but by enhancing their decision-making capabilities. For example, an autonomous medical diagnosis system is designed to assist physicians in making informed decisions rather than replace their expertise. This contrasts with other types of intelligent systems, such as self-driving cars, where the aim is to make the machine function independently of the user.

An intelligent system must also have the ability to learn from user interactions and explicit feedback, as well as utilize contextual information. The system should continuously develop, use, and maintain an evolving knowledge base. This evolution is driven not only by data sources but also by ongoing interactions with users. Figure 2.2 provides a high-level overview of an intelligent system (shown as a black box for now) and how it interacts with users and other systems.

2.2.2 Categories of intelligent systems

The distinction between supporting users and acting on their behalf defines two main categories of intelligent systems: intelligent autonomous systems and intelligent advisory systems (IASs) [2]. In an *intelligent autonomous system,* the machine performs tasks independently, effectively replacing the user in decision-making and execution. Key features of autonomous systems include the following:

- *Full automation*—The system operates without human input (or with minimal input), making all decisions based on its programming and sensory data.
- *Real-time decision-making*—The system must analyze data and make decisions in real time.
- *Adaptability*—Autonomous systems often need to adapt to changing environments and unexpected situations.

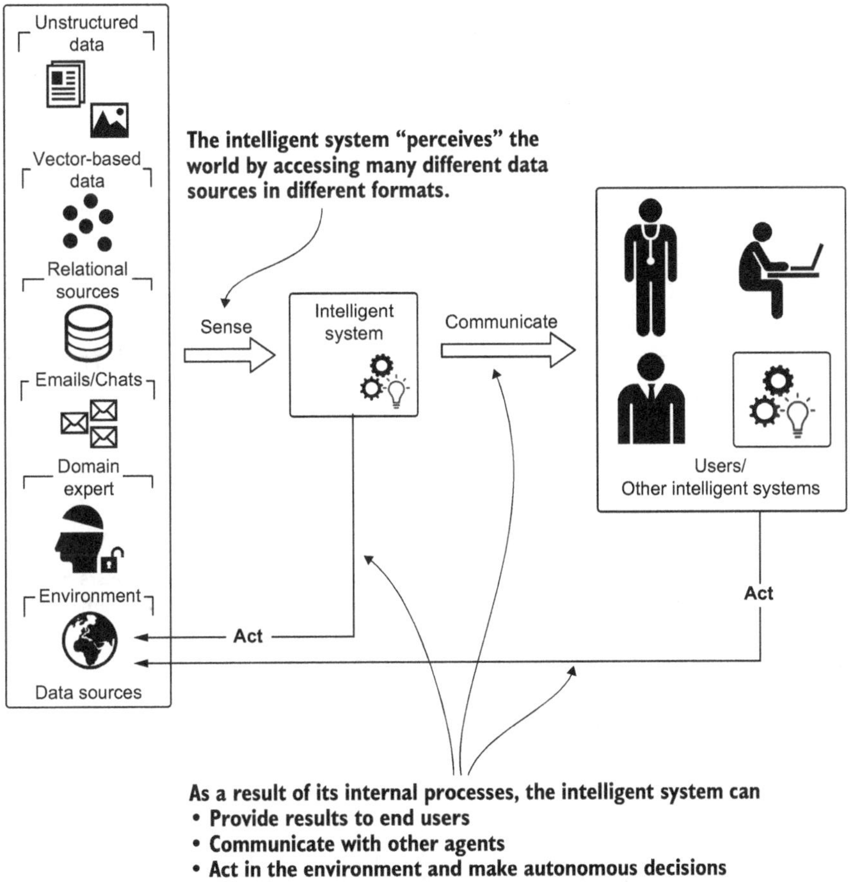

Figure 2.2 An intelligent system and its interactions with other elements. It acquires knowledge by observing the environment and ingesting data from existing sources. Internal processes provide results to the end user.

On the other hand, an *intelligent advisor system's* role is to provide information and recommendations. Key features of advisor systems include the following:

- *Decision support*—The system provides insights, suggestions, and recommendations to help users make informed choices, but it does not execute actions on its own.
- *Context awareness*—The system uses contextual information, such as user preferences or specific scenarios, to tailor its advice to the situation at hand.
- *User interaction*—These systems are designed for easy interaction, allowing users to explore options, ask questions, and receive detailed explanations to aid their decision-making.

Figure 2.3 illustrates the differences between these two types of intelligent systems.

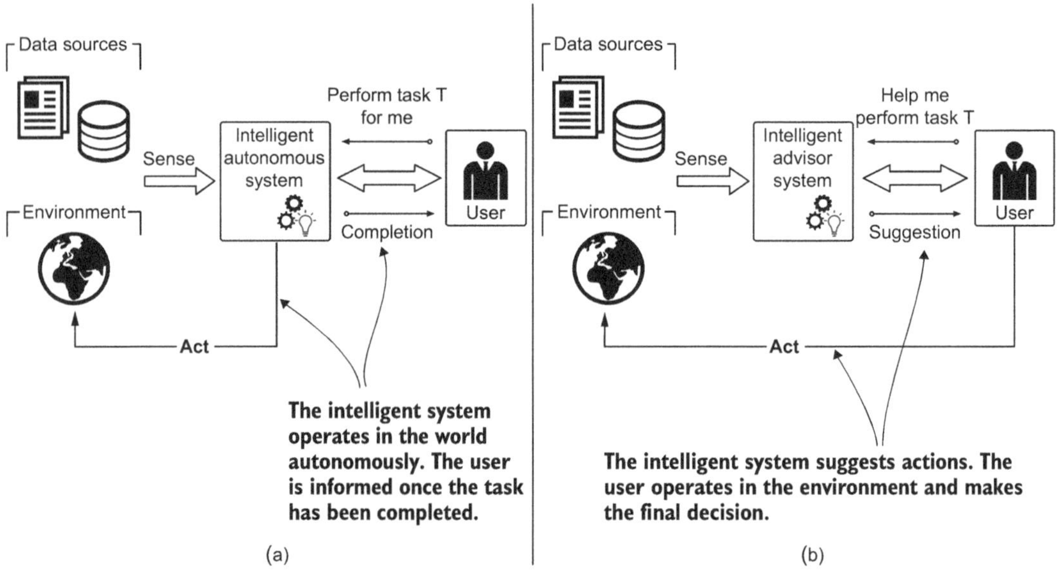

Figure 2.3 Differences between (a) an intelligent autonomous system and (b) an intelligent advisor system. The first acts on behalf of users, whereas the second only makes suggestions. In both cases, the intelligent system supports or helps the end user; it is not meant to replace the user.

We focus primarily on IASs, as their features align closely with the strengths of KGs that we have outlined previously: enhanced decision support, deep context awareness, and an interactive user experience. IASs allow us to fully exploit the capabilities of KGs, providing users with more powerful and effective decision-support tools. Examples of IASs can be found in various fields:

- In law enforcement, predictive policing systems analyze crime data to identify potential hotspots or forecast where crimes are likely to occur.
- In financial services, IASs analyze transaction patterns, flagging suspicious activities that could indicate fraud.
- In biomedical scenarios, these systems can provide a list of potential diagnoses and recommend treatment options based on available data.

It's important to note that in all these cases, although the systems offer valuable insights, the humans—using them—make the final decisions about what actions to take.

2.2.3 Characteristics of an intelligent system

An intelligent system must include four key characteristics that should drive both design and implementation:

- *A meaningful objective*—The system should exist for a specific, achievable purpose that is meaningful to end users. This objective must drive the entire development process.
- *The intelligent experience*—The system must present intelligent outputs to users in ways that achieve desired outcomes. This requires interfaces that adapt based on predictions, maximize value when intelligence is correct, and minimize costs when mistakes occur. The interface must also facilitate implicit and explicit user feedback.
- *Knowledge creation and update*—Intelligent behavior requires the capability to build, maintain, and reason with knowledge continuously. Combining LLMs and KGs enables proper handling of evolving knowledge and user feedback.
- *Orchestration*—Intelligent systems involve multiple algorithms and tools working together, with the output of one becoming input for another. This includes managing how the system acquires knowledge from sources, controls risk, and maintains quality throughout its lifecycle.

Continuing our design process, we need to consider key aspects that drive our architectural decisions:

- *Focus on autonomous advisor systems.* Our intelligent system should suggest actions rather than accomplish actions on behalf of users.
- *Use an established knowledge base.* This includes research papers, existing ontologies, and structured data sources rather than generic knowledge. The system shouldn't provide generic answers but should use domain-specific understanding refined by experts.
- *Learn from experience.* The system should extend its knowledge base using feedback from the results of suggested actions.

We now have all the elements to design our intelligent system, as summarized in figure 2.4. The next two sections focus on the key processes of an intelligent system:

- *Knowledge acquisition*—Collecting information from data sources, the environment, or domain experts
- *Reasoning*—Converting acquired knowledge into actionable expertise

Through these processes, we'll explain how intelligent system elements interact and compare how KGs and LLMs store, process, and use data.

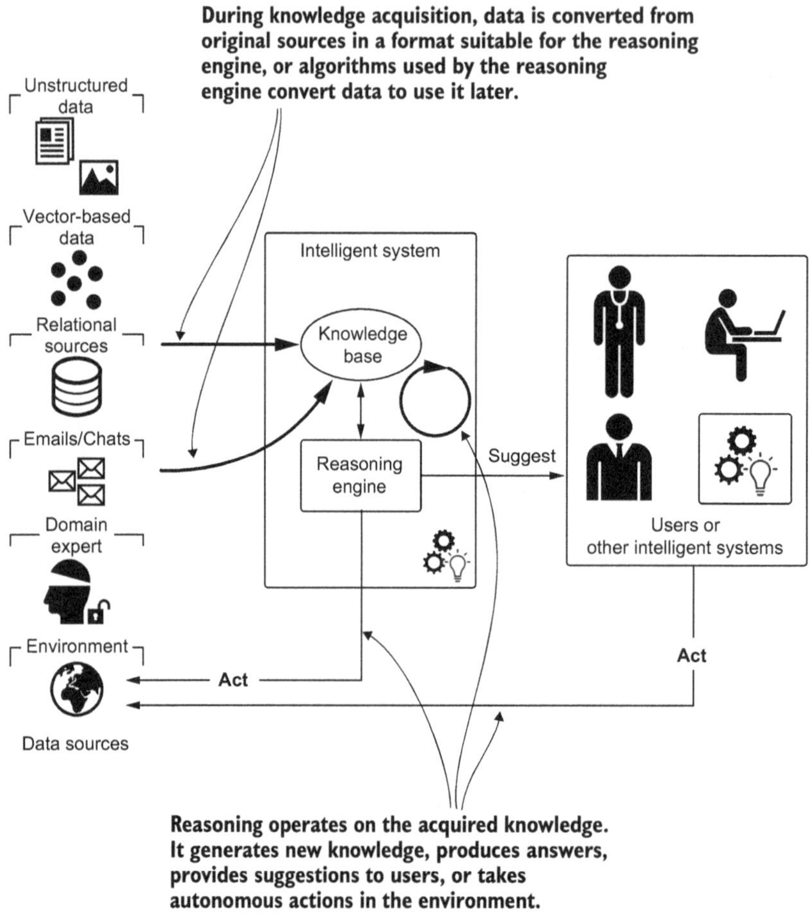

Figure 2.4 Extended model of an intelligent system. The focus is on the core components (the knowledge base and the reasoning engine) and the core processes (knowledge acquisition and reasoning).

2.3 Knowledge acquisition and representation

Knowledge acquisition enables the IAS to "learn" from existing data available within the domain where the system will be deployed, from user feedback, and from the environment. This process converts raw data into structured knowledge representations that are tailored to the system's requirements and used during the reasoning phase. The result is stored in one or more knowledge bases. How knowledge is acquired, represented, and stored depends on the underlying reasoning mechanisms, which is where LLMs and KGs diverge significantly. Figure 2.5 shows the components of our mental model covered in this section.

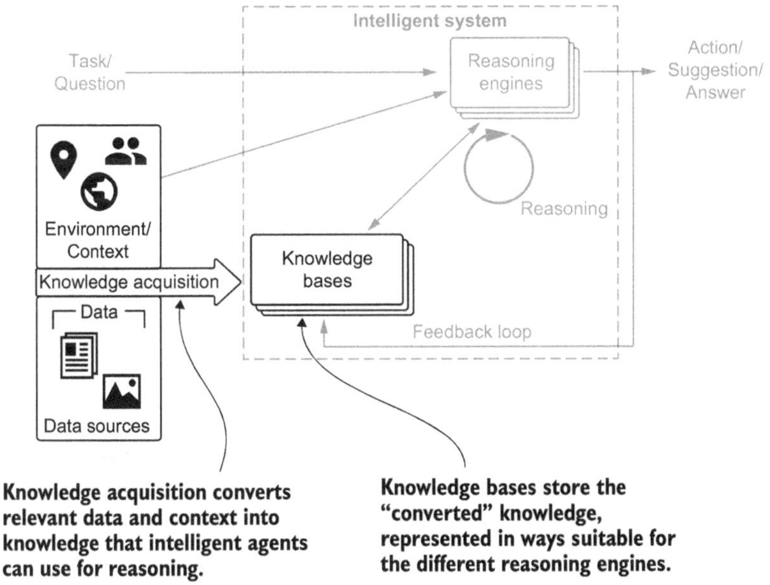

Figure 2.5 In this section, we focus on the knowledge acquisition part of our mental model. It allows the intelligent system to acquire data and convert it into knowledge.

For KGs, knowledge acquisition typically involves transforming raw, structured, or semistructured data into a graph-based format, where entities are represented as nodes and their relationships are captured as edges. The structure and semantics of the domain—defined by ontologies or schemas—are essential in guiding this transformation. The process often involves a domain expert to better understand the semantics of the data and the intrinsic relationships among entities. Converting heterogeneous data sources into a unified, explicit schema demands meticulous work to ensure that the resulting KG accurately reflects the domain it represents. However, this preparation pays off in terms of flexibility.

In contrast, LLMs acquire knowledge by ingesting vast amounts of unstructured text data, which is encoded into dense, high-dimensional vector spaces during training. Unlike KGs, LLMs do not require extensive data preparation (considering the enormous amount of data), and the process is mostly unsupervised; the main effort consists of selecting the data sources and cleaning them. Information is encoded as statistical patterns rather than as explicit relationships defined by schemas. This implicit approach allows LLMs to grasp subtle contextual meanings and complex linguistic relationships, but makes the knowledge opaque and difficult to inspect or modify.

Figures 2.6 and 2.7 compare the acquisition process for KGs and LLMs, respectively. There are clear differences in terms of model complexity and the role of domain experts.

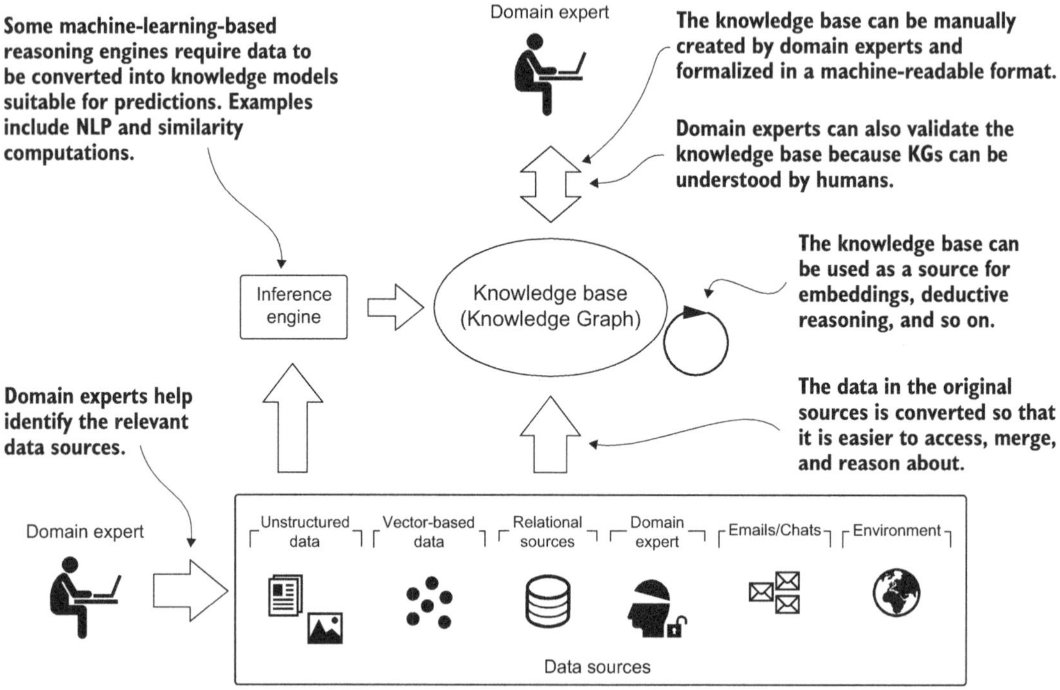

Figure 2.6 Knowledge acquisition for KGs: converting available data into an explicit knowledge representation through structured entities, relationships, and properties. This process involves a domain expert who identifies relevant data sources, supports the data model, and evaluates the results.

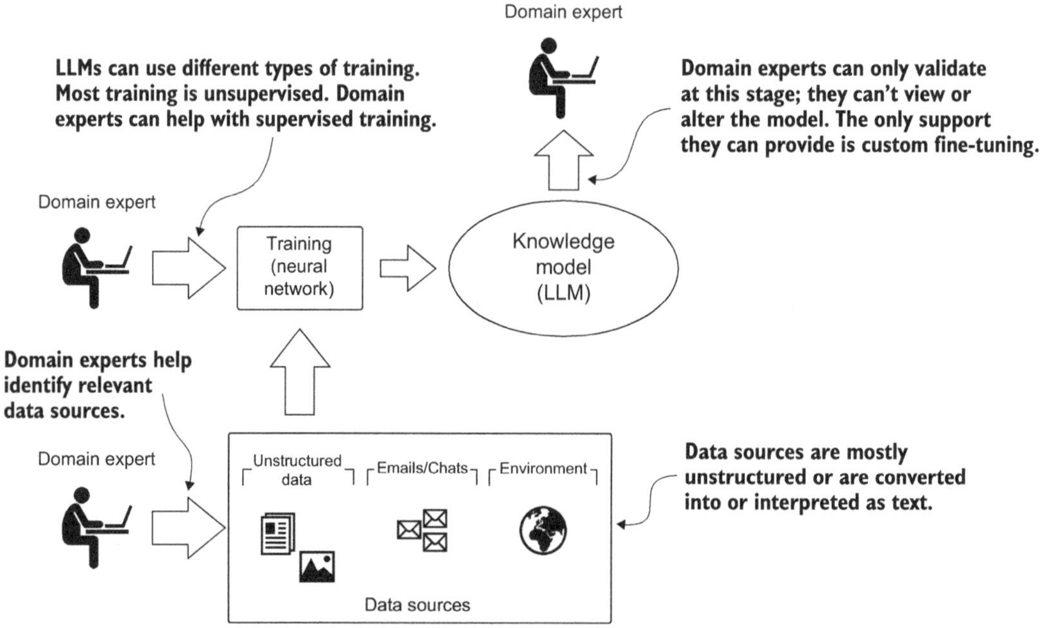

Figure 2.7 Knowledge acquisition for LLMs: converting text data into an implicit knowledge representation through statistical parameters. Domain experts are involved during data source selection and result evaluation.

A few key differences must be considered when designing systems that use both technologies:

- *Access*—LLMs store knowledge through implicit representation using billions of parameters in continuous vector spaces, making it opaque and inaccessible to humans. KGs use explicit knowledge representation through nodes, relationships, and properties that are directly interpretable by both humans and machines.
- *Updates*—Updating a KG involves adding, removing, or modifying nodes and relationships. Updating an LLM is far more complex, requiring retraining or fine-tuning the model.
- *Capabilities*—LLMs are inherently adept at understanding and generating human language. KGs depend heavily on how developers design their access patterns and domain schemas.

Although there are clear advantages and limitations to each method of knowledge acquisition and representation, these differences are also complementary. A *hybrid approach* to the development of intelligent systems can overcome the limitations of both, and they can empower each other by offering solutions for a wider set of tasks. This new paradigm embraces a broader spectrum of computational tasks and uses diverse forms of knowledge representations, from structured data models to numerical parameters. In this era, reasoning is no longer confined to formal inference mechanisms but also includes probabilistic, contextual, and pattern-based computations that LLMs excel at. This shift allows AI systems to reason with explicit, structured knowledge (as in traditional expert systems) and, at the same time, unstructured, ambiguous, and contextual knowledge derived from language and experience.

2.4 Reasoning

In an IAS, the reasoning engine delivers insights and suggestions. The user provides input by formulating a request that contains the desired goals and further information required. Figure 2.8 shows the reasoning component in our mental model.

We must consider some important open questions:

- *How do we deal with uncertainty?* Not all the information we have is true, accurate, or unequivocal. Reasoning accuracy depends on the certainty of the initial statements.
- *How can we infer some of the knowledge we need?* Under some circumstances, we can derive new information from the available data.
- *How can we abstract from what we have seen to a broader understanding of the domain?*

We'll describe the learning process with an example taken from Alessandro Negro's book, *Graph-Powered Machine Learning* [3]. Consider the implementation of a spam filter for email. A pure programming solution is to write a program that memorizes all emails labeled as spam by a human user and stores the result in a knowledge base. When a new email arrives, the pseudo-agent searches for a match in the knowledge base. If a match is found, the new email is rerouted to the spam folder. Otherwise, the

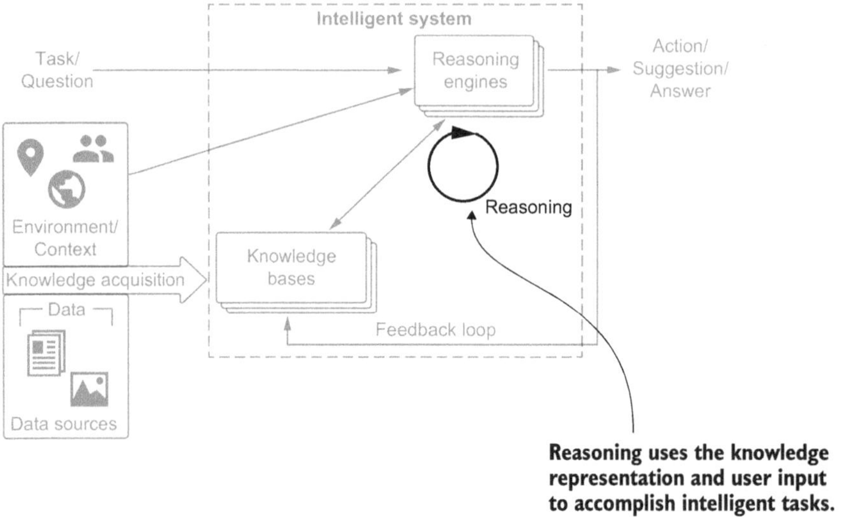

Figure 2.8 Reasoning uses the knowledge base(s) to accomplish the tasks that the intelligent system is designed to do for end users.

email passes through the filter untouched. This approach can work and, in some scenarios, can be useful. But it is not a proper learning process because it lacks the ability to generalize and to transform individual examples into a broader model. In this specific use case, this means the ability to label unseen emails even though they are not the same as the previously labeled emails. This process is also referred to as *inductive reasoning* or *inductive inference.*

Deductive and inductive reasoning

Deductive reasoning is a basic form of reasoning. It begins with a general statement or hypothesis and examines the possibilities to reach a specific, logical conclusion. For example, consider the reasoning: "All men are mortal. Alessandro is a man. Therefore, Alessandro is mortal." With deductive reasoning, the hypothesis must be correct. It is assumed that the premises, "All men are mortal" and "Alessandro is a man," are true. Therefore, the conclusion is logical and true.

Inductive reasoning makes broad generalizations from specific observations. It starts with data that includes samples of reality and then draws conclusions. For example, "The coin I pulled from the bag is a penny. The second and the third coins from the bag are pennies. Therefore, all the coins in the bag are pennies." Note that even if all the premises are true in the original statement, inductive reasoning can lead to false conclusions. Here's an example: "Harold is a grandfather. Harold is bald. Therefore, all grandfathers are bald." In this case, the conclusion does not follow logically from the statements.

Because ChatGPT and similar tools can mimic human conversation, people often think that they possess extensive reasoning capabilities. Let's look at a quick example. We used Claude.ai (https://claude.ai), which offers one of the best "reasoning" tools powered by LLMs, to verify our assumptions.

> **NOTE** The version of Claude.ai we tested is 3.5 Sonnet. Considering the speed of improvements, we're pretty sure that by the time this book is printed, running the same experiment will generate a different result.

We used the following prompt.

Listing 2.1 Prompt for checking reasoning capabilities

```
A farmer stands at the side of the river with a sheep. There is a boat with
enough room for one person and one animal. How can the farmer get himself and
the sheep to the other side of the river using the boat in the smallest
number of trips?
```

We selected this example because it is a simpler version of a well-known problem (which includes a wolf and a head of lettuce in addition to the farmer and the sheep), and we are confident that the training data used to train the LLM included many similar examples. So, we expect the probabilistic reasoning engine to go in the direction of the full problem instead of "understanding" what we asked for. The answer confirmed our assumption. Figure 2.9 is a snapshot of the results from Claude.ai.

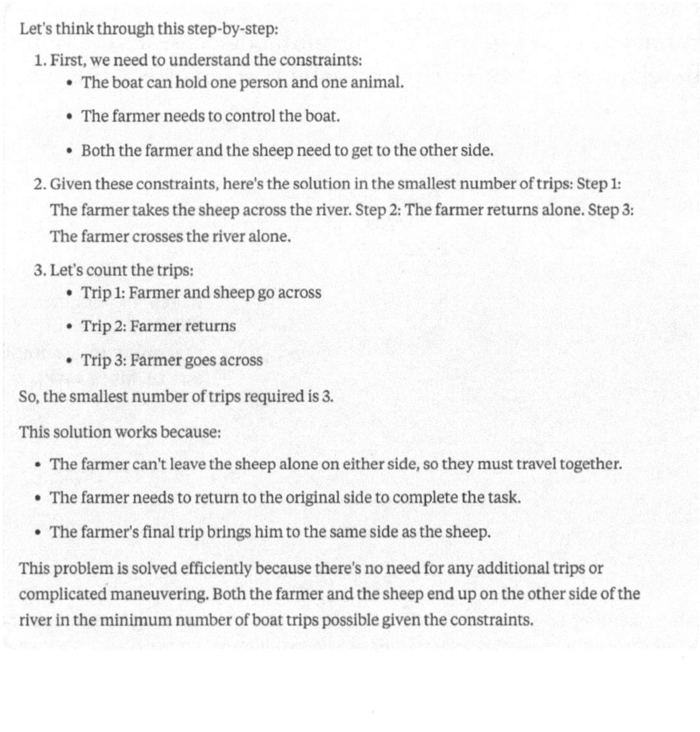
Let's think through this step-by-step:

1. First, we need to understand the constraints:
   - The boat can hold one person and one animal.
   - The farmer needs to control the boat.
   - Both the farmer and the sheep need to get to the other side.
2. Given these constraints, here's the solution in the smallest number of trips: Step 1: The farmer takes the sheep across the river. Step 2: The farmer returns alone. Step 3: The farmer crosses the river alone.
3. Let's count the trips:
   - Trip 1: Farmer and sheep go across
   - Trip 2: Farmer returns
   - Trip 3: Farmer goes across

So, the smallest number of trips required is 3.

This solution works because:

- The farmer can't leave the sheep alone on either side, so they must travel together.
- The farmer needs to return to the original side to complete the task.
- The farmer's final trip brings him to the same side as the sheep.

This problem is solved efficiently because there's no need for any additional trips or complicated maneuvering. Both the farmer and the sheep end up on the other side of the river in the minimum number of boat trips possible given the constraints.

Figure 2.9 Result from Claude.ai when we prompted it with the contents of listing 2.1

The answer contains some reasoning issues: there is no sense in the farmer going back and forth without sheep. The problem was solved completely after step 1, but because the problem formulation is very similar to (but not the same as) one from the data sources used during Claude.ai's training, the proposed solution is "probabilistically" the closest.

This example illustrates the limitations of LLMs in certain types of reasoning. Wu et al. [4] tested a suite of 11 different tasks: coding to drawing, logic to spatial, and chess to arithmetic. They observed interesting performance with counterfactual variants—as they deviated from the default or well-known tasks—like the farmer and the sheep without wolf and lettuce, but they found that performance substantially and consistently degraded compared to the default conditions. Although current LLMs possess some abstract task-solving skills, they often rely on narrow, nontransferable procedures.

Thus, as we said earlier, KGs and LLMs can be the foundation for different types of reasoning, complementing each other in intelligent systems. We can use KGs for tasks that require precise, rule-based reasoning and explicit knowledge representation, and LLMs for tasks involving pattern recognition, context understanding, handling ambiguity or incomplete information, and reasoning about graph structures and their derived metrics. However, neither approach inherently possesses common-sense reasoning capabilities comparable to those of humans, and they often fail to make intuitive leaps or understand the implicit context that would be obvious to a person. These limitations underscore the importance of carefully considering the strengths and weaknesses of each approach when designing intelligent systems and potentially developing a powerful hybrid IAS.

2.5 Reasoning engines

Let's extend our framework to explore how the knowledge base and reasoning engine interact in the development of an intelligent system (see figure 2.10). The depicted

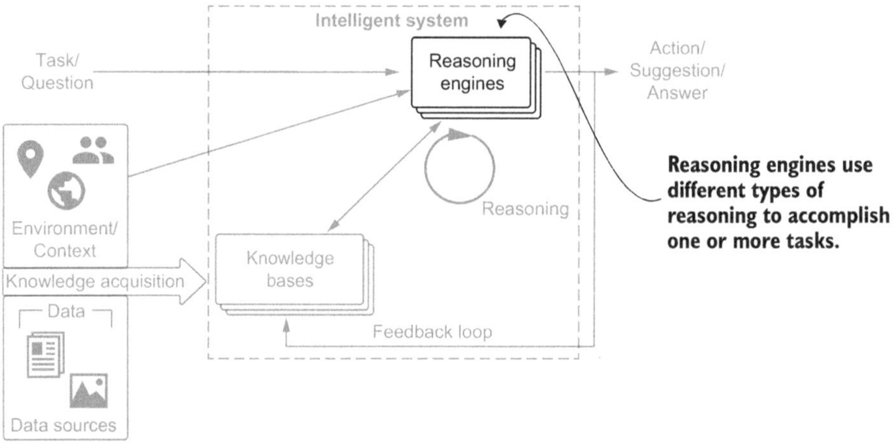

Figure 2.10 Multiple reasoning engines, each with different types of reasoning strategies, can contribute to delivering the tasks required to implement the intelligent system.

reasoning engine is generic; it can use a single type of reasoning—deductive, inductive, or otherwise—or a combination of reasoning strategies. Importantly, this engine not only reads from the knowledge base but also writes back to it. The actions (or suggestions) generated by the engine influence the environment, which in turn produces new observations. These observations are processed by the reasoning engine to build new knowledge, driving subsequent actions or suggestions. This feedback loop creates an iterative process, where the system continuously improves its ability to respond to environmental changes.

2.5.1 Limitations of a pure deductive reasoning engine

Let's look at an example of applying the deductive reasoning process in the context of automated medical diagnosis. Imagine a patient visiting a virtual doctor: our intelligent system. The system must propose a series of actions (e.g., medical tests, treatments, queries) to diagnose the illness and suggest a course of therapy.

This sequence of actions is computed using the knowledge base, which contains information about the costs and outcomes of potential actions, probabilistic relationships between diseases and symptoms, and the patient's preferences. The deductive reasoner can logically infer optimal actions when the knowledge base encodes all necessary data. In this idealized scenario, the deductive reasoner can outperform other reasoning methods.

However, a major limitation of deductive reasoning is that it requires a highly complete and accurate knowledge base, which is rarely available. In figure 2.11, the knowledge base is constructed by transforming data sources into logical statements that guide decision-making.

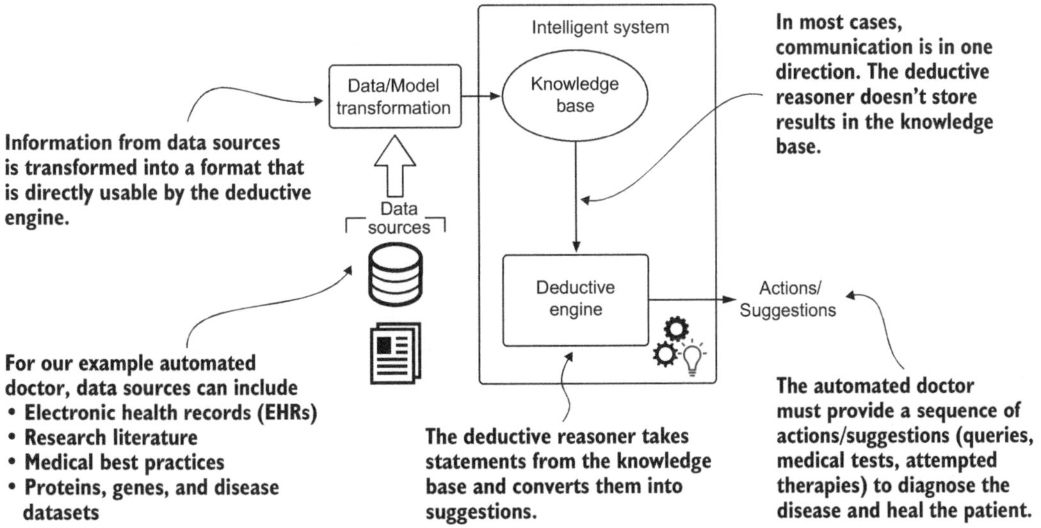

Figure 2.11 The deductive reasoner. The knowledge base is created by transforming data sources. The deductive reasoner uses logical statements applied to segments of the knowledge base to act or to provide suggestions.

2.5.2 Using inductive reasoning and ML

Inductive reasoning, powered by ML, addresses some of the limitations of purely deductive reasoning. Inductive reasoning can enhance the system in two key ways:

- By learning and building relevant ontologies and relationships, ML expands the knowledge base, enabling it to handle a broader range of cases.
- By providing inference under uncertainty, ML allows the system to generalize from incomplete data and make predictions even when not all information is available.

Figure 2.12 shows how an inductive reasoner works. The first step transforms raw data into a structured format, often with the help of ML algorithms. For example, natural language processing (NLP), powered by LLMs, converts unstructured text into structured data that can be incorporated into the knowledge base. This step can contribute to the creation or extension of a KG. The second step uses this knowledge to make

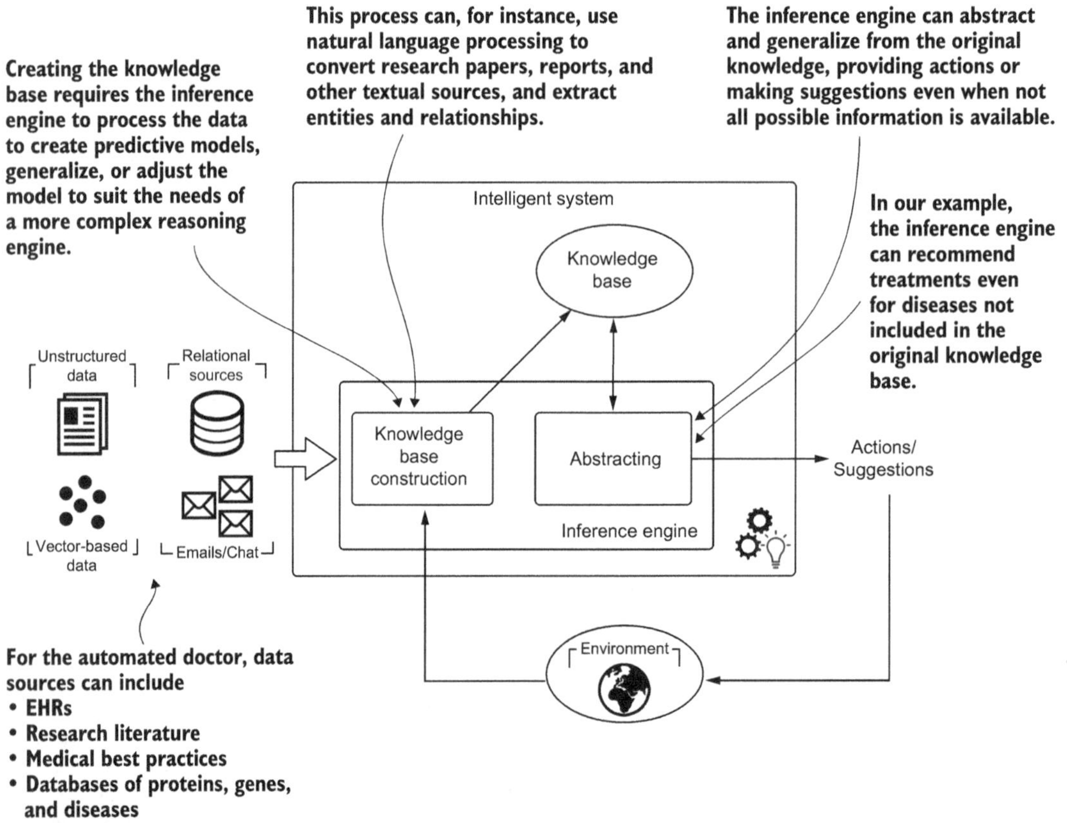

Figure 2.12 An inductive reasoner. Constructing the knowledge base requires more effort; it is not a simple transformation. This reasoning engine can abstract from the knowledge base and work under some level of uncertainty.

predictions or generate actions through inductive reasoning, which abstracts patterns from available observations.

In traditional ML approaches, this process often requires manually selecting features from the knowledge base to train prediction models. This can be a tedious and sometimes infeasible task, especially in complex domains.

2.5.3 The role of LLMs in the reasoning engine

Unlike purely deductive systems that require complete knowledge bases and explicit rules, LLMs can use their probabilistic reasoning capabilities to generate contextually relevant suggestions even when critical information is missing. Consider a medical scenario where a patient presents with nonspecific symptoms that could indicate anything from stress to serious neurological conditions. Traditional deductive reasoning would struggle with such an ambiguous presentation, especially when patient records are incomplete. An LLM, however, can draw on patterns learned from vast medical literature to evaluate multiple diagnostic possibilities simultaneously. The LLM's strength lies in its ability to reason probabilistically with uncertainty. It can weigh the likelihood of different conditions based on available data and, rather than providing a single definitive answer, recommend a prioritized diagnostic approach.

This probabilistic reasoning capability enables LLMs to bridge knowledge gaps that would halt a purely deductive reasoning process. When integrated with KG-based reasoning engines, an LLM acts as a reasoning layer that can interpret ambiguous inputs and provide nuanced recommendations that account for the inherent uncertainty in complex decision-making scenarios. This hybrid approach enables IASs to function effectively in real-world environments where information is often incomplete or uncertain.

2.6 A KG approach to IASs

Where do KGs fit in the development of IASs? The short answer is, *everywhere.* In recent years, academia and industry have used KGs extensively as a form of structured human knowledge [5–8]. In addition to this graph-based representation, several reasoning and analysis algorithms have been devised to derive insights from KGs.

The idea of using a graph to support decision-making processes is not new. Stokman and de Vries [9] anticipated that with knowledge-based systems, it would be possible to construct computer programs that advise professional users with a limited domain of expertise. In this context, they speculated that "The structuring of knowledge in a graph can be seen as the construction of a knowledge-based system integrating knowledge from different sources" [9].

In recent years, KGs have become a standard approach to merge distributed data sources into a single connected source of truth [10]. And with the advent of generative AI and LLMs, KGs can mitigate hallucinations and provide up-to-date data, among other benefits [11].

But simply viewing KGs as aggregators of knowledge overlooks the goal for which they were introduced: building intelligent systems. We consider this a *bottom-up approach* to KG construction. It begins with data from various sources, consolidates that data into a single source of truth, and then initiates the discovery process. It expects the data to tell a story without any idea of what the end user is looking for. Figure 2.13 summarizes this approach.

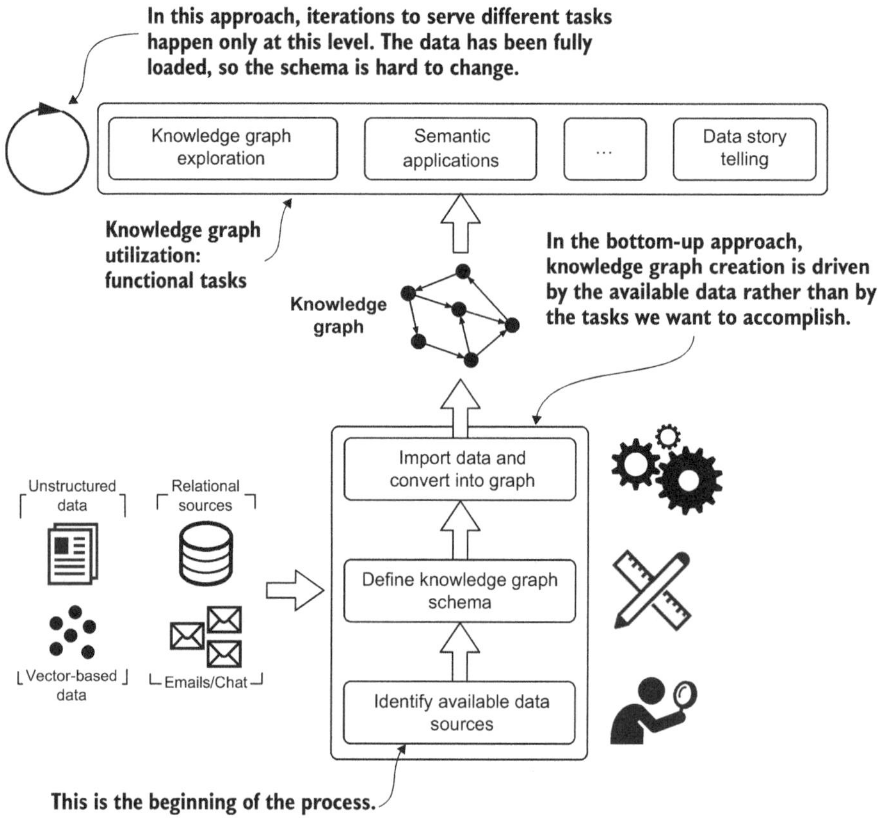

Figure 2.13 A bottom-up approach to KG creation. It begins with importing all the data, rather than first considering the functional tasks we want to achieve.

Our experience is that this bottom-up approach often leads to the failure of KG adoption. There are too many data sources, each with different structures and identifiers, and significant effort is required to normalize the data into a single homogeneous structure. Much of the content is task-specific and therefore not relevant to global thinking.

Developing intelligent agents requires us to represent knowledge (in our case, as a KG) in a way that is effective and capable of capturing and handling the intrinsic complexity of the domain in which the agent must operate. This approach should be driven by business objectives rather than by available data. Building on established ML project methodologies, CRISP-DM [12], we can use a purpose-driven approach for

KG construction. Figure 2.14 illustrates how a KG serves as the central knowledge representation in this process.

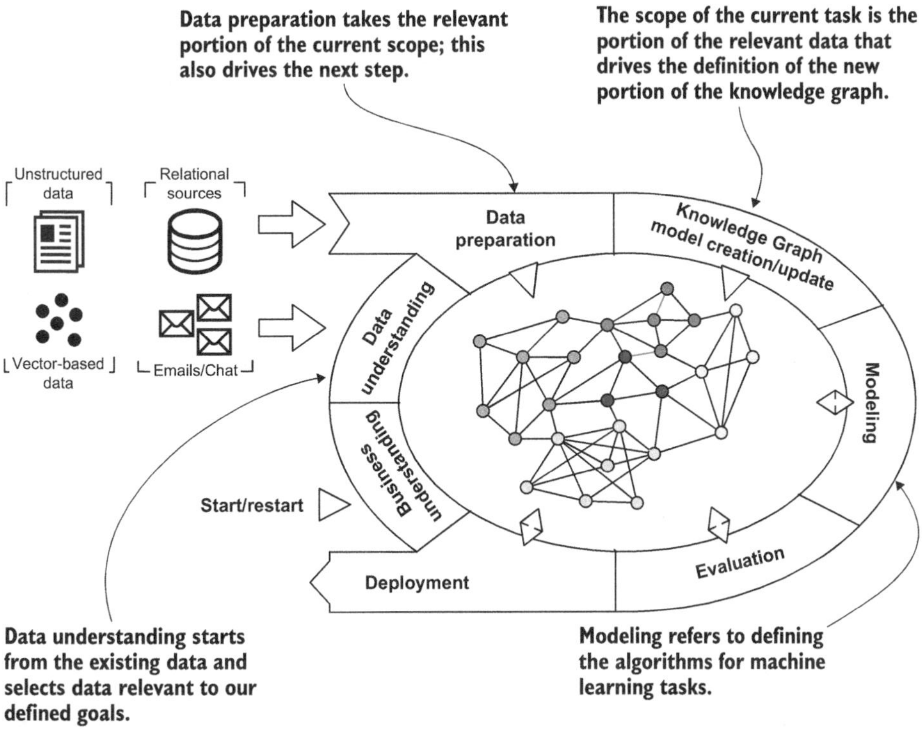

Figure 2.14 CRISP-DM revisited, applied to KG platforms. The KG is used as a model of the knowledge base for the intelligent system. It is the center of the revisited CRISP-DM process.

This approach emphasizes that everything starts from the business understanding. These goals drive the data understanding, allowing us to focus on the specific portion of the data we need rather than blindly importing all available data sources. This determines the requirements for defining the content and structure of the KG. In this context, the KG represents a self-sufficient, domain-specific, customizable source of truth that copies and transforms the data we need. During acquisition, LLMs extract relevant entities and relationships from unstructured data and provide generic understanding, such as sentiment analysis or topic identification.

In the modeling phase, we use and test one or more algorithms to reach specific goals; in the next phase, the results are evaluated. LLMs can be involved in reasoning on top of KGs to understand users' questions and provide answers in natural language. The output of these two phases is composed of a set of algorithms, a set of trained or pretrained models, and a report describing the tests and the overall quality of the trained models.

If everything goes well, we incorporate the graph schema and model, the pipelines for ingestion and post-processing, the algorithms, and the predictive models into a product and then deploy. Then a new round can start—but this time we do not start from an empty KG.

DEFINITION A *predictive model* is a formula for estimating an unknown value of interest: the *target*. It represents in an efficient format the result of the learning process on the training dataset, and we access it to perform the actual prediction.

In the second round, we work by difference and extension, ensuring that the results of the previous iteration are not affected. The schemaless approach for the graph allows for extensions with new nodes and relationship types, without compromising previous data and functionalities.

DEFINITION *Schemaless* refers to the flexibility of storing data in a database or a generic data structure with fewer (or no) constraints on how data items are formatted and related to each other. Graph databases are generally considered schemaless because their elements (nodes and relationships) and attributes can store practically everything.

In the book, we frequently use schemas to drive the process between scenarios and use cases. These schemas are repurposed, and the different phases are highlighted as examples of how this process works in practice.

Summary

- Intelligence is fundamentally about acquiring and applying knowledge, making knowledge representation and reasoning the core components of intelligent system architecture.
- Intelligent systems are categorized as either autonomous systems that act independently or advisory systems that support human decision-making.
- Knowledge acquisition differs between KGs and LLMs: KGs use explicit, structured representations requiring domain expertise but offering interpretability, whereas LLMs use implicit statistical patterns that capture language understanding but lack transparency.
- Hybrid systems combining KGs and LLMs use their complementary strengths: KGs provide structured reasoning and explicit knowledge, and LLMs handle ambiguity, context, and natural language understanding.
- LLMs enhance reasoning engines by bridging knowledge gaps and providing contextual interpretation, making intelligent systems more robust with incomplete or ambiguous information.
- Purpose-driven KG development starting from business objectives is more effective than bottom-up data integration strategies, which often lead to project failure.

Part 2

Building knowledge graphs from structured data sources

This part of the book addresses the complex but essential process of constructing KGs from disparate structured data sources—a fundamental step before enriching them with unstructured information and combining them with large language models (LLMs). Organizations maintain vast repositories of data, each with its own schema, structure, and storage format. The challenge is harmonizing this data into a coherent KG while preserving its semantic meaning and relationships. We'll guide you through this process, demonstrating how to transform diverse structured data sources into a unified knowledge representation.

A key theme is the importance of data quality and validation, because the quality of downstream applications depends on the reliability of the underlying knowledge representation. You'll learn how to verify data integrity, ensure accurate entity matching, and validate the semantic correctness of KGs.

Chapter 3 presents a healthcare example, constructing a KG that helps clinicians diagnose rare diseases based on patient symptoms. It introduces fundamental concepts like semantic integration through ontologies, compares KG technologies, and provides hands-on implementation guidance.

Chapter 4 explores the progression from simple networks to comprehensive multisource integration across biomedical applications. It demonstrates advanced analysis methodologies, including community detection algorithms and domain-specific metrics, and it introduces the integration of large language models for result interpretation and decision support.

The examples in these chapters demonstrate the technical aspects of KG construction and also illustrate how these principles can be applied to solve real-world problems in any domain.

3 Create your first knowledge graph from ontologies

This chapter covers

- Selecting the best KG technology based on use cases
- Constructing a KG to support clinicians' activities
- Performing analysis and ontology-based reasoning on top of a KG

KG construction is complex due to the need to extract and integrate information from data sources that differ in format (XML, CSV, JSON), storage technology (relational or document-oriented), information syntax (e.g., 2022-08-09 or 9 August 2022), and especially the meaning of the data. In healthcare, for instance, varied expressions that identify the same concept (type 2 diabetes versus ketosis-resistant diabetes), identical acronyms that define distinct concepts (PE as physical examination or pulmonary embolism), and information granularity (necrosis or lobular necrosis) are obstacles to data integration.

When constructing a KG, we aim for a unified, well-grounded, and meaningful representation of data from various sources, where individual pieces of information are integrated into a coherent view. Issues related to the meaning of data can be addressed using semantic integration. A common strategy is to adopt one or more ontologies as a reference schema and vocabulary for incoming data. An *ontology* lets you model data using a standard vocabulary that includes elements such as formal names, properties, categories, and relationships between entities described within the data.

The ontology acts as an intermediary between semantically heterogeneous information. A *mapping* bridges a data source's local schema to the ontology's reference schema. We can map each data element to concepts expressed by the ontology; these annotations bring together data elements from different origins.

This chapter offers guidelines for building a KG using a reference ontology, focusing on helping clinicians identify rare diseases. We highlight data understanding and preparation, ingesting and processing the Human Phenotype Ontology (HPO; https://hpo.jax.org/app/) and an HPO-annotated dataset. The HPO source provides information about the connections between diseases and their associated phenotypic abnormalities. These abnormalities represent observable physical or biochemical characteristics that deviate from typical human traits and may result from genetic mutations, environmental influences, or a combination of both. We also explore the differences among KG technologies and offer a blueprint for selecting the most suitable option. Finally, we outline a set of analyses, including ontology-based reasoning, to support clinicians in diagnosing rare diseases.

Figure 3.1 provides a mental model for this chapter. The center shows the steps to create a KG in our example context, and the bottom illustrates an abstract pipeline

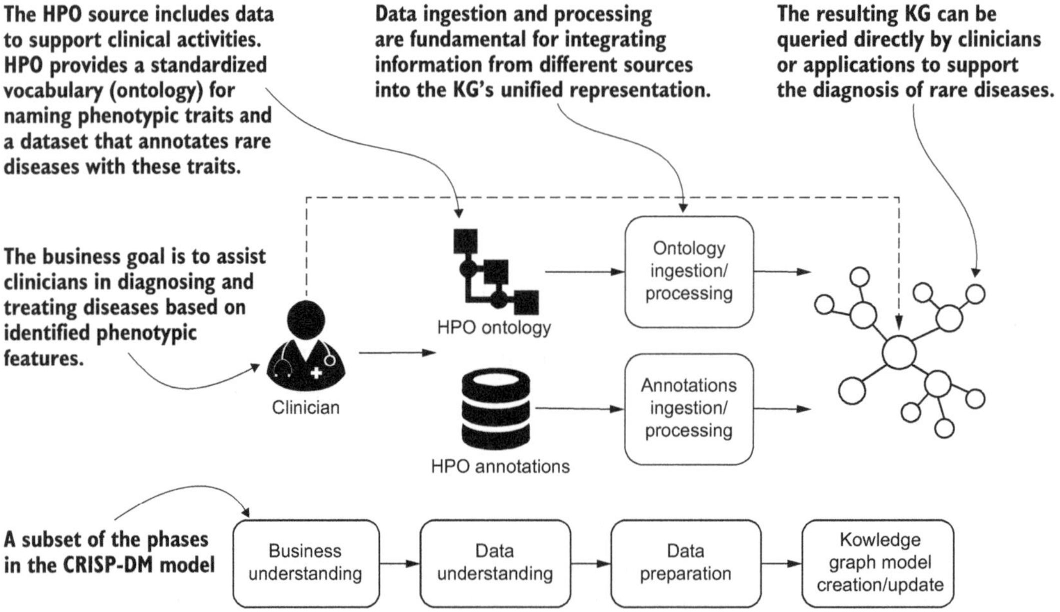

Figure 3.1 Mental model of the KG construction process as a specification of the CRISP-DM model, from understanding the business goal to defining the KG queries that support clinicians' activities

for constructing a KG that can be used in different scenarios. The components of this pipeline come from a version of the CRISP-DM model introduced in chapter 2 (and shown again in figure 3.2).

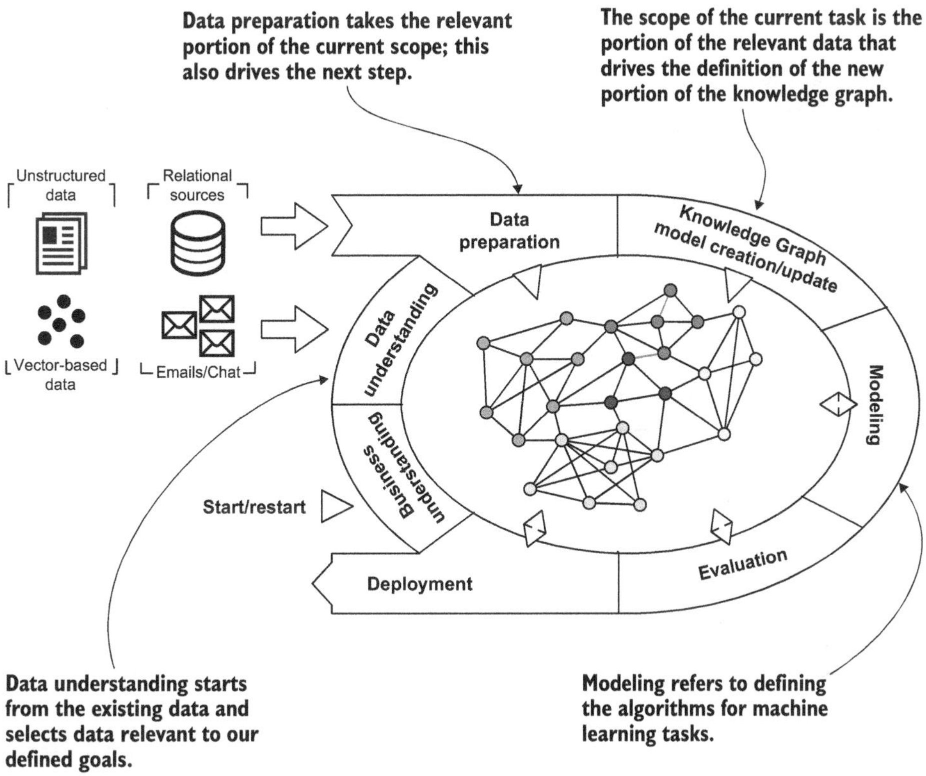

Figure 3.2 The CRISP-DM model adapted to KGs. A subset of these components, including business understanding, data understanding, data preparation, and KG model creation/update, are key phases described in this chapter.

3.1 Knowledge graph building: Warmup

Before creating a KG, we'll analyze the problem we want to solve, build an overview of the application domain, and scout for data.

3.1.1 Business and domain understanding

The target persona of our KG is the clinician: a healthcare professional who diagnoses and treats diseases. One of the clinician's most complex activities is correctly identifying a disease based on symptoms (phenotypic traits), particularly in the case of rare syndromes (see figure 3.3).

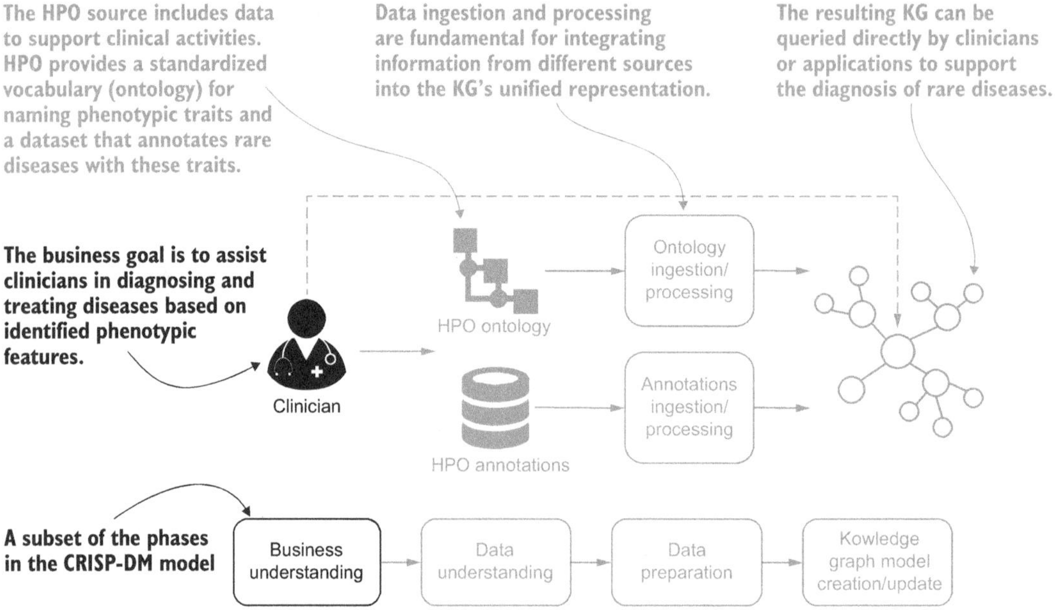

Figure 3.3 Understanding the business domain for creating a KG that supports clinicians' activities. This phase is not strictly related to the technical aspects, but it is fundamental for the next steps.

In addition to prescribing specific tests to reach a diagnosis, the clinician can use a structured knowledge base of available information. It should have these two features:

- *A contextual description of the phenotype domain*—For instance, phenotypic anomalies related to the same organs or systems should be explicitly connected.
- *Data describing the relationship between phenotypic anomalies and diseases.* This information must be tracked so clinicians can access the sources of the connections.

We want to build a KG that incorporates these features. To better understand the application domain, here are some definitions.

DEFINITION The *phenotype* of an individual with a disease can be said to be the sum of all of the phenotypic features manifested by that individual [1].

DEFINITION A *disease* is an entity characterized by (1) a set of causes for a specific condition, (2) a time course, (3) a group of phenotypic features, and (4) characteristic response to a particular treatment.

For example, the common cold is characterized by distinct phenotypic features, including fever and fatigue. The time course ranges from a couple of days to a week, and treatments such as aspirin can support healing.

But the clinician's work also involves gray areas. For instance, diabetes mellitus can be classified as a disease or as a phenotypic characteristic of other rare syndromes (see figure 3.4). We'll work on this use case as an example of how we can help clinicians handle this kind of uncertainty.

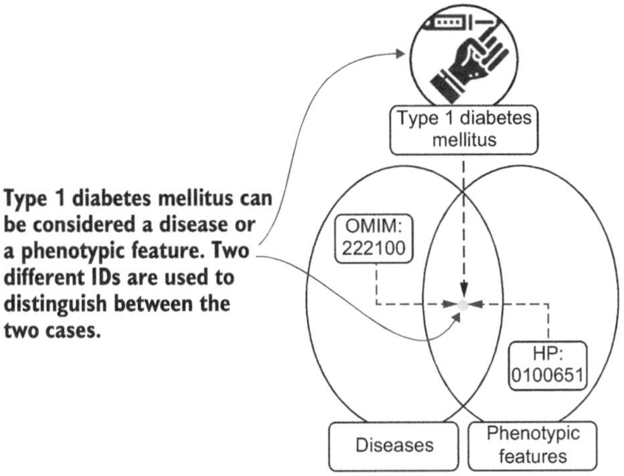

Figure 3.4 Type 1 diabetes mellitus can be considered either a disease or a phenotypic feature. Based on the context, two different IDs can be adopted.

3.1.2 Data understanding

Our data source is the Human Phenotype Ontology (HPO) repository. It provides two sets of information for our example (figure 3.5). The first, in an RDF/XML file called

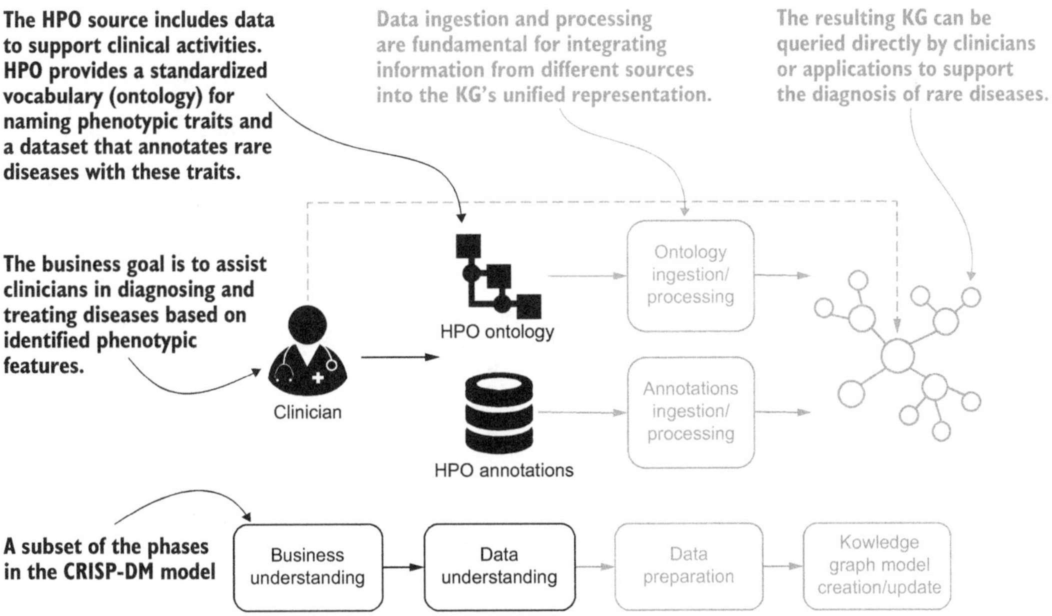

Figure 3.5 Understanding the data to support clinicians' activities. This explorative phase gets the key information needed to construct the KG.

hpo.owl (http://purl.obolibrary.org/obo/hp.owl), is an ontology that contains standardized information on phenotypic anomalies. This kind of standardization allows interoperability and lets us integrate data from multiple sources. Listing 3.1 shows part of the hpo.owl file related to Type I diabetes mellitus; the data is serialized to Turtle (Terse RDF Triple Language) for better readability.

Listing 3.1 Type I diabetes mellitus details in hpo.owl

```
obo:HP_0100651 a owl:Class ;
    rdfs:label "Type I diabetes mellitus" ^^xsd:string ;
    obo:IAO_0000115 "A chronic condition in which the pancreas produces
        little or no insulin…" ^^xsd:string ;
    oboInOwl:created_by "doelkens"^^xsd:string ;
    oboInOwl:creation_date "2010-12-29T06:37:55Z"^^xsd:string ;
    oboInOwl:hasDbXref "MSH:D003922"^^xsd:string,
        "SNOMEDCT_US:46635009" ^^xsd:string,
        "UMLS:C0011854" ^^xsd:string ;
    oboInOwl:hasExactSynonym "Diabetes mellitus Type I"^^xsd:string,
        "Juvenile diabetes mellitus" ^^xsd:string,
        "Type 1 diabetes",
        "Type I diabetes";
    oboInOwl:hasRelatedSynonym "Insulin-dependent diabetes
        mellitus"^^xsd:string ;
    oboInOwl:id "HP:0100651"^^xsd:string ;
    rdfs:comment "The onset of type 1 diabetes is typically during
        adolescence…" ^^xsd:string ;
    rdfs:subClassOf obo:HP_0000819 .
```

Defines Type I diabetes mellitus, identified by URI obo:HP_0100651, as an ontology class

Describes the disease in natural language

Shows metadata related to the author ("doelkens") of this entry

IDs of external data sources that refer to this form of diabetes

Defines Type I diabetes mellitus as a subclass of the phenotypic feature identified by the obo:HP_0000819 URI, which corresponds to diabetes mellitus

Reading an OWL file can be challenging. We can use the `rdflib` Python library to explore this file as a collection of triples, each of which includes a subject, a predicate, and an object, as shown in listing 3.2.

Listing 3.2 Processing an OWL file using the `rdflib` Python library

```
from rdflib import Graph, URIRef
g = Graph()
g.parse("hp.owl", format="xml")

g.bind("obo", "http://purl.obolibrary.org/obo/")
g.bind("rdf", "http://www.w3.org/1999/02/22-rdf-syntax-ns#")
g.bind("rdfs", "http://www.w3.org/2000/01/rdf-schema#")
g.bind("xsd", "http://www.w3.org/2001/XMLSchema#")

subject_uri = URIRef("http://purl.obolibrary.org/obo/HP_0100651")
filtered_statements = g.triples((subject_uri, None, None))
for subject, predicate, obj in filtered_statements:
```

```
print(
      f"({g.qname(subject)}, {g.qname(predicate)}, "
      f"{g.qname(obj) if isinstance(obj, URIRef) else obj})"
  )
print()
```

The output from this script is as follows (long strings have been truncated for clarity).

Listing 3.3 Sample OWL file shown as a set of triples

```
(obo:HP_0410050, rdf:type, owl:Class)

(obo:HP_0410050, owl:equivalentClass, N25507ac984704bd78a0effd951947a7f)

(obo:HP_0410050, rdfs:subClassOf, obo:HP_0011013)

(obo:HP_0410050, obo:IAO_0000115, A decrease in the level of…)

(obo:HP_0410050, dc:date, 2018-01-27T00:26:24+00:00)

(obo:HP_0410050, dcterms:creator, ns1:0000-0001-5208-3432)

(obo:HP_0410050, oboInOwl:hasExactSynonym, Decreased level of 1,5-AG…)

(obo:HP_0410050, oboInOwl:hasExactSynonym, Decreased level of 1,5-anhydro…)

(obo:HP_0410050, rdfs:label, Decreased level of 1,5 anhydroglucitol in serum)
```

The second set of information from HPO repository, contained in the tab-separated-values (TSV) file phenotype.hpoa, collects recognized, discovered, and annotated phenotypic features associated with different diseases, including rare syndromes. These annotations include modifiers that clarify the age of onset and the frequency of each feature related to the illness. The following listing shows a sample of this annotation file.

Listing 3.4 Sample of the phenotype.hpoa file

```
database_id    disease_name    qualifier    hpo_id    reference    evidence
onset    frequency    sex    modifier    aspect    biocuration

OMIM:222100    Diabetes mellitus, insulin-dependent-1
    HP:0410050    PMID:9357814;PMID:17659063;PMID:16731998
    PCS    30/30        P
    HPO:NicoleVasilevsky[2018-02-23];HPO:NicoleVasilevsky[2018-03-02]

OMIM:222100    Diabetes mellitus, insulin-dependent-1
    HP:0000103    OMIM:222100
    IEA                P    HPO:iea[2009-02-17]
```

This file includes the following fields:

- `database_id` (`OMIM:222100`)—Disease identifier from ontologies such as Online Mendelian Inheritance in Man (OMIM) and Orphanet.

- `disease_name (Diabetes mellitus, insulin-dependent-1)`—Disease name from the related ontology.
- `hpo_id (HP:0410050)`—HPO identifier of the related phenotypic abnormality.
- `reference (PMID:9357814;PMID:17659063.PMID:16731998)`—Source of information used for the annotation. This may be from an article indicated with the related PubMed ID (PMID).
- `evidence (PCS)`—Level of evidence supporting the annotation. PCS stands for published clinical study.
- `frequency (30/30)`—A count of patients affected within a group of people with a common statistical characteristic. 30/30 indicates that 30 of the 30 patients with the specified disease were found to have the phenotypic abnormality referred to by the HPO term.
- `aspect (p)`—Phenotypic aspect. P means phenotypic abnormality.
- `biocuration (HPO:NicoleVasilevsky[2018-02-23];HPO:NicoleVasilevsky [2018-03-02])`—research center or user making the annotation and the date on which the annotation was made.

For further details, see https://mng.bz/EwAo.

3.2 Understanding knowledge graph technologies

Now that we understand the data, the next phase involves ingesting and processing it from the available sources. But first, we will examine the different KG technologies so we can make an informed decision for our use case.

Two of the most popular approaches for creating KGs are the Resource Description Framework (RDF) and Labeled Property Graph (LPG). RDF is a standard framework, defined and regulated by the World Wide Web Consortium (W3C), for data exchange on the web. With RDF, each statement is composed of three elements: subject, predicate, and object (a triple). The subject is a node (vertex) in the graph, the predicate represents a relationship (edge), and the object is another node. This framework models a KG as a collection of statements, and we can use web technologies to represent, store, and exchange information. RDF is particularly suitable for creating ontologies that describe a specific domain of knowledge.

LPG provides a fast, query-based traversal of graph data and path analysis features. Efficiency of data storage and access is guaranteed by the structured information in the form of key–value pairs associated with nodes and relationships in the graph.

In RDF, relationships (triples) are defined globally, so metadata applied to a predicate affects all instances of that relationship throughout the graph. To address this limitation, RDF supports, for instance, named graphs, which let us treat groups of triples as a single entity and provide context-specific information. In contrast, LPG supports unique edges between nodes, allowing metadata and properties to be attached to individual relationships. This is a flexible model for representing edge-specific information. The RDF-DEV Community Group is working on an RDF* ("RDF-star") specification that lets users add properties to edges, reconciling the RDF and LPG technologies.

LPG can't express the advanced semantics of RDF. To address this issue, vendors such as Neo4j provide tools that can reduce the gap between RDF and LPG. The Neosemantics plugin lets us use RDF and its vocabularies (OWL, RDFS, SKOS, and others) in Neo4j to run basic inference. Other vendors, such as Amazon Neptune, use alternative strategies that let us execute Cypher queries (the query language of LPG graphs) on RDF data. The next section presents the limitations and opportunities of adopting RDF and LPG for our example use case.

3.2.1 RDF or LPG? A goal-driven discussion

To select the best technology for building a KG, we need a better understanding of the available information (in our case, the HPO ontology and the annotations data) and a clear goal. We mentioned that RDF is particularly suitable for creating ontologies; this is why the HPO ontology is serialized using RDF. The file extension of the HPO file is .owl. OWL stands for Web Ontology Language, and its primary goal is to enrich the semantic information available in RDF to support expressive class definitions and property definitions. OWL ontologies are widely used, and many LLMs, including GPT and Claude, have been trained on them, making it easier for these models to interpret and reason over OWL-based data.

The clinicians in our use case don't care how the knowledge is modeled: they are interested in an unambiguous representation of phenotypic features, possibly in a hierarchical structure. The core information in the annotated data often comes from the scientific literature and consists of cases in which a specific phenotypic feature is identified with a disease. For example, the entry that shows a connection between "Diabetes Mellitus, Insulin-dependent-1" (OMIM:222100) and "Decreased level of 1,5 anhydroglucitol in serum" (HP:0410050) was published in a clinical study entitled "A kinetic mass balance model for 1,5-anhydroglucitol: applications to monitoring of glycemic control" [3] (PMID: 9357814), created by Nicole Vasilevsky in February 2018. The best way to model it is to incorporate the details into a relationship between a disease and a phenotypic feature. Modeling data this way lets us create multiple relationships, each potentially representing a specific annotation characterized by a provenance and date.

Figure 3.6 illustrates how we can convert data from annotations in a table structure into an edge in the KG. The disease and the phenotypic feature are represented as nodes, and information about the annotation author, creation date, and source is specified as properties of the edge (`HAS_PHENOTYPIC_FEATURE` in the figure).

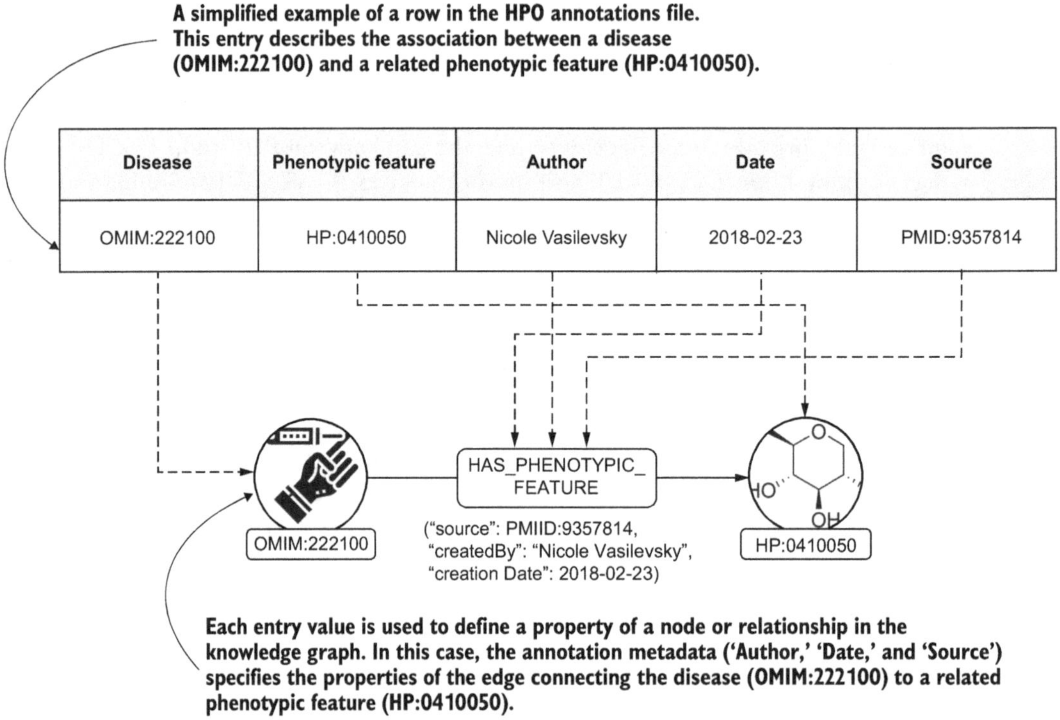

Figure 3.6 Data transformation from a table row to a KG edge. Information in the table is adapted to define the properties of nodes and edges in the KG.

Exercise

See if you can select the best technology to support clinicians' activities for the example use case. Here's a reminder of the primary requirements:

- The clinician's goal is to use available data to make informed decisions when diagnosing diseases, especially rare pathologies.
- Clinicians are not interested in a knowledge base that represents the entire clinical domain. They want to see cases in which anomalous phenotypic features (or combinations) can be associated with diseases that are not easy to detect. For this reason, they want information that reports such cases, including the provenance and date of the information.
- Using this metadata, clinicians want to easily compare all the cases in which a specific phenotypic feature is associated with a disease.

The selection of the right technology does not have a unique answer, but selecting the most suitable one will help you reach the defined goals in a more straightforward way. You can adapt this exercise to different domains and applications.

3.2.2 Representing edge properties with RDF and LPG

From our point of view, LPG is the best solution for representing the data, as it emphasizes information about an edge connecting a phenotypic feature and a disease. To clarify why LPG is the most suitable technology, let's make a concrete comparison between RDF and LPG. The goal is to retrieve all the information (including source, author, and creation date) related to an annotation. As we mentioned earlier, we can use different mechanisms to represent such data using RDF, as described in the following sections.

RDF: N-ARY RELATIONS

A standard approach to modeling data related to a specific edge is to adopt n-ary relations. Using this approach, we create a new concept to connect the data; in our example, this is defined as an annotation. Consider the RDF representation in listing 3.5 and the related SPARQL query in listing 3.6.

Listing 3.5 Example of n-ary relations

```
_:Annotation rdf:type :PhenotypicAnnotation ;
    :forDisease        OMIM:222100 ;
    :phenotypicFeature HP:0410050 ;
    :source            PMID:9357814 ;
    :createdBy         "Nicole Vasilevsky" ;
    :creationDate      "2018-02-23"^^xsd:date .
```

This RDF snippet represents a phenotypic annotation using the Turtle syntax. The annotation is expressed as a blank node (`_:Annotation`), which is an unnamed resource used to group related information without assigning it a global identifier. A blank node can be considered as a placeholder for something that exists but doesn't need a specific name, much like an anonymous object in programming.

The blank node is typed as a `:PhenotypicAnnotation` and links a disease (identified by an OMIM ID) to a phenotypic feature (from the HPO). Additional metadata includes the data source (a PubMed ID), the author of the annotation, and the creation date. This structure supports provenance tracking and semantic interoperability in biomedical datasets.

Listing 3.6 SPARQL query in the context of n-ary relations

```
SELECT ?source ?author ?date
WHERE {
    ?annotation a :PhenotypicAnnotation ;
        :forDisease OMIM:222100 ;
        :phenotypicFeature HP:0410050 ;
        :source ?source ;
        :createdBy ?author ;
        :creationDate ?date .
}
```

This SPARQL query retrieves metadata about a specific phenotypic annotation. It filters annotations by a given disease (`OMIM:222100`) and phenotypic feature (`HP:0410050`) and then returns the source of the information, the author who created the annotation, and the date it was created.

In many cases, data consumers can easily interpret and adapt to changes in the original schema. However, as the ontology evolves, its complexity may increase, potentially introducing challenges related to backward compatibility and long-term maintenance.

RDF: NAMED GRAPHS

RDF named graphs include a fourth element specifying that this statement is part of a named (sub)graph and can be considered a node of the RDF graph. Therefore, we can create new statements to attach the data related to the annotation. This approach is represented in listing 3.7, and the SPARQL query is defined in listing 3.8.

Listing 3.7 Example of a named graph

```
:Graph1 {
    OMIM:222100 :hasPhenotypicFeature HP:0410050 .
}

:Graph1
    :source PMID:9357814 ;
    :createdBy "Nicole Vasilevsky" ;
    :creationDate "2018-02-23"^^xsd:date .
```

This RDF example uses TriG syntax to define the named graph `:Graph1`. In simple terms, TriG lets you group RDF statements under a label (the named graph) and add metadata. In this graph, the triple asserts that the disease `OMIM:222100` has the phenotypic feature `HP:0410050`. Metadata about this assertion is attached to `:Graph1`, including the source (`PMID:9357814`), the creator (`"Nicole Vasilevsky"`), and the creation date.

Listing 3.8 SPARQL query in the context of a named graph

```
SELECT ?source ?author ?date
WHERE {
    GRAPH :Graph1 {
        OMIM:222100 :hasPhenotypicFeature HP:0410050 .
    }
    :Graph1 :source ?source ;
            :createdBy ?author ;
            :creationDate ?date .
}
```

This SPARQL query retrieves metadata about a specific phenotypic annotation stored in a named graph. It looks in graph `:Graph1` to find a triple asserting that

`OMIM:222100` has the phenotypic feature `HP:0410050`. It then queries the metadata about `:Graph1` and returns the source, the author, and the creation date.

Although named graphs are powerful for representing contextual metadata and provenance, they can add complexity. In particular, managing a large number of named graphs may lead to inefficiencies in data storage and exchange. Fine-grained updates to individual statements in named graphs can also be challenging.

RDF-STAR

As previously mentioned, RDF-star is an extension of RDF that narrows the gap between RDF and property graph models such as LPG. This approach is illustrated in the following two listings.

Listing 3.9 Example of RDF-star

```
<<OMIM:222100 :hasPhenotypicFeature HP:0410050>>
    :source PMID: 9357814 ;
    :createdBy "Nicole Vasilevsky" ;
    :creationDate "2018-02-23"^^xsd:date .
```

Listing 3.10 Example of a SPARQL-star query in the context of RDF-star

```
SELECT ?source ?author ?date {
    <<OMIM:222100 :hasPhenotypicFeature HP:0410050>>
        :source ?source ;
        :createdBy ?author ;
        :creationDate ? date .
}
```

RDF-star represents a step in attaching properties to edges and uses a more readable SPARQL query. However, its query performance must be improved; and, as noticed by Orlandi et al. [2], "The use of a new syntax extension requires a specific implementation of RDF engines and, therefore, limits the adoption of this approach."

Other methods exist for annotating RDF statements, such as reification and singleton properties. These methods are less used in real-world applications, where more scalable and maintainable alternatives like named graphs and n-ary relations are preferred.

LPG

The LPG approach represents annotation details directly within the relationship, using key–value pairs. An example of this modeling approach and the corresponding Cypher query are shown next.

Listing 3.11 Example LPG representation

```
(d { id: "OMIM:222100" })
-[:HAS_PHENOTYPIC_FEATURE {
       source: "PMID:9357814"
```

```
        createdBy: "Nicole Vasilevsky";
        creationDate: "2018-02-23}]->
(p { id: "HP:0410050" })
```

The two nodes represent entities: a disease (`OMIM:222100`) and a phenotype (`HP:0410050`). The relationship `:HAS_PHENOTYPIC_FEATURE` connects them and includes key–value pairs that describe the source of the annotation ("`PMID:9357814`"), the creator ("`Nicole Vasilevsky`"), and the date it was created ("`2018-02-23`").

Listing 3.12 Example Cypher query

```
MATCH (d)-[r:HAS_PHENOTYPIC_FEATURE]->(p)
WHERE d.id = "OMIM:222100" and p.id = "HP:0410050"
RETURN r.source, r.createdBy, r.creationDate
```

This Cypher query retrieves the metadata attached to the `:HAS_PHENOTYPIC_FEATURE` relationship between the disease and phenotype nodes. It matches the pattern in the graph, filters based on the node IDs, and returns the annotation details stored in the relationship.

As these examples demonstrate, the LPG model is well-suited for modeling metadata-rich relationships in a way that is expressive and accessible. For these reasons, we'll adopt LPG and Cypher as the core tools for building our KG system.

3.3 Building a knowledge graph

Let's get into the details of how to build our first KG. The process has two steps: loading the ontology and ingesting a data source using the ontology as a reference.

> **NOTE** To build the KG, you can run the code in the GitHub repository (https://github.com/alenegro81/knowledge-graphs-and-llms-in-action/tree/main/chapters/ch03) or test the Cypher queries in this section using the Neo4j browser. The code has been tested using Neo4j (version 5.20.0 Enterprise Edition, installed with the Neo4j Desktop 1.6.1 application), the APOC library (version 5.20.0), and the Neosemantics plugin (version 5.20.0). Details for installing Neo4j and its plugins are provided in online appendix B. We explain each query, but we assume you have a basic understanding of the Cypher query language. The results are derived from the HPO version available in February 2025.

3.3.1 Ontology ingestion and processing with neosemantics

Figure 3.7 illustrates the ontology ingestion and processing phase. The first step is to create and initialize the HPO database using the following command.

Listing 3.13 Creating the HPO database in Neo4j

```
CREATE DATABASE hpo IF NOT EXISTS
```

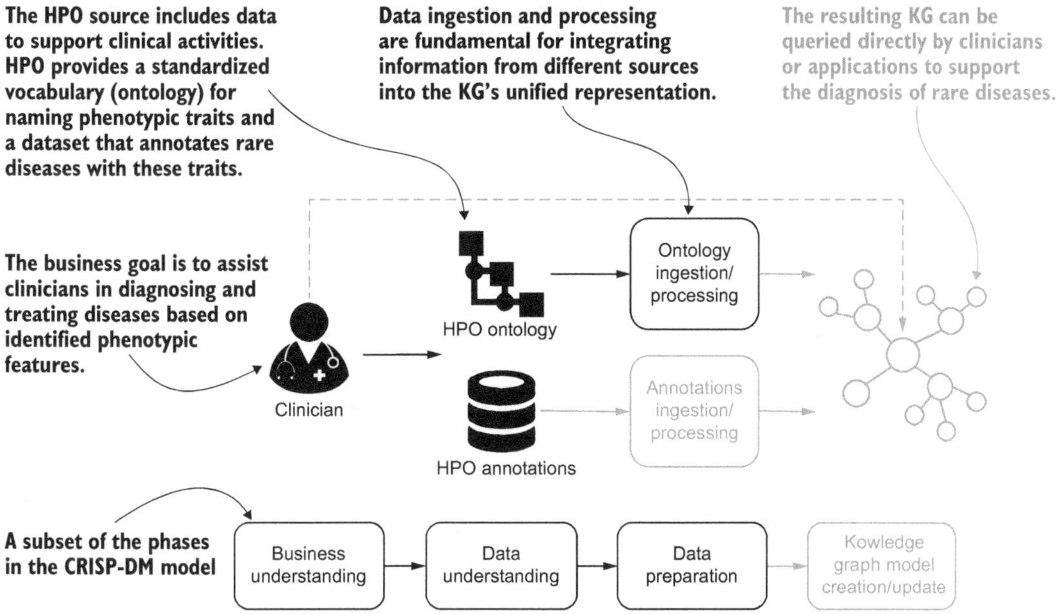

Figure 3.7 Ontology ingestion and processing

In the next listing, we establish constraints that ensure the uniqueness of the `uri` and `id` properties of the nodes labeled `Resource`. We also create indexes for the `id` properties of `HpoPhenotype` and `HpoDisease` nodes to enhance access to this information during the KG building phase and information retrieval. The `HpoPhenotype` and `HpoDisease` labels define our phenotypic abnormality and disease nodes.

Listing 3.14 Creating constraints and indexes

```
CREATE CONSTRAINT n10s_unique_uri IF NOT EXISTS FOR (r:Resource) REQUIRE
     r.uri IS UNIQUE;
CREATE CONSTRAINT IF NOT EXISTS FOR (n:Resource) REQUIRE (n.id) IS UNIQUE;
CREATE INDEX disease_id IF NOT EXISTS FOR (n:HpoDisease) ON (n.id);
CREATE INDEX phenotype_id IF NOT EXISTS FOR (n:HpoPhenotype) ON (n.id);
```

The second step defines an initial configuration for the Neosemantics component.

Listing 3.15 Configuring the Neosemantics plugin

```
CALL n10s.graphconfig.init();
CALL n10s.graphconfig.set({ handleVocabUris: "IGNORE" });
CALL n10s.graphconfig.set({ applyNeo4jNaming: True });
```

This configuration defines two main rules for importing data. The first rule ignores the namespaces in the import phase (namespaces can help keep track of distinct ontologies that use similar expressions.) The second rule encodes the relationship types in uppercase, following the standard representation of LPG relationships.

The next step is to load the HPO vocabulary.

Listing 3.16 Loading the HPO vocabulary into Neo4j

```
CALL n10s.rdf.import.fetch("http://purl.obolibrary.org/obo/hp.owl","RDF/XML");
```

During our tests, this command loaded 899,558 statements into Neo4j. Before processing and loading the annotation data, we can enrich our nodes with the `HpoPhenotype` label and the `id` property computed from the resource's original URI.

Listing 3.17 Enriching nodes

```
MATCH (n:Resource)
WHERE n.uri STARTS WITH "http://purl.obolibrary.org/obo/HP"
SET n:HpoPhenotype,
       n.id = coalesce(n.id,
     replace(apoc.text.replace(n.uri,'(.*)obo/',''),'_', ':'))
```

Sets n.id as HP:0000001

Let's review the current state of the KG. Listing 3.18 shows the code to retrieve a small portion of this graph, illustrated in figure 3.8. You can explore this by running the code in the Neo4j browser.

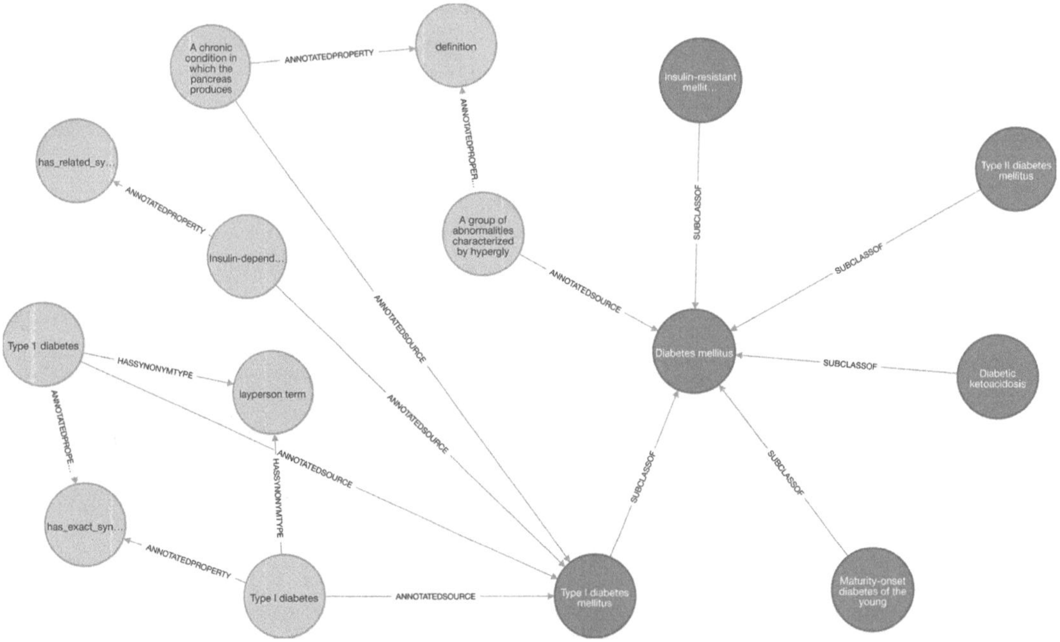

Figure 3.8 A portion of the HPO ontology loaded in the graph database using LPG as a storage model. We can distinguish between two types of information: ontological information (left) and domain-specific information related to phenotypic features (right).

Listing 3.18 Showing part of the KG at the current stage

```
MATCH path1=(n:HpoPhenotype)<-[:SUBCLASSOF]-(m:HpoPhenotype)
WHERE n.label = "Diabetes mellitus"
WITH path1
MATCH path2=(i:HpoPhenotype)<-[:ANNOTATEDSOURCE]-(j)
WHERE i.label in ["Diabetes mellitus", "Type I diabetes mellitus"]
WITH path1, path2, j
MATCH path3=(j)-[:ANNOTATEDPROPERTY|HASSYNONYMTYPE]-()
RETURN path1, path2, path3
```

WARNING The query in listing 3.18 will work only if you execute it while following the chapter instructions one step at a time. If you run the entire ingestion process using the repository code, the query will fail due to the final data cleaning phase.

The HPO ontology provides different types of information. The left side of figure 3.8 reports ontological information about the nature of the nodes, and the right side includes details on hierarchical connections related to diabetes mellitus.

3.3.2 Annotation ingestion and processing

To finish constructing the KG, we must ingest and process the annotations file. The phenotypic abnormalities in this file are connected to the associated diseases, whose terms come from other ontologies. Figure 3.9 shows the second phase of the data processing and modeling.

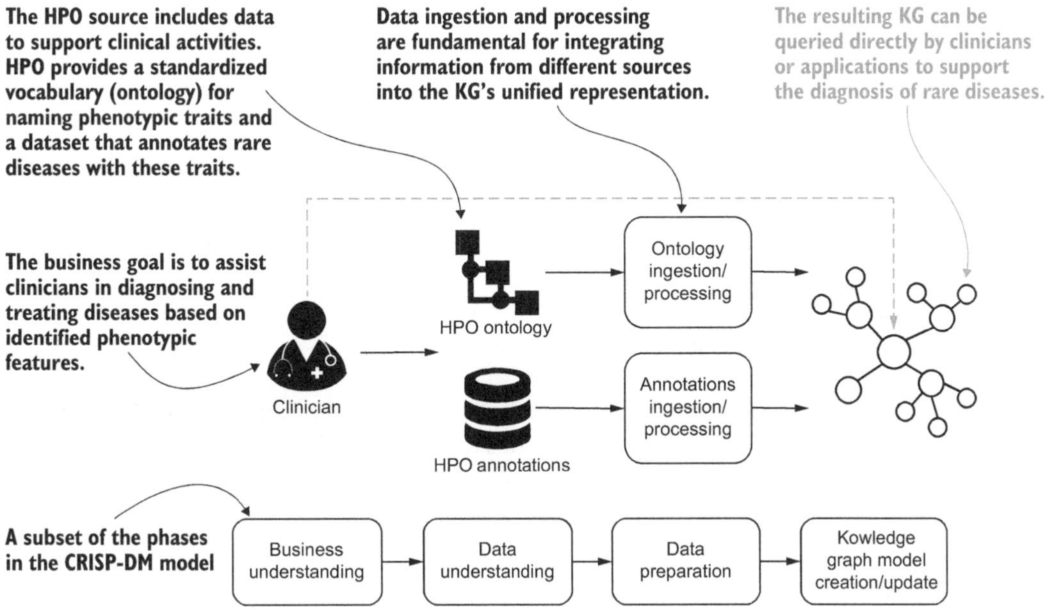

Figure 3.9 Ingesting and processing the annotation dataset to finalize the construction of the KG

Unlike the hpo.owl file generated using the RDF data model, our next file is provided in an HPO annotation (HPOA; https://mng.bz/NwQN) format that consists of tab-separated-values (TSVs). The HPOA file includes valuable information:

- An explicit association between a disease and multiple phenotypic features or abnormalities
- Evidence supporting this association, such as that it's inferred from an electronic annotation or from a published clinical study or traceable author statement
- The age of onset
- The frequency with which a disease and a phenotypic feature appear together
- Additional metadata that describes the ontology source

Working with this TSV file allows us to incorporate different file types based on existing knowledge. The Cypher queries in listings 3.19–3.24 let us load, process, and integrate information from the annotations file on GitHub. First we create disease nodes.

Listing 3.19 Creating `HpoDisease` nodes

```
LOAD CSV FROM 'https://mng.bz/qRyr' AS row
FIELDTERMINATOR '\t'
WITH row
SKIP 5
MERGE (dis:Resource:HpoDisease {id: row[0]})
ON CREATE SET dis.label = row[1];
```

Skips the first five rows of the file because they are file metadata

Next we create the relationships between disease nodes and phenotypic feature nodes.

Listing 3.20 Creating relationships between `HpoDisease` and `HpoPhenotype` nodes

```
LOAD CSV FROM 'https://mng.bz/qRyr' AS row
FIELDTERMINATOR '\t'
WITH row
SKIP 5
MATCH (dis:HpoDisease)
WHERE dis.id = row[0]
MATCH (phe:HpoPhenotype)
WHERE phe.id = row[3]
MERGE (dis)-[:HAS_PHENOTYPIC_FEATURE]->(phe)
```

Creating these relationships integrates information from the hpo.owl and phenotype.hpoa files. The following code queries the result of this integration process.

Listing 3.21 Finding associations

```
MERGE (dis:HpoDisease)-[:HAS_PHENOTYPIC_FEATURE]->(phe:HpoPhenotype)
RETURN dis.label, collect(phe.label)
LIMIT 3
```

The results of the query are reported in table 3.1.

Table 3.1 Sample associations between the `HpoDisease` and `HpoPhenotype` nodes

`HpoDisease` entry	Associated `HpoPhenotype` entries
Developmental and epileptic encephalopathy 96	Hydrops fetalis, Autosomal dominant inheritance, Death in infancy, Epileptic spasm, Primary microcephaly, EEG with burst suppression, Intellectual disability, profound, Small for gestational age, Epileptic encephalopathy, Neonatal respiratory distress, Tonic seizure
Pseudohyperkalemia, familial, 2, due to red cell leak	Generalized muscle weakness, Hyperkalemia, Periodic paralysis, Muscle spasm, Hemolytic anemia, Hand tremor, Autosomal dominant inheritance
Immunoglobulin kappa light chain deficiency	Chronic diarrhea, Recurrent infections, Recurrent respiratory infections, Absent circulating immunoglobulin kappa chain, Childhood onset, Diarrhea, Autosomal recessive inheritance

The following code adds relationship properties in the form of key–value pairs.

Listing 3.22 Adding properties to `HAS_PHENOTYPIC_FEATURE` relationships

```
LOAD CSV FROM 'https://mng.bz/qRyr' AS row
FIELDTERMINATOR '\t'
WITH row
SKIP 5
MATCH (dis:HpoDisease)-[rel:HAS_PHENOTYPIC_FEATURE]->(phe:HpoPhenotype)
WHERE phe.id = row[3] and dis.id = row[0]
FOREACH(_ IN CASE WHEN row[4] is not null THEN [1] ELSE [] END|
  SET rel.source = row[4])
FOREACH(_ IN CASE WHEN row[5] is not null THEN [1] ELSE [] END|
  SET rel.evidence = row[5])
FOREACH(_ IN CASE WHEN row[6] is not null THEN [1] ELSE [] END|
  SET rel.onset = row[6])
FOREACH(_ IN CASE WHEN row[7] is not null THEN [1] ELSE [] END|
  SET rel.frequency = row[7])
FOREACH(_ IN CASE WHEN row[8] is not null THEN [1] ELSE [] END|
  SET rel.sex = row[8])
FOREACH(_ IN CASE WHEN row[9] is not null THEN [1] ELSE [] END|
  SET rel.modifier = row[9])
FOREACH(_ IN CASE WHEN row[10] is not null THEN [1] ELSE [] END|
  SET rel.aspect = row[10])
FOREACH(_ IN CASE WHEN row[11] is not null THEN [1] ELSE [] END|
  SET rel.biocuration = row[11])
```

This is a flexible approach to enrich relationship information. This script matches existing nodes and relationships in the Neo4j graph and sets additional relationship properties based on the presence of values in each row of the input file. Each of the `FOREACH` blocks adds a new property to the relationship only if the corresponding column in the TSV is not null. This makes the script resilient to missing data and avoids overwriting values with nulls.

Next we incorporate the information from the following query to clarify the meaning of the properties associated with the relationships between diseases and phenotypic features.

Listing 3.23 Enriching HAS_PHENOTYPIC_FEATURE with more properties

```
CALL apoc.periodic.iterate(
  "MATCH (dis:HpoDisease)-[rel:HAS_PHENOTYPIC_FEATURE]->(phe:HpoPhenotype)
   RETURN rel",
  "SET rel.createdBy = apoc.text.regexGroups(
        rel.biocuration, 'HPO:(\\w+)\\['
      )[0][1],
   rel.creationDate = apoc.text.regexGroups(
        rel.biocuration, '\\[(\\d{4}-\\d{2}-\\d{2})\\]'
      )[0][1],
   rel.aspectName = CASE
     WHEN rel.aspect = 'P' THEN 'Phenotypic abnormality'
     WHEN rel.aspect = 'I' THEN 'Inheritance'
   END,
   rel.aspectDescription = CASE
     WHEN rel.aspect = 'P' THEN
       'Terms with the P aspect are located in the Phenotypic abnormality ' +
       'subontology'
     WHEN rel.aspect = 'I' THEN
       'Terms with the I aspect are from the Inheritance subontology'
   END,
   rel.evidenceName = CASE
     WHEN rel.evidence = 'IEA' THEN
       'Inferred from electronic annotation'
     WHEN rel.evidence = 'PCS' THEN
       'Published clinical study'
     WHEN rel.evidence = 'TAS' THEN
       'Traceable author statement'
   END,
   rel.evidenceDescription = CASE
     WHEN rel.evidence = 'IEA' THEN
       'Annotations extracted by parsing the Clinical Features sections ' +
       'of the Online Mendelian Inheritance in Man resource are assigned ' +
       'the evidence code IEA.'
     WHEN rel.evidence = 'PCS' THEN
       'PCS is used for information extracted from articles in the medical ' +
       'literature. Generally, annotations of this type will include the ' +
       'pubmed id of the published study in the DB_Reference field.'
     WHEN rel.evidence = 'TAS' THEN
       'TAS is used for information gleaned from knowledge bases such as ' +
       'OMIM or Orphanet that have derived the information from a ' +
       'published source.'
   END,
   rel.url = CASE
     WHEN rel.source STARTS WITH 'PMID:' THEN
       'https://pubmed.ncbi.nlm.nih.gov/' + apoc.text.replace(
         rel.source, '(.*)PMID:', ''
       )
```

```
    WHEN rel.source STARTS WITH 'OMIM:' THEN
      'https://omim.org/entry/' + apoc.text.replace(
        rel.source, '(.*)OMIM:', ''
      )
  END",
  {batchSize: 1000}
)
```

This query uses `apoc.periodic.iterate` to process and update the `HAS_PHENOTYPIC_FEATURE` relationships in batches. For example, it creates metadata from the `biocuration` property by extracting the curator and creation date using a regular expression. The query also adds properties to improve readability during graph exploration. The annotation file includes abbreviated versions of information related to `aspect` (`P` or `I` values) and `evidence` (`IEA`, `PCS`, or `TAS` values). To clarify this data, we add properties such as `aspectName`, which can have the value `'Phenotypic abnormality'` or `'Inheritance'`. The goal is to make it easier for humans to access information.

The final step in building the KG is to clean it by removing nodes and relationships that come from the ontology but are not necessary for our purposes.

Listing 3.24 Cleaning the KG by removing unnecessary nodes and relationships

```
CALL apoc.periodic.iterate(
    "MATCH (n:Resource) RETURN id(n) as id",
    "MATCH (n)
     WHERE id(n) = id AND
           NOT 'HpoPhenotype' in labels(n) AND
           NOT 'HpoDisease' in labels(n)
     DETACH DELETE n",
     {batchSize:10000})
YIELD batches, total return batches, total
```

3.4 Querying the data

Clinicians can now use the KG as a support tool for diagnosing rare diseases, beginning with the detection of phenotypic abnormalities in a patient. By entering specific traits, clinicians can query the KG to identify rare pathologies. This querying phase is the final step of our mental model and is shown in figure 3.10.

Imagine that a clinician sees a patient: a boy affected by Type 1 diabetes. The patient's clinical history is stored in the hospital database as an electronic health record (EHR). The hospital has embraced the KG paradigm change, so patient information is stored using the terms included in HPO and OMIM (an online catalog of genetic disorders and rare diseases). Type 1 diabetes is classified as a phenotypic feature and a disease, so the information is stored using two different identification codes:

- HP:0100651 (phenotypic feature): https://hpo.jax.org/app/browse/term/HP:0100651.
- OMIM:222100 (disease): https://www.omim.org/entry/222100.

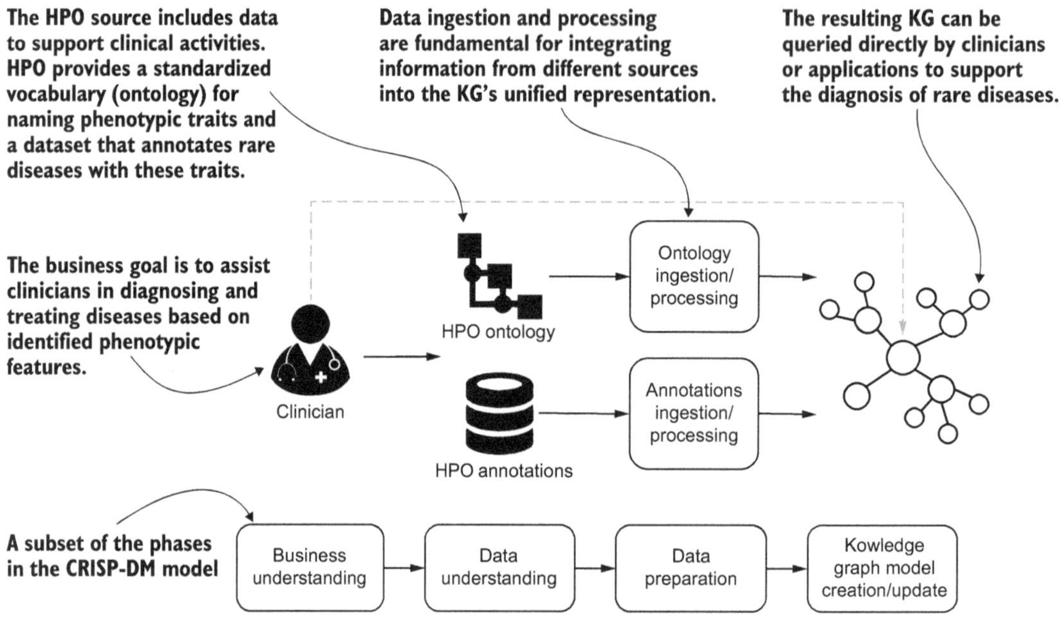

Figure 3.10 Querying the generated KG to support clinicians' activities

The clinician recognizes the typical phenotypic features of Type 1 diabetes in the patient, which can also be explored in the KG with the query in the following listing. Figure 3.11 shows the results.

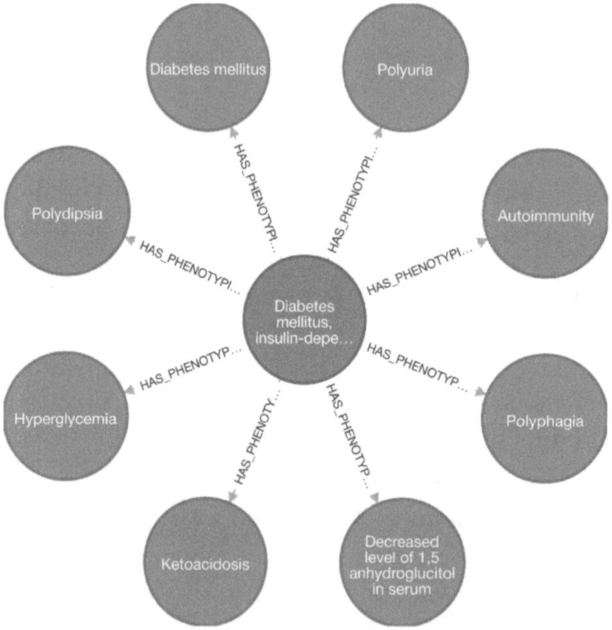

Figure 3.11 Result of a query that gets all the phenotype features related to Type 1 diabetes

Listing 3.25 Querying phenotypic features associated with Type 1 diabetes

```
MATCH path=(dis:HpoDisease)-[:HAS_PHENOTYPIC_FEATURE]->(phe:HpoPhenotype)
WHERE dis.id = "OMIM:222100"
RETURN path
```

The central node defines Type 1 diabetes, and the other nodes define the associated phenotypic features. However, during the medical examination, the clinician recognizes new symptoms classified as phenotypic features that are not directly connected to Type 1 diabetes:

- Growth delay: https://hpo.jax.org/app/browse/term/HP:0001510.
- Large knee: https://hpo.jax.org/app/browse/term/HP:0030866.
- Sensorineural hearing impairment: https://hpo.jax.org/app/browse/term/HP:0000407.
- Pruritus: https://hpo.jax.org/app/browse/term/HP:0000989.

The clinician wants to use the information in the KG to identify other pathologies connected to these phenotype features. To perform this task, the clinician runs the following query, which gives the results listed in table 3.2.

Listing 3.26 Finding diseases associated with specific phenotypic features

```
MATCH (phe:HpoPhenotype)
WHERE phe.label IN [
  "Growth delay",
  "Large knee",
  "Sensorineural hearing impairment",
  "Pruritus",
  "Type I diabetes mellitus"
]
WITH phe
MATCH path=(dis:HpoDisease)-[:HAS_PHENOTYPIC_FEATURE]->(phe)
UNWIND dis as nodes
RETURN
  dis.id as disease_id,
  dis.label as disease_name,
  collect(phe.label) as features,
  count(nodes) as num_of_features
ORDER BY num_of_features DESC, disease_name
LIMIT 5
```

Table 3.2 Top diseases matching clinician-identified phenotypic features

disease_id	disease_name	features	num_of_features
OMIM:619269	Ondontochondrodysplasia 2 with hearing loss and diabetes	Growth delay, Sensorineural hearing impairment, Pruritus, Large knee, Type I diabetes mellitus	5
OMIM:618500	Holoprosencephaly 12 with or without pancreatic agenesis	Sensorineural hearing impairment, Growth delay, Type I diabetes mellitus	3

Table 3.2 Top diseases matching clinician-identified phenotypic features *(continued)*

disease_id	disease_name	features	num_of_features
OMIM:614700	3-methylglutaconic aciduria, type VIII	Growth delay, Sensorineural hearing impairment	2
OMIM:616192	Alobar holoprosencephaly	Growth delay, Sensorineural hearing impairment	2
OMIM:602782	Alpha-Thalassemia/mental retardation syndrome, X-linked	Growth delay, Sensorineural hearing impairment	2

These results lead to a diagnosis of Ondontochondrodysplasia 2 with hearing loss and diabetes. Starting with these results, the clinician can conduct further investigations to determine the frequency with which these phenotypic features are associated with the disease and identify more potential sources of information.

Exercise

Extend the query in listing 3.26 to retrieve relationship properties including `evidence_name`, `evidence_description`, `source`, and `url`.

3.5 Reasoning over the KG

In the previous case, we showed how to obtain results from the information stored in the KG. However, one of the most powerful tools of a KG is inference, which uses deductive reasoning (see chapter 2) based on logical rules to derive results from implicit information. For example, consider this question: which diseases are characterized by an abnormality of the endocrine system?

Some annotations are explicitly connected to this phenotypic feature. But a clinician would also be interested in more specific phenotypic traits that involve the thyroid. For this purpose, we can use the hierarchical representation of HPO. The following query retrieves a subset of phenotypic features representing subclasses of endocrine system abnormalities (`id=HP:0000818`).

Listing 3.27 Finding subclasses of endocrine system abnormalities

```
MATCH (p:HpoPhenotype)<-[:SUBCLASSOF*1..3]-(n:HpoPhenotype)
WHERE p.id = "HP:0000818"
RETURN p,n
```

Finds all phenotype nodes (n) that are one to three subclass levels more specific than another phenotype node (p)

Using this hierarchical structure, we can infer annotations implicitly linked to the abnormalities of the endocrine system through the following Neosemantics procedure (listing 3.28). Table 3.3 shows a subset of the results.

Listing 3.28 Finding phenotypic features related to the abnormality subclasses

```
MATCH (cat:HpoPhenotype {label: "Abnormality of the endocrine system"})   <-- Finds the top-level phenotype node
CALL n10s.inference.nodesInCategory(cat, {
  inCatRel: "HAS_PHENOTYPIC_FEATURE",
  subCatRel: "SUBCLASSOF"})     <-- Gets diseases linked (directly or indirectly) to this phenotype
YIELD node as dis
WHERE dis.label IN [
  "Congenital atransferrinemia",
  "Deafness, autosomal recessive 4, with enlarged vestibular aqueduct",
  "Diabetes mellitus, transient neonatal, 1",
  "Edema, familial idiopathic, prepubertal",
  "Familial dysalbuminemic hyperthyroxinemia"
]     <-- Keeps only selected diseases for reproducible output
MATCH (dis)-[:HAS_PHENOTYPIC_FEATURE]->(phe:HpoPhenotype)   <-- Matches their phenotype features
RETURN dis.label as disease, collect(DISTINCT phe.label) as features
ORDER BY size(features) ASC, disease
```

Table 3.3 Subset of the results of annotations implicitly connected to the "Abnormality of the endocrine system" phenotypic feature. Phenotypic features that are direct or inferred subclasses of this phenotypic feature are highlighted in bold.

disease	features
Congenital atransferrinemia	Anemia, Abnormality of the pancreas, Recurrent infections, Arthritis, Abnormality of the cardiovascular system, **Hypothyroidism**
Deafness, autosomal recessive 4, with enlarged vestibular aqueduct	Enlarged vestibular aqueduct, Congenital onset, **Goiter**, Autosomal recessive inheritance, Incomplete partition of the cochlea type II, Sensorineural hearing impairment
Diabetes mellitus, transient neonatal, 1	**Transient neonatal diabetes mellitus**, Autosomal dominant inheritance, Dehydration, Hyperglycemia, Intrauterine growth retardation, Severe failure to thrive
Edema, familial idiopathic, prepubertal	**Diabetes mellitus**, Abnormality of the genitourinary system, Irritability, Vomiting, Autosomal dominant inheritance, Edema
Familial dysalbuminemic hyperthyroxinemia	**Abnormal circulating free T4 concentration**, **Abnormal thyroid-stimulating hormone level**, Autosomal dominant inheritance, Autosomal recessive inheritance, **Euthyroid hyperthyroxinemia**, **Increased circulating free T4 concentration**

These results demonstrate how reasoning over subclass relationships and phenotypic features can reveal meaningful disease associations within an ontology-driven graph. The use of the Neosemantics plugin highlights the power of semantic inference in enriching biomedical queries, enabling us to go beyond direct connections and tap into the structure of domain knowledge.

Summary

- KG construction is a complex process that requires a clear idea of the problem you want to solve, an understanding of the reference domain, and a phase that includes data scouting, exploration, and comprehension.
- The resulting KG must be a unified, well-grounded, meaningful representation of data from different sources, with individual pieces of information fused into a unique view.
- The Resource Description Framework (RDF) and Labeled Property Graph (LPG) are two of the most prominent technologies for building KGs.
  - The RDF data model focuses on knowledge representation and is particularly suitable for constructing ontologies.
  - The LPG approach provides fast, query-based traversal of graph data and path analysis, emphasizing the efficiency of data storage and access.
  - Understanding the differences between RDF and LPGs is crucial for selecting the best technologies for your specific purpose.

4 From simple networks to multisource integration

This chapter covers

- Building and integrating complex knowledge graphs
- Exploring examples of knowledge graphs
- Understanding analysis and query techniques
- Analyzing KG results with LLMs

This chapter extends our understanding of how to construct increasingly large and complex knowledge graphs (KGs) and use them to develop intelligent advisor systems (IASs). Whereas in chapter 3, we had a single knowledge base in the form of an ontology, from this point on, we will create KGs from multiple structured data sources that are available in graph-friendly formats. This approach will let us focus on graph modeling decisions, integration strategies, and analysis methods.

NOTE Appendix C on the book's website offers comprehensive guidance on ingesting and transforming raw data from multiple complex sources.

The examples in the following sections cover transforming structured and semistructured schemas and data formats into a homogeneous graph, reconciling and matching names and identifiers, post-processing techniques to merge entities and relationships, and analyzing the resulting KG to find relevant information. We use biomedical data sources, but the techniques and patterns are directly transferable to other domains.

LLMs play complementary but limited roles in this phase of the KG lifecycle. The structured nature of the data sources in this chapter (CSV files, relational databases, and APIs) means traditional data integration techniques will be the primary approach, with LLMs serving as auxiliary tools rather than core components of the construction pipeline.

4.1 Biomedical knowledge graphs and applications

Imagine that you are tasked with addressing one of these situations:

- Starting from known relationships between diseases and proteins, can we discover new connections?
- Can we discover meaningful relationships between micro-RNAs and diseases without expensive in vitro tests?
- What are the key processes involved in celiac disease (or another disease)?
- Is it possible to repurpose existing drugs without multiyear studies?
- How can we support precision medicine, which uses patient-specific information?

All of these tasks can be addressed by organizing existing biomedical knowledge in the form of graphs and determining whether the graphs contain the knowledge to answer complex questions.

Let's start by delimiting the context of our example domain. Biomedical science deals with the organs and systems of the human body, focusing primarily on diseases, gene expression, proteins, drugs, and related topics. As reported by Nicholson and Green [1], KGs can help researchers tackle biomedical problems such as finding new uses for existing drugs [2], diagnosing patients [3], identifying associations between diseases and biomolecules [4], identifying proteins' functions [5], prioritizing cancer genes, [6] and recommending safer drugs for patients [7, 8]. Each application has different business goals and, according to our CRISP-DM model, is built using different data sources.

For each type of application, we'll present a case study with the code to import and merge the source databases and then query and analyze the resulting graphs. This exercise will teach you how to select data sources to feed a KG and determine whether the information is sufficient to accomplish the required tasks. Figure 4.1 summarizes the various applications and the most relevant information stored as nodes and relationships.

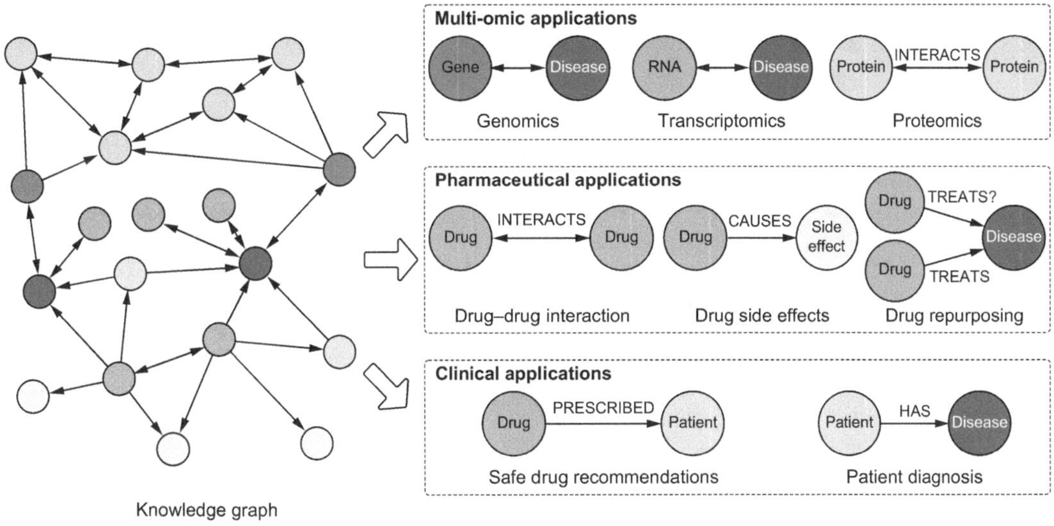

Figure 4.1 The primary types of biomedical applications for KGs, grouped by business goal. They have many data sources in common.

4.2 Multi-omic applications of KGs

Multi-omic refers to a biological analysis approach that uses many "omics" datasets, such as genomes, proteomes, and transcriptomes (see figure 4.2). The suffix *ome* in molecular biology means a totality: for instance, *genome* refers to all the genetic information of an organism.

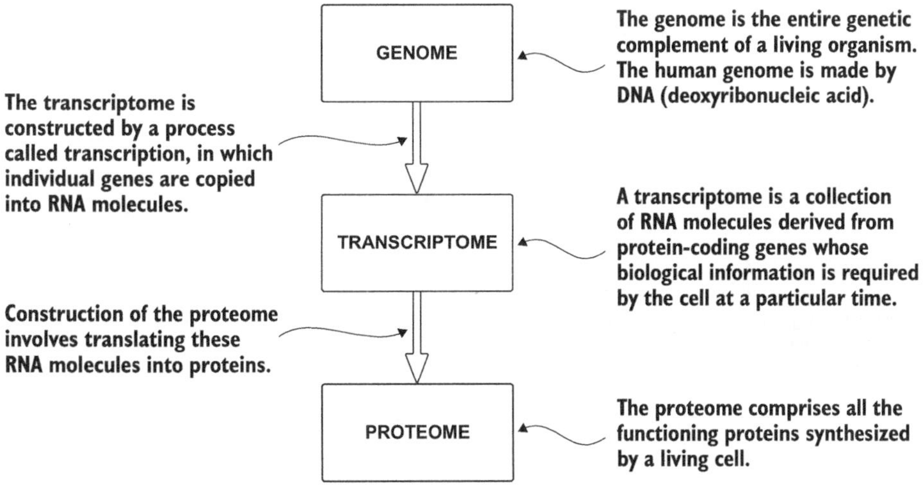

Figure 4.2 The three primary 'omics' data types used in biomedical KGs. Genome (DNA), transcriptome (RNA), and proteome (protein) data are biologically connected through transcription and translation.

> **Genome, transcriptome, and proteome**
>
> These terms and related concepts are used throughout this chapter:
>
> - *Genome*—The entire genetic complement of a living organism. Most genomes are made of DNA (deoxyribonucleic acid), but a few viruses have RNA (ribonucleic acid) genomes. DNA and RNA are polymeric molecules made up of chains of monomeric subunits called nucleotides.
> - *Transcriptome*—A collection of RNA molecules that direct the synthesis of the proteome. The transcriptome is constructed by the process called transcription, in which individual genes are copied into RNA molecules.
> - *Proteome*—The final product of genome expression that comprises all the functioning proteins synthesized by a living cell. It is the culmination of genome expression and also the starting point for the biochemical activities that constitute cellular life.

Many multi-omic applications use KGs to study the genome, how genes are expressed in the transcriptome, and how the products of those transcripts interact in the proteome. These include detecting miRNA-disease associations [4], gene–symptom prioritization [9], and predicting protein–protein interactions [10, 11, 12].

For example, Yang et al. [9] proposed a KG model to identify candidate genes associated with given symptoms. The researchers merged many heterogeneous data sources. To unify and integrate disease terms, they mapped the disease identifiers from the different databases to Unified Medical Language System (UMLS; https://www.nlm.nih.gov/research/umls/index.html) codes. Figure 4.3 shows the process.

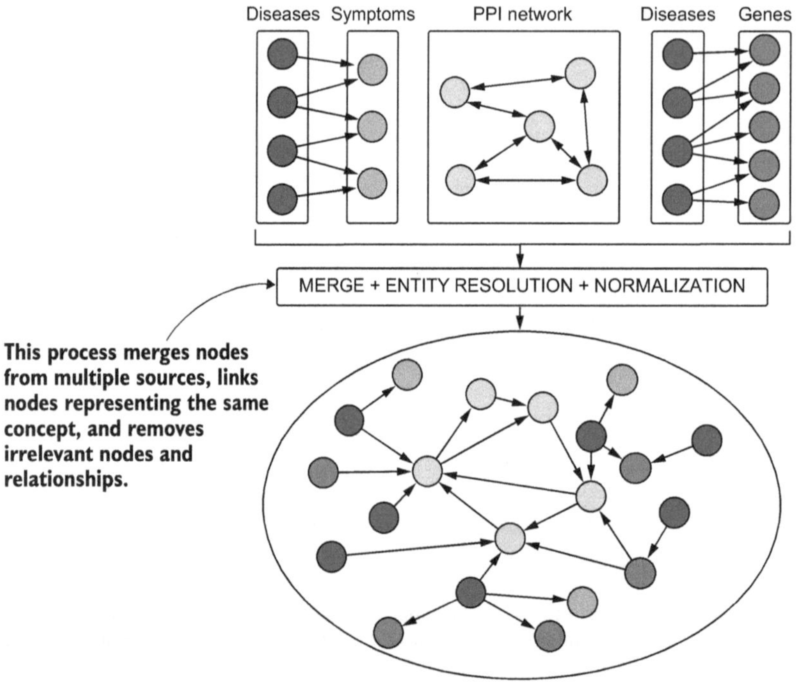

Figure 4.3 An extract from an image by Yang et al. [9], illustrating how the researchers combined data sources to create a holistic KG

In another case, protein–protein interaction (PPI) networks and protein–disease association have been successfully used in the computational discovery of disease pathways (groups of proteins associated with a specific disease) [12]. This is a perfect use case for developing IASs, where KGs play a key role, because trying to understand each disease protein in isolation cannot fully explain most human diseases. Let's look at how to construct and analyze this simpler type of KG before moving to more complex scenarios that require merging multiple data sources.

4.2.1 Creating a KG from the PPI and protein-disease networks

The goal is to discover disease pathways starting from known pathways. The approach proposed by Agrawal et al. [12] begins with a KG, as shown in Figure 4.4. Diseases are connected to associated known proteins, which are connected in the PPI network. For instance, figure 4.5 shows the connections between celiac disease[1] and relevant genes.

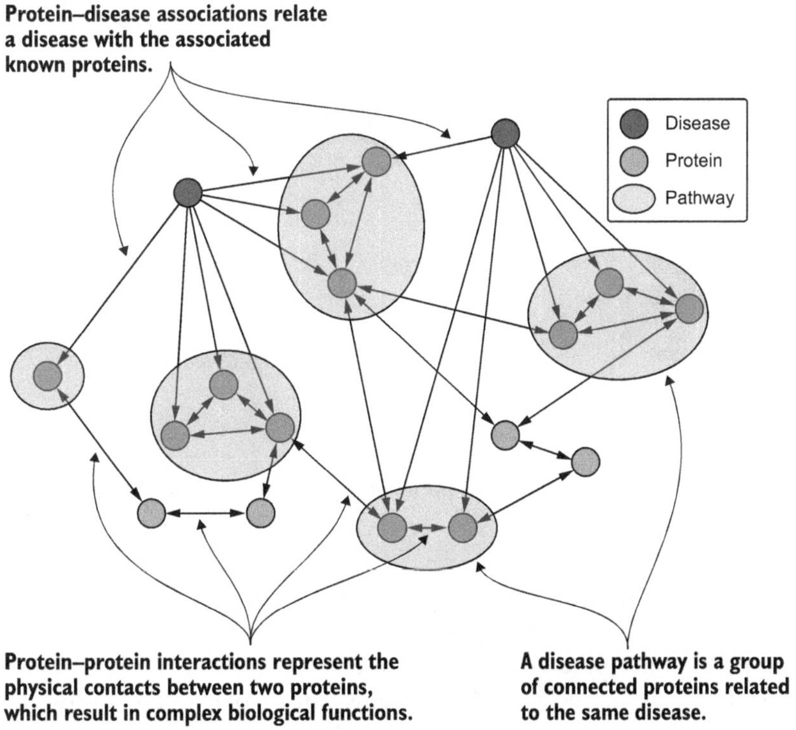

Figure 4.4 A disease pathway is a subgraph of the PPI network defined by a set of proteins associated with the disease.

1 One of the authors of this book, Alessandro, has a daughter affected by this disease. So, we can easily check the results without being experts.

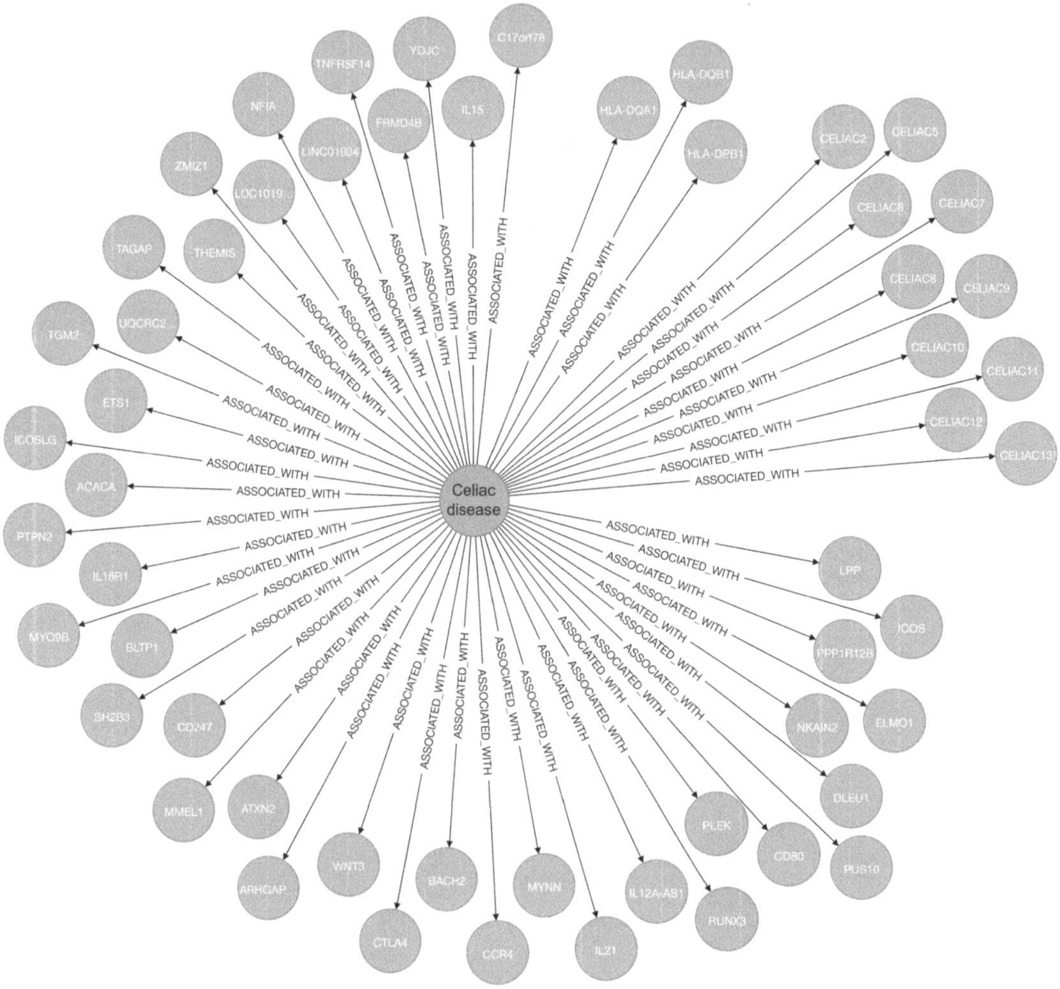

Figure 4.5 A small portion of the KG built by Agrawal [12]. We started from celiac disease and found the associated genes.

Now let's look at the discovery process to understand what we will do with this simple KG. Figure 4.6 shows the starting point and the result. We have a set of known pathways, and the IAS must predict and report a set of potential proteins and related pathways associated with the disease. The proteins can be part of an existing pathway or form a new one. The resulting KG is composed of a monopartite graph (the PPI network) and a bipartite graph (the disease–protein association network).

In this case, we have the data source we need: we can use *Disease Pathways in the Human Interactome* from the Stanford Network Analytics Project (SNAP; http://snap.stanford.edu/pathways/). Agrawal [12] created this simpler network starting from more complex data sources, and we can import and explore it. Then we will combine it with another dataset to make the resulting KG easier for humans to read.

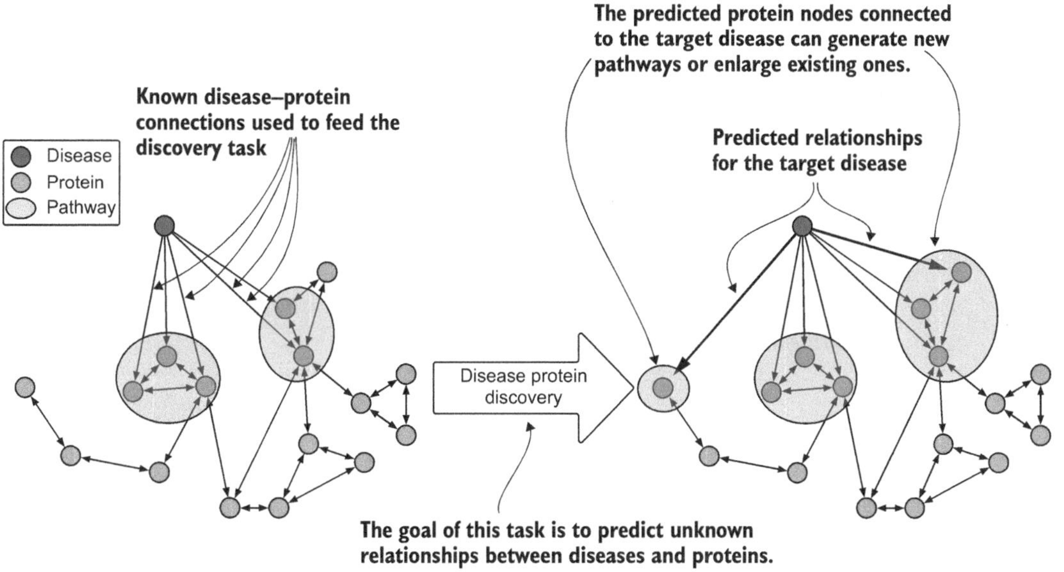

Figure 4.6 The discovery process to find proteins related to diseases

The following node key constraints ensure that all nodes with a particular label have an ID value and that it is unique.

Listing 4.1 Creating the constraints

```
CREATE CONSTRAINT protein_key IF NOT EXISTS FOR
     (n:Protein) REQUIRE (n.id) IS NODE KEY;
CREATE CONSTRAINT disease_key IF NOT EXISTS FOR
     (n:Disease) REQUIRE (n.id) IS NODE KEY;
```

If you aren't sure a constraint exists, add IF NOT EXISTS to ensure that it is created only if it doesn't exist.

The first file we'll import into our dataset is the human protein–protein interaction (PPI) network compiled by Menche et al. [13] and Chatr-Aryamontri et al. [14]. The resulting graph contains 342,354 experimentally documented interactions among 21,559 proteins in humans. Listings 4.2–4.4 assume that the files have been downloaded from SNAP, decompressed, and moved to a PPI directory in the import directory in Neo4j.

Listing 4.2 Importing the PPI network

```
:auto LOAD CSV FROM 'file:///PPI/bio-pathways-network.csv' AS line
CALL {
    WITH line
    MERGE (f:Protein {id: trim(line[0])})
    MERGE (s:Protein {id: trim(line[1])})
    MERGE (f)-[:INTERACTS_WITH]->(s)
} IN TRANSACTIONS OF 100 ROWS
```

> **Exercise**
>
> Run the necessary queries to verify the numbers of proteins and connections among them. Do this before the next step because it adds new proteins.

Next we'll import protein–disease associations in the form of tuples (u, d), where the alteration of protein u is linked to disease d. These associations come from DisGeNET (www.disgenet.org), a platform that centralizes knowledge about diseases. It contains more than 21,000 protein–disease associations divided among the 519 diseases that each have at least 10 disease proteins.

Listing 4.3 Importing pathways

```
:auto LOAD CSV WITH HEADERS
FROM 'file:///PPI/bio-pathways-associations.csv' AS line
CALL {
    WITH line
    WITH trim(line["Associated Gene IDs"]) AS proteins,
         trim(line["Disease Name"]) AS diseaseName,
         trim(line["Disease ID"]) AS diseaseId
    MERGE (d:Disease {id: diseaseId, name: diseaseName})
    WITH d, proteins
    UNWIND split(proteins, ",") AS protein
    WITH d, protein
    MERGE (p:Protein {id: trim(protein)})
    MERGE (d)-[:ASSOCIATED_WITH]->(p)
} IN TRANSACTIONS OF 100 ROWS
```

> **Exercise**
>
> Run some checks to verify the numbers. You should notice a change in the number of proteins. Can you identify the new proteins? Hint: Use the `NOT EXISTS` clause.

The last file we'll download from the SNAP dataset contains the disease categories. Diseases are subdivided into categories and subcategories using the Disease Ontology (https://disease-ontology.org/) and also mapped to UMLS codes. Of the 519 diseases pulled from DisGeNET, 290 have a UMLS code that maps to a code in the ontology. The dataset uses the second level of the ontology, which consists of 10 categories, including cancers (68 diseases), nervous system diseases (44), cardiovascular system diseases (33), and immune system diseases (21).

Listing 4.4 Importing disease classes

```
:auto LOAD CSV WITH HEADERS
➥FROM 'file:///PPI/bio-pathways-diseaseclasses.csv' AS line
CALL {
```

```
    WITH line
    WITH line["Disease ID"] as diseaseId, line["Disease Class"] as class
    MATCH (d:Disease {id:diseaseId})
    SET d.class = class
} IN TRANSACTIONS OF 100 ROWS
```

Exercise

After the import check, review the numbers for each disease's classes and the list of diseases without classes.

We've ingested the data from the SNAP dataset, but it uses codes to identify proteins. To improve readability, we can import gene information (https://ftp.ncbi.nih.gov/gene/DATA/gene_info.gz) from the NIH. After downloading the file, decompress it and move it to the same directory as the PPI.

Listing 4.5 Importing gene information

```
:auto LOAD CSV WITH HEADERS FROM 'file:///PPI/gene_info' AS line
     FIELDTERMINATOR '\t'
CALL {
    WITH line
    WITH trim(line["GeneID"]) AS proteinId, trim(line["Symbol"]) AS symbol,
    trim(line["description"]) AS description
    WITH proteinId, symbol, description
    MATCH (p:Protein {id:proteinId})
    SET p.name = symbol, p.description = description
} IN TRANSACTIONS OF 100 ROWS
```

4.2.2 High-level analysis of the resulting KGs

The next step is to inspect the KG, to evaluate the quality of the graph and explore the database. If you haven't been following along, you can download a Neo4j backup from https://mng.bz/5v7O. The next listing shows how to import this database using Neo4j 5.x.

Listing 4.6 Creating the PPI database from a Neo4j backup

```
# Add the following line to the neo4j.conf file
# dbms.databases.seed_from_uri_providers=URLConnectionSeedProvider
# then run the following command

CREATE DATABASE ppi OPTIONS { existingData: "use",
➥ seedUri: "https://mng.bz/5v7O"}
```

Our analysis of the graph starts with a generic evaluation of the PPI network. Our preferred algorithm for this type of evaluation is the *weakly connected component* (WCC): a community detection algorithm that finds disconnected subgraphs within a graph. To run this analysis, we will use the graph data science (GDS) library available on Neo4j (see online appendix B for installation instructions).

First we mark connected proteins using `INTERACTS_WITH`.

Listing 4.7 Marking proteins in the PPI network

```
MATCH (p:Protein)-[:INTERACTS_WITH]-()
SET p:PPIProtein
```

Now we need to create an in-memory representation of the graph, known as a *projection*.

Listing 4.8 Creating the graph projection in memory

```
call gds.graph.project(
    'ppi-graph',
    'PPIProtein',
    {
        INTERACTS_WITH: {
            orientation: 'UNDIRECTED'
        }
    }
)
```

- Name of the in-memory graph
- List of node types we would like to include. In this example, there is only one, but it can be a list.
- Here we have the list of relationships we would like to include in the analysis.

Once the subgraph has been created in memory, we can run the WCC algorithm using the following query.

Listing 4.9 Running the WCC on the PPI network

```
CALL gds.wcc.write('ppi-graph', { writeProperty: 'componentId' })
YIELD nodePropertiesWritten, componentCount, componentDistribution;
```

The results of the query are shown in table 4.1. Percentiles indicate the value below which a percentage of data points fall: for example, `p99: 21521` means that 99% of the connected components have fewer than 21,521 proteins.

Table 4.1 Summary results of the query in listing 4.9

nodePropertiesWritten	componentCount	componentDistribution
21559	27	{ "p99": 21521, "min": 1, "max": 21521, "mean": 798.481, "p90": 3, "p50": 1, "p999": 21521, "p95": 4, "p75": 2 }

The output of our algorithm shows that the proteins in the PPI network are highly connected. The 21,559 proteins in the graphs can be grouped into 27 non-overlapping subgraphs. Of those, one is very large, with 21,521 proteins. The other subgraphs are single nodes or islands of up to four components.

WCC assigns proteins to the same group just because they are connected. There may be groups of proteins connected more densely to each other than other proteins outside of this "community." To find them, we can use another graph clustering method: the Louvain modularity algorithm [15]. This is one of the fastest modularity-based algorithms and works well with large graphs. It reveals hierarchies of communities at different scales, which is useful for understanding the global functioning of a network. It works by maximizing the modularity score for each community—that is, how well groups have been partitioned into communities—by evaluating how much more densely connected the nodes are, compared to how connected they would be in a random network.

The next query runs the GDS implementation of Louvain on the same in-memory graph as earlier. If you have restarted the database or didn't run it before, you must execute the query in listing 4.8 before running this one.

Listing 4.10 Running Louvain on the PPI network

```
CALL gds.louvain.write('ppi-graph',
{ writeProperty: 'componentLouvainId' })
YIELD communityCount, modularity, modularities, communityDistribution
```

The results of this algorithm, shown in table 4.2, tell a different story than those in table 4.1.

Table 4.2 Summary results of the query in listing 4.10

communityCount	modularity	communityDistribution

48	0.5464241018027929	{
		"p99": 3533,
		"min": 1,
		"max": 3533,
		"mean":
		449.1458333333333,
		"p90": 1817,
		"p50": 3,
		"p999": 3533,
		"p95": 2336,
		"p75": 311
		}

We have some large communities with more than 3,500 proteins as well as smaller ones. The average size is around 450 proteins per community. The modularity score, which considers all the communities, is around 0.40 (40%). The next query lets us inspect the contents of the communities.

Listing 4.11 Inspecting the top 10 communities

```
MATCH (p:PPIProtein)
WITH p.componentLouvainId as communityId, count(p) as members
ORDER BY members desc
LIMIT 10
MATCH (p:PPIProtein)-[:INTERACTS_WITH]-(o)
WHERE p.componentLouvainId = communityId
WITH communityId, members, p.name as name, count(o) as connections
ORDER BY connections DESC
RETURN communityId, members, collect(name)[..20] as keyMembers
```

This query shows the top 20 most connected elements for each community identified by Louvain. The large cluster includes proteins like APP, NTRK1, GRB2, EGFR, and HSP90AA1; another includes ELAVL1, MOV10, NXF1, VCP, and SHMT2. A little googling (because we are not experts) shows that these groups make sense.

These algorithms are easy to use but generic: they treat each node and relationship the same way. Next we will introduce several techniques that are contextualized to our domain and goal, and that use the meaning of each node and each relationship. The book's code includes a library of these tools.

4.2.3 Domain-specific analysis of the PPI and disease KG

The earlier algorithms analyzed how the PPI network is structured. Now we'll consider subnetworks: the disease pathways. Translated into graph theory, given the PPI network, $G = (V, E)$, where nodes V represent proteins and edges E denote protein–protein interactions. The disease pathway for disease d is an undirected subgraph, $H_d = (V_d, E_d)$ of the PPI network specified by the set of proteins V_d associated with d and by the set of protein–protein interactions:

$$E_d = \{(u, v) | (u, v) \in E \ and \ u, v \in V_d\}$$

Using our graph, we can extract this subnetwork via a simple query.

Listing 4.12 Extracting disease pathways from the KG

```
MATCH (d:Disease {id:$id})-[:ASSOCIATED_WITH]->(p)
WITH collect(p) as proteins
UNWIND proteins as m0
UNWIND proteins as m1
OPTIONAL MATCH (m0)-[r:INTERACTS_WITH]->(m1)
RETURN DISTINCT m0, r, m1
```

This is a monopartite subnetwork, meaning it doesn't contain connections between proteins and diseases. Disease pathways related to different diseases can also overlap.

For certain measures, we need to consider how this subnetwork is connected to the rest of the PPI network. We can compute the pathway boundary

$$B_d = \{(u, v) | (u, v) \in E \text{ and } u \in V_d \text{ and } v \in V_d \backslash V\}$$

where $V_d \setminus V$ represents all nodes that are in the global set V but not in V_d, which translates to all nodes not associated with the target disease.

The measures we will consider characterize connectivity of disease proteins: both inside the disease pathways and outside, toward the other proteins in the PPI Network. Other metrics consider the distance and concentration in the pathways. All the measures are calculated for each disease, to characterize each one and find relevant patterns. They can also be collected, and their statistical information can give us a broader overview of the network and how it is distributed over different diseases.

LARGEST PATHWAY COMPONENT

The first measure is the relative *size of the largest pathway component.* This measure computes the fraction of disease proteins that lie in H_d's largest connected component

$$\text{relativeLargestCC}\,(d) = \frac{|\text{nodes}(\text{largestCC}(H_d))|}{|V_d|}$$

where nodes(largestCC(H_d)) returns the nodes in the largest WCCs of H_d. The code uses the `networkx` function in the next listing. (The complete code is available in the book's code repository in chapter/ch04/analysis/multiomic_analysis.py.)

Listing 4.13 Finding the size of the largest pathway component

```
class MultiOmicAnalysis(GraphDBBase):        <-- Python class created to analyze the PPI network. It extends a base class that contains the main functions for analyzing command-line arguments and handling connections with the Neo4j database.
    def __init__(self, argv, database):
        super().__init__(command=__file__, argv=argv)
        self.__database = database

    def load_hd(self, disease):        <-- Loads the disease pathway, which is a subgraph of the PPI network
        query = """
            MATCH (d:Disease {id:$id})-[:ASSOCIATED_WITH]->(p)
            WITH collect(p) as proteins
            UNWIND proteins as m0
            UNWIND proteins as m1
            OPTIONAL MATCH (m0)-[r:INTERACTS_WITH]->(m1)
            return distinct m0, r, m1
        """
        param = {"id": disease}
        return self.load_graph_and_get_nx_graph(query, param)

    def load_graph_and_get_nx_graph(self, query, param={}):        <-- Gets a query representing a subgraph and loads it as a networkx graph
        data = self.get_raw_data(query, param)
        G = networkx_utility.graph_undirected_from_cypher(data)        <-- Converts the query result into a networkx graph
        return G

    def get_raw_data(self, query, param):        <-- Returns a list of nodes and relationships for further processing
        with self._driver.session(database = self.__database) as session:
            results = session.run(query, param)
        return results.graph()
```

```
    def compute_largest_components(self, networkx_graph):
      largest_cc = max(nx.connected_components(networkx_graph), key=len)
      return largest_cc

if __name__ == '__main__':
  analysis = MultiOmicAnalysis(argv=sys.argv[1:], database="ppi")
  disease_id = 'celiac disease'
  networkx_graph = analysis.load_Hd(disease_id)
  nodes_count = networkx_graph.nodes.__len__()
  largest_cc = analysis.compute_largest_components(networkx_graph)
  relative_size_of_largest_cc =
    float(largest_cc_size.__len__())/nodes_count
```

Computes all connected components and returns the largest one

A disease to analyze (the full code analyzes all diseases)

Computes the relative size of the largest component, normalized over the total number of nodes

DENSITY

The second metric we'll calculate is the *density of the pathway*. As the name suggests, it measures how densely connected the proteins are in the disease pathways:

$$\text{density}(d) = \frac{2|E_d|}{|V_d|(|V_d| - 1)}$$

The denominator computes the number of possible edges, and the numerator considers the real edges. The resulting value is in [0; 1]: a higher density indicates that a higher fraction of all possible edges appear between nodes in H_d.

Listing 4.14 Calculating the density of the pathway

```
def compute_density(networkx_graph):
  nodes_count = networkx_graph.nodes.__len__()
  edges_count = networkx_graph.edges.__len__()
  density_pathway =
      2.0 * float(edges_count) / (nodes_count * (nodes_count - 1))

if __name__ == '__main__':
  analysis = MultiOmicAnalysis(argv=sys.argv[1:], database="ppi")
  disease_id = 'celiac disease'
  networkx_graph = analysis.load_hd(disease_id)
  density_pathway = compute_density(networkx_graph)
```

Computes the density for a disease represented by the related subgraph extracted from the full PPI network

CONDUCTANCE

The third metric is *conductance* [16]: the independence of the disease pathway (the subgraph) from the rest of the graph. It uses the edges connecting a node inside the subgraph with a node outside, regardless of direction:

$$\text{conductance}\ (d) = \frac{|B_d|}{(|B_d| + 2|E_d|)}$$

The resulting value is in [0; 1]: lower conductance means the pathway is a tighter-knit community, separated from the rest of the network.

Listing 4.15 Computing conductance

```
def compute_bd(self, disease):                          ◁ Computes Bd using
  query = """                                             a Cypher query
          MATCH (d:Disease {id:$id})-[:ASSOCIATED_WITH]->(p)
          WITH collect(p) as proteins
          MATCH (m0)-[r:INTERACTS_WITH]-(m1)
          WHERE m0 in proteins and not m1 in proteins
          RETURN count(DISTINCT r) as bd
  """
  param = {'id': disease}
  return self.get_data(query, param)["bd"][0]

def get_data(self, query, param={}):
  with self._driver.session(database=self.__database) as session:
    results = session.run(query, param)
    data = pd.DataFrame(results.values(), columns=results.keys())
  return data
```

Returns a pandas dataframe with columns representing the values returned; useful when a Cypher query returns values instead of nodes and relationships

```
if __name__ == '__main__':
  analysis = MultiOmicAnalysis(argv=sys.argv[1:], database="ppi")
  disease_id = 'celiac disease'
  networkx_graph = analysis.load_hd(disease_id)
  bd = analysis.compute_bd(disease_id)
  edges_count = networkx_graph.edges.__len__()
  conductance = float(bd) / (bd + 2 * edges_count)     ◁ Computes conductance
```

ANALYZING DISEASE PATHWAYS AND CLUSTERS

Now that we've computed metrics for each subgraph—the disease pathways—let's look at them as a whole. A common way to do so is to perform a frequency analysis that splits the results into buckets, as shown in figure 4.7.

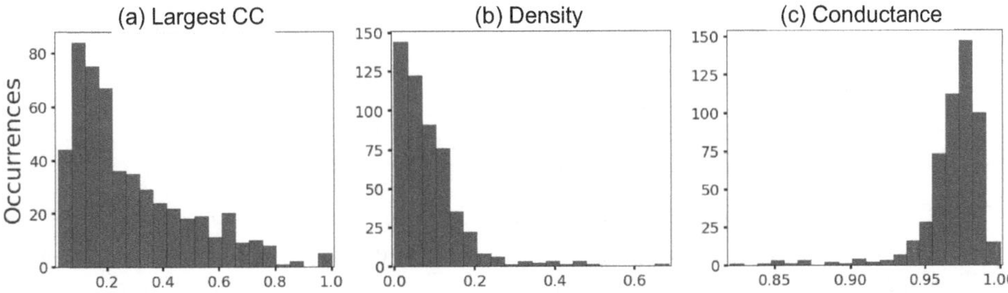

Figure 4.7 Distributions of the three key measures for disease pathways

We can see that disease pathways are fragmented in the PPI network, with a median of 16 connected components per disease and a median of only 21% of the proteins in the largest pathway component (figure 4.7a). Only about 10% of pathways have more than 60% of their proteins in the largest pathway component. The disease pathways are not well connected internally, with a median density of only 0.07 (the overall PPI network density is 0.0015), and 90% of diseases have a density below 0.17 (figure 4.7b). On the other hand, the disease pathways are well connected externally, with a median conductance of 0.96 (figure 4.7c).

These overlapping subgraphs obtained by considering disease pathways are very different from what we obtain by clustering using WCC or Louvain. To verify this theory, let's run the same measures on the clusters we computed using Louvain; the results are shown in figure 4.8.

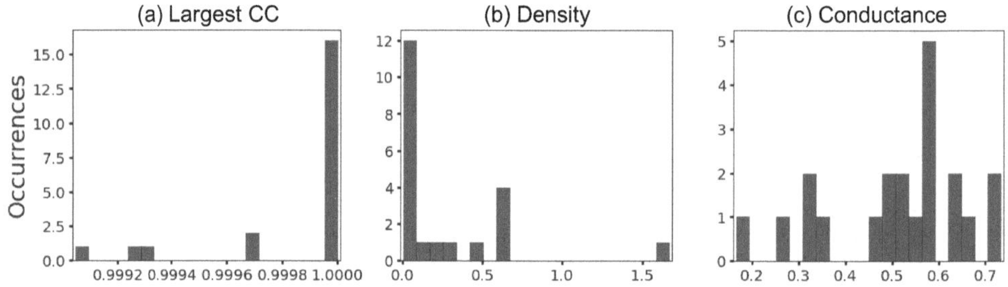

Figure 4.8 Distribution of the three key measures for the clusters obtained via the Louvain algorithm

These clusters tell us a different story. As expected, most of the proteins reside in a large, connected component (figure 4.8a). Density is related to the overall connectivity of the network, so the changes are only related to the different structures of the clusters. Conductance has improved: the clusters are better connected internally than externally.

The next section introduces the second type of applications (pharmaceuticals) and new algorithms for extracting information from KGs. We'll focus on edges and paths in addition to single nodes.

4.3 Pharmaceutical applications of KGs

The cost of developing a new therapeutic drug has been estimated at $1.4 billion [17]. The process typically takes 15 years from first compound to market [18], and the likelihood of success is remarkably low [19].

Drug analysis and repurposing can drastically reduce the duration, failure rates, and costs of approval. Such an analysis uses preexisting information on approved drugs, including toxicology profiling, preclinical models, clinical trials, and post-release surveillance. There are numerous examples where KGs have been used to predict drug interactions [20], identify molecular targets with which a drug might interact [21], and determine new diseases that can be treated with established drugs [22].

Dai et al. [21] used recommendation systems, in particular collaborative filtering, to infer drug–disease associations. Other researchers used these techniques to infer drug–target interactions [23, 24] and drug–disease treatments [25, 26]. Despite reported success, these approaches are limited to the drugs and diseases contained in the graph. Enriching the KG by combining these approaches with representations of chemical structures, biological processes, and other relevant knowledge might let researchers make predictions about novel compounds.

Himmelstein et al. [2] constructed a graph encoding knowledge from 29 public resources to connect compounds, diseases, genes, anatomies, pathways, biological processes, molecular functions, cellular components, pharmacological classes, side effects, and symptoms. They called the graph *Hetionet* (from "hetnet," short for "heterogeneous network"). The graph database is publicly available (https://het.io/) in a Neo4j format. So, for this example, we don't need to create a database from multiple sources, because the researchers did the work for us. Instead, we'll discuss the importance of a properly designed KG with a coherent schema, and ways to analyze the KG to evaluate the completeness of its information.

We've made a Neo4j 5.x backup for the database that you can download from https://mng.bz/648e. The following listing shows how to import it.

Listing 4.16 Creating the Het.io database

```
# Add the following line to the neo4j.conf file
# dbms.databases.seed_from_uri_providers=URLConnectionSeedProvider
# then run the following command

CREATE DATABASE hetionet OPTIONS { existingData: "use",
➥ seedUri: "https://mng.bz/648e"}
```

The imported KG consists of 47,031 nodes of 11 types and 2,250,197 relationships of 24 types. The nodes consist of 1,552 small-molecule compounds and 137 complex diseases, as well as genes, anatomies, pathways, biological processes, molecular functions, cellular components, perturbations, pharmacologic classes, drug side effects, and disease symptoms. The edges represent relationships between these nodes and encompass the collective knowledge produced by millions of studies over the last half century [2]. Figure 4.9 shows the full schema of the dataset.

For example, Compound–binds–Gene edges represent a compound binding to a protein encoded by a gene. Hetionet includes 11,571 edges, and for each, the reference is stored as a relationship attribute.

Exercise

Explore the imported graph and examine how the nodes are distributed across the different node types. Do the same for relationships. Be careful: the relationships can be more complex. Refer to the schema to make accurate queries.

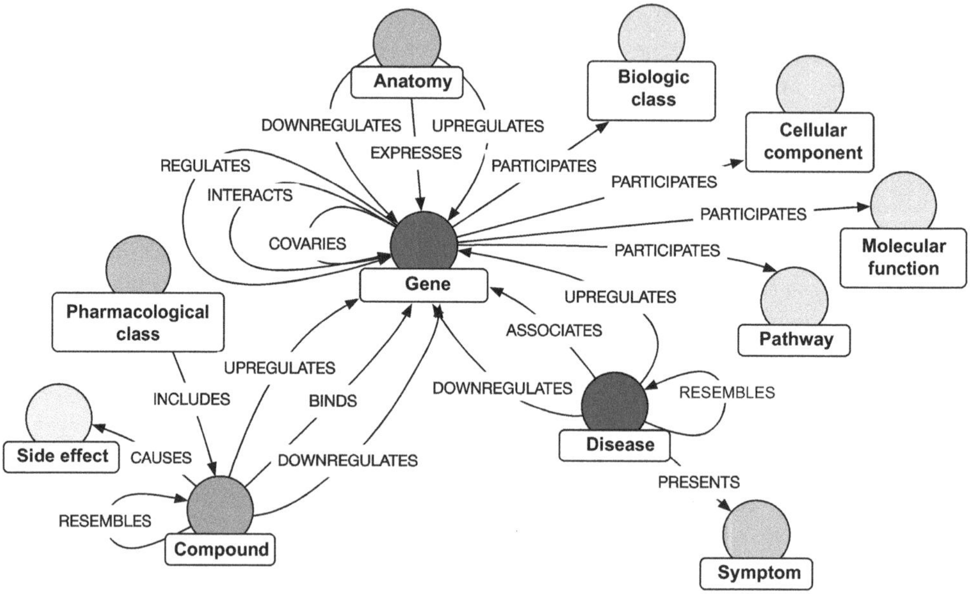

Figure 4.9 Het.io KG schema. The details of the nodes and relationships are available at https://mng.bz/EwgD.

Metapaths and degree-weighted path count (DWPC)

The path-exploration examples that follow use a new metric to order by relevance: *degree-weighted path count* (DWPC). It was introduced by Himmelstein [27], adapting an existing method originally developed for social network analysis, called PathPredict [28]. DWPC quantifies the prevalence of *metapaths* in Hetionet.

As shown in panel (a) of the following figure, a schema is represented using real nodes and existing relationships. A metapath, on the other hand, represents classes

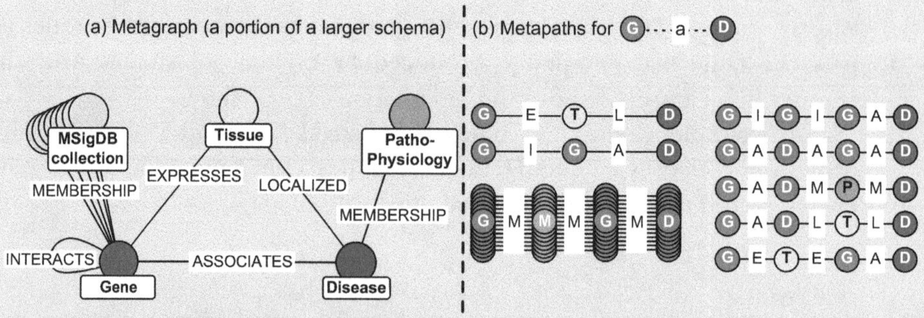

Metagraph (a) and metapath (b) excerpts for Hetionet. A metagraph describes the structure of the database, indicating the types of nodes and the types of relationships. Metapaths describe paths and indicate types of nodes and relationships.

sequence of nodes and relationships that describe potential real paths between a node of the first type and a node of the last type. We can "query" the schema, searching for patterns of connection among source types and destination types. For example, we can produce a list of possible metapaths for a generic pattern like (Gene)—a—(Disease) of max length 4, as shown in panel (b).

Again, note that these are descriptions of paths, not real instances of paths.

Now that we have explored the example KG, we can begin computing metrics. The simplest metapath-based metric is *path count* (PC): the number of paths, of a specified metapath, between the defined source and target nodes. PC does not adjust for the extent of graph connectivity along the path: each path has a value of 1. For example, figure 4.10a shows part of the KG where a specific gene, *IRF1*, relates to a specific disease, multiple sclerosis. All the paths belong to one of the potential metapaths for the generic pattern (Gene)—a—(Disease). In figure 4.10b, the paths related to each metapath are grouped. The first group has an intermediate node of type Tissue and only one path, so the PC is 1. The second group has another gene as intermediate node; in this group, the graph has three paths so the PC is 3.

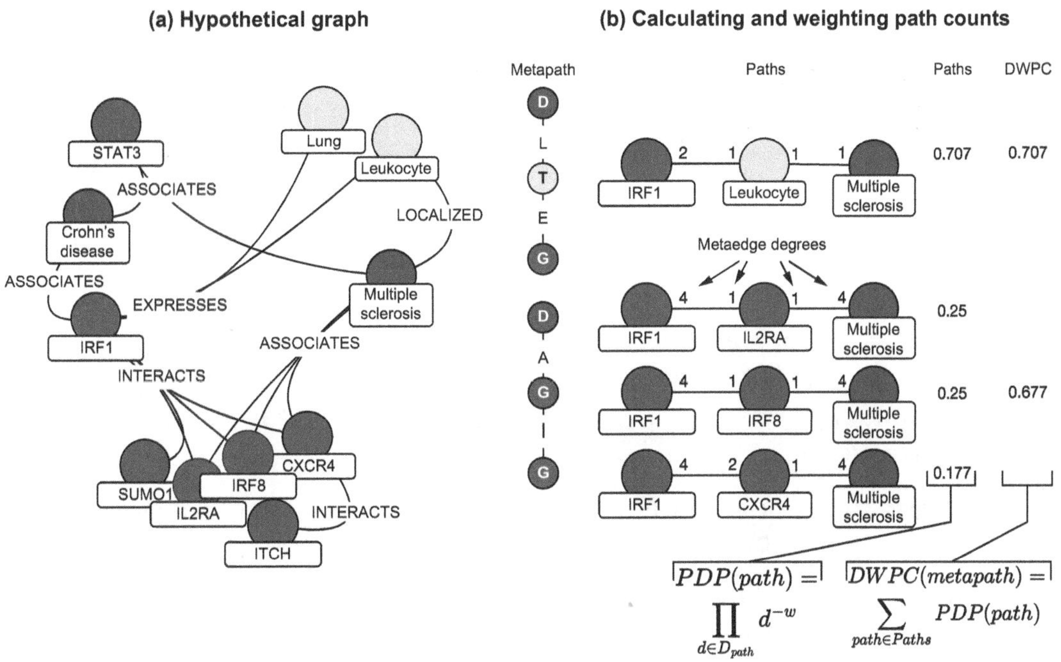

Figure 4.10 (a) Extracting paths based on a defined metapath, and (b) computing the path-degree product (PDP) and DWPC

DWPC, on the other hand, associates an individual value with each path, called the *path-degree product* (PDP). It is calculated using the following formula

$$\text{PDP}(\text{path}) = \prod_{d \in D_{\text{path}}} d^{-w}$$

and calculated as follows:

1. Extract all metaedge-specific degrees along the path (D_{path}), where each edge in the path contributes two degrees. In figure 4.10, the edge between IRF1 and IL2RA has the two degree values 4 and 1: IRF1 has four outgoing edges of type `INTERACTS`, and IL2RA has one incoming edge of type `INTERACTS`. The edge between IRF1 and CXCR4 has the degree values 4 and 2, because CXCR4 has two incoming edges of type `INTERACTS`.
2. Raise each degree to the $-w$ power, where $w \geq 0$ and is called the *damping exponent.*
3. Multiply all exponentiated degrees to yield the PDP.

Let's consider the path (IRF1)—[]—(CXCR4)—[]—(Muliple sclerosis) in figure 4.10. Suppose $w = 0.5$ Then the computation looks like this:

$$4^{-0.5} * 2^{-0.5} * 1^{-0.5} * 4^{-0.5} = 0.167 \cong 0.177$$

Figure 4.10 shows the values for the other paths. The DWPC equals the sum of the PDPs for the specific metapath:

$$\text{DWPC}_m(s, t) = \sum_{\text{path} \in \text{Paths}_m(s,t)} \text{PDP(path)}$$

These metrics evaluate path prevalence while also ignoring "well-known nodes"—a common issue during KG analysis.

4.3.1 Deep analysis of the Hetionet knowledge graph

At this stage, we have all the ingredients to perform a deep analysis of the Hetionet graph. We'll use Cypher queries and the DWPC metric to identify prominent gene ontology (GO) processes in a set of disease-associated genes.

NOTE The following analysis was inspired by the Thinklab project started by Daniel Himmelstein (https://think-lab.github.io/d/220/).

We'll use celiac disease (CD) again as an example. CD is a common (prevalence 1:100), chronic, immune-mediated enteropathy caused by intolerance to gluten that develops in genetically predisposed individuals. We can see the 48 genes associated with CD with the query `MATCH p = (:Disease {name: 'celiac disease'})-[rel: ASSOCIATES_DaG]-() RETURN p`.

Next we'll compute the DWPC between CD and each GO process in which at least two celiac-related genes participate. The results are further restricted to processes with at least five participating genes. Here's the Cypher query.

Listing 4.17 GO process enrichment for CD

```
MATCH path = (n0:Disease)-[:ASSOCIATES_DaG]-(n1)-[:PARTICIPATES_GpBP]-
➥ (n2:BiologicalProcess)
WHERE n0.name = 'celiac disease'
WITH
[
  size([(n0)-[:ASSOCIATES_DaG]-() | n0]),
  size([()-[:ASSOCIATES_DaG]-(n1) | n1]),
  size([(n1)-[:PARTICIPATES_GpBP]-() | n1]),
  size([()-[:PARTICIPATES_GpBP]-(n2) | n2])
]
AS degrees, path, n2
WITH
  n2.identifier AS go_id,
  n2.name AS go_name,
  count(path) AS PC,
  sum(reduce(pdp = 1.0, d in degrees| pdp * d ^ -0.4)) AS DWPC,
  size([(n2)-[:PARTICIPATES_GpBP]-() | n2]) AS n_genes
  WHERE n_genes >= 5 AND PC >= 2
RETURN
  go_id, go_name, PC, DWPC, n_genes
ORDER BY DWPC DESC
LIMIT 10
```

Searches for DaG-GpBP paths

Restricts to 'celiac disease' as source

Computes relationship-related degrees necessary for DWPC

Returns the GO process ID and name

Counts paths

Computes DWPC

Counts the genes in the GO process

Filters out GO processes with fewer than five generic genes involved and fewer than two celiac-related genes

When we ran it, the query returned the top 10 GO processes listed in table 4.3.

Table 4.3 Results of the query in listing 4.17

GO ID	GO name	PC	DWPC	# genes
GO:0031295	T cell costimulation	10	0.03347	75
GO:0031294	lymphocyte costimulation	10	0.03329	76
GO:0002507	tolerance induction	3	0.03276	12
GO:0050870	positive regulation of T cell activation	14	0.02925	201
GO:0034112	positive regulation of homotypic cell-cell adhesion	14	0.02902	205
GO:1903039	positive regulation of leukocyte cell-cell adhesion	14	0.02891	207
GO:0051249	regulation of lymphocyte activation	18	0.02763	381
GO:0002684	positive regulation of the immune system process	21	0.02718	880
GO:0022409	positive regulation of cell-cell adhesion	14	0.02716	242
GO:0050863	regulation of T cell activation	16	0.02701	290

The GO process with ID GO:0002684 has a high PC value and is connected to 880 genes. Ordering by PC, this process would be listed first. However, it is involved in many other processes, not just CD; ordering by DWPC, it is near the bottom of the results list. At the top is GO:0031295, "T cell costimulation," which is very relevant for the disease we are investigating.

Let's refine our search by considering more complex paths, including protein interaction relationships. The query in the next listing only considers associations between diseases and genes derived from genome-wide association studies (GWASs) [29, 30], which are less biased by existing knowledge. We also add protein interaction to the metapath to identify genes in the neighborhood of the interactome for CD. Finally, the query considers only genes that are upregulated in celiac-affected tissues.

Listing 4.18 Tissue-specific interactomics

```
MATCH path = (n0:Disease)-[e1:ASSOCIATES_DaG]-(n1)-[:INTERACTS_GiG]-(n2)-
➥ [:PARTICIPATES_GpBP]-(n3:BiologicalProcess)
WHERE n0.name = 'celiac disease'
  AND 'GWAS Catalog' in e1.sources
  AND exists((n0)-[:LOCALIZES_DlA]-()-[:UPREGULATES_AuG]-(n2))
WITH
[
  size([(n0)-[:ASSOCIATES_DaG]-() | n0]),
  size([()-[:ASSOCIATES_DaG]-(n1) | n1]),
  size([(n1)-[:INTERACTS_GiG]-() | n1]),
  size([()-[:INTERACTS_GiG]-(n2) | n2]),
  size([(n2)-[:PARTICIPATES_GpBP]-() | n2]),
  size([()-[:PARTICIPATES_GpBP]-(n3) | n3])
] AS degrees, path, n3 as target
WITH
  target.identifier AS go_id,
  target.name AS go_name,
  count(path) AS PC,
  sum(reduce(pdp = 1.0, d in degrees| pdp * d ^ -0.4)) AS DWPC,
  size([(target)-[:PARTICIPATES_GpBP]-() | target]) AS n_genes
  WHERE 5 <= n_genes <= 100 AND PC >= 2
RETURN
  go_id, go_name, PC, DWPC, n_genes
ORDER BY DWPC DESC
LIMIT 10
```

The query results are shown in table 4.4.

Table 4.4 Results of the query in listing 4.18

GO ID	GO name	PC	DWPC	# genes
GO:0031295	T cell costimulation	10	0.00665	75
GO:0031294	lymphocyte costimulation	10	0.00662	76

Table 4.4 Results of the query in listing 4.18 *(continued)*

GO ID	GO name	PC	DWPC	# genes
GO:0010560	positive regulation of glycoprotein biosynthetic process	6	0.00342	17
GO:0033689	negative regulation of osteoblast proliferation	4	0.00341	9
GO:1903020	positive regulation of glycoprotein metabolic process	6	0.00327	19
GO:0006573	valine metabolic process	5	0.00277	8
GO:0070884	regulation of calcineurin-NFAT signaling cascade	2	0.00277	19
GO:0010559	regulation of glycoprotein biosynthetic process	7	0.00272	35
GO:1903018	regulation of glycoprotein metabolic process	7	0.00257	40
GO:0070098	chemokine-mediated signaling pathway	9	0.00256	72

The results are even more specific. The first two are the same, but adding the protein interaction returned other disease-specific aspects, such as a strong dominance of processes related to glycoproteins. If we're interested in the "positive regulation of glycoprotein biosynthetic process" relationship, we can retrieve the paths behind the DWPC.

Listing 4.19 Finding the paths behind a DWPC

```
MATCH path = (n0:Disease)-[e1:ASSOCIATES_DaG]-(n1)-[:INTERACTS_GiG]-(n2)-
➥ [:PARTICIPATES_GpBP]-(n3:BiologicalProcess)
WHERE n0.name = 'celiac disease'
  AND n3.name = 'positive regulation of glycoprotein biosynthetic process'
  AND 'GWAS Catalog' in e1.sources
  AND exists((n0)-[:LOCALIZES_DlA]-()-[:UPREGULATES_AuG]-(n2))
RETURN path
```

The result is shown in figure 4.11.

Exercise

By modifying the queries, you can perform the same analysis on different diseases. Try running some and doing research to evaluate how much knowledge this KG captures. Thinklab offers many other interesting queries to explore.

As we've seen, KGs can capture knowledge that is easy to navigate and use. Our analysis provided a quantitative evaluation of the stored information.

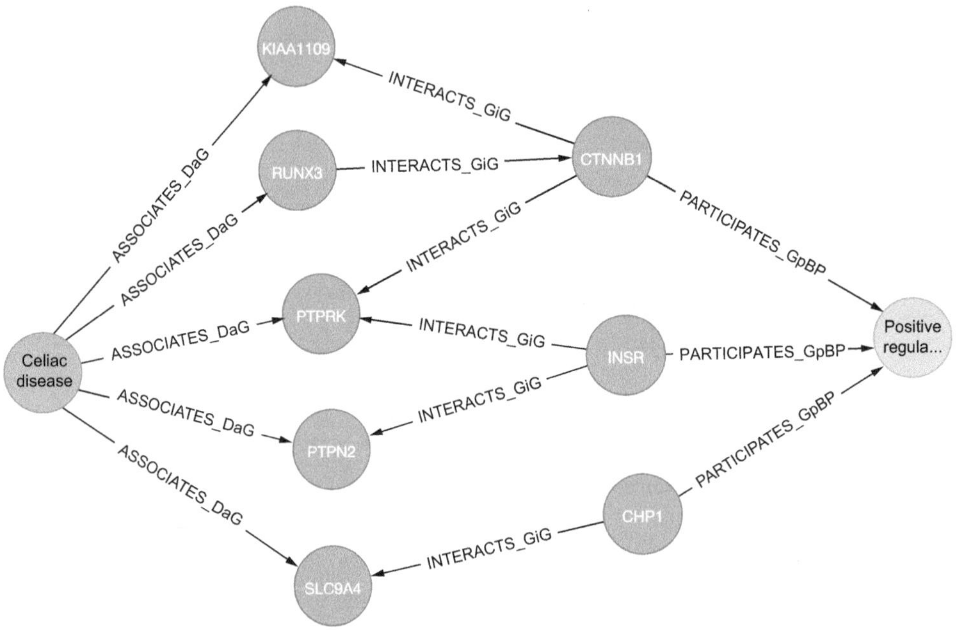

Figure 4.11 Result of the query in listing 4.19 showing the paths between CD and "positive regulation of glycoprotein biosynthetic process"

4.3.2 LLM-assisted interpretation of pathway analysis results

Although the DWPC-based queries provide quantitative rankings of biological processes, translating these results into clinically actionable insights requires domain expertise and contextual understanding. LLMs can serve as intelligent interpreters, helping to synthesize complex pathway analysis results into coherent biological narratives and clinical recommendations.

Let's demonstrate this using the GO process enrichment results from our CD analysis. The query returned processes like "T cell costimulation," "tolerance induction," and "positive regulation of glycoprotein biosynthetic process" with varying DWPC scores. An LLM can help interpret these findings in their broader biological context.

Listing 4.20 Example LLM analysis prompt

```
You are a biomedical research assistant analyzing gene ontology pathway
enrichment results for celiac disease. Please interpret the following
results from a knowledge graph analysis and provide insights for clinical
researchers:

QUERY RESULTS:
- T cell costimulation (DWPC: 0.03347, PC: 10, Genes: 75)
- lymphocyte costimulation (DWPC: 0.03329, PC: 10, Genes: 76)
- tolerance induction (DWPC: 0.03276, PC: 3, Genes: 12)
```

```
- positive regulation of T cell activation (DWPC: 0.02925, PC: 14, Genes: 201)
- positive regulation of glycoprotein biosynthetic process
➥(DWPC: 0.00342, PC: 6, Genes: 17)

CONTEXT: These pathways were identified through DWPC analysis of celiac
disease-associated genes in a protein-protein interaction network. DWPC
scores indicate pathway relevance while accounting for node degree bias.

ANALYSIS REQUEST:
1. Interpret the biological significance of these top-ranked pathways in
     celiac disease
2. Explain the relationship between these processes and celiac disease
     pathogenesis
3. Identify potential therapeutic implications
4. Highlight any unexpected findings that warrant further investigation
5. Suggest follow-up research questions based on these results
```

The LLM translates raw analytical results into a comprehensive analysis, explaining how T cell costimulation relates to CD's autoimmune nature, why tolerance induction appears disrupted, and how glycoprotein regulation connects to gluten intolerance mechanisms. This interpretation transforms results into actionable biological insights. The first part of the results obtained using Claude.ai Sonnet 4.0 (https://claude.ai/new) are shown in the next sidebar.

Partial Claude.ai results for biological significance of top-ranked pathways

T Cell and Lymphocyte Costimulation Pathways (DWPC: 0.03347 and 0.03329). These pathways represent the core immunological dysfunction in celiac disease. The high DWPC scores and substantial gene counts (75-76 genes) indicate that dysregulated costimulatory signaling is central to disease pathogenesis. In celiac disease, antigen-presenting cells present gliadin peptides to T cells through HLA-DQ2/DQ8 molecules, and aberrant costimulation leads to inappropriate T cell activation rather than tolerance.

Tolerance Induction (DWPC: 0.03276) Despite having fewer genes (12), this pathway shows a remarkably high DWPC score, suggesting it's highly interconnected within the celiac disease network. This likely reflects the fundamental breakdown of oral tolerance to dietary antigens - a hallmark of celiac disease pathogenesis.

Positive Regulation of T Cell Activation (DWPC: 0.02925) With 201 genes involved, this represents the broadest immunological dysregulation. The sustained T cell activation drives the chronic inflammatory response that characterizes celiac disease, leading to villous atrophy and clinical symptoms.

This approach demonstrates how LLMs can complement KG analytics by providing a contextual interpretation that transforms quantitative results into qualitative understanding, bridging the gap between computational analysis and applications.

4.4 Clinical applications of KGs

Clinical applications are still in the early stages of using KGs. In this case, the long-term goal is to use and analyze the KG to support patient care, primarily through precision medicine. The precision medicine initiative is a long-term research endeavor to understand how a person's genetics, environment, and lifestyle can help determine the best approach to prevent or treat diseases. Implementing precision medicine requires the integration of omics data, such as proteomics, genomics, transcriptomics, into the clinical decision-making process, which involves patient data, such as electronic health records (EHRs). The quantity and diversity of biomedical data, the spread of clinically relevant knowledge across multiple biomedical databases and publications, and privacy concerns pose challenges to data integration [31].

EHRs are designed to contain information from all clinicians involved in a patient's care. They can be challenging to interpret, there is considerable subjectivity, and information a clinician deems irrelevant may be omitted or not pursued, leading to missing information [32]. So, KGs used in clinical applications merge EHRs with multi-omics datasets, multiple ontologies, and other data sources. The key elements are nodes representing patients, drugs, and diseases; edges encode relationships such as a patient being treated with certain drugs or diagnosed with a disease.

Another example that uses EHRs and graphs is *patient journey mapping*, also called *patient experience mapping* [33]. This is a rapidly growing approach for better understanding how people enter, experience, and exit health services. It is often compared with *clinical pathways* [34], which establish the standard of care for a patient's clinical presentation with a specific disease and are often linked to a companion patient journey map. Figure 4.12 illustrates the scope of a single patient journey for a complex diseases like cancer.

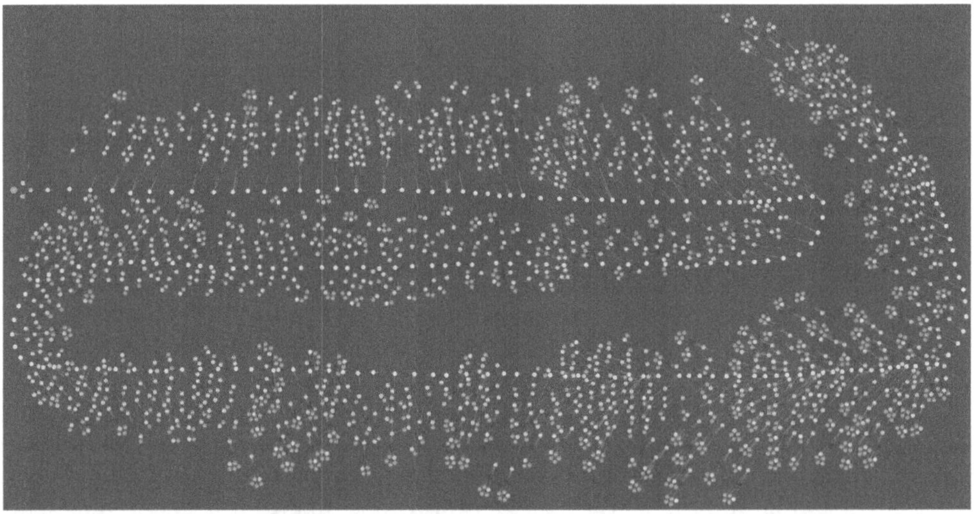

Figure 4.12 A single patient's clinical oncology journey (courtesy of David Hughes; https://www.graphable.ai/blog/patient-journey-mapping)

The community is working hard to find solutions to the privacy and security concerns related to using EHRs. Some approaches use a huge set of patient data to extract statistical information about diseases, symptoms, or treatment outcomes [32]. These statistical relationships, along with their related weights, are stored in the KG, but not the actual patient data. This increases the guarantee of privacy [35].

Another approach is to build a deidentified, generic clinical KG based on nonsensitive data, anonymized data, experimental results, and statistical information derived from real data. Patient EHR data is used only when strictly necessary and with patient consent.

The Clinical Knowledge Graph (CKG) from Albertos Santos et al [31] is a platform with a KG at its core. CKG harmonizes and integrates data by connecting 33 node labels with 51 relationship types (see figure 4.13). It enables queries that could give insights into altered functions, suggest drugs for regulated proteins, and reveal possible confounding factors.

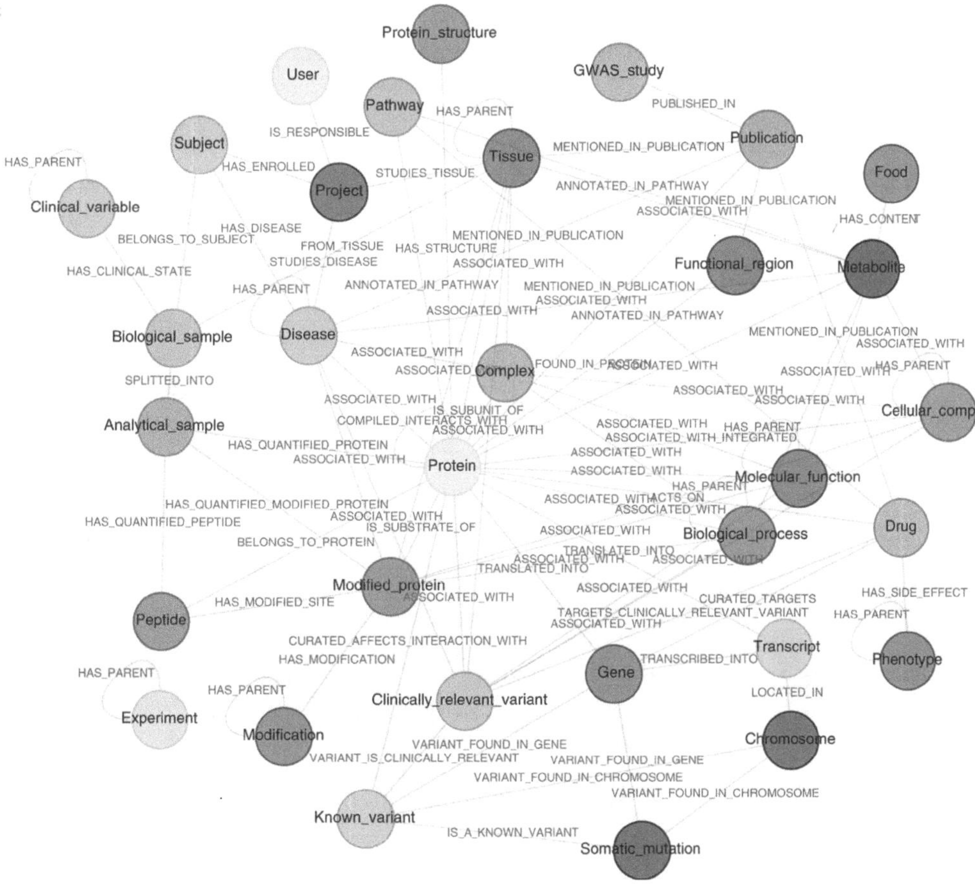

Figure 4.13 The schema for the Clinical Knowledge Graph (https://www.nature.com/articles/s41587-021-01145-6)

CKG is available in Neo4j format at https://github.com/MannLabs/CKG. We upgraded to the latest version available while writing this book, and you can import the provided dump (https://mng.bz/oZQZ) to your machine using the following code.

Listing 4.21 Importing the CKG database

```
# Add the following line to the neo4j.conf file
# dbms.databases.seed_from_uri_providers=URLConnectionSeedProvider
# then run the following

CREATE DATABASE ckg OPTIONS { existingData: "use",
➥ seedUri: "https://mng.bz/oZQZ"}
```

Let's run a query to show how simple it is to extract valuable insights from a KG like CKG. Suppose your current clinical study is targeting a set of proteins, and you are planning a clinical trial. A portion of the patients eligible for the trial suffer from cardiomyopathy-related diseases. You want to check whether known associations exist between your proteins and any cardiomyopathy-related disease.

Listing 4.22 Finding known protein–disease associations

```
WITH
  ['A1BG~P04217','A2M~P01023','ACACB~O00763',
   'ACTC1~P68032','ADIPOQ~Q15848','AGT~P01019',
   'AIFM2~Q9BRQ8','APOA2~V9GYM3'] as  proteins,      <-- Defines the list of proteins we are interested in
  3 as minScore,                                     <-- Defines the minimum association strength threshold
  "DOID:0050700" as parentDisease                    <-- Defines the target disease DOID
MATCH (protein:Protein)-[r]-(disease:Disease)        <-- Matches any type of protein–disease association
WHERE (
  (protein.name+"~"+protein.id) IN proteins) AND
  toFloat(r.score)> minScore  AND
  ((disease)-[:HAS_PARENT*0..]->(:Disease {id: parentDisease}))   <-- Matches any disease related to cardiomyopathy
RETURN
  (protein.name+"~"+protein.id) AS node1,
  disease.name+" <"+disease.id+">" AS node2,
  r.score AS weight, type(r) AS type,
  r.source AS source
ORDER BY weight DESC
```

The results in table 4.5 show a specific protein that is strongly associated with several types of intrinsic cardiomyopathies. This finding provides a specific starting point for possible further investigations.

NOTE DOID is the disease ontology identifier, as defined at www.disease-ontology.org.

Table 4.5 Protein–disease associations from the query in listing 4.22

node1	node2	weight	type	source
"ACTC1~P68032"	"intrinsic cardiomyopathy <DOID:0060036>"	5	"ASSOCIATED_WITH"	"DISEASES"
"ACTC1~P68032"	"left ventricular noncompaction <DOID:0060480>"	5	"ASSOCIATED_WITH"	"DISEASES"
"ACTC1~P68032"	"familial hypertrophic cardiomyopathy <DOID:0080326>"	5	"ASSOCIATED_WITH"	"DISEASES"
"ACTC1~P68032"	"hypertrophic cardiomyopathy <DOID:11984>"	5	"ASSOCIATED_WITH"	"DISEASES"
"ACTC1~P68032"	"dilated cardiomyopathy <DOID:12930>"	5	"ASSOCIATED_WITH"	"DISEASES"
"ACTC1~P68032"	"restrictive cardiomyopathy <DOID:397>"	5	"ASSOCIATED_WITH"	"DISEASES"

4.4.1 LLM-guided clinical decision support analysis

Clinical KGs contain complex relationships between patients, treatments, and outcomes that require careful interpretation. LLMs can help clinicians and researchers synthesize multidimensional clinical data into coherent treatment recommendations and research directions. Using our CKG analysis, which identified strong associations between the ACTC1 protein and various cardiomyopathies, an LLM can provide clinical context and decision support.

Listing 4.23 Example LLM clinical analysis prompt

```
You are a clinical informatics specialist analyzing protein-disease
associations from electronic health records integrated with biomedical
knowledge graphs. Provide clinical decision support based on these
findings:

CLINICAL SCENARIO: Research study targeting proteins in patients with
     cardiomyopathy-related diseases

KNOWLEDGE GRAPH FINDINGS:
- ACTC1~P68032 shows strong associations (score: 5.0) with:
  * Intrinsic cardiomyopathy (DOID:0060036)
  * Left ventricular noncompaction (DOID:0060480)
  * Familial hypertrophic cardiomyopathy (DOID:0080326)
  * Hypertrophic cardiomyopathy (DOID:11984)
  * Dilated cardiomyopathy (DOID:12930)
  * Restrictive cardiomyopathy (DOID:397)
```

```
TARGET PROTEIN LIST:
➥ ['A1BG~P04217','A2M~P01023','ACACB~O00763','ACTC1~P68032','ADIPOQ~Q15848',
➥ 'AGT~P01019','AIFM2~Q9BRQ8','APOA2~V9GYM3']

CLINICAL REQUEST:
1. Interpret the clinical significance of ACTC1's broad cardiomyopathy
   associations
2. What does this suggest about patient stratification for clinical trials?
3. Identify potential safety considerations for the research study
4. Recommend additional screening or monitoring protocols
5. Suggest companion biomarkers or genetic testing approaches
6. Propose modifications to inclusion/exclusion criteria based on these
   findings
```

This LLM-assisted analysis helps translate computational discoveries from KGs into practical clinical decision-making, informing patient care and research protocols. The results are too lengthy to include; you can use this prompt as an exercise with one of your favorite LLM tools.

> **NOTE** We do not suggest using results from LLMs without proper interpretation by physicians and researchers. Our purpose is to show how LLMs can convert complex data extracted from large KGs into interpretable insights. Remember, our goal is to empower humans via IASs, not to replace them!

Summary

- Knowledge graphs built from structured data sources require systematic integration of heterogeneous datasets. This process involves entity resolution, schema alignment, and data quality validation to create coherent and queryable knowledge representations.
- Clustering algorithms like weakly connected components (WCCs) and Louvain provide insights into the global structure and community organization of any multisource KG.
- Subgraph analysis measures like density, conductance, and relative size of largest connected components offer quantitative approaches to evaluate KG quality and completeness across domains.
- Advanced path-based metrics such as degree-weighted path count (DWPC) enable more sophisticated analysis of relationship patterns and entity relevance than simple path-counting approaches.
- Comprehensive KGs like Hetionet, the PPI network, and CKG serve as valuable testbeds for demonstrating integration techniques and analytical approaches.
- LLM-assisted interpretation of KG analysis results helps translate quantitative metrics into actionable domain-specific insights and research hypotheses.

Part 3

Building knowledge graphs from text

Transforming unstructured textual data into structured knowledge is an exciting frontier in the development of intelligent systems. This part of the book explores the combination of knowledge graphs (KGs) and large language models (LLMs) in extracting, structuring, and representing knowledge from text, demonstrating how these technologies complement each other to unlock value from unstructured information.

Unstructured text comprises 80% to 90% of enterprise data today. The integration of LLMs has revolutionized this domain, helping us understand and extract meaningful information from content in natural language and reducing the need for human labor. Combining these capabilities with traditional natural language processing (NLP) techniques and KG technologies lets us create systems that can understand context and maintain structured, verifiable knowledge representations.

Chapter 5 demonstrates converting text to KGs and introduces named entity recognition (NER) and relationship extraction using modern LLM-based methods. A case study shows how to extract structured knowledge from historical documents.

Chapter 6 focuses on the workflow from document processing and OCR scanning to graph analytics. We demonstrate a schema design and advanced techniques for data cleaning, entity resolution, and network analysis.

Chapter 7 explores named entity disambiguation (NED). A case study shows how to link entities to structured knowledge bases, enabling conceptual search and intelligent advisory systems.

Chapter 8 shows an approach to NED that combines LLMs with domain ontologies, enhancing the LLMs with structured domain knowledge for contextually aware disambiguation.

The techniques presented here demonstrate the synergy between traditional knowledge representation and modern AI capabilities, establishing the groundwork for building intelligent knowledge systems.

5 Extracting domain-specific knowledge from unstructured data

This chapter covers

- Building knowledge graphs from unstructured data
- Complexities of managing archives: the Rockefeller Archive Center example
- Using large language models to extract entities and relationships

Until now, we have discussed knowledge graphs (KGs) based on structured data such as tables, knowledge bases, and so forth, but what about unstructured data? Think about emails, chats, laws, research papers, news articles, social media, and more—the world is overflowing with information and knowledge in an unstructured form. Using these data sources could provide valuable information for your business.

The task of transforming unstructured data into knowledge consists of data ingestion and processing, various natural language processing (NLP) techniques, data enrichment, machine learning (ML) processing, and data modeling to build downstream applications. Conceptually, this process has two main challenges:

- *Knowledge representation* (as discussed in chapter 2) refers to how information is modeled so that computers (and humans) can access it autonomously to solve tasks. If properly designed, it speeds up processing by making concepts (re)usable and extendable. In this context, a KG represents an ordered and connected version of information that's otherwise isolated, distributed, and disorganized.
- *Knowledge learning* uses a combination of frameworks and technologies, such as NLP and large language models (LLMs), to mine insights from unstructured documents.

To illustrate the complexities involved in building KGs from textual data, this chapter dives into an example project and shows how to overcome some of the challenges of mining unstructured information.

5.1 The archives challenge

An archive covers a wide range of topics and concepts spanning current and historical data, and incorporates data sources of different complexities and linguistic styles. The data is typically unstructured, including sources such as books, reports, meeting minutes, grant assignments, and so on. In this chapter and the next, we will focus on a subset of historical data on the origins of modern scientific disciplines held by the Rockefeller Archive Center (RAC).

The RAC is not just a repository of historical and current documents; it is also a research center dedicated to the study of philanthropy and the research sectors influenced by American foundations, individual donors, and civil society organizations. It holds the records of more than 40 philanthropic foundations, research institutions, and cultural organizations, including the Rockefeller Foundation and the Ford Foundation, and makes them accessible to researchers worldwide.

The Rockefeller Foundation

The Rockefeller Foundation was founded in 1913 as one of the earliest major philanthropic institutions in the United States by John D. Rockefeller, his son, and their business advisor, Frederick Taylor Gates. Rockefeller was, in his epoch, the wealthiest American of all time: at his peak, he controlled 90% of oil production in the country. He was worried that his heirs might "dissipate their inheritances or become intoxicated with power" [1], so Gates encouraged the idea of creating "permanent corporate philanthropies for the good of Mankind." Toward that end, Rockefeller and other industrialists, including steel magnate Andrew Carnegie, defined the modern approach of targeted philanthropy and created the foundations that bear their names.

We aim to shed light on how grant-making processes function behind the scenes. To achieve this, we'll design a high-quality domain-specific knowledge extraction system, following the steps outlined in the mental model in figure 5.1.

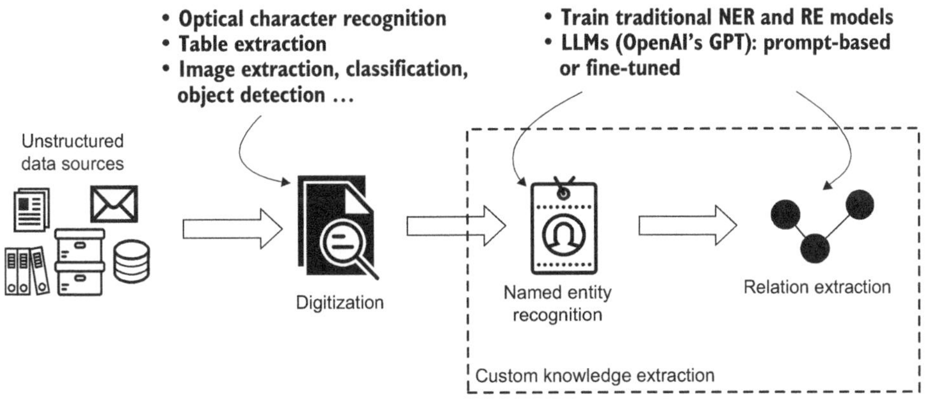

Figure 5.1 Path from domain-specific unstructured textual data to structured knowledge. Each step relies on state-of-the-art machine learning models, such as optical character recognition for document digitization, named entity recognition, and relation extraction systems.

The Rockefeller Foundation's process of selecting projects for funding relied on program officers who pinpointed areas of research worthy of grants. These officers developed deep knowledge about their specializations by building networks of researchers as well as searching for recommendations outside of those networks. They wrote notes about meetings, phone calls, and dinners in their diaries, often hastily and on typewriters, using shortcuts, abbreviations, and domain-specific nomenclature. These diaries represent a treasure trove of detailed knowledge as well as professional and personal observations. If mined and modeled properly, we could use this information to answer questions like these:

- Are there any patterns that typically precede the funding of an idea?
- Do granted projects tend to follow recommendations from influential scientists or previous grantees?
- How many internal discussions take place before a grant is awarded?
- Are there trends in funding subdisciplines? Do they change over time?

This chapter showcases how we can adjust state-of-the-art ML technologies to a specific domain and mine complex knowledge from unstructured data. In the following chapter, we use this extracted information to produce a KG and answer complex questions about relational information previously locked in unstructured documents.

5.2 Key concepts of knowledge extraction

Transforming textual data into structured KGs centers on two fundamental processes: identifying *entities* within the text and extracting the *relationships* that connect them. These interconnected components form the structural backbone of any KG. This section focuses on these building blocks of knowledge extraction.

5.2.1 Recognizing named entities

The first step from text (or other unstructured data source) to a KG is *named entity recognition* (NER). NER is an ML classification system trained to identify mentions of named entities in raw text and assign them to predefined categories. Recognizing named entities has many business use cases:

- Discovering insights by connecting documents from various data sources (for example, connecting people mentioned in financial documents with information from business registries)
- Improving a company's information management and data governance
- Laying the basis for a data compliance system
- Improving search capabilities
- Relating causes with effects (for example, weather conditions and flight delays)

Many open source NLP libraries offer models with generic entity categories (`Person`, `Location`, `Organization`, and so on) out of the box. However, these are rarely enough. For example, figure 5.2 shows an entry from the diary of Rockefeller Foundation

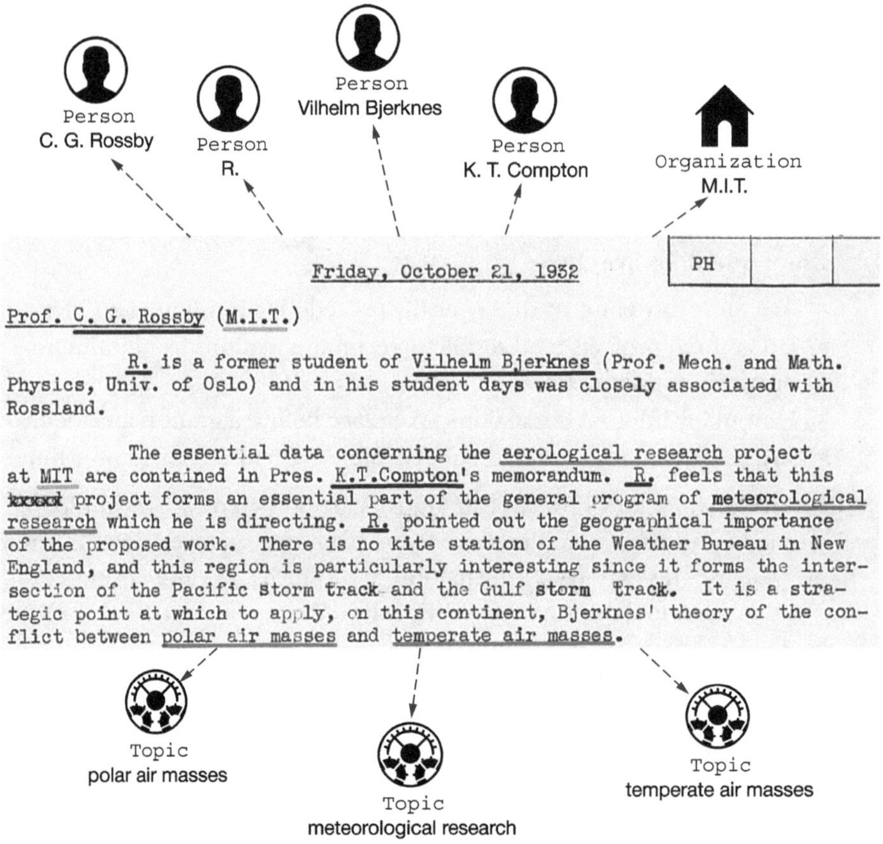

Figure 5.2 A snippet of Warren Weaver's diary entry with highlighted relevant named entities

program officer Warren Weaver. In this case, identifying mentions of people and organizations is important, but just as important is recognizing conversation topics. Further, a `Topic` entity can be one of three subtypes: a research `discipline`, a `technology`, or a `disease`.

The example diary entry mentions four topics of the `discipline` type: "aerological research," "meteorological research," "polar air masses," and "temperate air masses." A simple dictionary-based NER system would not be able to identify them. To handle this task, we need a custom entity-extraction system. And we can achieve that either by training a custom NER model or, as we'll see, by taking advantage of LLMs.

5.2.2 Extracting relations

The second step on our path from textual data to a KG is *relation extraction* (RE): identifying semantic relations between entity pairs within textual documents. For example, consider the following sentence: "Jane Austen, Victorian era writer, is currently employed by Google." This text mentions named entities of classes `PERSON` ("Jane Austen") and `ORGANIZATION` ("Google"), and those entities are closely related: one is the employee of the other. Capturing this relatedness is the making of a true KG.

NOTE There are many ways to model this kind of relationship, such as `Jane Austen - WORKS_FOR -> Google` and `EMPLOYS: Jane Austen <- EMPLOYS - Google`. The important thing is to be consistent across documents.

5.3 Building KGs with large language models

So far, we've discussed "traditional" NLP: building task-specific training datasets, identifying the best model architectures, fine-tuning the hyperparameters, and so on. Part of this process is improving the quality of the training data. Doing so is, to put it mildly, arduous.

In late 2022, OpenAI published its first models from the GPT-3.5 series, including a chatbot, ChatGPT, with astonishing capabilities: based on a question or a task description formulated in natural language, it can help you draft a letter, summarize an article, answer factual questions, translate a recipe, generate a specified image, write Python code, and much more. This type of generative model is called a *large language model*, built on the Transformer architecture [2]. Its key concept is transfer learning: the ability to reuse linguistic patterns and knowledge learned in a generic task (such as predicting randomly masked tokens) in another task (such as RE). This significantly reduces the training dataset size required for supervised learning. The same accuracy can be achieved with less human-labeled data because we don't have to train the model from scratch, but the weights learned on massive datasets are reused.

What makes LLMs exceptional is the model complexity (number of parameters) and the size and quality of the training corpus. Larger neural models (i.e., more trainable parameters) require fewer data samples to reach the same performance in terms of the test-set loss [3]. Not surprisingly, the more data the model has to learn from, the better it gets. But it's not just about data quantity, but also data quality. In traditional ML, the primary focus was often on identifying the best model architecture and fine-tuning its hyperparameters. This *model-centric* approach, in an extreme form, ignores potential data quality issues—and it should not be surprising that if we put in faulty data, we get faulty predictions. Over time, a *data-centric* paradigm [3] has gained traction, focusing on data engineering to improve the quality (and quantity) of data used to train high-complexity ML models. As a result, today's LLMs are so powerful that we can formulate a task in natural language (prompt engineering), and the model generates an answer. No model engineering is required.

Although LLMs in general, and OpenAI's GPT family of models in particular, have formidable capabilities, we must keep some limitations in mind when designing a system that depends on them. The most important for our example is *hallucinations*: the tendency of the model to make up "facts" and do false reasoning in cases when there is no justification for the response in the training data. For example, if we ask ChatGPT about the costs of NASA's SLS rocket, but its training data does not contain this sort of information, it will choose a random number and claim that this is the cost. The OpenAI team is working on limiting this behavior, but it remains an open issue at the time of writing.

Despite their achievements, we wouldn't call these models "AI"; there is a long way to go to achieve true artificial intelligence. Rather, we suggest using LLMs to build more comprehensive, cleaner KGs by asking them to extract high-quality named entities, relations, and properties; see the mental model in figure 5.3 as a reminder.

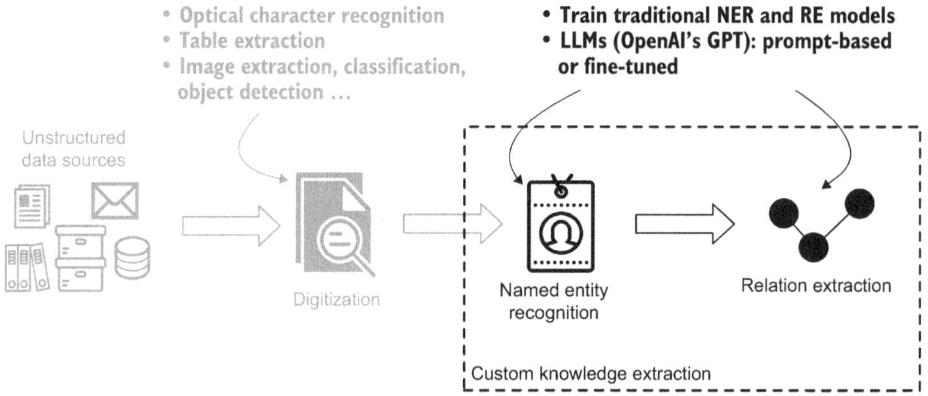

Figure 5.3 Mental model of transforming textual data into structured knowledge: NER and RE using an LLM

5.3.1 *Using LLMs*

LLMs can be used to help build KGs out of the box, via prompt-based inference, or we can fine-tune them to produce more accurate, stable output specific to our domain. LLMs typically perform well out of the box if we simply formulate the task in natural language and (optionally) provide an example. The task formulation is referred to as a *prompt*, and the iterative process of identifying the most performant prompt for the given task is called *prompt engineering*.

In this chapter, we are interested in text completion: we give the model a prompt, and it generates a text according to the context and task formulation in the prompt. Our goal is to use the power of GPT to identify entities and their relations from textual inputs. The process is outlined schematically in figure 5.4.

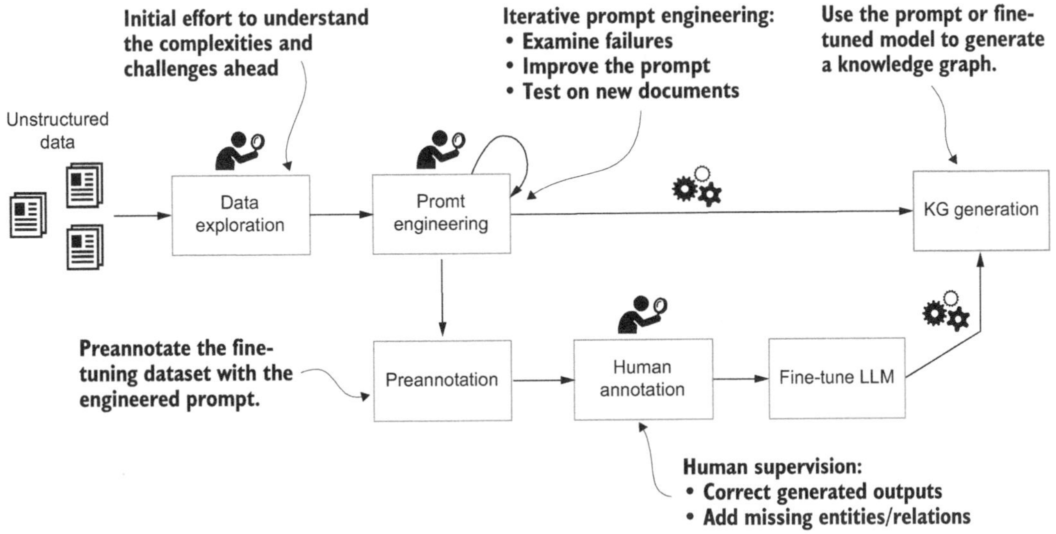

Figure 5.4 The two roles of LLMs in KG generation from textual data: the prompt-based approach (upper branch) and the fine-tuning approach (lower branch)

As usual in data science projects, we start with data exploration: we need to understand the domain we're dealing with, the challenges ahead, and reasonable expectations for the outcomes. For example, remember the diary entry earlier in this chapter? The interviewee, *C. G. Rossby*, was introduced by full name only at the beginning of the entry and was later referred to as "R." Therefore, we need to design our knowledge extraction system in a way that can resolve these uncommon ways of referencing people.

The next step is prompt engineering. Typically, it takes several iterations to identify the most valuable prompt: changing a few words can sometimes have a significant effect on performance. We need to describe the task as precisely as possible to limit ambiguity, which would give the model a chance to be too inventive in its answers.

After prompt engineering, we'll either be satisfied with the quality of the replies and proceed directly to KG generation, or we'll find that the task is too complex to rely purely on a prompt-based approach. In that case, we'll prepare a small training dataset consisting of prompts (limited to pure input documents without task descriptions) and expected outputs. (Our prompt engineering work won't be wasted because we can use it to preannotate the dataset before we have humans complete the annotations.) Once the dataset is ready, we can use OpenAI's API to *fine-tune* the model. If we are satisfied after the first iteration, we can use it to produce a KG. If it's not good enough yet, we can repeat the process: add more training data and try again. This process costs time and money, but we'll get a model that is specialized to our domain, providing more stable and accurate outputs.

5.3.2 Prompt engineering examples

Let's take a closer look at prompt engineering. The following prompt asks GPT to identify all entities and their relations.

Listing 5.1 Prompt version 1; identifying entities and relations

```
prompt_segments = dict()

prompt_segments['task'] =                    <-- General task formulation
"""You are an expert on constructing Knowledge
➥Graphs from texts using named entity recognition and relation extraction.
➥Given a prompt, identify as many entities and relations among them as
➥possible and output a list of relations in the format [ENTITY 1, ENTITY 1
➥TYPE, RELATION, ENTITY 2, ENTITY 2 TYPE].
➥The relations are directed, so the order matters."""

prompt_segments['example'] = "J.R.Smith (Prof. Phys.) is employed by MIT
➥and mentioned another scientist, Mary Hodge, who works on cyclotron
➥research."                                  <-- An example: especially useful for complex tasks such as RE

prompt_segments['example_output'] =                          <-- States the expected output
"""["J. R. Smith", "person", "has
➥title", "Professor of Physics", "title"]
["J. R. Smith", "person", "works for", "MIT", "organization"]
["J. R. Smith", "person", "talked about", "Mary", "person"]
["Mary", "person", "works on", "cyclotron", "occupation"]"""
```

We can deploy the prompt on a snippet of a diary entry using the following OpenAI API call.

Listing 5.2 OpenAI API call

```
import os
import time
from dotenv import load_dotenv
from openai import OpenAI
from listing_2 import prompt_segments

_ = load_dotenv()                  <-- Loads the OpenAI API key from the .env file

OPENAI_MODEL = "gpt-4o-mini"
```

```
def openai_query(client, prompt_segments: dict,
➥ query: str):
    messages = [
      {"role": "system", "content": prompt_segments['task']},
      {"role": "user", "content": prompt_segments['example']},
      {"role": "assistant", "content": prompt_segments['example_output']},
      {"role": "user", "content": query}
    ]

    t_start = time.time()
    response = client.chat.completions.create(model=OPENAI_MODEL,
    ➥ messages=messages, temperature=0., max_tokens=2000)
    print(response.choices[0].message.content)
    print(f"\nTime: {round(time.time() - t_start, 1)} sec\n")

    return response.choices[0].message.content


if __name__ == "__main__":
  client = OpenAI(api_key=os.environ['OPENAI_API_KEY'])

  text = """
  ➥ JOHNS HOPKINS UNIVERSITY Chemistry Department:
  ➥ Wednesday, November 9, 1932
  ➥ WW visits the Dept. with Dr. Frazer (Baker Prof. Chem.). There are 239
  ➥ undergraduate and 116 graduate students of chemistry, the latter group in-
  ➥ cluding holders of the special State fellowships in chemistry under the
  ➥ New Plan. D.H. Andrews (Prof.Chem.) is a physical chemist specializing in
  ➥ thermodynamics. He is not present at the time of WW's call, but one of his
  ➥ assistants explains his work. He is measuring specific heats of organic
  ➥ compounds by a straight calorimetric method. This work is in its early
  ➥ stages. He is also interested in making mechanical models of various atoms
  ➥ from which can be demonstrated the theory of the Raman spectra.
  ➥ J.B.Mayer (Assoc. in Chem.) is a former student of G. N. Lewis and works
  ➥ with Max Born at Gottingen summers. He specializes in the energetics of
  ➥ crystal lattices. His wife, last summer, prepared the new edition of
  ➥ Born's treatise on this subject. In Mayer's laboratory Mrs. Wintner, wife
  ➥ of the mathematician, is working on an experimental problem. Andrews says
  ➥ that Mayer is young and impresses one as an enthusiastic and able man.
  ➥ """

openai_query(client, prompt_segments, text)
```

Function to run the stateless ChatGPT API query

Specifies the model, temperature, and other parameters

Text to process

The results are encouraging. For example, the extracted relations featuring *D. H. Andrews* and *J. B. Mayer* are shown next.

Listing 5.3 GPT output of the prompt in listing 5.2

```
["D.H. Andrews", "person", "has title", "Prof. Chem.", "title"]
["D.H. Andrews", "person", "specializes in", "thermodynamics", "field"]
["D.H. Andrews", "person", "is measuring", "specific heats of organic
➥ compounds", "research"]
["D.H. Andrews", "person", "is interested in", "mechanical models of
➥ various atoms", "research"]
```

```
["D.H. Andrews", "person", "demonstrates", "theory of the Raman spectra",
➥"theory"]
["J.B. Mayer", "person", "has title", "Assoc. in Chem.", "title"]
["J.B. Mayer", "person", "is a former student of", "G. N. Lewis", "person"]
["J.B. Mayer", "person", "works with", "Max Born", "person"]
["J.B. Mayer", "person", "works at", "Gottingen", "location"]
["J.B. Mayer", "person", "specializes in", "energetics of crystal
➥lattices", "field"]
```

Impressive! D. H. Andrews is indeed a professor of chemistry, and he is involved in all the identified research topics. Similarly, for J. B. Mayer, we learn his title, specialization, and whom he studied under. We also have full names in these relations, even though the diary entry only mentions "Mayer" or "he." In traditional RE, an NER model would identify entity mentions ("Mayer"). Then we'd need to use the coreference resolution model to link "Mayer" and "he" to a full name, and finally use RE to obtain relations and resolved names. Here, due to the generative nature of LLMs, the coreference resolution is done implicitly: the model generates output based on its understanding of the document's entire context. Finally, notice that the titles were resolved from "Prof. Chem." and "Assoc. in Chem." to "Professor of Chemistry" and "Associate in Chemistry." The model deduced the correct full titles from their shortened versions—no traditional NER model could do that.

Now let's look at the entity relation types. Notice the extreme granularity (level of detail): `specializes in`, `is measuring`, `is interested in`, and `demonstrates` are all accurate, but is this output useful for a KG? They all represent the same concept. A human would probably assign them the same relation type, such as `works on`, but GPT provided us with four different types! And this was just from one short paragraph. Imagine what the KG schema would look like if we processed thousands of pages and then wanted to find answers to questions such as "Who works on research of organic compounds?" We would have to know and list all the semantically identical (or very similar) relation types in the Cypher query to avoid returning results that didn't represent the umbrella term `works on`. That would be impractical, to put it mildly.

The same is true for the node labels. The four research topics from this paragraph have been assigned three different labels: `field`, `research`, `theory`. In essence, they are correct. But what are they really? They are all research topics of Professor Andrews, so a human might call each one a `topic` or `occupation` and have a single corresponding node label in the graph for all of them.

Finally, did you notice that the output is missing Mayer's personality traits? Or that the model ignored the mention of "straight calorimetric method," a relation featuring the "theory of Raman spectra"? We decided to try again. We used the same prompt and model configuration to generate entities and relations from the same text, to test *prediction stability*: that is, whether the LLM would produce the same output the second time. The answer was no. For example, in our second round of output, *theory of Raman spectra*, correctly identified in the first run, was missing, along with *straight calorimetric method.* The model acknowledged that Andrews talked about Mayer's personality traits (we got the relation `["D.H. Andrews", "person", "describes", "J.B. Mayer",` "person"]) but didn't capture what he said about Mayer. This result demonstrates the issue of instability in predictions based solely on generic prompts of the style "Identify all entities and relations among them" when mining knowledge from documents to produce a KG for downstream analysis and tasks.

So, let's test a new version of the prompt, shown in listing 5.4. To address the normalization issue, we include lists of entity classes and relation types, including explanations of some of the underperforming relation types.

> **TIP** Instead of using these simple lists, we could state the full, authoritative KG schema here, but this approach leaves the door open for output that includes entities and relations we haven't thought of.

We also add two notes to the task description to help guide the model and improve prediction stability: one explaining the habit of referring to people by their initials, and the other mentioning aliasing for university and department names.

Listing 5.4 Prompt version 2: identifying specific entities and relations

```
prompt_segments = dict()

prompt_segments['task'] = """
...

Entities of interest: person, location, organization, date, occupation
➥(a.k.a. person's work, specialization, research discipline, interests,
➥occupation, technology).

➥Top relations of interest: "works for", "works with",
➥"student of" (link students with their teachers/advisors), "talked about"
➥(a person talking about another person), "talked with" (a person talking
➥with another person), "works on" (assignment of persons to
➥their occupation, work, specialization, research
➥discipline, interests etc.).

➥Note that persons are often first referenced by their full name, and
➥then mentioned only by their surname or initials, for example: "A. N.
➥Richards" becomes "Richards", "ANR", or just "R.".

➥Note that organizations (universities, their departments) are often
➥shortened, for example: "University of California" is written as "U. of
➥Cal." or just "U. Cal.", "Department of Physics" is written as "Dept.
    Phys."
➥etc."""

prompt_segments['example'] = "..."
prompt_segments['example_output'] = """..."""
```

- The same task description as in listing 5.1.
- List of the most important entity classes
- List of the most important relation classes
- Same as in listing 5.1

The results show that stating the entities and relations of interest in the prompt guides the LLM to produce more normalized output. The following are the extracted relations for *D. H. Andrews* and *J. B. Mayer.*

Listing 5.5 GPT output of the prompt in listing 5.4

```
["D. H. Andrews", "person", "has title", "Professor of Chemistry", "title"]
["D. H. Andrews", "person", "works on", "thermodynamics", "occupation"]
["D. H. Andrews", "person", "measures", "specific heats of organic
➥ compounds", "occupation"]
["D. H. Andrews", "person", "is interested in", "mechanical models of
➥ various atoms", "occupation"]
["D. H. Andrews", "person", "talked about", "Raman spectra", "occupation"]
["J. B. Mayer", "person", "has title", "Associate in Chemistry", "title"]
["J. B. Mayer", "person", "is a former student of", "G. N. Lewis",
➥ "person"]
["J. B. Mayer", "person", "works with", "Max Born", "person"]
["J. B. Mayer", "person", "specializes in", "energetics of crystal
➥ lattices", "occupation"]
```

All the topics related to work have the same entity label: `occupation`. Titles are provided in their full form: *Professor of Chemistry* and *Associate in Chemistry*. And we have a single instance of the `works on` relation, which is an improvement, although we still also have `measures` and `specializes in`. This time we have *Raman spectra* instead of *theory of Raman spectra*; both are correct, but at the very least we expect consistency across runs and documents. And where is the relation featuring the "straight calorimetric method"? Although these are great results after a few minutes of tweaking the prompt, we can do better.

Let's try one more iteration, this time expanding the example in the hope that it will provide clearer guidelines and prediction stability. The `works on` relations are important to us, so we add another mention of `occupation`. We also give an example of `student of` because the previous prompt failed on this relation.

Listing 5.6 Prompt version 3: more complex examples

```
prompt_segments = dict()

prompt_segments['task'] = """..."""

prompt_segments['example'] = "J.R.Smith, Prof. Phys. is employed by MIT and
➥ mentioned another colleague Mary Hodge, who studies along with her
➥ master's student John Smith radioisotopes produced by cyclotron."

prompt_segments['example_output'] = """["J. R. Smith", "person", "has
➥ title", "Professor of Physics", "title"]
["J. R. Smith", "person", "works for", "MIT", "organization"]
["J. R. Smith", "person", "talked about", "Mary Hodge", "person"]
["Mary Hodge", "person", "works for", "MIT", "organization"]
["John Smith", "person", "student of", "Mary Hodge", "person"]
["Mary Hodge", "person", "works on", "radioisotopes", "occupation"]
["Mary Hodge", "person", "works on", "cyclotron", "occupation"]"""
```

The same task formulation as in listing 5.1 (annotation on `prompt_segments['task']`)

Let's again inspect in detail the output related to *D. H. Andrews* and *J. B. Mayer*.

Listing 5.7 GPT output of the prompt in listing 5.6

```
["D. H. Andrews", "person", "has title", "Professor of Chemistry", "title"]
["D. H. Andrews", "person", "works for", "Johns Hopkins University
➥Chemistry Department", "organization"]
["D. H. Andrews", "person", "works on", "thermodynamics", "occupation"]
["D. H. Andrews", "person", "works on", "specific heats of organic
➥compounds", "occupation"]
["D. H. Andrews", "person", "works on", "calorimetric method",
➥"occupation"]
["J. B. Mayer", "person", "has title", "Associate in Chemistry", "title"]
["J. B. Mayer", "person", "works for", "Johns Hopkins University Chemistry
➥Department", "organization"]
["J. B. Mayer", "person", "student of", "G. N. Lewis", "person"]
["J. B. Mayer", "person", "works with", "Max Born", "person"]
["Max Born", "person", "works at", "Gottingen", "location"]
["J. B. Mayer", "person", "works on", "energetics of crystal lattices",
➥"occupation"]
```

Eureka! We achieved everything we wanted: a high level of stability in terms of assignment of entity and relation classes, and correct identification of all the relations we care about.

> **NOTE** This example illustrates what prompt evolution can look like. In the real project, we did a couple more iterations and changed the output format to JSON so that each entity and relation can have properties where relevant. That allowed us to extract more complex knowledge, such as the sentiment of each `TALKED_ABOUT` relation (stored as a property) as well as business titles (an attribute of the `WORK_FOR` relation). For the final version of the prompt used to generate the KG presented in this chapter, check out the book's code repository.

Note that we designed the prompts in this chapter for ChatGPT models and tested them on GPT-4o mini. By the time you read this book, newer models will be available. That's why we focus on fundamental principles rather than model specifics—you should be able to adapt the example prompts to the current state of the art.

5.3.3 Prompt engineering guidelines

LLMs are rapidly evolving, so there is no point in sharing technical guidelines that may quickly become obsolete. However, certain general learning points will be transferable to newer models. The key principles we discovered when working on the RAC project are summarized in the following good practices of prompt engineering.

Task description and domain-specific guidance

A well-explained task is very important for the quality and stability of the output. It is worth experimenting with different formulations and adding specifics of the current dataset, such as, in our example, referring to people by abbreviations and initials.

NAMING OF ENTITY AND RELATION CLASSES

In the prompt, include lists of the entity and relation classes you're most interested in. This helps clarify the task and provide more normalized outputs. The chosen terminology matters a lot! If you notice that an entity or relation class underperforms, try renaming it. For example, at first we called the subject of conversations in diary entries `Topic`, but we realized that this term was too generic to be used as an entity class. When we renamed it `Occupation`, otherwise identical prompts produced much more comprehensive and stable results.

COMPLEX AND REPRESENTATIVE EXAMPLES

In complex tasks such as entity RE, it is useful to provide an example of input and expected output as part of the prompt. It can be a condensed version of the actual text you need to process, containing examples of important entities and relations. Include complex linguistic formulations that appear in the dataset, and focus on relations that the model struggles with. Also make the example as representative as possible: be sure the example contains all of your key relation types.

LLM CONFIGURATION

Experiment with different LLMs and choose the best option for you. Also test their parameters, especially *temperature*. The higher the temperature, the more varied and creative the output produced (and the greater the propensity for hallucinations). Lower temperatures yield more deterministic output. So, creative tasks such as text generation are better performed with higher temperature values, whereas tasks such as code generation require a lower temperature (around 0.2). For fact-focused tasks such as extracting entities and relations from a document, we use temperature 0.

TESTING PREDICTION STABILITY

Remember that LLMs are generative models, so by definition, they can have and do have "moods": the same prompt can produce different results if run repeatedly on the same text. You can limit this behavior with careful prompt engineering (a non-ambiguous task formulation) and by setting very low values for temperature (as just discussed). If you choose a non-zero temperature, consider testing prediction stability by running the same prompt on the same test dataset multiple times and evaluating the overlap. If there's one thing you don't want when mining factual knowledge, it's unstable prediction behavior and low confidence in the resulting KG!

UNIT-TESTING THE PROMPT

Prompt engineering should be a quick, straightforward task, but sometimes it may take you a lot of iterations to get the result you want. So, just as with code development, consider setting up a simple unit-testing system: each time you update the prompt, add the text snippet and the expected output to the test list; and every few iterations, run this list of tests in bulk, calculate the success rate, and output the failures so you can inspect them. This way, you won't lose any achievements from previous iterations.

EYEBALLING A MINI-KG

Each time you reach a prompt milestone, we recommend deploying the prompt on a small sample of documents (a few dozen pages) and producing a KG. Why? Well, we humans are sensory creatures, and seeing and touching are sometimes more useful than assuming and imagining. We find that a quick look at a mini-KG can help us discover opportunities for improvement.

> **DEFINITION** Prompt engineering is an iterative process. When you've aggregated enough prompt improvements to feel as though you've made significant progress toward addressing the original task, you've reached a *prompt milestone.*

For example, while navigating the RAC graph, we noticed many organization names in abbreviated forms, such as *U. of PA*. GPT, given its significant general knowledge acquired during training, should be able to fill in the blanks and identify this as the University of Pennsylvania, if properly instructed. Similarly, we saw people's names abbreviated in the form *S.* And several people seemingly worked for the same organization, but it was just *Department of Physics*—which university? For the next iteration, we considered these failures and added complexity to the prompt example to guide GPT to give us the desired output.

Evaluation

When you're satisfied with the prompt, do a quantitative evaluation. Process a few dozen pages of text, nominate someone as quality assurance manager, and ask them to go through the predictions and mark them as correct, incorrect, or missing entities and relations. Then calculate per-class precision, recall, and F1 score for entities and relations.

The QA manager is well positioned to spot systemic failures that couldn't be identified when testing on a handful of examples. Another option is to use an LLM as a judge: instead of asking a human, give this task to another powerful LLM. It will make mistakes, but human-level performance is not 100% either. Whichever way you decide to go, a proper evaluation will give you confidence in the prediction quality before you spend time and money producing a KG from a big dataset, will serve as a basis for monitoring future model drift, and will give you one more chance to improve your prompt.

Initial explorative KG

To do prompt engineering, you need a minimal understanding of the data, its content, and the knowledge you want to extract from it. But we've seen many use cases where companies had only a vague idea of the content; they knew it must include something useful, but didn't know exactly what to mine—that is, what the KG schema should be. In such cases, you need to dive into the data and spend some time on exploration and understanding. This potentially long and tedious task can be streamlined if you design a quick generic entity and RE prompt (ask the LLM to extract all entities and relations, and give it short example to demonstrate the output format), produce a KG from a sample of documents, and then explore it, navigate it, and draw inspiration from it. Yes, it will be highly unnormalized, but it will help you quickly understand the content of the dataset, identify the kinds of entities and relations you can mine from it, and start prompt engineering.

BE AMBITIOUS

Think big! Don't assume that something would be too difficult for the LLM—just try it. Remember that LLMs are trained on a vast amount of data and have deep linguistic understanding and general knowledge. They can handle things like typos in names, deduce from the context that "Prof. Chem." is the title Professor of Chemistry, and figure out that a mention of "Stanford" means Stanford University rather than the name of a location or person. So when you provide an example in the prompt, be ambitious. Provide relations with full, clean entity names so you get a cleaner, more accurate KG from the start, reducing the need for entity cleansing and resolution during post-processing.

DON'T OVERTHINK

Prompt engineering is a simplistic technique called *zero-shot learning* (just a task description) or *one-shot learning* (when you provide one example). We expect a model pretrained on large amounts of data to perform well on a specific domain and tasks based on a task description and one or two examples. Despite the power of LLMs, this is challenging when we're dealing with complex reasoning tasks: there will always be imperfections because one-shot learning simply cannot prepare the model for all the complexities and ambiguities in the full dataset.

So our last bit of advice is this: don't overengineer and overthink prompt development. Do a couple of quick iterations, verify every milestone by producing and eyeballing a mini-KG to identify possible systemic failures and candidates for prompt improvements, and move on. When you get to the point that, despite all your best efforts, prompt engineering is not yielding satisfactory results, it's better to invest the remaining project time in fine-tuning the LLM rather than making never-ending prompt improvements.

5.3.4 KG building: Traditional NLP or LLMs?

At this point, you may be wondering how to determine whether to follow the traditional NLP path or the LLM path. Does traditional NLP have a place in the modern world of AI? Let's start by looking at the pros and cons of each approach.

Traditional NLP offers these advantages:

- *Prediction speed*—Smaller, simpler models generate faster predictions, even on a CPU.
- *Infrastructure simplicity and costs*—Simple and cheap infrastructure is enough to train and deploy models, often with no need for GPUs.
- *Prediction costs*—Due to the simpler, cheaper infrastructure, prediction costs are very low.
- *Security*—It's easier and cheaper to configure on-premises solutions for isolated secure deployments.

These are the disadvantages of traditional NLP:

- *In-house expertise*—Design, training, deployment, and maintenance require highly specialized data science expertise.
- *Complex NLP pipeline configuration*—Specialized, customized models are required: for example, NER, RE, coreference resolution, entity resolution, and disambiguation.
- *Data annotation complexity and cost*—Each model must be trained for your domain with your specific data, which requires building multiple high-quality training datasets. This process takes time, data science expertise, and infrastructure and software. The initial investment is very high, and the outcomes are not guaranteed, especially for complex tasks like RE.

LLMs have the following advantages:

- *Initial domain customization costs*—The road to production on your specific domain is much quicker thanks to transfer learning and prompt engineering.
- *Shallow learning curve*—You can quickly get started and build know-how without expert data scientists. Anyone with minimal technical skills can learn to do prompt engineering and fine-tuning.
- *All-in-one NLP*—No need to engineer a sequence of separate (but dependent) processing steps to achieve the goal; one pass through the data does it all.
- *Generative nature*—In addition to the simpler processing pipeline, the results are high quality thanks to transfer learning and the generative nature of LLMs. Their contextual and linguistic understanding and reasoning lead to cleaner, more accurate KGs than any traditional NLP model, right out of the box.
- *Simpler post-processing*—The generative nature and language understanding of LLMs mean less post-processing is required (cleansing, normalization, entity resolution).

LLMs also have some disadvantages:

- *Prediction speed*—Massive models imply much slower prediction speed, despite being served on powerful GPUs.
- *Infrastructure complexity*—Because GPUs are a must-have not just for training but also for prediction, infrastructure complexity and costs are higher.
- *Fine-tuning costs*—If prompt engineering is insufficient, the model must be fine-tuned. This means higher costs for preparing a training dataset, infrastructure, and prediction. (OpenAI charges 10 times more for running predictions with a custom model; even for on-premise deployments, you need to consider costs related to maintaining and managing model versions.)
- *Prediction costs on very large datasets*—For small to medium-sized datasets, using LLMs will probably be cheaper than the initial investment to create a custom traditional NLP pipeline. But the numbers can look quite different if you have a massive dataset.

- *Security/on-premises deployment costs*—If you work in a high-security domain, good luck, especially if you can't use a cloud provider and have to set up, deploy, and maintain your own GPU cluster.

NOTE These days, many closed source as well as open source LLMs are made available through hyperscalers such as Amazon Web Services, Azure, and Google Cloud Platform, which alleviates some of the pain points we just mentioned.

To answer the introductory question, "Does traditional NLP have a place in the modern world of AI?" we believe the answer is "Absolutely!" Despite foreseeing a great future for the use of LLMs with KGs, we believe substantial space remains for other technologies (such as NLP), especially considering security requirements, costs (massive datasets), and streaming scenarios (prediction speed). If you cannot use LLMs in production for some reason, consider using them for tasks such as training custom NLP models; use them to increase the efficiency of your data annotation process by doing preannotation based on quick prompt engineering.

Summary

- Producing KGs from unstructured textual data requires identifying custom domain-specific named entities and relations among them.
- With traditional NLP, a range of models, such as named entity recognition, relation extraction, and coreference resolution, must be trained and chained in a complex workflow. Training requires a high initial investment for building high-quality human-annotated training datasets, and specialized data science skills to train, evaluate, deploy, and monitor the models.
- LLMs, such as OpenAI's GPT, can be used out of the box with iterative prompt engineering (or fine-tuning) to build accurate, domain-specific KGs with much lower initial costs compared to traditional NLP.
- Traditional NLP and LLMs both have their pros and cons, depending on the concrete domain and business considerations. They can also coexist side by side, or one can be used to prepare a training dataset for the other.
- The generative nature of LLMs means that we get cleaner, more accurate KGs with minimal need for entity normalization and resolution.

6 Building knowledge graphs with large language models

This chapter covers

- Transforming an archive into a knowledge graph
- Graph modeling
- Data normalization and cleansing
- Entity resolution
- Analyzing the intellectual network

In the previous chapter, we discussed extracting complex relational knowledge from unstructured data using state-of-the-art machine learning (ML) technologies, including large language models (LLMs). Specifically, we looked at extracting knowledge from the historical typewritten documents of the Rockefeller Archive Center (RAC). As a brief reminder, these documents contain detailed descriptions of conversations between Rockefeller Foundation (RF) program officers and researchers from a wide range of universities and other institutions. The RF used the information collected during these meetings to decide whether to fund research projects. For a detailed description of the RAC use case and the goals of the project, revisit chapter 5.

As highlighted by the mental model in figure 6.1, we'll pick up where we left off: we've extracted the knowledge from the textual documents, and now we'll explore how to transform it into a KG and how to use the KG for the benefit of our organization.

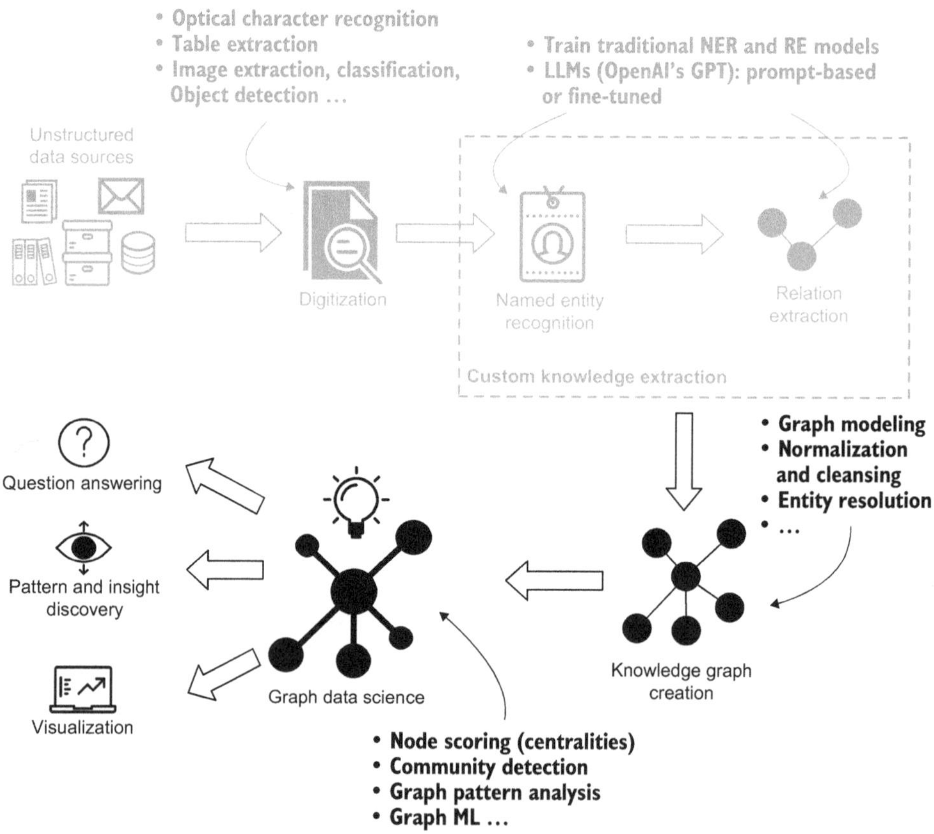

Figure 6.1 Path from domain-specific unstructured textual data toward KG insights. The steps rely on state-of-the-art ML models, such as optical character recognition for document digitization, named entity recognition and relation extraction systems, entity resolution, and GraphML.

6.1 Transforming an archive to a KG

Following is a list of challenges we still need to handle in this project:

- *Analog typewritten documents*—The analog documents need to be scanned and processed by an optical character recognition (OCR) system to produce a digital textual corpus. Various OCR technologies are available, including those from cloud providers like Amazon and Microsoft and the open source Tesseract OCR library.

- *Historical documents*—Many of the research disciplines discussed are no longer pursued. Therefore, there is no hope of compiling a named entity recognition (NER) dictionary or knowledge base comprehensive enough to be used as a reference for disambiguation and entity resolution.
- *Uncommon linguistic conventions*—The program officers had specific writing styles. For example, some of them referred to people and organizations with abbreviations, such as "S." instead of "J. R. Smith" or "U.Cal." instead of "University of California." None of the off-the-shelf coreference models we tested could resolve these shortened names into canonical forms. However, GPT was successful at implicitly performing NER, entity resolution and relation extraction (RE) tasks in response to our prompts.
- *Domain-specific named entities*—We're working with descriptions of research projects in the natural sciences domain. The primary custom-named entities are `Occupations` and include research disciplines, technologies, treatments, and diseases, and they vary in granularity. No traditional NER model is available for these entities (except for diseases). We can however implement a custom ML-based NER and then design, for example, an unsupervised entity resolution system to cluster semantically similar occupations, allowing for further downstream analyses.
- *High relational complexity*—The relational knowledge in these documents is dense and complex. A single page can contain dozens of relevant relations. It is vital to define the RE schema properly so we don't retrieve useless knowledge while potentially missing opportunities to achieve higher accuracy. This is especially important when training RE models by manually labeling large datasets, but also when using the RE schema to guide an LLM for this task.
- *KG normalization, cleansing, entity resolution, and disambiguation*—These tasks will require significant effort. For example, each document may use a different variant of the same name; some conversations have multiple participants who speak about their research in semantically similar, yet different, words; and conversations are often part of chains that take place over months or years. Unfortunately, this kind of analysis is outside of the scope of this book; here we will focus on producing and analyzing interaction networks.
- *Matching/linking unstructured data sources*—Ideally, we'd like to reconcile (match) knowledge extracted from the officer diaries with another data source—board of directors minutes—in a single KG. Doing so would let us identify which conversations resulted in which grants and answer questions such as, "Are there any patterns that typically precede the funding of an idea?" Again, this is outside the scope of this book, but it serves as an illustration of the possibilities that lie ahead when we use unstructured data sources.

Although they may seem daunting, we can call ourselves lucky to live in the LLM era. In the not-so-distant past, we would have had to spend significant resources to build traditional ML models and strategies to overcome these obstacles. Today, as we shall see in the remainder of this chapter, many of them can be solved with the right choice of a knowledge representation system, an LLM model, and prompt engineering.

6.1.1 Graph modeling

The KG schema of the RAC project is shown in figure 6.2 (simplified for this book). We will focus on one aspect the KG: *influence networks*. These are the relations among people interviewed by RF representatives, such as who talked with whom about who else.

We decided to design the graph in three layers:

- *Document-level layer*—The result of initial data ingestion. Each diary file is represented as a `File` node with properties such as file name, location, and author; and each `Page` node, as result of extraction from each file by the OCR model, with properties such as the final clean text of the page.
- *Metagraph layer*—Unmerged GPT entities (`Entity` nodes) and relations among them, as well as their linkage to the original page from which they were extracted.
- *KG layer*—Final, normalized, cleansed resolved entities (`Person`, `Title`, `Organization`, `Occupation`) and relations among them (`WORKS_ON`, `WORKS_FOR`, etc.).

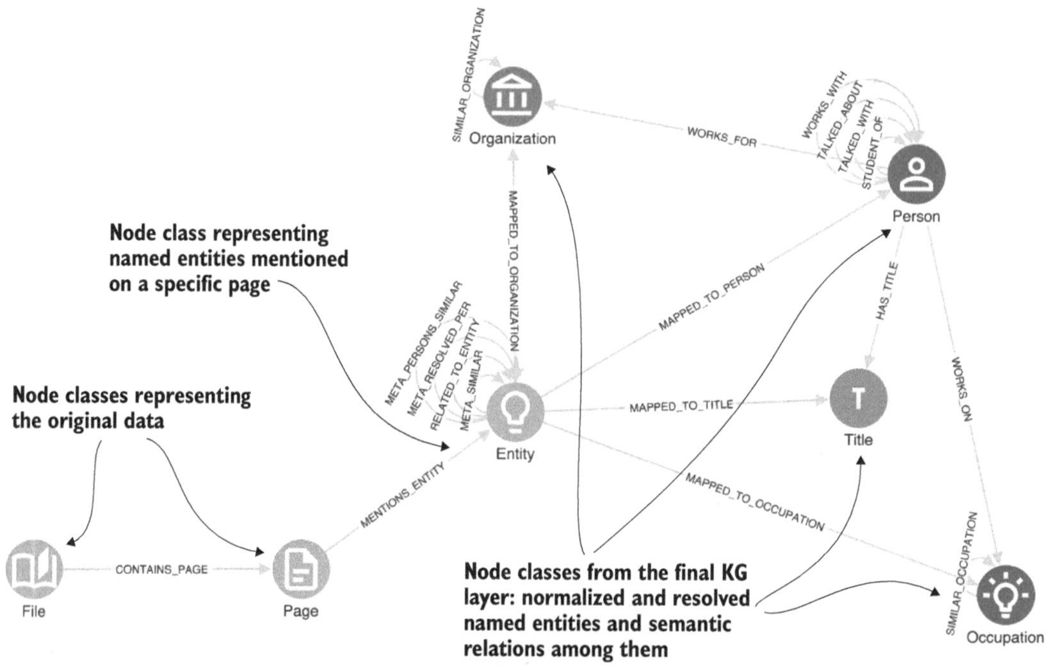

Figure 6.2 Simplified KG schema of the Rockefeller Archive Center project

As we've discussed, an LLM does its best to produce the desired output, but it cannot be used to produce a KG directly. First we need to perform the normalization and entity resolution steps, which are enabled by this schema.

6.1.2 Creating a metagraph

Let's briefly discuss how to create the metagraph. When dealing with texts longer than a few pages, the first step is to define a chunking strategy to avoid running into the max tokens limit or deteriorating processing quality for very long texts. Here we show the simplest approach: splitting by page.

> **NOTE** We had more than 10,000 pages for this project, but for this example, we selected a subset of 150 pages of Warren Weaver's diary. You can find the OCRed dataset and full ingestion code in the book's code repository. The documents are typewritten and date from 1939, so the digitization process may have misspelled some entity names.

After each page is processed, we create (not merge!) all the identified entity mentions (nodes called `Entity` in the schema with property `name`), link them to their page, and create their relations extracted from the given page (called `RELATED_TO_ENTITY` with the `type` property representing the relation class). This allows us to do normalization and entity resolution based on knowledge about each entity mention. Then, when creating the final KG, we can easily aggregate all the knowledge extracted about all the resolved entity mentions across all the pages while preserving the underlying information about the origin of these entities and relations. That will allow us to design the graph visualization platform in an easily explainable manner by being able to show on demand the original text snippets from which the selected entities and relations were identified. It is also useful for data scientists maintaining the KG system to be able to easily track the origin of nodes and relationships in the graph and, for example, fine-tune entity resolution as needed, because the final KG can be re-created anytime from the metagraph.

6.1.3 Normalization and cleansing

Once the metagraph is created, we can inspect statistics such as top entities per class, top relation classes, and so on. This gives us a quick overview of the structure of the knowledge. Plus, if we notice an opportunity to increase future graph connectivity, we'll implement it: for example, lowercasing entity names if case is irrelevant (such as `Occupations`). This type of normalization is important for ensuring data (KG) consistency and efficient integration across documents. Similarly, GPT occasionally included a person's title as part of their name, even though it was instructed to treat them separately, so we implemented a cleansing strategy that strips irrelevant tokens from people's names to avoid having the same person represented in the KG by multiple nodes (once with and once without the title). The Cypher queries to fix these cases are as follows.

Listing 6.1 Normalizing people and occupations

```
from neo4j import GraphDatabase

URI = "bolt://localhost:7687"
AUTH = ("neo4j", "password")
NEO4J_DB = "neo4j"

REMOVE_TITLES = ["dr.", "prof.", "dean", "president", "pres.", "sir",
➥ "mr.", "mrs."]
QUERY_NORM_PERSONS = """                    <-- Cleans Person names: removes titles/degrees
➥ MATCH (e:Entity {label: "Person"})
➥ WITH e, CASE WHEN ANY(title IN $remove_titles WHERE toLower(e.name)
➥ STARTS WITH title) THEN apoc.text.join(split(e.name, " ")[1..], " ")
➥ ELSE e.name END AS name
➥ SET e.name_normalized = name
➥ """
                                            Lowercases Occupation
QUERY_NORM_OCCUPATIONS = """             <-- entity names
➥ MATCH (e:Entity {label: "Occupation"})
➥ ET e.name_normalized = toLower(e.name)
➥ """

if __name__ == "__main__":
  with GraphDatabase.driver(URI, auth=AUTH) as driver:       Executes
    with driver.session(database=NEO4J_DB) as session:    <-- the queries
      print("Normalizing Person names")
      session.run(QUERY_NORM_PERSONS, remove_titles=REMOVE_TITLES)
      print("Normalizing Occupations")
      session.run(QUERY_NORM_OCCUPATIONS)
```

We create new node properties called `name_normalized`, which will be later used instead of unnormalized `name` properties when linking to final nodes in the KG layer.

6.1.4 *Graph-based entity resolution*

The generative nature of LLMs helps produce cleaner, more accurate KGs. One reason is that, unlike traditional NER and RE models, when properly guided by the prompt or fine-tuning, they return only full, clean entity names. Think of it as coreference resolution, a key task in the standard NLP pipelines, being performed implicitly, thus reducing the need for entity resolution.

Reducing, but not removing. We still need to be able to resolve entities across documents: is "Eleanor Smith" in one document the same person as "E. Smith" in another? A vital part of any KG creation process is thus entity resolution, or even entity disambiguation: linking each subject to a concrete concept in a knowledge base.

In this case, we'll take advantage of the graph structure and design a graph-based entity resolution system. A full discussion is out of the scope of this chapter, but we'll outline the general approach and an initial baseline. Most of the entity mentions in the metagraph layer have one or more relations to other mentions, most of which are useful for entity resolution. Think of the `WORKS_FOR` relations: if there is a high level of string similarity between two names ("Eleanor Smith" and "E. Smith"), and both work for the same university, that's a strong signal. Similarly, it is unlikely that people with identical or very similar names are working on the same research topic. If we can amass multiple signals of this type, our confidence in this resolution grows.

This approach relies on initially linking nodes in the metagraph layer based on their string similarities. We link two nodes with `META_SIMILAR` relationships if they have identical or very similar string representations. We also take advantage of domain knowledge when defining similarity thresholds. For example, we know that a person's name is composed of first name, middle name(s), and surname. Often, middle names are abbreviated or skipped; the same is true for first names. But relying only on surnames would result in lots of false positives. A combination of surname and at least the first name (or its abbreviation) gives us higher confidence that they could be the same person. We can use these considerations to define a set of rules for creating `META_SIMILAR` edges between nodes representing mentions of person names. Similar reasoning can be applied to other entities, such as `Organizations`.

> **TIP** Sometimes names include generic words. For example, the `Organization` names of many foundations include the keyword *Foundation*, so it would be counterproductive to create similarity links among them. It is important to analyze the situation and define a stopword list before creating `SIMILAR` relationships. Different datasets and domains will require adjusted approaches.

Enough hypothesizing: let's examine the concrete case shown in figure 6.3. We see three mentions of nuclear physicist Ernest Lawrence (who won the Nobel Prize for the invention of the cyclotron), on pages 26, 99, and 126: *Ernest Orlando Lawrence, Ernest O. Lawrence,* and *Lawrence.*

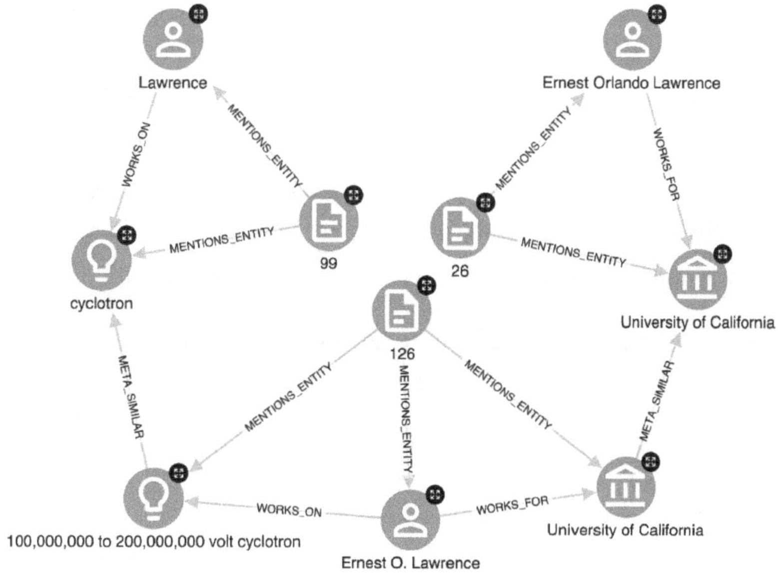

Figure 6.3 Graph-based entity resolution example

How do we know that these three names refer to the same person? There is a strong string similarity based on the rules and patterns we just discussed. We also see that *Ernest Orlando Lawrence* and *Ernest O. Lawrence* are three hops apart, because in both cases they are identified as employees of the University of California. Similarly, we can find a relation to the last mention, *Lawrence*, through the `WORKS_ON` relationships and the similarity between the `Occupations` *cyclotron* and *100,000,000 to 200,000,000 volt cyclotron*. But notice that *Ernest Orlando Lawrence* and *Lawrence* are six hops apart: this kind of traversal would be much harder in a relational database.

Would you like an even more "graphy" approach? How about taking advantage of the intellectual network relations—`TALKED_ABOUT` and `TALKED_WITH`—and running graph community detection algorithms, such as Louvain, to identify clusters of people who interact or, in general, are connected? The reasoning behind this is that *John Doe* working on *maritime research* in *Antarctica* will probably be part of a different interaction network than *John Doe* specializing in *cosmology*. Membership in communities provides another signal to help us decide whether they are the same person.

How about adding ML? One obvious option is to design a semantic similarity approach to identify similar `Occupations`. We can create `META_SIMILAR` links even when there is zero string similarity, but with topics that are highly related: for example, *fertility* and *human ovulation*. A frequent choice is to use embeddings provided by GPT and cluster them based on their similarities (we achieved very good results with an agglomerative clustering approach).

There are many options for graph-based entity resolution; we've just scratched the surface. To conclude our baseline approach for resolving people, we need these last few ingredients:

- Create `META_PERSONS_SIMILAR` relationships among person mentions that comply with the criteria we've defined (string similarity and relatedness through RE outputs).
- Run the weakly connected components (WCC) algorithm on the `META_PERSONS_SIMILAR` metagraph to identify groups of mentions that should be resolved to the same KG entity (final graph layer).
- For each WCC group, select a common name to represent it: we choose the longest one (in the previous example, that's *Ernest Orlando Lawrence*).
- Create the final KG layer with fully resolved entities.

These tasks are straightforward; see our code repository for the full flow.

6.2 Intellectual network analysis: The value of graphs

We've finally reached our goal: a KG. What now? How can we use it? At this point, the general value of KGs should be clear, so we'll explore an analytical aspect: graph data science.

Certain parts of the KG are suitable for graph analytics, especially the *intellectual network* of people (scientists) formed by `TALKED_ABOUT`, `TALKED_WITH`, `WORKS_WITH`, and `STUDENT_OF` relations. We used Neo4j's Graph Data Science library to analyze this network using graph algorithms such as PageRank, Eigenvector centrality, node degree, and betweenness centrality to identify the following:

- *Influencers*—People who stand out in terms of recommending other people's work
- *Influencees*—Popular targets of other people's referrals (or professional gossip)
- *Bridges*—Those who act as connectors among different communities of people

Different visualization styling options can be designed to help guide us in exploration and analysis.

Figure 6.4 is the largest connected component of the extracted intellectual network with styling based on betweenness centrality: nodes are bigger when more shortest paths among any pair of nodes pass through them. This styling highlights people

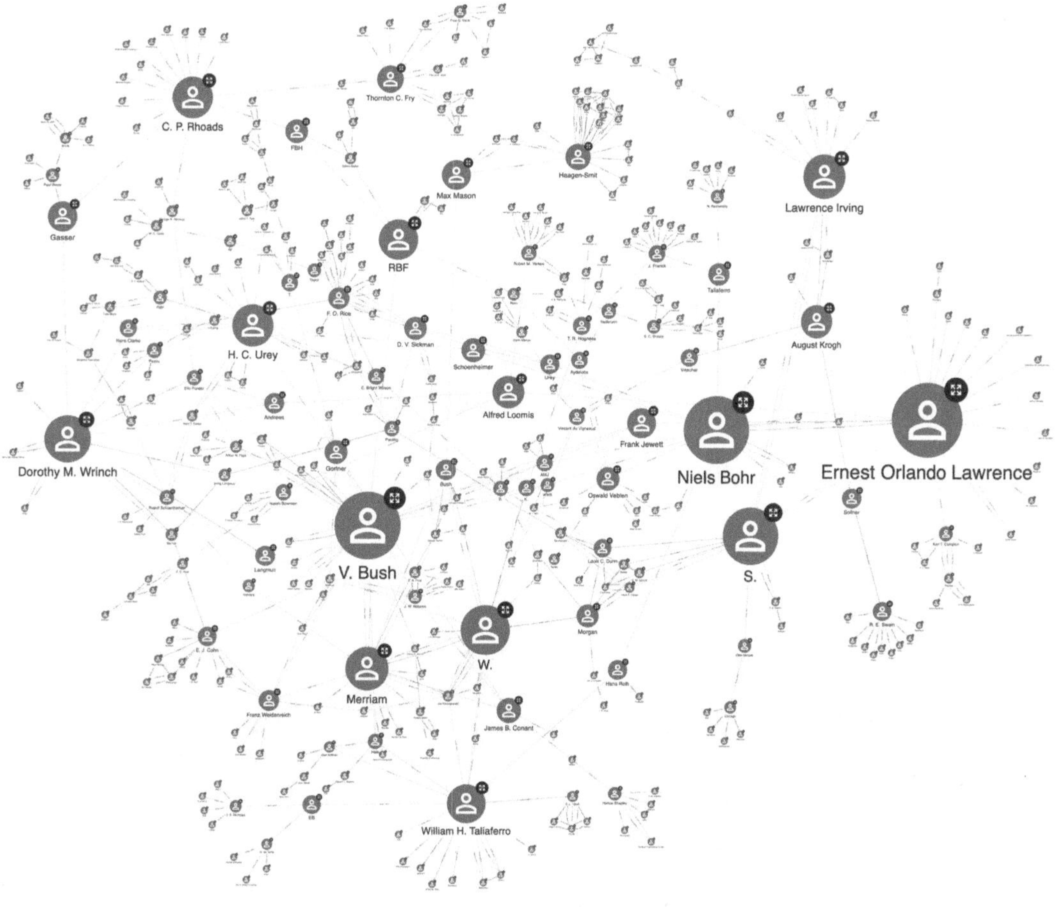

Figure 6.4 The intellectual influence network comprises the relations `TALKED_ABOUT`, `TALKED_WITH`, `WORKS_WITH`, and `STUDENT_OF`. Node styling is based on their betweenness centrality score.

acting as bridges among different subgraphs representing groups of researchers who'd otherwise be very loosely connected or even disconnected. Not surprisingly, famous scientists such as Niels Bohr (the father of atomic physics) and Ernest Lawrence (the inventor of a particle accelerator called cyclotron) are among them; but less famous people are also highlighted, which leads to other, potentially surprising, insights worth investigating.

We can also use our intellectual network to answer more focused questions, such as, "Who played an important role related to the cyclotron research and its funding?" This question can be answered with a simple few-hop query (listing 6.2).

Listing 6.2 Showing the influence network related to cyclotron research

```
MATCH path = ()<-[:WORKS_ON|WORKS_FOR]-(p2:Person)
➥-[:TALKED_ABOUT|TALKED_WITH|WORKS_WITH|STUDENT_OF*1..2]->
(p:Person)-[:WORKS_ON]->()-[:SIMILAR_OCCUPATION*0..1]-(o:Occupation)
WHERE o.name = toLower($occupation) AND
➥NOT ANY(x IN nodes(path1) WHERE x.name = "WW")
RETURN path
```

Within the matched path, we allow up to a two-hop distance between the person working on cyclotron research and some other person. That allows us to explore more complex referral patterns. The graph representation of this influence network of the cyclotron-related research is shown in figure 6.5, along with information such as occupations and university affiliations. The PageRank centrality calculated on the full influence network graph was used to scale the nodes. We see that besides Ernest Lawrence and Niels Bohr, other important people appear nearby, including Harlow Shapley, astronomer and head of Harvard College Observatory, and James B. Conant, organic chemist and 23rd president of Harvard University (Harvard built a cyclotron, which, after secret negotiations with General Leslie Groves, President Conant later sold to the U.S. government for $1 to help the development of the first nuclear bomb).

There is also an element of surprise. Notice the presence of Laurence Irving (with the first name misspelled by GPT as *Lawrence*—a mixup apparently caused by the presence of Ernest Lawrence on the same page), a pioneer in comparative physiology. Is it possible that he played a role in the influence network of the cyclotron invention? That would be unexpected. A closer look reveals that this is an example of failure in the RE task: he should not appear in this subgraph. This is an important reminder that LLMs are not magic; they do make mistakes, and sometimes silly ones. It is important to design a feedback loop in your KG applications so that analysts can validate or invalidate the content of the graph.

Let's conclude with one more example. Imagine that person with experience in a particular domain—in our case, project officer Warren Weaver—leaves their post, and someone new is hired. They're asked to handle a physics research project that spans

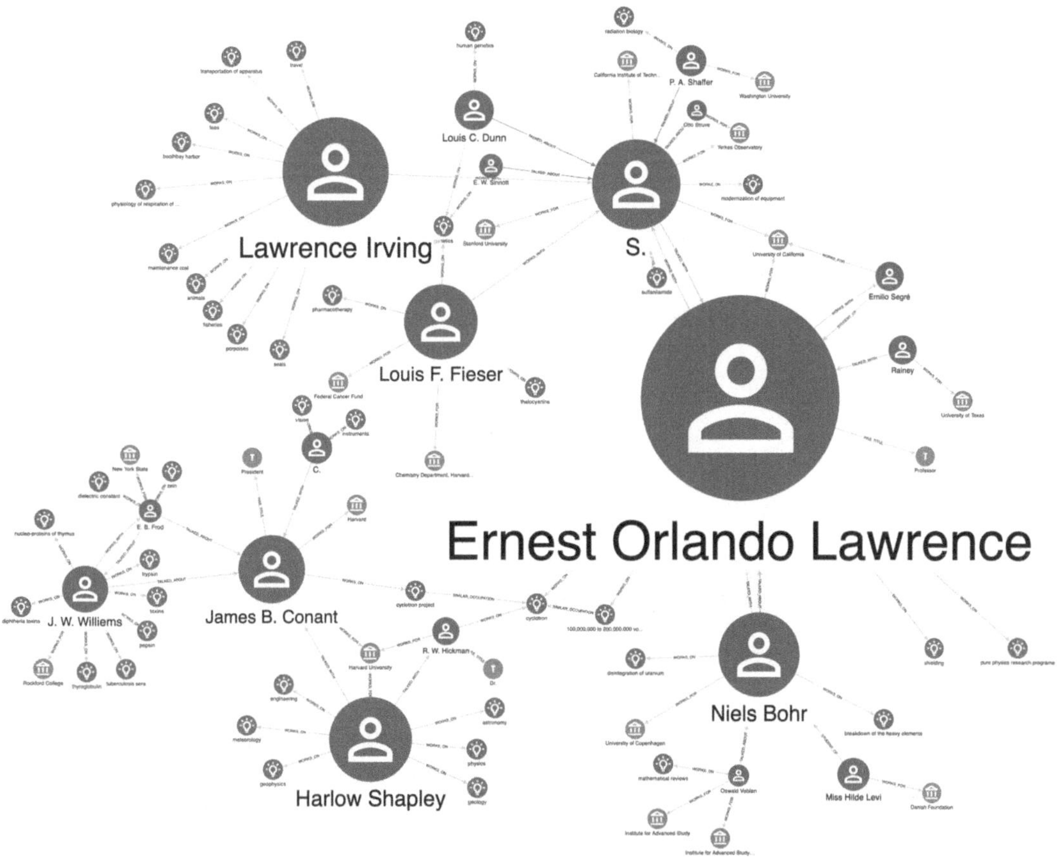

Figure 6.5 Influence network in the two-hop vicinity of the cyclotron research. The `Person` node sizes are based on global PageRank centrality to highlight popular nodes in the graph.

Johns Hopkins University and Harvard University. Which person should they approach first? They need to sound someone out informally, ideally a person with exposure to the physics domain at both Johns Hopkins and Harvard. The question can be answered by inspecting the relevant part of the influence network: we take all employees of both universities (`WORKS_FOR` relations) and search for any connections among them (relations `TALKED_ABOUT`, `TALKED_WITH`, `WORKS_WITH`, and `STUDENT_OF`) with, say, up to three hops, where at least one of the people works on physics research. The result is shown in figure 6.6.

If this were a bigger network, we could run a betweenness centrality algorithm on this subgraph to help us identify the important connectors, but in this case, it is a simple task. Only a handful of people stand out at first glance as useful connectors between the two universities. A good start could be Irving Langmuir (chemist,

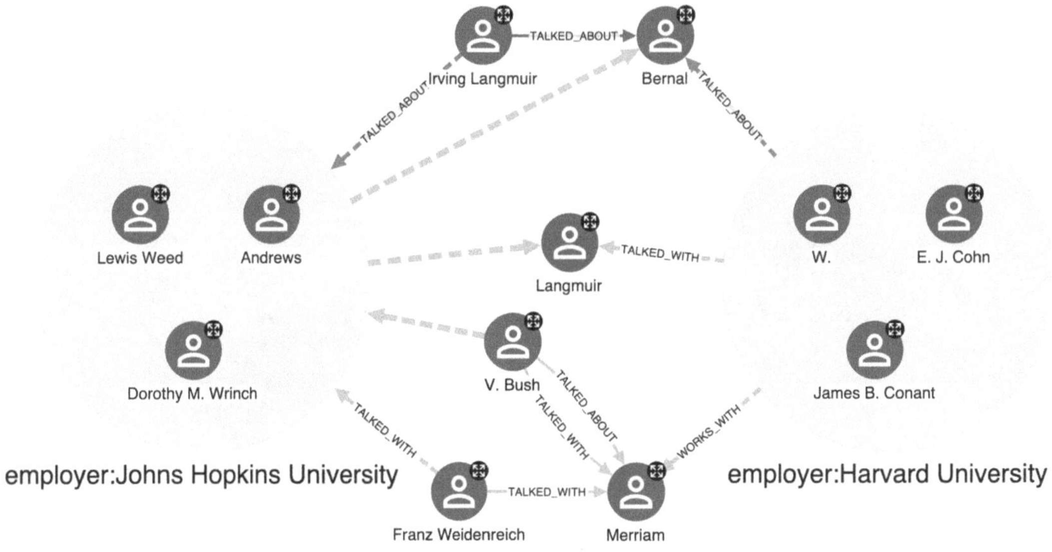

Figure 6.6 Physics research influence network connecting Johns Hopkins University and Harvard University, with no more than three hops between people

physicist, and engineer who won the Nobel Prize in Chemistry in 1932), who talked positively about Dorothy M. Wrinch (who studied insulin and protein structures using X-rays) and who has a direct one-hop link to both universities. Notice that two nodes represent this scientist, *Irving Langmuir* and *Langmuir*, because once his surname was mentioned on a page without additional relations that could be used during entity resolution. Moreover, by examining the properties of `TALKED_ABOUT` relationships that indicate sentiment, we discover that Bernal has a negative attitude toward Dorothy Wrinch, and Irving Langmuir has a negative attitude toward Bernal. To obtain balanced insight, we might want to interview both.

6.3 Next steps in the Rockefeller Archive Center project

The results in the previous section are based on only 150 pages from a much larger data source, but they demonstrate the impressive complexity of the KG. In a full production-quality project, we'd need to do more:

- *Improve knowledge extraction.* More iterations of prompt engineering or fine-tuning the LLM will improve the accuracy of the KG.
- *Handle multipage documents.* Each diary has hundreds of pages, but there is a token limit of how much data we can send to and retrieve from the LLM. In the RAC project, we used ChatGPT-3.5-Turbo to identify the boundaries of individual diary entries, which typically contain fewer than three pages, and process them simultaneously.

- *Perform entity resolution.* We can improve the baseline approach presented in this chapter, expand it to other entities, and complement it with entity disambiguation against WikiData or a similar knowledge base.
- *Add grants.* Mining details about grants awarded by the RF from board of directors minutes and linking the grants to conversations in the diaries will let us answer questions such as, "Do granted projects tend to run through recommendations of influential scientists or previous grantees?"
- *Perform entity resolution of* `Occupations`. These are named entities with varied granularity: for example, we have *nuclear physics*, *isotopes*, and *heavy nitrogen*, but both isotopes and heavy nitrogen are part of nuclear physics and heavy nitrogen is an isotope of nitrogen. To answer complex questions, we need to be able to link (resolve) them and thus gain access to the entire history of the given topic. We've gotten the best results by creating embeddings of `Occupations` (using SentenceBERT or GPT) and clustering them using agglomerative hierarchical clustering.
- *Create conversations.* We can create `Conversation` nodes by using high-quality RE and other information: a `Conversation` needs a date, an interviewer, interviewee(s), and a topic (`Occupations` of the interviewees). Once we have `Conversations`, we can identify their follow-up chains and link them to grants. Both tasks are achievable thanks to the unsupervised resolution of occupations.

Now the full extent of the RAC project is clear. Bleeding-edge knowledge mining from historical typewritten documents, reconciling unstructured data sources, entity resolution systems, graph modeling, graph data science, complex visualization, and styling—it's challenging, it's tough, and, most importantly, it's fun!

6.4 The value of knowledge graphs in the LLM era

You may wonder why, in the era of super-powerful Large Language Models, we build KGs instead of feeding these models our data and asking questions directly, without intermediate steps. The answer to this question is complex, and this book—our testament to KGs—is the big answer. But we can also provide a briefer answer, related to this chapter and summarized as follows:

- *Explainability*—Applications based on well-designed KGs have a huge advantage in being natively explainable. They give users the tools to inspect and verify the underlying data and reasoning, and they can be configured to handle conflicting sources of information while providing the entire chain of "thought" when required.
- *Demystification, or de-black-boxing*—People often view advanced ML models as black boxes that they are supposed to blindly trust. If we simply fine-tuned an LLM on our dataset and asked it questions, we would have no way to assess the confidence of the responses. And could we be sure that the "AI" wouldn't miss a crucial part of the information in our data? Instead, using the language understanding power of these models to extract specific factual information

from documents and produce a KG gives us confidence in the generated insights.

- *Democratization*—LLMs are massive beasts that are expensive to train and fine-tune. We can think of KGs as one way to democratize their use so that even organizations without massive funds can profit from them: we can use the expensive model only once to produce the KG, which we will then use for a long time (perhaps with occasional inexpensive batch updates) for downstream tasks and analyses.
- *Explorability*—Graphs let users view and touch their (relational) data from new angles. They provide global views as well as drill-down investigations. And KG visualization and explorability inspire people to hypothesize and then verify or disprove their theories.
- *Advanced analytics*—Perhaps most importantly, KGs empower data scientists and analysts to perform downstream graph-based analyses and ML while giving them full control over the generation of answers to user questions.

Summary

- Knowledge Graph schema design, a.k.a. graph modeling, ensures that information is stored optimally for the use case. A well-designed schema simplifies KG creation, entity and relation cleansing, normalization, and resolution, and ensures efficient downstream analyses and insight discovery.
- Extracting high-quality entity relations from textual documents helps us design an unsupervised graph-based entity resolution approach.
- Various graph data science and graph ML techniques can help us analyze patterns and draw insights from KGs without relying too heavily on black-box tools such as LLMs.

7 Named entity disambiguation

This chapter covers

- Combining named entity disambiguation with knowledge graph technologies
- Building a knowledge graph from multiple sources
- Performing advanced analysis

Natural language processing (NLP) techniques play a critical role in the automatic construction of knowledge graphs (KGs) from unstructured data. A key task in this process is named entity recognition (NER), which identifies mentions of relevant named entities in raw text. NER assigns these entities to predefined categories such as people, organizations, locations, or diseases. Although NER is an important component in building KGs, it doesn't give us a precise understanding of text in our application domain.

7.1 From recognition to disambiguation

Imagine developing an intelligent advisory system (IAS) to support the activities of stakeholders in the healthcare field. A critical attribute of such IASs is *interactivity*, which is the ability to exchange information with humans through multiple interactions. Features which enable this exchange include the following:

- Detecting meaningful entities in natural language
- Retrieving information about these entities from different knowledge sources

NER inference can't provide these features. For example, consider the following paragraph from a weekly bulletin released by the European Centre for Disease Prevention and Control (ECDC) [1]:

> *In the week of 13 April, Belize reported for the first time mosquito-borne Zika virus transmission. Update on the observed increase of congenital Zika syndrome and other neurological complications Microcephaly and other fetal malformations potentially associated with Zika virus infection.*

The term *Zika* appears three times in this short text. However, its meaning changes depending on the surrounding context. Assuming we can achieve high accuracy for this specific task, the output of an NER model will identify that the first instance refers to a *virus*. In contrast, the second and third instances refer to a *disease* entity. Do they represent the same disease? Apparently yes, because they both mention the term *Zika*. But we must be as accurate as possible in critical domains such as medicine. For some use cases, it is crucial to distinguish between the traditional Zika disease or infection (the third mention) and its congenital form (the second mention). Disambiguating such terms may be straightforward for a domain expert, but it becomes impractical when the volume of documents increases.

These problems are addressed by another NLP task: *named entity disambiguation* [2] (NED). The goal of the NED task is to automatically remove the uncertainty or ambiguity of the meaning of *Zika* by examining the context of each mention and connecting that mention to an entity in a knowledge base. An example of such a ground entity and its reference knowledge base is the *Congenital Zika virus infection* entity in the Unified Medical Language System (UMLS) [3]. This is different from the *Zika virus* and *Zika virus infection* entities, which are both also specified in UMLS. Figure 7.1 shows a screenshot from the UMLS website providing details about the *Zika virus* entity.

By mapping mentions of "Zika" in the raw text, we satisfy the IAS requirement related to detecting meaningful entities: in this case, a UMLS entity. But that is not all. Through this mapping, we implicitly created the conditions necessary to satisfy the second requirement of the IAS, which involves retrieving information from various knowledge sources. Starting from the detected UMLS entity, we can explore contextual knowledge in multiple biomedical ontologies related to the extracted entities. Medical ontologies allow us to retrieve, for instance, the connections between the disambiguated entities in our example. In some cases, they explicitly define a trivial relationship, such as specifying that *Zika virus* is the `CAUSATIVE_AGENT` of both syndromes. Other relationships are less trivial: for instance, the diseases Campylobacter infection

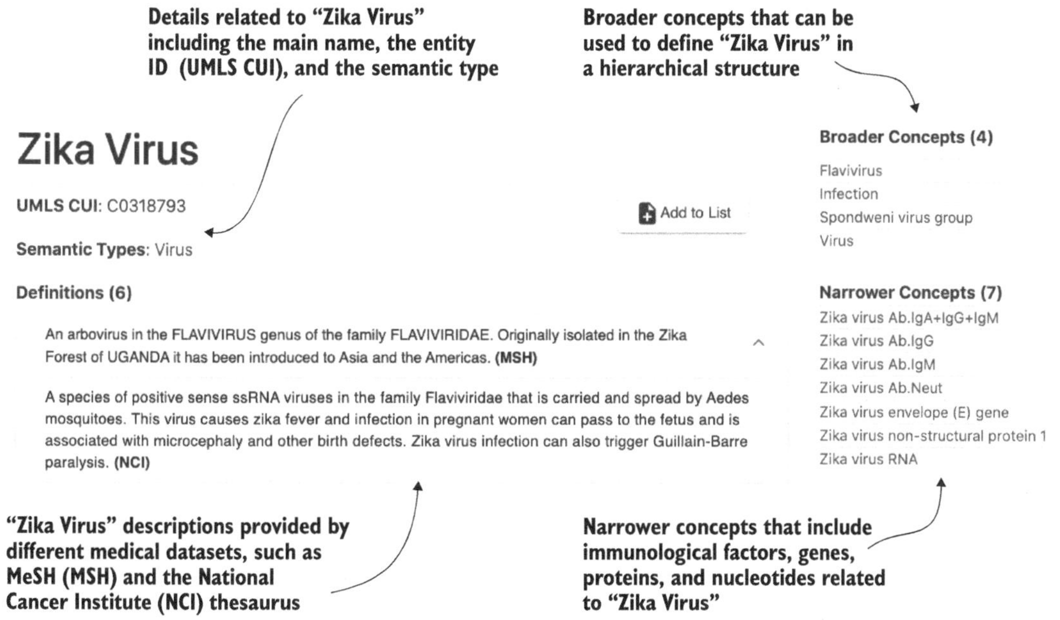

Figure 7.1 Screenshot from the UMLS website showing information about the *Zika Virus* entity. This information includes the name, the ID (concept unique identifier [CUI]), the semantic type, and a set of definitions, broader concepts, and narrower concepts.

and AIDS can be connected because the first affects the intestinal tract like a specific form of the second, known as *AIDS with intestinal malabsorption*.

This chapter demonstrates how to apply NED models to textual content in the healthcare domain. Drawing on our experience on a project conducted with the Directorate-General for Health & Food Safety (DG SANTE) of the European Commission, we first present an overview of the NED model with an example of disambiguation and interlinking with biomedical ontologies. Next, we introduce the documents and ontologies involved in the process. Finally, we show how to automatically construct a real-world KG that can extract and integrate information from multiple technical documents into a unified view.

> **Exercise**
>
> This exercise will help you identify different perspectives of NED. In the Zika example, we saw that a single term can refer to distinct entities based on the context. However, the opposite situation may also arise: in some cases, different terms can refer to the same entity. Can you spot an example? (Hint: Check the examples of medical entities mentioned in the chapter.) How is the KG useful in modeling these cases?

7.2 Understanding named entity disambiguation

Knowledge bases play a central role in collecting structured representations of entities in a specific domain. NER does not resolve the uncertainty related to mentions recognized as named entities, so we need to link mentions in the text to the correct entities in the reference knowledge base. This linking step is enabled by NED systems, which usually include three primary phases:

1. Candidate selection
2. Candidate ranking
3. Ontology integration

Figure 7.2 shows the mental model of a typical KG-based NED system.

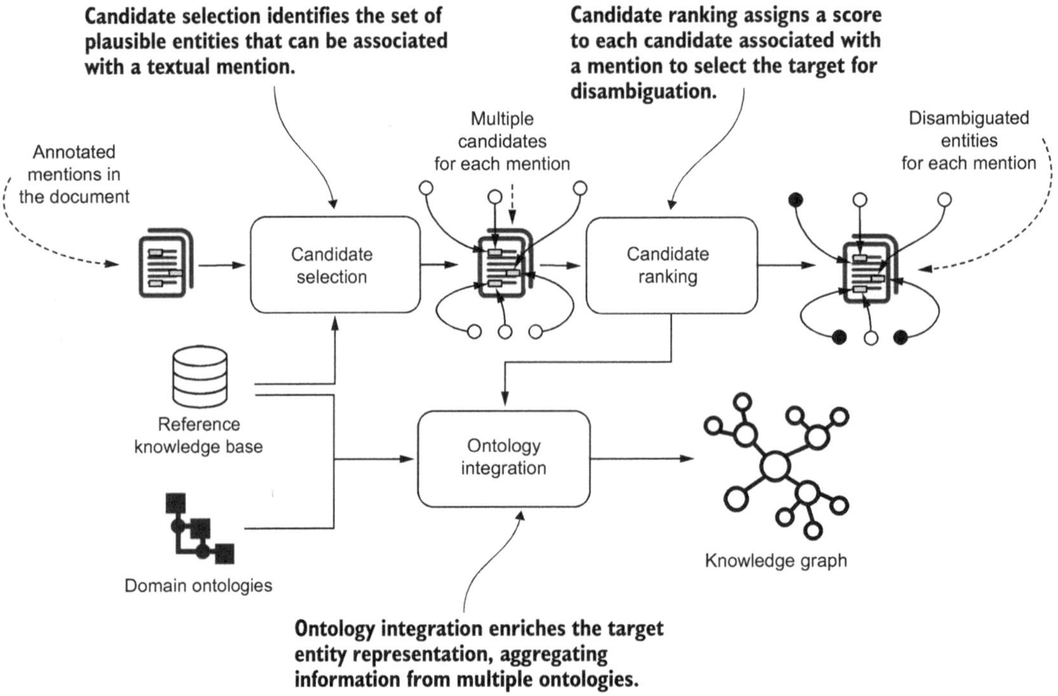

Figure 7.2 Architecture of the NED system, including the three main phases: candidate selection, candidate ranking, and ontology integration

Candidate selection identifies the best candidates for the recognized named entity mentions. This selection is performed against an existing knowledge base that includes useful structural information, enabling the precise identification of different entities. *Candidate ranking* assigns a score to each candidate based on the contextual information (words surrounding the recognized entity). The entity that achieves the best score represents the *target entity* of the detected mention.

We'll use a Python-based library called scispaCy [4] for disambiguating named entities. The model implemented in scispaCy can recognize named entities, select candidates against a knowledge base, and rank these candidates to identify the target entity. The following listing shows an example of a Python script using the scispaCy model.

Listing 7.1 Selecting and ranking candidates with the scispaCy model

```
import spacy
from scispacy.linking import EntityLinker

nlp = spacy.load("en_core_sci_md")
nlp.add_pipe("scispacy_linker",
             config={"resolve_abbreviations": True, "linker_name": "umls"})

linker = nlp.get_pipe("scispacy_linker")
linker_dict = linker.kb.cui_to_entity

doc = nlp("""In the week of 13 April, Belize reported for the first time
mosquito-borne Zika virus transmission. Update on the observed increase
of congenital Zika syndrome and other neurological complications
Microcephaly and other fetal malformations potentially associated with
Zika virus infection.""")
for ent in doc.ents:
  if "Zika" in ent.text:
    print("Recognized entity:", ent.text, ent.start_char, ent.end_char)
  print("Ranked target candidates:")
  for kb_ent in ent._.kb_ents:
    print('-', linker_dict[kb_ent[0]][0], linker_dict[kb_ent[0]][1])
```

Running this code retrieves a list of associated ranked candidates.

Listing 7.2 scispaCy model results for candidate selection and ranking

```
Recognized entity: Zika virus 75 85
Ranked target candidates:
- C0318793 Zika Virus                          <-- Target entity of the "Zika
- C0276289 Zika Virus Infection                    Virus" mention detected
- C4687930 Zika Virus Antibody Measurement         between characters 75 and 85.

Recognized entity: congenital Zika syndrome 135 159
Ranked target candidates:
- C4546023 Congenital Zika Syndrome            <-- Target entity of the "Congenital
                                                   Zika Syndrome" mention detected
Recognized entity: Zika virus infection 268 288    between characters 135 and 159.
Ranked target candidates:
- C0276289 Zika Virus Infection                <-- Target entity of the "Zika Virus
- C0318793 Zika Virus                              Infection" mention detected
- C4687930 Zika Virus Antibody Measurement         between characters 268 and 288.
```

Each recognized entity is associated with a list of candidates ranked using the scispaCy model score. The first result for each mention is the best one reached by the model: notice that a different UMLS entity ID is associated with each mention of "Zika." We can now obtain an annotated text in which each detected entity is linked to the UMLS knowledge base.

The final step before we can use the extracted information is *ontology integration*: incorporating knowledge from domain ontologies where the structural and contextual information of the extracted entities is integrated into a unique KG. The UMLS provides terminology, classification, and coding standards from multiple sources. This allows the creation of interoperable biomedical information systems whose information can be accessed and explored starting from another source. To better understand how the UMLS collects this information, here is a sample UMLS entry.

Listing 7.3 Sample entry from the UMLS entity file

```
C0276289|ENG|S|L0388876|VC|S0517846|Y|A2985635|8552019|3928002||
SNOMEDCT_US|PT|3928002|Zika virus disease|9|N|256|

C0276289|ENG|P|L13115709|PF|S16069662|N|A27369917||C128423||
NCI|PT|C128423|Zika Virus Infection|0|N|256|

C0276289|ENG|S|L0392793|VW|S16069660|Y|A26676017||M000613823|D000071243|
MSH|ET|D000071243|Zika Fever|0|N|256|
```

We've highlighted the most important fields for ontology integration: from left to right, the entity ID, the ontology, and the name associated with the entity ID in the ontology. As you can see from the first entry, the UMLS ID that represents the *Zika Virus Infection* entity is mapped to the ID 3928002 from the SNOMEDCT_US [5] ontology, which defines one of the possible names of this entity (*Zika virus disease*). SNOMEDCT_US, or Systematized Nomenclature of Medicine (SNOMED), is one of the most comprehensive, multilingual clinical terminologies, encompassing more than 450,000 concepts. It also provides a rich set of relationship types between these concepts, including interesting semantic connections from a clinical point of view, such as `CAUSATIVE AGENT` and `FINDING SITE`. Let's look at two file samples related to the SNOMED ontology, including the SNOMED entities/relationships descriptions and edges (or triples). The first is a sample of the SNOMED description file.

Listing 7.4 Samples from the SNOMED description file

```
84087010     20020131    1    900000000000207008    50471002
    en    900000000000013009    Zika virus    900000000000017005

8552019      20020131    1    900000000000207008    3928002
    en    900000000000013009    Zika virus disease    900000000000017005

367784012      20020131    1    900000000000207008    246075003
    en    900000000000013009    Causative agent    900000000000020002
```

You can see the SNOMED IDs and the related names. The file includes both IDs for entities and the relationship between the entities. In this sample, the first entry represents an entity (*Zika virus*), and the third entry represents a relationship (*Causative agent*).

Now, here is an entry from the edge file.

Listing 7.5 Sample from the SNOMED edge file

```
769900023      20020131     1     900000000000207008
    3928002              50471002     0     246075003
900000000000011006      900000000000451002
```

The highlighted values represent the triple elements, including the source ID for *Zika virus disease* (3928002), the target ID for *Zika virus* (50471002), and the relationship ID representing *Causative agent* (246075003).

By incorporating external ontologies, the NED model's output becomes the entry point for exploring and discovering information and building a KG that lets us bridge unstructured and structured knowledge in a unified view. Figure 7.3 shows an intuitive example of this KG, which includes all the previous pieces of information.

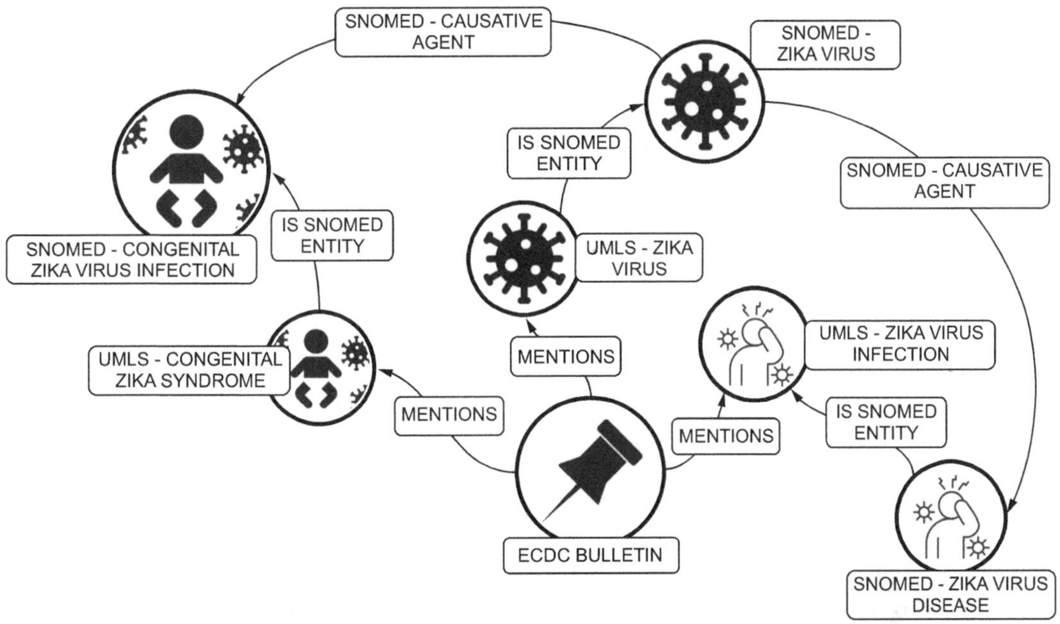

Figure 7.3 Example KG built by integrating information from the text processed with the scispaCy model, the UMLS, and the SNOMED ontologies

Our example KG will enable us to perform advanced analyses in a real-world scenario related to the definitions of healthcare standards and regulations associated with managing *substances of human origin* (SoHO) in the European Union. Figure 7.4 provides a mental model to illustrate the process described in this chapter, from business understanding to KG creation and querying. As discussed in other chapters, this mental model represents a specification of the CRISP-DM model adapted to KGs, as introduced in chapter 2.

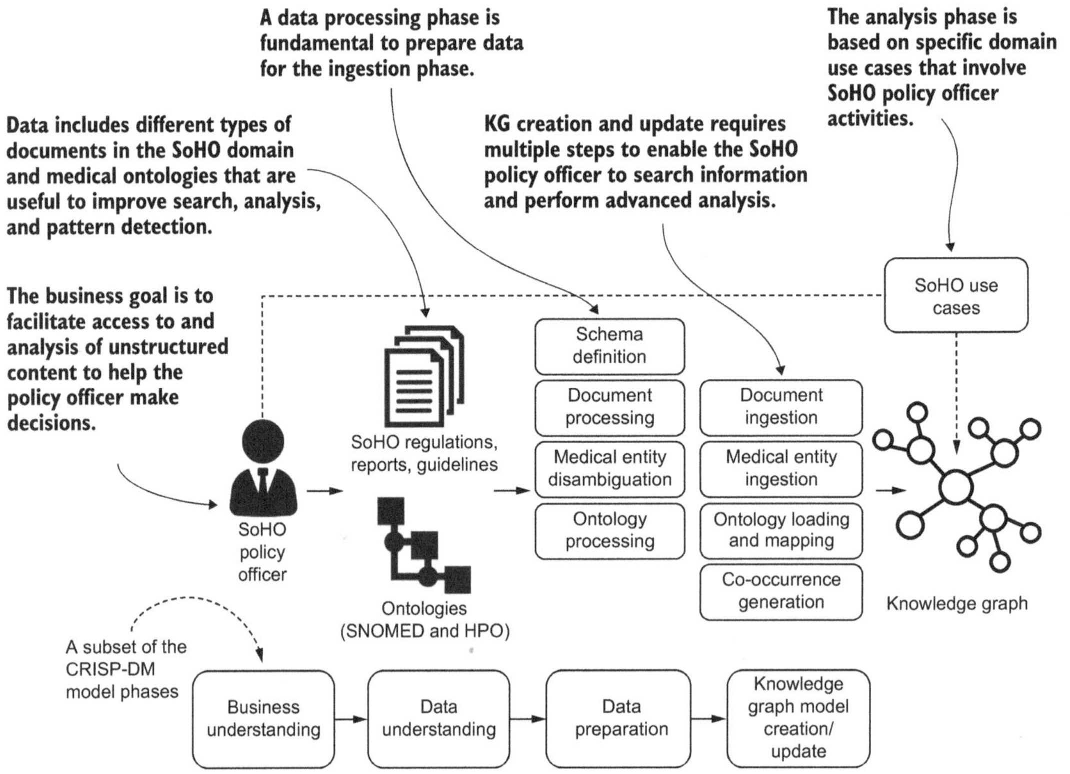

Figure 7.4 Mental model describing the KG construction process as a specification of the CRISP-DM model, from understanding the business goal to defining the KG queries useful for our analysis

Before we introduce the example business application, let's recap the opportunities and limitations of LLMs introduced in chapter 6, applied to the current case. LLMs represent a modern alternative to using scispaCy, but they must be combined with KG technologies to add value in this context.

7.3 Domain-based NED and LLMs

Earlier, we discussed how the capacity to detect concepts in textual content is an essential feature of an IAS that supports decision-making. For this reason, we did a simple experiment to test the ability of ChatGPT, the most prominent application based on LLM technologies, to reach this goal.

Here is the basic prompt we have defined based on our running example:

AN "In the week of 13 April, Belize reported for the first time mosquito-borne Zika virus transmission. Update on the observed increase of congenital Zika syndrome and other neurological complications Microcephaly and other fetal malformations potentially associated with Zika virus infection." Disambiguate all the medical entities you can detect.

The output from ChatGPT is the following:

- Zika virus
- Mosquito-borne transmission
- Congenital Zika syndrome
- Neurological complications
- Microcephaly
- Fetal malformations

NOTE ChatGPT is based on a generative model that is continuously evolving. For this reason, you can receive different responses even during similar tests and experiments.

As you can see from this initial result, the model does not perfectly recognize that the first "Zika" mention refers to a virus entity and the last refers to the virus infection. Considering the complexity of the medical domain, we need to be confident that the model "understands" the meaning of these expressions. From the NED perspective, we must check whether these entities are correctly mapped against the proper knowledge base. We defined a further prompt to test this aspect:

AN Can you assign UMLS ids to these extracted entities?

The answer was the following:

As an AI language model, I am not able to assign UMLS ids to extracted entities. However, UMLS Metathesaurus is a biomedical and health ontological resource that provides normalized names and mappings to concepts in various biomedical ontologies. It can be used to map extracted entities to their corresponding UMLS concepts and obtain their unique identifiers (UMLS ids). This requires domain-specific knowledge and expertise in utilizing the UMLS resources.

As you can tell, the UMLS knowledge base is not currently incorporated in the ChatGPT model. The last sentence is particularly critical: it suggests that we need to develop models characterized by domain-specific knowledge and expertise on UMLS resources. In our example, we'll combine NED technologies and KGs in an approach that includes these features and can be easily integrated into an IAS.

7.4 Business and domain understanding

Figure 7.5 depicts the business understanding step. Our real-world scenario is related to the definition of standards and regulations in the management of SoHO. These substances include blood, tissues, cells, and organs that can be used in various medical therapies. Treatments based on SoHO save lives (e.g., blood transfusions), improve the quality of life (e.g., kidney transplants), and even help create life (gametes and in vitro fertilization). The KG technology can respond to specific requirements in this scenario through features such as representation flexibility and harmonization of multiple sources in a unified view.

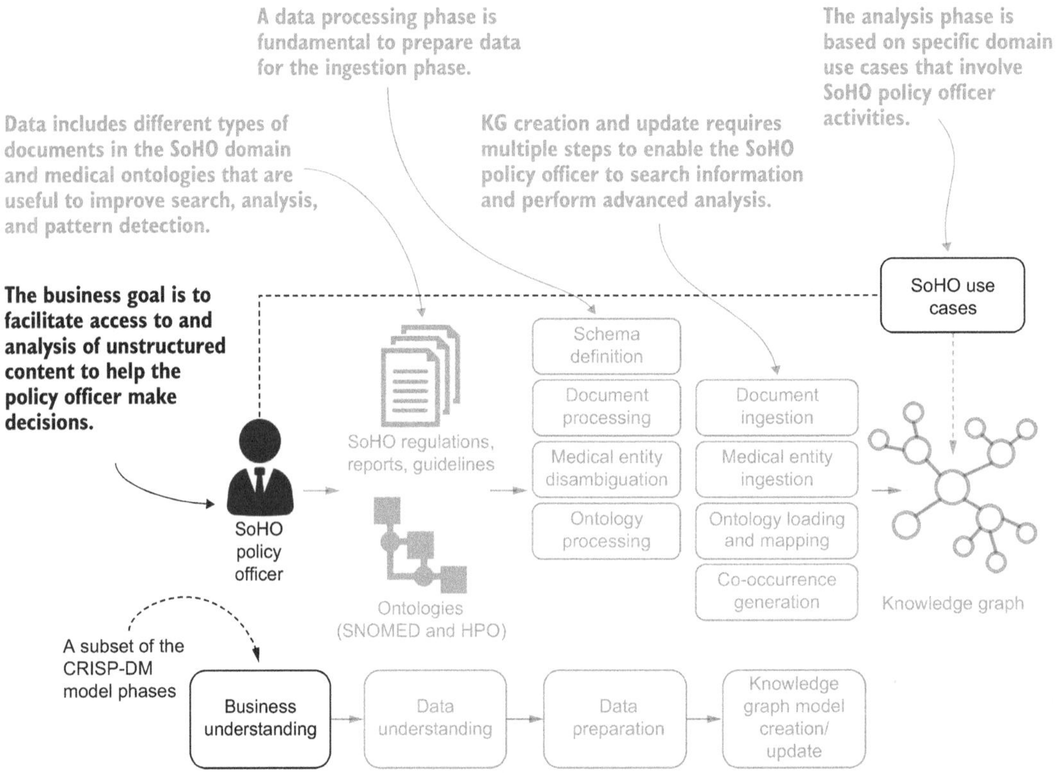

Figure 7.5 Business understanding clarifies the problems we want to solve. This phase is not strictly related to the technical aspects, but it is fundamental for the next steps.

7.4.1 Context

A critical area in the healthcare domain is the safety of patients undergoing blood transfusion, transplantation, and medical-assisted reproduction. From substance donation to the patient application, components such as blood, tissues, and cells (BTC) are used in treatments across the EU. Figure 7.6 illustrates the various aspects of this healthcare sector: beginning with donor evaluation, multiple dimensions can be analyzed, including procurement, quality criteria, distribution, traceability, and biovigilance.

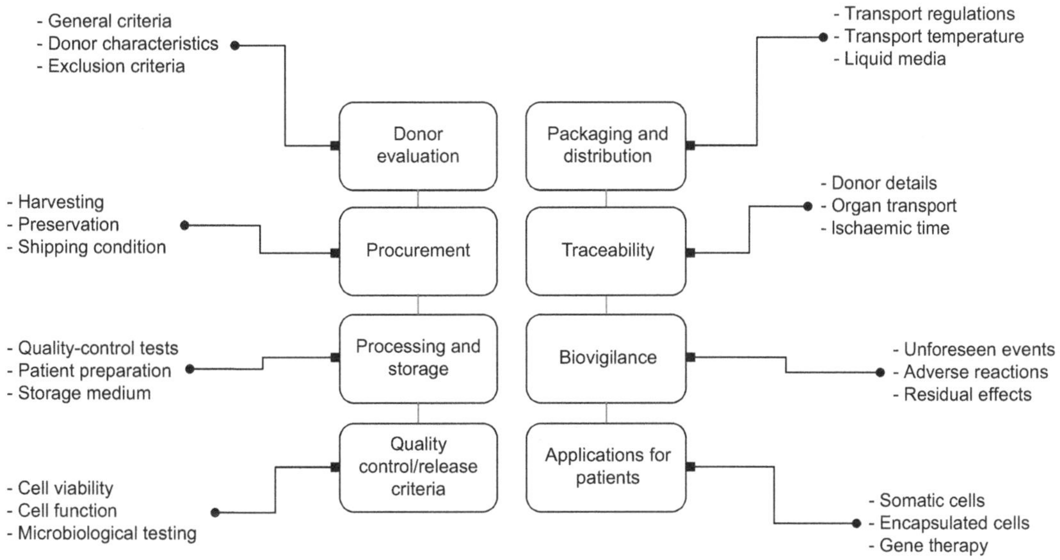

Figure 7.6 (Center) Steps in the SoHO supply chain. (Left and right) Characteristics of these phases.

The BTC sector relies on citizens for donations, but their availability is significantly reduced during public health crises, such as the COVID-19 pandemic. At the same time, BTC quality must be kept up to date with new methods for collecting, testing, and processing SoHO. New risks and technology trends will continue to emerge, so a legal framework is needed that is "effectively implemented, future proof, crisis resistant and agile enough" [6] to provide appropriate requirements continuously.

In 2022, the European Commission (EC) released a proposal for a regulation on standards and quality of SoHO for human applications. This proposal aims to ensure the safety of patients treated with SoHO therapies and protect them from avoidable and predictable risks. Of the alternatives explored, the best option identified by SoHO stakeholders was a joint regulation built on the expertise of bodies such as the European Centre for Disease Prevention and Control (ECDC) and the European Directorate for the Quality of Medicines & HealthCare (EDQM). These two agencies play complementary roles: the ECDC generally provides short reports related to health surveillance, responses to health threats, emerging trends, and the safety of SoHO; the EDQM releases detailed guidelines to address issues of quality and safety beyond the risks of communicable disease transmission and provides technical standards for the collection, processing, storage, and distribution of SoHO. The ability to extract useful information and contextual details from both kinds of textual documents is fundamental to identifying rules and rapidly updating regulations that guarantee the safety of patients and protect them from avoidable risks.

7.4.2 Use case definition

Let's imagine a health policy officer who must identify specific guidelines and possible risks related to the transplantation of pancreatic islets—also known as islets of Langerhans—and, in parallel, analyze the spread of the Zika virus in a particular region. As we will see, adopting NED and KG technologies can support this type of activity.

CONCEPTUAL SEARCH

Conceptual search is a retrieval method that enables users to find information based on meaning rather than exact keywords. It can reconcile different expressions that refer to the same entity (e.g., "pancreatic islets" and "islets of Langerhans") or distinguish between entities with similar names but different meanings.

STRUCTURED KNOWLEDGE-BASED SEARCH

A structured knowledge-based search retrieves information in the text by using the formalized knowledge structured in the domain ontologies. This information enables us to create nontrivial relationships between different pieces of text from multiple documents. For example, by navigating the ontology paths, the user can identify different types of disorders caused by diabetes, retrieve all the documents that mention these disorders, and obtain a complete overview of the relevant textual content.

KG-BASED INTERPRETABILITY AND DISCOVERY

Relationships or paths in the formalized knowledge in the ontologies can reflect essential information in textual content (interpretability) or provide insights with connections that enrich or complete the information in the text (discovery). For instance, from the interpretability perspective, type 1 diabetes (T1D) and islets of Langerhans entities co-occur because the former is a syndrome that affects the latter. From the discovery perspective, diseases such as AIDS and T1D can co-occur because some pathologies associated with T1D can involve the immune system.

UNCOVERING NEW KNOWLEDGE

More exciting examples emerge when knowledge of co-occurring entities is not yet formalized in ontologies but is available in the EDQM guidelines or related to discoveries in the field. For example, the pancreatic islets entity is mentioned along with information related to SoHO management (see figure 7.6). Moreover, SoHO stakeholders who are interested in unusual co-occurrences between communicable and non-communicable diseases, such as COVID-19 and diabetes mellitus, can consult ECDC bulletins in the same (graph-based) view to understand whether infections are increasing in a specific member state and make decisions about blocking the import of organs and tissue.

7.5 Understanding the data

Developing an IAS in the SoHO domain requires integrating heterogeneous information from various repositories into a unified source, combining both unstructured and semantically structured data (see figure 7.7). This section gives an overview of documents released by the EC and its agencies and the medical ontologies adopted in this context, such as SNOMED and the Human Phenotype Ontology (HPO).

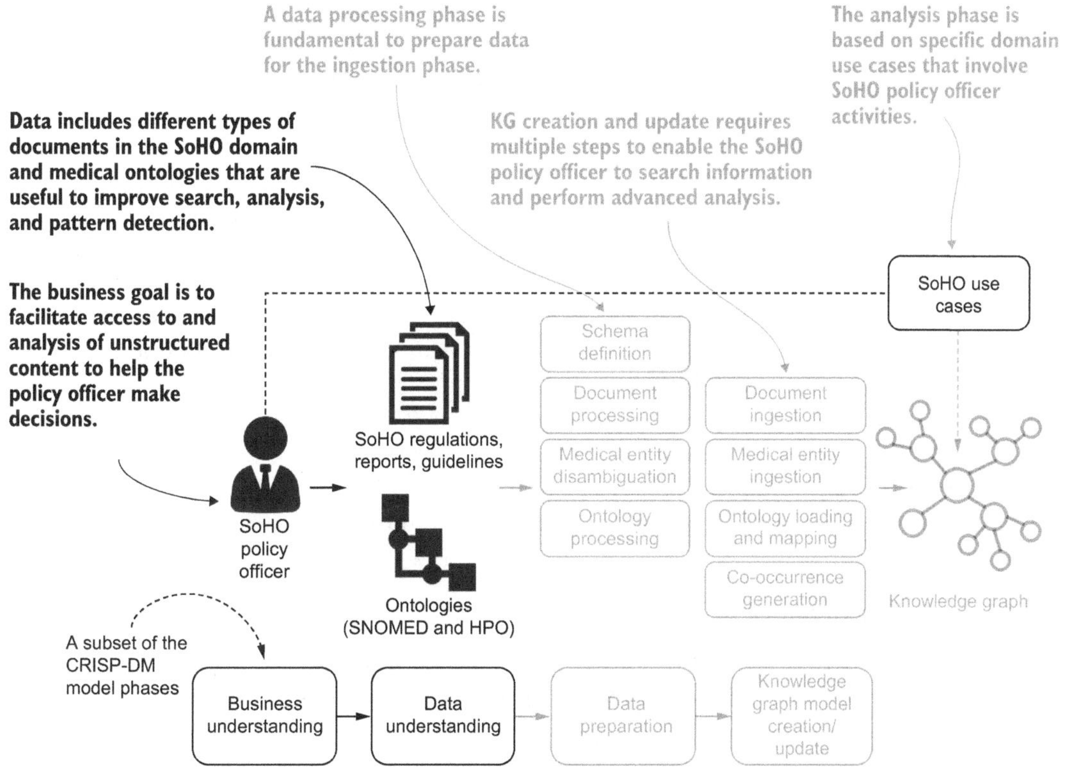

Figure 7.7 The data understanding step enables us to comprehend the characteristics of the available information. For the example scenario, the available data includes SoHO regulations, reports, and guidelines released by the EC and its agencies, as well as medical ontologies such as SNOMED and the HPO.

7.5.1 Unstructured data

Unstructured contents include several types of documents:

- Impact assessment reports in the BTC field and related regulatory proposals
- Reports on stakeholders' positions on the regulation proposal
- Guidelines and newsletters for SoHO management from the EDQM
- Reports and bulletins from the ECDC to monitor the progress of infectious diseases

Let's look at the characteristics of these documents to clarify the types of unstructured information that are processed and transformed into a KG. This will help you build intuition about potential use cases that can be based on these documents.

Impact assessment reports provided by the EC outline the political and legal context surrounding problems in the BTC field in the EU. They collect ideas to revise previous legislation, highlight problems such as interruptions in BTC supply, discuss new diseases and developments in science and technology, outline objectives for improving the BTC sector, analyze policy options, and propose regulations.

Regulation proposals are evaluated by stakeholders who provide position papers, lessons learned, and general comments. For instance, in a position paper, the International Society for Stem Cell Research (ISSCR) raised concerns about unproven cellular therapies and businesses making unsubstantiated claims for clinical effectiveness. The paper suggested that EU expert bodies must consult with other regulators and harmonize standards with international norms, and that consultations for guidance documents should be simplified to encourage feedback on new proposals.

Documents such as the "Guide to the Quality and Safety of Tissues and Cells for Human Application" [7] from the EDQM provide healthcare professionals with technical guidance. The guide presents minimum standards that align with EU directives, best practices consistent with current scientific knowledge, experts' opinions, and the results of international projects.

Weekly communicable disease threat reports (CDTRs) from the ECDC consolidate all data collected via epidemic intelligence activities related to infectious diseases that are significant to the EU. This summary also offers information on worldwide conditions and alterations in the epidemiology of communicable diseases that could impact Europe.

7.5.2 Domain ontologies

Chapter 3 introduced the adoption of ontologies as a reference schema for integrating different sources. For the scope of the scenario we are addressing, we use the UMLS, SNOMED, and HPO ontologies.

UNIFIED MEDICAL LANGUAGE SYSTEM (UMLS)

The UMLS is a meta-thesaurus composed of multiple controlled vocabularies in the biomedical domain. It provides a mapping structure among these vocabularies, simplifying translation among the various terminology systems. Our code examples use the 2022AA version of the UMLS.

For our scenario, we will use these two files:

- *MRCONSO.RRF*—A list of biomedical entities from multiple vocabularies. For each entity name, it includes the entity ID from which the name comes.
- *MRSTY.RRF*—A list of the semantic types categorizing the UMLS entities.

These files are formatted using delimiter-separated values (DSVs), and the separator is a vertical bar or pipe (|). So, they can be processed as traditional CSV files. Listings 7.6 and 7.7 show samples of MRCONSO.RRF and MRSTY.RRF.

Listing 7.6 Sample of the UMLS MRCONSO.RRF file

```
C0022131|ENG|P|L0022136|PF|S0054489|N|A2883106|130586015|78696007||
SNOMEDCT_US|SY|78696007|Islets of Langerhans|9|N|256|

C0022131|ENG|S|L7933100|PF|S9245679|Y|A15439829||76489||
FMA|SY|76489|Insulae pancreaticae|0|N|256

C0022131|ENG|S|L0826072|PF|S0870037|N|A0928304||||
RCD|PT|XaIIj|Endocrine pancreatic structure|3|N|256|

---

C0011311|ENG|P|L0011312|VC|S0000287|Y|A2872183|63434017|38362002||
SNOMEDCT_US|SY|38362002|Dengue fever|9|N|256|

C0011311|ENG|S|L0286841|VO|S14576929|N|A24118377||M0005831|D003715|
MSH|PM|D003715|Break Bone Fever|0|N|256|

C0011311|ENG|S|L0294785|VW|S4069775|Y|A4402397||||
ICPC2ICD10ENG|PT|MTHU021113|dandy fever|3|N|256|

---

C0018681|ENG|S|L0290365|PF|S0362835|N|A2926207|41994011|25064002||
SNOMEDCT_US|SY|25064002|Cephalgia|9|N|2304|

C0018681|ENG|S|L1406212|VO|S1680379|Y|A1641924||M0009824|D006261|
MSH|PM|D006261|Cranial Pains|0|N||

C0018681|ENG|P|L0018681|PF|S0046854|N|A24679981|||HP:0002315|
HPO|PT|HP:0002315|Headache|0|N|256|
```

MRCONSO.RRF aggregates information on ontologies, codes, and entity names related to medical entities. Each entry is identified by the UMLS ID located in the first column of each row; we need this for NED because the scispaCy model provides disambiguation results using these IDs. Listing 7.6 shows a set of rows related to *Islets of Langerhans*, *Dengue fever*, and *Cephalgia* (headache).

Ontologies

Codes and names associated with the entities in this example are located in the following sources:

- SNOMED, https://www.nlm.nih.gov/healthit/snomedct/us_edition.html
- Foundational Model of Anatomy (FMA), http://si.washington.edu/projects/fma
- Read Codes (RC), http://www.connectingforhealth.nhs.uk/systemsandservices/data/readcodes/
- Medical Subject Headings (MSH), https://www.nlm.nih.gov/mesh/

(continued)

- International Classification of Primary Care, 2nd edition; International Classification of Diseases, Tenth Revision (ICPC2ICD10ENG), https://www.who.int/standards/classifications/other-classifications/international-classification-of-primary-care
- HPO, https://hpo.jax.org/app/

Next, this listing shows how *Islets of Langerhans, Dengue Fever,* and *Headache* are categorized in UMLS.

Listing 7.7 Sample of the UMLS MRSTY.RRF file

```
C0022131|T023|A1.2.3.1|Body Part, Organ, or Organ Component|AT19674993|256|
C0011311|T047|B2.2.1.2.1|Disease or Syndrome|AT41932582|256|
C0018681|T184|A2.2.2|Sign or Symptom|AT17639733|256|
```

For each entry in MRCONSO.RRF the MRSTY.RRF file provides a semantic type code and name. Here, "Body Part, Organ, or Organ Component" (T023), "Disease or Syndrome" (T047), and "Sign or Symptom" (T184) correspond to semantic types of *Islets of Langerhans, Dengue Fever,* and *Cephalgia*, respectively.

SYSTEMATIZED NOMENCLATURE OF MEDICINE (SNOMED)

SNOMED encompasses more than 450,000 concepts and relationship types between them. It is provided using the UMLS free license and can be downloaded from https://www.nlm.nih.gov/healthit/snomedct. We used the SNOMED version released on 01 September 2022.

For our scenario, we will use these two files:

- *sct2_Description_Full-en_US1000124_20220901.txt*—All the entity names (and aliases) and relationships formed in the triplet file that define the relationships between entities
- *sct2_Relationship_Full_US1000124_20220901.txt*—A set of triplets (plus other metadata) that defines all the relationships between the SNOMED entities. Each entity and relationship is identified using a numerical code.

These files use a TSV format. Listings 7.8 and 7.9 provide samples.

Listing 7.8 Sample from the SNOMED description file

```
130586015    20020131    1    900000000000207008    78696007
en    900000000000013009    Islets of Langerhans    900000000000017005
63434017    20020131    1    900000000000207008    38362002
en    900000000000013009    Dengue fever    900000000000017005
41993017    20020131    1    900000000000207008    25064002
en    900000000000013009    Cephalalgia    900000000000020002
```

Here we see how information is initially provided by the data source from which UMLS has been generated. The SNOMED entry includes the code and name for *Islets of Langerhans*, *Dengue fever*, and *Cephalalgia*, respectively. The next listing shows how these can be either source or target entities in semantic relationships.

Listing 7.9 Sample from the SNOMED relationship file

```
169174023    20020131    1    900000000000207008    360555004
78696007    0    116680003    900000000000011006    900000000000451002

182243021    20020131    1    900000000000207008    20927009

38362002    0    116680003    900000000000011006    900000000000451002
424787021    20020131    1    900000000000207008    54012000
25064002    0    116680003    900000000000011006    900000000000451002
```

In this case, *Islets of Langerhans*, *Dengue fever*, and *Cephalalgia* are target entities of an `IS_A` relationship (ID 116680003). The source entities are *Endocrine pancreas cell* (ID 360555004), *Dengue hemorrhagic fever* (ID 20927009), and *Posttraumatic headache* (ID 54012000), respectively.

Human Phenotype Ontology (HPO)

The HPO ontology [8] is released as an RDF/XML file called hpo.owl (http://purl.obolibrary.org/obo/hp.owl). It contains standardized information on phenotypic anomalies. The next listing shows a subset of the file related to T1D; the data is serialized from RDF/XML to Turtle (Terse RDF Triple Language) for improving readability.

Listing 7.10 T1D details in hpo.owl

```
obo:HP_0100651 a owl:Class ;
    rdfs:label "Type I diabetes mellitus" ^^xsd:string ;
    obo:IAO_0000115 "A chronic condition in which the pancreas produces
        little or no insulin..." ^^xsd:string ;
    oboInOwl:created_by "doelkens"^^xsd:string ;
    oboInOwl:creation_date "2010-12-29T06:37:55Z"^^xsd:string ;
    oboInOwl:hasDbXref "MSH:D003922"^^xsd:string,
        "SNOMEDCT_US:46635009" ^^xsd:string,
        "UMLS:C0011854" ^^xsd:string ;
    oboInOwl:hasExactSynonym "Diabetes mellitus Type I"^^xsd:string,
        "Juvenile diabetes mellitus" ^^xsd:string,
        "Type 1 diabetes",
        "Type I diabetes";
    oboInOwl:hasRelatedSynonym "Insulin-dependent diabetes
        mellitus"^^xsd:string ;
    oboInOwl:id "HP:0100651"^^xsd:string ;
    rdfs:comment "The onset of type 1 diabetes is typically during
        adolescence..." ^^xsd:string ;
    rdfs:subClassOf obo:HP_0000819 .
```

Defines T1D (URI obo:HP_0100651) as an ontology class

Describes the disease in natural language

Metadata related to the author ("doelkens") of this entry

IDs of external data sources that refer to T1D

Defines T1D as a subclass of the phenotypic feature identified by the obo:HP_0000819 URI, which corresponds to diabetes mellitus

7.6 Building a SoHO knowledge graph

Constructing the KG and developing use cases on top of this source of truth involves these steps:

1. Define the KG schema.
2. Process and ingest documents.
3. Disambiguate and ingest medical entities.
4. Process, load, and map ontologies.
5. Generate co-occurrence relationships.

Figure 7.8 shows the key steps for building KGs that involve data preparation and ingestion.

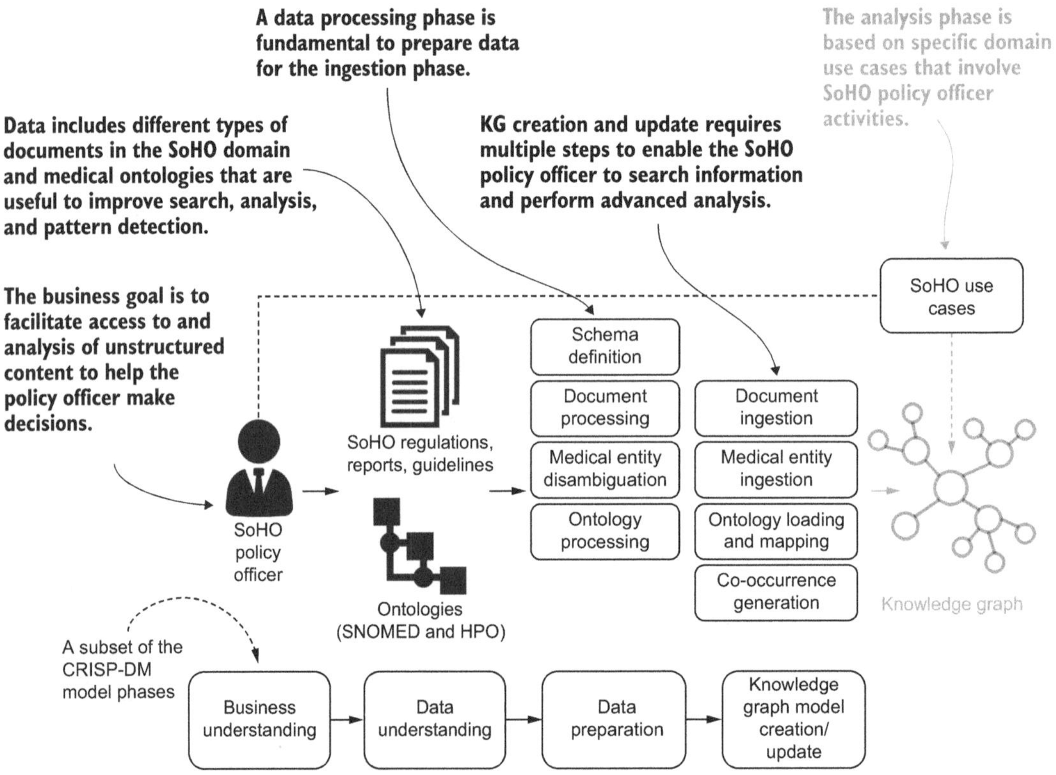

Figure 7.8 Preparing data and creating and updating the KG are critical technical steps. The data preparation step involves processing the available data, and the KG creation and/or update step uses the output of this process to generate the database for the analysis phase.

At this point, you have two choices for how to proceed in this section. First, you can build the KG from scratch following each of these steps. Alternatively, if your goal is to understand the main ideas to construct the KG and then focus on the use cases (section 7.7), you can begin with an intermediate version of the KG, which includes documents processed using scispaCy. In this case, begin with section 7.6.1 and then skip to section 7.6.4 to load the ontologies and map their nodes to the extracted medical entities. The full code for building the KG combines Python scripts and Cypher queries, and is available on the book's code repository.

7.6.1 Defining the schema

Defining the schema is a theoretical step that defines a graph-based model for our data, which will help us with the use cases in section 7.7. Figure 7.9 illustrates the schema that models the primary components (nodes and relationships) of the KG we will construct.

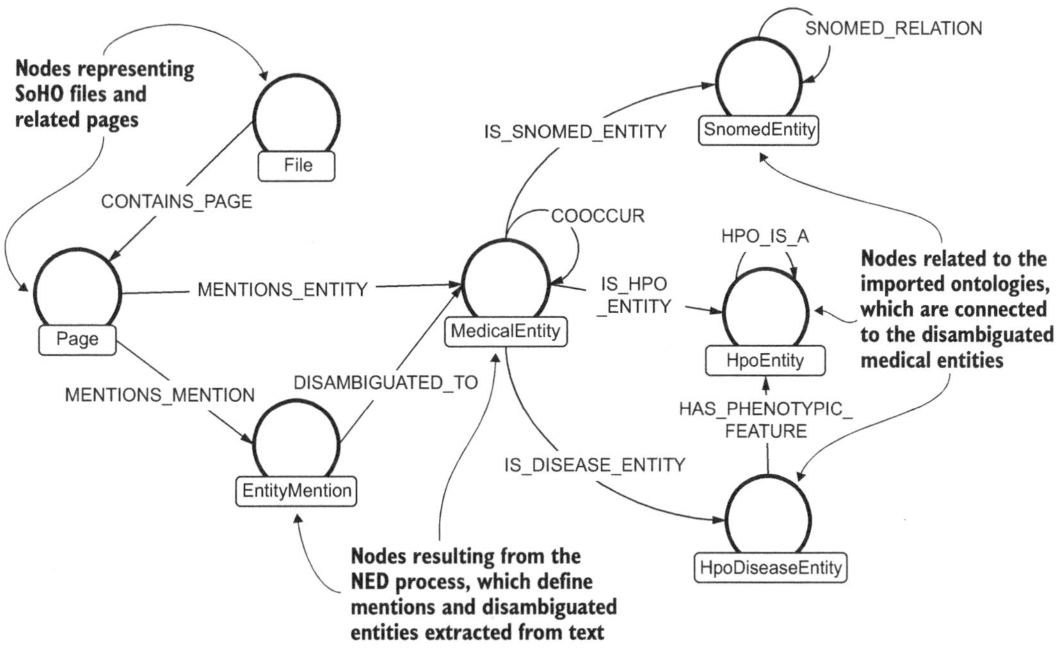

Figure 7.9 KG schema, including relevant node labels and relationship types, to enable multiple types of analyses

Ingested documents are structured in a graph by connecting the `File` node and related `Page` nodes. Each `Page` is linked to a collection of `EntityMention` nodes that define all the recognized entities in the text. These `EntityMention` nodes are disambiguated and connected to `MedicalEntity` nodes. The `DISAMBIGUATED_TO` relationship lets us model cases in which mentions with the same string refer to different entities and, on the other hand, entities characterized by different strings point to the same entity. For example, as we saw earlier, the term "Zika" can refer to multiple entities, whereas "AIDS" and "Acquired Immunodeficiency Syndrome" are two different expressions of the same entity. The `MENTIONS_ENTITY` relationship connects the `Page` node and the disambiguated `MedicalEntity` node.

The remaining nodes and relationships map the extracted `MedicalEntity` to `SnomedEntity`, `HpoEntity`, and `HpoDiseaseEntity`. To specify this mapping, we defined the following relationships: `IS_SNOMED_ENTITY`, `IS_HPO_ENTITY`, and `IS_DISEASE_ENTITY`. Now that we've defined the KG schema, we can begin to ingest data.

7.6.2 Processing and ingesting documents

In this phase, we ingest documents and model the related content in a graph-based structure. Most of the documents available for our purpose are released in PDF or DOCx format. So, before loading the data into Neo4j, we extracted the raw content using the Amazon Textract OCR service and processed the result. To reconstruct the full text, we created Python scripts for managing documents with different structures, such as one-column or two-column documents. Figure 7.10 shows the key aspects of this preparation phase for reconstructing the full text from PDF and DOCx documents.

NOTE Amazon Textract (https://aws.amazon.com/textract/) is a machine learning service provided by AWS that automatically extracts text, handwriting, and data from scanned documents.

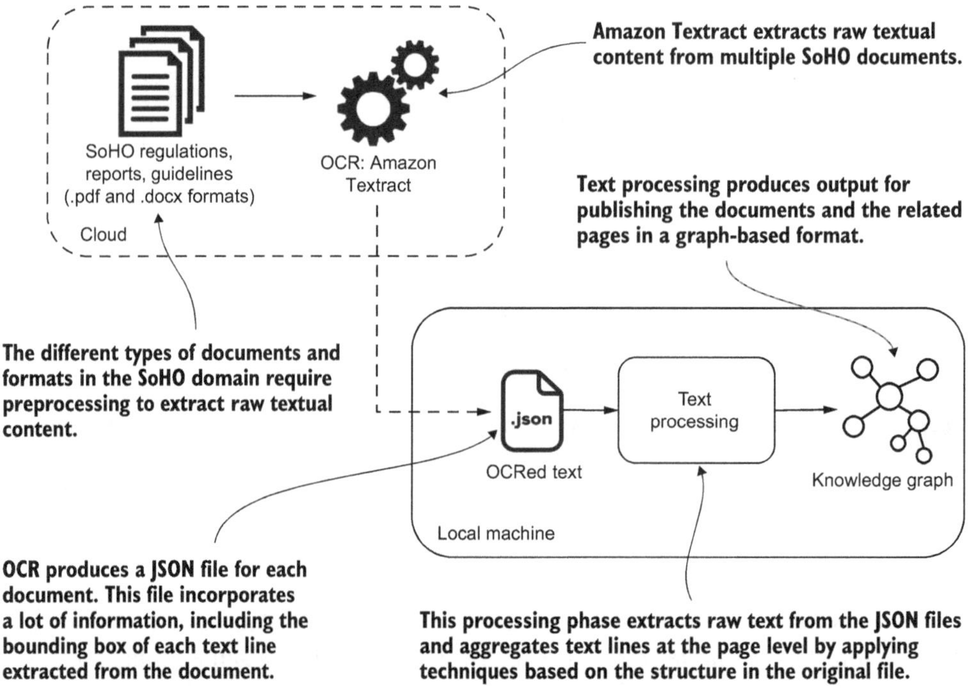

Figure 7.10 We extracted the text from the SoHO documents using Amazon Textract.

You will need to run the text processing script on your local machine to reconstruct the full text of the pages, and then load the results into the KG. The full code implementation is available in the book's code repository. Listing 7.11 shows the Cypher query to ingest raw text or processed documents, and structure this information in a graph-based format.

Listing 7.11 Loading textual content into Neo4j

```
[...]
class DocsImporter:
[...]

  def set_constraints(self):
    queries = ["CREATE FULLTEXT INDEX pageText FOR (n:Page) ON EACH [n.text]"]

    for q in queries:
      self.connection.query(q, db=self.db)

  def load_docs(self):
    with open(self.docs_file) as json_file:
      docs = json.load(json_file)

    query = """
      MERGE (f:File {id: $name})
      SET f.type = $type, f.path = $name
      WITH f

      UNWIND $pages as page
      MERGE (p:Page {id: replace($name, '.pdf', '') + '_' + page.page_idx})
      SET p.page_idx = page.page_idx,
          p.text = page.text

      MERGE (f)-[:CONTAINS_PAGE]->(p)
      """

    for i in tqdm(docs):
      name = i['name']
      type = i['type']
      pages = i['pages']
      self.connection.query(query,
                            parameters={'name': name,
                                        'type': type,
                                        'pages': pages},
                            db=self.db)
```

When we finish this process, files and page texts have been loaded into the KG.

7.6.3 Disambiguating and ingesting medical entities

The next phase extracts and disambiguates medical entities by processing documents directly from the JSON file generated by the OCR, storing the results in a Python dictionary, and then loading the results into Neo4j. A sample of the outcome of this processing is shown next.

Listing 7.12 Python dictionary resulting from document processing

```
{'id': 'sample_dataset-PublicUse/ECDC Documents/west nile virus/EU-summary
➥-report-trends-sources-zoonoses-2013_120',
'ents': [{'sentenceIndex': 0,
   'value': 'zoonoses',
   'lemma': 'zoonosis',
   'label': 'ENTITY',
   'beginCharacter': 60,
   'endCharacter': 68,
   'selected_ned_id': 'C0043528',
   'selected_ned_name': 'Zoonoses',
   'selected_ned_definition': 'Diseases of non-human animals that may be
   ➥transmitted to HUMANS or may be transmitted from humans to non-human
   ➥animals.',
   'selected_ned_aliases': ['Zoonotic Disease',
    'Zoonosis, NOS',
    'Zoonoses',...],
   'selected_ned_types_id': ['T047'],
   'selected_ned_types': ['Disease or Syndrome']...
}
```

These results store details related to the extracted entities, including the sentence index and the position of the mentions in the text, by specifying the start and end characters. In addition to information entities such as types and aliases, these details will be used to perform advanced queries, as discussed in section 7.7. Now we can load the results into Neo4j.

Listing 7.13 Loading NED data

```
[...]
class NLPImporter(BaseImporter):
[...]

  def load_nlp_res(self):
    print("Loading data into Neo4j...")
    with open(self.file,'rb') as file:
    processed_pages = pickle.load(file)

    query = """
            UNWIND $rows as item

            MATCH (page:Page)                              <-- Matches node pages that are not yet processed
            WHERE page.id = item.id AND NOT page:NEDProcessed
            SET page:NEDProcessed
            WITH page, item

            UNWIND item.ents as entity
            MERGE (
              mention:EntityMention {
                name_normalized: toLower(
                  apoc.text.join(
                    apoc.text.split(trim(entity.value), "\\s+"), " "
                  )
```

```
        )
      }                    Creates entity mention nodes
    )                      and connects them to pages
    ON CREATE SET
      mention.name = apoc.text.join(
        apoc.text.split(trim(entity.value), "\\s+"), " "
      )
    MERGE
(page)-[s:MENTIONS_MENTION {from_model: "ned"}]->(mention)

    ON CREATE SET s.start_chars= [entity.beginCharacter],
                s.end_chars= [entity.endCharacter],
                s.sentence_index = [entity.sentenceIndex],
                s.type = toLower(entity.label)
    ON MATCH SET s.start_chars = s.start_chars + entity.beginCharacter,
                s.end_chars = s.end_chars + entity.endCharacter,
                s.sentence_index = s.sentence_index +
                ➥entity.sentenceIndex
    WITH page, mention, entity

    FOREACH(medical in entity |
    MERGE (dis:MedicalEntity {id: medical.selected_ned_id})
    ON CREATE SET dis.name=
    ➥apoc.text.join(apoc.text.split(trim(medical.selected_ned_name),
    ➥"\\s+"), " "),
                dis.type_id = medical.selected_ned_types_id,
                dis.types = medical.selected_ned_types,
                dis.type = medical.selected_ned_types[0],
                dis.original_mention = medical.value,
                dis.definition = medical.selected_ned_definition,
                dis.aliases = medical.selected_ned_aliases,
                dis.start_chars= [entity.beginCharacter],
                dis.end_chars= [entity.endCharacter],
                dis.sentence_index = [entity.sentenceIndex]
    ON MATCH SET dis.start_chars = dis.start_chars +
    ➥entity.beginCharacter,
                dis.end_chars = dis.end_chars + entity.endCharacter

    MERGE (mention)-[r:DISAMBIGUATED_TO]->(dis)
    SET r.confidence = medical.selected_ned.confidence

    MERGE (page)-[t:MENTIONS_ENTITY]->(dis)
    ON CREATE SET t.sentence_index = [medical.sentenceIndex]
    ON MATCH SET t.sentence_index = t.sentence_index +
    ➥medical.sentenceIndex)

    """

  self.load_in_batch(query, processed_pages, len(processed_pages),
  ➥chunk_size=1)
```

Adds properties, including start and end chars, to relationships connecting pages and mentions

Merges medical entity nodes extracted using the scispaCy tool

Adds properties, including aliases and semantic types, to the medical entity nodes

Connects medical entity nodes to entity mentions

Connects medical entity nodes to pages

This query stores the results of scispaCy processing in Neo4j. First it creates the `EntityMention` nodes, which are connected to the `Page` nodes. Then it creates the `MedicalEntity` nodes, enriches them with UMLS data, and connects the medical entities to `EntityMention` and the `Page` nodes. As we mentioned earlier, we kept both the

`EntityMention` and the disambiguated `MedicalEntity` in the graph to improve flexibility in representing data.

7.6.4 Processing, loading, and mapping ontologies

In this phase, we load UMLS, SNOMED, and HPO ontologies into the KG. The UMLS serves as the entry point to access specific information across multiple ontologies. For this reason, we first load the SNOMED and HPO ontologies and then map each entity from them to UMLS.

INGESTING SNOMED

The following listing creates nodes and relationships in Neo4j from sct2_Relationship_Full_US1000124_20220901.txt.

Listing 7.14 Ingesting SNOMED: loading relationships

```
[...]
class SnomedRelationshipsImporter(BaseImporter):
  [...]
  def set_constraints(self):
    queries = [
        (
            "CREATE CONSTRAINT IF NOT EXISTS FOR (n:SnomedEntity) "
            "REQUIRE n.id IS UNIQUE"
        ),
        (
            "CREATE INDEX snomedNodeName IF NOT EXISTS "
            "FOR (n:SnomedEntity) ON (n.name)"
        ),
        (
            "CREATE INDEX snomedRelationId IF NOT EXISTS "
            "FOR ()-[r:SNOMED_RELATION]-() ON (r.id)"
        ),
        (
            "CREATE INDEX snomedRelationType IF NOT EXISTS "
            "FOR ()-[r:SNOMED_RELATION]-() ON (r.type)"
        ),
        (
            "CREATE INDEX snomedRelationUmls IF NOT EXISTS "
            "FOR ()-[r:SNOMED_RELATION]-() ON (r.umls)"
        ),
    ]


    for q in queries:
      self.connection.query(q, db=self.db)

  def import_snomed_rels(self):
    query = """
       UNWIND $batch as item
       MERGE (e1:SnomedEntity {id: item.sourceId})
       MERGE (e2:SnomedEntity {id: item.destinationId})
       MERGE (e1)-[:SNOMED_RELATION {id: item.typeId}]->(e2)
       FOREACH(ignoreMe IN CASE WHEN item.typeId = '116680003'
```

Annotations:
- Extends the BaseImporter class, which contains the base importing functionalities
- Defines constraints and indexes on SNOMED entities and properties
- Imports SNOMED relationships using a parametric query

```
➥THEN [true] ELSE [] END|
      MERGE (e1)-[:SNOMED_IS_A]->(e2)
    )
    """
```

Creates the SNOMED_IS_A relationship type to track hierarchical connections between entities

```
size = self.get_csv_size(snomedRels_file)
self.batch_store(snomed_rels_query, self.get_rows(snomedRels_file),
➥size=size)
```

Gets the size of the file (default implementation in the BaseImporter class)

Loads the SNOMED data in batches (implementation in the BaseImporter class)

SNOMED includes hundreds of relationships. To keep the graph schema as simple as possible, we decided to create a unique `SNOMED_RELATION`, and we store the relationship name as a `type` property. In listing 7.14 we create a `SNOMED_IS_A` relationship to define the hierarchical connections; we will see shortly why this choice is handy to propagate information from the root to the leaf nodes.

Now that we have ingested the nodes and relationships to shape the graph, we need to enrich this structure by adding names and aliases. The following class extracts information from sct2_Description_Full-en_US1000124_20220901.txt.

Listing 7.15 Ingesting SNOMED: loading names and aliases

```
[...]
class SnomedNamesImporter(BaseImporter):
  [...]

  def import_snomed_names(self, snomedNames_file):
        snomed_names_concepts_query = """
        UNWIND $batch as item
        MATCH (e1:SnomedEntity)
        -[r:SNOMED_RELATION {id: item.conceptId}]->
        (e2:SnomedEntity)
        WHERE item.conceptId <> '116680003' AND r.id = item.conceptId
        SET r.type = CASE
                WHEN r.type IS NULL THEN item.termAsType
                ELSE r.type END,
            r.aliases = CASE
                WHEN item.termAsType IN r.aliases THEN r.aliases
                ELSE coalesce(r.aliases,[]) + item.termAsType END
        """

        snomed_names_entities_query = """
        UNWIND $batch as item
        MATCH (e:SnomedEntity {id: item.conceptId})
        SET e.name = CASE
                WHEN e.name IS NULL THEN item.term
                ELSE e.name END,
            e.aliases = CASE
                WHEN item.term in e.aliases THEN  e.aliases
                ELSE coalesce(e.aliases, []) + item.term END
        """
        size = self.get_csv_size(snomedNames_file)
```

Adds the relationship name in the type property

Adds relationship aliases

Adds the node name

Adds node aliases

```
        self.batch_store(
          snomed_names_concepts_query,
          self.get_rows(snomedNames_file),
         size=size)
        self.batch_store(
          snomed_names_entities_query,
          self.get_rows(snomedNames_file),
          size=size)

[...]
```

This class adds names and aliases to the nodes and relationships loaded into the graph. The next step involves propagating information from the root nodes to all subnodes, down to the leaf nodes. The first-level nodes represent the archetypal entities of SNOMED in the medical domain, such as diseases, body structures, substances, and events. These root nodes define the semantic types of the entities available in SNOMED. However, this information is implicit in the data we ingested because for each other entity, there are only names and aliases in the original data. Therefore, we need a mechanism to transfer this information through the ontology's tree structure; this way, we can easily detect that a deep entity is a disease or a product. Figure 7.11 clarifies this propagation mechanism.

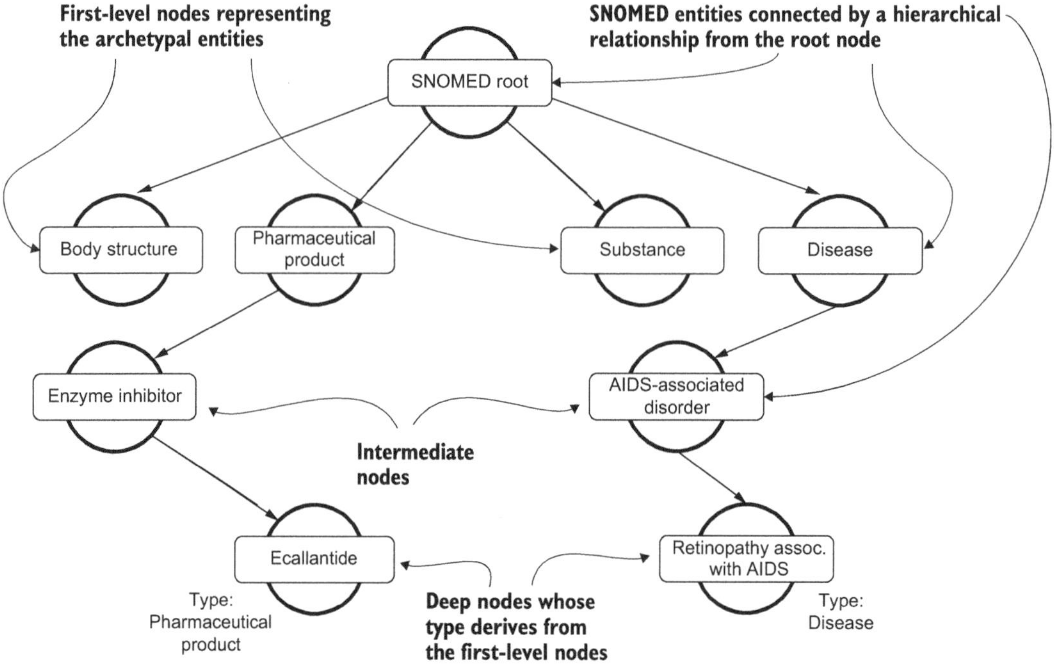

Figure 7.11 A sample of the hierarchical structure of the SNOMED ontology. Using this hierarchical structure, nodes located on a deeper level, such as *Ecallantide* and *Retinopathy associated with AIDS*, can be categorized using the information from the first-level nodes, such as *Pharmaceutical product* and *Disease*, which represent the archetypal entities of the ontology.

The next listing retrieves all nodes, following the hierarchical structure to propagate information from first-level nodes to deeper nodes.

Listing 7.16 Ingesting SNOMED: propagating labels from first-level nodes

```
[...]
class SnomedLabelPropagator():
[...]

  def get_rows(self):
    propagation_query = """
      MATCH p=(n:SnomedEntity)<-[:SNOMED_IS_A]-(m:SnomedEntity)
      WHERE n.id= "138875005" // Root node
      WITH distinct m as first_node

      CALL apoc.path.expandConfig(first_node, {        <-- Uses expandConfig to set the
              relationshipFilter: '<SNOMED_IS_A',          rules for traversing the hierarchy
                minLevel: 1,
                maxLevel: -1,
                uniqueness: 'RELATIONSHIP_GLOBAL'
            }) yield path

     UNWIND nodes(path) as other_level              <-- Gets the nodes resulting
     WITH first_node, collect(DISTINCT other_level) as uniques    from this traversal process
             UNWIND uniques as unique_other_level
             WITH first_node,unique_other_level
             WHERE not first_node.name in
     coalesce(unique_other_level.type,[])

             RETURN unique_other_level.id as id, first_node.name as label   <-- Returns all the
            """                                       nodes characterized by a specific type

    with self._driver.session(database=self._database) as session:
      result = session.run(query=propagation_query)
      for record in iter(result):
         yield dict(record)
[...]
```

The SNOMED_IS_A relationship propagates the semantic types through the tree structure by using the hierarchical connections between entities.

INGESTING HPO

The following listings outline the primary steps for ingesting the HPO ontology. More details, including the creation of the proper indices, are discussed in chapter 3 and included in the Cypher code in the book's repository. First we import the HPO ontology using the Neosemantics plugin.

Listing 7.17 Ingesting HPO: loading the ontology

```
CALL n10s.rdf.import.fetch("http://purl.obolibrary.org/obo/hp.owl","RDF/XML");
```

The HPO ontology is available in the RDF/XML format, and it is converted into a Neo4j graph structure to be processed using Cypher.

Next, we add the HPO label to nodes representing phenotypic feature entities.

Listing 7.18 Ingesting HPO: adding the `HpoEntity` label to phenotypic features

```
MATCH (n:Resource)
WHERE n.uri STARTS WITH "http://purl.obolibrary.org/obo/HP"
SET n:HpoEntity,
 n.id = coalesce(n.id, replace(apoc.text.replace(n.uri,'(.*)obo/',''),'_', ':'));
```

Now we need to process the annotation file that describes the connections between the phenotypic features and diseases. To make this step more efficient, we use the following query to load the disease entities as graph nodes.

Listing 7.19 Ingesting HPO: creating `HpoDiseaseEntity` nodes

```
LOAD CSV FROM 'https://github.com/obophenotype/human-phenotype-
➥ontology/releases/latest/download/phenotype.hpoa' AS row
FIELDTERMINATOR '\t'
WITH row
SKIP 5
MERGE (dis:Resource:HpoDiseaseEntity {id: row[0]})
ON CREATE SET dis.label = row[1];
```

The next step is to create the relations between the available phenotypic features and disease nodes.

Listing 7.20 Ingesting HPO: relations between `HpoEntity` and `HpoDiseaseEntity`

```
LOAD CSV FROM 'https://github.com/obophenotype/human-phenotype-ontology/
➥releases/latest/download/phenotype.hpoa' AS row
FIELDTERMINATOR '\t'
WITH row
SKIP 5
MATCH (dis:HpoDiseaseEntity)
WHERE dis.id = row[0]
MATCH (phe:HpoEntity)
WHERE phe.id = row[3]
MERGE (dis)-[:HAS_PHENOTYPIC_FEATURE]->(phe)
```

The following query establishes the connection between the disambiguated entities extracted from the text and the ontology nodes.

Listing 7.21 Integrating SNOMED through the UMLS

```
MATCH (m:MedicalEntity)
WITH m
MATCH (d:SnomedEntity)
WHERE m.id in d.umls_ids
WITH m, d
MERGE (m)-[:IS_SNOMED_ENTITY]->(d)
```

We perform an analogous process for the HPO ontology (see the full code for more details). The next query connects `MedicalEntity` nodes and the `HpoDiseaseEntity` nodes from the HPO annotation file.

Listing 7.22 Connecting `MedicalEntity` and `HpoDiseaseEntity` nodes

```
MATCH (m:MedicalEntity)
WITH m
MATCH (d:HpoDiseaseEntity)
WHERE m.id in d.umls_ids
WITH m, d
MERGE (m)-[:IS_DISEASE_ENTITY]->(d)
```

In the next section, we generate the co-occurrence relationship between entities located in the same sentence.

7.6.5 Generating entity co-occurrences

Identifying co-occurrences of medical entities in the text is a fundamental step in enabling advanced use cases that combine unstructured knowledge from textual content with structured knowledge in domain ontologies. The query in listing 7.23 creates a new relationship called `COOCCURR` between medical entities identified in the same sentence.

DEFINITION *Co-occurrence* refers to the projection of `Page` nodes onto `Entity` nodes.

Listing 7.23 Creating co-occurrence relationships at the sentence level

```
CALL apoc.periodic.iterate(
  "MATCH (n:Page) WHERE exists( (n)-[:MENTIONS_ENTITY]->(:MedicalEntity) )
  RETURN n",
  "MATCH (n)-[r:MENTIONS_ENTITY]->(m:MedicalEntity)
  WITH n, r.sentence_index as sentences, m
  UNWIND sentences as sentence
  WITH n, sentence, collect(distinct m) as entities

  UNWIND range(0, size(entities)-2) as i
  UNWIND range(i+1, size(entities)-1) as j

  WITH n, sentence, entities, i, j
  MATCH (m1) WHERE id(m1) = id(entities[i])
  MATCH (m2) WHERE id(m2) = id(entities[j])

  WITH n, sentence, entities, i, j, m1, m2
  MERGE (m1)-[s:COOCCURR]-(m2)
  ON CREATE SET s.count = 1,
       s.sentences = [sentence]
  ON MATCH SET s.count = s.count + 1,
   s.sentences = s.sentences + sentence",
{batchSize: 50})
```

This query produces more than 25,000 relationships in the KG, making explicit the connections between medical entities located in the same sentence. As we will discuss next, analyzing the ontology connections between co-occurring entities lets us discover the established knowledge related to these entities and uncover new information that is not yet established in biomedical ontologies.

7.7 KG-based use cases

In this section, code examples will show how we handle the following use cases using KGs in combination with NED:

- Conceptual search
- Structured knowledge-based search
- KG-based interpretability and discovery
- Uncovering new knowledge

Figure 7.12 includes the analysis step related to the use cases defined in this application domain.

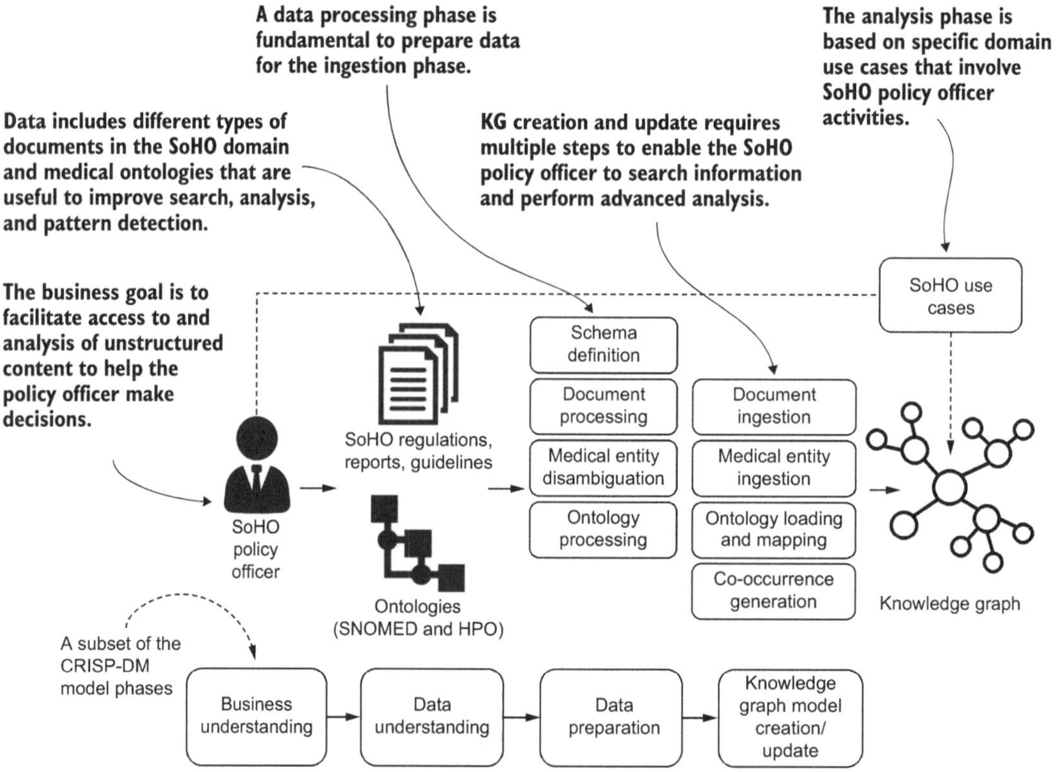

Figure 7.12 After generating the KG, we can perform analyses by applying defined use cases to address business problems and provide solutions based on the KG.

NOTE Your query results may vary slightly from those shown in the chapter due to differences in environments, Neo4j indexing behavior, data pipeline ingestion order, and the nondeterministic aspects of entity extraction performed by scispaCy.

7.7.1 Conceptual search

Conceptual search is related to the capacity to reconcile—and return to the user—different expressions with the same meaning or distinguish similar terms that refer to distinct entities. Performing a conceptual search can help us expand or focus the search for specific documents and the related portions of text that mention the entity. Figure 7.13 provides a high-level comparison of conceptual search and traditional full-text search.

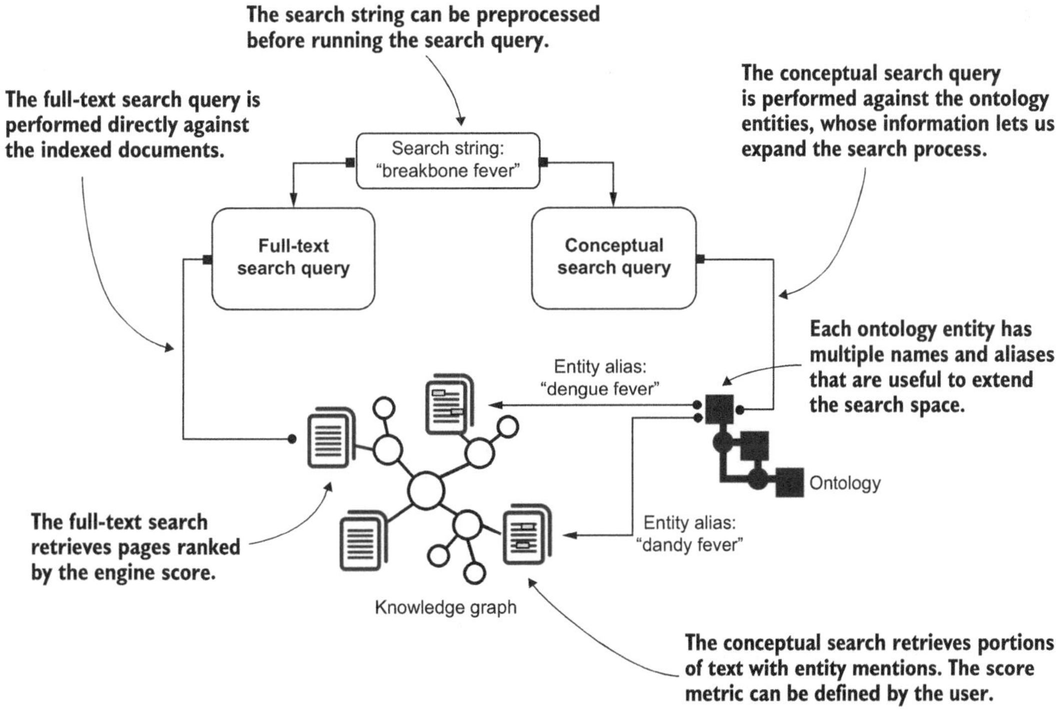

Figure 7.13 Differences between traditional full-text search and conceptual search. The full-text search query is performed directly on the set of documents, whereas the conceptual search query uses information from ontologies to expand the search space before searching the documents.

Let's examine the effect of conceptual search starting from a traditional full-text search. The following search query tries to retrieve all documents mentioning "breakbone fever."

Listing 7.24 Full-text search query with "breakbone fever" as the input string

```
CALL db.index.fulltext.queryNodes("PageText", "breakbone fever")
YIELD node, score
WITH node as p, score as score
MATCH (f:File)-[:CONTAINS_PAGE]->(p)
RETURN f.id as `File ID`, p.page_idx as `Page index`, score as Score
LIMIT 5
```

Table 7.1 shows the results of the full-text search ordered by score value. The first column lists the document path, the second column shows the page index in the document, and the third column reports the score computed by the full-text search algorithm.

Table 7.1 The top five pages retrieved by a full-text search for "breakbone fever"

File ID	Page index	Score
sample_dataset-PublicUse/ECDC Documents/west nile virus/emerging-vector-borne-diseases_annual-epidemiological-report-2014.pdf	5	2.12
sample_dataset-PublicUse/ECDC Documents/west nile virus/emerging-vector-borne-diseases_annual-epidemiological-report-2014.pdf	4	2.09
sample_dataset-PublicUse/ECDC Documents/zika virus/Communicable-disease-threats-report-26-mar-2016.pdf	10	2.08
sample_dataset-PublicUse/ECDC Documents/ebola/communicable-disease-threats-report-13-19-mar-2016.pdf	9	2.08
sample_dataset-PublicUse/ECDC Documents/zika virus/Communicable-disease-threats-report-26-mar-2016.pdf	10	2.08

This type of search identifies keywords in a set of documents by using fuzzy logic. In this case, "breakbone" is never mentioned in the text, but the term "fever" appears multiple times in the high-scored documents. Nevertheless, we are interested in identifying documents that mention this specific disease or, eventually, the causative agent of this disease.

In the UMLS knowledge base, the code C0011311 identifies this entity, which can appear in various forms, including "dengue fever," "dungero," and "dandy fever." So, we next run the following query to retrieve all medical entities identified by the scispaCy model whose alias is "breakbone fever."

Listing 7.25 Finding mentions of the entity whose alias is "breakbone fever"

```
MATCH (f:File)-[:CONTAINS_PAGE]->(p)
      -[r:MENTIONS_MENTION]->(m)-[:DISAMBIGUATED_TO]->(e)
WHERE "breakbone fever" IN [x IN e.aliases | toLower(x)]
```

Filters nodes by checking if the alias "breakbone fever" (in lowercase) exists among aliases of the entity

```
UNWIND range(0, size(r.start_chars) - 1) AS mention
WITH f, p, e, m, r, mention
RETURN DISTINCT
  f.id AS `File ID`,
  p.page_idx AS `Page index`,
  apoc.text.join(
    collect(
      substring(
        p.text,
        apoc.coll.max([r.start_chars[mention] - 100, 0]),
        r.end_chars[mention] - r.start_chars[mention] + 200
      )
    )[0..3],
    '\n\n'
  ) AS `Mention contexts`,
  size(collect(m.name)) AS `Number of mentions`
ORDER BY `Number of mentions` DESC
LIMIT 5
```

Iterates over each mention index in the list of start characters to handle multiple mentions per page

Calculates a starting index for the substring, ensuring that it doesn't go below zero by subtracting 100 from the start position

Determines the length of the text snippet by computing the difference between the end and start of the mention and adding 200 for extra context

Limits the collected context snippets to the first three for each file–page combination to keep the output concise

Table 7.2 shows the top-scored pages from our conceptual search and an example of a paragraph that mentions the UMLS entity representing breakbone fever, listed by the number of mentions.

Table 7.2 Top-scored pages retrieved using "breakbone fever" as an entity alias

File ID	Page index	Mention context	Number of mentions
sample_dataset-PublicUse/ECDC Documents/hepatitis-a/communicable-disease-threats-report-feb-24-2018.pdf	11	"[...] In 2017, Cambodia reported over 3,200 suspected **dengue** cases."	22
sample_dataset-PublicUse/ECDC Documents/ebola/communicable-disease-threats-report-17%20may-2014.pdf	11	"[...] Singapore has reported more than 1000 **dengue** cases nationally from January to April this year, which is 15 per cent fewer cases compared with [...]"	20
sample_dataset-PublicUse/ECDC Documents/ebola/Communicable-disease-threats-report-19-jul-2014.pdf	12	"[...] An epidemic of **dengue fever** in Malaysia has now infected nearly 47,000 people, which is more than double the number of cases [...]"	20
sample_dataset-PublicUse/ECDC Documents/ebola/communicable-disease-threats-report-21-jun-2014.pdf	13	"[...] Cuba has recorded 67 imported cases of **dengue fever** up to 8 June, according to media quoting the Cuban government."	20
sample_dataset-PublicUse/ECDC Documents/west nile virus/communicable-disease-threats-report-21-jun-2014.pdf	12	"[...] Oceania: As of 13 June 2014, 1 762 suspected **dengue cases** have been reported in Solomon Islands since January 2014."	19

Comparing the results with those from the full-text search, we see that the most relevant pages are completely different. Let's try to update the conceptual search query to show and explore the full result set (remove the `LIMIT` clause). The first result from the full-text query is located at the 19th position in the conceptual search query. This specific document has 17 mentions of the UMLS entity, whereas the top-scored result of the conceptual search query includes 22 mentions of the C0011311 UMLS entity.

Adopting conceptual search has a huge effect on our application domain. We can retrieve more precise and detailed information compared to the full-text search: in addition to the document path and the page index, we can identify the portion of text that mentions the entity and the number of occurrences of this entity on the page. Thus, conceptual search enables other features that improve the explainability of the retrieved document. Because the NED model lets us identify the position of the detected entity in the text, we can eventually perform precise debugging tests to identify the cases in which the model did not perform as expected.

Conceptual search also enhances the search process in scenarios where a word or expression has different meanings based on context. For example, the word "islands" has a traditional meaning, but it takes on a completely different semantic context when used in the expression "islands of Langerhans." A traditional full-text search might lead to irrelevant results referring to land masses surrounded by water. By using the conceptual search mechanism, we can filter out these results and broaden the search scope to include other expressions, such as "pancreatic islets," to capture more relevant content. As we discuss next, the core concept of conceptual search can be expanded by linking pages that include medical entities connected through ontology relationships.

7.7.2 Structured knowledge-based search

Using structured knowledge-based search, we can retrieve information from text by using formalized knowledge organized in domain ontologies and create nontrivial relationships between different pieces of text across multiple documents. We've already seen how we can aggregate information referring to the same concept, such as dengue fever or pancreatic islets, regardless of ambiguous or multiple names. However, by using the knowledge embedded in ontologies like SNOMED, we can aggregate and connect unstructured content driven by ontology relationships. For instance, given the importance of donations of cells like the islets of Langerhans, it would be beneficial to aggregate all text that mentions diseases that can affect these cells and thus compromise the donation process. Figure 7.14 shows a mental model of the difference between a conceptual search query and a structured knowledge-based query.

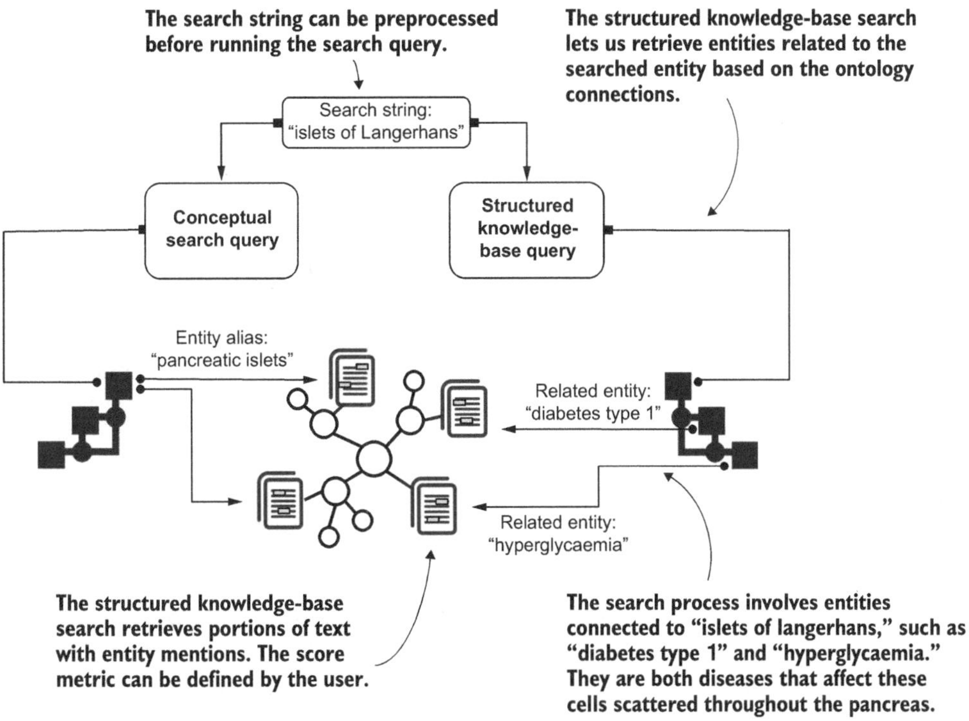

Figure 7.14 Differences between conceptual search and structured knowledge-based search. In this case, the search process involves medical entities connected by ontology relationships to the entity detected in the search query. Starting from the "islets of Langerhans" search, the system searches for "diabetes type 1" and "hyperglycaemia," which are two diseases that can affect the islets of Langerhans.

The following query retrieves portions of text that mention diseases that can affect the islets of Langerhans.

Listing 7.26 Getting text about diseases that can affect the islets of Langerhans

```
MATCH (m1:MedicalEntity)-[:IS_SNOMED_ENTITY]->(s1:SnomedEntity)
<-[r1:SNOMED_RELATION]-(s2:SnomedEntity)
<-[:IS_SNOMED_ENTITY]-(e:MedicalEntity)
WHERE m1.name = "Islets of Langerhans" AND r1.type = "FINDING_SITE"
WITH e
MATCH path = (f:File)-[:CONTAINS_PAGE]->(p)
-[r:MENTIONS_MENTION]->(m)-[:DISAMBIGUATED_TO]->(e)
UNWIND range(0, size(r.start_chars) - 1) AS mention
```

Filters for SNOMED entities related to "Islets of Langerhans" by the FINDING_SITE relationship type

Iterates over each mention instance using indices from start_chars, allowing multiple mentions per relation

Computes a start index for context extraction, backing up 100 characters without going below 0

Calculates an end index up to 100 characters beyond the mention without exceeding the page text length

```
WITH f, p, r, e, mention,
     apoc.coll.max([r.start_chars[mention] - 100, 0]) AS start,
     apoc.coll.min([r.end_chars[mention] + 100, size(p.text)]) AS end
WITH f, p, r, e, mention, substring(p.text, start, end - start) AS context
WITH f, p,
     collect(DISTINCT e.name) AS `Mentioned entities`,
     collect(context)[0..3] AS contexts
RETURN DISTINCT
  f.id AS `File ID`,
  p.page_idx AS `Page index`,
  `Mentioned entities`,
  apoc.text.join(contexts, '\n\n') AS `Mention contexts`
ORDER BY size(`Mentioned entities`) DESC
LIMIT 5
```

Extracts a substring of the page text from the calculated start to end position as the context window

Limits the collected context windows to the first three mentions

Gathers a deduplicated list of medical entity names mentioned on the page

A subset of the results of this query are shown in table 7.3.

Table 7.3 Textual content about diseases that can affect the islets of Langerhans

File ID	Page index	Mentioned entities	Mention contexts
sample_dataset-PublicUse/ EDQM Documents/BTC/ guide-to-the-quality-and-safety-of-organs-for-transplantation-7th-edition.PDF	137	`Diabetes Mellitus, Metabolic Syndrome X`	"Metabolic syndrome, arterial hypertension, diabetes mellitus, albuminuria (see below) and other chronic kidney diseases or systemic disease [...]"
sample_dataset-PublicUse/ EDQM Documents/BTC/ guide-to-the-quality-and-safety-of-organs-for-transplantation-7th-edition.PDF	144	`Hyperglycemia, Diabetes Mellitus, Non-Insulin-Dependent`	" [...] Many patients with severe head trauma become hyperglycaemic and require insulin therapy, despite normal pancreatic function and no history of diabetes. [...] On the other hand, manifestation of diabetes mellitus type II is possible at an age of over 50-65 years."

In listing 7.26, we extend the logic of the conceptual search query, taking a collection of entities from the ontology as input and retrieving the related details in the documents. One of the most interesting results is from page 144 of *Guide to the Quality and Safety of Organs for Transplantation,* 7th ed., reported in column 4 of table 7.3. This page mentions *Hyperglycemia,* which is explicitly connected to the *Islets of Langerhans* entity through the `FINDING_SITE` relationship, in the context of managing a potential donor who has suffered head trauma. This sentence is located in a section dedicated to pancreas donation focused on donor-maintenance protocols. This critical information would not have been retrieved through the conceptual search mechanism. However, we used the connection of the *Hyperglycemia* medical entity to the starting point of our search (*Islets of Langerhans*) to reach this information. The other results mention different forms of diabetes mellitus, which is particularly relevant in the donation of pancreatic islets.

A structured knowledge-based search can also be performed by using the longest paths in an ontology. Let's consider the Zika virus example. This virus can be categorized as a Togavirus, and it is transmitted to humans via species of arthropods that feed on blood, especially insects and arachnids. Suppose we are interested in all diseases mentioned in the document that are caused by a Togavirus. We can explore a path that concatenates multiple `CAUSATIVE_AGENT` relationships in the SNOMED ontology, using the results to acquire the desired documents; figure 7.15 shows an example.

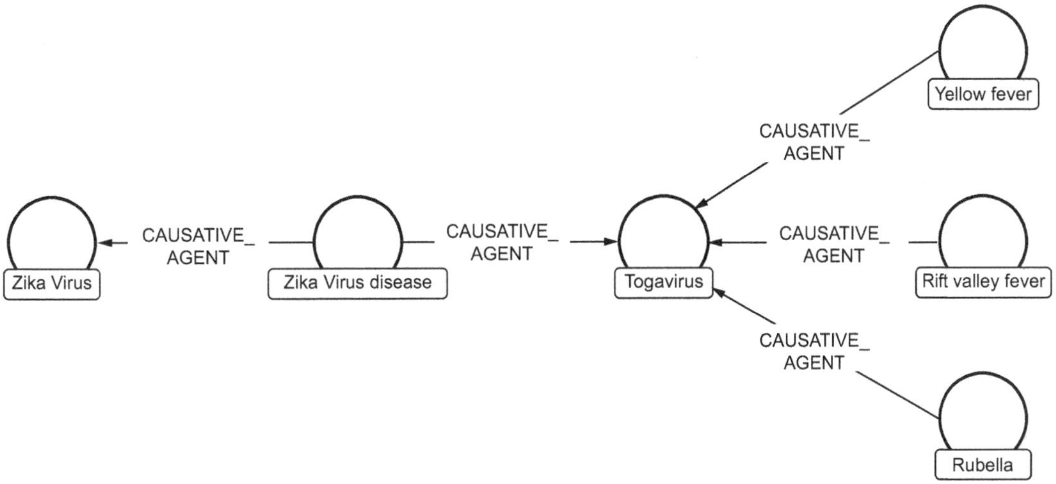

Figure 7.15 SNOMED ontology paths including only the `CAUSATIVE_AGENT` relationship. Navigating this subset of relationships is particularly useful for identifying diseases carried by the same virus types.

We can expand the search to involve entities such as *Yellow fever*, *Rift valley fever*, and *Rubella* that do not have a direct connection with the entity specified in the search query (*Zika virus*). Listing 7.27 shows the query to use these complex paths for retrieving relevant documents. This example is particularly exciting for our application domain because we can retrieve documents mentioning similar diseases based on the type of virus they have in common.

Listing 7.27 Getting documents mentioning diseases caused by Togaviruses

```
MATCH (m1:MedicalEntity)-[:IS_SNOMED_ENTITY]->(s1:SnomedEntity)
-[r1:SNOMED_RELATION*3..3]-(s2:SnomedEntity)
      <-[:IS_SNOMED_ENTITY]-(e:MedicalEntity)
WHERE m1.name = "Zika Virus"
```

Traverses three SNOMED_RELATION hops to discover indirectly related medical entities

```
AND all(x IN r1 WHERE x.type = "CAUSATIVE_AGENT")
WITH DISTINCT e

MATCH path = (f:File)-[:CONTAINS_PAGE]->(p)
-[r:MENTIONS_MENTION]->(m)-[:DISAMBIGUATED_TO]->(e)
WITH f, e, collect(p.page_idx) AS pages_list
RETURN DISTINCT
  f.id AS `File ID`,
  pages_list,
  collect(DISTINCT e.name) AS `Mentioned entity`
ORDER BY size(`Mentioned entity`) DESC
LIMIT 5
```

Filters paths where all three relationships are CAUSATIVE_AGENT, to ensure semantic consistency

Collects indices from all pages in which the entity is mentioned

The results of this query are listed in table 7.4.

Table 7.4 Documents and pages mentioning diseases caused by Togaviruses

File ID	Pages	Mentioned entities
sample_dataset-PublicUse/ECDC Documents/west nile virus/TER-Mosquito-surveillance-guidelines.pdf	10	*Murray valley encephalitis, Japanese Encephalitis, Venezuelan equine encephalomyelitis, Encephalomyelitis, Eastern Equine, Ross river virus infection*
sample_dataset-PublicUse/ECDC Documents/ebola/ebola-preparedness-belgium.pdf	38	*Yellow Fever, Rift Valley Fever, West Nile Fever, Dengue Fever, Chikungunya Fever*
sample_dataset-PublicUse/ECDC Documents/west nile virus/communicable-disease-threats-report-18-august-2019-updated-26-august-2019.pdf	1	*Rubella, Yellow Fever, Japanese Encephalitis, Dengue Fever, Chikungunya Fever*
sample_dataset-PublicUse/ECDC Documents/ebola/communicable-disease-threats-report-18-august-2019-updated-26-august-2019.pdf	1	*Rubella, Yellow Fever, Japanese Encephalitis, Dengue Fever, Chikungunya Fever*
sample_dataset-PublicUse/ECDC Documents/west nile virus/communicable-disease-threats-report-15-december-2018.pdf	1	*Yellow Fever, Dengue Fever, Mosquito-Borne Diseases, Chikungunya Fever*

This use case is particularly useful for automatically retrieving relevant information using ontology connections. Starting from the entity mentioned in the search string, we can navigate between multiple pieces of text that mention entities related to this search entity, opening new possibilities to enrich the user experience in an IAS system.

7.7.3 KG-based interpretability and discovery

Starting from the co-occurrence of entities in the same sentence, KG-based interpretability and discovery lets us analyze how these entities are connected in the ontologies and what the nature of this connection is. In some cases, the ontology connections reflect the reason for the co-occurring entities in a specific sentence (interpretability). This analysis can also validate co-occurring entities against an ontology. And other cases, ontology connections add knowledge that expands the information provided by the sentence (discovery).

To better understand the value of this use case, consider listing 7.28, which includes sentences from the document entitled "Proposal for a Directive of the European Parliament and of the Council Setting Standards of Quality and Safety for the Collection, Testing, Processing, Storage, and Distribution of Human Blood and Blood Components and Amending Council Directive 89/381/EEC." In this document, "AIDS" and "Hepatitis" co-occur two times.

Listing 7.28 Sentences where *AIDS* and *Hepatitis* co-occur

```
SENTENCE 1: The reasons why they should not donate which put recipients at
risk, such as unsafe sexual behaviour, HIV/ AIDS, hepatitis, drug
addiction and the use and abuse of drugs;

[...]

SENTENCE 2: Infectious diseases persons suffering or having suffered from
- Babesiosis
- Hepatitis B (HBsAg confirmed positive)
- Hepatitis C
- Hepatitis, infectious (of unexplained aetiology)
- HIV/AIDS
```

"AIDS" and "Hepatitis" appear close to each other in these sentences because they both represent a risk factor in the donation process: they are infectious diseases. This information is directly encoded in SNOMED, and expressed by different ontology paths. The following listing shows a subset.

Listing 7.29 Paths connecting entities, interpretability perspective

```
(AIDS)-[:PATHOLOGICAL_PROCESS]->(Infectious disease)
<-[:DUE_TO]-(Hepatitis due to infection)
-[:IS_A]->(Inflammatory disorder of liver)

(AIDS)-[:PATHOLOGICAL_PROCESS]->(Infectious disease)
<-[:DUE_TO]-(Viral hepatitis)
-[:IS_A]->(Inflammatory disorder of liver)
```

These ontology paths define connections between these two entities and encode the meaning of the co-occurrence of "AIDS" and "Hepatitis" (which is labeled "Inflammatory disorder of liver" in the SNOMED ontology). We also validate the extracted entities against the ontology, which enables us to understand why these entities were extracted in the same sentence.

Other types of SNOMED paths reveal interesting connections between AIDS and hepatitis. For example, the first SNOMED path in the next listing shows that AIDS is related to a disorder defined as "Hepatomegaly associated with AIDS" that affects the liver. The second entry reports that a specific form of hepatitis called "Lupus hepatitis" involves the immune system as "AIDS."

Listing 7.30 Paths connecting entities, discovery perspective

```
(AIDS)<-[:ASSOCIATED_WITH]-(Hepatomegaly associated with AIDS (disorder))
-[:FINDING_SITE]->(Liver)
<-[:FINDING_SITE]-(Inflammatory disorder of liver)

(AIDS)-[:HAS_DEFINITIONAL_MANIFESTATION]->(Immune system finding)
<-[:HAS_DEFINITIONAL_MANIFESTATION]-(Lupus hepatitis)
-[:IS_A]->(Inflammatory disorder of liver)
```

The ontology supports us in understanding why a pair of medical entities appear in the sentence and lets us discover new details related to this pair. Figure 7.16 illustrates integrating domain ontologies into a KG built from natural language content; it shows "Dengue" and "Zika virus" as examples of co-occurrence.

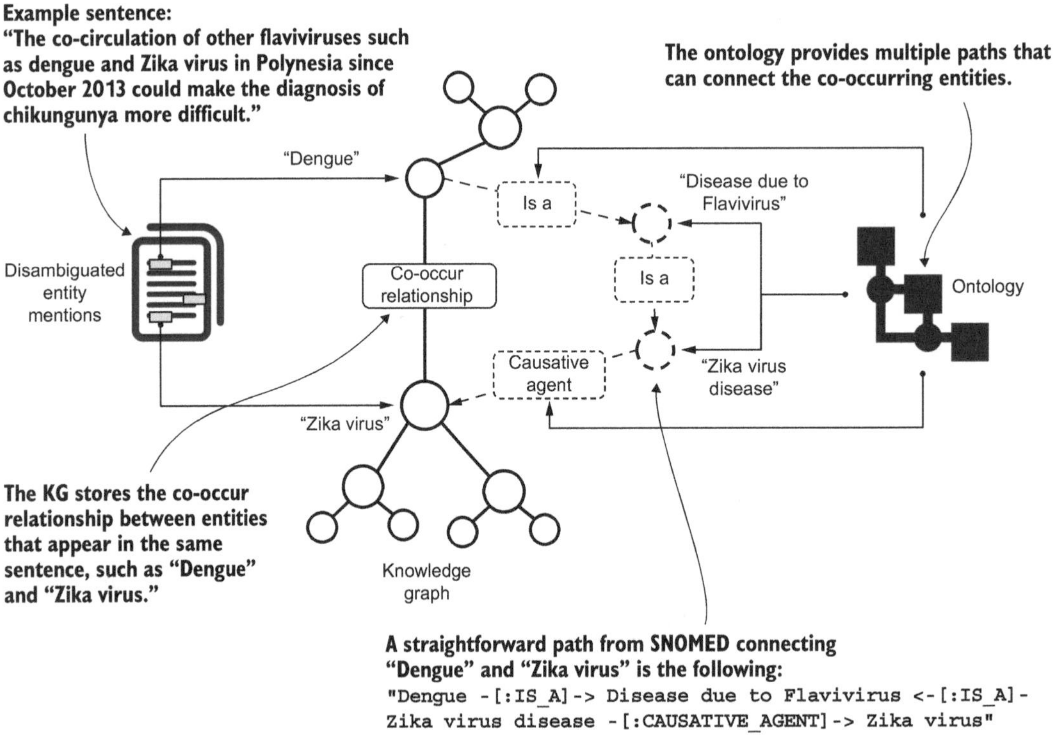

Figure 7.16 Mental model describing the KG-based interpretability and discovery process. Co-occurring entities in the text can be connected by multiple paths in the SNOMED ontology.

Let's dive into the details and see how to apply practical solutions in the SoHO domain to enable interpretability and discovery with a real KG. The following listing retrieves the top five entity types that co-occur with "Zika virus."

Listing 7.31 Retrieving the top entity types co-occurring with "Zika virus"

```
MATCH (m1:MedicalEntity)-[r:COOCCURR]-(m2:MedicalEntity)
WHERE m1.id= "C0318793"
RETURN m2.type as `Entity Type`, count(m2.type) as `Number of co-occurrences`
ORDER BY count(m2.type) DESC
LIMIT 5
```

This query computes the number of co-occurring entity types to identify the most relevant ones. The results are shown in table 7.5.

Table 7.5 Top entity types co-occurring with "Zika virus"

Entity	Number of co-occurrences
Geographic Area	255
Qualitative Concept	132
Disease or Syndrome	125
Functional Concept	106
Finding	98

Most of the results include `Geographic Area`. This is related to the fact that "Zika virus" is often mentioned in bulletins that report the spread of communicable diseases. Other categories, such as `Qualitative Concept` and `Functional Concept`, include broader concepts that in most cases are not relevant for our example. For this reason, we will focus on the co-occurring `Disease or Syndrome` entities. The next query finds co-occurring entities and the portion of text from which this co-occurrence was extracted.

Listing 7.32 Getting co-occurring disease entities with context

```
MATCH (n1:MedicalEntity)-[r:COOCCURR]-(n2:MedicalEntity)
WHERE n1.id = "C0318793" AND n2.type = "Disease or Syndrome"    <-- Filters for entities co-occurring with "C0318793" (Zika virus) and restricts to those of type "Disease or Syndrome"
WITH n1, r, n2
ORDER BY r.count DESC
MATCH (f:File)-[:CONTAINS_PAGE]->(p:Page)
      -[r1:MENTIONS_MENTION]->(m1)-[:DISAMBIGUATED_TO]->(n1),
      (p)-[r2:MENTIONS_MENTION]->(m2)-[:DISAMBIGUATED_TO]->(n2)
WHERE r1.sentence_index = r2.sentence_index    <-- Ensures that both entities were mentioned in the same sentence on the page
WITH f, p, r1, r2, n2
RETURN DISTINCT
  f.id AS `File ID`,
  p.page_idx AS `Page index`,
```

```
n2.id AS `Co-occurring entity id`,
n2.name AS `Co-occurring entity name`,
CASE
  WHEN r1.end_chars[0] > r2.start_chars[0]
  THEN substring(p.text, r2.start_chars[0],
  ➥r1.end_chars[0] - r2.start_chars[0])
  ELSE substring(p.text, r1.start_chars[0],
  ➥r2.end_chars[0] - r1.start_chars[0])
END AS `Mentions context`
```

Captures the co-occurrence span

Ensures that the context window always runs from the earlier to the later character position

Table 7.6 reports a subset of the results; you can analyze the full result set by running the query in listing 7.32.

Table 7.6 Disease entities that co-occur with "Zika virus" and context

File ID	Page index	Co-occurring entity ID	Co-occurring entity name	Mentions context
sample_dataset-PublicUse/ ECDC Documents/zika virus/ Communicable-disease-threats-report-23-apr-2016.pdf	8	C0009450	Communicable Diseases	"COMMUNICABLE DIS-EASE THREATS REPORT Countries and territories with reported confirmed autochthonous cases of Zika virus"
sample_dataset-PublicUse/ ECDC Documents/ebola/ Communicable-disease-threats-report-01-jul-2017.pdf	17	C0009450	Communicable Diseases	"COMMUNICABLE DIS-EASE THREATS REPORT Zika: No mosquito-borne Zika virus"
sample_dataset-PublicUse/ ECDC Documents/zika virus/ Questions and answers about Zika virus disease.pdf	4	C0276289	Zika Virus Infection	"Zika virus disease Risk of transmission in Europe What is the risk to Europe? The main risk to the EU is related to an infected traveller intro-ducing the virus to an area with mosquitoes that are able to transmit Zika virus"
sample_dataset-PublicUse/ ECDC Documents/west nile virus/Communicable-disease-threats-report-2-jul-2016.pdf	1	C0018378	Guillain-Barre Syndrome	"Zika virus is a cause of microcephaly and Guillain-Barre syndrome"
sample_dataset-PublicUse/ EDQM Documents/BTC/ optimal-use-of-clotting-factors-and-platelets-european-symposium-proceedings-wildbad-kreuth-initiative-iv-freising-germany.PDF	300	C0011311, C0008055	*Dengue Fever, Chikungunya Fever*	"chikungunya and dengue virus infections in France and overseas departe-ments, and emerging pathogens such as Zika virus"

The entities *Zika virus* and *Communicable Diseases* (UMLS ID C0009450) occur many times in the same sentence. This is because many of the ingested bulletins have a similar structure, such as "COMMUNICABLE DISEASE THREATS REPORT Zika: No mosquito-borne Zika virus [...]." However, other co-occurrence examples are more relevant for interpretability and discovery. For instance, *Zika virus* often co-occurs with the following entities: *Zika Virus Infection* (UMLS ID C0276289), *Dengue Fever* (UMLS ID C0011311), and *Chikungunya Fever* (UMLS ID C0008055).

The co-occurrence with *Zika Virus Infection* is understandable. However, the semantic connection between these two entities is directly available in the SNOMED ontology. The following query uses the corresponding SNOMED IDs and labels to show the SNOMED connection between *Zika virus disease* (SNOMED ID 3928002) and *Zika virus* (SNOMED ID 50471002).

Listing 7.33 Getting paths between *Zika virus disease* and *Zika virus*

```
MATCH (s1), (s2)
WHERE s1.id = "3928002" AND s2.id = "50471002"
WITH s1, s2, allShortestPaths((s1)-[:SNOMED_RELATION*1..8]-(s2)) AS paths
UNWIND paths AS path
WITH relationships(path) AS path_edges,
     nodes(path) AS path_nodes
WITH
  [n IN path_nodes | n.name] AS node_names,
  [r IN path_edges | COALESCE(r.type, 'IS_A')] AS rel_types,
  [n IN path_edges | startnode(n).name] AS rel_starts
WITH [i IN range(0, size(node_names) - 1) |
  CASE
    WHEN i = size(node_names) - 1
    THEN '(' + node_names[i] + ')'
    WHEN node_names[i] = rel_starts[i]
    THEN '(' + node_names[i] + ')' + '-[:' + rel_types[i] + ']->'
    ELSE '(' + node_names[i] + ')' + '<-[:' + rel_types[i] + ']-'
  END
] AS string_paths
RETURN DISTINCT apoc.text.join(string_paths, '') AS `Extracted paths`
```

Finds shortest paths (up to eight hops) between two SNOMED concepts using SNOMED_RELATION

Uses the relationship type (default "IS_A") to ensure valid labeling

Retrieves the name of the starting node for each relationship to determine the relationship direction

Completes the path string

Indicates that the relationship is outgoing from the current node

Indicates that the relationship is incoming to the current node

This query returns all the shortest paths between *Zika virus* and *Zika virus disease* in a pretty-printed format. The result is shown next.

Listing 7.34 Paths connecting *Zika virus disease* and *Zika virus*

```
(Zika virus disease)-[:CAUSATIVE_AGENT]->(Zika virus)
```

In this case, the SNOMED ontology provides a relationship that clearly "interprets" the meaning of this co-occurrence. Such a connection reflects the linguistic and conceptual proximity of the disease and its causative agent in clinical and epidemiological texts. In our scenario, we provide graph-based augmented information, which makes explicit why these co-occurring entities can be validated.

As reported in table 7.6, the *Zika virus* medical entity also co-occurs with another disease, *Dengue Fever.* We can explore the ontology paths connecting these two entities by running the query in listing 7.33 and replacing the `WHERE` clause with `s1.id="38362002" AND s2.id="50471002"`. The results are as follows.

Listing 7.35 Paths connecting *Dengue* and *Zika virus*

```
(Dengue)-[:IS_A]->(Disease due to Flavivirus)
<-[:IS_A]-(Zika virus disease)-[:CAUSATIVE_AGENT]->(Zika virus)

(Dengue)-[:IS_A]->(Mosquito-borne flavivirus fever)
<-[:IS_A]-(Zika virus disease)-[:CAUSATIVE_AGENT]->(Zika virus)

(Dengue)-[:IS_A]->(Viral disease)
<-[:IS_A]-(Zika virus disease)-[:CAUSATIVE_AGENT]->(Zika virus)

(Dengue)-[:PATHOLOGICAL_PROCESS_(ATTRIBUTE)]->(Infectious process
➥ (qualifier value))
<-[:PATHOLOGICAL_PROCESS_(ATTRIBUTE)]-(Congenital Zika virus infection)
-[:CAUSATIVE_AGENT]->(Zika virus)

(Dengue)-[:CAUSATIVE_AGENT]->(Arthropod-borne organism)
<-[:CAUSATIVE_AGENT]-(Zika virus disease)
-[:CAUSATIVE_AGENT]->(Zika virus)

(Dengue)-[:PATHOLOGICAL_PROCESS_(ATTRIBUTE)]->(Infectious process
➥ (qualifier value))
<-[:PATHOLOGICAL_PROCESS_(ATTRIBUTE)]-(Zika virus disease)
-[:CAUSATIVE_AGENT]->(Zika virus)

(Dengue)-[:PATHOLOGICAL_PROCESS]->(Infectious disease)
<-[:PATHOLOGICAL_PROCESS]-(Zika virus disease)
-[:CAUSATIVE_AGENT]->(Zika virus)

(Dengue)-[:CAUSATIVE_AGENT]->(Togavirus)
<-[:CAUSATIVE_AGENT]-(Zika virus disease)
-[:CAUSATIVE_AGENT]->(Zika virus)
```

Multiple paths connect *Dengue* and *Zika virus,* including key entities such as *Viral disease* and *Infectious disease* that allow us to interpret why these diseases co-occur in the same sentence (see the last row of table 7.6). In addition, entities such as *Disease due to Flavivirus, Togavirus,* and *Mosquito-borne flavivirus fever* provide insights into how *Dengue* and *Zika virus* are connected, regardless of the sentence in which they are mentioned.

This validation process can be extended to other biomedical ontologies, including the HPO. For example, the results of the following query demonstrate how co-occurrence patterns between phenotypic features (e.g., *Renal cell carcinoma, Leukemia*) and associated disease entities (e.g., *von Hippel-Lindau syndrome, Colorectal cancer,*

RETINOBLASTOMA) can be systematically extracted and validated. This approach enables the identification of clinically relevant phenotype–disease associations grounded in document-level evidence.

Listing 7.36 Finding HPO disease entities that co-occur with phenotypic features

```
MATCH (d:HpoDiseaseEntity)<-[:IS_DISEASE_ENTITY]-(n1:MedicalEntity)
      -[r:COOCCURR]-(n2:MedicalEntity)-[:IS_HPO_ENTITY]->(h:HpoEntity)
WHERE EXISTS((d)-[:HAS_PHENOTYPIC_FEATURE]->(h))
 AND n2.id in ["C0007134", "C0376545"]
WITH n1, n2, d, h

MATCH (f:File)-[:CONTAINS_PAGE]->(p:Page)
      -[r1:MENTIONS_MENTION]->(m1)-[:DISAMBIGUATED_TO]->(n1),
      (p)-[r2:MENTIONS_MENTION]->(m2)-[:DISAMBIGUATED_TO]->(n2)
WHERE r1.sentence_index = r2.sentence_index
WITH f, p, r1, r2, n1, n2, d, h

RETURN DISTINCT
  f.id AS `File name`,
  p.page_idx AS `Page index`,
  h.label AS `HpoEntity name`,
  d.label AS `HpoDiseaseEntity name`,
  CASE
    WHEN r1.end_chars[0] > r2.start_chars[0]
    THEN substring(p.text, r2.start_chars[0], r1.end_chars[0]
    - r2.start_chars[0])
    ELSE substring(p.text, r1.start_chars[0], r2.end_chars[0]
    - r1.start_chars[0])
  END AS `Mentions context`
```

Selects pairs of medical entities where n1 co-occurs with a fixed subset of phenotype entities and is linked to a disease d that has the phenotype h

Filters the results to mentions that appear in the same sentence

Extracts the surrounding text to form a co-occurrence snippet

Ensures the correct ordering for text extraction

Unlike earlier examples, here we specify that one medical entity must be a disease and the other a phenotypic feature indexed in the HPO annotation file. The results of this query are listed in table 7.7.

Table 7.7 HPO disease entities co-occurring with phenotypic features

File ID	Page index	HPO name	HpoDisease name	Mentions context
sample_dataset-PublicUse/EDQM Documents/BTC/guide-to-the-quality-and-safety-of-organs-for-transplantation-7th-edition.PDF	275	Renal cell carcinoma	von Hippel-Lindau syndrome	"[...] von Hippel-Lindau syndrome could be considered (preferably for the heart donation) when inappropriate risks associated with RCC [...]"
sample_dataset-PublicUse/EDQM Documents/BTC/guide-to-the-quality-and-safety-of-organs-for-transplantation-7th-edition.PDF	228	Renal cell carcinoma	Colorectal cancer	[...] "RCCs, two neuroendocrine carcinomas, one breast cancer, one colorectal cancer [...]"

Table 7.7 HPO disease entities co-occurring with phenotypic features *(continued)*

File ID	Page index	HPO name	`HpoDisease` name	Mentions context
sample_dataset-PublicUse/BTC key docs/CELEX-_52002PC0319_EN_TXT.pdf	12	Leukemia	RETINOBLAS-TOMA	"[...] retinoblastoma, melanoma of the anterior pole, haematological neo-plasm [...]"

This use case has practical applications for analysts, who can derive interesting patterns from co-occurring entity types. For example, in the case of multiple co-occurring diseases, we can verify which ontology paths connect these diseases. On the other hand, the absence of interesting paths between co-occurring entities signals new knowledge that is not encoded in biomedical ontologies; we discuss this case next.

7.7.4 *Uncovering new knowledge*

In a context that changes quickly due to research advancements, some knowledge in the text has not yet been consolidated in medical ontologies. As a consequence, entities that co-occur in the same sentence may not have a direct match in terms of interpretability and discovery in the domain ontologies.

Instead of using the ontology to enrich the information of the KG, we can use a KG built from textual content to suggest new facts that can be integrated into the ontology. This use case allows us to identify new patterns in the text that can be useful in the medical domain. To identify this type of pattern, let's recap the diseases that co-occur most with *Zika virus* by running the following query.

Listing 7.37 Finding the top diseases co-occurring with "Zika virus" in text

```
MATCH (n1:MedicalEntity)-[r:COOCCURR]-(n2:MedicalEntity)
WHERE n1.id= "C0318793" and n2.type = "Disease or Syndrome"
RETURN n2.name, r.count
ORDER BY r.count DESC
LIMIT 5
```

The results are shown in table 7.8.

Table 7.8 Top diseases co-occurring with *Zika virus*

Disease entity	Occurrences
Communicable Diseases	606
Zika Virus Infection	520
Dengue Fever	206
Guillain-Barre Syndrome	195
Chikungunya Fever	155

In the results, several diseases are associated with the *Zika virus* entity. Among them, Guillain-Barre Syndrome stands out because, unlike the others, it is not a vector-borne disease. This makes its co-mention potentially unexpected and clinically significant, suggesting a possible complication rather than mere co-endemicity.

For this reason, it is helpful to get further details by exploring the textual content that mentions both Zika virus and Guillain–Barre syndrome. We can reuse the query in listing 7.32 by replacing the first `WHERE` clause with `n1.id= "C0318793" AND n2.id = "C0018378"`, which are the UMLS ids of Zika virus and Guillain–Barre syndrome, respectively (we also removed from the results the "Co-occurring entity id" and the "Co-occurring entity name" fields because they are not useful in this case). The cleaned results of this query, obtained by removing redundant results, are shown in table 7.9.

Table 7.9 Text mentioning both Zika virus and Guillain-Barre syndrome

File ID	Page index	Mentions context
sample_dataset-PublicUse/ECDC Documents/ebola/communicable-disease-threats-report–20-feb-2016.pdf	3	"Zika and potential complications published on 12 February 2016, six countries have reported an increase in the incidence of cases of micro-cephaly (Brazil) and Guillain-Barre syndrome"
sample_dataset-PublicUse/ECDC Documents/zika virus/zika-virus-rapid-risk-assessment-11-april-2016.docx.pdf	2	"Zika virus epidemic, health services and practi-tioners should be alerted to the possible occur-rence of neurological syndromes (Guillain-Barre syndrome)"
sample_dataset-PublicUse/ECDC Documents/ebola/communicable-disease-threats-report-16-june-2019.pdf	3	"Guillain-Barre is known to be triggered by bac-terial infections, respiratory viruses, entero-viruses, and arboviruses such as dengue and Zika"

The results state that Zika virus is one of the causes of Guillain–Barre syndrome. So, we expect ontologies such as SNOMED to include a fact such as `Guillain-Barre syndrome-[:CAUSATIVE_AGENT]->Zika virus`. Let's check by running the query in listing 7.33 and replacing *Zika virus disease* (SNOMED ID 3928002) with *Infectious neuronitis* (the SNOMED term for Guillain–Barre syndrome; SNOMED ID 40956001) in the `WHERE` clause. The following listing shows a subset of the results: multiple SNOMED ontology paths connect these entities, but most of these paths do not represent meaningful connections between.

Listing 7.38 Paths connecting *Zika virus* and *Infectious neuronitis*

```
(Zika virus)<-[:CAUSATIVE_AGENT]-(Congenital Zika virus infection)
-[:PATHOLOGICAL_PROCESS_(ATTRIBUTE)]->(Infectious process (qualifier value))
<-[:PATHOLOGICAL_PROCESS_(ATTRIBUTE)]-(Reactivation of hepatitis B viral
     hepatitis (disorder))
-[:ASSOCIATED_MORPHOLOGY]->(Inflammation)
<-[:ASSOCIATED_MORPHOLOGY]-(Infectious neuronitis)
```

```
(Zika virus)<-[:CAUSATIVE_AGENT]-(Zika virus disease)
-[:CAUSATIVE_AGENT]->(Togavirus)
<-[:CAUSATIVE_AGENT]-(Mosquito-borne flavivirus encephalitis)
-[:ASSOCIATED_MORPHOLOGY]->(Inflammation)
<-[:ASSOCIATED_MORPHOLOGY]-(Infectious neuronitis)
```

In the first entry, *Zika virus* is connected to *Infectious neuronitis* because Zika virus is the causative agent of *Congenital Zika virus infection*, which is an infectious process. The issue is that the *Infectious process* (qualifier value) node is connected to multiple contagious processes, such as *Reactivation of hepatitis B viral hepatitis* (disorder). This disorder is associated with inflammation, which is also a morphological manifestation of *Infectious neuronitis.* Similar reasoning can be applied to the second entry in listing 7.38. These paths were retrieved because they include hub nodes, such as *Infectious process* (qualifier value) and *Inflammation,* which are connected to a massive number of nodes related to infectious processes.

One solution is to filter out paths that include these hub nodes. To do so, we can use graph data science algorithms provided by the Neo4j Graph Data Science Library (GDS), which offers tools to compute the centrality of a node in the graph. To run this algorithm, the first step is to create a graph projection that includes the relevant set of nodes and relationships to perform our analysis. In this case, we want to focus on the SNOMED ontology graph, and we can run the following code.

Listing 7.39 Creating a projection on the SNOMED ontology

```
CALL gds.graph.project(
  'snomedGraph',
  'SnomedEntity',
  'SNOMED_RELATION'
)
YIELD
  graphName AS graph,
  relationshipProjection AS knowsProjection,
  nodeCount AS nodes,
  relationshipCount AS rels;
```

After generating the projection, we can run the degree algorithm in streaming mode to retrieve the most-connected nodes and use this result to filter out paths that are not relevant for our purpose.

Listing 7.40 Filtering out hub nodes

```
CALL gds.degree.stream('snomedGraph')
YIELD nodeId, score
WITH gds.util.asNode(nodeId).name AS name, score AS degree
ORDER BY degree DESC
LIMIT 350
WITH collect(name) AS hub_nodes          <-- Collects the top 350 high-degree
                                             nodes (central hubs)
```

```
MATCH (s1), (s2)
WHERE s1.id = "3928002" AND s2.id = "40956001"
WITH s1,
     s2,
     allShortestPaths((s1)-[:SNOMED_RELATION*1..8]-(s2)) AS paths,
    hub_nodes
UNWIND paths AS path
WITH relationships(path) AS path_edges,
nodes(path) AS path_nodes,
hub_nodes
WITH
[n IN path_nodes | n.name] AS node_names,
[r IN path_edges | COALESCE(r.type, 'IS_A')] AS rel_types,
[n IN path_edges | startnode(n).name] AS rel_starts,
hub_nodes
WHERE NOT any(x IN node_names WHERE x IN hub_nodes)
WITH [i IN range(0, size(node_names) - 1) |
CASE
WHEN i = size(node_names) - 1
THEN '(' + node_names[i] + ')'
WHEN node_names[i] = rel_starts[i]
THEN '(' + node_names[i] + ')' + '-[:' + rel_types[i] + ']->'
ELSE '(' + node_names[i] + ')' + '<-[:' + rel_types[i] + ']-'
END
] AS string_paths
RETURN DISTINCT apoc.text.join(string_paths, '') AS `Extracted paths`
```

Finds all shortest paths (1–8 hops) between the two SNOMED concept nodes (annotates `hub_nodes`)

Defaults the relationship type to "IS_A" if it's missing (annotates `rel_types`)

Retrieves the name of the source node for each relationship to determine directionality in the final string (annotates `rel_starts`)

Excludes any path that passes through a hub node (annotates `WHERE NOT any(...)`)

Marks the end of the path (annotates the first `THEN`)

Renders a forward (outgoing) relationship between the current node and the next (annotates the second `THEN`)

Renders a backward (incoming) relationship from the next node to the current one (annotates `ELSE`)

This query combines the nodes' degree computation with the detection of relevant paths connecting two entities. Paths that include nodes with a higher degree are excluded from the results. The next listing shows the results after this filtering process.

Listing 7.41 Revised paths connecting *Zika virus disease* and *Infectious neuronitis*

```
(Zika virus disease)-[:IS_A]->(Viral disease)
<-[:IS_A]-(Erythema multiforme caused by virus (disorder))
-[:PATHOLOGICAL_PROCESS_(ATTRIBUTE)]->(AI - autoimmune)
<-[:PATHOLOGICAL_PROCESS_(ATTRIBUTE)]-(Infectious neuronitis)

(Zika virus disease)-[:IS_A]->(Disease due to Flavivirus)
<-[:IS_A]-(Acute hepatitis C)
-[:IS_A]->(Acute inflammatory disorder)
<-[:IS_A]-(Infectious neuronitis)

(Zika virus disease)<-[:ASSOCIATED_FINDING]-(Presumptive recent Zika
     negative)
-[:IS_A]->(Context-dependent finding (context-dependent category))
<-[:IS_A]-(History of Guillain Barre syndrome (situation))
-[:ASSOCIATED_FINDING]->(Infectious neuronitis)
```

```
(Zika virus disease)-[:IS_A]->(Viral disease)
<-[:IS_A]-(Common cold)-[:IS_A]->(Acute inflammatory disorder)
<-[:IS_A]-(Infectious neuronitis)

(Zika virus disease)-[:IS_A]->(Viral disease)
<-[:IS_A]-(VHF - Viral haemorrhagic fever)
-[:IS_A]->(Acute inflammatory disorder)
<-[:IS_A]-(Infectious neuronitis)

(Zika virus disease)<-[:ASSOCIATED_FINDING]-(Presumptive recent Zika
     positive)
-[:IS_A]->(Context-dependent finding (context-dependent category))
<-[:IS_A]-(History of Guillain Barre syndrome (situation))
-[:ASSOCIATED_FINDING]->(Infectious neuronitis)

(Zika virus disease)-[:IS_A]->(Viral disease)
<-[:TEMPORALLY_FOLLOWS]-(Transient paroxysmal cold hemoglobinuria)
-[:PATHOLOGICAL_PROCESS_(ATTRIBUTE)]->(AI - autoimmune)
<-[:PATHOLOGICAL_PROCESS_(ATTRIBUTE)]-(Infectious neuronitis)

(Zika virus disease)-[:IS_A]->(Viral disease)
<-[:DUE_TO]-(Erythema multiforme caused by virus (disorder))
-[:PATHOLOGICAL_PROCESS_(ATTRIBUTE)]->(AI - autoimmune)
<-[:PATHOLOGICAL_PROCESS_(ATTRIBUTE)]-(Infectious neuronitis)

(Zika virus disease)-[:IS_A]->(Viral disease)
<-[:AFTER]-(Transient paroxysmal cold hemoglobinuria)
-[:PATHOLOGICAL_PROCESS_(ATTRIBUTE)]->(AI - autoimmune)
<-[:PATHOLOGICAL_PROCESS_(ATTRIBUTE)]-(Infectious neuronitis)
```

This time, we retrieved a result set of 9 entries, compared to the 11,185 paths detected with the base query. However, the results still include general entities such as *Viral disease*, which connects *Zika virus disease* to random viral diseases that can be used to connect *Zika virus disease* to *Infectious neuronitis*. In other words, a direct connection between these entities is not encoded in the SNOMED ontology. This is a typical example in which the co-occurrence of entities defined in the KG can potentially be used to enrich a domain ontology in a virtuous circle.

This mechanism can be exponentially enhanced by extracting meaningful relationships from the text. In this approach, the starting point is represented by the extracted relationships, which are more specific than the co-occurrence connection; see figure 7.17.

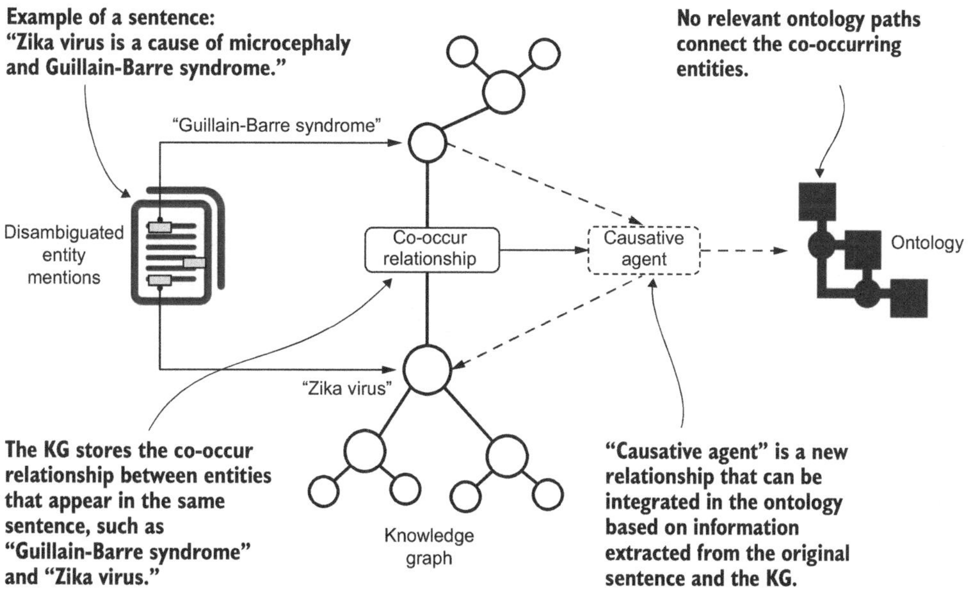

Figure 7.17 Mental model describing the process of uncovering new knowledge. In this case, "Zika virus" and "Guillain-Barre syndrome" appear multiple times in the same sentences, but the medical ontologies do not provide any relevant connections between these entities.

Summary

- Named entity disambiguation (NED) lets us connect entities mentioned in the text to a reference knowledge base.
- Combining NED with KG technologies opens new opportunities to develop advanced services in critical domains.
- Constructing a KG requires multiple steps, including defining the schema, ingesting documents, disambiguating entities from these documents, integrating domain ontologies, mapping extracted entities, and generating co-occurrence relationships between entities located in the same sentence.
- Advanced analysis can be performed on the KG to support different use cases in the application domain: conceptual search, structured knowledge-based search, KG-based interpretability and discovery, and uncovering new knowledge.

8 NED with open LLMs and domain ontologies

This chapter covers

- Understanding the limitations of traditional NED tools
- Combining general-purpose LLMs and domain ontologies for NED
- Performing multistep disambiguation with shortest-paths detection, path-to-text translation, and textual paths summarization

Chapter 7 is focused on named entity disambiguation (NED), highlighting the role of scispaCy, a specialized natural language processing (NLP) tool built on the spaCy framework. This tool is designed to process documents and publications by providing pretrained models in the biomedical domain.

8.1 Understanding limitations of traditional NED systems

scispaCy incorporates vocabularies and ontologies, such as the Unified Medical Language System (UMLS), that provide canonical entities useful for disambiguating mentions in the text. However, this approach has some limitations:

- It is designed for a particular application domain: the biomedical field.
- It presents challenges in expanding and updating the reference knowledge base to incorporate new entities and terms.
- It fails to fully use the extensive information available in the knowledge base.
- It doesn't use the existing relationships and paths between entities for the disambiguation task.

To understand the effect of this last point, let's recap the example we discussed at the beginning of chapter 7, which used this quote from the European Centre for Disease Prevention and Control (ECDC):

> *In the week of 13 April, Belize reported for the first time mosquito-borne Zika virus transmission. Update on the observed increase of congenital Zika syndrome and other neurological complications Microcephaly and other fetal malformations potentially associated with Zika virus infection.*

scispaCy uses the contextual words surrounding the term "Zika" to detect the three correct disambiguated entities. The results are shown in the following listing.

Listing 8.1 Candidate selection and ranking with scispaCy

```
Recognized entity: Zika virus 75 85
Ranked target candidates:
- C0318793 Zika Virus
- C0276289 Zika Virus Infection
- C4687930 Zika Virus Antibody Measurement

Recognized entity: congenital Zika syndrome 135 159
Ranked target candidates:
- C4546023 Congenital Zika Syndrome

Recognized entity: Zika virus infection 268 288
Ranked target candidates:
- C0276289 Zika Virus Infection
- C0318793 Zika Virus
- C4687930 Zika Virus Antibody Measurement
```

Target entity "Zika Virus" detected between characters 75 and 85

Target entity "Congenital Zika Syndrome" detected between characters 135 and 159

Target entity "Zika Virus Infection" detected between characters 268 and 288

But now let's test the following slightly different example that doesn't include surrounding words such as "congenital" and "syndrome":

> *Zika belongs to the Flaviviridae virus family, and it is spread by Aedes mosquitoes. Individuals affected by Zika disease and other syndromes like chikungunya fever often experience symptoms like viral myalgia, infectious edema, and infective conjunctivitis. Severe outcomes of Zika are due to its capacity to cross the placental barrier during pregnancy, causing microcephaly and congenital malformations.*

Compared to the previous example, there are no words supporting the disambiguation phase. Let's look at the scispaCy output.

Listing 8.2 Candidate selection and ranking with the scispaCy model

```
Recognized entity: Zika 0 4
Ranked target candidates:
- C0276289 Zika Virus Infection
- C0318793 Zika Virus
- C4687930 Zika Virus Antibody Measurement

Recognized entity: Zika disease 109 121
Ranked target candidates:

Recognized entity: Zika 278 282
Ranked target candidates:
- C0276289 Zika Virus Infection
- C0318793 Zika Virus
- C4687930 Zika Virus Antibody Measurement
```

The model disambiguates "Zika" as the entity "C0276289 Zika Virus Infection" in the first and the third sentences, but it doesn't detect a target entity for the mention in the second sentence.

This chapter addresses these limitations with a novel approach that uses open large language models (LLMs) and domain ontologies. Unlike domain-based tools such as scispaCy, this approach can be used in other application domains in which we can use rich ontologies.

8.2 Ingesting the domain ontology

To drive the disambiguation process, we will use the SNOMED (Systematized Nomenclature of Medicine) ontology introduced in chapter 7. As a reminder, SNOMED is a multilingual clinical terminology repository encompassing more than 450,000 concepts and a rich set of relationship types. For our example scenario, we will again use these two files: sct2_Description_Full-en_US1000124_20220901.txt (entity names and aliases, and relationships between entities) and sct2_Relationship_Full_US1000124_20220901.txt (numerical codes identifying entities and relationships).

NOTE For examples from these files, see section 7.5.2.

Figure 8.1 illustrates the SNOMED hierarchical structure and the propagation of information through the nodes. Listings 8.3–8.5 do the following, respectively: create nodes and relationships in Neo4j from sct2_Relationship_Full_US1000124_20220901.txt, extract names and aliases from sct2_Description_Full-en_US1000124_20220901.txt, and follow the hierarchical structure to propagate information from first-level nodes to deeper nodes.

NOTE For annotated versions of these listings and more details, see section 7.6.4. The complete example code is available in the book's online repository.

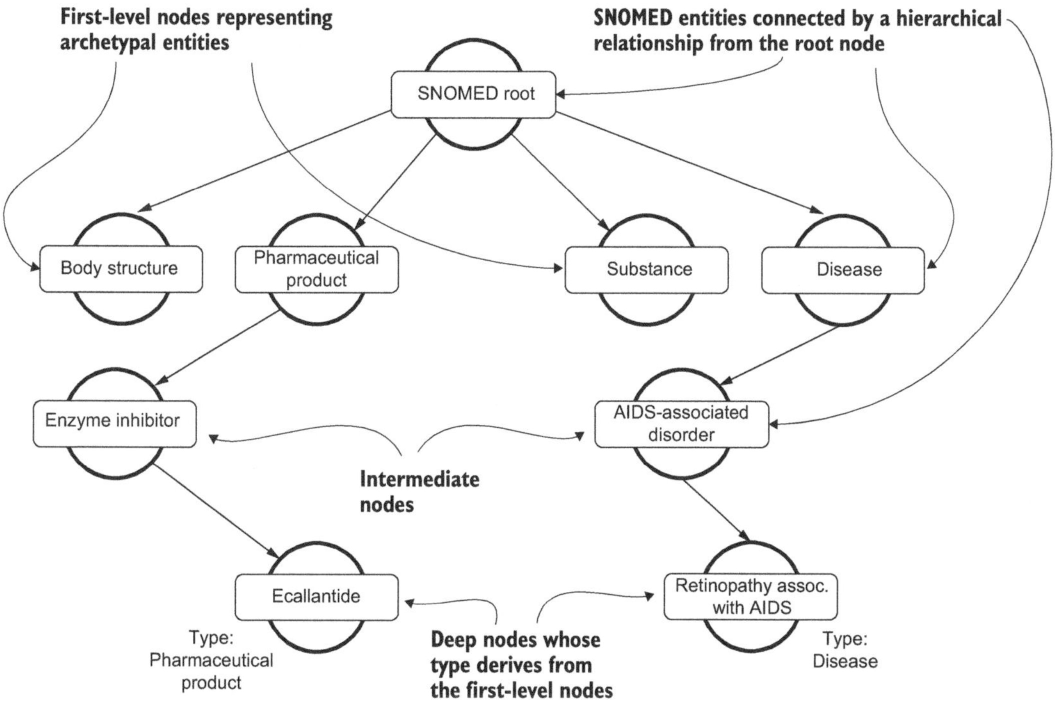

Figure 8.1 A sample of SNOMED's hierarchical structure. Nodes on deeper levels can be categorized using information from first-level nodes, which are the ontology's archetypal entities.

Listing 8.3 Ingesting SNOMED: loading relationships

```
[...]
class SnomedRelationshipsImporter(BaseImporter):
  [...]
  def set_constraints(self):
    queries = [
        (
            "CREATE CONSTRAINT IF NOT EXISTS FOR (n:SnomedEntity) "
            "REQUIRE n.id IS UNIQUE"
        ),
        (
            "CREATE INDEX snomedNodeName IF NOT EXISTS "
            "FOR (n:SnomedEntity) ON (n.name)"
        ),
        (
            "CREATE INDEX snomedRelationId IF NOT EXISTS "
            "FOR ()-[r:SNOMED_RELATION]-() ON (r.id)"
        ),
        (
            "CREATE INDEX snomedRelationType IF NOT EXISTS "
            "FOR ()-[r:SNOMED_RELATION]-() ON (r.type)"
        ),
        (
```

```
            "CREATE INDEX snomedRelationUmls IF NOT EXISTS "
            "FOR ()-[r:SNOMED_RELATION]-() ON (r.umls)"
        ),
    ]


    for q in queries:
      self.connection.query(q, db=self.db)

  def import_snomed_rels(self):
    query = """
       UNWIND $batch as item
       MERGE (e1:SnomedEntity {id: item.sourceId})
       MERGE (e2:SnomedEntity {id: item.destinationId})
       MERGE (e1)-[:SNOMED_RELATION {id: item.typeId}]->(e2)
       FOREACH(ignoreMe IN CASE WHEN item.typeId = '116680003'
       ➥THEN [true] ELSE [] END|
         MERGE (e1)-[:SNOMED_IS_A]->(e2)
       )
       """

size = self.get_csv_size(snomedRels_file)
self.batch_store(snomed_rels_query, self.get_rows(snomedRels_file),
     size=size)
```

Listing 8.4 Ingesting SNOMED: loading names and aliases

```
[...]
class SnomedNamesImporter(BaseImporter):
  [...]

  def import_snomed_names(self, snomedNames_file):
        snomed_names_concepts_query = """
        UNWIND $batch as item
        MATCH (e1:SnomedEntity)
        -[r:SNOMED_RELATION {id: item.conceptId}]->
        (e2:SnomedEntity)
        WHERE item.conceptId <> '116680003' AND r.id = item.conceptId
        SET r.type = CASE
                WHEN r.type IS NULL THEN item.termAsType
                ELSE r.type END,
            r.aliases = CASE
                WHEN item.termAsType IN r.aliases THEN r.aliases
                ELSE coalesce(r.aliases,[]) + item.termAsType END
        """

        snomed_names_entities_query = """
        UNWIND $batch as item
        MATCH (e:SnomedEntity {id: item.conceptId})
        SET e.name = CASE
                WHEN e.name IS NULL THEN item.term
                ELSE e.name END,
            e.aliases = CASE
```

```
                WHEN item.term in e.aliases THEN  e.aliases
                ELSE coalesce(e.aliases, []) + item.term END
        """
        size = self.get_csv_size(snomedNames_file)
        self.batch_store(
          snomed_names_concepts_query,
          self.get_rows(snomedNames_file),
         size=size)
        self.batch_store(
          snomed_names_entities_query,
          self.get_rows(snomedNames_file),
          size=size)
[...]
```

Listing 8.5 Ingesting SNOMED: labeling propagation from first-level nodes

```
[...]
class SnomedLabelPropagator():
[...]

  def get_rows(self):
    propagation_query = """
      MATCH p=(n:SnomedEntity)<-[:SNOMED_IS_A]-(m:SnomedEntity)
      WHERE n.id= "138875005" // Root node
      WITH distinct m as first_node

      CALL apoc.path.expandConfig(first_node, { // #A
              relationshipFilter: '<SNOMED_IS_A',
                minLevel: 1,
                maxLevel: -1,
                uniqueness: 'RELATIONSHIP_GLOBAL'
            }) yield path

     UNWIND nodes(path) as other_level // #B
     WITH first_node, collect(DISTINCT other_level) as uniques
             UNWIND uniques as unique_other_level
             WITH first_node,unique_other_level
             WHERE not first_node.name in
     coalesce(unique_other_level.type,[])

             RETURN unique_other_level.id as id, first_node.name as label - C
            """

    with self._driver.session(database=self._database) as session:
     result = session.run(query=propagation_query)
     for record in iter(result):
        yield dict(record)
[...]
```

The `SNOMED_IS_A` relationship has been used to propagate the semantic types through the tree structure by using the hierarchical connections between entities.

8.3 Setting up the model with Ollama and Llama 3.1 8B

In previous chapters, we explored how to use OpenAI APIs to perform NLP tasks. Now, we extend that knowledge by deploying a NED system locally using Ollama and Llama 3.1 8B (released by Meta).

Ollama is an open source tool that lets users run LLMs directly on their local machines. By running models locally, we gain full control over our data while reducing latency and dependency on external providers. Llama 3.1 8B is an open source LLM with 8 billion parameters. It supports a context length of up to 128,000 tokens and is optimized for multilingual information processing. It is also designed for efficient deployment on consumer-grade hardware.

To deploy the Llama 3.1 8B model on your local machine, you will first need to download and install Ollama. The tool is compatible with macOS, Linux, and Windows, and the installation files are available at https://ollama.com/. Ollama offers both command-line and graphical user interface (GUI) options; we used the following command-line instructions to download and deploy Llama 3.1 8B for our NED system.

Listing 8.6 Ollama commands to download and install Llama 3.1 8B

```
ollama serve
ollama pull llama3.1:latest
```

Ollama offers built-in compatibility with the OpenAI Chat Completions API, so we can interact directly with our locally deployed model using Python code like that in previous chapters. This simplifies the process of integrating the model into our NED system. The next listing shows the Python class needed to interact with our model.

Listing 8.7 Running our Llama 3.1 8B model in Python

```
from openai import OpenAI

class LLM_Model():
    def __init__(self, url='http://localhost:11434/v1', key="default"):
        self.client = OpenAI(
          base_url= url,            # Default URL through which the model is served
          api_key = key,            # "api_key" is required for the OpenAI Chat Completions API but is not used for open models.
        )

    def generate(self, messages):
        response = self.client.chat.completions.create(
            model="llama3.1:latest",     # Specifies llama3.1:latest, downloaded by Ollama
            messages=messages,
            temperature=0,
            max_tokens=4000,
            top_p=1,
            frequency_penalty=0,
            presence_penalty=0,
        )
        # It assumes as response the ChatGPT API format
        return response.choices[0].message.content
```

NOTE We obtained our results for the example, generated using the prompts in the following sections, in October 2024 using the latest version of the Llama 3.1 model.

Using a general-purpose model like Llama 3.1 for NED will demonstrate the potential of LLMs to perform well in niche areas when combined with domain-specific ontologies. In the next section, we break down this process and show how the system can interpret and disambiguate entities in complex biomedical texts, facilitating information extraction and analysis.

8.4 End-to-end NED process

Figure 8.2 shows the mental model describing our example's NED process from the input document to the disambiguated mentions. The process begins with an input document containing unstructured text, which is analyzed by an LLM-based named entity recognition (NER) component. Here, the LLM identifies and labels relevant biomedical entities in the input text using the knowledge embedded in the domain ontology. For instance, a term like "Zika" can be recognized as a *Disease* concept according to SNOMED. This step transforms raw text into structured data, which will be processed in subsequent stages.

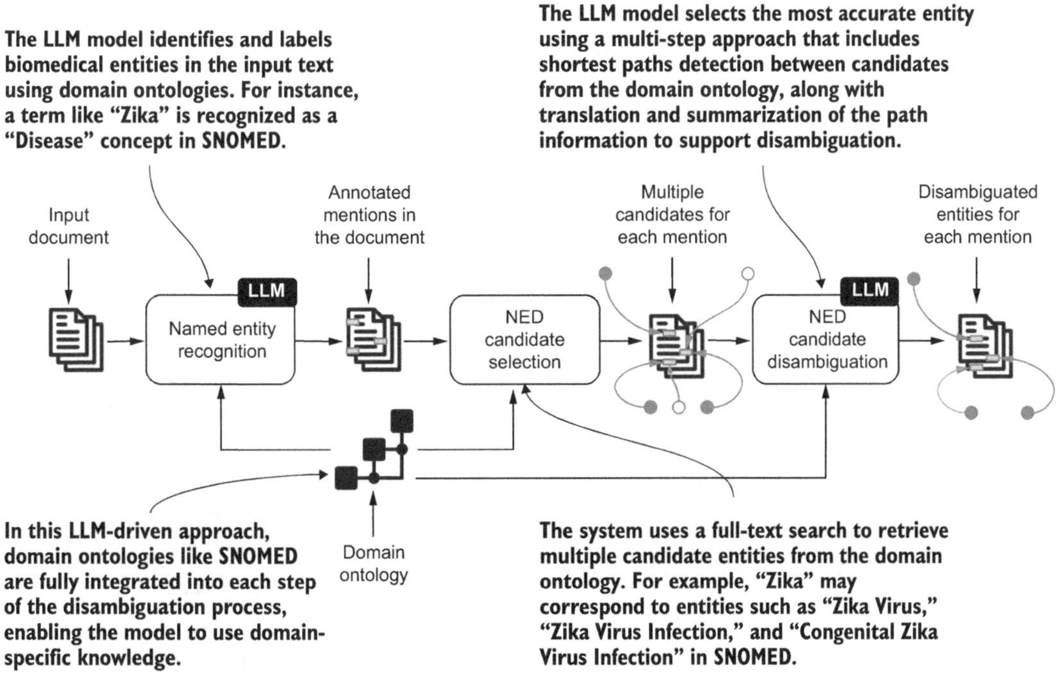

Figure 8.2 Workflow for a NED system designed to use LLMs and domain-specific ontologies, such as SNOMED, for biomedical text processing. Each stage of this workflow involves interactions to accurately disambiguate entities in the input text.

Next, the system moves to the NED candidate selection (CS) stage. A full-text search mechanism generates a list of possible matches for each identified entity mention. For instance, the term "Zika" may correspond to several entities in SNOMED, such as *Zika Virus, Zika Virus Infection,* and *Congenital Zika Virus Infection.* This step sets up a pool of potential disambiguation targets; the system will evaluate them in the following phase to find the most accurate match.

In the final stage, NED candidate disambiguation (CD), the LLM refines its selection to determine the most precise entity match for each mention. A multistep approach identifies the shortest path between candidates in the ontology structure; it then translates and summarizes relevant path details to support disambiguation with contextual knowledge and ensure that each entity mentioned in the input document is mapped accurately to its corresponding disambiguated entity in the ontology.

This LLM-driven approach integrates domain-specific ontologies at each step of the disambiguation process. By incorporating the hierarchical and relational structures of the ontology, the model can make more informed decisions about entity classification and disambiguation, especially in complex cases where terms may have multiple meanings or associations.

8.4.1 Named entity recognition

The goal of NER is to identify and classify named entities mentioned in unstructured text into predefined categories, such as diseases, organisms, and procedures. As discussed in previous chapters, one practical approach is to use prompt engineering, where the types of entities we are interested in are explicitly defined in the prompt. Often, a data scientist or data engineer works with a domain expert to identify and define these entities.

In our scenario, we incorporate SNOMED's structured medical knowledge to enable the LLM to perform more precise and contextually aware entity recognition in biomedical texts. Figure 8.3 illustrates the input and output of the NER.

NER requires us to retrieve all the predefined categories from the ontology. The following query retrieves the categories from SNOMED.

Listing 8.8 Retrieving predefined categories from SNOMED

```
MATCH (n:SnomedEntity)
UNWIND n.type as named_entity
WITH DISTINCT named_entity, count(named_entity) as num_of_entities
ORDER BY num_of_entities DESC
RETURN collect(named_entity) as named_entities
```

We can use the results from this query in our prompt for the NER task. Listing 8.9 is a simplified version of the prompt messages we defined for this purpose; the full prompt is in code repository.

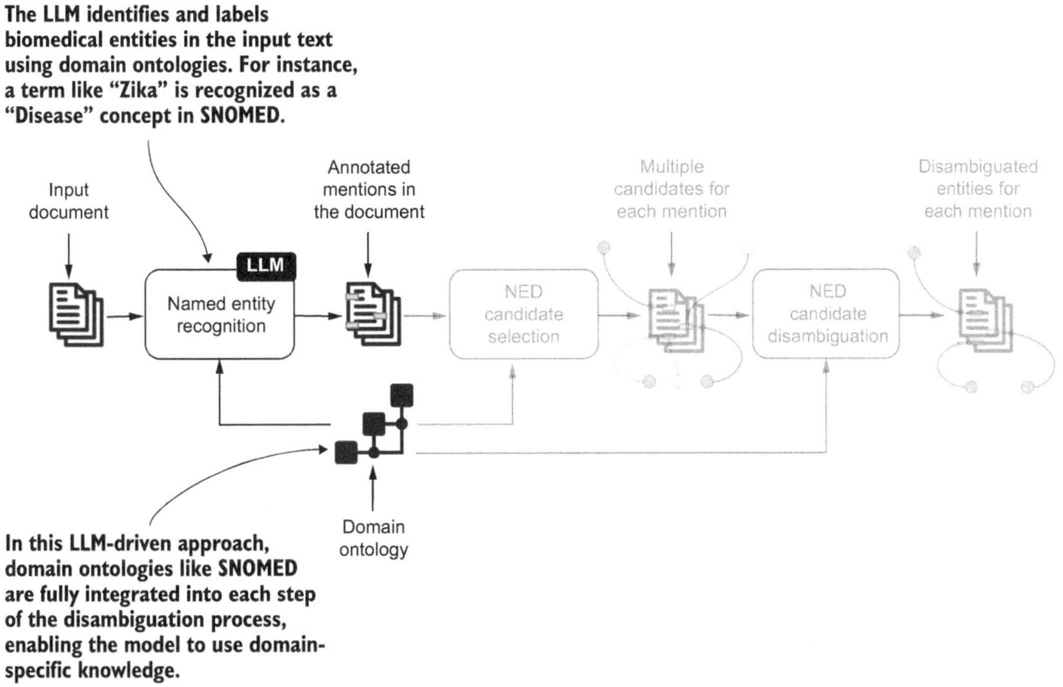

Figure 8.3 The first stage of NED is NER. In our scenario, named entities are derived directly from the ontology. In SNOMED, categories are defined by the ontology's first-level nodes, whose information is propagated to all the other nodes.

Listing 8.9 Simplified prompt for NER

```
system = """You are an assistant capable of extracting named entities in the
➥medical domain.
Your task is to extract ALL single mentions of named entities from the text.
You must only use one of the pre-defined entities from the following list:
{named_entities}.
No other entity categories are allowed.
For each sentence, extract the named entities and present the output in
valid JSON format""".format(named_entities=named_entities))

input = """Risk factors for rhinocerebral mucormycosis include poorly
controlled diabetes mellitus and severe immunosuppression."""

assistant = [
  {
    "sentence": """Risk factors for rhinocerebral mucormycosis include
 poorly controlled diabetes mellitus and severe immunosuppression.""",
    "entities": [
      {
        "id": 0,
        "mention": "Risk factors",
```

```
          "label": "Events"
        },
        {
          "id": 1,
          "mention": "rhinocerebral mucormycosis",
          "label": "Disease"
        },
        {
          "id": 2,
          "mention": "poorly controlled diabetes mellitus",
          "label": "Disease"
        },
        {
          "id": 3,
          "mention": "severe immunosuppression",
          "label": "Qualifier value"
        }
      ]
    }
]
```

This prompt is structured as follows:

- *System instruction*—The system message says to extract occurrences of named entities that belong to categories in the medical domain from the SNOMED ontology, avoiding irrelevant or out-of-scope categories.
- *Input text*—In this example, the input text discusses risk factors for a medical condition (rhinocerebral mucormycosis), listing conditions such as diabetes mellitus and immunosuppression that are medical terms which need to be recognized.
- *Assistant output*—The system responds with structured JSON output that contains the following fields:
  - `sentence`—The system processes text sentence by sentence to ensure that it analyzes each unit of meaning individually.
  - `entities`—The output includes an array of identified entities. Each entry contains an ID to uniquely identify the entity in the sentence, a mention of the named entity found in the text (e.g., "rhinocerebral mucormycosis"), and a label that classifies the entity according to a SNOMED category, such as *Disease*.

Here's an example of input text passed to the LLM instructed with the NER prompt.

Listing 8.10 User message for NER

```
user = """Severe outcomes of Zika are due to its capacity to cross the
placental barrier during pregnancy, causing microcephaly
and congenital malformations""".
```

And here is a subset of the results generated by Llama 3.1.

Listing 8.11 NER output from the sentence in listing 8.10

```
{
  "sentence": """Severe outcomes of Zika are due to its capacity to cross
the placental barrier during pregnancy, causing microcephaly
and congenital malformations. """,
  "entities": [
    {
      "id": 0,
      "mention": "Zika",
      "label": "Organism",
      "start": 19,
      "end": 22
    },
    {
      "id": 1,
      "mention": "microcephaly",
      "label": "Clinical finding (finding)",
      "start": 105,
      "end": 116
    },
    {
      "id": 2,
      "mention": "congenital malformations",
      "label": "Clinical finding (finding)",
      "start": 122,
      "end": 145
     }
   ]
}
```

From this result, we can identify and classify three distinct entities:

- "Zika"—Identified as an *Organism*, with its position in the sentence spanning from character 19 to 22.
- "Microcephaly"—Labeled a *Clinical finding (finding)*, indicating that it is a medical condition. This mention appears from character 105 to 116.
- "Congenital malformations"—Also labeled a *Clinical finding (finding)*. It is located between characters 122 and 145 in the sentence.

LLMs have trouble accurately detecting the starting and ending characters of mentions in a sentence. For this reason, we generated the `start` and `end` fields in post-processing with the following Python function.

Listing 8.12 Python function to compute starting and ending characters of a mention

```
def find_all_mention_indices(self, string, substring):
  indices = []
  start_index = 0
```

```
    while True:
      start_index = string.find(substring, start_index)

      if start_index == -1:
        break  # No more occurrences found

      end_index = start_index + len(substring) - 1
      indices.append((start_index, end_index))

      # Move start_index forward to search for the next occurrence
      start_index += len(substring)

    return indices
```

This function identifies the position of the mention, which is information recognized by traditional NER systems.

8.4.2 Candidate selection

The second phase of the NED process is CS, which identifies relevant entities or concepts that could match the intended meaning of each identified named entity. Figure 8.4 illustrates the input and output of this phase, highlighting how candidate entities are selected.

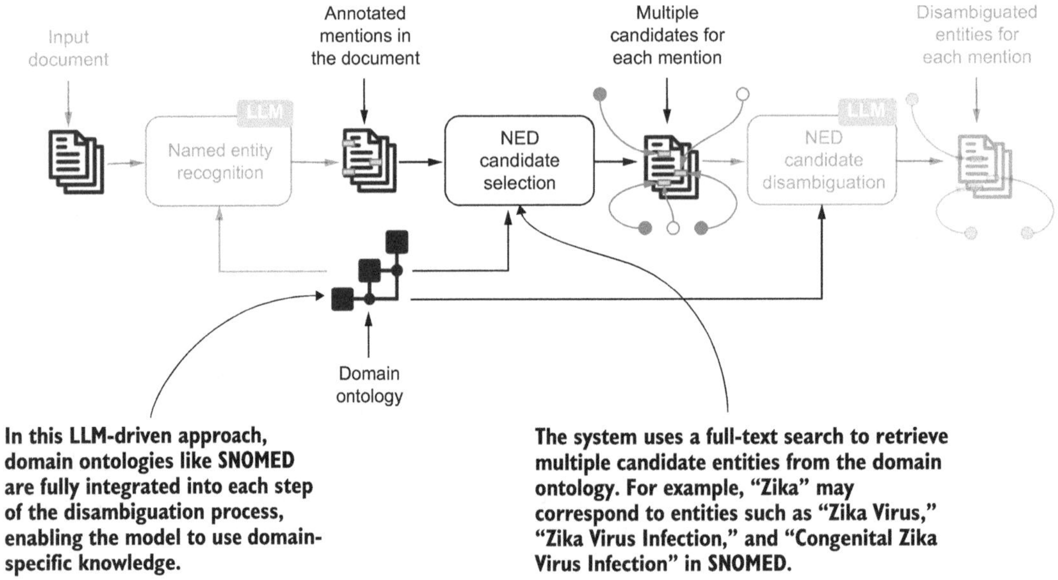

Figure 8.4 The second stage of NED is candidate selection. For each entity mention detected in the previous step, this stage retrieves potential candidates that may refer to it.

As shown in the following listing, the input for CS consists of the mentions annotated in the input text by the NER process, along with the domain ontology. The output is a list of one or more candidate entities associated with each mention.

We do not use the LLM in this step for two reasons. First, we want to retrieve candidates directly from the domain ontology rather than rely on knowledge embedded in the LLM. Second, the size of the ontology prevents us from loading it in its entirety in a prompt. So, to perform CS efficiently, we use Neo4j's full-text search capabilities, which can identify strings in the ontology that closely match each mention.

Listing 8.13 Python class for CS

```
class CandidateSelection:
[...]
  def full_text_query(self):
    query = """
            CALL db.index.fulltext.queryNodes("names", $fulltextQuery,
            ➥{limit: $limit})
            YIELD node
            WHERE node:SnomedEntity AND ANY(x IN node.type
            ➥WHERE x IN $labels)
            RETURN distinct node.name AS candidate_name, node.id
            ➥AS candidate_id
            """

    return query

  def generate_full_text_query(self, input):
    full_text_query = ""
    words = [el for el in input.split() if el]

    if len(words) > 1:
      for word in words[:-1]:
        full_text_query += f" {word}~0.80 AND "
        full_text_query += f" {words[-1]}~0.80"
    else:
      full_text_query = words[0] + "~0.80"

    return full_text_query.strip() [...]
```

We specify the `$labels` parameter to reduce the query's search space. These labels are collected from the output of the NER phase, forcing the system to identify only a subset of entities that are relevant to the type of entities mentioned.

NOTE Although the full-text search mechanism offers a viable solution, it can be enhanced by incorporating a vector-based search to retrieve additional candidates that may not be identified through text matching.

The JSON result of the query when we pass "Zika" as an input term is shown next.

Listing 8.14 Example of updated NED results from the CS step

```
{
  "id": 0,
  "mention": "Zika",
  "label": "Organism",
  "start": 19,
  "end": 22,
  "candidates": [
    {
      "snomed_id": "50471002",
      "name": "Zika virus"
    },
    {
      "snomed_id": "3928002",
      "name": "Zika virus disease"
    },
    {
      "snomed_id": "762725007",
      "name": "Congenital Zika virus infection"
    }
  ]
}
```

The `candidates` field includes a list of potential matches or candidates the system found for each mention. Each candidate represents a possible interpretation of the mention based on SNOMED. The following fields characterize each candidate:

- `snomed_id`—The unique identifier for the concept in SNOMED
- `name`—The name of the medical entity associated with the `snomed_id`

In this case, the candidates are "Zika virus" (50471002), "Zika virus disease" (3928002), and "Congenital Zika virus infection" (762725007). These candidates represent possible medical meanings of "Zika" in clinical terminology, setting the stage for further refinement in the disambiguation phase.

8.4.3 Candidate disambiguation

The final phase of the NED process is CD (see figure 8.5). We apply a strategy that uses contextual information provided by other medical entities co-occurring with the target entities in a sentence. By cross-referencing these entities with the structured knowledge in the domain ontology, we can verify and refine the selected candidates to determine the most accurate match.

For example, consider a sentence that mentions both "Zika" and "microcephaly." The presence of "microcephaly" alongside "Zika" provides valuable context: it suggests an association with *Congenital Zika virus infection*, given that this infection is known to cause microcephaly. The disambiguation process can use this co-occurrence to prioritize *Congenital Zika virus infection* over other potential meanings of "Zika" (such as a general virus or an unrelated term).

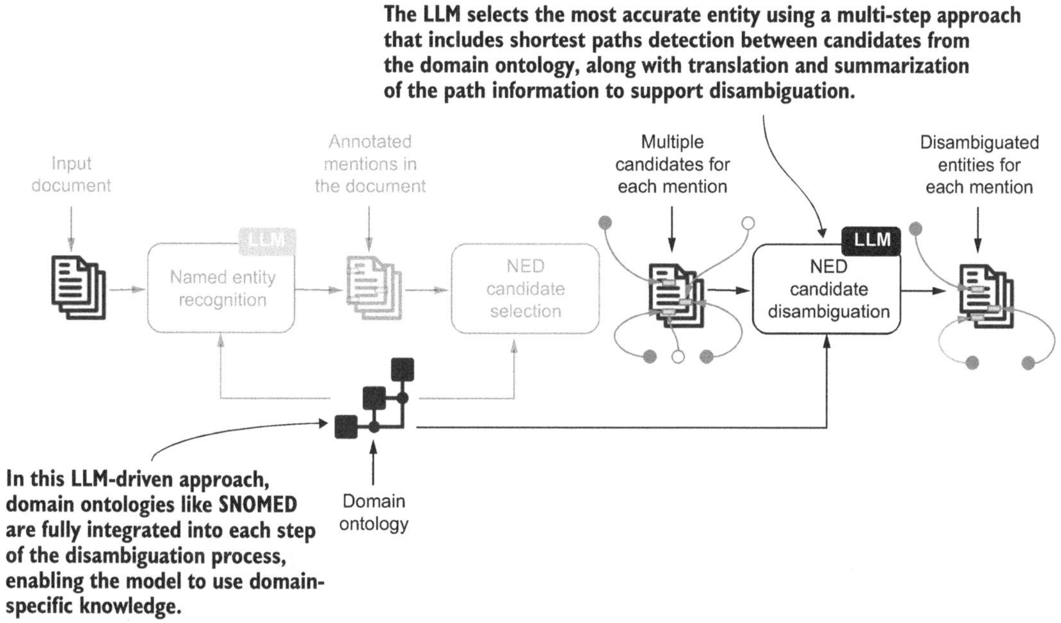

Figure 8.5 The third stage of NED is the candidate disambiguation. The goal is to select the best match among all the possible candidates identified in the previous step, by combining graph-based algorithms (shortest-path detection) and LLMs.

To generate disambiguated entities for each mention identified in the input document, we perform three steps:

1. *Detecting shortest paths*—We identify the minimal-length paths between the candidate entities associated with different mentions in a sentence. By mapping these connections, we establish potential relationships that help clarify the intended meaning of each mention.
2. *Translating paths to text*—To use the LLM's strengths in processing textual information, we translate each graph path that connects candidate entities into natural language sentences. This transformation enables the LLM to interpret relational information in a format it processes effectively.
3. *Summarizing textual paths*—We summarize all textual information derived from the translated paths into a synthetic explanation. This summary captures the essence of the relationships and supports the LLM in making more accurate disambiguation decisions.

Figure 8.6 provides an overview of these steps in the disambiguation process. LLMs empower the path-to-text translation and textual path summarization steps, enabling them to interpret and condense relational information effectively. Shortest-path detection, discussed next, uses Neo4j's Graph Data Science (GDS) library to identify connections between candidates.

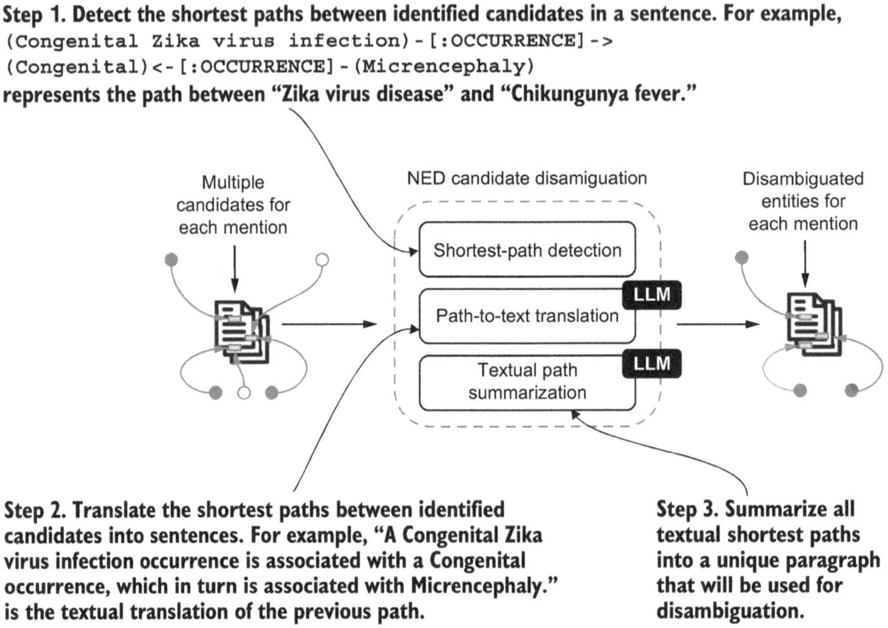

Figure 8.6 NED CD steps: (1) detecting the shortest paths between all the candidates related to the entity mentions in the sentence; (2) translating detected paths into natural language sentences; (3) summarizing those sentences into useful text for disambiguation

DETECTING SHORTEST PATHS

The goal of this step is to detect the shortest path between all the possible candidates associated with each medical entity mention identified during the CS phase. The following listing shows the query to perform this operation.

Listing 8.15 Python class for extracting relevant path from the SNOMED ontology

```
class PathExtraction():
  def __init__(self, model, store, candidates, named_entities):
    self.model = model
    self.store = store
    self.candidates = candidates
    self.named_entities = named_entities
  [...]

  def get_co_occs_query(self, s1_id, s2_id):
    query = f"""
      CALL gds.degree.stream('snomedGraph')
      YIELD nodeId, score
      WITH gds.util.asNode(nodeId).name AS name, score AS degree
      ORDER BY degree DESC
      LIMIT 350
      WITH collect(name) as hub_nodes
      MATCH (s1), (s2)
```

```
        WHERE s1.id="{s1_id}" AND
              s2.id="{s2_id}"
        WITH s1,
             s2,
             allShortestPaths((s1)-[:SNOMED_RELATION*1..2]-(s2)) AS paths,
             hub_nodes
        UNWIND paths AS path
        WITH relationships(path) AS path_edges, nodes(path) as path_nodes,
             hub_nodes
        WITH [n IN path_nodes | n.name] AS node_names,
             [r IN path_edges | r.type] AS rel_types,
             [n IN path_edges | startnode(n).name] AS rel_starts,
             hub_nodes
        WHERE not any(x IN node_names WHERE x IN hub_nodes)
        WITH [i in range(0, size(node_names)-1) | CASE
        WHEN i = size(node_names)-1
        THEN "(" + node_names[size(node_names)-1] + ")"
        WHEN node_names[i] = rel_starts[i]
        THEN "(" + node_names[i] + ")" + '-[:' + rel_types[i] + ']->'
        ELSE "(" + node_names[i] + ")" + '<-[:' + rel_types[i] + ']-' END]
        ➥ as string_paths
        RETURN DISTINCT apoc.text.join(string_paths, '') AS `Extracted paths`
    """.format(s1_id=s1_id, s2_id=s2_id, named_entities=named_entities)
    return query
[...]
```

The critical steps of this query are as follows:

- *Degree calculation*—The query first retrieves nodes with the highest "degree" (number of relationships) from the graph using `CALL Gds.Degree.Stream`. These nodes represent highly connected hub nodes, which will later be excluded to focus on more meaningful, less generic connections.
- *Shortest-path search*—The query finds all shortest paths between two entities, `s1` and `s2`, based on their IDs, limiting the path length to one or two hops (relationships). The relationships between these nodes are filtered to exclude "hub" nodes and avoid generic or overly broad relationships.
- *Path transformation*—Once paths are identified, the query unwinds them and collects both the nodes and relationships involved in each path. It then formats these paths into readable strings that show the direction and types of relationships (e.g., `(n1)-[:REL_TYPE]->(n2)`).

The next listing shows an example of detected paths.

Listing 8.16 Paths detected using the Neo4j GDS library

```
[
  {
    "id": 1,
    "path": "(Congenital Zika virus infection)-[:OCCURRENCE]->(Congenital)
    ➥ <-[:OCCURRENCE]-(Micrencephaly)"
  },
  {
```

```
    "id": 2,
    "path": "(Congenital Zika virus infection)-[:OCCURRENCE]->(Congenital)
   ➥<-[:OCCURRENCE]-(Acrocephaly)"""
  },
  {
    "id": 3,
    "path": "(Congenital Zika virus infection)-[:OCCURRENCE]->(Congenital)
   ➥<-[:OCCURRENCE]-(Multiple congenital malformations)"
  },
  {
    "id": 4,
    "path": "(Congenital Zika virus infection)-[:OCCURRENCE]->(Congenital)
   ➥<-[:OCCURRENCE]-(Congenital malformation)"
  },
  {
    "id": 5,
    "path": "(Congenital Zika virus infection)-[:OCCURRENCE]->(Congenital)
   ➥<-[:OCCURRENCE]-([X]Other congenital malformations)"
  },
  {
    "id": 6,
    "path": "(Micrencephaly)-[:OCCURRENCE]->(Congenital)
   ➥<-[:OCCURRENCE]-(Multiple congenital malformations)"
  },
  {
    "id": 7,
    "path": "(Micrencephaly)-[:OCCURRENCE]->(Congenital)
   ➥<-[:OCCURRENCE]-(Congenital malformation)"
  },
  {
    "id": 8,
    "path": "(Micrencephaly)-[:OCCURRENCE]->(Congenital)
   ➥<-[:OCCURRENCE]-([X]Other congenital malformations)"
  },
  {
    "id": 9,
    "path": "(Acrocephaly)-[:OCCURRENCE]->(Congenital)
   ➥<-[:OCCURRENCE]-(Multiple congenital malformations)"
  },
  {
    "id": 10,
    "path": "(Acrocephaly)-[:IS_A]->(Craniosynostosis syndrome)
   ➥-[:IS_A]->(Congenital malformation)"
  },
  {
    "id": 11,
    "path": "(Acrocephaly)-[:PATHOLOGICAL_PROCESS_(ATTRIBUTE)]
   ➥->(Pathological developmental process)
   ➥<-[:PATHOLOGICAL_PROCESS_(ATTRIBUTE)]-(Congenital malformation)"
  },
  {
   "id": 12,
   "path": "(Acrocephaly)-[:OCCURRENCE]->(Congenital)
  ➥<-[:OCCURRENCE]-(Congenital malformation)"
```

```
  },
  {
  "id": 13,
  "path": "(Acrocephaly)-[:OCCURRENCE]->(Congenital)
  ➥<-[:OCCURRENCE]-([X]Other congenital malformations)"
 }
]
```

In this JSON output, each entry contains an ID and a path, and each path shows a relational link between biomedical entities based on their co-occurrence in ontology paths. Here are the details:

- *Congenital Zika virus infection paths*—Many paths begin with *Congenital Zika virus infection* linked to various congenital conditions, such as *Micrencephaly*, *Acrocephaly*, and *Multiple congenital malformations*, through the relationship type `[:OCCURRENCE]`. This implies that *Congenital Zika virus infection* is associated with these conditions, possibly as a cause or occurrence.
- *Shared congenital condition*—*Congenital* is a common node linking multiple congenital conditions like *Micrencephaly* and *Acrocephaly*. This central node indicates that these conditions share a similar occurrence attribute.
- *Alternative relationships*—Some paths use relationships like `[:IS_A]` and `[:PATHOLOGICAL_PROCESS_(ATTRIBUTE)]`, showing hierarchical or attribute-based relationships. For instance, *Acrocephaly* is classified under *Craniosynostosis syndrome*, which is linked to *Congenital malformation*.

TRANSLATING PATHS TO TEXT

This step translates graph paths into sentences, which allows LLMs to process complex relational data in a format they are optimized to understand: natural language. This transformation makes it easier for the model to interpret connections between entities, providing context that aids in distinguishing between similar terms. The following is a simplified version of the prompt for translating paths into sentences.

Listing 8.17 Simplified version of the prompt for translating paths into sentences

```
system = """You are an assistant capable of translating a Neo4j graph path
➥into a clear sentence.
Use the exact entity names from the path while generating the sentence.
The sentences will assist a large language model (LLM) in disambiguating
➥biomedical entities.
Ensure the output is a valid JSON with no extraneous characters."""

input = {
  "path": "
  ➥(Hypertension)-[:RISK_FACTOR_FOR]->(Cardiovascular Disease)
  ➥<-[:ASSOCIATED_WITH]-(Myocardial Infarction)"
}

assistant = {
  "sentence": "Hypertension is a risk factor for cardiovascular
  ➥disease. Myocardial infarction is also associated with cardiovascular
```

```
➥disease, indicating that hypertension may increase the risk of
➥experiencing a myocardial infarction through its connection to
➥cardiovascular disease."
}
```

Here are the details of the prompt:

- *System instruction*—The system translates Neo4j graph paths into clear, human-readable sentences.
- *Input graph paths*—In this case, the input consists of a graph path from a Neo4j database, which might represent complex relationships.
- *Assistant output*—The system responds with a valid JSON structure showing the generated sentence.

Each graph path is translated into a single, clear sentence, as shown in the following listing.

Listing 8.18 Results of the path's translation into natural language

```
[{
  "sentence": "A Congenital Zika virus infection occurrence is associated
  ➥with a Congenital occurrence, which in turn is associated with
  ➥Micrencephaly."
 },
 {
  "sentence": "A Congenital Zika virus infection occurrence is associated
  ➥with a Congenital occurrence, which in turn is associated with an
  ➥Acrocephaly occurrence."
 },
[...],
 {
  "sentence": "Micrencephaly occurs in Congenital and Multiple congenital
  ➥malformations also occur in Congenital."
 },
 {
  "sentence": "Micrencephaly occurs in Congenital and is also an occurrence
  ➥of Congenital malformation."
 },
 [...],
 {
  "sentence": "Acrocephaly occurs in Congenital and Other congenital
  ➥malformations also occur in Congenital."
 }]
```

These JSON entries make the graph paths accessible for an LLM to interpret and use for disambiguation.

SUMMARIZING TEXTUAL PATHS

Before executing the final disambiguation of the selected candidates, we need to summarize the sentences representing the translated graph paths. Doing so reduces the "cognitive load" for the model (fewer tokens), making it easier to interpret entity relationships and select the most accurate candidate without being overwhelmed by excessive detail. The next listing shows a simplified version of the prompt.

Listing 8.19 Simplified prompt for summarizing textual paths

```
system = """You are an assistant that can summarize multiple sentences
➥derived from ontology paths into a short summary. This summary will be
➥used to support a named entity disambiguation task.
Ensure the output is a valid JSON with no extraneous characters."""

input = {
  "sentences": [
    {
      "id": 1,
      "sentence": "Hypertension is a risk factor for cardiovascular
      ➥disease. Myocardial infarction is also associated with cardiovascular
      ➥disease, indicating that hypertension may increase the risk of
      ➥experiencing a myocardial infarction through its connection to
      ➥cardiovascular disease."
    },
    {
      "id": 2,
      "sentence": "Diabetes mellitus is a complication that arises from
      ➥an endocrine disorder. Diabetic retinopathy is also associated with
      ➥endocrine disorders, suggesting that diabetes mellitus can lead to the
      ➥development of diabetic retinopathy through its link to endocrine
      ➥dysfunction."
    },
    {
      "id": 3,
      "sentence": "Asthma is associated with respiratory disorders.
      ➥Allergic rhinitis is also linked to respiratory disorders, which
      ➥implies that individuals with asthma may also experience allergic
      ➥rhinitis due to their common association with respiratory
      ➥conditions."
    },
    {
      "id": 4,
      "sentence": "Osteoporosis leads to bone weakness. Bone fractures
      ➥are a result of bone weakness, indicating that osteoporosis can
      ➥increase the likelihood of bone fractures due to the weakened state
      ➥of the bones."
    }
  ]

assistant = {
  "context": "Hypertension is a risk factor for cardiovascular disease,
  ➥which in turn increases the likelihood of experiencing a myocardial
  ➥infarction. Similarly, diabetes mellitus is linked to endocrine disorders,
  ➥potentially leading to complications such as diabetic retinopathy. Asthma
  ➥and allergic rhinitis are both associated with respiratory disorders,
  ➥suggesting a common link between these conditions. Finally, osteoporosis
  ➥weakens bones, making individuals more susceptible to bone fractures."
}
```

Here are the details of the prompt:

- *System instruction*—The system is instructed to summarize sentences derived from ontology paths, retaining all identified entities in the summaries. The output should be formatted as a valid JSON object, with each summary provided as a string under the key `context`.
- *Input sentences*—The input consists of multiple sentences, each containing relationships between medical conditions and their effects or associations.
- *Assistant output*—The system responds with a single summarized sentence for each group of related entities in a valid JSON format.

The output structure summarizes the core relationships in the input sentences, preserving the critical entities and relationships (listing 8.20).

Listing 8.20 Results of the summarization phase

```
{"context": "A Congenital Zika virus infection occurrence is associated
➥with various congenital malformations, including Micrencephaly,
➥Acrocephaly, Multiple congenital malformations, and Other congenital
➥malformations. These conditions all share a common link to the Congenital
➥entity."}
```

This result provides the LLM with a distilled version of complex relational information, allowing it to focus on the most relevant context for disambiguation.

DISAMBIGUATION

In the final stage, we combine all the ingredients for the disambiguation, including the selected candidates and the textual details provided by the summarization phase. The next listing shows the prompt for the disambiguation.

Listing 8.21 Prompt for final disambiguation

```
system = """You are an assistant specialized in entity disambiguation.
Your task is to identify and accurately disambiguate the entities
➥mentioned in a given sentence, relying heavily on the contextual entities
➥present in surrounding sentences:
1. Original Sentence: The sentence that contains ambiguous entities that
need to be resolved.
2. Candidate Entities: A list of potential entities extracted from the
sentence, with each entity having multiple possible meanings or labels.
3. Contextual Sentences: A collection of related or surrounding sentences
that provide additional context for disambiguating the mentioned entities.
Your objective is to use the entities mentioned in the contextual sentences
➥as the primary source of information to disambiguate the entities in the
➥original sentence. Analyze the candidate entities for each ambiguous
➥mention and select the one that aligns best with both the context and the
➥meaning provided by the contextual sentences. The output must be a valid
➥JSON."""
```

```
input = {
  "sentence": "Asthma and allergic rhinitis are commonly addressed
  ➥together in treatment protocols, given their shared underlying
  ➥inflammatory processes in allergic individuals.",
  "candidates": [
    {
      "id": 1,
      "candidates": [
        {
          "snomed_id": "233681001",
          "name": "Extrinsic asthma with asthma attack"
        },
        {
          "snomed_id": "195967001",
          "name": "Asthma"
        },
        {
          "snomed_id": "266361008",
          "name": "Intrinsic asthma"
        },
        {
          "snomed_id": "266364000",
          "name": "Asthma attack"
        },
        {
          "snomed_id": "270442000",
          "name": "Asthma monitored"
        },
        {
          "snomed_id": "170642006",
          "name": "Asthma severity"
        },
        {
          "snomed_id": "170643001",
          "name": "Occasional asthma"
        },
        {
          "snomed_id": "170644007",
          "name": "Mild asthma"
        },
        {
          "snomed_id": "170645008",
          "name": "Moderate asthma"
        }
      ]
    }
  ],
"context":"Asthma is associated with respiratory disorders. Allergic
➥rhinitis is also linked to respiratory disorders, which implies that
➥individuals with asthma may also experience allergic rhinitis due to their
➥common association with respiratory conditions."}

  }
```

```
assistant = {
  "entities": [
    {
      "id": 1,
      "disambiguation": {
        "snomed_id": "195967001",
        "name": "Asthma"
      }
    },
    {
      "id": 2,
      "disambiguation": {
        "snomed_id": "61582004",
        "name": "Allergic rhinitis"
      }
    }
  ]
}
```

Here are the details of the prompt:

- *System instruction*—The system is directed to identify and accurately disambiguate ambiguous entities. It must analyze each entity in the original sentence and select the candidate that best aligns with the contextual meaning provided by the summarized contextual information, prioritizing entities that align with these contextual details.
- *Input structure*:
  - *Original sentence*—The primary sentence contains ambiguous entities that require disambiguation.
  - *Candidate entities*—A list of potential SNOMED entities for each mention, each with multiple possible interpretations or labels.
  - *Contextual sentences*—Additional sentences that provide context to help clarify the meaning of each ambiguous entity in the original sentence.
- *Assistant output*:
  - `id`—A unique identifier for the entity mention
  - `disambiguation`—An object with the selected SNOMED entity, including `snomed_id` and `name`, that best matches the contextual information

We achieved the following result by passing the LLM the input sentence "Severe outcomes of Zika are due to its capacity to cross the placental barrier during pregnancy, causing microcephaly and congenital malformations."

Listing 8.22 Results of the disambiguation process

```
{
  "entities": [
    {
      "id": 0,
```

```
      "disambiguation": {
        "snomed_id": "762725007",
        "name": "Congenital Zika virus infection"
      }
    },
    {
      "id": 1,
      "disambiguation": {
        "snomed_id": "204030002",
        "name": "Micrencephaly"
      }
    },
    {
      "id": 2,
      "disambiguation": {
        "snomed_id": "116022009",
        "name": "Multiple congenital malformations"
      }
    }
  ]
}
```

Each entity is matched to the most relevant concept in the SNOMED ontology, allowing for precise identification and classification based on contextual information.

8.5 Conclusions

Thus chapter provided an in-depth exploration of a NED system that uses open LLMs and domain-specific ontologies. By integrating domain ontologies like SNOMED with open and general-purpose LLMs such as Llama 3.1 8B, we can address some of the limitations of traditional NLP tools in the biomedical domain, such as scispaCy. Our flexible approach can adapt across application domains: using Neo4j's GDS library for shortest-path detection and full-text search, combined with the disambiguation power of LLMs, enables a robust system for identifying and accurately disambiguating entities in complex texts. Through techniques like path-to-text translation and textual path summarization, we improved the LLM's ability to process relational data in a natural language format, enhancing its capacity to distinguish between similar entities. This framework lays the groundwork for future applications of LLMs in domain-specific NED tasks.

Summary

- Named entity disambiguation is essential for accurately identifying and distinguishing entities in complex domains.
- Traditional NLP tools such as scispaCy can't be used in diverse domains and can't use the relationships between entities, and their reference knowledge can't be extended and updated.
- Combining general-purpose LLMs and domain ontologies allows us to address these problems: LLMs can be driven by the continuously updated knowledge incorporated by the ontology, and use its relational structure.

- We deployed a flexible end-to-end process for NED, including multiple phases involving LLMs and domain ontologies.
- To take full advantage of the capabilities of LLMs combined with the graph dimension of domain ontologies, disambiguation is divided into three stages: detecting shortest paths, translating paths to text, and summarizing text paths.
- Future NED applications can use this framework and adapt to other domains characterized by rich ontologies describing the relational nature of their entities.

Part 4

Machine learning on knowledge graphs

This part of the book explores how representation learning and graph neural networks can transform the static knowledge contained in graphs into dynamic, learnable features:

- Neural-network-based representations capture the complexity of graph structures and their entities.
- Structured information can be effectively encoded in vector spaces.
- Flexible feature representations support downstream tasks, from classification to link prediction.
- Interpretation of learned embeddings allows automated knowledge extraction.

Chapter 9 introduces the fundamental concepts and motivations for applying machine learning (ML) to KGs, establishing why graph-based approaches better reflect real-world dependencies and how they can be applied to computational tasks.

Chapter 10 illustrates manual and semiautomated approaches to feature engineering in graph-based ML, demonstrating how graph metrics and structural patterns can be captured and utilized.

Chapter 11 shows how graph neural networks can automatically learn optimal representations from graph structures.

Chapter 12 demonstrates these concepts in action through two real-world implementations that showcase how graph neural networks can tackle business challenges while maintaining interpretability.

Many representation learning techniques mirror approaches used in modern language models. This parallel highlights the broader theme of our book: the combination of structured knowledge representation with advanced ML techniques.

9 Machine learning on knowledge graphs: A primer approach

This chapter covers

- Understanding machine learning on knowledge graphs
- Exploring common machine learning tasks performed on graphs
- Understanding the role of node and relationship representations

Building knowledge graphs is a crucial step in developing intelligent systems. It enables us to acquire holistic knowledge from multiple and diverse data sources, representing it in a way that supports exploration, navigation, and more advanced analytics. So far, we have seen how to query a graph and extract relevant information, how to navigate through nodes and relationship types, and even how to extract statistical information to validate the import process and evaluate the "quality" of the knowledge stored in the KG. These are all important steps in building *intelligent advisory systems* (IASs).

In an IAS, "advising" provides insights that users cannot extract on their own. For example, how can a researcher efficiently navigate a vast KG containing diseases, proteins, genes, and compounds to identify potential opportunities for repurposing drugs? Or, how can a clinician combine patients' symptoms and DNA sequences with literature, clinical trials, and standard protocols to develop personalized treatment plans? There are many such scenarios. And most, if not all, require using machine learning (ML) algorithms that take the knowledge in the graphs as input.

Chapters 9–12 delve into the realm of ML on KGs. We'll extend our previous book [1] with new algorithms and theories. These, in the last few years, have been improved (in particular graph neural networks [GNNs]) and tested on graphs (such as LLMs). We'll also discuss new libraries that are stable and performant enough to be considered in a production environment.

9.1 Machine learning on graphs: Why?

We begin by giving you a clear understanding of why executing ML on (knowledge) graphs can be valuable (with and without LLMs) and why this approach is sometimes the optimal—or even the only feasible—choice. The key reasons can be summarized as follows:

- *Data representation*—Data used or produced by real-world applications has diverse forms, from matrixes and tensors to sequences and time series [2]. Graphs provide a universal data representation; many kinds of data from a wide variety of systems can be transformed into graphs.
- *Problem modeling*—A huge number of problems can be addressed as a small set of computational tasks on graphs. For example, detecting anomalous nodes and suggesting medications for patients can be summarized as problems of node classification, and making recommendations and identifying interactions are essentially problems of relationship prediction.
- *Data item dependency*—Traditional ML algorithms assume that data items are independent and identically distributed. But in many real-world use cases, data items are intrinsically connected, and ignoring these relationships can lead to incomplete or wrong results. Storing data as graphs, which naturally store relationships, and applying computational tasks on those graphs can give better results [3].

ML techniques like GNNs together with LLMs create powerful IASs by combining the GNN's ability to detect complex structural patterns with the LLM's natural language understanding and generation capabilities. For example, in personalized medicine, GNNs process patient similarity networks and biological pathway graphs, while LLMs synthesize medical literature and clinical guidelines to explain treatment rationales in clear medical terminology. This GNN–LLM integration enables the system to identify complex patterns and explain them in context-appropriate language, making insights accessible and actionable for end users.

You want to use the best tool possible to achieve your final goal and solve your business problem. ML is inherently a problem-driven discipline; so for many of the scenarios we'll consider, ML on graphs will be the best arrow in your bow.

9.2 Machine learning on graphs: What?

Classical ML algorithms can be categorized in different ways. The most common approach differentiates them according to the type of data and the task they solve, classifying them as supervised or unsupervised:

- In a *supervised* algorithm, data is partially labeled: the output is known for certain data items, and the goal is to predict the labels for the remaining data. A typical example of this learning process is a spam filter. The learner requires labels, such as "spam" and "not spam" (the significant information), in the training dataset for each data item (emails). It learns from these labels how to classify an email.
- In an *unsupervised* algorithm, the data is fully unlabeled, and the goal is to extract insights and patterns from it, such as clusters from a set of data points or communities from a graph.

ML on graphs is no different, but in this case the supervised and unsupervised categories are not necessarily the most useful [4], even though they remain valid: for example, node classification can be considered a supervised task (even though it isn't, exactly), and community detection is unsupervised. Instead, ML tasks on graphs are generally divided into these two categories (see figure 9.1):

- *Node-focused tasks*—The entire dataset is represented as one graph, with nodes and relationships as the data points.
- *Graph-focused tasks*—The data consists of a set of graphs, and each data point is an entire graph.

In this section, we will go through the most important and well-studied ML tasks on graph data. We'll outline the primary tasks in each category, focusing on those that you're likely to find the most useful.

9.2.1 Node classification

Suppose you manage a social network with millions of users. Among these users are a substantial number of bots. Detecting these bots is important because they could violate the network's terms of service, spread fake news, or be irrelevant targets for marketing campaigns. Manually identifying them is infeasible. Ideally, you want a model that can differentiate users as either bots or legitimate users, given a small set of manually labeled examples. This is a classic example of a node classification task: for each unlabeled node u in graph V, the goal is to predict the label y_u, when we are only given the known labels on a training set of nodes V_{train} that is a small subset of V.

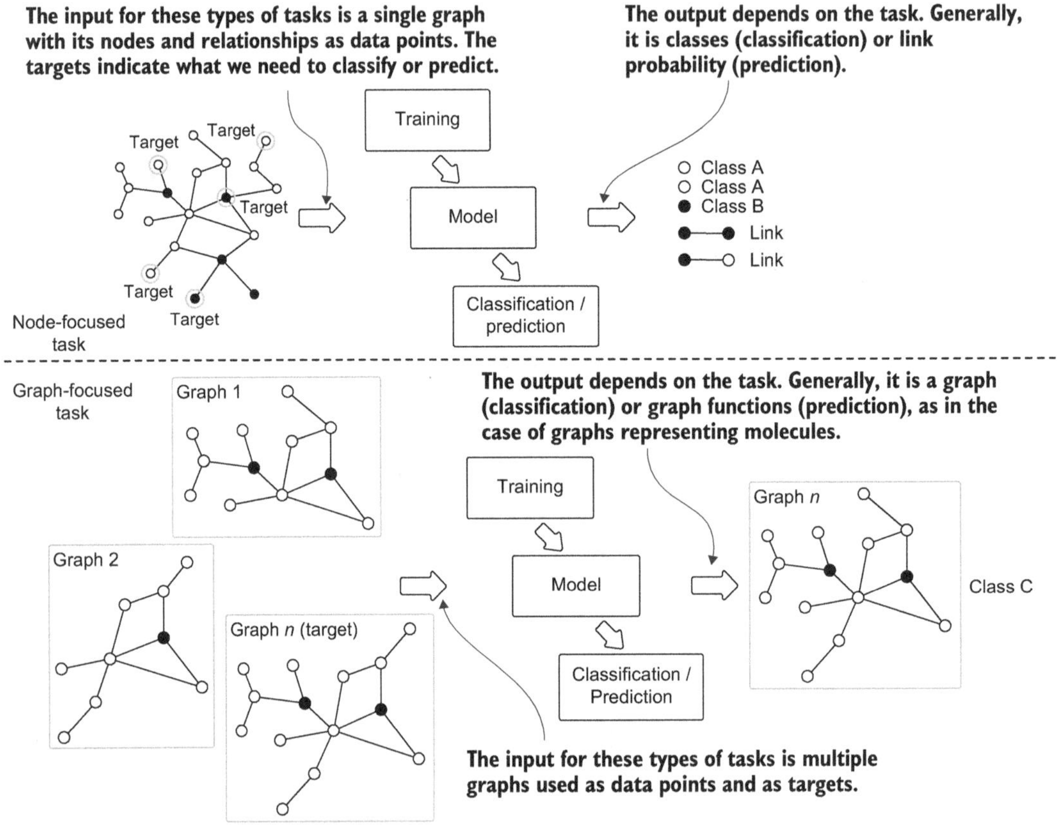

Figure 9.1 Node-focused and graph-focused tasks are represented in terms of expected input and output during training and prediction.

Other examples of node classification include classifying the function of proteins in the interactome [4] and classifying the topic of documents based on hyperlinks or citation graphs [5]. It is a powerful tool during the implementation of an IAS, helping with identification and decision-making. Figure 9.2 delineates the principal components and phases of node classification.

At first glance, node classification seems to be a straightforward variant of standard supervised classification, but there are distinct differences. Notably, the nodes in a graph are not *independent and identically distributed* (i.i.d.). Typically, in constructing supervised ML models, we assume that each data point is statistically independent of all other data points. If this is not the case, we may need to clarify the dependencies among all of our input points. Similarly, we assume that the data points are identically distributed, to ensure that our model can effectively generalize to unseen data points. But node classification shatters this i.i.d. assumption. Instead of modeling a set of i.i.d. data points, we're modeling an interconnected network of nodes.

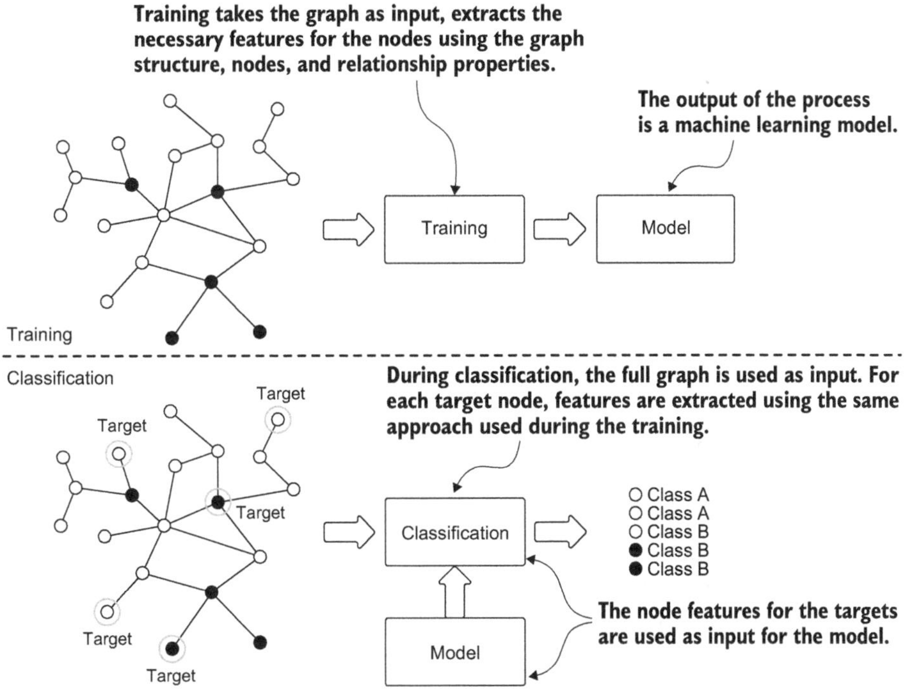

Figure 9.2 The typical flow of node classification. Like many supervised ML tasks, it has two phases: training and prediction (which, in this case, translates into classifying unclassified nodes).

Different graph types exhibit various relationship patterns that challenge the i.i.d. assumption. In social networks, *homophily* illustrates this interconnectedness: nodes influence each other through their relationships, exhibiting shared interests, attributes, and behaviors with their neighbors [6]. This violation of the i.i.d. assumption means that effective models must consider both node features and their network relationships when making predictions [7]. In protein interaction networks, structural equivalence becomes crucial—nodes with similar neighborhood structures tend to share functional properties [8]. *Heterophily* presents another pattern where nodes preferentially connect to those with different characteristics, further demonstrating how real-world data often violates i.i.d. assumptions. These principles underscore why treating nodes as independent data points fails to capture the rich relational information encoded in graphs. Successful node classification requires modeling both node attributes and their complex interdependencies.

Is node classification supervised or unsupervised?

Many researchers agree that node classification is *semisupervised* [9] because when we train node classification models, we usually have access to the full graph, including all the unlabeled (e.g., test) nodes. The only thing we are missing is the labels of

(continued)

the test nodes. However, we can still use information about the test nodes (e.g., knowledge of their neighborhood in the graph) to improve our model during training. This is different from the usual supervised setting, in which unlabeled data points are unobserved during training.

The general term for models that combine labeled and unlabeled data during training is *semisupervised learning*, so, understandably, this term is often used for node classification tasks. It is important to note, however, that standard formulations of semisupervised learning require the i.i.d. assumption, which does not hold for node classification. We still struggle with this definition. This shows why ML tasks on graphs do not easily fit classical categories!

Node classification can be expanded to assign multiple labels to a single node. For instance, Flickr (www.flickr.com), an image-hosting platform, uses graphs and multilabel node classification to address users' interests. In addition to hosting photos, Flickr serves as an online social community where users can follow each other, thus forming a network through these user connections. Moreover, Flickr users can subscribe to interest groups; these memberships signify user interests and can serve as user labels. Users can subscribe to numerous groups, so each user may be associated with multiple labels. A multilabel node classification problem on graphs can help predict potential groups that users might be interested in but haven't yet subscribed to; Tang and Liu [10] provide datasets related to such Flickr user behaviors.

9.2.2 *Link prediction (a.k.a. relationship prediction)*

Link prediction is a fundamental task in graph-based ML that identifies potential future connections between nodes. Consider a comprehensive database of research papers from domains such as healthcare (PubMed, https://pubmed.ncbi.nlm.nih.gov; MedRxiv, www.medrxiv.org), COVID-19 research (CORD-19, https://mng.bz/JwGQ), broad scientific research (Web of Science, https://mng.bz/qRPz), or computer science (DBLP, https://dblp.org). From these sources, we can construct a co-authorship graph in which authors represent nodes and edges represent their collaboration on at least one paper. The link prediction task then involves forecasting likely future collaborations between authors who haven't yet worked together.

This predictive approach extends naturally to other critical domains, such as law enforcement and security applications. Figure 9.3 illustrates the two primary phases of a typical link prediction task.

In many real-world applications, graphs are not complete because of missing edges. This incompleteness is usually due to one of two reasons. First, sometimes connections exist but are not observed or recorded—or, in certain cases, they are kept hidden by the key actors in the network. And second, many graphs are naturally evolving; for example, in an academic collaboration graph, an author can always build new collaboration relations with other authors by writing a new article. Inferring or

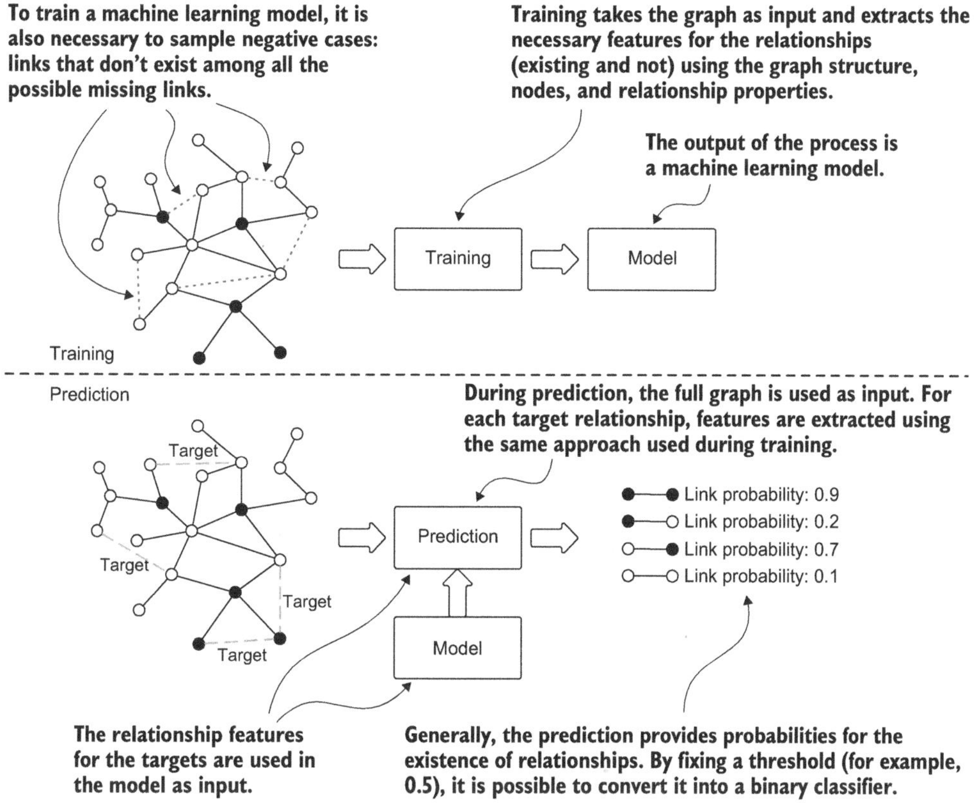

Figure 9.3 Typical link prediction flow. It has two phases. During the training phase, the graph is used as input, and the model is trained to determine whether a link exists. During the prediction phase, the model provides an output for each pair of nodes representing the target relationship to predict. It provides an existence probability for each.

predicting these missing edges can benefit many IASs, helping with friend recommendations [11, 12], product recommendations, KG completion [13], predicting drug side effects [14], inferring new facts in a relational database [15], discovering protein–protein interactions [16], analyzing criminal intelligence [17], and many more.

Names for the link prediction task

This task is known as *link prediction*, *graph completion*, or *relational inference*, among other names, depending on the application domain. *Link prediction* typically pertains to predicting the existence of a connection between two nodes, regardless of the relationship type (which is consistently the same and predetermined). Conversely, the term *relationship prediction* is generally used when we want to pinpoint not just the existence but also the type of relationships. In this book, we'll use these terms interchangeably.

Like node classification, link prediction is typically approached as a semisupervised learning task. Although specific links between node pairs may be missing, we can use both existing examples of connections and rich node-level information to predict potential relationships. This semisupervised nature allows us to use known patterns in the graph structure along with node attributes to infer likely missing or future connections between nodes.

9.2.3 Clustering and community detection

Imagine that you obtain a catalog of research papers from any of the sources mentioned in the previous section. You generate a collaborative graph connecting researchers who have coauthored papers. On inspecting this network, you're unlikely to observe a dense "hairball" where collaborations are equally probable among everyone. Instead, the graph is probably partitioned into distinct clusters of nodes grouped by such elements as research area, institution, or geographic factors. The propensity for two researchers from the same university to collaborate is higher than that of colleagues situated remotely. Similarly, two researchers in the same field are more likely to reference other researchers in that sphere than in an unrelated domain. This natural clustering behavior forms the theoretical foundation for community detection algorithms, which aim to identify these inherent groupings in the network structure (see figure 9.4).

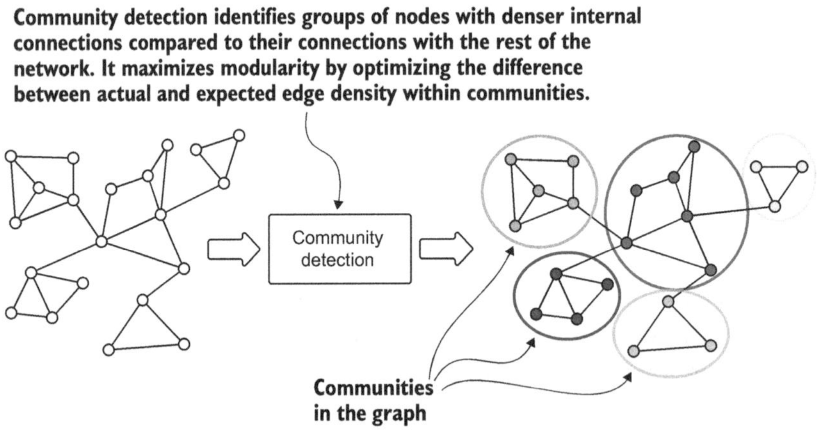

Figure 9.4 Flow of community detection. The input is a graph, and the output is a mapping between nodes and groups (circled in the image).

Community detection uncovers latent group structures in a graph using only the network's topology and relationships. This task has diverse real-world applications, from identifying functional modules in genetic interaction networks [18] to detecting fraudulent user groups in financial transaction networks [19].

One of the most powerful applications of graph clustering is in graph description and summarization. By identifying densely connected regions, clustering provides a higher-level view of the network's organization. This capability is particularly valuable when dealing with large-scale graphs that defy direct visualization or comprehensive manual analysis, effectively providing a structural summary of complex network relationships.

Names for the community detection task

The terms *community detection* and *graph clustering* are often used interchangeably in network analysis, but they differ fundamentally from traditional clustering algorithms like K-means and DBSCAN. K-means partitions *n* data points into *k* clusters by iteratively assigning each point to the nearest cluster center (centroid) and updating these centers; *k* must be specified in advance. DBSCAN (density-based spatial clustering of applications with noise) groups together points that are closely packed (points with many nearby neighbors) while marking points in low-density regions as outliers; it doesn't require specifying the number of clusters beforehand.

The key distinction lies in the data structure: traditional clustering algorithms work with independent data points in vector space, whereas graph clustering specifically handles interconnected data in which relationships between nodes are crucial to determining group membership. We'll use these terms interchangeably, as they refer to the same task when applied to graphs.

Graph clustering is generally unsupervised, requiring no prelabeled information to identify community structures. However, some clustering approaches, such as label propagation [20], can incorporate existing labels to guide community assignment, bridging the gap between supervised and unsupervised learning in graph analysis.

The three previous algorithms belong to the category of node-focused tasks. Next, we'll look at one that is graph-focused.

9.2.4 Graph classification

Consider the task of predicting the toxicity and solubility of chemical molecules. These properties emerge not just from individual atoms but also from how these atoms are connected to form the molecule. We can represent each molecule as a graph, where atoms serve as nodes and chemical bonds as edges [21]. This graph representation allows us to apply graph classification techniques to predict multiple molecular properties simultaneously. As illustrated in figure 9.5, graph classification can systematically analyze the atomic composition and structural patterns to categorize previously unlabeled molecules based on properties such as solubility and toxicity.

Whereas node classification predicts labels for individual nodes in a single graph, graph classification deals with datasets containing multiple independent graphs, each representing a complete sample (such as a molecule). In graph classification, each graph serves as an i.i.d. data point with its label: for instance, whether a molecule is toxic.

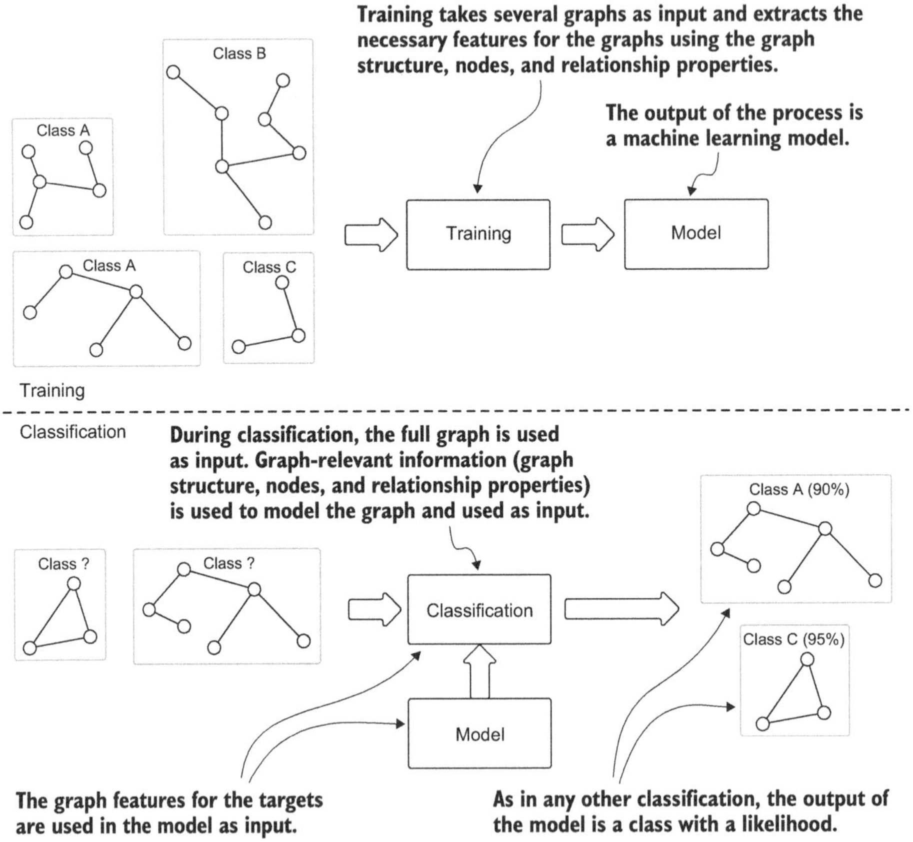

Figure 9.5 Flow of graph classification. Like many supervised tasks, it has two phases. During training, it trains different graphs with related classes to recognize the class of each. And during prediction, the model predicts the class of a graph.

The goal of graph classification is to learn a mapping from entire graphs to their associated labels using a training set of labeled graphs. Similarly, graph clustering at the graph level extends traditional unsupervised clustering to categorize entire graphs rather than nodes. The primary challenge in these graph-level tasks lies in developing features that effectively capture both the internal structure of each graph and the properties of its components.

Graph clustering has many real-world applications, such as in IASs. For example, enzymes are a type of protein. Proteins can be represented as graphs, where amino acids are nodes, and edges between two nodes can be created if they are less than a certain distance apart. After the training, given a protein, the graph classification algorithm can predict whether it is an enzyme. Another example is a malware classifier: the task in this case is to build a classification model to detect whether a computer program is malicious by analyzing a graph-based representation of its syntax and data flow [22].

9.3 Machine learning on graphs: How?

At this point, we understand why ML on graphs has emerged as a distinct branch of research and the complexities these algorithms can address. Now we'll explore our implementation options. Generally, solutions can be developed in two directions, as summarized in figure 9.6. The first approach uses algorithms specifically designed for graphs, such as collective classification [23]. These specialized algorithms directly process the graph structure, simultaneously considering both node features and neighborhood relationships to make predictions. The second approach transforms the graph problem into a traditional ML task by first converting graph structures into feature vectors. This feature engineering step allows us to use the entire ecosystem of existing ML algorithms, including modern deep learning techniques. The main challenge then shifts to defining appropriate features that capture the essential characteristics of nodes, edges, and, in the case of graph classification, the entire graph structure.

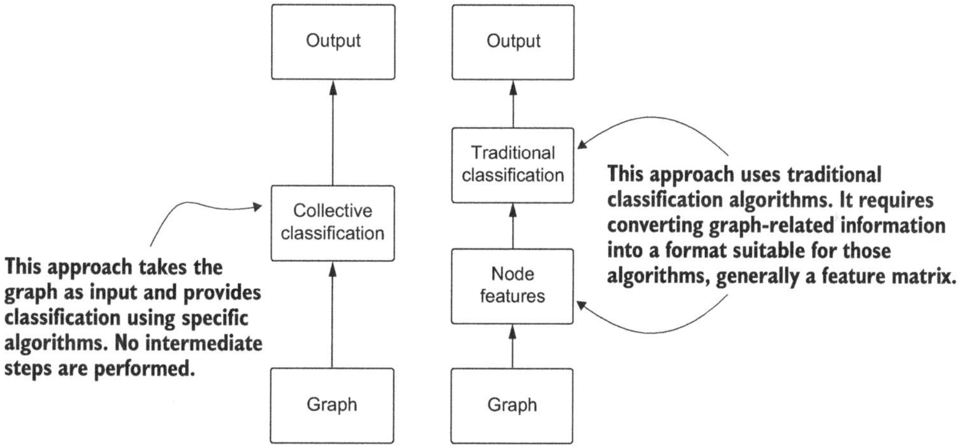

Figure 9.6 A graph-based classification approach (collective) versus traditional algorithms for classification

In this part of the book, we focus on feature engineering for graphs. We begin by exploring manual feature extraction methods, demonstrating their thoroughness but also their tedious nature. We then progress to semiautomated approaches before diving into GNNs as a powerful solution for automated feature learning. GNNs excel at capturing both structural patterns and node properties, making them particularly valuable for incomplete KGs. We'll examine how GNNs create meaningful vector embeddings that encode graph knowledge in ways that directly benefit downstream ML tasks such as classification (for node classification, for example).

9.3.1 Node classification and link prediction

Figure 9.7 shows the high-level training process for node classification and link prediction. As a result of this training, a prediction model is created: it is the output of this phase and the input of the next phase. Figure 9.8 shows the steps of the prediction process, which takes the existing nodes and relationships and predicts classes and missing links.

NOTE The featurization process used during training must be the same as that used for making predictions. Otherwise, the prediction phase will not function correctly.

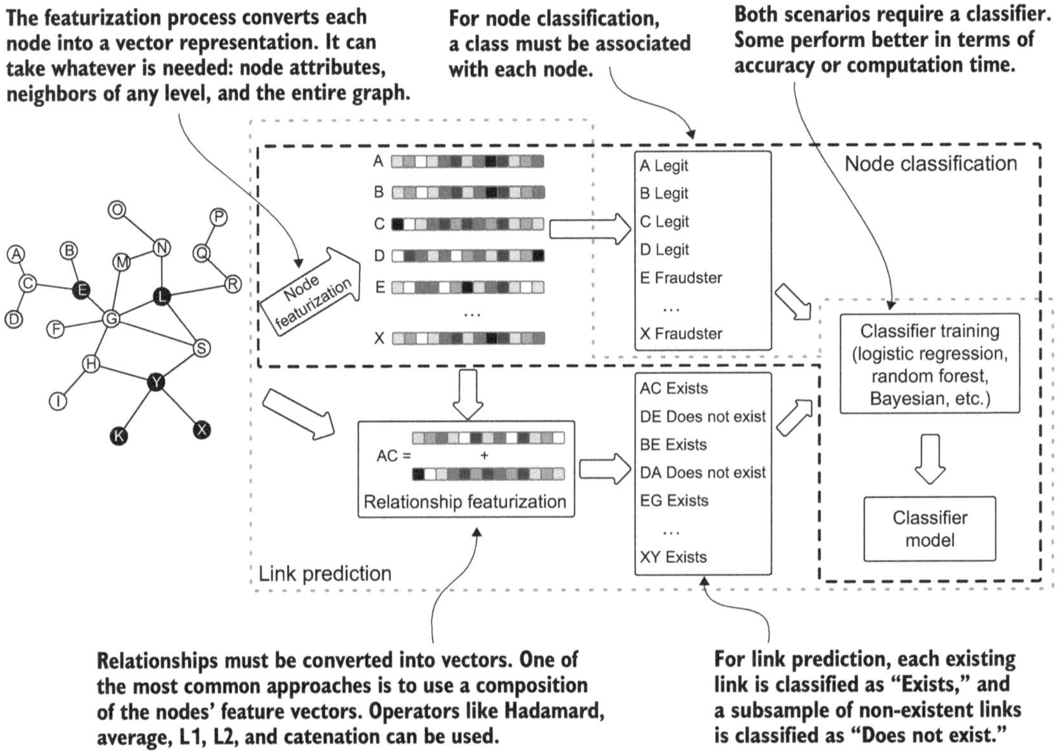

Figure 9.7 Training flow for node classification and link prediction. A critical step is the featurization of nodes and relationships. When this process is finished, the vectors can be passed to a classic algorithm. Both node classification and link prediction can be seen as classification tasks.

Let's put these principles into practice with a simple example. Suppose you would like to classify nodes in a network. For learning purposes, we will use a small graph: the famous Zachary Karate Club [24]. The graph documents the relationships among 34 members of a karate club, tracking interactions between pairs of members outside the

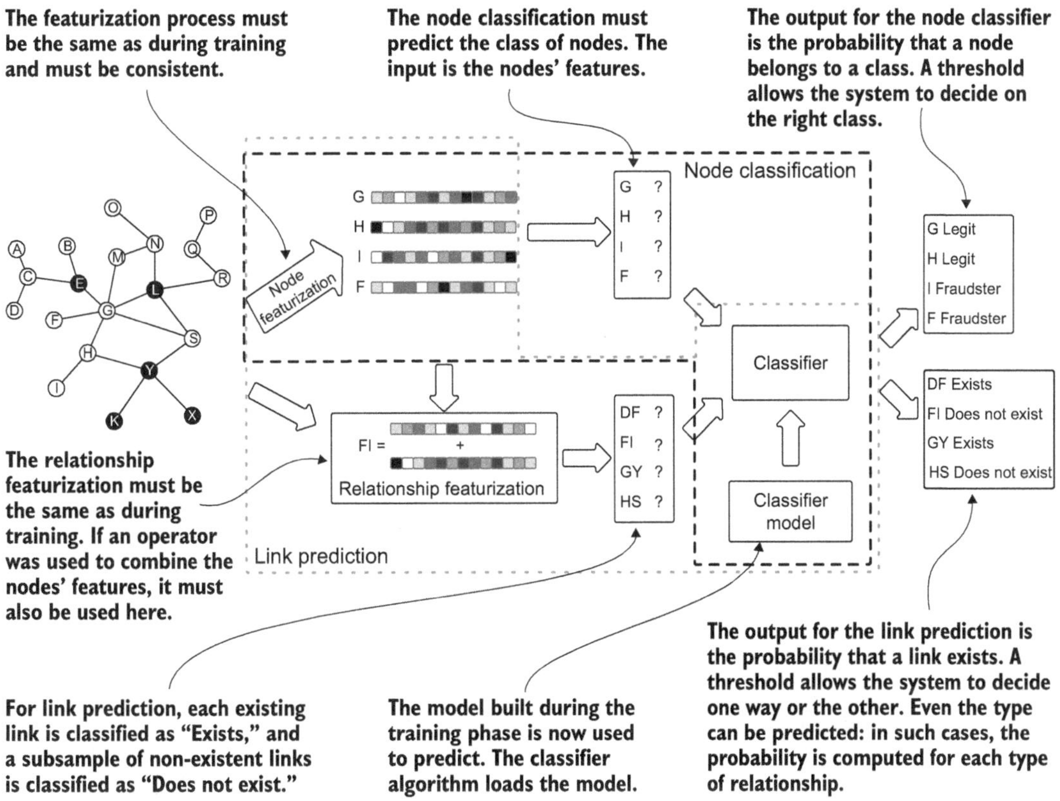

Figure 9.8 Prediction flow for node classification and link prediction. The featurization process should be the same as during training. The classifier model built previously is used in this phase to make predictions.

club. A dispute between the administrator, "John A," and the instructor, "Mr. Hi" (pseudonyms), caused the club to divide into two factions.

After the club's split, each member (represented as a node) either became affiliated with the instructor's new club (Mr. Hi) or remained with the administrator's original club (John A). This real-world outcome provides us with ground-truth labels: each node is labeled according to which club the member ultimately joined. Our node classification task is to predict these club affiliations using only the friendship network structure that existed before the split, demonstrating how network patterns can predict social behavior. We'll explain, using simple code, the entire flow described in figures 9.7 and 9.8.

Let's inspect the network first and then analyze it. For this example, we won't store anything in Neo4j. The network is very small, and it is available out of the box in many network analysis tools, as well as in Networkx (https://networkx.org), which is the tool we will use. The following listing shows how to import the necessary packages and load the karate club graph.

Listing 9.1 Creating and drawing a karate club network

```
import networkx as nx
import matplotlib.pyplot as plt

G = nx.karate_club_graph()                    <- Loads the karate club graph
draw_and_save_graph_picture(G)

def draw_and_save_graph_picture(G):           <- Displays the graph onscreen and saves it in PNG and SVG formats
    set_club_colors(G)
    layout_position = nx.spring_layout(G, k=8 / math.sqrt(G.order()))
    colors = [n[1]['color'] for n in G.nodes(data=True)]
    nx.draw_networkx(G, pos=layout_position, node_color=colors)
    plt.axis('off')
    plt.savefig("Karate_Graph.svg", format="SVG", dpi=1000)
    plt.savefig("Karate_Graph.png", format="PNG", dpi=1000)
    plt.show()

def set_club_colors(G):                       <- Assigns a color to each node group
    for node in G.nodes(data=True):
        color = '#00fff9'
        if node[1]['club'] == 'Mr. Hi':
            color = '#e6e6fa'
        node[1]['color'] = color
```

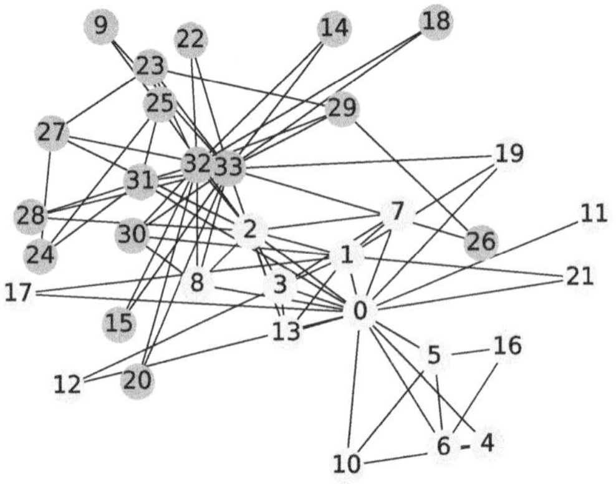

Figure 9.9 The karate club graph produced by the code in listing 9.1, with the shades of the nodes representing the club the member ultimately joined

The resulting network is shown in figure 9.9. The nodes are two different shades, representing the club each member ultimately joined after the split.

As described in figures 9.7 and 9.8, the first step is creating a vector representation of each node that will serve as input for classification algorithms during training and prediction. Chapters 10 and 11 will explore sophisticated embedding techniques in detail; here, let's start with a simple approach: representing each node by its degree (the number of connections it has to other nodes). This feature captures a node's connectivity in the network. The next listing computes the degree of each node in the graph.

Listing 9.2 Representing each node by its degree

```
def compute_degree_embeddings(G):
                                                                    <- Computes the embedding for each node
    embeddings = np.array(list(dict(G.degree()).values()))
    embeddings = [[i] for i in embeddings]      <- Converts an element in the list into a single-value embedding
    return embeddings
```

> **Exercise**
>
> Although this technique is foundational, the degree of a node may not offer substantial help in classifying nodes for our goal. As an exercise, try using two other metrics: the degree of Mr. Hi's neighbors and the degree of John A's neighbors. They provide more insight for the algorithm to discern the group to which a node belongs. The solution is shown later in this chapter.

Before the advent of GNNs, Node2Vec [25] was a prominent technique for autonomous representation learning that computed node embeddings based purely on network structure. The following listing shows how to generate these structure-aware node embeddings using the Node2Vec algorithm.

Listing 9.3 Using Node2Vec as an embedding technique

```
def compute_complex_embeddings(G):
    node2vec = Node2Vec(
             G,
             dimensions=64,
             walk_length=30,
             num_walks=200,
             workers=4,
             seed=0)                 <-- Node2Vec library constructor
                                         precomputes probabilities and
                                         generates random walks.

    model = node2vec.fit(
             window=10,
             min_count=1,
             batch_words=4,
             seed=0)                 <-- Computes embeddings

    embeddings = [model.wv.get_vector(i) for i in G.nodes]
    return embeddings
```

This code does the following:

1. It initializes Node2Vec by specifying that a 64-dimensional vector should represent each node. The algorithm then performs 200 random walks through the graph, each visiting 30 nodes. For efficiency, it uses four parallel processes, and a random seed ensures reproducible results.
2. The model is trained using parameters inspired by Word2Vec: it considers 10 nodes before and after each walk sequence, includes all nodes in the training (even those visited once), and processes words in small batches.
3. It extracts the learned embeddings for each node in the graph, returning a list of vector representations in which each vector captures the node's structural role in the network. These embeddings can be used as input features for downstream ML tasks like node classification or link prediction.

Listings 9.2 and 9.3 compute the embedding for the full graph, so we don't need to compute it separately for the training set and then for prediction. The following listing shows an example of a training function that uses logistic regression as a classifier.

Listing 9.4 Training function

```
def train(self, train_dataset):
    node_embeddings = train_dataset.embeddings.values.tolist()
    node_labels = train_dataset.label.values.tolist()

    self.scaler = StandardScaler().fit(node_embeddings)
    scaled_embeddings = self.scaler.transform(node_embeddings)

    clf = LogisticRegressionCV(
        random_state=0,
        solver='liblinear',
        multi_class='ovr',
        max_iter=1000)
    self.model = clf.fit(scaled_embeddings, node_labels)
```

- node_embeddings is a matrix in which each row contains the vector representation (embedding) of a node.
- node_labels is a vector containing the class label for each node, aligned with node_embeddings.
- Standardizes the embeddings to have zero mean and unit variance
- Initializes a logistic regression classifier with cross-validation for automatic parameter tuning
- Trains the classifier using the standardized embeddings and their corresponding labels

This training process introduces two important ML concepts: feature standardization and logistic regression. *Feature standardization* is essential when working with multiple node features that operate on different scales. In our example, node degrees may range from single digits to thousands, and other metrics operate on different scales. By using `StandardScaler` to transform all features so they have zero mean and unit variance, we ensure that each feature contributes proportionally to the model's decisions, regardless of its original scale.

> **Why feature scaling matters**
>
> ML algorithms often rely on Euclidean distance calculations between data points. Without proper scaling, features with larger numerical ranges will dominate these calculations, regardless of their actual importance. For example, if node degree ranges from 1 to 1,000 and centrality measures range from 0 to 1, the degree will overwhelm the influence of centrality in distance-based calculations. This can lead to biased predictions and reduced model accuracy, as the model becomes overly sensitive to features simply because of their scale rather than their predictive power.

Logistic regression, despite its name, is a classification algorithm that excels at binary prediction tasks [25]. Here, it estimates the probability of a node belonging to a particular class. The algorithm transforms linear combinations of features into probabilities between 0 and 1 using the logistic function, making it ideal for our node classification task. For instance, in the karate club example, it predicts the probability of each member joining either the instructor's or administrator's club.

This implementation demonstrates a key advantage of our approach: by converting graph data into feature vectors through embeddings and proper scaling, we can use well-established ML algorithms. As shown in the following listing, the subsequent evaluation phase tests this model's accuracy by comparing predicted labels with actual outcomes for a held-out set of test nodes.

Listing 9.5 Making a prediction and comparing it with the actual value

```
def evaluate(self, test_dataset):
    test_embeddings = test_dataset.embeddings.values.tolist()
    true_labels = test_dataset.label.values.tolist()

    scaled_test_embeddings = self.scaler.transform(test_embeddings)

    predicted_labels = self.model.predict(scaled_test_embeddings)

    print("True labels:\t\t", true_labels)
    print("Predicted labels:\t", list(predicted_labels))

    # Calculate performance metrics
    metrics = precision_recall_fscore_support(true_labels,
    ➥predicted_labels, average='weighted')
    print('Precision:', metrics[0], 'Recall:', metrics[1], 'f-score:',
    ➥metrics[2])
    conf_matrix = confusion_matrix(true_labels, predicted_labels)
    print("Confusion Matrix:\t", conf_matrix)
```

- test_embeddings is a matrix in which each row contains the vector representation of a test node.
- true_labels contains the class labels for test nodes, aligned with test_embeddings.
- Standardizes test embeddings using the same scaler fitted on training data
- Predicts class labels for each test node using the trained model
- Calculates precision, recall, and F1-score by comparing predicted labels against true labels
- Generates a confusion matrix to visualize prediction accuracy across different classes

This function is useful for evaluating the quality of the predictive model. Our example has a very small network and just two labels, but the code also works for bigger graphs and multiple labels.

At this point, we have all the ingredients to perform the training and the evaluation of our node classification task. Listing 9.6 uses all the components (functions) from previous listings and prints the results. Switching from one embedding to the other just requires commenting and uncommenting the desired embedding function.

Listing 9.6 The full node classification process

```
G = nx.karate_club_graph()
draw_and_save_graph_picture(G)
```

```
labels = np.asarray([G.nodes[i]['club'] != 'Mr. Hi' for i in G.nodes])
    .astype(np.int64)                                    <-- Retrieves the label for each node and
                                                             assigns a value of 0 or 1 depending
#embeddings = compute_degree_embeddings(G)               <-- on the group it belongs to
embeddings = compute_complex_embeddings(G)
                                                             Select the embedding to
df = pd.DataFrame({                                          test by uncommenting the
        'nodeId': G.nodes,                                   option you wish to try.
        'embeddings': embeddings,
        'label': labels                                  Creates a DataFrame that includes the nodeId,
})                                                   <-- the full embedding, and the node labels

train, test = train_test_split(df, test_size=0.4, random_state=0)   <--

classifier = EvaluateEmbedding()                                     Divides the
classifier.train(train)               Invokes the functions          DataFrame into two
classifier.evaluate(test)             to create and evaluate         frames by randomly
                                                                     splitting the dataset
```

After running the code with the two different embedding techniques, we can see the different results in the following listing.

Listing 9.7 Results for the two embeddings

```
RESULTS WITH MORE SIMPLE EMBEDDINGS USING DEGREE

Gold:      [0, 1, 1, 0, 0, 1, 1, 0, 0, 1, 1, 1, 1, 0]
Predicted:     [1, 1, 0, 1, 0, 1, 0, 1, 0, 0, 0, 0, 1, 0]

Precision: 0.44642857142857145
Recall: 0.42857142857142855
f-score: 0.42857142857142855            Confusion matrix for first run: three true
                                        negatives (top-left), three false positives
Confusion Matrix:     [[3 3]            (top-right), five false negatives (bottom-left),
                       [5 3]]       <-- and three true positives (bottom-right)

RESULTS WITH MORE COMPLEX EMBEDDINGS USING NODE2VEC
Gold:      [0, 1, 1, 0, 0, 1, 1, 0, 0, 1, 1, 1, 1, 0]
Predicted:     [0, 0, 0, 1, 1, 1, 1, 0, 0, 0, 1, 1, 1, 0]

Precision: 0.6530612244897959
Recall: 0.6428571428571429
f-score: 0.6446886446886447
                                       Confusion matrix for second run: four
Confusion Matrix:     [[4 2]           true negatives, two false positives, three
                       [3 5]]      <-- false negatives, and five true positives
```

The results from both runs demonstrate relatively poor and inconsistent performance. Multiple executions of these scenarios show significant volatility in the outcomes, with *f*-scores fluctuating widely between 30% and 70%. Given that logistic regression is a well-established and proven algorithm, this instability suggests that the limitation lies not in the classification method but in our feature engineering approach. The high variance in results indicates that our simple node representation, based solely on degree, fails to capture the complex network patterns necessary for reliable node classification. The same is true with Node2Vec.

Let's improve our feature engineering by using homophily. Instead of using only node degree, which simply counts total connections, we can create a richer node representation by considering the social context of these connections. For each node, we'll create a three-element vector containing the total degree (total connections), the "Mr. Hi degree" (connections to the instructor's group), and the "officer degree" (connections to the administrator's group). This approach, shown in the next listing, capitalizes on homophily by assuming that a node's group membership is likely influenced by the group affiliations of its neighbors.

Listing 9.8 Computing featurization based on three types of degrees

```
def compute_specific_degree_embeddings(G):
    clubs = nx.get_node_attributes(G, "club")
    mr_hi_degree =
        [[clubs[c] for c in G.neighbors(i)].count('Mr. Hi') for i in
        G.nodes()]
    officer_degree =
        [[clubs[c] for c in G.neighbors(i)].count('Officer')
        for i in G.nodes()]
    degree = list(dict(G.degree()).values())
    embeddings =
        [[degree[i], mr_hi_degree[i], officer_degree[i]] for i in G.nodes]
    return embeddings
```

Calculates mr_hi_degree, taking into account only neighbors that belong to the Mr. Hi group

Calculates officer_degree, taking into account only neighbors that belong to the Officer group

Computes the degree in the traditional way, considering all nodes

Combines the three values into a single vector for each node

Now that we have a new function, we just need to change listing 9.6 to point to the new embedding function. The results are presented in the next listing.

Listing 9.9 Results with the vectors made using three degrees

```
Gold:     [0, 1, 1, 0, 0, 1, 1, 0, 0, 1, 1, 1, 1, 0]
Predicted:     [0, 1, 1, 0, 0, 1, 1, 0, 0, 1, 1, 1, 1, 1]

Precision: 0.9365079365079365
Recall: 0.9285714285714286
f-score: 0.9274255156608098

Confusion Matrix:    [[5 1]
                      [0 8]]
```

The results are much better. You can run this multiple times, and the results will be very stable and always close to 100%.

This experiment, although simple, demonstrates several principles for building effective IASs using ML on graphs:

- *Feature engineering is critical.* The way we represent nodes and relationships fundamentally impacts the success of graph-based ML tasks, with domain-informed features often outperforming simple metrics like degree centrality.

- *Autonomous embeddings require careful tuning.* Methods like Node2Vec, although powerful, don't guarantee optimal results. Parameters must be thoughtfully configured to avoid generating overly homogeneous node representations. As an exercise, run the experiment using lower values of `walk_length` and `num_walks`.
- *Domain understanding matters.* Knowledge of underlying graph dynamics and network properties like homophily can guide better feature engineering strategies that are often more effective than generic approaches.

These insights will serve as foundations as we explore more sophisticated approaches to graph representation learning in subsequent chapters.

9.3.2 Graph classification

The approach to feature engineering, discussed before for node classification and link prediction, is similar for graph classification. But instead of extracting features for nodes, most algorithms compute or extract a set of features for the entire graph—and, of course, we have multiple graphs as input. Figure 9.10 shows the high-level process.

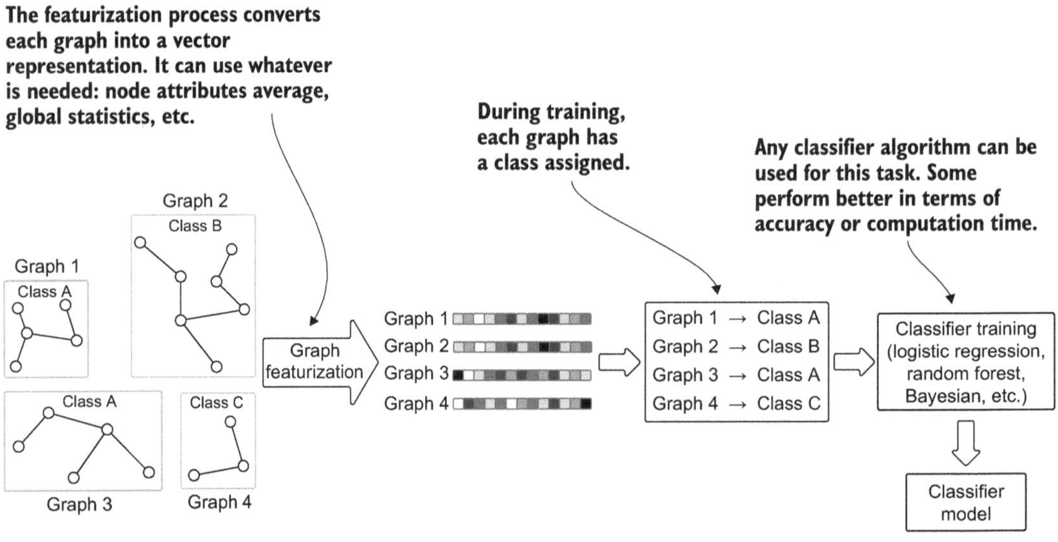

Figure 9.10 High-level training process for graph classification. The output is a classifier model that has been trained on the known classes of different graphs.

Once the model has been trained, it is used as an input for the prediction phase together with the unclassified graphs. Figure 9.11 shows the key steps and actors of the prediction.

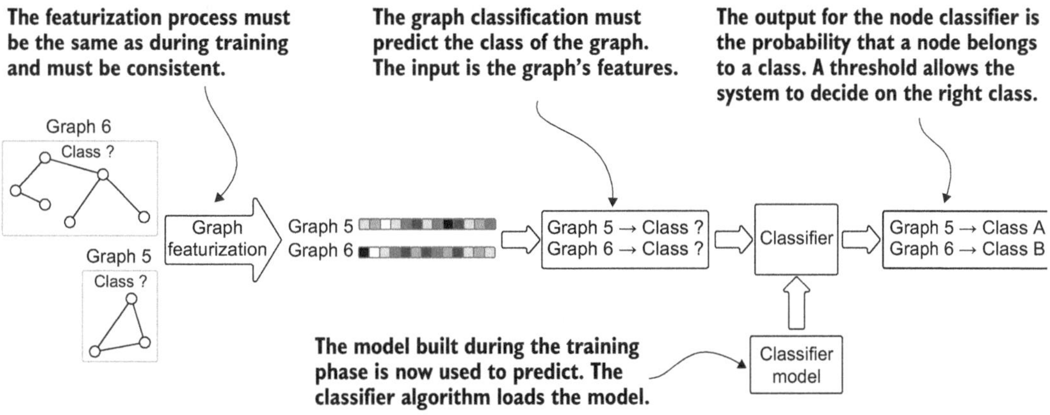

Figure 9.11 High-level prediction process for graph classification. The outputs are the classes assigned to the unlabeled graphs.

Again, it is clear that feature extraction for nodes, relationships, and graphs is a vital aspect of the process because it forms the inputs for training and prediction. The final quality of the output, including accuracy and overall performance, largely depends on the quality of these features and the precise tuning of downstream algorithm parameters. Chapter 10 and much of the rest of the part 4 will focus on this task and using the results of this process effectively.

9.3.3 *Graph clustering*

Not all ML tasks on graphs require the steps shown in the previous sections. In the case of graph clustering, for example, the input is the entire graph (or a subgraph), and the algorithms use nodes and relationships to extract communities (see figure 9.12).

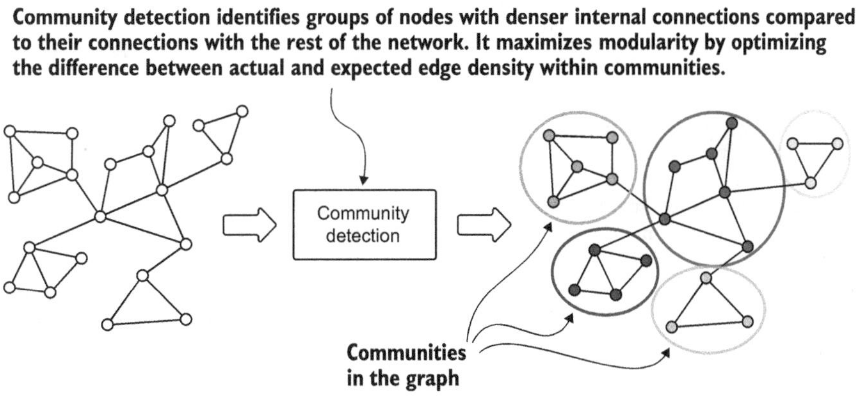

Figure 9.12 High-level graph clustering process. This is an example of a pure graph algorithm approach that doesn't require an intermediate transformation into a vector representation or other format.

For this task, there is no feature extraction because graph algorithms use node relationships, their directions, and their weights to split the graph. Certain algorithms, such as weakly connected component (WCC), use a fixed mechanism and consider only independent subgraphs. Other methods, such as the Louvain and label propagation algorithms, optimize certain outcomes, such as modularity. We discussed Louvain in chapter 4; let's quickly introduce label propagation.

The *label propagation algorithm* (LPA) [20] is a fast method for detecting communities in a network. It propagates labels throughout the network, and at the end, nodes with the same labels are considered to belong to the same community. LPA doesn't guarantee consistent output, due to its randomness; therefore, running it multiple times on the same network may produce slightly different communities.

To show how the process works, we'll use the same karate club graph and run Louvain on it using the following code.

Listing 9.10 Running Louvain on the karate club network

```
import math
import time
import networkx as nx
import matplotlib.pyplot as plt

def set_club_colors(G):
    for node in G.nodes(data=True):
        color = '#00fff9'
        if node[1]['club'] == 'Mr. Hi':
            color = '#e6e6fa'
        node[1]['color'] = color

def draw_and_save_graph_picture(G, i=0):
    set_club_colors(G)
    layout_position = nx.spring_layout(G, k=8 / math.sqrt(G.order()))
    colors = [n[1]['color'] for n in G.nodes(data=True)]
    nx.draw_networkx(G, pos=layout_position, node_color=colors)
    plt.axis('off')
    plt.savefig("Karate_Graph_" + str(i) + ".svg", format="SVG", dpi=1000)
    plt.savefig("Karate_Graph_" + str(i) + ".png", format="PNG", dpi=1000)
    plt.show()

if __name__ == '__main__':
    start = time.time()
    G = nx.karate_club_graph()
    draw_and_save_graph_picture(G)
    communities = nx.community.louvain_communities(G, seed=123)   # Computes communities using Louvain
    i = 1
    for community in communities:                # Draws multiple graphs, one for each community
        subGraph = G.subgraph(community)
        draw_and_save_graph_picture(subGraph, i)
        i += 1

    end = time.time() - start
    print("Time to complete:", end)
```

This code identifies four communities, as shown in figure 9.13. We immediately see that the algorithm did a great job identifying groups of nodes which are well connected with other nodes in the same community and loosely connected with nodes outside. Each community is pretty much homogeneous, with nodes belonging to the same group (as indicated by the shades of the nodes). Only in one case do we have a spurious node (number 8), which is in a community with nodes that are all from the other group. Maybe this person is in the wrong group!

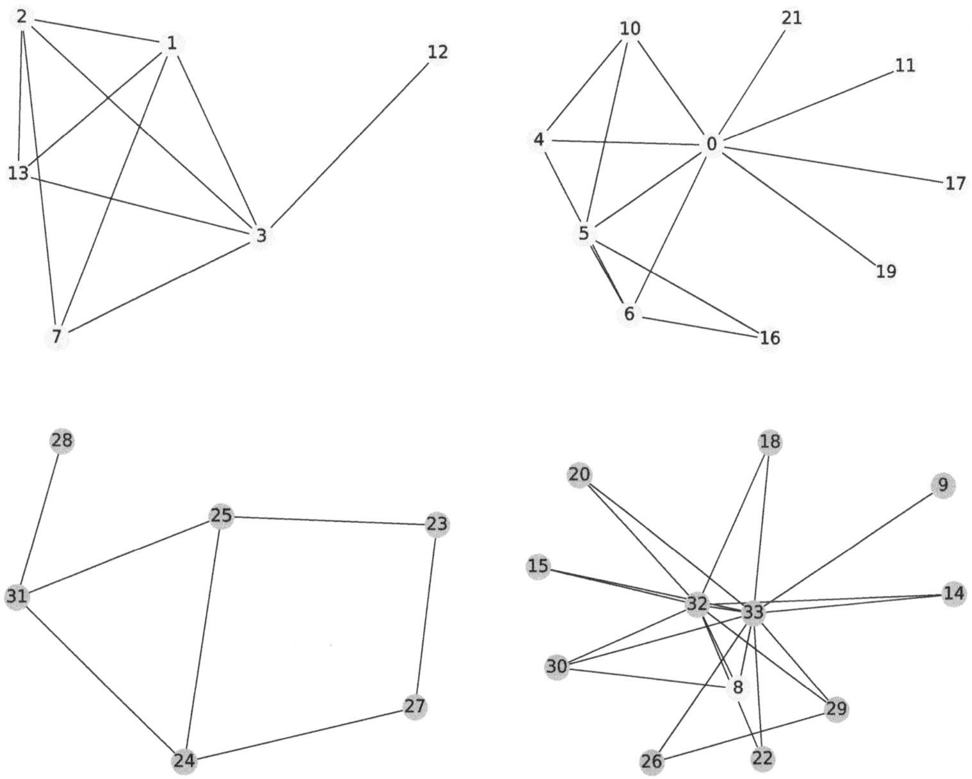

Figure 9.13 The result of the community detection algorithm applied to the karate club network. The algorithm identified four communities. All but one contain only members of the same groups. There is one spurious node, but it is well connected to other people belonging to a different group.

Two aspects distinguish this task from those we've covered previously. First, there's no requirement for representation transformation. The entire graph serves as the input, and the algorithm directly interacts with the nodes and relationships. And second, there's no training phase. This task follows an unsupervised approach. It takes the graph and generates the output without using any examples of labels, etc.

Summary

- Machine learning on graphs naturally handles interconnected data, provides universal data representation, and enables the modeling of complex problems through a limited set of computational tasks.
- Unlike traditional ML, which assumes independent and identically distributed data points, graph-based approaches use connections and dependencies between nodes, better reflecting real-world relationships and patterns.
- ML tasks on graphs fall into two main categories: node-focused (like node classification and link prediction), where tasks are performed on a single graph, and graph-focused (like graph classification), where each graph is a separate data point.
- Node classification and link prediction are typically semisupervised tasks, using both labeled and unlabeled data, along with the graph's structural information. Community detection is usually unsupervised and operates directly on the graph structure.
- Feature engineering plays a critical role in these tasks.
- Node embeddings can be generated through various approaches, from manual feature engineering to automated techniques like Node2Vec. However, autonomous embeddings require careful tuning to avoid generating overly homogeneous representations.
- The success of graph-based ML often depends on finding the right balance between automated feature learning, domain knowledge incorporation, and appropriate algorithm selection for the task at hand.

10 Graph feature engineering: Manual and semiautomated approaches

This chapter covers

- Manual feature engineering techniques for nodes and relationships in graphs
- Combining domain expertise with semiautomated extraction in a graph representation
- Real-world applications of feature engineering

The success of machine learning (ML) on graphs depends on a fundamental challenge: how to effectively represent graph elements (nodes, relationships, and entire graphs) as vectors that ML algorithms can process. This representation step, often called vectorization or featurization, determines how well our models can learn and make predictions.

Although modern ML algorithms—from traditional approaches like logistic regression and random forests to sophisticated deep learning models—are well-established, they can't directly process graph structures. Instead, they require numerical input vectors. The quality of these vectors directly affects the performance of any downstream task, whether it's classifying nodes, predicting relationships, or analyzing entire graphs.

This chapter explores the art and science of creating these vector representations, progressing from manual to automated approaches. We start with manual feature engineering, crafting interpretable features based on domain knowledge and graph properties. This hands-on approach, although time-consuming, provides insights into what makes representations effective and helps us understand why certain features work better than others.

We'll gradually introduce more automated techniques. However, the more automated our feature extraction becomes, the less interpretable the features tend to be. This creates a spectrum:

- *Manual features* are highly interpretable but labor-intensive to create (quickly introduced in chapter 9 and discussed in depth in this chapter).
- *Semiautomated features* strike a balance between interpretability and efficiency (also covered in this chapter).
- *Fully automated features* are efficient to generate but harder to interpret (discussed in chapters 11 and 12).

In traditional datasets, features are direct measurements from the real world. For example, a weather prediction dataset may include measurable attributes like precipitation, temperature range, and wind speed. During model training, we use rows where we know both the features (measured attributes) and the label (actual weather). For prediction, we apply our trained model to new data where we only have the features and need to determine the weather label.

But in graph-based ML, we must construct our features from the graph structure itself. Instead of physical measurements, we need to capture meaningful properties of nodes, relationships, or entire graphs as numerical values.

There are two fundamental approaches to creating these graph-based features:

- *Feature engineering*, which we introduced in the previous chapter, relies on manually designed features based on graph properties and domain knowledge. These features are highly interpretable but time-consuming to create, and they may not capture all relevant patterns for complex tasks. Common examples of graph-based features include node degree, clustering coefficients, and centrality measures.
- *Representation learning*, in contrast, automatically learns feature representations from the graph structure. This approach requires minimal human intervention and can adapt to specific tasks through training. It often captures complex patterns more effectively than manual engineering, but it typically produces features that are harder to interpret. This approach will be covered in the next two chapters.

Understanding the challenges and limitations of feature engineering will help us appreciate why representation learning has become increasingly important. Manual feature engineering remains valuable for two key reasons. First, it produces interpretable features that humans can understand and validate. Second, it provides insights into what makes graph representations effective, informing the design of automated approaches.

Another significant advantage of manually extracted features is their compatibility with large language models (LLMs) for autonomous reasoning about graphs. Because these features are based on well-understood graph algorithms and properties, LLMs can effectively interpret and reason about them.

In this chapter, we'll explore three practical approaches to feature engineering, each drawn from real-world consulting projects. These examples demonstrate both the power and limitations of manual feature extraction in graph-based ML.

10.1 Manual node features

Suppose we have a network of people: that is, a graph with nodes that represent people and relationships that represent any connection among these individuals (see figure 10.1). Among these people are some recognized fraudsters. We don't have a full list of them, so our work is to classify nodes to recognize the unrecognized fraudsters or determine the risk of people being victims of fraudulent activities.

The network includes two types of nodes: black nodes represent known fraudsters (nodes D, E, F, and I), and white nodes represent legitimate users or unidentified nodes. All connections between nodes are represented as undirected edges. The following listing shows how to create this network using Python and NetworkX.

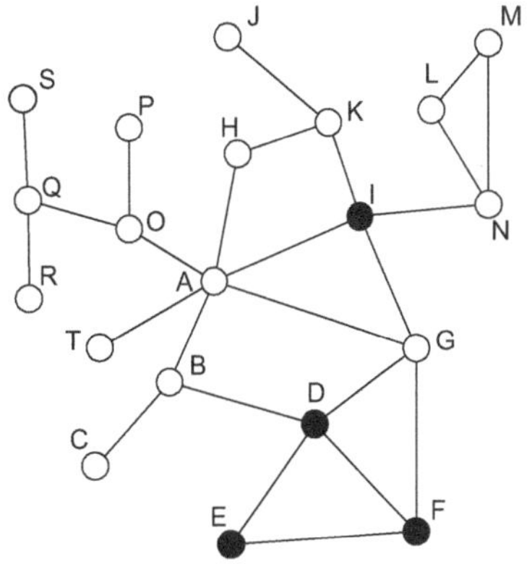

Figure 10.1 An example social network in which white nodes represent legitimate individuals or those whose status as fraudsters is unknown, and black nodes represent known fraudsters

Listing 10.1 Creating the fraud detection network example

```
import networkx as nx
import matplotlib.pyplot as plt

def create_fraud_network():
    G = nx.Graph()                                  <-- Initializes the empty undirected graph

    fraudsters = ['D', 'E', 'F', 'I']               <-- Fraudulent nodes (black in figure 10.1)

    # Add all nodes first
    nodes = ['A', 'B', 'C', 'D', 'E', 'F', 'G', 'H', 'I', 'J',
             'K', 'L', 'M', 'N', 'O', 'P', 'Q', 'R', 'S', 'T']   <-- Defines all nodes in the network

    G.add_nodes_from(nodes)

    for node in G.nodes():
        G.nodes[node]['is_fraudster'] = node in fraudsters   <-- Sets the fraudster attribute for each node, based on the list
```

```
    edges = [
            ('A', 'B'), ('A', 'G'), ('A', 'H'), ('A', 'I'), ('A', 'O'),
            ('A', 'T'), ('B', 'D'), ('B', 'C'), ('D', 'E'), ('D', 'F'),
            ('D', 'G'), ('E', 'F'), ('F', 'G'), ('G', 'I'), ('H', 'K'),
            ('I', 'K'), ('I', 'N'), ('K', 'J'), ('L', 'M'), ('L', 'N'),
            ('N', 'M'), ('O', 'P'), ('O', 'Q'), ('Q', 'R'), ('Q', 'S')
    ]                                           <-- Defines all edges
                                                    in the network
    G.add_edges_from(edges)
                                          Returns the
    return G                          <-- complete graph
```

You can use this network for all the subsequent analyses we perform in the chapter by using the following call.

Listing 10.2 Example use

```
G = create_fraud_network()        <-- You can use this graph object with
                                      any of our metric calculations.
degree_metrics = compute_degree_metrics(G)
triangle_metrics = compute_triangle_metrics(G)   Example metrics that we define later
```

Our goal is to implement a classifier that, given a node, will say whether it is a fraudster. Generally, this task is accomplished by using well-known classical classification algorithms, such as logistic regression, Bayesian classifier, decision tree, random forest, and so on. They are all supervised algorithms, so during training, the input is a set of features associated with each data point (nodes, in this case) and a label (here, fraudster/not fraudster). After the training builds a ML model, the classifier will be able to assign labels with a certain likelihood.

To use such algorithms, we have to "represent" each node as a set of features that can be used during training and prediction as good indicators, as illustrated in figure 10.2. We can extract a lot of interesting information for each node:

- *Local features* are those we can extract considering the node's one-hop neighborhood or *ego-centered network* (*egonet*)—that is, a particular node and its immediate neighbors. The center of the egonet is the *ego*, and the surrounding nodes are the *alters*. These local features can also consider an *n*-order neighborhood around the ego node, considering nodes that are *n* hops from that node.
- *Global features* measure the role of each node in the entire network or a great portion of it (not in the egonet or an *n*-order neighborhood). In this category fall centrality metrics like betweenness centrality, closeness centrality, PageRank, and Eigenvector centrality. These measures capture a node's influence in the network and how the node can be influenced by others. (If you are not familiar with these centrality algorithms, we recommend our earlier book, *Graph-Powered Machine Learning* [1], or [2] as a reference.)

We'll use metrics to identify features representing each node. We'll also customize some to improve the classification's final quality and demonstrate how the featurization process can be tailored to our needs. Our approach will progress from local to global metrics, starting with features based on immediate neighbors before examining network-wide patterns. In each case, we'll define the metric and its significance, present code for automated extraction, and display the results in a table.

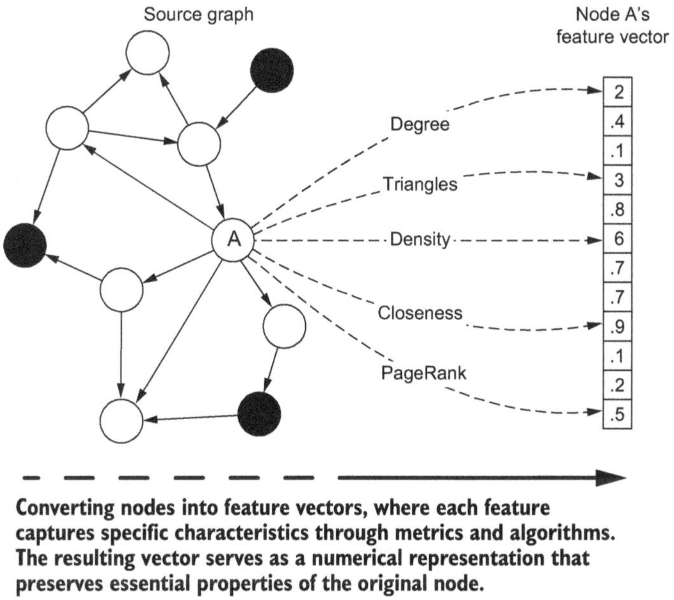

Figure 10.2 Node feature extraction: using metrics and graph algorithms to transform nodes into numerical feature vectors that capture key characteristics

We'll build these features incrementally, showing how each new metric adds a dimension to our node representations. This systematic approach allows us to capture increasingly complex patterns of network structure and node behavior.

10.1.1 Degree

The degree of a node represents how many neighbors the node has. In our example case, we want to distinguish between the number of fraudulent and legitimate direct neighbors. These are called *fraudulent* and *legitimate degrees* (which we shorten to fraud degree and legit degree). These two measures, together with the global degree, provide a better representation of the node's direct connections. For example, if I have 10 direct neighbors who are all fraudulent, the chances that I am a fraudster are higher than if all my neighbors were legit. The following listing computes these values in a generic graph.

Listing 10.3 Computing types of node degrees in a fraud detection network

```
def compute_degree_metrics(G):
    degree_metrics = {}
```

Initializes a dictionary to store degree metrics for each node

```
    for node in G.nodes():
        neighbors = list(G.neighbors(node))
        total_degree = len(neighbors)

        fraud_degree = sum(1 for neighbor in neighbors
                          if G.nodes[neighbor].get('is_fraudster', False))

        legit_degree = total_degree - fraud_degree

        degree_metrics[node] = {
            'total_degree': total_degree,
            'fraud_degree': fraud_degree,
            'legit_degree': legit_degree
        }

    return degree_metrics

def get_node_degrees(G, node):
    metrics = compute_degree_metrics(G)
    return metrics.get(node, {
        'total_degree': 0,
        'fraud_degree': 0,
        'legit_degree': 0
    })
```

Calculates the total number of neighbors (total degree)

Counts neighbors marked as fraudsters using the node attribute is_fraudster

Calculates the legit degree as total minus fraudulent neighbors

Returns a dictionary containing all degree metrics for each node

Gets degree metrics for a specific node

This code assumes that the graph has nodes marked with an `'is_fraudster'` boolean attribute to identify fraudulent nodes. Table 10.1 contains the related values. For example, node D has a total of four direct neighbors, of which two are fraudulent and two are legitimate.

Table 10.1 Global degree, fraud degree, and legit degree of the fraud graph in figure 10.1

Node	A	B	C	D	E	F	G	H	I	J
Total degree	6	3	1	4	2	3	4	2	4	1
Fraud degree	1	1	0	2	2	2	3	0	0	0
Legit degree	5	2	1	2	0	1	1	2	4	1
Node	**K**	**L**	**M**	**N**	**O**	**P**	**Q**	**R**	**S**	**T**
Total degree	3	2	2	3	3	1	3	1	1	1
Fraud degree	1	0	0	1	0	0	0	0	0	0
Legit degree	2	2	2	2	3	1	3	1	1	1

> **Exercise**
>
> Compute the values yourself manually, and check them to verify that the concepts are clear. These are very simple measures to compute; later, the others will require to be run by code.

10.1.2 Triangles

In graph theory, a *triangle* is a subgraph that consists of three nodes which are all connected. So, if we have three nodes—A, B, and C—they form a triangle if relationships exist between the couples A-B, A-C, and B-C (see figure 10.3).

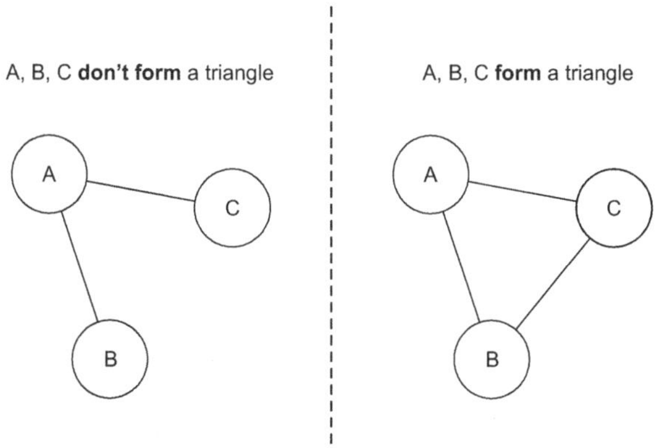

Figure 10.3 Examples of three connected nodes: if each node is connected to the other two, they constitute a triangle.

The presence of triangles in a node's egonet is an indication that the target node has strong connections with its neighbors. Think about the people close to you: your friends are probably also friends with each other. That's why triangles reveal the influential effect of a closely connected group of individuals. Consider a node and two alters forming a triangle. In our example, if both alters are fraudulent, we can conclude that the triangle is fraudulent, and vice versa. If only one alter is fraudulent, the triangle is called *semifraudulent*.

The following code computes the total number of triangles and the fraudulent, legitimate, and semifraudulent triangles in our graph.

Listing 10.4 Computing triangle metrics in a fraud detection network

```
import networkx as nx

def compute_triangle_metrics(G):
    triangle_metrics = {}                   <- Initializes a dictionary to store triangle metrics for each node

    for node in G.nodes():
        triangles = []
        neighbors = list(G.neighbors(node))

        for i in range(len(neighbors)):
            for j in range(i + 1, len(neighbors)):
                if G.has_edge(neighbors[i], neighbors[j]):    <- Finds triangles by checking whether two neighbors of the target node are connected
                    triangles.append((neighbors[i], neighbors[j]))
```

```
        total_triangles = len(triangles)
        fraud_triangles = 0
        legit_triangles = 0
        semi_fraud_triangles = 0

        for n1, n2 in triangles:
            n1_fraud = G.nodes[n1].get('is_fraudster', False)
            n2_fraud = G.nodes[n2].get('is_fraudster', False)

            if n1_fraud and n2_fraud:
                fraud_triangles += 1
            elif not n1_fraud and not n2_fraud:
                legit_triangles += 1
            else:
                semi_fraud_triangles += 1

        triangle_metrics[node] = {
            'total_triangles': total_triangles,
            'fraud_triangles': fraud_triangles,
            'legit_triangles': legit_triangles,
            'semi_fraud_triangles': semi_fraud_triangles
        }

    return triangle_metrics

def get_node_triangles(G, node):
    metrics = compute_triangle_metrics(G)
    return metrics.get(node, {
        'total_triangles': 0,
        'fraud_triangles': 0,
        'legit_triangles': 0,
        'semi_fraud_triangles': 0
    })
```

Initializes counts

Classifies each triangle based on the fraud status of the two other nodes

Counts a triangle as fraudulent if both other nodes are fraudsters

Counts a triangle as legit if both other nodes are legit

Counts a triangle as semifraudulent if one other node is fraudulent and one is legit

Returns a dictionary containing all triangle metrics for each node

Gets triangle metrics for a specific node

Table 10.2 contains the values for our fraudulent graph.

Table 10.2 The triangle measures of the fraud graph in figure 10.1

Node	A	B	C	D	E	F	G	H	I	J
Total triangles	1	0	0	2	1	2	2	0	1	0
Fraud triangles	0	0	0	1	1	1	1	0	0	0
Legit triangles	0	0	0	0	0	0	0	0	1	0
Semifraud triangles	1	0	0	1	0	1	1	0	0	0
Node	**K**	**L**	**M**	**N**	**O**	**P**	**Q**	**R**	**S**	**T**
Total triangles	0	1	1	1	0	0	0	0	0	0
Fraud triangles	0	0	0	0	0	0	0	0	0	0
Legit triangles	0	1	1	1	0	0	0	0	0	0
Semifraud triangles	0	0	0	0	0	0	0	0	0	0

Exercise

Again, compute the values yourself, and check them to be sure the concepts are clear.

10.1.3 Density

Density is another measure that indicates how nodes can influence each other. It measures the extent to which nodes in a graph are connected. Given a fully connected graph of N nodes, the following formula computes the total number of possible edges:

$$\binom{N}{2} = \frac{N(N-1)}{2}$$

In this case, each node is connected to every other node in the network. The density measures the portion of these possible edges that are observed in the actual graph. So, if M is the number of edges in the graph, the density of the entire network can be computed with the following formula:

$$d = \frac{M}{\binom{N}{2}} = \frac{2M}{N(N-1)}$$

We can also compute the density for each node considering the density of its egonet. For example, suppose node A is the target node. Its egonet has 7 nodes, so the total number of possible edges in the egonet is $7(7-1)/2 = 21$. The number of observed edges is 7, and $d = 7/21 = \sim 0.33$. In this example, the calculation is simple; the next listing contains the code for when things get more difficult. This measure, due to its nature, does not include specific values related to the fraud domain we are considering (there is no fraud density, or legit density).

Listing 10.5 Computing egonet density in a fraud detection network

```
import networkx as nx

def compute_density_metrics(G):
    density_metrics = {}                          # Initializes a dictionary to store density values for each node

    for node in G.nodes():
        neighbors = list(G.neighbors(node))
        egonet_nodes = neighbors + [node]         # Creates an egonet by getting the node's neighbors plus the node itself

        N = len(egonet_nodes)                     # Gets the number of nodes in the egonet

        if N < 2:  # Handle special case where egonet is too small
            density_metrics[node] = 0.0
            continue
```

```
        M = 0
        for i in range(len(egonet_nodes)):
            for j in range(i + 1, len(egonet_nodes)):
                if G.has_edge(egonet_nodes[i], egonet_nodes[j]):
                    M += 1

        max_possible_edges = (N * (N - 1)) / 2
        density = M / max_possible_edges

        density_metrics[node] = round(density, 2)

    return density_metrics

def get_node_density(G, node):
    metrics = compute_density_metrics(G)
    return metrics.get(node, 0.0)
```

Counts the actual number of edges (M) in the egonet

Calculates maximum possible edges N(N – 1)/2 in the egonet

Rounds the density to two decimal places

Calculates the density as ratio of actual edges to maximum possible edges

Returns the dictionary containing density values for all nodes

Gets the density value for a specific node

Running this listing on our example graph gives the values in table 10.3.

Table 10.3 Density measures of the fraud graph in figure 10.1

Node	A	B	C	D	E	F	G	H	I	J
Density	0.33	0.5	1	0.6	1	0.83	0.6	0.66	0.5	1
Node	**K**	**L**	**M**	**N**	**O**	**P**	**Q**	**R**	**S**	**T**
Density	0.5	1	1	0.66	0.5	1	0.5	1	1	1

The measures we have seen so far use the egonet of a node to compute values. The measures that follow consider the entire network during computation.

10.1.4 Geodesic (or shortest) path

The *geodesic path* or *shortest path* represents the minimum distance between two nodes. We can use this measure and customize it to the specific needs of our domain to identify features that could be the input for downstream algorithms.

In our example, we want to know whether there are paths between fraudulent nodes and legitimate nodes, how long they are, and how many of these the network contains. If more paths exist between two nodes, and those paths are short, there is a higher chance that fraudulent behavior will affect the target node. Based on these considerations, we decide to take the shortest path to a fraudulent node (the geodesic path). We also need to know the number of fraudulent nodes surrounding a node at a certain distance, so we consider the number of paths with one, two, or three hops to any fraudulent node.

This time, before showing the code, let's start with some examples that can be computed manually. Node A is connected to node I via a single hop (direct connection). The geodesic distance is, hence, 1. There are no other direct connections to other fraudulent nodes: the number of one-hop paths is one. There are four two-hop paths—A-G-I, A-B-D, A-G-D, and A-G-F—and so on; see table 10.4.

Table 10.4 Geodesic paths of the fraud graph in figure 10.1

Node	A	B	C	D	E	F	G	H	I	J
Geodesic paths	1	1	2	0	0	0	1	2	0	2
1-hop paths	1	1	0	2	2	2	3	0	0	0
2-hop paths	4	3	1	8	4	7	5	2	6	1
3-hop paths	18	13	3	19	15	17	25	4	9	0
Node	**K**	**L**	**M**	**N**	**O**	**P**	**Q**	**R**	**S**	**T**
Geodesic paths	1	2	2	1	2	3	3	4	4	2
1-hop paths	1	0	0	1	0	0	0	0	0	0
2-hop paths	0	1	1	0	1	0	0	0	0	1
3-hop paths	9	1	1	8	4	1	1	0	0	4

Our network is straightforward, and computing even the three-hop paths is not complicated. But for real networks, manual computation is infeasible and not practical.

Calculating geodesic paths is computationally expensive. Various algorithms are available, and one of the best for our case is Dijkstra's.

> **NOTE** *Dijkstra's algorithm* finds the shortest path between nodes in a graph by iteratively selecting the unvisited node with the smallest tentative distance, calculating distances through it to each unvisited neighbor, and marking the node as visited. The algorithm efficiently builds up the shortest path tree one vertex at a time [3].

Listing 10.6 contains the code to automatically extract the features related to the geodesic distance. It uses the library `networkx`, which has an implementation of the Dijkstra algorithm from a single source. Even Neo4j, in the current GDS library (https://github.com/neo4j/graph-data-science), has a couple of Dijkstra implementations, one of which computes the shortest paths between a source node and all nodes reachable from that node.

Listing 10.6 Computing geodesic path metrics in a fraud detection network

```
import networkx as nx
from collections import defaultdict

def compute_geodesic_metrics(G, max_hops=3):
    path_metrics = {}

    fraudster_nodes = [n for n, attr in G.nodes(data=True)
                       if attr.get('is_fraudster', False)]

    for node in G.nodes():
        if G.nodes[node].get('is_fraudster', False):
```

- `path_metrics = {}` — Initializes a dictionary to store path metrics for each node
- `fraudster_nodes = ...` — Identifies all fraudulent nodes in the graph

```
            geodesic_path = 0                          ◁ If the node is fraudulent, the distance
            hop_counts = defaultdict(int)                to the nearest fraudster is 0.
        else:
            paths_to_fraudsters = []                   ◁ For nonfraudulent nodes, calculates
            hop_counts = defaultdict(int)                paths to all fraudsters

            for fraudster in fraudster_nodes:
                try:
                    path = nx.shortest_path(G, node, fraudster)     ◁ Uses Dijkstra's algorithm (via
                    path_length = len(path) - 1                       networkx) to find the shortest
                    paths_to_fraudsters.append(path_length)           path to each fraudster

                    if path_length <= max_hops:
                        hop_counts[path_length] += 1    ◁ Counts the number of
                except nx.NetworkXNoPath:                 paths for each hop
                    continue                              distance up to max_hops

            geodesic_path = min(paths_to_fraudsters)
              if paths_to_fraudsters else float('inf')  ◁ Finds the shortest path
                                                          length to any fraudster
        path_metrics[node] = {
            'geodesic_path': geodesic_path,
            '#1-hop_paths': hop_counts[1],
            '#2-hop_paths': hop_counts[2],             Stores metrics, including
            '#3-hop_paths': hop_counts[3]              shortest path and count of
        }                                            ◁ paths at each hop distance

    return path_metrics                ◁ Returns a dictionary containing
                                         all path metrics for each node
def get_node_paths(G, node):
    metrics = compute_geodesic_metrics(G)
    return metrics.get(node, {
        'geodesic_path': float('inf'),
        '#1-hop_paths': 0,
        '#2-hop_paths': 0,
        '#3-hop_paths': 0            Gets path metrics
    })                             ◁ for a specific node
```

This implementation computes the geodesic distance from the starting node to fraudster nodes only and up to a predefined distance.

10.1.5 Closeness

Closeness centrality represents how "close" a node is to all other nodes. It measures the mean distance from a node to all other nodes in the network, where the distance between nodes is computed as the geodesic or shortest path (described in the previous section) between them. Given a network with N nodes, the mean geodesic distance or "farness" from node i to the other nodes is computed as follows:

$$g(v_i) = \frac{\sum_{j=1\ (j \neq i)}^{N} d(v_i,\ v_j)}{N - 1}$$

Let's examine each part:

- The numerator $\Sigma_{j=1 (j \neq i)}^{N} d(v_i, v_j)$ adds up all the shortest path distances:
  - $d(v_i, v_j)$ represents the shortest path distance between node v_i and another node, v_j.
  - The summation goes from $j = 1$ to N, covering all nodes in the network. $j \neq i$ in the sum indicates that we skip the distance to the node itself (which would be 0).
- The denominator $(N - 1)$ represents the following:
  - N is the total number of nodes in the network.
  - We subtract 1 because we don't include the distance from a node to itself.
  - This gives us the number of other nodes in the network.

Thus this formula calculates the average by adding up all the shortest paths from node v_i to every other node and dividing by the number of other nodes. A lower $g(v_i)$ value indicates that the node is generally closer to other nodes in the network, whereas a higher value suggests it tends to be farther away.

For example, if a node has many direct connections, its shortest paths to other nodes will tend to be small, resulting in a lower $g(v_i)$ value. This indicates the node is well-connected and centrally positioned in the network. In the fraud use case, when a fraudulent node has a low value for $g(v_i)$, fraud may spread easily through the network and contaminate other nodes faster.

Closeness centrality is the inverse of farness because we assign higher values to nodes that are more central in the network. The formula is as follows:

$$\text{closeness centrality}(v_i) = \left(\frac{\Sigma_{j=1\ (j \neq i)}^{N} d(v_i,\ v_j)}{N - 1} \right)^{-1}$$

Two problems can arise. First, the values of the closeness centralities for all the nodes in the network may be close together, so we often have to look at the decimal places to see the differences. Second, when a node cannot reach another (no path exists between the two), the distance between them is infinite. To overcome this problem, closeness centrality excludes the distances to nodes that cannot be reached. So, when the closeness centrality is computed for a node, the calculation doesn't use the full network—it only uses the portion of the network reachable from that node.

The following code computes the closeness centrality for a network represented using a `networkx` graph.

Listing 10.7 Computing closeness centrality in a fraud detection network

```
import networkx as nx
from collections import defaultdict

def compute_closeness_metrics(G):
    closeness_metrics = {}
```

Initializes a dictionary to store closeness values for each node

```
        for node in G.nodes():
            total_distance = 0
            reachable_nodes = 0

            shortest_paths = nx.single_source_shortest_path_length(G, node)

            for other_node, distance in shortest_paths.items():
                if other_node != node:
                    total_distance += distance
                    reachable_nodes += 1

            n = len(G.nodes()) - 1
            if reachable_nodes > 0 and n > 0:
                closeness = (reachable_nodes / n) * (reachable_nodes /
                    total_distance)
            else:
                closeness = 0.0

            closeness_metrics[node] = round(closeness, 2)

        return closeness_metrics

    def get_node_closeness(G, node):
        metrics = compute_closeness_metrics(G)
        return metrics.get(node, 0.0)

    def analyze_closeness_distribution(G):
        metrics = compute_closeness_metrics(G)
        values = list(metrics.values())

        stats = {
            'max_closeness': max(values),
            'min_closeness': min(values),
            'avg_closeness': sum(values) / len(values),
            'most_central_node': max(metrics.items(), key=lambda x: x[1])[0],
            'least_central_node': min(metrics.items(), key=lambda x: x[1])[0]
        }

        return stats
```

Annotations:
- Uses networkx to calculate shortest paths to all nodes
- Excludes self
- Counts reachable nodes and sums up the distances
- Total nodes minus self
- Calculates the normalized closeness centrality considering disconnected components
- Rounds the closeness to two decimal places
- Returns a dictionary containing closeness values for all nodes
- Gets closeness value for a specific node
- Analyzes the distribution of closeness values

The code first determines the shortest paths from a target node to all other nodes in the network using `networkx`'s path-finding algorithms. This step gives us the fundamental distances needed for the centrality calculation.

However, real-world networks may not be fully connected. To handle this common scenario, the code incorporates a normalization strategy that considers only the reachable nodes. This approach prevents disconnected components from distorting the centrality values while still providing meaningful measurements for partially connected networks.

The computation of closeness centrality follows the formula we introduced earlier. To make the results more practical and interpretable, we've included analytical capabilities that help understand the distribution of closeness values across the network.

This can be particularly valuable when trying to identify nodes that serve as central points in the network's structure.

By processing each node this way, we obtain a comprehensive view of how central each node is relative to the rest of the network, with values normalized between 0 and 1 for easier comparison and analysis (see table 10.5). This implementation strikes a balance between theoretical correctness and practical applicability, making it suitable for both research and real-world applications.

Table 10.5 Closeness metrics of the fraud graph in figure 10.1

Node	A	B	C	D	E	F	G	H	I	J
Closeness	0.5	0.39	0.28	0.35	0.26	0.33	0.43	0.37	0.45	0.26
Node	**K**	**L**	**M**	**N**	**O**	**P**	**Q**	**R**	**S**	**T**
Closeness	0.34	0.26	0.26	0.34	0.40	0.29	0.31	0.24	0.24	0.34

Node A is the most closely connected to all other nodes in the network. Nodes R and S are the farthest away from all other nodes.

10.1.6 Betweenness

Betweenness centrality helps us understand a node's importance in a network from a different perspective than closeness centrality. Whereas closeness measures how quickly a node can reach others, betweenness measures how often a node acts as a bridge between other nodes. Specifically, it quantifies the number of times a node appears on the shortest paths between other pairs of nodes.

For any pair of nodes in a network, information or influence likely flows along the shortest path between them. If a particular node frequently appears on these shortest paths, it has high betweenness centrality and thus potentially controls the flow of information among many other nodes. Mathematically, the betweenness centrality of a node v is calculated as

$$\text{betweenness}(v) = \sum_{s,t\ (s \neq t \neq v)} \frac{\sigma_{st}(v)}{\sigma_{st}}$$

where σ_{st} represents the total number of shortest paths between nodes s and t, and $\sigma_{st}(v)$ represents the number of those paths that pass through node v. As shown in the next listing, this sum is taken over all pairs of nodes s and t where neither is equal to v.

Listing 10.8 Computing betweenness centrality in a fraud detection network

```
import networkx as nx
from collections import defaultdict

def compute_betweenness_metrics(G, normalized=True):
    betweenness_metrics = {}        <-- Initializes a dictionary to store betweenness values for all nodes
```

```
    betweenness = nx.betweenness_centrality(
        G,
        normalized=normalized,
        endpoints=False
    )

    for node in G.nodes():
        betweenness_metrics[node] = round(betweenness[node], 3)

    return betweenness_metrics

def analyze_betweenness_distribution(G):
    metrics = compute_betweenness_metrics(G)
    values = list(metrics.values())

    return {
        'max_betweenness': max(values),
        'min_betweenness': min(values),
        'avg_betweenness': sum(values) / len(values),
        'key_bridges': [node for node, score in metrics.items()
                       if score > sum(values) / len(values)]
    }

def get_node_betweenness(G, node):
    metrics = compute_betweenness_metrics(G)
    return metrics.get(node, 0.0)

def identify_potential_bottlenecks(G, threshold=0.5):
    metrics = compute_betweenness_metrics(G)

    bottlenecks = {node: score for node, score in metrics.items()
                  if score > threshold}
    return bottlenecks
```

Calculates betweenness using networkx's implementation

Rounds values to three decimal places for readability and stores them

Returns a dictionary containing betweenness values for all nodes

Identifies nodes with above-average betweenness as key bridges

Gets the betweenness value for a specific node

Identifies potential bottlenecks based on a threshold

The code uses `networkx`'s betweenness centrality algorithm while adding practical functionality for analysis and interpretation. The computed betweenness values are normalized by default, meaning they are scaled to fall between 0 and 1, making them easier to compare across different networks. A value closer to 1 indicates that the node appears on many shortest paths and thus has a high potential for controlling information flow.

Looking at the results in table 10.6, we see interesting patterns. Node A, with a betweenness centrality of 104, appears to be a crucial bridge in the network, potentially controlling the flow of information among many other nodes. In contrast, nodes C, E, J, L, M, P, R, S, and T all have betweenness values of 0, indicating that they don't act as bridges between any pairs of nodes.

The implementation includes additional analytical tools that help identify potential bottlenecks and key bridges in the network. These can be useful when trying to understand vulnerabilities in the network structure or identify nodes that might require additional monitoring in a fraud detection context.

Table 10.6 Betweenness metrics of the fraud graph in figure 10.1

Node	A	B	C	D	E	F	G	H	I	J
Betweenness	104	24.67	0	13.83	0	6.167	35.3	9	65	0
Node	**K**	**L**	**M**	**N**	**O**	**P**	**Q**	**R**	**S**	**T**
Betweenness	20	0	0	34	63	0	35	0	0	0

10.1.7 PageRank

PageRank is a powerful metric that measures node importance based on the structure of incoming connections. Originally developed by Google's founders to rank web pages, it has proven valuable in many other network analysis contexts, including fraud detection. Unlike simpler centrality measures, PageRank considers not just the quantity of connections but also their quality: a node connected to other highly ranked nodes will receive a higher PageRank score.

In our fraud detection context, we can adapt PageRank in two interesting ways. First, we'll compute a base PageRank that considers all connections equally. Then we'll compute a fraud-weighted PageRank where connections from known fraudulent nodes carry more weight. This dual approach, shown in the following listing, will help us understand both a node's general importance in the network and its specific relationship to fraudulent activity [4].

Listing 10.9 Computing PageRank variations for fraud detection

```
import networkx as nx
import numpy as np

def compute_pagerank_metrics(G, fraud_weight=2.0, damping_factor=0.85):
    pagerank_metrics = {}                    # Initializes a dictionary to store both PageRank variations

    base_pagerank = nx.pagerank(
        G,
        alpha=damping_factor,
        personalization=None,
        weight=None
    )                                        # Calculates standard PageRank using networkx implementation

    fraud_personalization = {}
    for node in G.nodes():                   # Creates a personalization dictionary that gives higher weight to fraudulent nodes
        if G.nodes[node].get('is_fraudster', False):
            fraud_personalization[node] = fraud_weight
        else:
            fraud_personalization[node] = 1.0

    fraud_pagerank = nx.pagerank(
        G,
        alpha=damping_factor,
        personalization=fraud_personalization,
        weight=None
    )                                        # Calculates fraud-weighted PageRank using personalization
```

```
    for node in G.nodes():
        pagerank_metrics[node] = {
            'pagerank_base': round(base_pagerank[node], 3),
            'pagerank_fraud': round(fraud_pagerank[node], 3)
        }                                          <-- Stores both PageRank
                                                       values for each node
    return pagerank_metrics    <-- Returns a dictionary
                                   containing all
                                   PageRank metrics
def get_node_pagerank(G, node):
    metrics = compute_pagerank_metrics(G)
    return metrics.get(node, {
        'pagerank_base': 0.0,
        'pagerank_fraud': 0.0       Gets the PageRank values
    })                          <-- for a specific node
```

The results for each node in our example graph are shown in table 10.7.

Table 10.7 PageRank metrics of the fraud graph in figure 10.1

Node	A	B	C	D	E	F	G	H	I	J
$PageRank_{base}$	0.108	0.057	0.023	0.068	0.036	0.051	0.067	0.04	0.07	0.024
$PageRank_{fraud}$	0.087	0.063	0.018	0.168	0.114	0.145	0.109	0.023	0.094	0.011
Node	**K**	**L**	**M**	**N**	**O**	**P**	**Q**	**R**	**S**	**T**
$PageRank_{base}$	0.06	0.041	0.041	0.057	0.066	0.026	0.75	0.028	0.028	0.022
$PageRank_{fraud}$	0.039	0.016	0.016	0.034	0.02	0.005	0.011	0.003	0.003	0.012

Node A has the highest base PageRank (0.108), indicating its general importance in the network structure. However, when we look at the fraud-weighted PageRank, node D emerges as the most significant (0.168), suggesting that it has stronger connections to fraudulent activity despite not having the highest base PageRank.

This divergence between base PageRank and fraud-weighted PageRank can provide valuable insights. Nodes that show a significant increase in their fraud-weighted PageRank compared to their base PageRank might warrant closer investigation, as they have more substantial connections to known fraudulent nodes than their overall network position suggests.

10.1.8 Prediction

We could continue extracting features, but at this point it should be clear how the process works. The process should be iterative; features can change and increase until the classifier reaches the quality of prediction you feel is enough. In this section, we will use the features extracted so far and perform a prediction using the same algorithm (logistic regression) we used in chapter 9. The following listing extracts a vector of features for each node and prepares the dataset for the next step.

Listing 10.10 Creating node features

```
import pandas as pd
import numpy as np
def create_node_features_dataset(G):
    degree_metrics = compute_degree_metrics(G)
    triangle_metrics = compute_triangle_metrics(G)
    density_metrics = compute_density_metrics(G)
    path_metrics = compute_geodesic_metrics(G)
    closeness_metrics = compute_closeness_metrics(G)
    betweenness_metrics = compute_betweenness_metrics(G)
    pagerank_metrics = compute_pagerank_metrics(G)

    features_dict = {}
    for node in G.nodes():
        features_dict[node] = {
            'total_degree': degree_metrics[node]['total_degree'],
            'fraud_degree': degree_metrics[node]['fraud_degree'],
            'legit_degree': degree_metrics[node]['legit_degree'],

            'total_triangles': triangle_metrics[node]['total_triangles'],
            'fraud_triangles': triangle_metrics[node]['fraud_triangles'],
            'legit_triangles': triangle_metrics[node]['legit_triangles'],
            'semi_fraud_triangles':
     triangle_metrics[node]['semi_fraud_triangles'],

            'density': density_metrics[node],
            'geodesic_path': path_metrics[node]['geodesic_path'],
            'paths_1hop': path_metrics[node]['#1-hop_paths'],
            'paths_2hop': path_metrics[node]['#2-hop_paths'],
            'paths_3hop': path_metrics[node]['#3-hop_paths'],
            'closeness': closeness_metrics[node],
            'betweenness': betweenness_metrics[node],
            'pagerank_base': pagerank_metrics[node]['pagerank_base'],
            'pagerank_fraud': pagerank_metrics[node]['pagerank_fraud'],

            # Label
            'is_fraudster': G.nodes[node]['is_fraudster']
        }

    # Convert to DataFrame
    df = pd.DataFrame.from_dict(features_dict, orient='index')

    return df
```

Computes all metrics for each node

Creates a comprehensive feature set for each node

Converts to a pandas DataFrame for easier manipulation

Now that we have our features for each node in a pandas DataFrame, we can split them and use part during training and part to validate the quality of the trained model, as shown in the following listing.

Listing 10.11 Training a fraud classifier and evaluating its accuracy

```
from sklearn.model_selection import train_test_split
from sklearn.linear_model import LogisticRegression
from sklearn.preprocessing import StandardScaler
from sklearn.metrics import classification_report, confusion_matrix

def train_fraud_classifier(G):
    df = create_node_features_dataset(G)

    X = df.drop('is_fraudster', axis=1)        # Separates features (X)
    y = df['is_fraudster']                     # from labels (y)

    X_train, X_test, y_train, y_test = train_test_split(    # Splits the data into
        X, y, test_size=0.2, random_state=42, stratify=y    # training (80%) and
    )                                                       # testing (20%) sets

    scaler = StandardScaler()
    X_train_scaled = scaler.fit_transform(X_train)    # Scales the features to
    X_test_scaled = scaler.transform(X_test)          # normalize their ranges

    clf = LogisticRegression(random_state=42, max_iter=1000)    # Trains the logistic
    clf.fit(X_train_scaled, y_train)                            # regression classifier

    y_pred = clf.predict(X_test_scaled)    # Calculates feature
                                           # importance
    feature_importance = pd.DataFrame({
        'feature': X.columns,
        'importance': abs(clf.coef_[0])                      # Collects all
    }).sort_values('importance', ascending=False)            # evaluation metrics

    results = {
        'classification_report': classification_report(y_test, y_pred),
        'confusion_matrix': confusion_matrix(y_test, y_pred),
        'feature_importance': feature_importance,
        'model': clf,
        'scaler': scaler        # Makes
    }                           # predictions

    return results
```

The stratified split (obtained by setting the parameter `stratify` to `yes`) ensures that both training and testing sets maintain the same proportion of fraudulent and legitimate nodes as the original dataset. `StandardScaler` ensures that all features are on the same scale, which is important for logistic regression. The feature importance analysis helps us understand which metrics are most useful for detecting fraudulent nodes.

With the model in our hands, we are now ready to predict the chance of a node being a fraudster by using the following function.

Listing 10.12 Function to predict the class of a node using a training model

```
def predict_fraud_probability(G, node, trained_results):
    df = create_node_features_dataset(G)
    node_features = df.loc[node].drop('is_fraudster')     # Gets node features

    scaled_features = trained_results['scaler'].transform(
        node_features.values.reshape(1, -1)
    )                                                      # Scales features

    fraud_prob =
        trained_results['model'].predict_proba(scaled_features)[0][1]    # Gets the probability

    return fraud_prob
```

All the functions are in place. Now we can run a simple analysis and a test to reveal the five most important features that indicate whether a node represents a fraudster or a legitimate person.

Listing 10.13 Obtaining the results of the entire process

```
G = create_fraud_network()
results = train_fraud_classifier(G)          # Creates and analyzes the network

print("Classification Report:")
print(results['classification_report'])      # Prints a classification report

print("\nConfusion Matrix:")
print(results['confusion_matrix'])           # Prints a confusion matrix

print("\nTop 5 Most Important Features:")
print(results['feature_importance'].head())  # Shows the top five most important features

node_of_interest = 'A'
prob = predict_fraud_probability(G, node_of_interest, results)
print(f"\nFraud probability for node {node_of_interest}: {prob:.3f}")    # Example: Gets the fraud probability for a specific node
```

We will not look at the results, as they were obtained from a sample graph that was too small to be statistically relevant. But this process can also be applied to larger, more realistic graphs. An advantage of this approach is that even though the process was complex and required extensive feature design and careful consideration, it is fully under your control, and each extracted feature is easy to explain just by looking at the graph. This increases the transparency of the process and is why this method is valid when, for example, the database has a limited size or when explainability is important.

10.2 Manual relationship features

After exploring how to represent nodes through structural features, we now turn our attention to another fundamental challenge in graph ML: how to represent relationships between nodes. Although nodes are the primary elements in a graph, the connections between them often hold information that we need to capture and analyze.

Imagine a scenario in which we want to predict potential interactions between elements in a graph. This is where relationship prediction (also known as link prediction) comes into play. Whether we're trying to predict if two proteins might interact, if a customer might be interested in a product, or if a drug could treat a disease, we're essentially asking the same question: given two nodes, how likely is it that a relationship exists between them?

Similar to node classification, relationship prediction requires us to transform graph elements into features that ML algorithms can process. However, instead of representing individual nodes, we need to capture the characteristics of potential connections between nodes. This can be approached as a binary classification task (predicting whether a relationship exists or not) or as a multiclass classification task (predicting the type of relationship that might exist).

To demonstrate these concepts, we'll explore a practical application in drug repurposing: finding new uses for existing drugs. This task can be modeled as a link prediction problem between drugs (also referred more formally as compounds) and diseases, where we aim to predict potential therapeutic relationships. Through this example, we'll examine different strategies for creating meaningful representations of relationships in graphs, building on the concepts we explored for node feature engineering. Figure 10.4, taken from chapter 9, compares the two tasks—node classification and link prediction—and anticipates how the representation of two nodes can be combined to obtain the representation of a relationship.

The key difference in node classification is that we use a node pair as input to indicate the link we want to predict or use during training. Thus for the link prediction to be accurate, we need an effective way to represent the possible connections between the node pair used as input. We can use two distinct approaches:

- *Node-based combination*—We derive the relationship representation by combining the feature vectors of the source and target nodes. For example, if we have node representations [1,2,3] and [4,5,6], we might combine them through operations like concatenation or element-wise multiplication to represent their potential connection. This is the case presented in figure 10.4.
- *Path-based features*—Instead of relying on node features, we characterize relationships by analyzing the ways nodes are connected in the graph. Each feature represents a distinct path pattern between nodes, such as the number of two-hop paths or the presence of specific metapaths, creating a vector that captures the structural context of the relationship.

Node-based combinations work well with node embeddings, whereas path-based features excel at capturing complex network patterns. Let's examine each in detail.

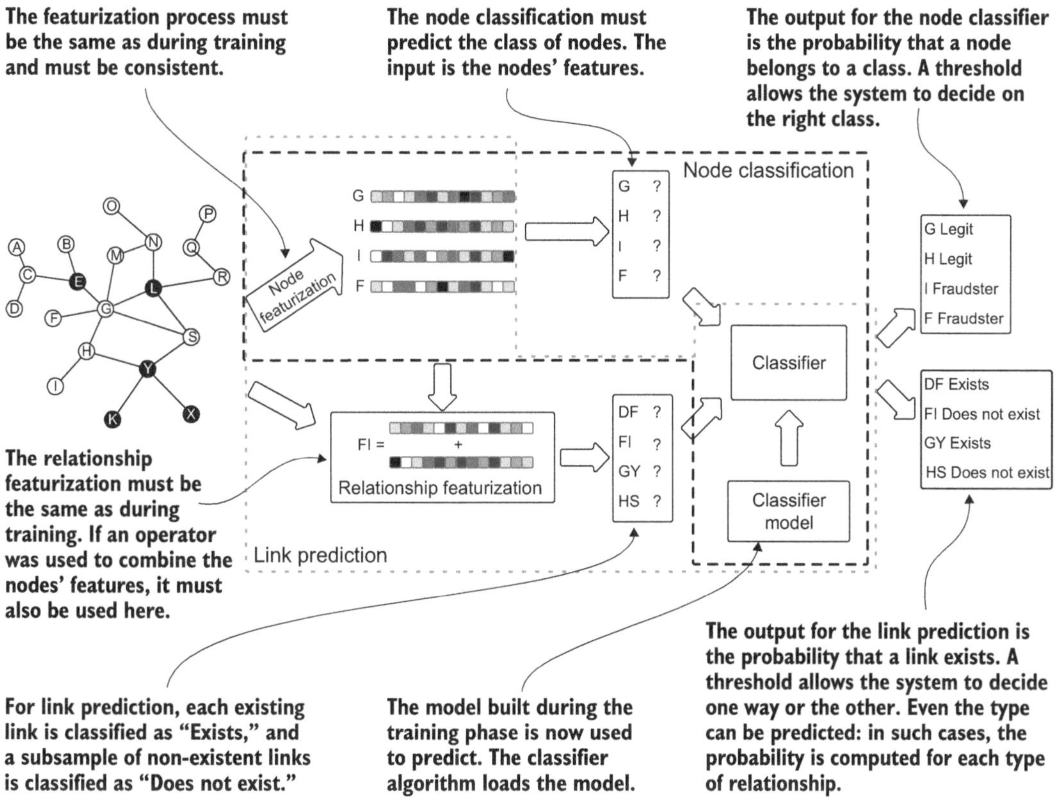

Figure 10.4 A typical relationship prediction, compared with the node classification process

10.2.1 Node-based representation

The most straightforward approach is to combine the feature representations of the two nodes that may be connected. Each node has a set of features that describe it (like a fingerprint), and we want to merge these features to describe what a connection between them might look like. This combination should work for any pair of nodes, whether they're connected in our graph or not. This is important because when we're predicting links, we need to evaluate both existing and potential connections.

The following are the most common techniques used to combine vectors with link prediction in mind:

- *Catenate*—Joins two vectors end to end. For vectors **u** and **v** of length n, it creates a new vector of length $2n$ by placing the elements of **u** followed by the elements of **v**. For example, if **u** = [1,2] and **v** = [3,4], their concatenation is [1,2,3,4]. This preserves all original information but doubles the dimension of the resulting vector.
- *Average*—Creates a new vector by taking the element-wise average (mean) of the two input vectors. For each position i, it computes $(\mathbf{u}[i] + \mathbf{v}[i])/2$. This

maintains the original dimension while capturing the central tendency between the two vectors. For example, if **u** = [2,4] and **v** = [4,8], their average is [3,6].

- *L1 (Manhattan distance)*—Computes the absolute difference between corresponding elements of the two vectors. For each position *i*, it calculates |**u**[*i*] – **v**[*i*]|. This captures how different the vectors are at each dimension and is useful for measuring dissimilarity. For example, if **u** = [1,4] and **v** = [3,1], their L1 combination is [2,3].
- *L2 (Euclidean distance)*—Computes the squared difference between corresponding elements. For each position *i*, it calculates $(\mathbf{u}[i] - \mathbf{v}[i])^2$. Like L1, it captures differences between vectors but emphasizes larger differences due to the squaring operation. For example, if **u** = [1,4] and **v** = [3,1], their L2 combination is [4,9].
- *Hadamard (element-wise product)*—Multiplies the corresponding elements of the two vectors. For each position *i*, it computes **u**[*i*] × **v**[*i*]. This operation is particularly useful when values in both vectors represent related quantities that should be combined multiplicatively. For example, if **u** = [2,4] and **v** = [3,1], their Hadamard product is [6,4].

The following listing shows how to implement each of these methods.

Listing 10.14 Combining two node representations into one link representation

```
def catenate(u, v):
    return u + v

def operator_avg(u, v):
    return (u + v) / 2.0

def operator_l1(u, v):
    return np.abs(u - v)

def operator_l2(u, v):
    return (u - v) ** 2

def operator_hadamard(u, v):
    return u * v
```

The quality of the link prediction depends directly on the quality of the nodes' representation. The composition technique also influences the final quality. There is no generic rule to help you with the selection, so a benchmark can give you an indication of which is the right approach for your scenario.

10.2.2 Path-based features

Some techniques describe the node pair representation, considering the source and destination nodes but not using their representation (or not using them exclusively). Many of these techniques require manual work to properly represent the relationships.

The manual process of representation is generally domain-specific, so it requires some understanding of the domain and the goal we want to achieve. As an example, like in chapter 4, we'll consider biomedical knowledge graphs and how they can help in drug discovery or repurposing. We will again use the Hetionet dataset, which integrates information from 19 public databases containing more than 50,000 nodes representing drugs, diseases, genes, and symptoms.

NOTE If you are following along with all the examples, you should already have the database. If not, go back to chapter 4 to see how to create it.

Himmelstein et al. [5] made significant advances in drug repurposing using the Hetionet dataset. Through computational analysis, they established more than 2 million relationships among these elements. And their work yielded practical results: they identified existing drugs used for depression and alcoholism that showed potential for treating smoking addiction and epilepsy. Let's examine their methodological approach at a high level.

Consider the Hetionet schema presented in chapter 4, repeated here in figure 10.5. The goal is to train a ML model to translate the network connectivity of a

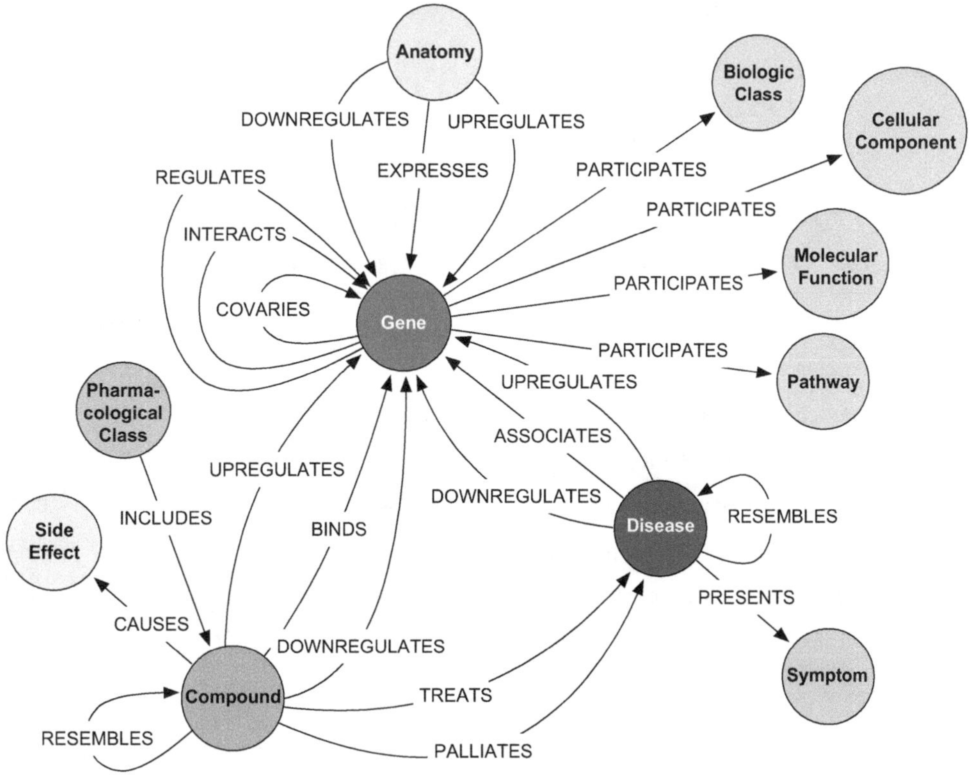

Figure 10.5 The Hetionet schema as it was presented in chapter 4

compound and a disease into a probability of treatment [6, 7]. To create a representation of each node pair—only compounds and diseases—that reflects the network connectivity between the nodes, the researchers evaluated all the metapaths that traverse from compound to disease and have lengths of 2 to 4. Figure 10.6 is a reminder of the concepts of metagraphs and metapaths, using examples between genes and diseases.

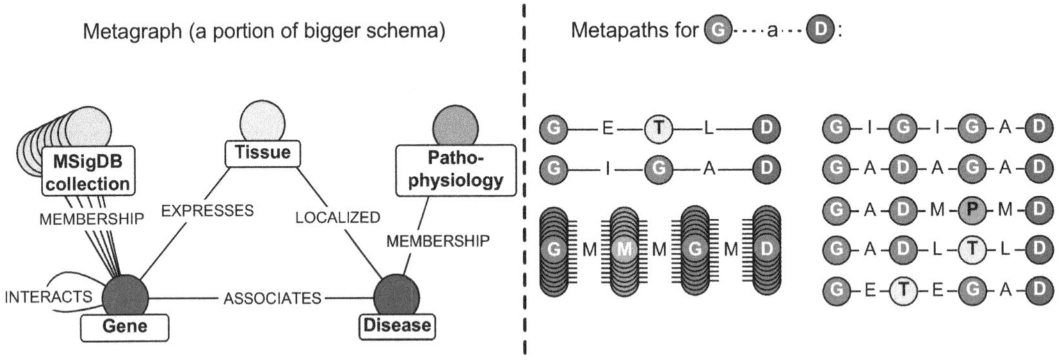

Figure 10.6 Metagraph and metapath examples from Hetionet

Starting from the schema in figure 10.5, some of the metapaths between *Compound* and *Disease* are listed in table 10.8. These metapaths represent just a subset of possible paths between compounds and diseases. They form features for each compound–disease pair, regardless of whether a direct connection exists.

Table 10.8 Examples of metapaths connecting drugs to diseases [5]

Metapath	Length	Abbr.
Compound–binds–*Gene*–associates–*Disease*	2	CbGaD
Compound–downregulates–*Gene*–upregulates–*Disease*	2	CdGuD
Compound–resembles–*Compound*–treats–*Disease*	2	CrCtD
Compound–binds–*Gene*–binds–*Compound*–treats–*Disease*	3	CbGbCtD
Compound–binds–*Gene*–expresses–*Anatomy*–localizes–*Disease*	3	CbGeAlD
Compound–binds–*Gene*–interacts–*Gene*–interacts–*Gene*–associates–*Disease*	4	CbGiGiGaD
Compound–binds–*Gene*–participates–*Pathway*–participates–*Gene* –associates–*Disease*	4	CbGpPWpGaD

For example, considering the compound *metformin* and the disease *type 2 diabetes*, we need to compute the value for each metapath (CbGaD, CdGuD, CrCtD, etc.); see figure 10.7. The simplest approach would be to count distinct path instances between the compound and disease. However, simply counting paths can be misleading if nodes with very high connectivity dominate the counts. For example, if a gene is involved in many biological processes, it will naturally appear in more paths, but this doesn't necessarily indicate stronger or more meaningful relationships between compounds and diseases.

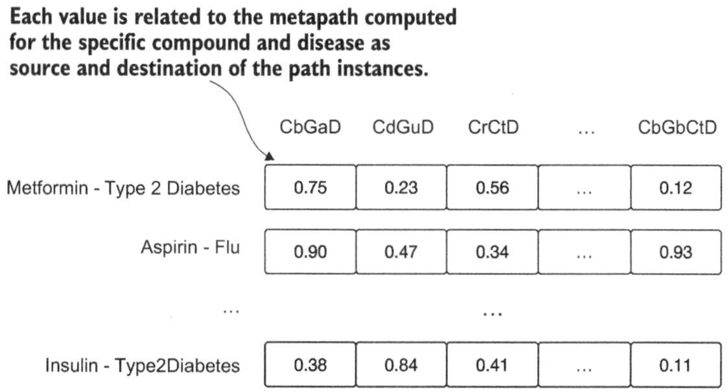

Figure 10.7 Metapath-based feature definition for the relationships between drugs and diseases

To address this bias, we use the degree-weighted path count (DWPC; discussed in more detail in chapter 4), which applies a damping factor based on node degrees. When we calculate DWPC,

- Each path is weighted inversely to the degrees of intermediate nodes
- Nodes with many connections contribute less to the final score
- The damping effect helps highlight more specific, focused biological pathways.

For instance, suppose we have two paths between metformin and type 2 diabetes:

- One through a highly connected gene (degree 100)
- Another through a more specific gene (degree 10)

The second path will contribute more significantly to the DWPC score, better reflecting potential biological significance. This approach has proven particularly effective in drug repurposing, as it helps identify meaningful therapeutic relationships while reducing noise from hub nodes in the biological network.

The next listing computes the DWPC between metformin and type 2 diabetes for the CbGaD (Compound–binds–Gene–associates–Disease) metapath using Neo4j.

Listing 10.15 DWPC between metformin and type 2 diabetes for CbGaD

```
MATCH path = (c:Compound)-[:BINDS_CbG]-(g)-[:ASSOCIATES_DaG]-(d:Disease)
WHERE c.name = 'Metformin' AND d.name = 'type 2 diabetes mellitus'
WITH
[
  count{(v)-[:BINDS_CbG]-()},
```

```
    count{()-[:BINDS_CbG]-(g)},
    count{(g)-[:ASSOCIATES_DaG]-()},
    count{()-[:ASSOCIATES_DaG]-(d)}
]
AS degrees, path, d
WITH
  d.identifier AS disease_id,
  d.name AS disease_name,
  count(path) AS PC,
  sum(reduce(pdp = 1.0, d in degrees| pdp * d ^ -0.4)) AS DWPC
RETURN
  disease_id, disease_name, PC, DWPC
```

Running it on our Hetionet database, we get the value 0.0007. We will use this value for the feature CbGaD in the vector for the *Metformin–Type 2 Diabetes* pair.

> **Exercise**
>
> Run the query in listing 10.15 for other compounds and diseases, considering existing and non-existent direct connections. Then change the query to test other metapaths.

Listings 10.16 and 10.17 provide two more examples.

Listing 10.16 DWPC value for CbGeAlD

```
MATCH path = (c:Compound)-[:BINDS_CbG]-(g:Gene)<-[:EXPRESSES_AeG]-
[CA](a:Anatomy)<-[:LOCALIZES_DlA]-(d:Disease)
WHERE c.name = 'Metformin' AND d.name = 'type 2 diabetes mellitus'
WITH
[
  count{(c)-[:BINDS_CbG]-()},
  count{()-[:BINDS_CbG]-(g)},
  count{(g)<-[:EXPRESSES_AeG]-()},
  count{()-[:EXPRESSES_AeG]-(a)},
  count{(a)<-[:LOCALIZES_DlA]-()},
  count{()-[:LOCALIZES_DlA]-(d)}
] AS degrees, path, d
WITH
  d.identifier AS disease_id,
  d.name AS disease_name,
  count(path) AS PC,
  sum(reduce(pdp = 1.0, d in degrees| pdp * d ^ -0.4)) AS DWPC
RETURN disease_id, disease_name, PC, DWPC
```

Listing 10.17 DWPC value for CbGpPWpGaD

```
MATCH path = (c:Compound)-[:BINDS_CbG]-(g1:Gene)-[:PARTICIPATES_GpPW]-
    >(pw:Pathway)<-[:PARTICIPATES_GpPW]-(g2:Gene)-[:ASSOCIATES_DaG]-
    (d:Disease)
WHERE c.name = 'Metformin' AND d.name = 'type 2 diabetes mellitus'
```

```
WITH
[
  count{(c)-[:BINDS_CbG]-()},
  count{()-[:BINDS_CbG]-(g1)},
  count{(g1)-[:PARTICIPATES_GpPW]->()},
  count{()-[:PARTICIPATES_GpPW]->(pw)},
  count{(pw)<-[:PARTICIPATES_GpPW]-()},
  count{()<-[:PARTICIPATES_GpPW]-(g2)},
  count{(g2)-[:ASSOCIATES_DaG]-()},
  count{()-[:ASSOCIATES_DaG]-(d)}
] AS degrees, path, d
WITH
  d.identifier AS disease_id,
  d.name AS disease_name,
  count(path) AS PC,
  sum(reduce(pdp = 1.0, d in degrees| pdp * d ^ -0.4)) AS DWPC
RETURN disease_id, disease_name, PC, DWPC
```

Computing the DWPC values for all possible compound–disease pairs across all potential metapaths would be computationally expensive and could lead to noisy or misleading results. To address this challenge, Himmelstein and colleagues [5] developed a two-step approach to reduce complexity and eliminate features that might be irrelevant or potentially harmful to the model's performance:

1. *Metapath reduction*—They developed a statistical method to identify the most significant metapaths by analyzing their frequency in known treatment-versus-nontreatment relationships. This analysis reduced the number of relevant metapaths from 1,026 to 709 while maintaining high predictive power.
2. *Pair selection*—They further refined the analysis by using domain knowledge and degree-based probabilistic analysis to identify the most promising compound–disease pairs. This reduction not only decreased computational overhead but also improved classifier performance by focusing on the most relevant pairs.

Although combining node representations (as discussed earlier) offers a simpler approach, it often performs poorly with manually extracted node features. As we'll explore later, this approach becomes more effective when working with automatically extracted features.

Using LLMs for graph feature engineering

LLMs, as we have seen many times throughout the book, can provide support in complex tasks. Graph feature engineering is one of them. LLMs excel at tasks that require understanding complex patterns and translating them into executable code. This is especially valuable when working with graph databases, where crafting queries often requires a deep understanding of both the domain and the query language. For instance, in our drug repurposing case, LLMs can do the following:

- *Query generation*—LLMs can translate high-level descriptions of metapaths into optimized Cypher queries.

(continued)

- *Feature engineering*—They can suggest relevant patterns and relationships that might not be immediately obvious.
- *Code generation*—They can help create the necessary infrastructure to execute and process query results.

For example, suppose we want to generate Cypher queries for multiple metapaths in our drug repurposing network to extract features for our relationships representation. Here's an effective prompt we can use with an LLM:

AN You are a graph database expert specializing in Neo4j and Cypher queries. I'm working on a drug repurposing project and need help generating queries for metapath analysis.

I'll provide you with:

- The graph schema (obtained from apoc.meta.schema())
- An example of the query for CbGaD
- A list of metapaths between Compound and Disease nodes
- Sample compound and disease names for testing

For each metapath:

- Generate a Cypher query that computes both Path Count (PC) and Degree-Weighted Path Count (DWPC, using damping factor 0.4)
- Include degree calculations for each node in the path
- Return disease_id, disease_name, PC, and DWPC

The schema is:

{Shema definition here or as attachment}

An example of the query for DWPC is:

```
MATCH path = (c:Compound)-[:BINDS_CbG]-(g)-[:ASSOCIATES_DaG]-
             (d:Disease)
WHERE c.name = 'Metformin' AND d.name = 'type 2 diabetes mellitus'
WITH
[
  count{(v)-[:BINDS_CbG]-()},
  count{()-[:BINDS_CbG]-(g)},
  count{(g)-[:ASSOCIATES_DaG]-()},
  count{()-[:ASSOCIATES_DaG]-(d)}
]
AS degrees, path, d
WITH
  d.identifier AS disease_id,
  d.name AS disease_name,
  count(path) AS PC,
  sum(reduce(pdp = 1.0, d in degrees| pdp * d ^ -0.4)) AS DWPC
RETURN
  disease_id, disease_name, PC, DWPC
```

> Please generate queries for these metapaths:
> - CbGaD (Compound-binds-Gene-associates-Disease)
> - CdGuD (Compound-downregulates-Gene-upregulates-Disease)
> - Use {source compound} as the compound and {destination disease} as the disease.

This is an example of a prompt you can use to generate Cypher queries; then you can write the Python code to generate the final representation. You can change the prompt to return results that are immediately useful, but our goal was to plant the seed for how you can use LLMs creatively.

10.3 Semiautomated feature extraction

In sections 10.1 and 10.2, we explored manual feature engineering for both nodes and relationships, demonstrating how domain knowledge can guide the creation of meaningful representations. We saw how careful selection of structural metrics and domain-specific patterns can create effective features for tasks like fraud detection and drug repurposing. But although this manual approach provides deep insights, it comes with significant challenges: it requires extensive domain expertise, is time-consuming to implement, and needs to be customized for each new use case.

What if we could maintain the benefits of manual feature engineering—interpretability, reliability, predictability—while automating much of the feature selection process? This is where ReFeX (Recursive Feature eXtraction) [8] comes in, offering a middle ground between fully manual feature engineering and the complex neural network approaches we'll explore in chapters 11 and 12. ReFeX automatically identifies and extracts relevant structural features from graphs. Unlike black-box neural approaches, ReFeX's process is transparent and produces interpretable features that domain experts can understand and validate. This transparency is particularly valuable when we need to explain why certain predictions were made—imagine a fraud detection system where we need to justify why an account was flagged as suspicious.

Another advantage of ReFeX is its consistency across different graphs. The features it generates can be compared meaningfully between different networks or even different snapshots of the same network over time—something that is rarely possible with more complex neural approaches. This property makes ReFeX particularly valuable for applications where we need to track how graph structures evolve or compare patterns across different networks.

To demonstrate these benefits, we'll first examine how ReFeX works by manually calculating its features on a small example. Then we'll see how it can be applied to larger, real-world scenarios where manual feature engineering would be impractical.

ReFeX works by recursively generating local and egonet features from the graph structure, automatically capturing many of the metrics we previously calculated manually. The key advantages of this approach are as follows:

- *Efficiency*—Automated extraction of recursive structural features
- *Consistency*—Systematic approach to feature generation
- *Interpretability*—Generated features that maintain clear structural meaning
- *Scalability*—Ability to handle larger graphs while maintaining feature quality

However, human oversight remains essential in this process. Domain experts can

- *Validate* the relevance of generated features
- *Incorporate* domain knowledge to guide feature selection
- *Understand* and explain the features' contribution to fraud detection
- *Modify* the feature extraction process based on specific requirements

This hybrid approach sets the stage for our later discussion of fully automated feature learning methods, where we'll see how deep learning techniques can extract features without human intervention, trading interpretability for potentially more sophisticated pattern recognition.

ReFeX computes features by recursively combining local (node-based) features with features coming from the node's neighborhood (egonet-based). In this way, the algorithm produces the regional features—capturing "behavioral" information—that represent the kind of nodes to which a given node is connected, as opposed to the identity of those nodes. It is who you know, or who you relate to, that matters in mining across different graphs.

The ReFeX process is based on two fundamental rules:

- *Structural*—The construction of feature matrix F should not require additional attribute information on nodes or links.
- *Effective*—Good node features should (1) help us predict node attributes when such attributes are available and (2) be transferable across graphs (e.g., when the graph changes over time).

The ideal feature set should help with data mining tasks. Typical tasks include node classification (after we are given some labels), de-anonymization of the graph nodes, and transfer learning. Figure 10.8 represents, in a very simple way, the input and the output of the process.

ReFeX operates on the pure structural aspects of the graph—nodes and relationships—without considering node labels or types. This focus on topology allows the algorithm to identify structural patterns. The feature extraction process occurs in three main stages:

1 *Local feature extraction* focuses on immediate node characteristics. The primary metric at this level is the node degree, including both weighted and unweighted variants. When working with directed graphs, ReFeX computes

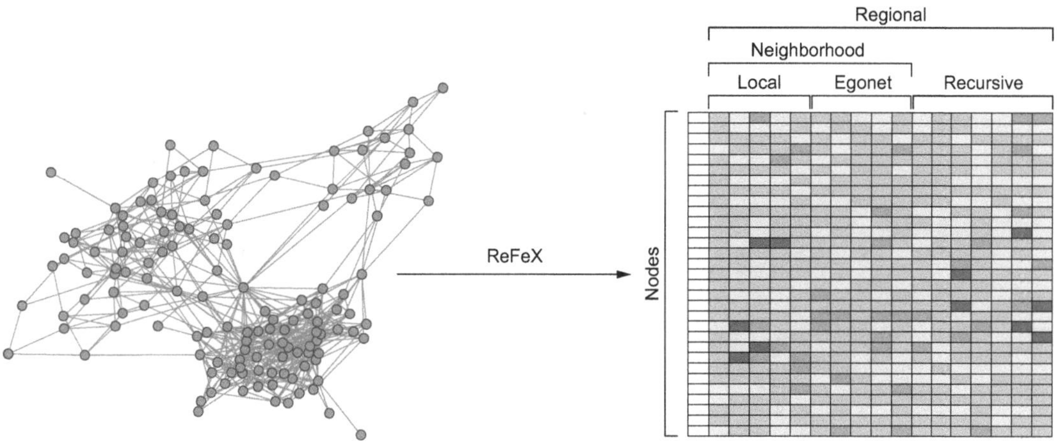

Figure 10.8 ReFeX converts each node into a vector representing the node's topological feature at different scales [8].

both in-degree and out-degree separately. For weighted graphs, it calculates the weighted degree as the sum of incident edge weights, providing a more nuanced view of node connectivity.

2 *Examination of egonet features* analyzes each node's immediate neighborhood. At this level, ReFeX computes metrics including the number of incoming egonet edges, outgoing egonet edges, and total egonet edges. When working with weighted graphs, it also calculates weighted variants of these metrics to capture the strength of connections within the ego network.
3 *Recursive feature extraction* aggregates existing features through the recursive application of summary statistics. This process uses combinations of aggregation functions (sum/mean) to capture increasingly complex structural patterns. For example, a feature like degree(sum)(mean)(mean)(sum) can capture regional structural patterns that extend beyond the immediate neighborhood. In directed graphs, ReFeX computes these recursive features separately for incoming and outgoing paths, providing a comprehensive view of directional patterns in the network.

The recursive nature of the algorithm can generate an exponentially growing number of features. To manage this complexity, ReFeX uses several pruning techniques:

- *Correlation analysis*—Identifies and eliminates highly correlated feature pairs
- *Logarithmic binning*—Maps feature values to discrete intervals for efficient comparison
- *Threshold-based pruning*—Removes features that differ by less than a specified threshold

10.3.1 Performing ReFeX manually

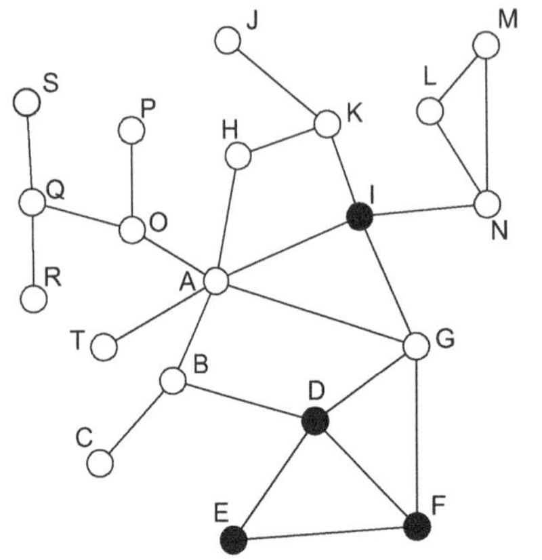

Figure 10.9 Our simple fraudulent network. In this case, the colors of the nodes will be ignored, because ReFeX doesn't consider node types.

Let's apply ReFeX manually to the small graph database shown in figure 10.9. We are considering an undirected and unweighted graph for simplicity, and we won't perform any pruning steps. Table 10.9 shows the degree of each node.

Table 10.9 Degree of the nodes in figure 10.9

Node	Degree
A	6
B	3
C	1
D	4
E	2
...	...

These results are the same as in section 10.1.1. This is not a directed graph, so we can't compute the in-degree and out-degree.

The next step is to consider the egonet for each node. For example, for node A, the egonet is composed of A itself and its neighbors: B, G, H, I, O, and T. The total number of nodes in the egonet is seven (A plus its six neighbors). The total number of internal edges is seven (six edges connecting A to its neighbors, plus one edge between G and I). The total number of in/out egonet edges is nine (these are edges that connect nodes in A's egonet to nodes outside: B→C,D; G→D,F; H→K; I→K,N; O→P,Q). Table 10.10 lists the total values for each of the nodes.

Table 10.10 Details of the egonet structure for the nodes in figure 10.9

Node's egonet	# of nodes	# of internal edges	# of in/out edges
A	7	7	9
B	4	3	5
C	2	1	1
D	5	6	4
E	3	3	3
...	...	...	...

The final step in ReFeX involves recursive feature aggregation, a multiphase process that progressively captures broader network characteristics. The algorithm aggregates features from increasingly distant neighborhoods at each iteration, creating a more comprehensive view of each node's structural context. Figure 10.10 illustrates this process using our example graph.

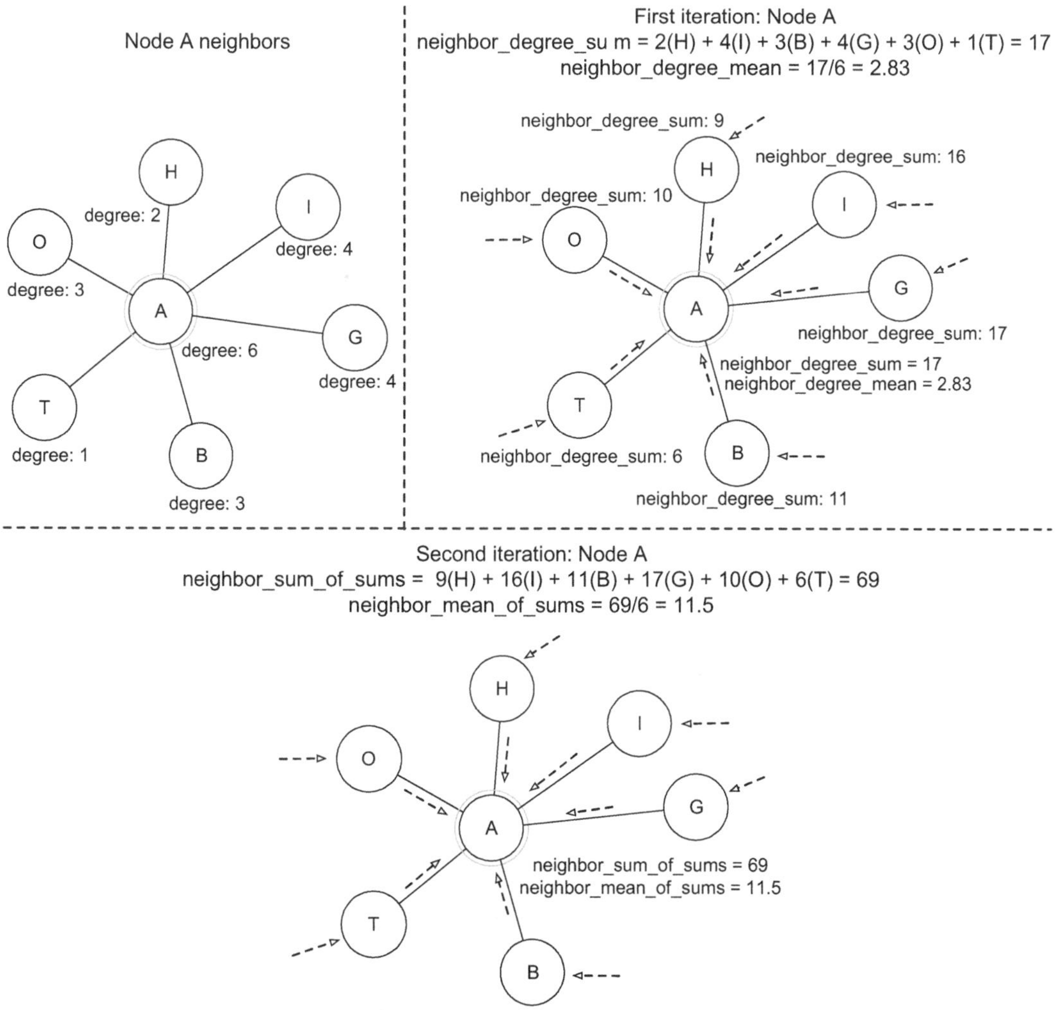

Figure 10.10 Illustration of a few iterations of the ReFeX process. At each iteration, each node passes its values (degree, previous sums, etc.) to the neighbors, which will aggregate.

Let's walk through the process using node A as our example:

1. First iteration:
   - Node A has six neighbors (H, I, G, B, T, O).
   - Local features: degree(A) = 6

- First aggregation using the SUM operator:

$$\text{sum(neighbor\_degrees)} = \text{degree}(H) + \text{degree}(I) + \text{degree}(G) + \text{degree}(B) + \text{degree}(T) + \text{degree}(O)$$

$$\text{sum(neighbor\_degrees)} = 2 + 4 + 4 + 3 + 1 + 3 = 17$$

2 Second iteration:
   - Uses the aggregated values from the first iteration.
   - Each neighbor now carries its first-iteration sum (agg).
   - Second aggregation:

$$\text{sum(neighbor\_aggregates)} = \text{agg}(B) + \text{agg}(G) + \text{agg}(H) + \text{agg}(I) + \text{agg}(O) + \text{agg}(T)$$

$$\text{sum(neighbor\_aggregates)} = 11 + 17 + 9 + 16 + 10 + 6 = 69$$

Additionally, ReFeX can use the MEAN operator for aggregation. For node A, this would give

- First iteration:

$$\text{mean(neighbor\_degrees)} = (3 + 4 + 2 + 4 + 3 + 1)/6 = 17/6 \approx 2.83$$

- Second iteration:

$$\text{mean(neighbor\_aggregates)} = (11 + 17 + 9 + 16 + 10 + 6)/6 = 69/6 = 11.5$$

Table 10.11 shows the results for node A after these iterations (before pruning).

Table 10.11 Features computed for node A

Feature type	Feature	Value
Local feature	Degree	6
Egonet feature	Number of edges in the egonet	7
Recursive feature, first iteration	Sum of neighbor degrees	17
	Mean of neighbor degrees	2.83
Recursive feature, second iteration	Sum of neighbor sums	69
	Mean of neighbor sums	11.5

10.3.2 Performing ReFeX automatically with code

The full implementation of the algorithm is available in the book's code repository. The following listing shows the most relevant part of the code.

Listing 10.18 ReFeX implementation (key parts)

```
import networkx as nx
import numpy as np
from collections import defaultdict
from sklearn.preprocessing import StandardScaler

class ReFeX:
    def __init__(self, max_iterations=2, correlation_threshold=0.95):
        self.max_iterations = max_iterations
        self.correlation_threshold = correlation_threshold

    def extract_features(self, G):
        features = self._extract_local_features(G)

        egonet_features = self._extract_egonet_features(G)
        features = np.column_stack((features, egonet_features))

        for iteration in range(self.max_iterations):
            new_features = self._generate_recursive_features(G, features)
            features = np.column_stack((features, new_features))
            features = self._prune_features(features)
        return features

    def _extract_local_features(self, G):
        """Extract local (node-level) features"""
        n_nodes = G.number_of_nodes()
        features = np.zeros((n_nodes, 3))

        for idx, node in enumerate(G.nodes()):
            # Degree features
            features[idx, 0] = G.degree(node)

            # In-degree and out-degree for directed graphs
            if G.is_directed():
                features[idx, 1] = G.in_degree(node)
                features[idx, 2] = G.out_degree(node)
            else:
                features[idx, 1] = features[idx, 2] = G.degree(node)

        return features

    def _extract_egonet_features(self, G):
        n_nodes = G.number_of_nodes()
        features = np.zeros((n_nodes, 3))
        for idx, node in enumerate(G.nodes()):
            ego = nx.ego_graph(G, node, radius=1)
            features[idx, 0] = ego.number_of_nodes()
            features[idx, 1] = ego.number_of_edges()
            features[idx, 2] = nx.density(ego)

        return features

    def _generate_recursive_features(self, G, current_features):
        n_nodes = G.number_of_nodes()
```

Initializes ReFeX with an iteration limit and correlation threshold

Extracts basic node-level features (degrees) and uses them to initialize the feature matrix

Adds features based on egonet properties

Generates and adds recursive features iteratively

Removes redundant features based on correlation

Computes local features including degree metrics

Calculates egonet-based features for each node

Generates recursive features using sum and mean aggregations

```
        n_features = current_features.shape[1]
        new_features = np.zeros((n_nodes, n_features * 2))

        for idx, node in enumerate(G.nodes()):
            neighbors = list(G.neighbors(node))
            if not neighbors:
                continue

            neighbor_feats =
               current_features[[list(G.nodes()).index(n) for n in neighbors]]
               new_features[idx, :n_features] = np.sum(neighbor_feats, axis=0)
               new_features[idx, n_features:] = np.mean(neighbor_feats,
               axis=0)
        return new_features

    def _prune_features(self, features):      <-- Identifies highly correlated features for removal, and removes them
        scaler = StandardScaler()
        scaled_features = scaler.fit_transform(features)      <-- Standardizes features

        corr_matrix = np.corrcoef(scaled_features.T)      <-- Computes the correlation matrix

        to_remove = set()
        for i in range(corr_matrix.shape[0]):      <-- Finds highly correlated features
            for j in range(i + 1, corr_matrix.shape[1]):
                if abs(corr_matrix[i, j]) > self.correlation_threshold:
                    to_remove.add(j)

        keep_features = list(set(range(features.shape[1])) - to_remove)      <-- Keeps uncorrelated features
        return features[:, keep_features]      <-- Returns a pruned feature matrix
```

Exercise

The book's code repository contains the complete code, which connects to a Hetionet database available in Neo4j. Give it a try.

ReFeX represents a significant step toward automated feature extraction, occupying an important middle ground between manual feature engineering and fully autonomous representation learning techniques. Its focus on pure graph structure provides an excellent foundation for understanding more complex approaches and demonstrates how structural patterns alone can capture meaningful characteristics of nodes and their neighborhoods. Although ReFeX automates feature extraction, it maintains transparency and interpretability; its computations can be traced and verified step by step, making it an invaluable tool for practitioners who need to understand and validate their feature engineering process. And ReFeX's deterministic nature ensures consistency: identical inputs will always produce identical outputs. This predictability is particularly valuable in production environments where reproducibility is essential. Moreover, when the graph structure changes, ReFeX allows for selective recomputation of affected features rather than requiring a complete regeneration of the feature matrix. This efficiency makes it particularly suitable for dynamic graph environments.

However, ReFeX also has limitations. Its reliance on structural features means it cannot directly incorporate node attributes or edge types. And although pruning helps manage computational complexity, it sometimes requires human oversight to ensure optimal feature selection.

In the next chapter, we'll see how modern autonomous representation learning techniques address these limitations while sacrificing some of the interpretability and deterministic nature that make ReFeX valuable for certain applications. Understanding ReFeX's strengths and limitations will provide essential context for appreciating the innovations and trade-offs introduced by these more advanced methods.

Summary

- Manual and semimanual feature engineering in graphs provides a foundation for ML tasks, balancing interpretability with automation.
- Manual feature engineering combines local metrics with global measures to create meaningful node representations that capture both immediate connections and broader network patterns.
- Combining node metrics helps identify patterns while maintaining interpretable decision-making processes.
- Relationship representation can be approached through node-based combinations (concatenation, averaging, distances) or path-based features (metapaths, structural patterns).
- Node-based relationship representation can use various combination methods: concatenation, averaging, L1/L2 distances, and Hadamard product.
- Path-based features capture structural patterns between nodes through metapath analysis.
- DWPC (degree-weighted path count) provides a sophisticated approach to measuring connection relevance while accounting for node degrees.
- Domain expertise guides feature engineering in both node and relationship representation, from metric selection to validation of results.
- Semiautomated approaches like ReFeX offer a middle ground by automatically generating interpretable features while preserving the option to incorporate domain knowledge.
- The choice between manual and semiautomated approaches depends on interpretability needs, computational resources, and available domain expertise.
- Feature pruning and selection remain essential in both approaches, requiring careful consideration of correlation and relevance to specific ML tasks.

11 Graph representation learning and graph neural networks

This chapter covers

- Understanding graph representation learning and its role in scaling machine learning on graphs
- Automating feature engineering with deep learning
- Understanding graph embeddings and their applications
- Working with graph neural networks

In chapters 9 and 10, we explored the fundamental concepts of machine learning (ML) on graphs, demonstrating how these techniques can solve complex tasks like node classification, link prediction, and community detection. We showed how manual feature engineering can effectively capture graph properties and relationships to power downstream ML tasks. These approaches provide insights into what makes graph-based ML work, offering transparency into how our models make decisions.

However, even simple classification tasks require significant effort to design and implement effective features. Manual approaches excel at interpretability and help build intuition, but they face significant challenges when scaled to real-world knowledge graphs (KGs) containing millions of nodes and relationships.

Graph representation learning (GRL) offers a powerful solution to these scalability challenges. Rather than relying on human expertise to design features, GRL uses *deep learning* (DL) techniques to automatically learn optimal representations—called *embeddings*—directly from the graph structure and node attributes. These learned representations capture patterns and similarities that would be difficult or impossible to specify manually. The *embedding process* transforms nodes, edges, and subgraphs into dense vector representations that preserve the graph's structural and semantic properties while being readily consumable by standard ML algorithms.

Graph neural networks (GNNs) have emerged as a particularly effective framework for learning these representations. By iteratively aggregating and transforming information from neighboring nodes, GNNs can automatically discover relevant features for downstream tasks while handling the unique challenges of graph-structured data. This chapter shows how GRL and, in particular, GNNs enable ML on graphs to scale to real-world applications.

We'll explore the technical details of these approaches, but our focus remains practical: understanding when and how to effectively apply these tools to build better intelligent advisor systems. By combining the intuitions developed through manual feature engineering with automated representation learning, we can build graph-powered ML systems that are both scalable and interpretable.

11.1 Embeddings in graph representation learning

When we look at the history of GRL, we can see a fascinating evolution that mirrors the broader development of ML. This field, which focuses on teaching computers to understand and work with graph-structured data, has grown through three generations, each building on the insights and achievements of its predecessors [1]:

1. *The first generation* emerged from traditional mathematics and computer science, focusing on what we now call traditional graph embedding. Imagine trying to take a complex three-dimensional object and create a faithful two-dimensional drawing of it—this was essentially the challenge these early researchers faced. They approached graphs through the lens of classical dimensionality reduction, trying to find ways to represent complex graph structures in simpler, more manageable forms while preserving their essential properties.
2. *The second generation* marked a revolutionary shift, sparked by breakthroughs in natural language processing. Just as word2vec showed us how to capture the meaning of words in numerical vectors, Node2Vec demonstrated that we could do the same with nodes in a graph. Rather than just reducing complexity, we were now capturing meaningful relationships and patterns in our numerical representations.
3. *The third and current generation* has embraced the power of DL, particularly through GNNs. Think of how DL transformed image recognition by automatically learning to identify features from raw pixels—GNNs do something similar

for graphs, automatically learning to understand complex patterns of relationships and interactions.

To harness the power of graph embeddings in real-world applications, we need to understand their fundamental characteristics and how these properties influence their performance in different scenarios. In the following sections, we'll explore the key dimensions that define graph embeddings, from the geometric spaces they occupy to how they capture local and global graph properties.

11.1.1 Understanding graph embeddings: From discrete to continuous

Imagine that you're trying to describe the layout of a city to someone who's never been there. You could list every street and intersection (like a discrete graph representation made by nodes and relationships), or you could draw a map with coordinates for each location (like a continuous embedding made by numbers). The map makes it much easier to understand relationships between locations and do useful calculations about the distance between points [2]. Figure 11.1 depicts the node embedding problem.

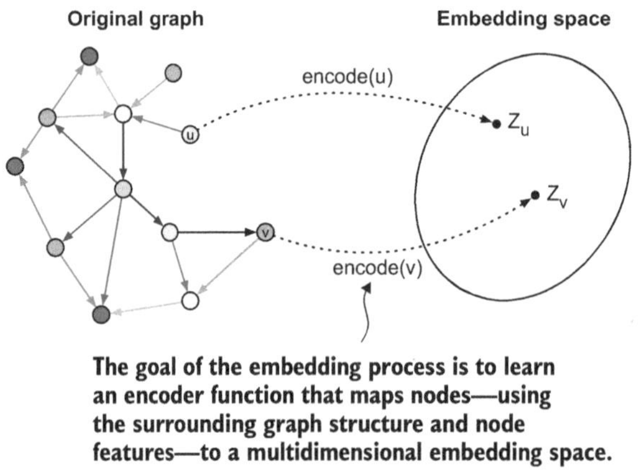

Figure 11.1 The node embedding problem. The goal of the task is to learn an encoding function, encode(*x*), that maps nodes to a multidimensional embedding space. These embeddings are optimized so that distances in the embedding space reflect relevant aspects of the original graph, such as the relative positions of the nodes.

This is what graph embeddings do: they transform discrete graph structures into continuous vector representations. But why is this transformation so valuable? Let's explore this through the different aspects of embedding approaches.

THE GEOMETRY OF EMBEDDINGS: BEYOND FLAT SPACES

To understand why geometric spaces matter in graph embeddings, we first need to recognize a fundamental challenge in ML: different types of data have different inherent structures. When we work with images or text, the data has a regular, predictable structure. Every pixel in an image has eight neighbors, and every word in a text has one word before and one after it. This regularity allows us to use well-established techniques like convolutional neural networks for images or recurrent neural networks for text [3].

However, in a graph, each node may have a different number of connections and neighborhood structure than its neighbors. This irregularity means we can't directly apply the same techniques we use for regular structured data. We need approaches that can handle this variability, which brings us to the question of geometric spaces.

Figure 11.2 shows the difference between a Euclidean space and a non-Euclidean space. Most ML models, including many graph embedding approaches, operate in Euclidean space: distances are measured with straight lines, and the Pythagorean theorem holds. Euclidean space is particularly effective for data where relationships are uniform and don't change based on position or scale. When we embed something in Euclidean space, we represent it as a vector of coordinates, and the distance between two points is calculated using the standard Euclidean distance formula: the square root of the sum of squared differences between coordinates.

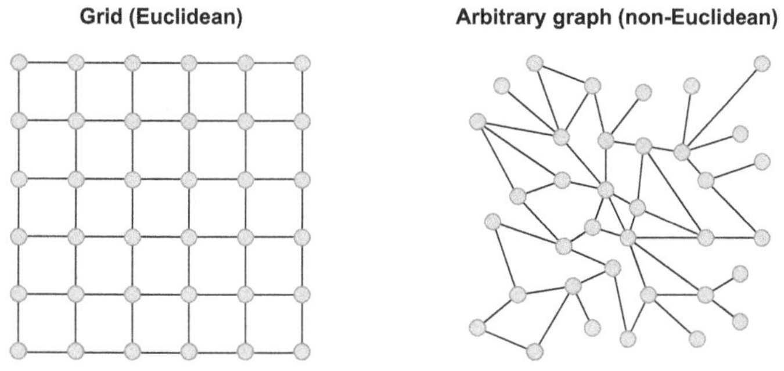

Figure 11.2 Euclidean vs. non-Euclidean space [3]. Pixels in an image are all equally distant from each other and have eight neighbors (except those on the border). In a graph, the number of neighbors can vary enormously from one node to another.

Researchers have discovered that some types of graph structures, particularly hierarchical ones, can be represented more effectively in non-Euclidean spaces, especially hyperbolic spaces. The key difference lies in how space itself behaves: in Euclidean space, the amount of space available grows polynomially as you move outward from a center point (see figure 11.3); but in hyperbolic space, the available space grows exponentially as you move outward, like a tree that branches out more at each level.

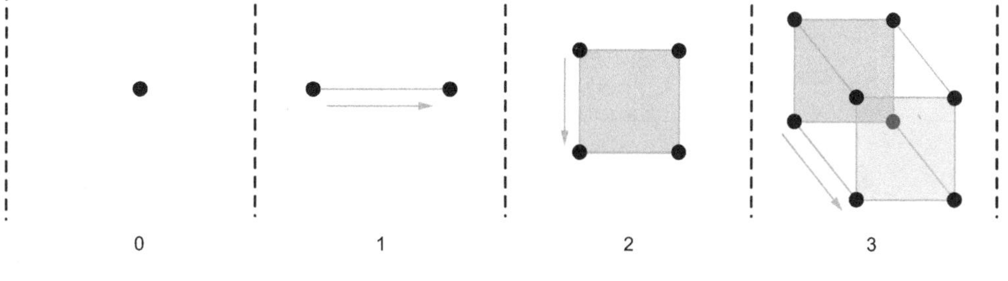

Figure 11.3 Euclidean space grows polynomially as we increase the number of dimensions. Moving from 2D to 3D to 4D and beyond, the available space increases according to a polynomial relationship with the dimension. For example, a unit square in 2D has an area of 1, a unit cube in 3D has a volume of 1, and a unit hypercube in 4D has a hypervolume of 1. Still, the total space available along each axis increases polynomially rather than exponentially.

Consider these practical implications for embeddings. In Euclidean space,

- Vectors are straightforward coordinate points, like (0.5, 0.3).
- Distances grow linearly with coordinate differences.
- The space between points remains constant regardless of their position.
- Most ML models assume this space, making it the default choice for many applications.

In hyperbolic space,

- Vectors are still represented as coordinates, but they behave differently.
- Distances grow exponentially as points approach the boundary of the space.
- The same coordinate difference represents larger distances near the boundary.
- Special distance formulas must be used to calculate similarities between points.

The choice of geometric space becomes particularly important when we know our graph has certain structural properties. For instance, many real-world graphs exhibit a hierarchical structure: think of corporate organizations, biological taxonomies, or internet network topology. In these cases, hyperbolic embeddings may preserve the graph's structure more faithfully than Euclidean embeddings.

It's important to understand that the Euclidean space works well for many applications. We should consider non-Euclidean embeddings only when we have strong evidence that our graph structure would benefit from their properties. When we do use non-Euclidean embeddings, we need to be mindful of how this affects our entire pipeline—from how distances are calculated to how we visualize and interpret the results. This geometric perspective is part of a broader field called *geometric deep learning* (GDL), which studies how to apply DL techniques to data with nonstandard geometric structures. Understanding these geometric spaces helps us choose the right tools for our graph problems and interpret the results appropriately.

LOCAL VS. GLOBAL: UNDERSTANDING POSITIONAL AND STRUCTURAL EMBEDDINGS

The distinction between positional and structural embeddings reflects a fundamental question in graph analysis: what aspects of the graph structure are most important to preserve? Let's explore this through an example of a social network [3]:

- *Positional embeddings* are like preserving the *absolute* positions of people in a social network. If we think of a friend group, positional embeddings would maintain information about who is central to the entire network, who bridges different communities, and how many steps it takes to get from one person to another. These embeddings use techniques like matrix factorization and random walks to capture global properties.
- *Structural embeddings* focus on *relative* positions or local patterns. Two people might be far apart in the network, but if they have similar friendship patterns (like both being the organizers of their respective friend groups), structural embeddings would represent them similarly. This is where GNNs excel, as they can learn to recognize and preserve these local patterns of connectivity.

Positional embeddings, with their focus on preserving global graph structure, have proven valuable for unsupervised tasks where the overall network topology matters most, such as link prediction (where understanding global connection patterns helps predict missing edges) and clustering (where knowing a node's position in the broader network helps identify communities). On the other hand, structural embeddings, particularly those generated by GNNs, excel in supervised tasks. Their ability to capture local neighborhood patterns makes them especially effective for node classification (where similar local structures often indicate similar labels) and whole graph classification (where local patterns can define graph-level properties).

Recent advances in the field have begun to blur these traditional boundaries. New architectures like positional GNNs have emerged, incorporating global positional information into the typically local-focused GNN framework. Furthermore, theoretical work has revealed deeper connections between these two perspectives, suggesting that positional and structural embeddings may capture complementary aspects of graph structure.

Learning strategies: Transductive vs. inductive approaches

The choice between transductive and inductive learning approaches reflects an important question in ML: how should models handle new, unseen data? This distinction is particularly important in graph learning, where new nodes and edges frequently appear [3]:

- *Transductive learning* is like learning to solve a specific puzzle: you can get very good at it, but your knowledge may not transfer to a different puzzle. In graph terms, transductive approaches learn embeddings for a fixed set of nodes, optimizing them directly for the known graph structure. This works well for static graphs where you don't expect new nodes to appear. Transductive methods allow us to infer new information between nodes analyzed during training. For example, when working with partially labeled nodes, we can classify unlabeled nodes based on the patterns learned from the known structure. Similarly, we can predict new edges between graph nodes that were observed during the training process.
- *Inductive learning* is like learning the general strategies for solving puzzles. Instead of memorizing specific patterns, inductive approaches learn rules that can be applied to new situations. This makes them useful for dynamic graphs. Node features are used in inductive GRL methods to learn embeddings with parametric mappings. The learning goal is achieved by optimizing such parametric mappings instead of directly optimizing the embeddings. This means the learning mappings can be applied to any node, even those that were not seen during training.

Consider a recommendation system for an e-commerce platform. A transductive approach works well for recommending existing products to existing users based on their past interactions. However, when a new user joins the platform (or a new product is offered), we need an inductive approach that can generate meaningful embeddings for this new user based on their initial interactions and profile information.

THE ROLE OF SUPERVISION IN LEARNING EMBEDDINGS

The distinction between supervised and unsupervised learning in graph embeddings reflects different levels of available information and different goals for the embedding process:

- *Unsupervised learning* in graph embeddings is like trying to understand the social dynamics of a group by watching who talks to whom, without knowing anything about the content of their conversations. The goal is to discover natural patterns and structures in the graph data. This approach relies on the assumption that the graph structure alone contains valuable information—which is often true!
- *Supervised learning* is like having additional context about the interactions we observe. This additional information helps guide the learning process toward specific goals.

11.1.2 Real-world applications and examples

Let's explore how these aspects of graph embeddings come together in real-world applications:

- *Social network analysis*—Consider a large social network like LinkedIn. Here, structural embeddings identify users with similar professional roles across different industries, while positional embeddings help understand who the key influencers and bridge-builders are in the network. The platform needs inductive learning capabilities to handle new users and may use supervised learning with job titles and skills to improve recommendation accuracy.
- *Biological networks*—In protein interaction networks, the choice of geometry is critical. The hierarchical organization of biological systems often benefits from hyperbolic embeddings. The need to constantly incorporate new discoveries makes inductive learning essential, and the availability of experimental data enables supervised learning approaches to improve prediction accuracy.
- *Medical knowledge graphs*—Consider a KG representing medical knowledge. The hierarchical nature of medical terminology (from broad categories to specific conditions) makes hyperbolic embeddings particularly appropriate. Structural embeddings help identify similar concepts across different branches of medicine, and supervised learning with expert-labeled data helps ensure accurate relationships between concepts.

Through these examples, we can see how different embedding approaches combine to solve real-world problems. The choice of embedding strategy isn't just a technical decision—it reflects our understanding of the problem structure and our goals for the solution.

11.2 The encoder–decoder model

The encoder–decoder model provides a powerful and unified way to understand how graph embedding methods work. Think of it like a translation system: first the model converts (encodes) graph information from one form into more compact, standardized representations, and then it translates (decodes) those representations to reconstruct meaningful graph properties [2] (see figure 11.4). In the context of graphs, this means transforming the discrete graph structure into continuous vector representations that preserve the important characteristics of the original graph.

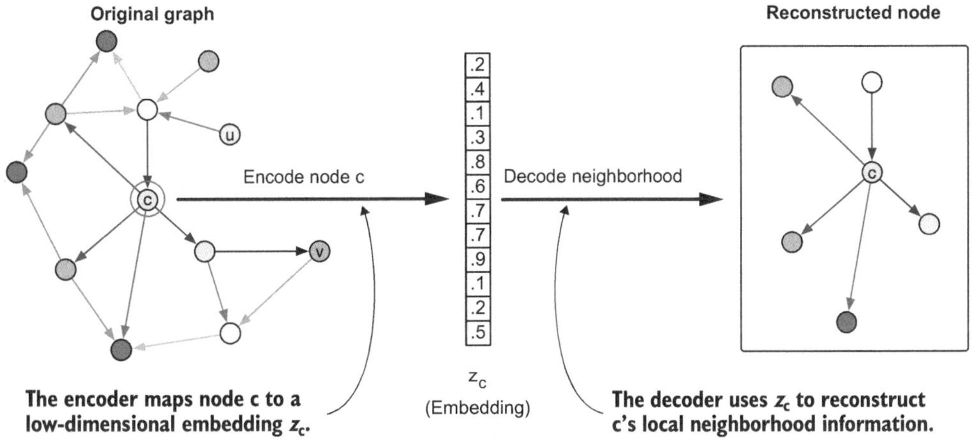

Figure 11.4 Overview of the encoder–decoder approach. The encoder maps node c to a low-dimensional embedding z_C. The decoder then uses z_C to reconstruct c's local neighborhood information.

11.2.1 The encoder: Converting graph structure to vectors

The encoder takes the raw graph data—its structure and any additional features—and converts it into dense vector representations (embeddings) for each node. The encoder takes two key inputs:

- The graph structure, represented as an adjacency matrix that shows how nodes are connected
- Node features, which provide additional information about each node's characteristics

What makes the encoder interesting is its flexibility: different methods can encode different aspects of the graph. Some focus on preserving the global structure and relative positions of nodes, whereas others prioritize capturing local neighborhood patterns. The encoder can be as simple as a lookup table that assigns each node a vector, or as sophisticated as a neural network that processes both structure and features.

11.2.2 The decoder: Reconstructing graph properties

The decoder takes the embeddings created by the encoder and attempts to reconstruct important properties of the original graph. This reconstruction ensures that the embeddings have captured meaningful information. The decoder's task varies depending on what aspects of the graph we want to preserve:

- For methods focused on graph structure, the decoder may try to predict whether nodes are connected in the original graph.
- To capture node similarity, it may reconstruct measures of neighborhood overlap between nodes.
- In cases with additional supervision, the decoder can predict node labels or other properties.

This reconstruction task serves as a training signal. By trying to minimize the difference between the decoder's predictions and the actual graph properties, we can optimize the encoder to learn better representations.

11.2.3 The power of the framework

What makes the encoder–decoder framework particularly valuable is its ability to unify many different approaches to GRL. Whether we're looking at matrix factorization methods, random walk-based approaches, or GNNs, they can all be understood as different ways of implementing this basic encode–decode pattern. The framework also helps us understand the trade-offs involved in different methods. For instance, simpler encoders may be more computationally efficient but capture less complex patterns, whereas more sophisticated neural network-based encoders can learn richer representations but require more data and computation to train effectively. The encoding–decoding perspective provides a lens through which we can analyze, compare, and improve methods for learning representations of graph-structured data.

11.2.4 Node2Vec: An example of an encoder–decoder framework

Consider the karate club network we worked with in chapter 9, where nodes represent club members and edges represent friendships between them. The club split into two groups following a dispute between the instructor (node 0) and the club administrator (node 33). This makes it a perfect example to understand how Node2Vec [4] works within the encoder–decoder framework.

THE ENCODING PROCESS IN NODE2VEC

First, Node2Vec's encoder needs to transform each club member (node) into a numerical vector that captures their position and role in the friendship network. Here's how it does this:

1. *Random walk generation*—The encoder starts by taking "walks" through the friendship network. Let's say we start at the instructor (node 0). A walk might look like $0 \rightarrow 1 \rightarrow 2 \rightarrow 3$, representing a path through friends of friends. Node2Vec can adjust how it explores the network by balancing between going

broad (exploring different social circles in the club) and going deep (staying within tight-knit groups of friends).

2. *Vector creation*—Based on these walks, the encoder creates a vector for each member that captures their social context. Members who frequently appear near each other in these walks (close friends or in the same social circles) will get similar vector representations.

THE DECODING PROCESS

The decoder takes these vectors and reconstructs information about the friendship network. For any two members *i* and *j*, the decoder tries to predict how likely they are to be friends based on their vector representations. It does this using the *softmax function*, which essentially asks, "Given member *i*'s vector, how likely are we to see member *j* nearby in our random walks?"

This encoding–decoding process reveals interesting patterns in the karate club network:

- *Community structure*—Members who ended up in the same faction after the split tend to get similar vector representations. The vectors capture not just direct friendships but also broader community affiliations.
- *Bridge members*—Members with friends in both factions get vector representations that reflect their intermediate position. These vectors help identify potential mediators in the conflict.
- *Leadership roles*—The instructor and administrator get distinct vector representations that reflect their central but opposing positions in the network. Their vectors capture their roles as community leaders through their connection patterns.

THE POWER OF THE FRAMEWORK

The encoder–decoder framework helps us understand why Node2Vec works:

- The encoder's random walks capture both local friendships and broader social structures.
- The decoder's prediction task ensures that the vectors preserve meaningful social relationships.
- Together, they create representations that can predict both friendships and faction membership.

This example shows how the encoder–decoder framework helps us understand and improve real-world network analysis. The following listing shows how to apply Node2Vec to the karate club network.

Listing 11.1 Applying Node2Vec embedding to the karate club network

```
import networkx as nx
import numpy as np
from node2vec import Node2Vec
import matplotlib.pyplot as plt
from sklearn.manifold import TSNE
```

```
G = nx.karate_club_graph()

faction_labels = {
    0: 0, 1: 0, 2: 0, 3: 0, 4: 0, 5: 0, 6: 0, 7: 0, 8: 0,
    9: 1, 10: 1, 11: 0, 12: 0, 13: 0, 14: 1, 15: 1, 16: 0,
    17: 0, 18: 1, 19: 0, 20: 1, 21: 0, 22: 1, 23: 1, 24: 1,
    25: 1, 26: 1, 27: 1, 28: 1, 29: 1, 30: 1, 31: 1, 32: 1,
    33: 1
}
nx.set_node_attributes(G, faction_labels, 'faction')

node2vec = Node2Vec(
    G,
    dimensions=16,
    walk_length=10,
    num_walks=20,
    p=1,
    q=1,
    workers=4
)

model = node2vec.fit(window=5)

def decode_similarity(model, node1, node2):
    return model.wv.similarity(str(node1), str(node2))

def visualize_graph_and_embeddings(model, G):
    embeddings = np.zeros((len(G.nodes()), model.vector_size))
    for i, node in enumerate(G.nodes()):
        embeddings[i] = model.wv[str(node)]

    tsne = TSNE(n_components=2, random_state=42)
    node_pos_2d = tsne.fit_transform(embeddings)

    fig, axes = plt.subplots(1, 2, figsize=(18, 8))

    # Left plot: original graph
    pos = nx.spring_layout(G, seed=42)
    colors = ['red' if G.nodes[node]['faction'] == 0 else 'blue'
              for node in G.nodes()]
    nx.draw(
        G,
        pos,
        ax=axes[0],
        with_labels=True,
        node_color=colors,
        node_size=500,
        font_size=10
    )
    axes[0].set_title("Original Karate Club Graph")

    # Right plot: node embeddings
    axes[1].scatter(node_pos_2d[:, 0], node_pos_2d[:, 1], c=colors, s=100)
    for i, node in enumerate(G.nodes()):
        axes[1].annotate(str(node), (node_pos_2d[i, 0],
            node_pos_2d[i, 1]), fontsize=9)
    axes[1].set_title("Node2Vec Embeddings (t-SNE)")
```

Loads the karate club network

Defines faction labels (0 for instructor, 1 for administrator)

Assigns faction attributes to network nodes

Configures Node2Vec with embedding parameters

Trains the Node2Vec model

Computes similarity between node embeddings

```
    plt.tight_layout()
    plt.show()                          <-- Visualizes the original graph and
                                            node embeddings in 2D space
print("Similarity between instructor (0) and their close ally (1):",
      decode_similarity(model, 0, 1))
print("Similarity between instructor (0) and administrator (33):",
      decode_similarity(model, 0, 33))          <-- Prints similarity scores
                                                    between key nodes
visualize_graph_and_embeddings(model, G)    <-- Generates and
                                                displays an
def analyze_community_structure(model, G):      embedding
    instructor_allies = []                      visualization
    administrator_allies = []

    for node in G.nodes():
        if node not in [0, 33]:
            sim_to_instructor = decode_similarity(model, node, 0)
            sim_to_administrator = decode_similarity(model, node, 33)

            if sim_to_instructor > sim_to_administrator:
                instructor_allies.append(node)
            else:
                administrator_allies.append(node)

    return instructor_allies, administrator_allies    <-- Analyzes the community
                                                          structure based on embeddings

instructor_group, administrator_group = analyze_community_structure(model, G)
print("\nPredicted instructor's faction:", sorted(instructor_group))
print("Predicted administrator's faction:", sorted(administrator_group))
                                                    <-- Prints predicted
                                                        faction assignments
```

This implementation demonstrates the aspects of the encoder–decoder framework that we just discussed. Run it! The t-SNE visualization shows how the encoded vectors cluster nodes by faction, and the similarity calculations between some important nodes demonstrate how the decoded embeddings can predict relationships in the original graph. You can see how members close to the instructor (node 0) have different embedding patterns than those close to the administrator (node 33), reflecting the real social dynamics that led to the club's split.

11.3 Shallow embeddings: A first approach to graph representation

The simplest way to understand graph embeddings is through *shallow embeddings*. These represent the most straightforward implementation of the encoder–decoder framework, but their simplicity comes with important limitations that have driven the development of more sophisticated approaches [2].

11.3.1 Understanding shallow embeddings

In shallow embedding methods, the encoder performs a simple operation: it acts as a lookup table, directly mapping each node to its vector representation. Think of it like assigning each person in a social network a unique "coordinate" in a high-dimensional space. This is similar to how a dictionary works: each word (node) has its own dedicated entry (vector).

In the encoder–decoder framework, this approach can be understood as follows:

- The encoder maintains a matrix where each row corresponds to a node's embedding vector. When asked to encode a node, it returns the corresponding row from this matrix. This is why we call these embeddings "shallow"—there's no deep processing or transformation of the input, just a direct lookup operation.
- The decoder takes these embedding vectors and tries to reconstruct important properties of the graph, such as whether two nodes are connected or how similar their neighborhoods are. This reconstruction process helps optimize the embedding vectors during training to capture meaningful patterns in the graph structure.

Let's consider a concrete example. In the karate club network we discussed earlier, a shallow embedding approach would create a separate vector for each club member. These vectors would be adjusted during training so that members who interact frequently end up with similar vectors and those who rarely interact end up with dissimilar vectors.

11.3.2 Limitations of shallow embeddings

Although shallow embeddings have achieved success in many applications, they face several important limitations:

- *Parameter inefficiency*—Shallow embeddings require a separate vector for each node in the graph. This means the number of parameters grows linearly with the number of nodes, making them impractical for very large graphs. For instance, in a social network with millions of users, we would need millions of embedding vectors.
- *No parameter sharing*—Shallow embeddings don't share parameters between nodes. This means they can't use common patterns or structures that may appear in different parts of the graph. In the karate club example, if two members play similar roles in different social circles, the model has to learn these patterns independently for each member rather than recognize and reuse the pattern.
- *Feature blindness*—These methods don't take advantage of node features or attributes. If we knew additional information about each club member (like age, interests, or role), shallow embeddings wouldn't have a natural way to incorporate this information into the representations.
- *Transductive nature*—Shallow embeddings are inherently transductive: they can only generate embeddings for nodes that were present during training. If a new member joins the club, we can't automatically generate an embedding for them because they weren't part of the original lookup table. We would need to retrain the entire model to incorporate new nodes.

These limitations have motivated the development of more sophisticated approaches, particularly GNNs, which we'll explore in section 11.6. These advanced methods learn to generate embeddings based on both graph structure and node features, enabling inductive learning and better parameter sharing.

Despite their limitations, shallow embeddings remain important both historically and practically. They help us understand the fundamental challenges of GRL and provide a baseline against which we can compare more sophisticated approaches. Their simplicity also makes them useful in situations where the graph is relatively small and static, and when computational resources are limited.

11.4 Embeddings in knowledge graphs

In our previous sections, we explored how to learn embeddings for simple graphs where edges represent a single type of relationship between nodes. However, real-world graphs often have much richer structures, in particular those we are addressing in this book for implementing an intelligent advisor system. Think of a biomedical KG where nodes represent drugs, diseases, genes, and proteins, with dozens of different types of relationships connecting them. These multirelational graphs require more sophisticated approaches to embedding.

In this section, we'll extend our discussion of shallow embeddings to handle these complex KGs. We need to introduce new techniques to handle the multiple types of relationships; this is particularly important for tasks like KG completion, where we predict missing relationships between entities.

Consider a biomedical KG in which we have *entities* (*Aspirin*, *Inflammation*, *Headache*, *COX-2*) and *relationships* (`TREATS`, `INHIBITS`, `CAUSES`). In a simple graph, we may just care about whether entities are connected. However, in a KG, the type of connection matters significantly. We need to be able to capture the following:

- (*Aspirin*, `TREATS`, *Headache*)
- (*Aspirin*, `INHIBITS`, *COX-2*)
- (*Inflammation*, `CAUSES`, *Headache*)

Our embedding approach must encode not just whether entities are related but also *how* they are related. So, we need a way to measure how well our embeddings capture the graph structure (the loss function) and a way to handle different types of relationships between nodes (the multirelational decoder). Let's explore how these components work together to create effective graph representations.

11.4.1 Loss function

Think of a *loss function* as a teacher grading a student's work. Just as a teacher needs clear criteria to evaluate performance, we need ways to measure how well our embeddings capture the graph's structure. However, designing an effective loss function for graph embeddings presents some challenges.

The simplest approach may seem to be directly comparing our predicted connections with the actual graph structure using something like mean squared error. But this approach faces two practical limitations:

- *Computational efficiency*—In a graph with millions of nodes, comparing every possible pair of nodes becomes computationally impossible. For example, in a social network with 1 million users, we'd need to evaluate nearly a trillion potential connections.
- *Sparsity*—Most real-world graphs are sparse, meaning most nodes aren't connected to each other. A social media user may have hundreds of friends, but this is tiny compared to the millions of total users. Our loss function needs to handle this imbalance effectively.

To address these challenges, modern approaches typically use *negative sampling with cross-entropy loss*. Here's how this loss function works:

$$\mathcal{L} = \sum_{(u,\tau,v)\in\varepsilon} -\log(\sigma(\text{DEC}(z_u, \tau, z_v))) - \gamma\mathbb{E}_{v_n \sim p_{n,v}(v)}[\log(\sigma(-\text{DEC}(z_u, \tau, z_{v_n})))]$$

Let's understand each element.

- Basic components:
  - $\mathcal{L}$—The total loss we're trying to minimize
  - Σ—Sum over all existing edges in our KG
  - σ—The sigmoid function, which converts scores to probabilities between 0 and 1
  - DEC—Our decoder function that scores how likely a relationship is
  - γ—A balancing parameter (gamma) that controls the importance of negative samples
- Node and relationship elements:
  - u—The head node (e.g., "Aspirin")
  - τ (tau)—The relationship type (e.g., "TREATS")
  - v—The tail node (e.g., "Headache")
  - z_u—The embedding vector for node u
  - z_v—The embedding vector for node v
- The positive part:

$$-\log(\sigma(\text{DEC}(z_u, \tau, z_v)))$$

  - DEC(z_u, τ, z_v)—Computes a score for the true relationship
  - σ(...)—Converts this score to a probability
  - –log(...)—Makes the loss larger when we give low probabilities to true relationships

- The negative part:

$$-\gamma \mathbb{E}_{v_n \sim p_{n,v}(v)} [\log(\sigma(-\text{DEC}(z_u, \tau, z_{v_n})))]$$

  - v_n—A negative sample (e.g., *COX-2* when sampling alternatives for *Headache*)
  - $P_{n,v}(V)$—The distribution we use to sample negative examples
  - $\mathbb{E}$—Expected value over negative samples
  - –DEC(...)—Negative score for false relationships
  - γ—Multiplier to control the importance of negative samples

Let's look at a practical example. Suppose we're trying to learn embeddings for our biomedical KG. We have a fact: "aspirin treats headache." Our loss function needs to do the following:

- *Reward true facts.* The first term encourages the decoder to give a high score to real relationships. In our example, it should give a high score to (*Aspirin*, `TREATS`, *Headache*).
- *Penalize false facts.* The second term involves "negative sampling"—we randomly sample entities that aren't known to have this relationship. For example, we may sample (*Aspirin*, `TREATS`, *COX-2*) and (*Aspirin*, `TREATS`, *Inflammation*).

The loss function encourages the decoder to give low scores to these negative samples.

The parameter γ balances these two objectives. Think of it as deciding how much we care about correctly identifying false relationships compared to correctly identifying true ones. In practice, because KGs are usually sparse (most possible relationships don't exist), we typically want $\gamma > 1$ to emphasize correctly identifying false relationships.

This loss function is computationally efficient because instead of checking all possible relationships, we only need to look at the true relationships and a small sample of negative ones. In practice, we may use 5–10 negative samples for each true relationship.

THE ART OF NEGATIVE SAMPLING IN KGS

The effectiveness of negative sampling depends heavily on how we choose these negative examples. At its core, negative sampling is about teaching our model to distinguish between relationships that should exist and those that shouldn't. However, this isn't as straightforward as it may seem.

The simplest approach is to randomly sample nodes from the graph to create negative examples. For instance, if we have the true relationship (*Aspirin* `TREATS` *Headache*), we might create negative samples like (*Aspirin* `TREATS` *Laptop*) and (*Aspirin* `TREATS` *Mountain*). This approach is computationally efficient, but it has two main limitations:

- *False negatives*—We may accidentally sample relationships that exist in our KG. Some systems address this by checking and filtering out such accidental true relationships.

- *Overly simple examples*—Many random samples are obviously wrong and don't help our model learn meaningful patterns.

To address these limitations, researchers have developed more sophisticated sampling strategies:

- *Type-constrained sampling*—Instead of sampling any random node, we only sample nodes that make semantic sense for the relationship. For example, when creating negative samples for a `TREATS` relationship, we only sample diseases as potential targets, not arbitrary entities. This forces the model to learn more subtle distinctions.
- *Adversarial sampling*—We generate challenging negative examples. Instead of random sampling, we identify examples that are likely to be confused with true relationships, helping the model develop a more nuanced understanding.

We can also sample negative examples by replacing either the subject or object of a relationship (or both). For example, given "Aspirin TREATS Headache," we could create negative samples by:

- Replacing the treatment—"Sunlight TREATS Headache"
- Replacing the condition—"Aspirin TREATS Happiness"
- Replacing both—"Sunlight TREATS Happiness"

In practice, considering replacing either the source or the destination helps prevent biases, especially in KGs where relationship direction matters.

11.4.2 Multirelationship decoder

Once we have our loss function, we need decoders that can handle different types of relationships. These decoders need to capture various patterns that appear in KGs:

- *Symmetric vs. asymmetric relations*—Some relationships, like `similar_to`, are symmetric (if A is similar to B, then B is similar to A). Others, like `causes`, are asymmetric (if A causes B, it doesn't mean B causes A).
- *Compositional patterns*—Sometimes relationships can be composed. For example, if drug A treats disease B, and disease B is a type of disease C, we may infer that drug A treats disease C.
- *Inverse relations*—Some relationships have natural inverses. If A `contains` B, then B is `part_of` A.

Let's look at three main approaches to building such decoders:

- *Translation-based* (TransE [5])—This is one of the most intuitive approaches. Each relationship is represented as a vector that "translates" one entity into another. In our medical example, if we add the `TREATS` vector to the *Aspirin* vector, we should get close to the *Headache* vector.
- *Matrix-based* (RESCAL [6])—This expressive approach represents each relationship as a matrix that transforms entity vectors. Although powerful, it requires

more parameters: for a graph with 1,000 entities and 100 relationship types, we'd need millions of parameters just for the relationships.

- *Semantic matching* (DistMult [7], ComplEx [8])—These decoders measure similarity between entities while taking the relationship type into account. ComplEx is particularly interesting because it uses complex numbers to handle asymmetric relationships elegantly.

The choice of decoder significantly impacts what kinds of patterns your model can learn. TransE, for example, is great at capturing compositional patterns but struggles with many-to-one relationships. ComplEx handles asymmetric relationships well but may not capture compositional patterns as effectively.

This framework of sophisticated loss functions and multirelational decoders forms the foundation for modern KG embeddings. In the next sections, we'll see how these ideas extend to even more powerful approaches using GNNs.

11.5 Message passing and graph neural networks

Although shallow embeddings provide an effective starting point for learning graph representations, they face limitations when dealing with large-scale graphs or when we need to capture complex patterns of relationships. GNNs offer a more sophisticated approach through a mechanism called *neural message passing*, which allows nodes to iteratively learn from their neighborhoods. Let's explore how this powerful framework works.

11.5.1 The message-passing framework: A neural conversation

Think of message passing in a GNN as a sophisticated conversation happening across the graph. Just as humans share and process information through conversations with their social circles, nodes in a graph share and update information through structured interactions with their neighbors. This "neural conversation" happens in rounds, with each round allowing information to travel one step further through the graph.

The key insight of message passing is that nodes can learn not just from their immediate connections but also from the broader graph structure through iterative updates. During each iteration of message passing, every node does the following:

1. Collects messages from its neighbors
2. Processes these messages to extract relevant information
3. Updates its own representation based on the processed messages

This process is formalized through two key functions:

- `AGGREGATE`—Collects and combines messages from neighboring nodes
- `UPDATE`—Uses the aggregated messages to update the node's representation

Figure 11.5 summarizes this concept [2].

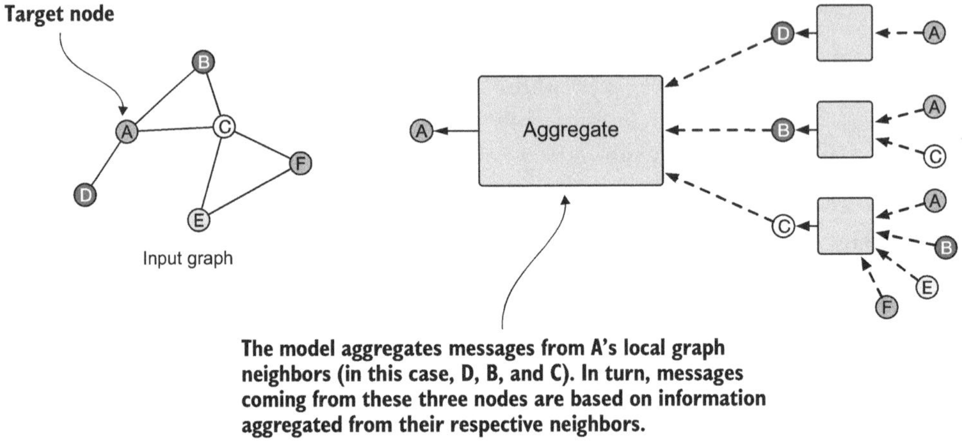

Figure 11.5 Example of how a single node aggregates messages from its local neighborhood in the message-passing model. Notice that the computation graph of the GNN forms a tree structure by unfolding the neighborhood around the target node.

For example, in a social network analyzing user interests, the message-passing process may work like this:

1. A user's initial representation includes their explicitly stated interests.
2. In the first round, they receive messages about their friends' interests.
3. In the second round, they get information about their friends-of-friends' interests.
4. After several rounds, each user's representation captures patterns of interests in their broader social circle.

11.5.2 Motivation and intuition: Why message passing works

The power of message passing comes from its ability to capture both local and global patterns in the graph structure. After k iterations of message passing, each node's representation contains information from its k-hop neighborhood. This progressive gathering of information serves two important purposes:

- *Structural information*—The message-passing process naturally encodes the graph's topology. For example, in a molecular graph, after several rounds of message passing, an atom's representation may encode information about being part of a benzene ring or other molecular structures.
- *Feature-based information*—Message passing also allows nodes to learn from the features of their neighbors. In a citation network, for instance, a paper's representation will gradually incorporate information from related papers, helping us better understand its place in the broader academic landscape.

11.5.3 The basic GNN model

Let's look at how we can implement this message-passing framework in practice. The basic GNN model defines the update rule for each node u at iteration k as

$$h_u^{(k)} = \sigma\left(W_{\text{self}}^{(k)} h_u^{(k-1)} + W_{\text{neigh}}^{(k)} \sum_{v \in \mathcal{N}(u)} h_v^{(k-1)} + b^{(k)}\right)$$

where

- $h_u^{(k)}$ represents node u's representation at iteration k.
- $W_{\text{self}}{}^{(k)}$ and $W_{\text{neigh}}{}^{(k)}$ are trainable parameter matrices.

NOTE These parameters can be shared across GNN message-passing iterations or trained separately for each layer (iteration).

- σ is a nonlinear activation function (like ReLU or tanh).
- The summation $\Sigma_{v \in \mathcal{N}(n)} h_v^{(k-1)}$ runs over all neighbors v of node u.
- $b^{(k)}$ is the bias term, which is often omitted (if used, it can be shared across multiple iterations or trained differently for each layer).

This basic model is analogous to a standard neural network layer but operates on graph-structured data. The primary difference is that instead of processing fixed-size inputs, it can handle varying numbers of neighbors through the summation operation.

We can define the basic GNN formula by splitting the two components of the `AGGREGATE` and `UPDATE` functions to match the mental model:

$$m_{\mathcal{N}(u)}^{(k-1)} = \text{AGGREGATE}^{(k-1)}\left(\left\{h_v^{(k-1)}, \forall\, v \in \mathcal{N}(u)\right\}\right) = \sum_{v \in \mathcal{N}(u)} h_v^{(k-1)}$$

$$\text{UPDATE}\left(h_u^{(k)}, m_{\mathcal{N}(u)}^{(k-1)}, b^{(k)}\right) = \sigma\left(W_{\text{self}}^{(k)} h_u^{(k-1)} + W_{\text{neigh}}^{(k)} m_{\mathcal{N}(u)}^{(k-1)} + b^{(k)}\right)$$

11.5.4 Message passing with self-loops

An important variation of the basic neural message-passing framework adds self-loops to the graph. In this approach, instead of having separate `AGGREGATE` and `UPDATE` steps, we treat each node as its neighbor during the aggregation process. This simplifies the message-passing equation to

$$h_u^{(k)} = \text{AGGREGATE}^{(k-1)}\left(\left\{h_v^{(k-1)}, \forall\, v \in \mathcal{N}(u) \cup \{u\}\right\}\right)$$

The self-loop approach offers several advantages:

- Simpler implementation due to combining the `AGGREGATE` and `UPDATE` steps
- Often helps prevent overfitting through parameter sharing
- Can improve model stability during training

However, this simplification comes with a trade-off: by treating a node's information the same as its neighbors', we lose flexibility in how nodes can combine their current state with neighborhood information.

The choice between standard message passing and the self-loop variant often depends on the specific application and the type of patterns we want our model to learn. For tasks where the distinction between a node's features and its neighbors' features is critical, the standard approach may be more appropriate. For tasks where this distinction is less important, the self-loop variant can offer a simpler and more robust solution. Chapter 12 includes examples that use this approach instead of `AGGREGATE` and `UPDATE`.

11.6 Generalized aggregation and update methods

The message-passing framework we explored earlier provides a powerful mental model for understanding how GNNs process and learn from graph-structured data and feature information. However, this framework can be significantly enhanced by introducing specialized methods for aggregating neighborhood information and updating node representations. In this section, we'll explore these generalizations and how they can improve GNN performance.

Just as traditional neural networks have evolved from simple perceptrons to sophisticated architectures with skip connections, attention mechanisms, and normalization layers, GNNs can benefit from similar architectural innovations. The challenge is adapting these ideas to respect the unique properties of graph-structured data, particularly the irregular connectivity patterns and varying neighborhood sizes that characterize real-world graphs.

Architectural enhancements for GNNs

Skip connections, also known as *residual connections*, create shortcuts in neural networks by allowing information to bypass one or more layers. In GNNs, skip connections help preserve node features from earlier layers, preventing the over-smoothing problem where node representations become too similar after multiple message-passing steps. They enable deeper GNN architectures by maintaining gradient flow during training.

Attention mechanisms allow a model to dynamically focus on different parts of the input by assigning varying importance weights. In GNNs, attention mechanisms help nodes selectively aggregate information from their neighbors by weighting neighbor contributions differently, based on their relevance to the current task. This enables more sophisticated message passing that can capture complex node relationships.

Normalization layers help stabilize neural network training by controlling the distribution of layer outputs. In GNNs, normalization is particularly important because nodes can have widely varying numbers of neighbors. Layer normalization and batch normalization help manage these differences by scaling features appropriately, leading to more stable training and better model convergence.

Let's examine two areas where the basic GNN framework can be enhanced: neighborhood aggregation and node-state updates. These enhancements address common challenges in graph learning, such as capturing complex neighborhood patterns, handling varying neighborhood sizes, and maintaining stable training dynamics.

11.6.1 Neighborhood normalization

A fundamental challenge in processing graph-structured data is handling neighborhoods of different sizes. A naive approach to aggregating neighborhood information can lead to numerical instabilities and make it difficult for the model to learn effectively across varying scales.

Neighborhood normalization techniques address this challenge by scaling the aggregated information based on neighborhood properties. The simplest form of normalization is to take the mean of neighbor features rather than their sum. The following formula performs the aggregation by computing the mean:

$$m_{\mathcal{N}(u)}^{(k-1)} = \frac{\sum_{v \in \mathcal{N}(u)} h_v^{(k-1)}}{|\mathcal{N}(u)|}$$

where $h_v^{(k\text{-}1)}$ is the feature vector coming from the neighbor v, and the denominator $|\mathcal{N}(u)|$ represents the number of neighbors of u. The sum operates on vectors, so each item is summed with the others in the same position.

More sophisticated normalization schemes can offer better performance. For example, the symmetric normalization approach popularized by Kipf and Welling [9] in their graph convolutional network uses the following formula:

$$m_{\mathcal{N}(u)}^{(k-1)} = \sum_{v \in \mathcal{N}(u)} \frac{h_v^{(k-1)}}{\sqrt{|\mathcal{N}(u)|\,|\mathcal{N}(v)|}}$$

This symmetric normalization is particularly effective in scenarios where both the source and target nodes' degrees should influence the message strength. For instance, in citation networks, this normalization reduces the impact of highly cited papers that may otherwise dominate the message-passing process. A paper cited thousands of times across diverse fields shouldn't necessarily have a stronger influence than more specialized, relevant citations.

The choice of a normalization scheme can significantly impact model performance. Consider these practical implications:

- *Mean normalization* (simple averaging) helps ensure that nodes with different numbers of neighbors can be compared on a similar scale.
- *Symmetric normalization* accounts for both sender and receiver node properties, which can be important in directed graphs or graphs where node importance varies significantly.

- Some applications may benefit from learned normalization factors that the model can adjust during training.

On the other hand, after normalization, it can be hard to use the learned embedding to distinguish between nodes of different degrees, making the normalization a lossy operation. Usually, normalization is most helpful in tasks where node feature information is far more useful than structural information or where there is a very wide range of node degrees that can lead to instabilities during optimization.

11.6.2 Neighborhood attention

Normalization helps handle varying neighborhood sizes, but it treats all neighbors equally within their normalized contributions. However, not all relationships in a graph carry equal importance. For example, in a social network, some friendships may be more relevant than others for predicting a user's interests. This is where attention mechanisms come into play.

Attention allows a GNN to learn which neighbors are most relevant for a given task by assigning learnable weights to different neighborhood relationships. The first GNN model to apply this style of attention was Veličković et al.'s graph attention network [10], which uses attention weights to define a weighted sum of the neighbors:

$$m_{N(u)}^{(k-1)} = \sum_{v \in N(u)} \alpha_{u,v} h_v^{(k-1)}$$

where α_{wv} denotes the attention on neighbor $v \in \mathcal{N}(u)$ when we are aggregating information at node u. In the original paper, the attention weights are defined as

$$\alpha_{u,v} = \frac{\exp\left(a^T\left[W h_u \bigoplus W h_v\right]\right)}{\sum_{v' \in N(u)} \exp\left(a^T\left[W h_u \bigoplus W h_{v'}\right]\right)}$$

where **a** is a trainable attention vector, W is a trainable matrix, and $\oplus$ denotes the concatenation operation.

The GraphSAGE framework [11] provides a practical example of how attention can be integrated into the aggregation process. This implementation uses attention to weight the importance of different neighbors during the aggregation step.

Attention mechanisms can be particularly valuable when the importance of neighbors varies significantly based on the task or context, when the graph contains noisy or irrelevant connections, or if the model needs to capture complex, nonlinear relationships between nodes.

11.6.3 Multihead attention and transformer connections

The attention mechanisms we've discussed share deep connections with transformer architectures that have revolutionized natural language processing and, more recently, become the backbone of LLMs. Understanding these connections can provide valuable insights into both the design and capabilities of modern GNNs.

Just as transformers process sequences of words by allowing each word to attend to all other words in a sentence, graph attention networks allow each node to selectively attend to its neighbors. However, a single attention mechanism may not be sufficient to capture all relevant patterns in the data. This insight led to the development of multihead attention in both domains.

In the context of GNNs, multihead attention works by maintaining several independent attention mechanisms that operate in parallel. Each attention head can learn to focus on different aspects of the neighborhood relationships. For instance, in a molecular graph, one head may learn to focus on chemical bond types while another captures spatial arrangements. Here's how this can be implemented.

Listing 11.2 Multihead attention implementation

```
class MultiHeadGraphAttention(nn.Module):
    def __init__(self, input_dim, num_heads):
        super().__init__()
        self.num_heads = num_heads
        self.head_dim = input_dim
        self.attention_heads = nn.ModuleList([
            GraphAttentionHead(self.head_dim)
            for _ in range(num_heads)
        ])                                          # Initializes multiple attention heads, each processing a slice of the input dimension

    def forward(self, node_features, neighbor_features):
        node_chunks = torch.chunk(node_features,
                                  self.num_heads, dim=-1)   # Splits node features into chunks for parallel processing by different heads
        neighbor_chunks = torch.chunk(neighbor_features,
                                      self.num_heads, dim=-1)   # Splits neighbor features into chunks for parallel processing by different heads
        head_outputs = []
        for i, head in enumerate(self.attention_heads):
            head_out = head(node_chunks[i], neighbor_chunks[i])   # Applies each attention head to its corresponding feature chunk
            head_outputs.append(head_out)

        return torch.cat(head_outputs, dim=-1)   # Concatenates outputs from all heads to form the final node representation
```

The parallel with transformer architecture becomes even clearer when we consider the fundamental operation in both cases. In transformers, the attention mechanism computes query (`Q`), key (`K`), and value (`V`) matrices to determine attention weights, as shown in the following listing.

Listing 11.3 Attention mechanism in transformer architecture

```
class TransformerStyleGraphAttention(nn.Module):
   def __init__(self, feature_dim):
       super().__init__()
       self.query_transform = nn.Linear(feature_dim, feature_dim)
       self.key_transform = nn.Linear(feature_dim, feature_dim)
       self.value_transform = nn.Linear(feature_dim, feature_dim)   # Initializes linear transformations for query, key, and value projections
```

```
    def forward(self, node_features, neighbor_features):
        Q = self.query_transform(node_features)
        K = self.key_transform(neighbor_features)
        V = self.value_transform(neighbor_features)        <-- Transforms input features into query, key, and value representations

        attention_scores = torch.matmul(Q, K.transpose(-2, -1))
        attention_scores = attention_scores / math.sqrt(K.size(-1))
        # Computes scaled dot-product attention_scores between query and keys

        attention_weights = F.softmax(attention_scores, dim=-1)
        attended_values = torch.matmul(attention_weights, V)
        # Applies softmax to get attention_weights and compute the weighted sum of values

        return attended_values        <-- Returns the attention-weighted node representations
```

This transformer-style attention in GNNs offers several advantages:

- *Scale and efficiency*—Like transformer models, this attention mechanism can efficiently process large neighborhoods by parallelizing computations.
- *Flexible feature learning*—Each attention head can specialize in capturing different types of relationships or patterns in the graph structure.
- *Interpretability*—The attention weights can provide insights into which neighbor relationships are most important for different tasks.

The connection to transformers also extends to how these models handle different scales of information. Just as transformers use positional encodings to capture sequence position information, some GNN architectures incorporate structural or positional encodings to capture graph topology. The following listing shows an example.

Listing 11.4 Including structural encoding to capture graph topology

```
class StructuralGraphTransformer(nn.Module):
  def __init__(self, feature_dim, num_heads):
      super().__init__()
      self.structural_encoding = nn.Embedding(max_degree, feature_dim)
      self.attention = MultiHeadGraphAttention(feature_dim, num_heads)
      # Initializes an embedding layer for structural encodings and multihead attention

  def forward(self, node_features, neighbor_features, degrees):
      structural_features = self.structural_encoding(degrees)
      enhanced_features = node_features + structural_features
      # Enhances node features with learnable structural information based on node degrees

      return self.attention(enhanced_features, neighbor_features)
      # Applies multihead attention using the structurally enhanced features
```

This convergence between GNNs and transformer architectures has important implications for the future of graph learning. As LLMs continue to advance, we can expect more cross-pollination of ideas between these domains. For instance, recent work has explored using LLMs to generate natural language descriptions of graph structures and using graph structures to enhance language understanding in LLMs.

11.6.4 Generalized update methods

The update phase of message passing is as important as aggregation but often receives less attention. The way we update node representations using the aggregated information can significantly impact a GNN's performance. Let's explore several powerful approaches to the update step.

Skip connections in GNNs

One of GraphSAGE's key innovations was the introduction of skip connections in the update phase. Similar to residual connections in traditional DL, skip connections in GNNs help preserve information across message-passing layers. Here's how GraphSAGE implements this concept.

Listing 11.5 `update` function in the GraphSAGE algorithm

```
class GraphSAGEUpdate(nn.Module):
    def __init__(self, input_dim, hidden_dim):
        super().__init__()
        self.update_nn = nn.Linear(input_dim * 2, hidden_dim)    # Initializes a neural network for transforming concatenated features

    def forward(self, node_features, aggregated_neighbor_features):
        combined = torch.cat([node_features, aggregated_neighbor_features],
        dim=1)    # Concatenates node and aggregated neighbor features

        updated = self.update_nn(combined)
        return F.relu(updated)    # Applies the nonlinear transformation and activation function
```

This concatenation-based update serves several purposes:

- *Information preservation*—By concatenating the node's previous state with aggregated neighborhood information, the network maintains access to the node's original features.
- *Feature separation*—The model can learn which aspects of the original node features and neighborhood information are most relevant for the task.
- *Gradient flow*—Skip connections provide additional paths for gradient flow during backpropagation, helping to train deeper GNN architectures.

Gated updates

Inspired by recurrent neural networks, *gated update* mechanisms provide finer control over how node representations are updated (see the next listing). These mechanisms are particularly valuable when nodes need to selectively incorporate neighborhood information.

Listing 11.6 Implementing gated updates

```
class GatedGraphUpdate(nn.Module):
    def __init__(self, feature_dim):
        super().__init__()
        self.update_gate = nn.Linear(feature_dim * 2, feature_dim)
        self.transform = nn.Linear(feature_dim * 2, feature_dim)    # Initialize gate and transform networks for feature updating.
```

```
    def forward(self, node_features, aggregated_features):
        gate_input = torch.cat([node_features, aggregated_features], dim=1)
        update_gate = torch.sigmoid(self.update_gate(gate_input))    # A

        combined = torch.cat([node_features, aggregated_features], dim=1)
        candidate = torch.tanh(self.transform(combined))              # B

        return (1 - update_gate) * node_features + update_gate * candidate   # C
```

A: Computes update gate values to control information flow

B: Generates candidate features through nonlinear transformation

C: Applies a gated update mechanism to combine old and new features

The gating mechanism allows the model to dynamically decide how much of the original node representation to preserve and how much new neighborhood information to incorporate. This is particularly useful in scenarios where some nodes should maintain more stable representations across layers, the relevance of neighborhood information varies across nodes, or the graph contains noisy or irrelevant connections.

JUMPING KNOWLEDGE NETWORKS

Another powerful update strategy involves maintaining representations from multiple layers and combining them adaptively. This approach, known as *jumping knowledge networks*, allows the model to capture multiscale structural information (listing 11.7).

Listing 11.7 Implementing jumping knowledge

```
class JumpingKnowledge(nn.Module):
    def __init__(self, feature_dim, num_layers):
        super().__init__()
        self.lstm = nn.LSTM(
            input_size=feature_dim,
            hidden_size=feature_dim,
            batch_first=True
        )                                                  # A

    def forward(self, layer_representations):
        stacked = torch.stack(layer_representations, dim=2)     # B
        batch_size, num_nodes, num_layers, feature_size = stacked.shape
        reshaped = stacked.reshape(batch_size * num_nodes,
                                   num_layers, feature_size)     # C
        output, _ = self.lstm(reshaped)                          # D
        last_output = output[:, -1, :]                           # E
        final_output = last_output.reshape(batch_size, num_nodes, -1)   # F
        return final_output
```

A: Initializes long short-term memory (LSTM) for combining multilayer representations

B: Stacks representations from different layers, with layers as the third dimension

C: Reshapes to combine batch and nodes dimensions for LSTM processing

D: Processes node representations through LSTM, treating layers as time steps

E: Extracts features from the final layer

F: Reshapes back to separate batch and nodes dimensions in the final output

This approach offers several advantages. Different nodes can effectively use information from different numbers of hops away, and the model can combine local and global structural information. And by maintaining access to earlier layer representations, the model can avoid the loss of distinctive node features.

Practical considerations

When implementing these update mechanisms, we need to consider several factors:

- *Computational efficiency*—More complex update mechanisms generally require more computation time and memory.
- *Task requirements*—Different tasks may benefit from different update strategies.
- *Graph properties*—The structure and characteristics of the input graph can influence which update mechanism is most appropriate.

For example, in a citation network where papers need to balance their content with influences from cited works, a gated update mechanism may be most appropriate. In contrast, for a molecular graph where atomic properties are influenced by multiscale structural patterns, a jumping knowledge approach could be more suitable.

These update mechanisms represent different approaches to balancing the preservation of node-specific information with the incorporation of neighborhood context. In practice, the choice of update mechanism can be as important as the choice of aggregation strategy, and the two components should be designed to complement each other.

In chapter 12, we'll see how these update mechanisms can be combined with the aggregation strategies we discussed earlier to create powerful GNN architectures for specific applications. We'll explore how different combinations of these components perform on real-world tasks and provide practical guidance for choosing the right update mechanism for your specific use case.

11.7 The synergy of GNNs and LLMs

GNNs and LLMs are powerful paradigms in modern AI, each with strengths that become more potent when they are combined thoughtfully. As we have seen in this chapter, GNNs excel at processing structured graph data through message passing between nodes, capturing local neighborhood information, and global graph topology. They are particularly effective at tasks like node classification and link prediction because they can aggregate features from neighboring nodes and encode graph structures. However, GNNs typically struggle with processing rich textual information associated with nodes and edges.

LLMs, on the other hand, demonstrate remarkable capabilities in understanding and generating natural language text. They can process long sequences of text, capture semantic relationships, and even exhibit reasoning abilities. However, they are fundamentally designed to work with sequential data and don't naturally handle the complex structural relationships present in graphs.

LLMs can be combined with GNNs in three primary ways [13]:

- *LLMs as predictors*—In this approach, LLMs serve as the final component for making predictions or generating outputs. The graph structure can be encoded into a sequence format that LLMs can process, or the LLM architecture can be modified to handle graph structures directly. This approach is particularly powerful when the task requires combining structural understanding with complex reasoning or natural language generation. For example, in a KG-based question-answering system, a GNN might first process the graph structure, and then an LLM could generate natural language answers based on both the graph embeddings and the question context.

- *LLMs as encoders*—Here, LLMs are used to process textual information associated with nodes or edges, creating rich feature representations that are then passed to GNNs for structural processing. This approach uses LLMs' text understanding capabilities while maintaining GNNs' ability to process graph structures. For instance, in a scientific citation network, an LLM could encode paper abstracts into meaningful vectors, which a GNN could then use to model citation relationships and predict future citations.
- *LLMs as aligners*—This approach uses LLMs alongside GNNs, aligning their outputs through techniques like contrastive learning and mutual training. The two models work in parallel, with each handling its specialized domain (text or structure) and their outputs being combined or aligned for the final task. This is particularly useful in scenarios where maintaining separate but aligned representations of both textual and structural information is beneficial, such as in multimodal KGs where both the connection patterns and the textual content carry important information.

The key to successful integration lies in understanding the complementary strengths of each technology and designing architectures that use these strengths appropriately for the task at hand. As both GNNs and LLMs continue to evolve, we expect to see even more sophisticated ways of combining their capabilities to build more powerful and intelligent systems for KG applications.

Summary

- Graph representation learning automates feature engineering by transforming nodes and edges into dense vector representations. Its evolution spans three generations: traditional dimensionality reduction, word2vec-inspired approaches, and modern GNNs.
- Graph embeddings can be either positional (preserving global structure) or structural (capturing local patterns), each suited for different tasks.
- The selection of an embedding method should consider data characteristics, computational resources, and specific application requirements.
- The choice between transductive and inductive approaches depends on whether new nodes are expected to join the graph.
- Geometric spaces matter: some graph structures are better represented in non-Euclidean spaces, particularly for hierarchical data.
- The encoding–decoding process works like a translation system, converting graph data into vectors and then back to meaningful patterns.

- The encoder–decoder framework unifies different embedding approaches by separating graph encoding from property reconstruction.
- Shallow embeddings provide a simple but important baseline through their lookup-table approach to graph representation.
- Message passing in GNNs enables automatic feature discovery through iterative information aggregation from neighboring nodes.
- Multihead attention enables GNNs to process different types of node relationships in parallel, similar to transformers.
- Neighborhood normalization and attention mechanisms help handle varying neighborhood sizes and relationship importance.
- Skip connections and gated updates improve information flow across multiple GNN layers, preventing feature loss.
- LLMs complement GNNs by providing three integration paths: as predictors, encoders, or aligners for graph tasks.

12 Node classification and link prediction with GNNs

This chapter covers

- Using graph neural networks in real-world scenarios
- Building a node classification system
- Building a link prediction system

This chapter explores how to use graph neural networks (GNNs) for node classification and link prediction. These tasks represent fundamental challenges in graph-based machine learning (ML) and are central to many real-world applications.

First we'll discuss the application of GNNs for node classification, with a focus on anti-money laundering (AML) applications. By representing financial transactions as a graph, GNNs can be used to identify suspicious patterns, classify nodes as licit or illicit, and aid in combating financial fraud. Then we focus on link prediction in recommendation systems. We will use a GNN-based approach to predict potential user–movie interactions based on ratings. By learning embeddings for users and movies and using the links between them, we can recommend movies to users based on their preferences. Despite their different tasks and application domains, we can address both scenarios with same end-to-end framework, illustrated in figure 12.1.

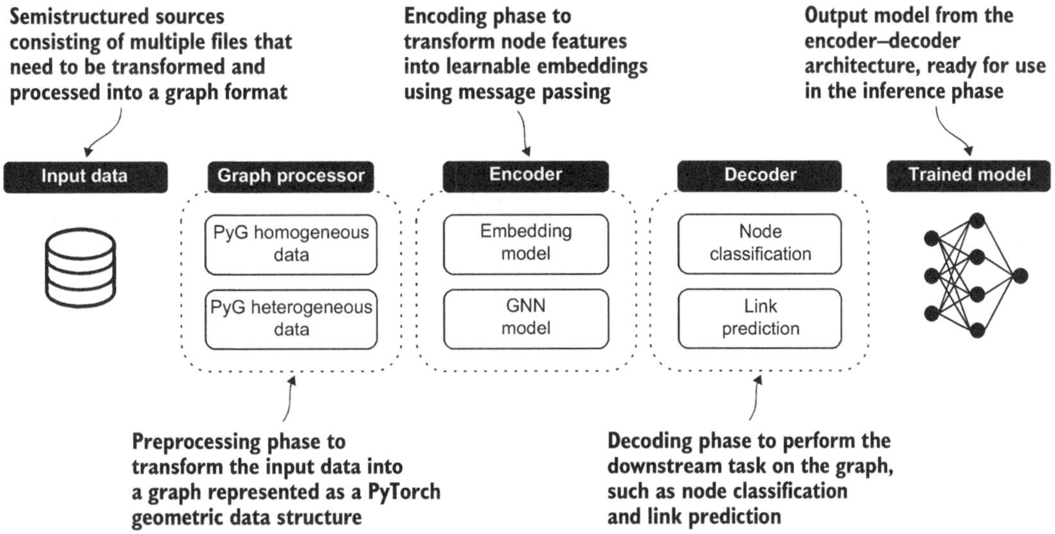

Figure 12.1 End-to-end framework to develop a GNN-based system that can be adopted for multiple tasks and application domains. The input data is usually a collection of semistructured sources describing different objects and interactions between them. The goal is to process the data and produce a graph that becomes the input for an encoder–decoder architecture. In our scenarios, the encoder uses a GNN model, and the decoder is based on a function that allows us to optimize the model for a specific downstream task. The output of this framework is a trained model that can be adopted for the inference phase.

Throughout the chapter, we compare the performance of different GNN architectures: Graph convolutional networks (GCNs) [1], GraphSAGE (SAGE) [2], and graph attention networks (GATs) [3]. These models are developed using the PyTorch Geometric (PyG) library and are evaluated using metrics such as precision, recall, and F1-score. Insights from confusion matrices and visualizations of metric trends further illustrate the trade-offs and capabilities of these approaches in real-world scenarios. By the end of this chapter, you will have a comprehensive understanding of how to apply GNNs to solve node classification and link prediction tasks, equipping you with the tools to use graph-based ML for diverse applications.

12.1 Node classification for anti-money laundering applications

Node classification is a critical task in graph-based ML and is suitable for various application domains, including combating financial crimes. In the context of AML, financial transactions can be modeled as graphs, where nodes represent accounts or entities and edges represent transaction relationships.

This section focuses on using GNNs to detect licit and illicit nodes in financial transaction networks provided by the Elliptic dataset. Figure 12.2 shows the end-to-end model for applying GNNs in node classification, where each block is characterized by a specific implementation to satisfy the requirements of our task.

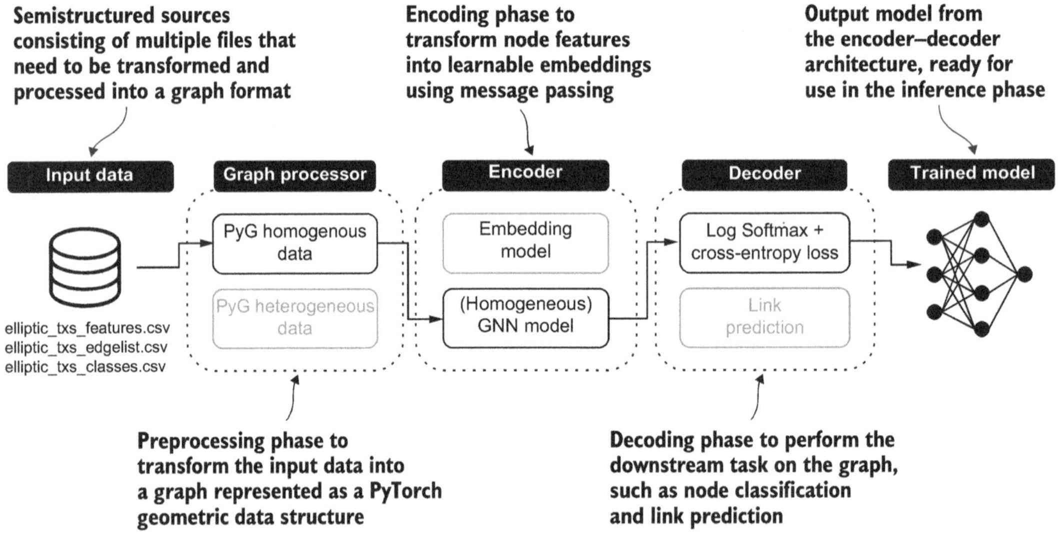

Figure 12.2 End-to-end framework tailored for node classification in the context of AML. Transaction data and node labels are transformed into a homogeneous graph structure. The encoder, a homogeneous GNN, learns node embeddings by capturing its local graph structure. The decoder classifies nodes as licit or illicit by using a log softmax function and cross-entropy loss, producing a trained model for detecting suspicious activities.

12.1.1 Input data

We will use the Elliptic dataset to explore the potential of GNNs in detecting licit and illicit nodes in financial transaction networks. The Elliptic dataset is a time-series graph comprising over 200,000 Bitcoin transactions (nodes), 234,000 directed payment flows (edges), and 166 node features derived from anonymized data.

The dataset is provided across three files. As of January 2025, these files provide the following information:

- *elliptic_txs_features.csv*—A 167-column file with 203,769 rows. The first column lists all node IDs, and the remaining columns represent anonymized features associated with each node. Data from this file is stored in the `features` variable.
- *elliptic_txs_edgelist.csv*—A 2-column file containing 234,355 rows corresponding to the number of edges in the network. The first column lists node IDs

representing transaction sources, and the second column lists node IDs representing transaction targets. Data from this file is stored in the `edges` variable.

- *elliptic_txs_classes.csv*—A 2-column file containing 203,769 rows corresponding to the number of nodes in the network. The first column lists all node IDs, and the second column specifies the label associated with each node: 1, 2, or unknown. Data in this file is stored in the `classes` variable.

In this dataset, the classes defining licit, illicit, and unknown nodes are distributed as shown in table 12.1.

Table 12.1 Distribution of licit, illicit, and unknown classes associated with nodes

Class	Labels	Counts	Percentage
Unknown	Unknown	157205	77.15%
Licit	2	42019	20.62%
Illicit	1	4545	2.23%

The next step preprocesses the CSV files to assign a more compact numerical representation to our data. Then we'll create structures to make our financial transactions graph suitable for the GNN model.

12.1.2 Graph processor: Data preparation

The preprocessing phase is critical for achieving a compact numerical representation of the original data and preparing our financial transaction graph structure for the GNN learning phase. Let's start with processing information in the `edges` variable. Table 12.2 shows a sample of the original data: the txId1 column lists the IDs of the source nodes, and txId2 lists the IDs of the target nodes.

Table 12.2 Sample of data stored in the `edges` variable showing source nodes (txId1 column) and target nodes (txId2 column)

txId1	txId2
230425980	5530458
232022460	232438397
230460314	230459870
230333930	230595899
232013274	232029206

The code in the following listing assigns each node a new incremental ID and creates an updated version of the edge data using these IDs.

Listing 12.1 Assigning a new incremental ID to nodes and updating `edges` data

```
tx_id_mapping = {tx_id: idx for idx, tx_id in enumerate(features['txId'])}
edges_with_features = edges.assign(
    Id1=edges['txId1'].map(tx_id_mapping),
    Id2=edges['txId2'].map(tx_id_mapping),
)
edges_with_features = edges_with_features.dropna(subset=['Id1', 'Id2'])
edges_with_features = edges_with_features.astype({
    'Id1': 'int64',
    'Id2': 'int64',
})
```

- Creates a dictionary between the original ID and the new incremental ID, starting from the node features file
- Maps source and target nodes to incremental IDs
- Only keeps edges where both the source and the target exist in the mapping
- Ensures that the new IDs are integers (map can yield floats if NaNs were present)

Table 12.3 shows a sample of the output of this process, stored in the `edges_with_features` variables.

Table 12.3 Edge data with the new incremental IDs associated with each node involved in a transaction

txId1	txId2	Id1	Id2
230425980	5530458	0	1
232022460	232438397	2	3
230460314	230459870	4	5
230333930	230595899	6	7
232013274	232029206	8	9

Starting from the new IDs, we can create `edge_index`, a tensor describing the edges in the graph. Here's how to create this structure.

Listing 12.2 Creating an `edge_index` tensor using the incremental node IDs

```
edge_index = torch.tensor(
    edges_with_features[['Id1', 'Id2']].values.T,
    dtype=torch.long
)
```

A sample of the `edge_index` tensor is shown next.

Listing 12.3 Sample of the `edge_index` tensor

```
tensor([[ 0, 2, 4, ..., 201921, 201480, 201954], [ 1, 3, 5, ..., 202042,
     201368, 201756]])
```

Next, let's process the original node features data structure by creating a new tensor, where each row corresponds to the incremental ID generated in the previous step. This step allows us to prepare the node features for the learning phase by dropping the original node IDs.

Listing 12.4 Creating a node feature tensor by dropping the original node ID

```
node_features = torch.tensor(
    features.drop(columns=['txId']).values,
    dtype=torch.float
)
```

The output is stored in the `node_features` tensor with size [203769, 166]. The first dimension of this tensor corresponds to the number of nodes, and the second dimension corresponds to the number of features.

As we mentioned, the index of each row of this matrix corresponds to the incremental ID created in the previous step. In other words, the 0th row of the `node_features` tensor corresponds to the set of features associated with node 0, whose original ID is 230425980.

The final step is to transform the original labels in the dataset into a numerical representation. To obtain this result, we use the `LabelEncoder` class of the scikit-learn library.

Listing 12.5 Transforming original node classes into a numerical representation

```
from sklearn.preprocessing import LabelEncoder
le = LabelEncoder()
class_labels = le.fit_transform(classes['class'])
original_labels = le.inverse_transform(class_labels)
node_labels = torch.tensor(class_labels, dtype=torch.long)
```

- `le = LabelEncoder()`: Creates an instance of LabelEncoder
- `class_labels = ...`: Assigns numerical labels to each class and converts the categorical labels into corresponding numerical labels
- `original_labels = ...`: Converts the numerical labels (class_labels) back into their original categorical labels, based on the mapping created in fit_transform
- `node_labels = ...`: Converts the class_labels list into a PyTorch tensor

The output is a new `node_labels` tensor with size 203769, where label 0 corresponds to the licit nodes ("1" in the original datasets), label 1 corresponds to the illicit nodes ("2" in the original dataset), and label 2 corresponds to unknown nodes ("unknown" in the original dataset). Next, we'll build our graph data as input for GNN models using PyG.

12.1.3 Graph processor: Homogeneous PyG graph

We can now build our graph data structure using PyG features. Figure 12.3 provides an overview of the steps applied by the graph processor: a preparation phase, the construction of a PyG Data object, and the creation of training, validation, and testing datasets.

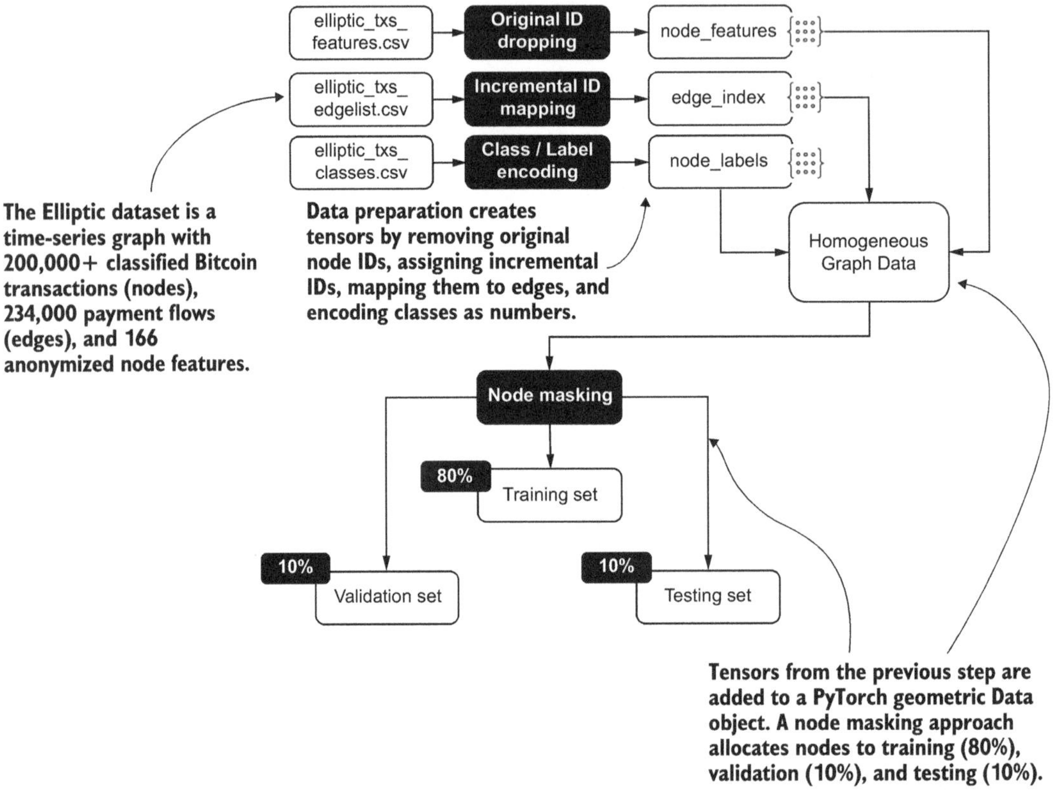

Figure 12.3 Overview of data processing applied to the Elliptic dataset. Source data is preprocessed to create node features, edge indices, and encoded labels. These tensors are incorporated into a PyG `Data` object, where a node masking approach partitions the nodes into training (80%), validation (10%), and testing (10%) sets.

The first step is to use the result of the preprocessing phase (`node_features`, `edge_index`, `node_labels`) to create a PyG `Data` object.

Listing 12.6 Creating a PyG `Data` object from the data preparation results

```
from torch_geometric.data import Data
data = Data(x=node_features,
            edge_index=edge_index,
            y=node_labels)
```

The PyG `Data` object incorporates the features of the nodes, the information on the edges, and the label associated with each node. The next step is to apply a mask to this object, which specifies the nodes to be used during the training and evaluation phases.

Considering that our GNN models need to learn which nodes are licit and which are illicit, we need to "make visible" only the nodes with known labels to our model. To do so, we can run the following code.

Listing 12.7 Preparing a mask filter to retrieve only known node labels

```
known_mask = (data.y == 0) | (data.y == 1)
unknown_mask = data.y == 2
```

- `known_mask`: Tensor of elements corresponding to nodes labeled 0 (licit) or 1 (illicit), set to True
- `unknown_mask`: Tensor of elements corresponding to nodes labeled 2 (unknown), set to False

The tensor of valid nodes (`known_mask`) is used to define the dimensions of the training, validation, and testing sets.

Listing 12.8 Dimension of the training, validation, and testing datasets

```
import numpy as np
num_known_nodes = known_mask.sum().item()
permutations = torch.randperm(num_known_nodes)
train_size = int(0.8 * num_known_nodes)
val_size = int(0.1 * num_known_nodes)
test_size = num_known_nodes - train_size - val_size
total = train_size + val_size + test_size
```

- `num_known_nodes`: Counts the True values in known_mask and converts the resulting scalar tensor into a Python integer
- `permutations`: Creates a permutation of indices
- `train_size`: Computes the size of the training dataset (80% of nodes)
- `val_size`: Computes the size of the validation dataset (10%)
- `test_size`: Computes the size of the test dataset (10%)
- `total`: Verifies that the total sizes add up to the original number of known nodes

Using the dimension of the results stored in the `total` variable, we determine the number of observations: that is, the number of labeled nodes to be included in the training, validation, and testing datasets. The results are summarized in table 12.4.

Table 12.4 Dimensions of the training, validation, and testing datasets, based on the number of labeled nodes

Dataset	Number of nodes	Percentage
Training	37,251	80%
Validation	4,656	10%
Testing	4,657	10%

Using the following code, we create the training, validation, and testing index masks on the PyG Data object based on the dimensions established in the previous step.

Listing 12.9 Training, validation, and testing masks on the PyG Data object

```
train_mask = torch.zeros(data.num_nodes, dtype=torch.bool)
val_mask = torch.zeros_like(train_mask)
test_mask = torch.zeros_like(train_mask)
nonzero_indices = known_mask.nonzero(as_tuple=True)[0]
train_indices = nonzero_indices[permutations[:train_size]]
```

- `train_mask`: Initializes the training set mask (all node indices are marked as False by default)
- `val_mask`: Initializes the validation set mask
- `test_mask`: Initializes the testing set mask
- `train_indices`: Fills training set indices with a uniquely shuffled batch of True values from known_mask

```
val_indices = nonzero_indices[
  permutations[train_size:train_size + val_size]
]
test_indices = nonzero_indices[permutations[train_size + val_size:]]
train_mask[train_indices] = True
val_mask[val_indices] = True
test_mask[test_indices] = True
data.train_mask = train_mask
data.val_mask = val_mask
data.test_mask = test_mask
```

Fills validation set indices with a non-overlapping batch of True values from known_mask

Fills testing set indices with another distinct, non-overlapping batch of True values from known_mask

Sets the training set indices to True in the training set mask

Sets the validation set indices to True in the validation set mask

Sets the testing set indices to True in the testing set mask

Table 12.5 shows the dataset's statistics to clarify how the data is split for training and evaluation. In this scenario, we can directly check the balance of licit and illicit information in each dataset.

Table 12.5 Training, validation, and testing dataset size and class distribution for each dataset

Dataset	Total count	Licit	Licit (%)	Illicit	Illicit (%)
Training	37,251	33,645	90.32	3,606	9.78
Validation	4,656	4,193	90.06	463	9.88
Testing	4,657	4,181	89.78	476	9.45

We performed the splitting process for the classification task manually by defining multiple scripts. In section 12.2.3, we will see that the PyG library provides features to help us split the dataset. Let's now discuss the end-to-end architecture to build our node classification system.

12.1.4 Encoder–decoder architecture

Chapter 11 introduced the encoder–decoder architecture. Figure 12.4 provides an overview of the steps involved in training a GNN model on a downstream task.

The following listing shows the implementation of a Python class to define an encoder–decoder for node classification.

Listing 12.10 Encoder–decoder implementation for node classification

```
import torch
import torch.nn.functional as F

class NodeClassifier(torch.nn.Module):
    def __init__(self, gnn_model):
        super().__init__()
        self.gnn = gnn_model

    def forward(self, x, edge_index):
        x = self.gnn(x, edge_index)
        return F.log_softmax(x, dim=1)
```

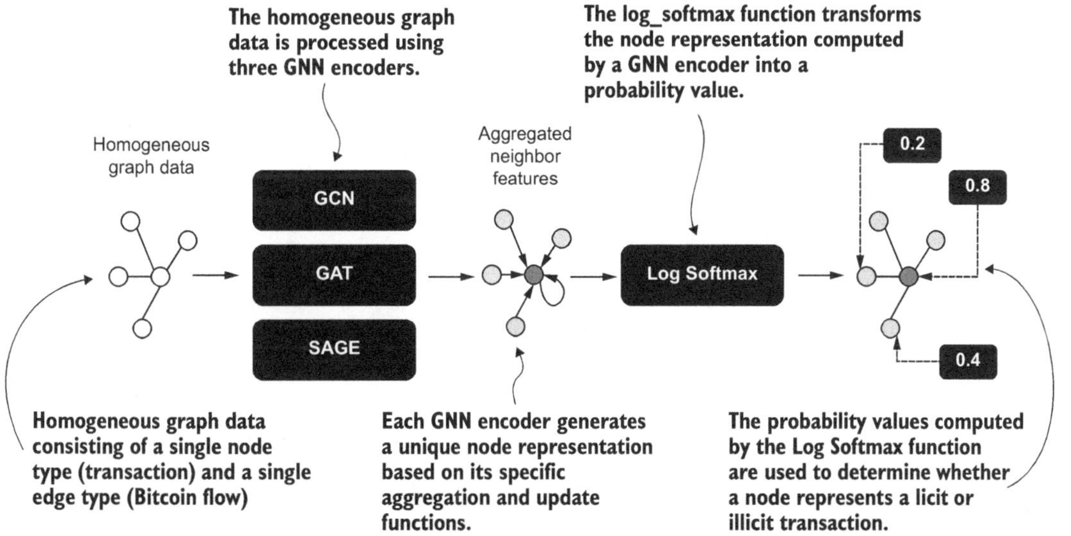

Figure 12.4 Overview of the main steps of the encoder–decoder architecture. Homogeneous graph data, consisting of transactions (nodes) and Bitcoin flows (edges), is processed using three GNN encoders: GCN, GAT, and SAGE. Each encoder generates unique node representations by aggregating neighbor features. Then these representations are transformed into probability values, which are used to classify transactions as licit or illicit.

The `forward` method of the `NodeClassifier` class includes an encoding phase performed by a GNN to update the node representation with information from its neighbors and a decoding phase executed by the `log_softmax` function provided by PyTorch, which produces a probability value associated with each node. Such a probability value will be used to establish whether a node is licit or illicit. Let's see the implementation of these components in detail.

THE ENCODER

The encoder component uses a homogeneous GNN to perform the message-passing process (see chapter 11). This means the encoder is designed to handle homogeneous graphs containing a single type of node and edge, such as those provided in financial transaction networks. To compare the behavior of different GNN encoders, in the following listing we define a base graph model that specifies the shared characteristics of these encoders.

Listing 12.11 Base graph model to define a general GNN encoder

```
import torch
import torch.nn.functional as F

class BaseGraphModel(torch.nn.Module):
    def __init__(self, input_dim,
                       hidden_dim,
                       out_dim,
                       conv_layer,
                       **conv_kwargs):
```

Defines the model's initialization, including the input, hidden, and output dimensions; type of convolution layer; and arguments that may be passed to the convolutional layer

```
        super(BaseGraphModel, self).__init__()
        self.conv1 = conv_layer(input_dim, hidden_dim, **conv_kwargs)
        self.conv2 = conv_layer(hidden_dim, out_dim, **conv_kwargs)

    def forward(self, x, edge_index):
        x = self.conv1(x, edge_index)
        x = F.relu(x)
        x = self.conv2(x, edge_index)
        return x
```

Calls the superclass initializer to set up the model

Initializes the first graph convolution layer with input and hidden dimensions

Initializes the second graph convolution layer with hidden and output dimensions

Defines the forward pass function for the model

Applies the first convolution layer to the input features and edge indices

Applies the ReLU activation function to introduce nonlinearity

Applies the second convolution layer to the transformed features

Returns the final node features after processing

This base class shows a two-layer architecture in which any GNN implementation provided by PyG can be used for neighborhood aggregation and node update operations (convolution). The `**conv_kwargs` argument lets us pass extra parameters that may be required for specific GNN implementations. Consider the implementation of our SAGE model in the next listing.

Listing 12.12 SAGE model implemented from the base class

```
from torch_geometric.nn import SAGEConv

class SAGE(BaseGraphModel):
    def __init__(self, input_dim, hidden_dim, out_dim):
        super(SAGE, self).__init__(
            input_dim=input_dim,
            hidden_dim=hidden_dim,
            out_dim=out_dim,
            conv_layer=SAGEConv
        )
```

The `SAGEConv` layer from PyG does not require additional parameters, so initializing our SAGE model is straightforward. This code creates a GNN model with two `SAGEConv` layers.

Other GNN models require an extension of our base class. Consider the implementation of the GAT model, shown in the following listing.

Listing 12.13 GAT model implemented by extending the base class

```
from torch_geometric.nn import GATConv

class GAT(BaseGraphModel):
    def __init__(self, input_dim,
                 hidden_dim,
                 out_dim,
                 num_heads=8,
                 add_self_loops=True):
```

Initializes the GAT model

```
concat_hidden_dim = hidden_dim * num_heads    ◁ Adjusts hidden dimensions
                                                 for concatenation across
                                                 multiple attention heads
conv1 = GATConv(                              ◁ Defines the first GATConv
    in_channels=input_dim,                       layer with multihead
    out_channels=hidden_dim,                     attention and parameters
    heads=num_heads,
    add_self_loops=add_self_loops
)
                                              Defines the second GATConv
conv2 = GATConv(                              ◁ layer for the final output
    in_channels=concat_hidden_dim,
    out_channels=out_dim,                     Sets heads=1, specifying that the final
    heads=1,                                  ◁ layer uses a single attention head
    add_self_loops=add_self_loops,            Sets concat=False, disabling
    concat=False                              ◁ concatenation for the final output
)
                                              Initializes the parent class
super(BaseGraphModel, self).__init__()        ◁ without automatic layer setup
self.conv1 = conv1                            ◁ Assigns the first GATConv
                                                 layer to self.conv1
self.conv2 = conv2                            ◁ Assigns the second
                                                 GATConv layer
                                                 to self.conv2
```

In this case, we must reimplement the convolutional layers to include the additional parameters required by the `GATConv` layer implemented in PyG.

THE DECODER

The decoder component uses PyTorch's `log_softmax` function to transform the neural network's output—specifically, the output of the GNN encoder—into probability values. Unlike the standard `softmax` function, `log_softmax` improves the stability of the learning process by mitigating the effects of extremely small or large numbers during the probability computation.

In this context, the `log_softmax` function works in tandem with PyTorch's `CrossEntropyLoss` function. This function combines the logarithm of softmax probabilities with the negative log-likelihood loss, providing an efficient approach to classification tasks. For example, in an AML system, the GNN encoder might analyze transaction data to detect suspicious behavior, and each node could be assigned a probability for different categories, such as licit or illicit.

The `log_softmax` function ensures that these probabilities are numerically stable and interpretable, and the `CrossEntropyLoss` function measures how well the model's predictions match the actual labels. If the model predicts a high probability for illicit but the node is labeled licit, the loss function identifies the error and optimizes the model to improve accuracy.

12.1.5 Evaluation and analysis

In our analysis, we compared three end-to-end models for node classification. Each model uses a different GNN encoder: GCN, GAT, or SAGE. Table 12.6 shows the number of parameters and the total training time in seconds for each model; we achieved these results after 400 epochs on a T4 Colab machine.

NOTE When you run the code examples, your results may differ slightly from those shown in the text. This is normal behavior in machine learning, where algorithms often incorporate randomness (for example, in initialization or sampling). Such variability does not indicate an error in your code.

Table 12.6 Number of parameters and total training time for each encoder

Encoder	Parameters	Training time (s)
GCN	2,723	19.02
GAT	22,025	43.45
SAGE	5,427	36.71

The results indicate that the GCN model is the most efficient, the GAT model is the least efficient, and the SAGE model falls between the other two. As you can guess, the training time is directly connected to the number of parameters. In section 12.1.4, we clarified that the GAT model incorporates an attention mechanism that introduces learnable coefficients for the neighborhood edges which increase the number of learning parameters.

PRECISION, RECALL, AND F1-SCORE

To explore the generalization capabilities of these models, we can evaluate their performance on precision, recall, and F1-score metrics. In the context of node classification for AML, these metrics allow us to answer the following questions:

- *Precision*—When the model says a node is licit or illicit, how often is it right?
- *Recall*—Of all the existing licit and illicit nodes, how many did the model correctly find?
- *F1-score*—How well does the model balance being accurate when it makes a prediction and finding as many correct nodes as possible?

Figure 12.5 shows plots of GCN, GAT, and SAGE performance across these metrics on the validation dataset during the training phase. The vertical axis shows the metric values, and the horizontal axis indicates the number of epochs.

We obtained these results using the `sklearn` library's built-in scoring functions for precision, recall, and F1-score. These scoring functions provide the `average` parameter to manage imbalanced datasets, such as ours, where licit nodes are much more numerous than illicit ones. We decided to use the `weighted` average because it provides a performance metric that reflects the data distribution and is suitable for general evaluation.

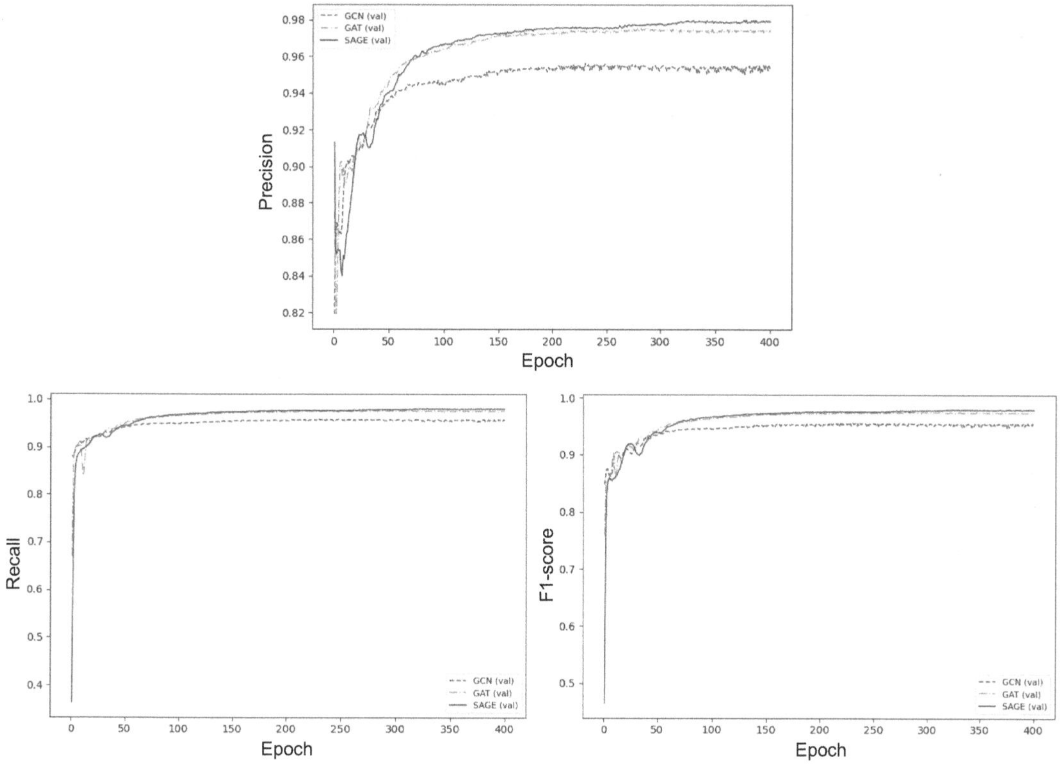

Figure 12.5 Performance of GCN, GAT, and SAGE across precision, recall, and F1-score on the validation dataset during the training phase

Let's answer our earlier questions in the context of the AML scenario for detecting licit and illicit nodes:

- *Precision*—When the models predict whether a node is licit or illicit, the SAGE model is the most accurate, maintaining consistently high precision throughout the training phase. This indicates that SAGE minimizes false positives and makes more reliable predictions about licit and illicit nodes. The GAT model also performs well in this regard, closely tracking SAGE. The GCN model demonstrates the lowest precision, often misclassifying licit and illicit nodes, especially in earlier epochs.
- *Recall*—The models perform similarly in identifying all actual licit and illicit nodes, with all three achieving close recall values as training progresses. This means GCN, GAT, and SAGE can effectively detect almost all licit and illicit nodes. However, recall alone does not account for false positives, so it must be combined with precision to understand overall model performance.

- *F1-score*—This score reflects how well the models balance precision and recall in detecting licit and illicit nodes. The SAGE model achieves the highest value, proving that it finds the right balance: it identifies most licit and illicit nodes and minimizes incorrect predictions. The GAT model is nearly as strong as SAGE, showing only a minor difference. Due to its lower precision, the GCN model struggles to achieve high scores despite its high recall, indicating weaker overall performance in balancing these metrics.

CONFUSION MATRICES

Beyond the overall behavior, we can conduct a more specific evaluation to distinguish the performance of these models on licit nodes from their performance on illicit nodes. To do so, we can use a *confusion matrix* that breaks down classification performance compared to the previously defined metrics by showing the counts of correct and incorrect predictions for each class (licit or illicit). Figure 12.6 shows the confusion matrices of the GCN, GAT, and SAGE models on the testing dataset.

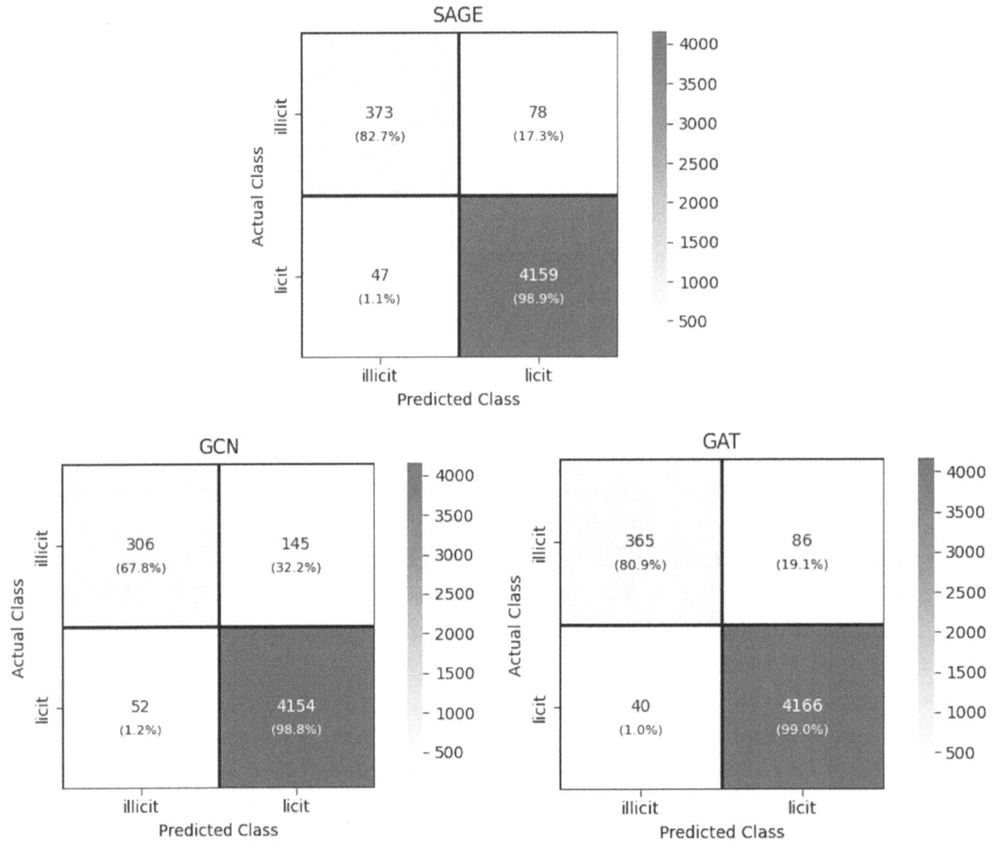

Figure 12.6 Confusion matrices to understand the performance of GCN, GAT, and SAGE models on each class (licit or illicit)

Overall, SAGE performs best, correctly classifying most licit and illicit nodes with minimal misclassifications. The GAT model also performs strongly, coming close to SAGE in accuracy, but with slightly higher misclassifications in the illicit class. The GCN model exhibits the weakest performance, with lower precision and recall for illicit nodes, indicating challenges in distinguishing these nodes compared to the other models. Let's analyze the behavior of each model in detail:

- *GCN*—This model shows moderate performance in classifying licit and illicit nodes. It correctly classifies about 68% of illicit nodes and about 99% of licit nodes. However, about one-third of illicit nodes are misclassified as licit, highlighting the struggle to identify illicit nodes correctly. On the licit side, about 1% of licit nodes are incorrectly predicted as illicit, showing better accuracy in predicting licit nodes. This imbalance indicates that although GCN effectively identifies licit nodes, its precision for illicit nodes requires improvement.
- *GAT*—This model outperforms GCN by correctly classifying about 81% of illicit and about 99.5% of licit nodes. It reduces misclassification for the illicit class compared to GCN: about one in five illicit nodes are misclassified as licit, whereas only 40 licit nodes are misclassified as illicit. This improvement demonstrates that GAT provides a more reliable balance across both classes.
- *SAGE*—This model achieves the highest performance among the three. It correctly classifies about 83% of illicit nodes and about 99% of licit nodes. Its misclassification rates are the lowest: fewer than 1 in 5 illicit nodes are misclassified as licit (88), and only around 50 licit nodes are misclassified as illicit.

Based on the overall analysis, the SAGE model's superior balance, higher accuracy for both licit and illicit nodes, and minimal misclassifications make it the most effective and reliable choice. It is particularly well suited for applications where detecting illicit nodes is critical, such as AML, while maintaining high accuracy for licit nodes.

12.2 Link prediction for movie recommendations

Link prediction is pivotal in graph-based ML and is particularly relevant for applications like recommendation systems. By using graph structures, we can model interactions and preferences as links between entities—in this case, representing the relationships between users and movies.

This section explores the use of GNNs to predict user–movie links, using the MovieLens dataset as a data source; figure 12.7 illustrates the end-to-end framework. The goal is to evaluate the ability of GNNs to suggest relevant movies while avoiding irrelevant recommendations, thereby enhancing the recommendation process.

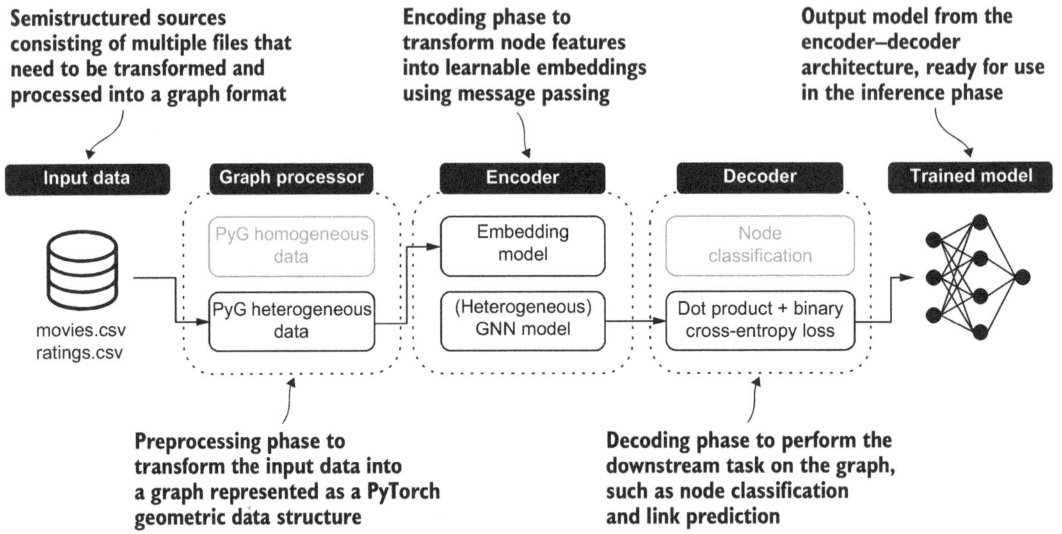

Figure 12.7 End-to-end framework for link prediction in the context of recommendation systems. Interaction/preference data is transformed into a heterogeneous graph structure that includes two types of nodes: users and movies. The encoder, a heterogeneous GNN, learns node embeddings by capturing its local graph structure. The decoder predicts the existence of links between users and movies by using a dot-product operation combined with a binary cross-entropy loss to produce a trained model for suggesting relevant movies to users.

12.2.1 Input data

We will use the small version of the MovieLens dataset to explore the capabilities of GNNs in performing link prediction for recommendation purposes. This version of the MovieLens dataset includes 100,000 ratings and 3,600 tag applications applied to 9,000 movies by 600 users. As of January 2025, the raw data is available at https://files.grouplens.org/datasets/movielens/ml-latest-small.zip and includes the following files:

- *movies.csv*—A CSV file with 9,742 rows and 3 columns. The columns define the ID of the movie, the title of the movie, and the genres, respectively.
- *ratings.csv*—A CSV file with 100,836 rows and 4 columns. The columns define the ID of the user, the ID of the movie, the rating, and a timestamp.

We will focus on a subset of the available columns for the link prediction task. In the case of movies.csv, we will use the `movieId` and `genres` columns. Table 12.7 shows a sample of this file with this subset of columns. The movie is identified by an incremental ID starting from 1, and its genre is provided as a collection of categorical strings separated by the pipe character (|).

Table 12.7 Sample of the `movieId` and `genres` columns from the movies.csv file

movieId	genres
1	Adventure|Animation|Children|Comedy|Fantasy
2	Adventure|Children|Fantasy
3	Comedy|Romance
4	Comedy|Drama|Romance
5	Comedy

In the ratings.csv file, we will consider only the `userId` and `movieId` columns. Table 12.8 provides a sample. Each row defines the rating of a specific movie (identified by the same ID used in the movies.csv file) from a particular user identified by an incremental ID.

Table 12.8 Sample of the `userId` and `movieId` columns from the ratings.csv file

userId	movieId
1	1
1	3
1	6
1	47
1	50

12.2.2 Graph processor: Data preparation

As in the node classification task, we have to prepare the data to achieve a compact numerical representation of the original data and a rating graph structure for the GNN learning phase. Let's start by processing the movies.csv file. The main goal is transforming the genre information into something numerically processable (a vector of features), as in the following listing.

Listing 12.14 Transforming genre information into a vector of features

```
movies_df = pd.read_csv(movies_path, index_col='movieId')
genres = movies_df['genres'].str.get_dummies('|')
movie_feat = torch.from_numpy(genres.values).to(torch.float)
assert movie_feat.size() == (9742, 20)
```

- Reads the movie dataset and loads it in memory (line 1)
- Separates genres and transforms them into binary indicators (line 2)
- Creates a new tensor where the binary representation of genres is a set of features attached to movies (line 3)
- Checks the consistency of the number of genres with the original representation (line 4)

A sample of the output stored in the `movie_feat` variable is shown in table 12.9. In this representation, each movie is associated with a feature vector containing 0s and 1s, where a value of 1 in a specific column indicates that the movie belongs to the corresponding genre.

Table 12.9 Vector of features for movie genres

`movieId`	Action	Adventure	Drama	Horror
1	0	1	0	0
2	0	1	0	0
3	0	0	0	0
4	0	0	1	0
5	0	0	0	0

In our example, the movie with ID 1 can be categorized as an Adventure movie, and the movie with ID 4 is categorized as a Drama movie. Multiple genre values can be associated with the same movie.

We need to create an `edge_index` tensor that describes the connections between users and movies (listing 12.15). The first step is to map the original IDs of movies and users to incremental IDs starting from 0. Then, we can create the `edge_index` using the new IDs.

Listing 12.15 Generating the `edge_index` tensor from user and movie IDs

```
ratings_df = pd.read_csv(ratings_path)        # Reads the rating file and loads it in memory

unique_user_id = ratings_df['userId'].unique()
unique_user_id = pd.DataFrame(data={
    'userId': unique_user_id,
    'mappedID': pd.RangeIndex(len(unique_user_id)),
})                                            # Creates a new data frame with a mapping from the original user IDs to the [0, num_user_nodes) range

unique_movie_id = pd.DataFrame(data={
    'movieId': movies_df.index,
    'mappedID': pd.RangeIndex(len(movies_df)),
})                                            # Creates a new data frame with a mapping from the original movie IDs to the [0, num_movie_nodes) range

ratings_user_id = pd.merge(
    ratings_df['userId'],
    unique_user_id,
    left_on='userId',
    right_on='userId',
    how='left'
)
ratings_user_id = torch.from_numpy(ratings_user_id['mappedID'].values)    # Stores the new source user IDs of the ratings into a new data frame
```

```
ratings_movie_id = pd.merge(
    ratings_df['movieId'],
    unique_movie_id,
    left_on='movieId',
    right_on='movieId',
    how='left'
)
ratings_movie_id = torch.from_numpy(ratings_movie_id['mappedID'].values)

edge_index_user_to_movie = torch.stack([ratings_user_id, ratings_movie_id],
     dim=0)
```

Stores the new target movie IDs of the ratings into a new data frame

Creates the edge_index by stacking the source and target data frames

The output of ID mappings for users and movies, along with the `edge_index` tensor, is shown in the following listing.

Listing 12.16 Output of ID mapping, and a sample of `edge_index`

```
Mapping of user IDs to consecutive values:
==========================================
   userId  mappedID
0       1         0
1       2         1
2       3         2
3       4         3
4       5         4

Mapping of movie IDs to consecutive values:
===========================================
   movieId  mappedID
0        1         0
1        2         1
2        3         2
3        4         3
4        5         4

Final edge indices pointing from users to movies:
=================================================
tensor([[   0,     0,     0,  ...,  609,   609,   609],
        [   0,     2,     5,  ..., 9462,  9463,  9503]])
```

The size of the edge index tensor is [2, 100836], and the second element corresponds to the number of ratings in the dataset. After the preprocessing phase, we can finally create our PyG graph structure to represent ratings as interactions between users and movies.

12.2.3 Graph processor: Heterogeneous PyG graph

Figure 12.8 provides an overview of the steps applied by the graph processor. They include a preparation phase, the construction of a PyG HeteroData object, the creation of training, validation, and testing datasets, and the preparation of the mini-batches.

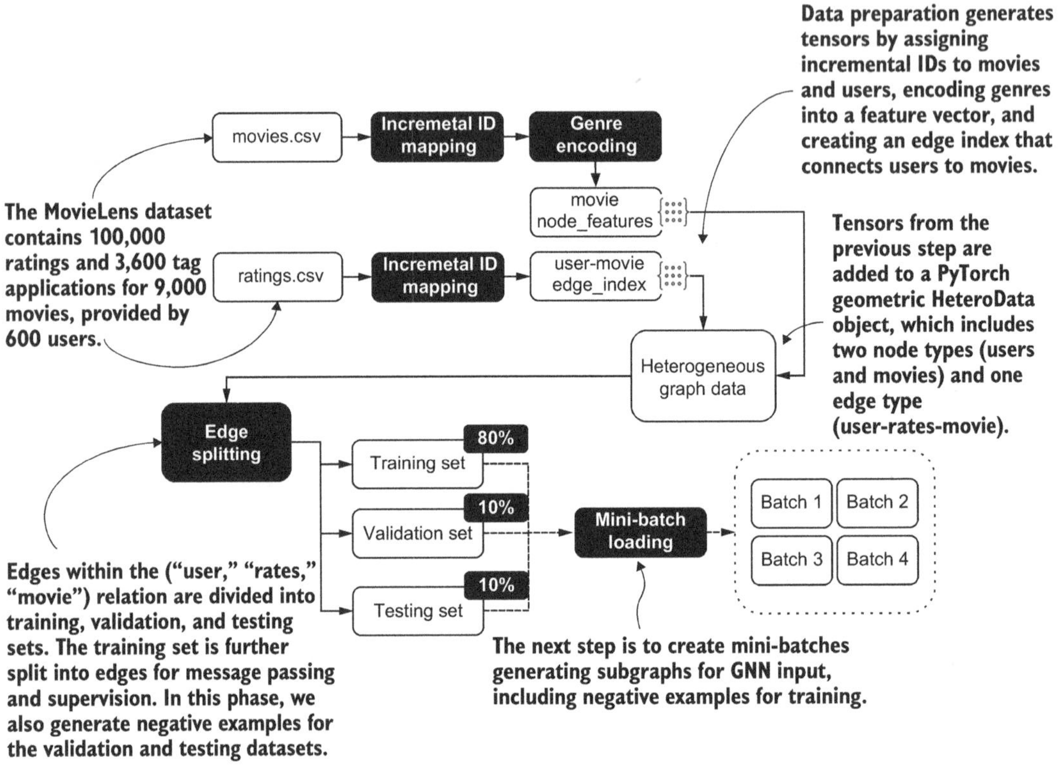

Figure 12.8 The data processing pipeline for the MovieLens dataset, including incremental ID mapping, genre encoding, and edge creation. The heterogeneous graph data comprises two node types (users and movies) and one edge type (user-rates-movie). Edges are split into training (80%), validation (10%), and testing (10%) sets, with negative examples generated for validation and testing. A mini-batch loader then prepares subgraphs for GNN input, ensuring scalability for large graphs that exceed memory capacity.

In our scenario, we have two types of nodes: users and movies. We construct our graph using PyG's `HeteroData` to represent information about these nodes. Unlike the `Data` class used in homogeneous graphs, which assumes a single node type and a single edge type, `HeteroData` allows us to differentiate features for each node type and associate the `edge_index` with a specific relationship: in this case, the `rates` relationship. The next listing constructs the PyG `HeteroData` object using the result of the preprocessing phase, which consists of the `movie_feat` generated with the related genres and the `edge_index`.

Listing 12.17 Building the PyG `HeteroData` object

```
from torch_geometric.data import HeteroData
data = HeteroData()
data["user"].node_id = torch.arange(len(unique_user_id))
data["movie"].node_id = torch.arange(len(movies_df))
```

```
data["movie"].x = movie_feat
data["user", "rates", "movie"].edge_index = edge_index_user_to_movie
data = T.ToUndirected()(data)
```

In this case, we have to add reverse edges to make explicit the GNN message passing from users to movies and vice versa.

After generating the graph, we can split the rating edges into training, validation, and testing datasets, as shown in the next listing. Our main goal is to avoid overlapping between these datasets in terms of links. In the context of node classification, we performed this spitting operation manually to separate the nodes, but in this case, we use the built-in PyG `transforms.RandomLinkSplit` function.

Listing 12.18 Creating training, validation, and testing datasets

```
import torch_geometric.transforms as T

transform = T.RandomLinkSplit(
    num_val=0.1,
    num_test=0.1,
    disjoint_train_ratio=0.3,
    neg_sampling_ratio=2,
    add_negative_train_samples=False,
    edge_types=("user", "rates", "movie"),
    rev_edge_types=("movie", "rev_rates", "user"),
)
```

- `num_val=0.1`: Defines the percentage of validation edges (10%)
- `num_test=0.1`: Defines the percentage of testing edges (10%)
- `disjoint_train_ratio=0.3`: Defines the percentage of edges for supervision (30%) and message passing (70%)
- `neg_sampling_ratio=2`: Defines the number of negative samples (2) for each existing edge in the validation and testing datasets
- `add_negative_train_samples=False`: Establishes no negative training samples (False) in the training dataset
- `edge_types`: Defines the existing edges for message passing and training
- `rev_edge_types`: Defines the reverse edges for message passing but not for training

The `transforms.RandomLinkSplit` function randomly partitions the edges in the `("user", "rates", "movie")` relation into training, validation, and test edges. Compared to traditional dataset splitting, in the case of GNNs we have to consider other factors. For example, the `disjoint_train_ratio` parameter further subdivides the training edges into two distinct groups:

- Edges used for message passing, stored in the `edge_index` variable
- Edges used for supervision, stored in the `edge_label_index` variable

The difference between these two types of edges is reflected in the following training data structure.

Listing 12.19 Details of the training data

```
Training data:
==============
HeteroData(
  user={
    node_id=[610]
  },
  movie={
```

```
    node_id=[9742],
    x=[9742, 20]
  },
  (user, rates, movie)={
    edge_index=[2, 56469],
    edge_label=[24201],
    edge_label_index=[2, 24201]
  },
  (movie, rev_rates, user)={
    edge_index=[2, 56469]
  }
)
```

The size of the training set is 80,669, which corresponds to 80% of 100,836 (the total number of edges). However, the training `HeteroData` reports a value corresponding to 56,469 (70% of 80,669) for `edge_index` and a value of 24,201 (30% of 80,669) for `edge_label_index`. It is important to remember that these edge sets are disjointed to avoid overlap between the edges used for message passing and those used for supervision.

Moreover, in the context of a heterogeneous graph, the reverse edges are specified with the `rev_edge_types` parameter. Reverse edges are used for message passing but not for training the link prediction model. The following HeteroData objects illustrate the structure of our validation and testing datasets.

Listing 12.20 Details of the validation and testing dataset

```
Validation data:
================
HeteroData(
  user={
    node_id=[610]
  },
  movie={
    node_id=[9742],
    x=[9742, 20]
  },
  (user, rates, movie)={
    edge_index=[2, 80670],
    edge_label=[30249],
    edge_label_index=[2, 30249]
  },
  (movie, rev_rates, user)={
    edge_index=[2, 80670]
  }
)

Test data:
================
HeteroData(
  user={
    node_id=[610]
  },
```

```
  movie={
    node_id=[9742],
    x=[9742, 20]
  },
  (user, rates, movie)={
    edge_index=[2, 90753],
    edge_label=[30249],
    edge_label_index=[2, 30249]
  },
  (movie, rev_rates, user)={
    edge_index=[2, 90753]
  }
)
```

The dimensions shown in this listing let us understand which edges are used for message passing and which for evaluating the model's goodness on the validation and testing datasets. For the validation dataset, the `edge_index` size is 80,670, equal to the number of edges in the training dataset. The `edge_label_index` size is 30,249, which is equivalent to 10,083 (10% of 100,836), resulting in 20,166 negative edges generated by `RandomLinkSplit`.

In this context, the 80,670 training edges are used for message passing, and the 30,249 edges are used to evaluate the model for the link prediction task on the validation dataset. An analogous principle is used for the testing set: the edges used for message passing (90,753) include the training (80,670) and validation edges (10,083).

After splitting the dataset, the next step is to define a mini-batch loader capable of producing subgraphs suitable for input into our GNN. Although this step may not be essential for small-scale graphs, it is important to use GNNs on larger graphs that exceed CPU or GPU memory capacity.

For this purpose, we use the `loader.LinkNeighborLoader` component of PyG to select a sample of edges from the set of input edges. As shown in the following listing, it constructs a subgraph from all the nodes in this list by sampling the number of neighbors in each iteration.

Listing 12.21 Sampling the number of neighbors in each iteration

```
from torch_geometric.loader import LinkNeighborLoader

edge_label_index = train_data["user", "rates", "movie"].edge_label_index
edge_label = train_data["user", "rates", "movie"].edge_label

train_loader = LinkNeighborLoader(
    data=data,
    num_neighbors=[20, 10],
    neg_sampling_ratio=2,
    edge_label_index=(("user", "rates", "movie"), edge_label_index),
    edge_label=edge_label,
    batch_size=128,
    shuffle=True
)
```

- `num_neighbors=[20, 10]`: Samples at most 20 neighbors in the first hop and at most 10 neighbors in the second hop
- `neg_sampling_ratio=2`: Defines the ratio of negative samples (2:1) for each existing edge created in the batch
- `batch_size=128`: Sets the batch size in terms of the number of edges
- `shuffle=True`: Random order of edges

Note that this process is also performed on the validation and testing datasets. After describing the data preparation phase, we can understand the architecture for addressing the link prediction task.

12.2.4 Encoder–decoder architecture

The link prediction system is also based on an encoder–decoder architecture. However, the architecture discussed in this section comprises specific components based on the characteristics of the input data (a heterogeneous graph structure) and the downstream task to be performed (link prediction for recommendation); figure 12.9 provides an overview of the steps involved. The following listing implements the encoder–decoder architecture in this scenario.

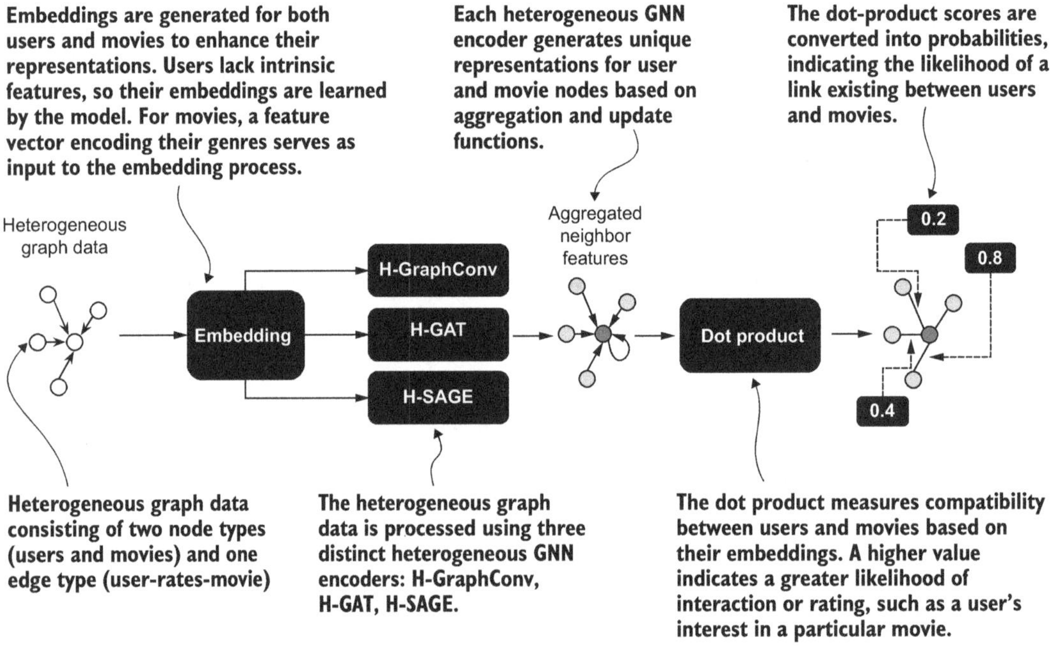

Figure 12.9 Pipeline for processing heterogeneous graph data in a link prediction system for movie recommendations. The data consists of users and movies as node types and user–movie ratings as edges. Embeddings are generated, with user embeddings learned by the model and movie embeddings initialized from genre features. The data is processed using three heterogeneous GNN encoders (H-GraphConv, H-GAT, and H-SAGE), which aggregate neighbor features to generate node representations. A dot product then quantifies the compatibility between users and movies, with higher scores indicating a greater likelihood of interaction. The scores are finally converted into probabilities representing the likelihood of a link between users and movies.

Listing 12.22 Encoder–decoder architecture for link prediction

```
class MovieLensLinkPredictor(torch.nn.Module):
    def __init__(self, gnn_model, data, hidden_channels):
```

```
        super().__init__()

        self.embedding = MovieLensEmbedding(
            data["user"].num_nodes,
            data["movie"].num_nodes,
            hidden_channels
        )

        self.gnn = gnn_model(
            data.metadata(),
            hidden_channels,
            hidden_channels,
            hidden_channels
        )

        self.classifier = DotProduct()

    def forward(self, data):
        x_dict = self.embedding(data)
        x_dict = self.gnn(x_dict, data.edge_index_dict)
        pred = self.classifier(
            x_dict["user"],
            x_dict["movie"],
            data["user", "rates", "movie"].edge_label_index
        )
        return pred
```

Initializes the embedding representation for user and movie nodes using the MovieLensEmbedding class

Initializes the model architecture (a heterogeneous version of modified GraphGCN, GAT, and SAGE)

Initializes the final layer (decoder), which performs a dot-product operation of user and movie embeddings

Performs forward propagation and computes the prediction

The `forward` method of `MovieLensLinkPredictor` shows the propagation of the data into the encoding–decoding process. The encoding phase combines two steps to enhance user and movie data representation:

- *Embedding generation*—This step generates embeddings for both users and movies to improve the expressiveness of their features. Because users are not associated with intrinsic features, their embeddings are learned from the model. For movies, a feature vector encoding their genres is used as input to the embedding process, providing a meaningful starting representation for each movie node.
- *Heterogeneous GNN model*—The embeddings are updated using a heterogeneous GNN model. This model uses the graph structure to refine node representations by aggregating information from neighboring nodes. Specifically, user embeddings are updated with information from the movies they interact with, and movie embeddings are updated with information from the users who have interacted with them. This bidirectional information exchange ensures that the embeddings effectively capture the relational structure of the graph.

The decoding phase uses the learned embeddings to make predictions. This is implemented using a dot-product operation, where the embeddings of user and movie nodes are combined to compute a similarity score. This score represents the likelihood of a link (rating) between a user and a movie. The dot product enables the model to predict user–movie relationships based on the learned embedding. Let's now analyze the encoder and decoder implementations in our link prediction system.

THE ENCODER

As introduced at the beginning of this section, the encoder component has two steps: the first generates the embedding, and the second applies the heterogeneous GNN model. The embedding generation step is shown next.

Listing 12.23 Class for the embedding generation

```
import torch

class MovieLensEmbedding(torch.nn.Module):
    def __init__(self, user_input_dim, movie_input_dim, out_dim):
        super().__init__()
        self.movie_lin = torch.nn.Linear(20, out_dim)
        self.user_emb = torch.nn.Embedding(user_input_dim, out_dim)
        self.movie_emb = torch.nn.Embedding(movie_input_dim, out_dim)

    def forward(self, data):
        return {
            "user": self.user_emb(data["user"].node_id),
            "movie": self.movie_lin(data["movie"].x) +
                     self.movie_emb(data["movie"].node_id),
        }
```

We apply different embedding generation approaches for the user and movie features. We use a single-step approach for users, creating an embedding matrix with rows equal to the total number of user nodes (`user_input_dim`) and columns defined by the `out_dim` parameter. In this context, users do not have any initial features associated with them, and their embeddings are learned solely from this matrix during training.

For movies, we use a two-step approach. First we apply a linear transformation to the input features, represented as a 20-dimensional vector encoding movie genres. Then we combine the output of this transformation with an embedding layer. This method enhances the expressiveness of the initial features, allowing the model to capture both learned embeddings and transformed feature representations.

The second step of the encoding phase uses a heterogeneous GNN. This means that, unlike the node classification in a financial transaction graph, the encoder is designed to manage multiple types of nodes and edges (see the following listing).

Listing 12.24 Implementation of a heterogeneous base encoder

```
import torch
from torch_geometric.nn import to_hetero

class HeteroBaseModel(torch.nn.Module):
    def __init__(self, metadata, input_dim, hidden_dim, out_dim, base_model):   # Defines the model's initialization
        super(HeteroBaseModel, self).__init__()   # Calls the superclass initializer to set up the model
```

Initializes the base homogeneous model with the specified input, hidden, and output dimensions

Converts the base homogeneous model into a heterogeneous model using the provided metadata

```
        self.base_model = base_model(input_dim, hidden_dim, out_dim)
        self.hetero_model = to_hetero(self.base_model, metadata=metadata)

    def forward(self, x_dict, edge_index_dict):
        return self.hetero_model(x_dict, edge_index_dict)
```

Defines the forward pass function for the heterogeneous graph model

Propagates the heterogeneous node features and edge indices through hetero_model to produce embeddings for each node type

This heterogeneous base class includes more ingredients than the homogeneous version. First, it uses the PyG `to_hetero()` function to automatically convert our base GNN homogeneous model into a heterogeneous GNN model, which is then used for the aggregation operation. This function requires two parameters: a base GNN model and a set of metadata. To improve our intuition for using the base GNN model, consider the following implementation of the heterogeneous version of our SAGE model.

Listing 12.25 Implementation of the `HeteroSAGE` model

```
class HeteroSAGE(HeteroBaseModel):
    def __init__(self, metadata, input_dim, hidden_dim, out_dim):
        super(HeteroSAGE, self).__init__(
            metadata,
            input_dim,
            hidden_dim,
            out_dim,
            SAGE
        )
```

In this case, the initialization of the `HeteroSAGE` class requires as an argument the `SAGE` class we adopted for processing the homogenous graph in the context of financial transactions. Recall that this `SAGE` class is a GNN model composed of two `SAGEConv` layers provided by the PyG library.

The structure of `HeteroSAGE` and all other heterogeneous models is based on their corresponding homogeneous versions and applied to each type of edge in the heterogeneous graph. In our scenario, for the characteristics of the tasks and the data, we have a single edge type: `("user", "rates", "movie")`. However, most complex scenarios have multiple edge types, and we can decide which convolution layer applies to each of them.

The `metadata` method of the `HeteroData` object provided by PyG defines the set of edge and node types, which is the second argument passed to the `to_hetero()` function. Thus, we can inform the hetero GNN model about which edge types are used for applying the neighborhood's feature aggregation. In other words, the convolution operation is driven by the nodes and edges specified in the metadata.

THE DECODER

The decoder component computes the dot product between user and movie embeddings, derived from the GNN encoder, to determine compatibility between users and movies. The dot product quantifies this compatibility based on the respective learned feature representations. A higher dot-product value indicates a stronger likelihood of interaction or rating, such as the potential user's interest in a particular movie.

This decoding function is paired with the `F.binary_cross_entropy_with_logits` function from PyTorch, which integrates the sigmoid activation and binary cross-entropy loss. The sigmoid activation converts dot-product scores into probabilities, making them interpretable as the likelihood of link existence. The binary cross-entropy loss then measures the difference between these predicted probabilities and the actual interaction labels, driving the model's optimization to enhance recommendation accuracy.

12.2.5 Evaluation and analysis

In our analysis, we compared three end-to-end models for link prediction. Each model uses a different GNN encoder: GCN, GAT, and SAGE. Table 12.10 shows the number of parameters and the total training time in seconds for each end-to-end model; we achieved these results after 55 epochs on a T4 Colab machine.

NOTE Our GCN implementation corresponds to different PyG operators depending on the graph type. For homogeneous graphs, we used `GCNConv`, the canonical GCN layer with degree normalization. For heterogeneous graphs, we used `GraphConv`, a closely related variant that integrates more naturally with the `HeteroConv` wrapper. `GCNConv` is not directly applicable to heterogeneous graphs because it assumes a single node and edge type, whereas `GraphConv` supports separate root and neighbor transformations required in the heterogeneous setting.

Table 12.10 Number of parameters and training time for the link prediction models using different GNN encoders

Encoder	Parameters	Training time (s)
GCN	713,408	826
GAT	1,066,880	956
SAGE	713,408	777

The results indicate that the SAGE model is the most efficient, the GAT model is the least efficient, and the GCN model falls between the other two. The number of model parameters is significantly higher than in the models used for node classification. This is the case for several reasons, including adding an embedding layer to improve the expressiveness of user and movie features and using heterogeneous GNN models to process our data. As you can guess, the number of parameters directly affects training time, which is much higher than it is for node classification with the same infrastructure.

PRECISION, RECALL, AND F1-SCORE

To evaluate the performance of GCN, GAT, and SAGE models in a link prediction task for movie recommendations, we can analyze their behavior using the same metrics we adopted for the node classification task:

- *Precision*—When the model predicts a link between a user and a movie (e.g., recommending a movie), how often is that prediction correct?
- *Recall*—Out of all the user–movie links (e.g., movies a user might like), how many does the model identify successfully?
- *F1-score*—How effectively does the model balance precision (being accurate in its recommendations) and recall (finding as many relevant recommendations as possible)?

Figure 12.10 shows the trend of these metrics on the validation dataset during the model's training.

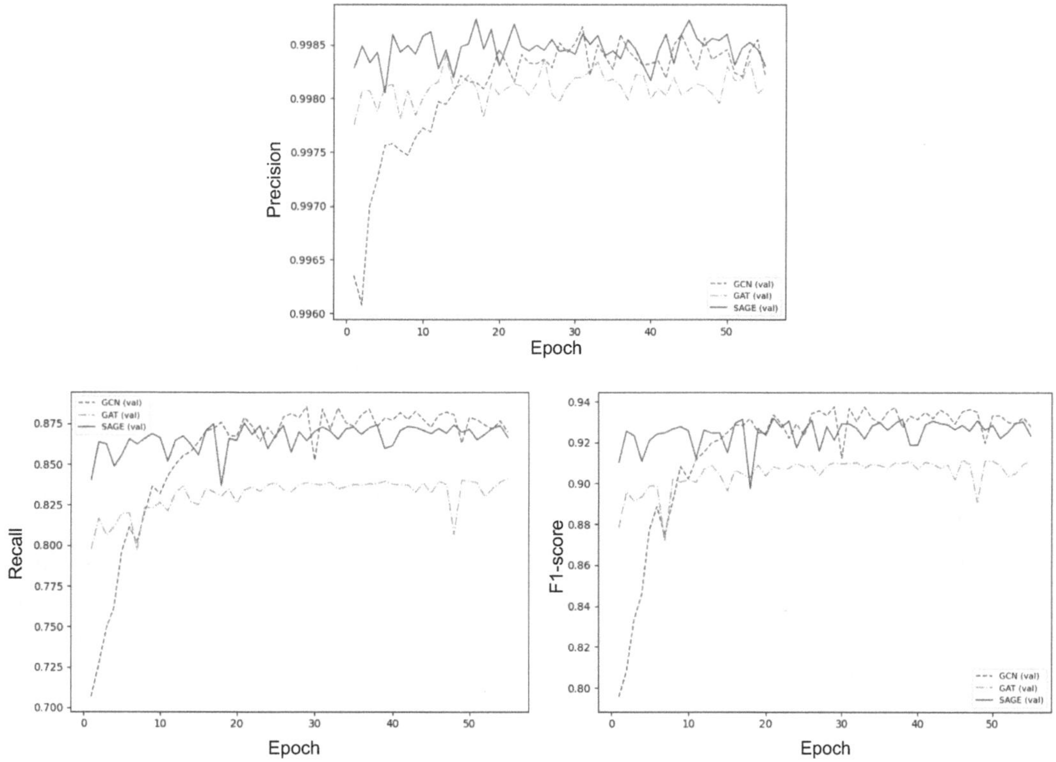

Figure 12.10 Trend of precision, recall, and F1-score of the GNN models on the validation dataset during training

Let's answer our earlier questions in the context of link prediction for recommendations:

- *Precision*—When the models predict whether a user would rate a movie (link exists), the SAGE model demonstrates the highest precision. SAGE is the most reliable in minimizing false positives, effectively predicting whether a user will interact with a movie by rating it. For movie recommendation tasks, this translates to fewer irrelevant recommendations, where users are unlikely to rate a suggested movie. The GCN model performs slightly worse but maintains high precision, making it a good alternative when reliability is essential. The GAT model exhibits the lowest precision, with more significant variability across epochs, suggesting that it makes more incorrect predictions about user engagement (i.e., predicting that users will rate movies they are unlikely to rate).
- *Recall*—In identifying actual user–movie links (i.e., all movies a user would rate), the GCN model achieves the highest recall. This indicates that GCN is the most comprehensive at identifying movies a user might engage with, successfully capturing the most true ratings. The SAGE model follows closely, with slightly lower recall, meaning it misses slightly more movies that users would rate compared to GCN. However, the GAT model struggles with recall, missing a significant portion of actual user–movie links, which reduces its ability to provide comprehensive recommendations.
- *F1-score*—The SAGE model achieves the highest F1-score, striking the best balance between providing accurate recommendations and ensuring coverage of user preferences. This makes SAGE particularly effective for predicting which movies a user would rate while minimizing irrelevant predictions. The GCN model performs well, benefiting from its high recall, but its slightly lower precision weakens its overall balance. Due to its lower precision and recall, the GAT model struggles to achieve competitive F1-scores, making it less reliable in capturing the full range of user–movie interactions.

CONFUSION MATRICES

Figure 12.11 shows the confusion matrices of the GCN, GAT, and SAGE models on the testing dataset, providing detailed insights into how effectively each model predicts user ratings. SAGE demonstrates strong performance in identifying non-existent links, correctly predicting 94.6% of movies that users would not rate (true negatives: 19,084). However, SAGE identifies 71.5% of movies users would actually rate (true positives: 7,211) while missing 28.5% of true ratings (false negatives: 2,872). This indicates that although SAGE is effective at filtering out movies users are unlikely to rate, it occasionally overlooks potential ratings. Significantly, SAGE minimizes false positives (1,082, or 5.4%), which means it rarely recommends movies users are unlikely to engage with, ensuring highly precise rating predictions.

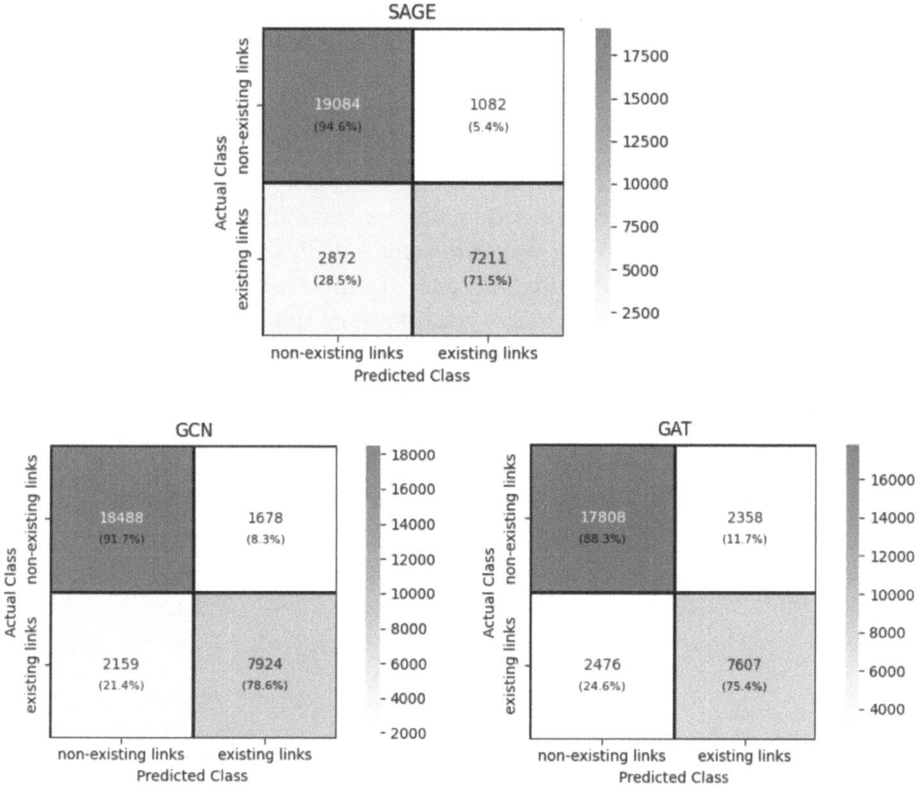

Figure 12.11 Confusion matrices of GCN, GAT, and SAGE models on the testing dataset

The GCN model provides a strong balance between identifying movies that users would and would not rate. It successfully identifies 91.7% of movies that users would not rate (true negatives: 18,488) and captures 78.6% of actual ratings (true positives: 7,924). GCN has a lower proportion of missed ratings (false negatives: 2,159) than SAGE, but has a slightly higher rate of false positives (1,678, or 8.3%). This means GCN is better at finding potential ratings but occasionally suggests movies that users may not rate.

The GAT model correctly predicts 88.3% of movies that users would not rate (true negatives: 17,808) and identifies 75.4% of actual ratings (true positives: 7,607). However, its false negative count (2,476, or 24.6%) is higher than that of GCN, meaning it misses more movies that users would rate. Additionally, its false positive count (2,358, or 11.7%) is the highest, indicating a greater likelihood of recommending movies users are unlikely to engage with.

These results show that although all three models perform well in predicting user ratings to varying degrees, SAGE stands out for its precision, ensuring that users are less likely to receive irrelevant movie suggestions. GCN offers the best balance between capturing potential ratings and avoiding irrelevant recommendations. GAT tends to over-recommend movies that user may not rate.

Summary

- Graph neural networks address fundamental challenges in graph-based ML tasks, such as node classification and link prediction.
- Despite differences in task domains, we can define a general encoder–decoder framework comprising multiple steps, which processes graph-structured data into a model suitable for inference. In this framework, the encoder is a GNN architecture such as a graph convolutional network (GCN), a graph attention network (GAT), or GraphSAGE (SAGE). The decoder applies task-specific functions to the learned representations.
- The ability of GNNs to capture complex relationships in graph data makes them highly valuable for real-world problems and versatile across diverse domains, such as fraud detection and recommendation systems.

Part 5

Information retrieval with knowledge graphs and LLMs

The integration of KGs with LLMs reaches its practical culmination in this final part of the book, where we explore how to use these combined technologies for accurate and reliable information retrieval. We'll focus on the practical implementation of systems that use KGs as ground truth to enhance LLM capabilities while preventing hallucinations.

Chapter 13 explores the integration of KGs with LLMs through retrieval augmented generation (RAG), showing how graph RAG systems can use structured data and language understanding to provide more accurate and transparent responses.

Chapter 14 illustrates how to build sophisticated question-answering systems that emulate domain expert reasoning to create contextually aware solutions. We demonstrate systematic approaches to intent detection, schema translation, and expert knowledge embedding.

Chapter 15 brings together all these concepts in a complete, working implementation using LangGraph and Streamlit. We demonstrate how to build a modular pipeline in which specialized agents handle different aspects of question processing while maintaining system observability and extensibility.

These chapters provide you with the practical knowledge to implement production-ready systems that combine the strengths of KGs and LLMs, serving as a comprehensive guide for organizations looking to deploy reliable, knowledge-grounded AI solutions.

13 Knowledge graph–powered retrieval-augmented generation

This chapter covers

- Making LLMs useful as AI agents
- Using retrieval augmented generation to ground LLMs using context
- Building a KG-powered RAG system

The year 2023 was marked by AI upheaval. Data scientists and ML engineers working in the natural language processing (NLP) domain were not just given a new toy: their work lives were turned upside down. The release of OpenAI's GPT-3.5 model at the end of 2022 marked a transformative change. Suddenly we didn't need to spend months or years building custom training datasets and models for each specific downstream task. With a little clever prompt engineering, almost anyone could build NLP applications.

But although LLMs are powerful, they are far from a magic solution for every problem. A lot of work remains to be done to make them useful in production enterprise-grade scenarios. This realization led to the concept of AI agents, related implementation libraries, and LLM operations (LLMOps).

The topics we'll discuss in this chapter are illustrated in the mental model in figure 13.1. Parts 2 and 3 of the book showed how to transform private data into a KG; now we'll explore how to build a chatbot that uses this KG as an input.

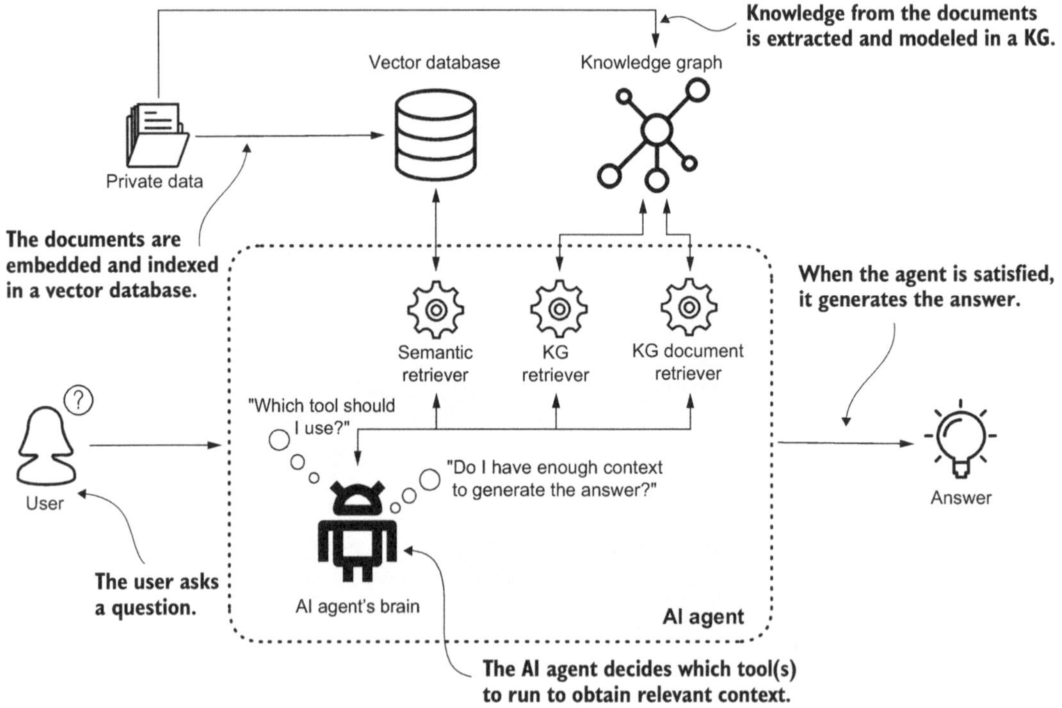

Figure 13.1 An AI agent design for KG-powered question answering. The agent has multiple tools at its disposal, which use external data sources such as a vector database and a KG to provide the necessary context for the user's question.

13.1 AI agents

AI agents [1] represent a significant evolution in the capabilities of modern intelligent systems. At their core, AI agents are autonomous entities designed to perform specific complex tasks by interacting with their environment. Unlike traditional software programs that follow a predetermined set of instructions, AI agents exhibit a level of autonomy, adaptability, and "intelligence," enabling them to make decisions, learn from experience, and respond to changing conditions in real time.

Consider a fully functional chatbot. We can start with a simple question: "What is the capital of France?" Pretty much any LLM at the top of the current model leaderboard will promptly and correctly reply, "The capital of France is Paris." Great! It works! But is this the kind of question that will generate a satisfactory return on investment, justifying the immense costs of building and running a model with hundreds of billions of parameters? Probably not. Those kinds of questions and tasks are much more complex; they typically require at least one of the following:

- *Advanced multistep reasoning capabilities*—Think of deduction tasks such as solving mathematical puzzles, or an adaptable system that needs to adjust the original execution plan based on what outputs are provided by intermediate steps.
- *Understanding of deep relational patterns among concepts*—Think of analyzing a social network where you'd like to identify influencers of certain discussion topics, or a supply chain challenge where you are tasked to pinpoint and remedy bottlenecks.
- *Access to the latest, often external and nonpublic data, not seen by the model during training*—This is often referred to as the *knowledge cutoff* of LLMs: the fact that these models are so large that they cannot be retrained often enough to be able to answer questions such as "What is the weather forecast for tomorrow?" not to mention questions related to sensitive internal data, especially when you need to handle multiple personas with different access rights.

Imagine a content writing assistant that helps users write articles, blog posts, or even social media posts. How would we approach this task as humans? First, we would likely research the requested topic by studying articles, blog posts, and books and pulling basic facts from knowledge bases such as Wikipedia. Then we'd write the first draft, ask a friend or colleague to do a review, and make final improvements before publication. This process is reflected in the design of an intelligent system to perform the task. For this system, we'd build several AI agents: a Researcher, multiple Writers (depending on what's being written), and a Reviewer. You can think of a multiagent system as being like a role-playing game, where the different agents (players) assume different specialized roles and communicate with each other to achieve a goal.

13.2 Chatting with the LLM

Now that we understand the concept of AI agents, it is time to look at a practical example. Let's consider the simplest possible scenario: a chatbot agent where the user fluently communicates with an LLM. After asking an initial question, the user can decide to follow up on it in a conversational manner. To build such an agent, we need only two things: access to a pretrained LLM, and memory to remember the full set of questions and answers so that we get a conversational experience. Such an agent can be written as a simple class, like the one in the following listing.

Listing 13.1 A conversational AI agent with memory

```
import os
from openai import OpenAI
from dotenv import load_dotenv

_ = load_dotenv()
```

```
class Agent:
    def __init__(self, model: str = "gpt-4o-mini", system: str = None):
        self.model = model
        self.system = system
        self.messages = list()                    <-- Instance variable as memory: it holds the full message history.
        self.client = OpenAI(api_key=os.environ['OPENAI_API_KEY'])

        if self.system is None or len(self.system) == 0:
            self.system = "You are an AI assistant providing straightforward
            ➥ concise answers."
        self.messages.append({"role": "system", "content": self.system})

    def __call__(self, message: str) -> str:
        self.messages.append({"role": "user",     <-- When we ask the agent a question, it is appended to the memory.
        ➥ "content": message})
        answer = self.execute()
        self.messages.append({"role": "assistant",   <-- The answer is also appended to the memory before being returned to the user.
        ➥ "content": answer})
        return answer

    def execute(self) -> str:
        completion = self.client.chat.completions.create(
                        model=self.model,
                        temperature=0,
                        messages=self.messages)
        return completion.choices[0].message.content


if __name__ == "__main__":
    agent = Agent()

    q = "Who are the top influencers of cyclotron     <-- First question
    ➥ funding?"
    print(f"> Question: {q}\n> Answer: {agent(q)}")

    q = "And in the context of the 1930s, related to the    <-- Follow-up question; the agent is aware of the previous question–answer pair.
    ➥ Rockefeller Foundation?"
    print(f"> Question: {q}\n> Answer: {agent(q)}")
```

The agent is initialized by model version, a system message frames its scope, and the OpenAI API key is provided as an environment variable through the .env file. The instance variable `messages` represents the agent's memory and holds the full message history. We could also run the agent in Jupyter to get a more interactive experience, or ideally add a UI layer to make it more like a real conversation, but here we use it from a standard Python script for simplicity. We ask an initial question followed by a clarification; the output is shown next.

Listing 13.2 Output of the conversation from listing 13.1

```
> Question: Who are the top influencers of cyclotron funding?
> Answer: The top influencers of cyclotron funding typically include
government agencies, research institutions, private foundations, and
industry stakeholders. Key players may include:
```

```
1. **National Institutes of Health (NIH)** - Provides significant funding
for medical research involving cyclotrons.
2. **Department of Energy (DOE)** - Supports research related to nuclear
science and particle accelerators.
3. **National Science Foundation (NSF)** - Funds various scientific
research projects, including those using cyclotrons.
4. **Private Foundations** - Organizations like the Wellcome Trust and the
Gates Foundation may fund related research.
5. **Universities and Research Institutions** - Institutions with cyclotron
facilities often seek grants and partnerships for funding.
6. **Pharmaceutical Companies** - They may invest in cyclotron technology
for drug development, particularly in radiopharmaceuticals.

These entities influence funding through grants, partnerships, and
collaborative research initiatives.
> Question: And in the context of the 1930s, related to the Rockefeller
Foundation?
> Answer: In the context of the 1930s, the Rockefeller Foundation played a
significant role in funding scientific research, including advancements in
nuclear physics and cyclotron development. Key influencers related to
cyclotron funding during this period included:

1. **John D. Rockefeller Jr.** - As a prominent philanthropist, he
supported various scientific initiatives through the foundation.
2. **Vannevar Bush** - An influential engineer and science administrator
who advocated for government and private funding in scientific research.
3. **Ernest O. Lawrence** - The inventor of the cyclotron, whose work
received support from the Rockefeller Foundation and other entities,
helping to advance particle accelerator technology.

The Rockefeller Foundation's funding helped establish research programs and
facilities that contributed to the development of cyclotrons and related
scientific fields during the 1930s.
```

The answer to the first question is correct, but very generic. The follow-up question that clarifies the context gets a better response; we see two familiar names (recall the KG we built in chapters 5 and 6): Ernest O. Lawrence and Vannevar Bush. Not surprisingly, out-of-the-box models cannot provide specific answers unless they see the data we expect the generated answer to be based on. We will learn more about this shortly.

We could build agents from scratch this way by adding more complexity, but fortunately we don't have to—because hand in hand with the current AI boom came the development of an entire engineering ecosystem around it.

13.3 Challenges in the production environment

Developing a useful real-world agent is complex and must consider several challenges and concerns related to LLMs:

- *Hallucinations, also known as "making stuff up"*—LLMs are trained to predict the most likely next token in the sequence, a process that inherently makes them susceptible to producing plausible-sounding but fabricated facts. This is particularly true when they are prompted about subjects not included in their training data. Despite lacking the knowledge, the model will still perform the task it was trained for: it will generate the most likely output given its experience encoded in billions of parameters. The response will be coherent and fully convincing, but partially or completely inaccurate.

- *Freshness, also known as the "knowledge cutoff"*—LLMs are trained on a vast amount of data, which makes them powerful but extremely expensive to train. Therefore, retraining happens only once or twice a year, so LLMs can't provide accurate responses regarding (not-so-)recent developments.
- *Transparency*—We get a coherent answer to our question, but without any insight into how it was generated. Information sources and reliability, reasoning processes, confidence level, and so on are concerns when developing enterprise solutions.
- *Data privacy*—Training models using potentially personal and private sensitive data without leaking it is a concern in many applications. And in many organizations, different groups of people have different data access privileges.
- *Cost*—Training, deploying, and maintaining the best current AI models come with significant costs, both financial and environmental. The computational power required for training large models is immense, leading to high energy consumption and substantial carbon footprints. This makes them accessible primarily to well-funded companies. The proliferation of smaller, specialized LLMs is reducing their expense, but it remains a significant consideration.
- *Ethical concerns and biases*—Because models learn from datasets that may contain prejudiced or harmful content, the models can inadvertently reproduce or amplify stereotypes, misinformation, and discriminatory viewpoints, raising serious ethical issues about their deployment and impact on society.

To address these issues, we need to move beyond a simplistic "question in, response out" scenario, which means building agents with greater complexity. For example, to address the freshness concern, we'd like to equip our conversational agent with tools that allow it to retrieve and use information from external sources, such as downloading the latest weather forecast data, news articles, or content from an up-to-date knowledge base—such as a knowledge graph. This is the topic of the remainder of this chapter.

13.4 Chatting with the AI about private data

LLM models have limited knowledge of specialized domains. In these cases, we need a way to make them experts on our domain and our private (often sensitive or secret) data, while preserving their superior language understanding capabilities and general knowledge.

Think of our Rockefeller Archive Center use case discussed in chapters 5 and 6. We built a KG that tracks grant-awarding processes that took place at the Rockefeller Foundation in the 1930s. This KG captures the awarded grants with relevant information such as grant amounts, research topics, universities, and researchers, along with behind-the-scenes conversations that took place between Foundation representatives and grant applicants prior to grant approval (i.e., who talked with whom about what). We thus have an influence network available, built from proprietary data never published before in its entirety, which allows us to accurately answer questions such as "Who were the influencers of cyclotron research funding?"

In chapters 5 and 6, we saw how to design a traditional KG-based system for such a use case through well-tuned graph visualization and dashboards. Now the exciting question is, can we develop an AI interface to deliver the same value to a broad range of users without requiring them to speak the Cypher query language, read and interpret charts and tables, or manipulate and navigate graph data structures? This is a job for AI agents using a pretrained LLM and multiple context-retrieval tools in a process called *retrieval-augmented generation* (RAG).

13.4.1 Retrieval-augmented generation

RAG [2] is a technique developed to address limitations of pretrained generative models, including those we mentioned earlier (hallucinations, freshness, transparency, and data privacy). It combines the knowledge and language understanding capabilities of pretrained LLMs with additional context relevant to the question, retrieved from an external data source: a structured database or an unstructured dataset (text, images).

In practice, a RAG agent is coded as a combination of an LLM, a prompt guiding the agent's steps, and one or more tools, which are essentially functions that retrieve question-relevant external information. The model is then asked to generate the answer, given the combination of the user's question and the provided external information as a context. Think of asking for tomorrow's weather forecast. An out-of-the-box model cannot answer this question unless we allow it to call a tool that polls a weather forecast API. At this point, the AI can generate an accurate answer by combining its language understanding skills with external, accurate, up-to-date information.

In this sense, RAG is a grounding technique: instead of letting the model go wild (hallucinations), we limit its scope for answer generation to the provided context, thus significantly reducing the chance that it will make things up.

NOTE We can never fully get around the fact that these models are probabilistic. They're trained to predict the most probable next token in a sequence, so even if we use a technique like RAG, they can still go astray. This is important to keep in mind when designing intelligent systems: instead of replacing humans, the systems should augment them. We believe that keeping humans in the loop through a feedback validation or supervision mechanism is essential for any product we build.

Let's explore an example. In the early days of RAG, the context came almost exclusively from a database of textual documents, as illustrated in figure 13.2. Documents were chunked into smaller portions (for example, paragraphs) and mapped into fixed-length vectors called *embeddings*, which captured their semantics. The embeddings were then stored and indexed in a vector database. The process of generating and storing embeddings for the Rockefeller Archive Center use case is shown in the following listing.

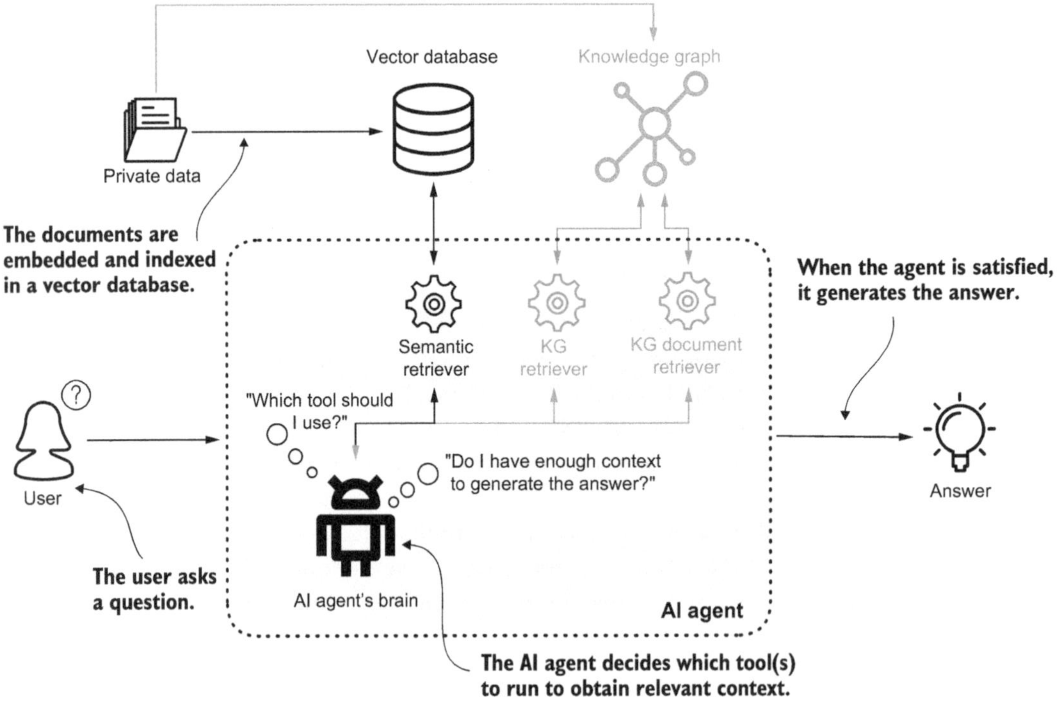

Figure 13.2 Vector search-based retrieval augmented generation. Documents are embedded into dense vector representations and indexed in a vector database. When a user asks a question, it is also embedded, and the most similar documents are retrieved from the database. The agent then generates the final answer.

Listing 13.3 Transforming documents into embeddings

```
import os
from langchain_community.vectorstores import Neo4jVector
from langchain_openai import OpenAIEmbeddings
from dotenv import load_dotenv

_ = load_dotenv()


if __name__ == "__main__":
    vector_index = Neo4jVector.from_existing_graph(
        embedding=OpenAIEmbeddings(),
        url=os.environ['NEO4J_URL'],
        username=os.environ['NEO4J_USER'],
        password=os.environ['NEO4J_PWD'],
        database=os.environ['NEO4J_DB'],
```

Creates embeddings and a vector index using specified nodes, properties, and an AI model

```
        index_name='embeddings',
        node_label="Page",
        text_node_properties=['text'],
        embedding_node_property='embedding'
    )

    q = "What is known about cyclotron research?"
    resp = vector_index.similarity_search_with_score(q,
    ➥ k=2)
    for r in resp:
        print(f"------\nScore: {r[1]}")
        print(r[0].page_content)
```

Semantic similarity search: returns the top two documents for a given question

Here we use the LangChain library, which enables us to build AI-based systems with support for various models, databases, information retrieval tools, and others. The code retrieves the texts from `Page` nodes, uses the specified embedding model to vectorize them, and stores the vectors back to the Neo4j DB. When a question is asked, it is embedded using the same model, and the most similar text chunks are retrieved. The shortened output is as follows.

Listing 13.4 The top two text chunks most similar to the question

```
------
Score: 0.9180829524993896

text: Tuesday, January 31, 1939 (Cont'd)
The reproduction cost of the large cyclotron would involve about $30,000
for the magnet, $15,000 for the power supply, and $30,000 for the cyclotron
chamber, accessories, controls, etc. Lawrence is already thinking about the
next step. He believes that his present "large" machine will be duplicated
several other places: but if it is wholly successful he wants to go on to
build a hundred million volt machine ...

------
Score: 0.9157187938690186

text: Dr. R. J. Van de Graaff, Massachusetts Institute of Physics. Van de
Graaff gives WW the whole history and philosophy of his scientific career
to date. The physical universe being composed of particles, G. decided to
study particles ...
Although he speaks with complete modesty and with complete generosity
relative to the cyclotron development, he is inclined to think that his
type of generator promises to offer relative advantage ...
```

The first document is highly relevant to the question. The second-highest-ranking document also mentions the cyclotron, although it resembles a sales pitch by Van de Graaff in favor of his (now-famous) generator.

13.4.2 Vector-based RAG limitations

We have seen how to transform out-of-the-box pretrained LLMs into useful conversational assistants capable of answering questions about private data using RAG agents based on vector search. What's next? Is this the best we can do?

Although RAG in its vector-search form is useful, it has some challenges and shortcomings:

- *Limited reasoning due to context fragmentation*—By providing a list of matching document chunks, we implicitly encode in the process a tendency to treat documents independently, thus potentially missing more complex multihop relationships among the documents as well as the entities mentioned in them. This also exposes the limitations of our chunking strategy: what if the information we need started in a previous chunk and continues in the current one? Will both be retrieved, in the right order and ranked high? Simple chunking probably won't perform well; we have to put much more thought into its design to mitigate at least some of the issues.
- *Scalability*—This approach is computationally expensive with larger corpora, often forcing us to use more efficient but less accurate approximate search algorithms.
- *Embedding limitations*—The attempt to encode the semantics of a document in a single dense vector leads to oversimplification: failure to capture important fine-grained semantics and domain-specific nuances. Another limitation is the possibility of sparsity in the training dataset of the embedding model (i.e., certain terms being underrepresented). This leads to inaccurate embedding representations and lower retrieval accuracy. Finally, reliance on static (precomputed) vectors makes RAG less adaptive to new or evolving knowledge and nomenclature.
- *Noise in retrieval*—Vector search can return loosely related or completely irrelevant documents, which leads to *distraction* [3]: too much noise, especially in longer contexts, can confuse the model and result in degradation of output quality. The key is to provide context with as high a density of relevant information as possible.
- *Misses in retrieval*—Just as embedding limitations and the use of approximate vector similarity search can lead to noise, they can also cause the opposite: failure to include the most relevant documents. And if we don't provide all the facts, we cannot obtain a fully correct answer, no matter how good the AI model is. Misses can also result from questions such as "What are the key research topics in this dataset?" The answer will be misleading because the vector similarity search will return chunks that are the most semantically similar to the question, rather than providing comprehensive data needed to generate the expected answer.

Let's illustrate these limitations with an example. Suppose our question is, "How is Lauritsen related to cyclotron research?" Intuitively, we expect that the most similar documents will, at the very least, mention Lauritsen by name. Wrong. That is not how embeddings work. They encode the overall meaning of a text and represent it with a condensed summary. They can't guarantee that the most similar document will even mention the entity we ask about! The semantic similarity of a question and a document can pick up on another linguistic meaning or pattern. And indeed, when we embed this question and find the three most similar documents based on cosine similarity, only one of the documents includes "Lauritsen" (and "cyclotron"); the other two mention only "cyclotron" and are therefore irrelevant to the question, even though they have nearly the same similarity score as the first document. Table 13.1 gives an overview of the top three documents.

Table 13.1 Top three documents most similar to the question "How is Lauritsen related to cyclotron research?" and an indication of whether they mention "Lauritsen " and "cyclotron"

Document	Cosine similarity	Lauritsen	Cyclotron
"Tuesday, January 3, 1939. Professor Karl Lark-Horovitz, Purdue University. The Van de Graaff machine at Purdue was built in two or three months and is now operating, producing 600 micro-amperes at 850 kilovolts. Thus as a neutron generator it is equivalent to several pounds of radium. The Purdue group has devised ..."	**0.906**	**True**	**True**
"Tuesday, May 2, 1939. Dr. Irving Langmuir, General Electric Company. L. very strongly favors continued support for Dr. Dorothy Wrinch. He bases this primarily on two considerations. First, and giving due recognition to the fact that W. is a difficult person whose scientific behavior is not always what it should be, L. considers it unquestionably true that W. has been responsible for stimulating ..."	**0.903**	**False**	**True**
"Dr. Dorothy M. Wrinch, April 3, 1939 (continued). In connection with the X-ray structure problem Langmuir obtained from Clowes some money which W. used for computing. She is not sure that she should have accepted funds from elsewhere, but WW assures her that ..."	**0.902**	**False**	**True**

How can we overcome these limitations? Our answer will come as no surprise to readers of this book: bring KGs into the picture. The graph-based approach to RAG is commonly referred to as *Graph RAG*. Besides mitigating or even completely solving the challenges related to vector-based RAG, this approach has additional benefits. The KG acts as a central knowledge repository, integrating not just raw texts but also various document metadata and high-confidence structured data sources (tables, CSVs, ontologies, and so on), which together unlock a wider range of use cases. Because KGs represent knowledge in a human-accessible format, they are easy to keep up to date. And domain experts can validate existing knowledge or enter new knowledge, thus directly affecting the AI system's output quality. This increased transparency results in greater user confidence.

13.4.3 Graph RAG

The development of synergies between KGs and LLMs is happening quickly [4]. The Rockefeller Archive Center KG is a good example of an LLM-augmented KG: we built it using prompt engineering on top of OpenAI's ChatGPT model, which extracted entities and relations and also completed the identified information using the model's internal knowledge. The resulting KG is a combination of a text-attributed graph and a text-paired graph [5] (see figure 13.3).

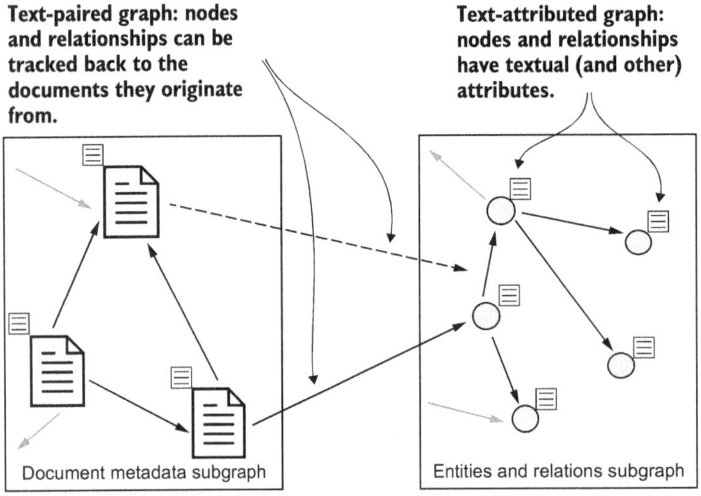

Figure 13.3 The Rockefeller Archive Center KG combines a text-attributed graph and a text-paired graph. Documents are represented as nodes, each with properties representing metadata such as author, type of document, and date. The extracted entities and relationships are traceable back to the original documents, which enables us to design a KG-based document selection tool for AI agents.

A *text-attributed graph* is a graph with nodes and relationships that have textual attributes, and a *text-paired graph* is a graph whose nodes, relationships, and graphs are associated with the documents that are their descendants. The design of our example KG enables us to implement a Graph RAG system that takes advantage of several aspects of data and knowledge modeling:

- *Metadata*—The documents typically have associated metadata such as publication date, type, source, author, and so on. All this information is available in the KG as properties and relationships, and can be used—in addition to the content—to design a context retrieval system. For example, communities can be identified in the graph of documents, and each community can be represented by a summary or by the most recent document (such as the most up-to-date version of a law or regulation).
- *KG retriever*—A KG is a great context resource. The nodes and typed relationships provide condensed, accurate, up-to-date information that an LLM can use to generate responses. A model can take the user's question and the KG's schema and generate a Cypher query to retrieve the information it needs. A KG retriever tool can also take as input the entities the user is asking about and return a subgraph that connects them (e.g. through all shortest paths), leaving it up to the final LLM to use whatever part of the data it deems relevant.
- *KG-enhanced document retriever*—If our KG is a text-paired graph, we can use it as a document retriever, which is more accurate than one based on vector search. For example, we can use it to retrieve only documents that mention all the

entities the user asked about, and eliminate one of the vector-search failures we discussed earlier. Or if we need more detailed information about a relationship than a KG can provide, we can retrieve only documents that mention this relationship, thus avoiding the distraction phenomenon.

- *Combined retrieval*—Sometimes questions span multiple data sources. For such cases, we can design an AI agent that breaks the question into two parts: one that retrieves the KG information (the KG retriever) and another that uses this information to find the most relevant documents. Both contexts are merged before the final answer is generated. For example, consider this question: "What are this year's transactions of the head of criminal group X?" It would be surprising to find that the financial documents contain "Head of X" as that person's title, so we need to extract that name from a KG built by a law enforcement agency and then use it to search the financial documents database.

Now that we understand what Graph RAG is about, let's implement a simple agent on top of the Rockefeller Archive Center KG (see figure 13.4). Our Graph RAG agent will have three tools at its disposal: the KG retriever, the KG-enhanced document retriever, and a semantic retriever (vector search tool) as a backup in case the other tools fail to return valuable context.

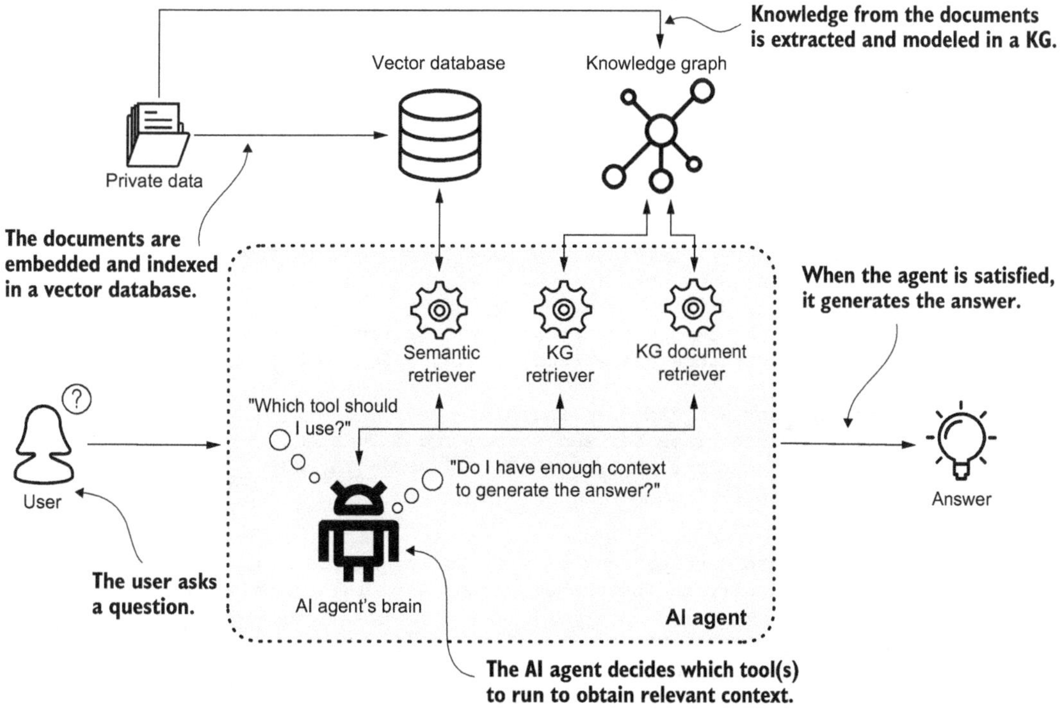

Figure 13.4 KG-powered RAG agent with a grounding in external data sources: the KG and a vector database

The complete code is available in the book's GitHub repository. Here we'll focus on the KG-enhanced document retriever, which is implemented as a parametrized tool for the use case of identifying documents where a specific relation between two entities is discussed. It will let us answer questions such as "What did person X say about person Y?"

Listing 13.5 KG-enhanced document retriever tool for a Graph RAG agent

```
from pydantic import BaseModel, Field
from langchain_community.graphs import Neo4jGraph

RE_SELECTOR_QUERY = """MATCH (p:Page)-                    <-- Precanned document
➥ [:MENTIONS_ENTITY]->(m1:Ent...                             selection query
WHERE e1.name = "{e1}" ...
...
RETURN DISTINCT p.id AS id, p.text AS text
"""

                                             Initializes the Neo4j
graph = Neo4jGraph(                      <-- database connection
        url=os.environ['NEO4J_URL'],
        username=os.environ['NEO4J_USER'],
        password=os.environ['NEO4J_PWD'],
        database=os.environ['NEO4J_DB']
    )
                                                    Definition of the input schema
class REDiarySelectorInput(BaseModel):          <-- (function arguments) of the new tool
    entity_source: str = Field(description="Source entity of the
    ➥relationship as mentioned in the question.")
    entity_source_class: str = Field(description=
      "Class of the source entity of the relationship. "
      "Available option is only one, 'Person'.")

 entity_target: str = Field(description="Target entity of the
 ➥relationship as mentioned in the question.")
 entity_target_class: str = Field(description=
      "Class of the target entity of the relationship. "
      "Available options are Person, Organization, Occupation and Title.")

 relationship: str = Field(description=
      "Relationship class between source and target entity. "
      "Available options: TALKED_ABOUT, TALKED_WITH, WORKS_WITH, WORKS_ON,
      ➥HAS_TITLE")


def kg_doc_selector(entity_source: str, entity_source_class: str,
➥entity_target: str, entity_target_class: str, relationship: str) ->
➥List[AnyStr]:                                           <-- KG-enhanced document
    query = RE_SELECTOR_QUERY.format(e1=entity_source,       retriever function
      e1_class=entity_source_class,
      e2=entity_target, e2_class=entity_target_class,
      rel_class=relationship)
 print(f"kg_doc_selector's query:\n{query}\n")
```

```
try:
    res = graph.query(query)
    print(f"kg_doc_selector found {len(res)} matching documents")
except Exception as e:
    print(f"Cypher execution exception: {e}")
    return []
   return [x['text'] for x in res[:3]]
```

The tool takes as input the two entities mentioned in the question, their classes (for example, `Person`), and the relationship type; these are provided by the AI agent based on the user's question. The main selector function uses them to complete a precanned Cypher query, which is executed against the Neo4j database, and the documents are returned to the agent.

> **NOTE** We could also design a more generic tool in which the document retriever Cypher query is generated automatically based on the question. However, doing so would introduce another possible point of failure when the Cypher queries are complex. That's why numerous Graph RAG systems in production contain a variety of KG-related tools, many of which are based on precanned Cypher queries for types of questions that are frequently repeated.

13.4.4 Reasoning agents

It's time to integrate everything into a single agent. The LangChain library provides several precanned agents that make this very easy. We have multiple tools with no clear execution order, so we'll use a ReAct (Reason and Act) agent [6] that integrates reasoning and acting capabilities to improve problem-solving in complex environments. The ReAct framework iteratively reasons about tasks to take, acts, and observes the outcomes in a dynamic feedback loop, refining its approach based on real-time outcomes.

The agent takes the original question within the constraints of the tools we provide it with, plans the next task (tool to execute), executes it, and reasons about the outcome. If the obtained information is not satisfactory, it acts using another tool. When it obtains contextual information that it deems sufficient to answer the original question, it ends the loop. The following shortened code defines such an agent.

Listing 13.6 ReAct agent implementing the Graph RAG approach

```
from langchain.tools import StructuredTool
from langchain.agents import create_structured_chat_agent, AgentExecutor
from langchain_openai import ChatOpenAI
from tools import REDiarySelectorTool, kg_doc_selector, REDiarySelectorInput
from definitions import KG_SCHEMA

tools = [                                    # Collects all tools definitions in one list
    StructuredTool.from_function(
        func=kg_doc_selector,                # Previously defined function to be transformed into a proper tool format
        name="KG-based-document-selector",
        args_schema=REDiarySelectorInput,    # Argument schema, which enables the agent to understand what inputs it needs to provide to this tool
```

```
        description=f"Use it for document (diary
        ➥ entries) retrieval when the question asks for detailed information
        ➥ regarding interaction between two entities ... Full KG
        ➥ schema:\n{KG_SCHEMA}"
    ),
    <KG RETRIEVER>,
    <VECTOR SEARCH>
]

llm = ChatOpenAI(model="gpt-4o-mini", temperature=0)
prompt = hub.pull("hwchase17/structured-chat-agent")

agent = create_structured_chat_agent(llm, tools, prompt)
agent_executor = AgentExecutor(agent=agent, tools=tools, max_iterations=5,
➥ return_intermediate_steps=True, verbose=True)

question = "What did August Krogh say about Lawrence Irving?"
response = agent_executor.invoke({"input": question})
```

Vector search-based retrieval tool (backup)

Tool description containing the KG schema, which allows the agent to determine which tool to use

KG retriever structured tool for questions that don't require original texts

Defines the agent and its executor by binding together the model, the agent's prompt, and the tools

The structured ReAct agent supports passing multiple input parameters to its tools. The tools have appropriately chosen names and descriptions to help the model determine which tool to call in which situation. Pay attention to these descriptions when you design an agent: if you write them well, you can significantly improve the stability and predictability of your system. Don't hesitate to overwrite the default prompts provided in various agents and tools by LangChain if the system doesn't behave as consistently as you expect. Always test, test, test repeatedly, even with the same setup and input question; this process can reveal insights into how to improve your application.

This example is only an illustration of how to build KG-powered Graph RAG systems—we do not suggest that it is a production-ready system. We could make several improvements, such as developing a document re-ranking strategy for the vector-search tool, adding a Cypher self-correction loop to the KG retriever, or incorporating tools to support other typical user questions. For more details, see [7].

13.4.5 Let's chat with our KG

Now that our Graph RAG agent is ready, let's put it to the test. Imagine that you are a researcher visiting the Rockefeller Archive Center to get information about Dorothy M. Wrinch (1894–1976), a mathematician and biochemical theorist. Her work is fairly well known, but you want to know how she was perceived by her colleagues in her time. You could find her in the KG, look at incoming `TALKED_ABOUT` relationships, and drill down until you find the documents from which they were extracted and read them. Alternatively, you can use your new agent: figure 13.5 shows what happens when you ask it "What did her fellow researchers say about Dorothy M. Wrinch?"

> **NOTE** When you try this yourself, you may see different outputs, depending on which version of OpenAI's GPT model or other model provider you're using.

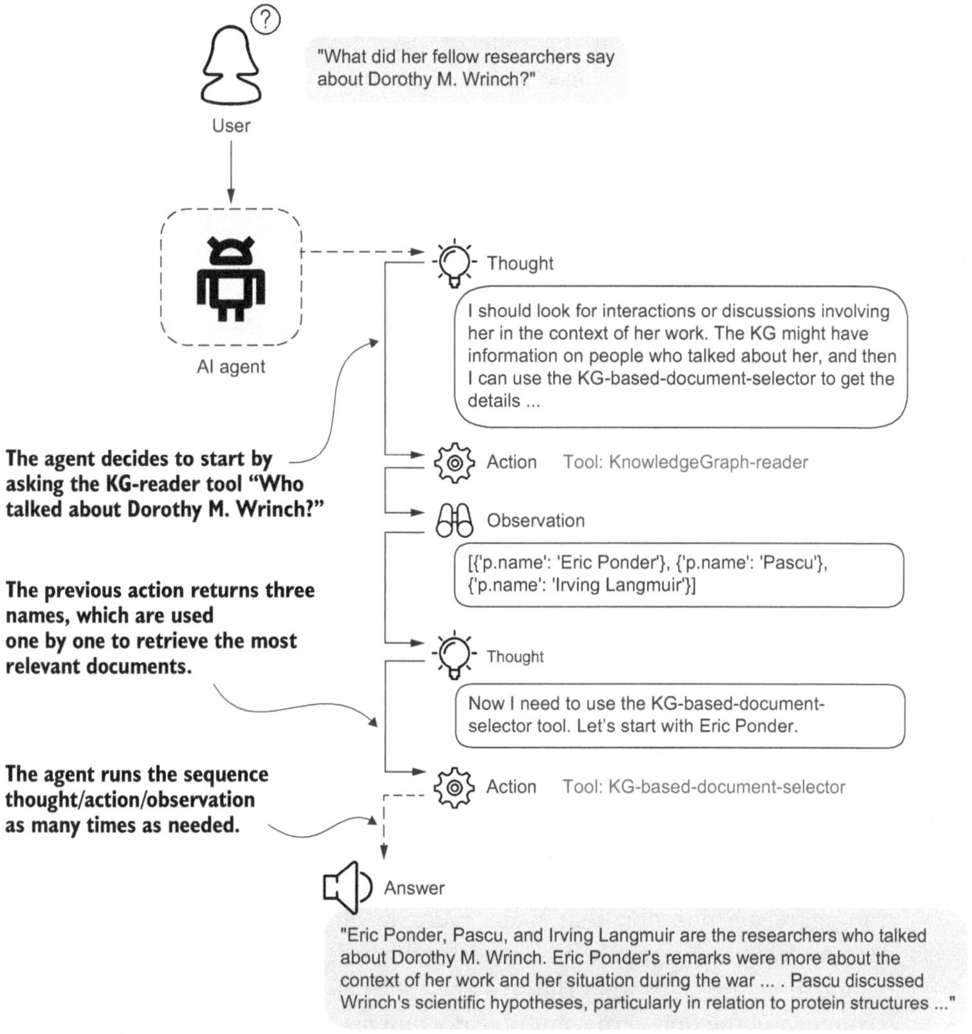

Figure 13.5 Example of our Graph RAG agents' internal steps. The agent starts with a thought that leads it to use the KG retriever to obtain a list of people who talked about Dorothy M. Wrinch. For each of them, it uses the KG-enhanced document retriever to identify the relevant documents. Finally, the agent uses all of this as a context for generating the final answer.

The agent takes into account all the tools it has available. It correctly realizes that the best course of action is to first retrieve from the KG the list of people who talked about Wrinch and then use the specialized KG-enhanced document retriever to obtain relevant documents providing details of what was said. The agent takes a total of four Thought/Action/Observation steps. The final answer, generated based on all the context retrieved, is impeccable: straight to the point and factual, clearly grounded in private documents provided to it.

Table 13.2 demonstrates two more questions. The first is a variant of the one about Dorothy M. Wrinch, but this time the agent can use the KG-enhanced document retriever tool directly because we ask about two specific people. If we asked the same question to an out-of-the-box LLM, either we'd get an answer like "There is no specific information available about what August Krogh said about Lawrence Irving" or the LLM would hallucinate an answer. With our Graph RAG system, however, we get accurate insight into their relationship.

Table 13.2 Graph RAG question-and-answer examples

Question	Graph RAG answer
"What did August Krogh say about Lawrence Irving?"	"August Krogh spoke with enthusiasm about Scholander's work on the physiology of respiration of deep diving animals in Norway and expressed the importance of getting Scholander and Lawrence Irving together. Krogh noted that Irving had done excellent work and could provide Scholander with facilities in the United States that were not available in Norway. They explored the possibility of working at Boothbay Harbor, Maine, and potentially with porpoises at aquatic zoos in Florida."
"Are there any shared research topics between Harvard University and Johns Hopkins University?"	"The shared research topics between Harvard University and Johns Hopkins University are astronomy and climatology."

Structured KG content is sufficient to answer the second question. The KG retriever tool generates a correct Cypher query (a bit clumsy, but correct), so the answer is straightforward and accurate. In contrast, if we wanted to answer this question purely based on a vector search, we would have to provide a large set of documents as a context and hope they contained the complete answer. That's because it is an example of an aggregate question that spans multiple documents: some diary entries discuss research done by people at Harvard, others describe topics at Johns Hopkins, but none directly discuss what Harvard and Johns Hopkins have in common. KGs excel at connecting the dots across multiple documents, and as a side benefit, they reduce the risk of the distraction phenomenon and hallucination, making predictions faster and cheaper (less context data is needed).

We can use a wide range of approaches to improve the accuracy, reliability, and stability of RAG systems. For example, we can add self-correction loops so the model generates the Cypher query first and then asks the LLM to double-check it and potentially correct the query in the follow-up step. Or we can add a more advanced document-reranking step after the initial context selection to improve its relevance and limit its size. In the next chapter, we will dive deeper into the topic of Cypher generation.

Summary

- An essential core of any AI agent is a combination of an LLM model functioning as the agent's brain, a prompt guiding the model, and a set of tools that allow the agent to interact with the outside world.

- Retrieval augmented generation (RAG) is a framework for building intelligent systems, such as AI agents, by combining generative models and information retrieval. As such, it addresses inherent LLM issues such as hallucinations, freshness, transparency, and data privacy.
- Vector-based RAG systems suffer from multiple shortcomings, such as limited reasoning capabilities, scalability issues, and inaccuracies in retrieval, including noise and missed relevant information.
- Graph RAG integrates KGs with LLMs to reinforce the reasoning capabilities and precision of information retrieval by using the structured relational multi-hop patterns within the KGs. KGs also provide more control and transparency for the question-answering process.
- Methods for integrating KGs into RAG systems are determined by the graph design. The most useful KGs combine text-attributed and text-paired graphs, which enable us to use both well-curated, structured knowledge and documents along with their metadata.

14 Asking a KG questions with natural language

This chapter covers

- Understanding the limitations of RAG in complex scenarios
- Building an advanced question-answering system that mimics domain expertise on KGs
- Transforming query results into meaningful, actionable summaries

In this chapter, we will explore how to build an advanced system that can answer questions effectively. Using a law enforcement example as our guide, we'll compare the retrieval-augmented generation (RAG) approach and our new "expert emulation" method for capturing the expertise of skilled information retrieval.

The framework we'll develop rests on several pillars:

- Understanding and properly routing different types of user questions
- Extracting and representing domain knowledge in a form that LLMs can use effectively
- Implementing expert-like reasoning patterns for query construction

- Ensuring that results are presented in meaningful, actionable ways

This framework is designed to integrate with a front-end layer, ensuring that the question-answering system can be presented to end users through a graphical interface. This integration-first approach influences many of our design decisions throughout the chapter, from how we structure query responses to how we handle data visualization.

This chapter walks through each of these components, using examples to illustrate the key concepts and design decisions; chapter 15 will provide a hands-on implementation guide, complete with an end-to-end example in a practical setting. By the end of these two chapters, you'll have both a deep understanding of the underlying concepts and the knowledge needed to implement an expert-emulated question-answering system for your own knowledge graphs.

Throughout this chapter, we'll use examples from law enforcement, but the principles and patterns we discuss can be adapted to any domain where expert knowledge needs to be systematically applied to complex data structures. Whether you're working in healthcare, finance, or scientific research, the framework will provide a solid foundation for building intelligent question-answering systems that use domain expertise.

14.1 Querying a knowledge graph in the policing domain

Imagine that you are an experienced analyst in a large law enforcement agency. Every day, you face the challenge of making sense of diverse and often overwhelming data streams. The policing domain is inherently complex and dynamic, with a mission to investigate crimes, prevent criminal activities, and protect the community. Your work sits at the heart of this mission.

The policing ecosystem encompasses a wide range of roles and responsibilities. Frontline officers respond to incidents and collect on-the-ground information, detectives and investigators connect the dots to solve cases, forensic experts analyze evidence, and analysts like you uncover patterns and trends from disparate data sources. Each role contributes vital pieces to the puzzle, and their collective efforts drive the interconnected processes in law enforcement.

A simple crime report can set off a cascade of activities: interviews, evidence collection, database searches, and more. Each step in this chain generates and consumes data, making it vital to integrate and organize this information effectively. Recognizing the need for a unified approach, your agency has invested in building a KG: a single source of truth that structures and connects roles, processes, and data. In this section, we will concentrate on extracting information, uncovering knowledge, and deriving insights from a fully constructed, ready-to-query KG.

14.1.1 Enabling domain experts with knowledge graphs

Seasoned analysts possess sharp intuition, a deep contextual understanding, and the ability to discern patterns in complex scenarios. In policing, these qualities often outweigh technical expertise when it comes to interpreting data and making impactful decisions.

Despite this, querying KGs is traditionally seen as a task requiring deep technical skills—skills that are outside the typical toolkit of domain experts. However, empowering analysts like you to interact directly with KGs opens immense possibilities:

- *Using expertise*—You, as a domain expert, bring unparalleled contextual knowledge to the table. This enables you to frame nuanced and insightful queries, driving highly accurate and relevant data retrieval.
- *Timely decisions*—Direct access to KGs eliminates bottlenecks, allowing you to make quicker decisions: a necessity in critical fields like law enforcement, where time is often of the essence.
- *Overcoming technical barriers*—Most domain experts, although masters of their fields, lack the technical training to write complex queries for KGs. Removing this barrier expands the accessibility of these tools.
- *Resource efficiency*—By reducing reliance on IT teams or data scientists to generate queries, you free up technical resources for other priorities, making workflows more efficient and collaborative.
- *Skill specialization*—Your focus is on mastery of your domain, not on becoming a technical expert. Enabling intuitive KG interaction ensures that your energy remains devoted to what you do best.
- *New perspectives*—When you can engage directly with data, your unique perspective allows for the discovery of innovative insights and applications that technical users might overlook.
- *Enhanced problem-solving*—With the ability to explore data hands-on, you can uncover creative approaches to solving problems, tailored to your domain's needs.
- *Maximizing ROI*—KGs represent a significant investment. Ensuring their full use by empowering analysts maximizes their value and impact.
- *Cross-functional collaboration*—Easy access to KGs fosters collaboration across teams, bridging gaps between technical and nontechnical stakeholders by creating a shared platform for data access.
- *Shared understanding*—By enabling broader access to KGs, organizations promote a unified approach to data analysis and problem-solving, building alignment across roles and disciplines.

By breaking down these barriers, the potential of KGs can be unlocked, bringing insights and practical solutions to the forefront.

14.2 RAG for KG querying: Capabilities and challenges

It's important to remember that LLMs generate answers based on the data collected during their training phase. Although LLMs can answer questions that require specialized expertise, their utility diminishes for users who are already experts in their field.

Consider the types of questions a law enforcement official might ask an LLM. In this context, it's hard to think of questions beyond basic inquiries like, "What is the legal definition of probable cause?" or "How should an officer properly collect and preserve evidence at a crime scene?" The responses that an LLM can generate are likely to be of little use to trained professionals.

To be beneficial, an LLM should provide access to information that personnel can use to expedite their processes, whether those involve suspect identification, organized crime network analysis, or other complex tasks. The most popular approach to answering questions grounded in the data available to an organization, such as a law enforcement agency, is RAG, as we discussed in chapter 13.

Yet RAG faces critical limitations when retrieval is incomplete. To illustrate this, we'll examine how removing a single piece of context from a working example leads to opposite conclusions.

14.2.1 RAG effectiveness with complete context

Let's start with RAG working effectively when all relevant context is retrieved. Consider a request like "Generate a summary of witness statements related to CASE123." There is little chance that an LLM alone can effectively handle this request because the model has no prior knowledge of that specific case. Without any contextual information, the LLM cannot access the details necessary to provide a meaningful response. However, if we integrate that question with a list of all witnesses connected to CASE123, the situation changes significantly. It transforms into a straightforward summarization task, and LLMs excel at this type of work. When questions are accompanied by relevant contextual content, LLMs can generate richer and more pertinent answers.

To demonstrate this concept, Listing 14.1 shows a sample set of witness statements that would typically be retrieved from a case database and provided as context to the LLM.

Listing 14.1 Sample witness statements for LLM prompt context

```
1. Witness A, a barista at a local coffee shop, says: "The person who came in
   that day was wearing a unique jacket with a distinctive logo on the left
   sleeve. They ordered a latte and when they went to pay, they used their
   right hand to take out their wallet. I noticed that their left hand had a
   small bandage on the index finger."

2. Witness B, a neighbor who saw the perpetrator leaving the scene, says: "I
   didn't get a good look at their face, but I did notice that they were
   carrying a bag in their right hand. They seemed to be in a hurry and were
   walking quickly."

3. Witness C, a security guard at a nearby building, says: "I reviewed the
   security footage and I noticed that the person of interest was holding a
   phone up to their ear with their left hand while they were walking. They
```

```
   seemed to be talking to someone and were carrying a bag in their right
   hand."

4. Witness D, a friend of the victim, says: "When I went to visit my friend,
   I noticed that some of their belongings had been moved around. I remember
   that a book on their bookshelf was out of place, but I can't recall
   anything unusual about it."

5. Witness E, a police officer who responded to the scene, says: "We found a
   footprint at the scene that we believe belongs to the perpetrator. The
   print shows that the person was wearing a shoe with a distinctive tread
   pattern on the sole, but we cannot determine which foot made the print.
```

Using these witness statements, let's build a prompt to test this idea. We'll use a reusable template, and the portions in curly brackets will be replaced with the relevant witness statement content and the question itself.

AN You are a detective assistant helping answer the detective's question

[Witness statements]

{{ witness_statements }}

[Question]

{{ question }}

If we use the prompt to ask the LLM to "summarize the witness statements," the model provides these results:

Here's a summary of the witness statements:

Physical Characteristics:

- Unique jacket with a distinctive logo on the left sleeve (Witness A)
- Small bandage on the left index finger (Witness A)

Actions and Behaviors:

- Used right hand to take out wallet (Witness A)
- Carrying a bag in right hand (Witnesses B and C)
- Held phone up to ear with left hand while walking (Witness C)
- Seemed to be in a hurry and walking quickly (Witness B)

Scene Evidence:

- Footprint with distinctive tread pattern, but unclear which foot made the print (Witness E)
- Book on bookshelf was out of place, but no other unusual details (Witness D)

The model understood the task and delivered a concise and relevant summary of the key details from the witness statements.

Now, let's ask whether the witness statements include anything related to a lead we are following. For example, if we use the prompt to ask "Is the perpetrator left-handed?"

the model's gives the following response. The output provides a detailed analysis of the relevant witness details, concluding that there is some evidence suggesting the suspect may be left-handed.

Let's analyze the witness statements to determine if the perpetrator is left-handed.

Witness A mentions that the perpetrator used their right hand to take out their wallet, which suggests that they might be right-handed. However, Witness A also notes that the perpetrator had a small bandage on the index finger of their left hand, which could indicate an injury. This doesn't necessarily imply that the perpetrator is left-handed, but it's worth considering.

Witness C says that the perpetrator was holding a phone up to their ear with their left hand while walking, which suggests that they might be left-handed. This is strong evidence pointing towards the perpetrator being left-handed.

Witness B and Witness E's statements don't provide any direct information about the perpetrator's handedness. Witness D's statement is also not relevant to this question.

Based on the available evidence, I would say that it's likely that the perpetrator is left-handed. The fact that they used their left hand to hold the phone to their ear in Witness C's statement is a strong indication of this. However, it's important to keep in mind that people can be ambidextrous or have varying degrees of handedness, so we shouldn't make any definitive conclusions just yet. Further investigation is needed to confirm our suspicions.

In this case, the LLM generated an answer that is consistent with the content we provided—the witness statements—and directed us to relevant pieces of information. This capability allows the LLM to assist in uncovering insights that may be critical to the investigation.

Now suppose the case in question is a murder investigation, and we want to find any connections between the victim and known criminal organizations. Given that people may be reluctant to discuss local criminal activities openly, the witness statements may not be useful. To obtain meaningful answers, we need more contextual information, and this is where LLMs can be particularly effective.

Additional context may include the victim's criminal record, prior convictions, personal history, associations or relationships, social media profiles, or any officer reports mentioning the victim or their family. This content must be retrieved from the respective sources, filtered for relevance, and then provided as context along with our question to the LLM. This retrieval, filtering, and contextual augmentation is what RAG aims to accomplish.

14.2.2 RAG fragility with incomplete retrieval

RAG is a highly effective approach with a wide range of applications. However, it comes with its own set of challenges. The success of RAG is closely tied to the effectiveness of the retrieval process.

LLMs cannot generate accurate answers if they are not provided with sufficient context; therefore, for RAG to produce a meaningful response, the retrieval process must be capable of locating the correct information.

Now let's see what happens with the same question but incomplete retrieval. Suppose we did not have a statement from witness C. We again ask the model "Is the perpetrator left-handed?" The following listing shows the response. Compare it to the previous response, and you can see how strongly it depends on the context provided: the absence of a single witness statement is enough to lead the model to the opposite conclusion!

Based on the witness statements, I think we can make an educated inference about the perpetrator's handedness.

Witness A, the barista, mentions that when the person went to pay, they used their right hand to take out their wallet. This suggests that the perpetrator is likely right-handed.

Additionally, Witness B, the neighbor, states that the perpetrator was carrying a bag in their right hand when they were leaving the scene, which further supports the idea that the perpetrator is right-handed.

There is no concrete evidence in the statements to suggest that the perpetrator is left-handed. The fact that Witness A mentions a bandage on the index finger of the perpetrator's left hand could be unrelated to their handedness.

So, based on the available information, it seems more likely that the perpetrator is right-handed rather than left-handed.

Figure 14.1 illustrates this process. Even though the AI agent confidently processes the available information, the incomplete context—caused by the retriever failing to identify critical documents—leads to wrong conclusions. This visualization emphasizes a key limitation of RAG systems: their outputs are only as good as their retrieval step, regardless of the model's confidence in its response.

In addition, RAG performs better when our sources of information can be divided into "passages" that contain fine-grained, independent pieces of information—essentially, many small blocks of information that can be used to construct a highly relevant context. But in practice, answers often span multiple documents, and the retrieval process may not capture all of them. Furthermore, some documents may be relevant even if they do not contain the specific answer we are searching for, which adds a layer of complexity to the task for the LLM.

When the retrieved passages lack the appropriate level of granularity, or if the retriever fails to accurately assess relevance, the context provided to the LLM becomes fragmented. This fragmented context can push the model toward incorrect assumptions, often leading it to generate plausible but inaccurate details. To address these challenges, we need an approach that captures the nuanced insight an expert would apply when querying a KG, combining structured retrieval with context-aware reasoning.

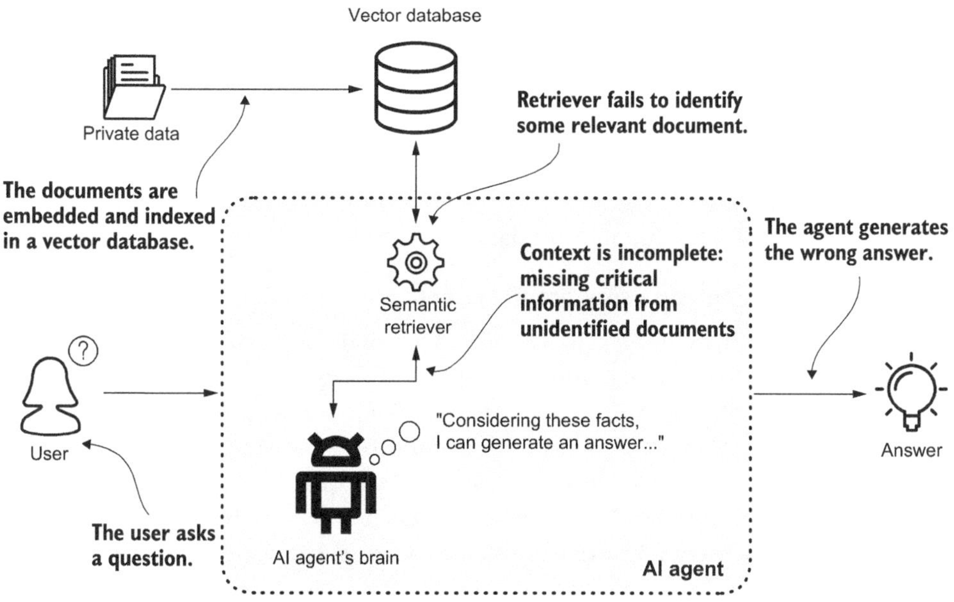

Figure 14.1 RAG system limitations. A RAG system can produce incorrect answers when the retriever fails to identify critical documents.

14.3 Schema-based approach for querying KGs

We have seen that RAG can sift through millions of documents to provide a pertinent and rich answer, provided the retriever delivers a comprehensive contextual picture to the LLM. Let's take a moment to scale this problem down to a more manageable size, say a dozen documents. Imagine that we ask a group of experts a question, but constrain them to apply a "human-powered" RAG-like approach. First they review the documents, marking any paragraphs that contain similar content or pertain to the same domain. From these, they select a dozen paragraphs that are the most relevant, which serve as a context. Once they have their context, they set aside everything else they have read and attempt to answer the question using only the selected pieces of information and their common sense, making assumptions if necessary.

This process is not impressive. Even though these are domain experts, when they're forced to work within RAG-like constraints, their approach lacks the depth and rigor that their genuine expertise would normally demand.

What would an expert do in this scenario? Imagine that we have a KG, and we need to answer a specific question. The first step is to understand the schema, which acts as the blueprint of the graph. For example, if the question involves people, it will likely involve a node labeled *Person*.

Understanding the schema is important because it allows us to convert specific requests like "show me the red Camaros seen in this area at that time" into a precise traversal. This traversal might involve entities and relationships such as "Person—Owns_car—Car—Captured_by—ANPR (automatic number plate recognition).

The traversal can then be refined by applying constraints, such as requiring the car to be red, the model to be Camaro, and the ANPR camera to be located in a specific area and time frame. Deciding which nodes and relationships to select, as well as how to apply these constraints, is guided by the schema. Understanding the schema allows experts to write formal queries that pinpoint the specific information they are seeking, even amid vast amounts of data.

14.3.1 Understanding and using graph schemas

Understanding a graph schema—the data modeler's structured interpretation of the domain—is like understanding the layout of a city before navigating through it: it lets us identify where specific types of information are stored and how they are linked. Figure 14.2 shows an example of the mental process an expert would follow when translating a natural-language question into a formal Cypher query. This translation process demonstrates how a solid understanding of the schema—knowing which nodes exist, their properties, and how they're connected—is fundamental to constructing effective graph queries.

When we receive a query like "show me the red Camaros seen in this area at that time," the initial step is to map the concepts mentioned in the query (e.g., red Camaros, area, time) to their corresponding nodes and relationships in the graph schema. This involves identifying the following:

- *Entities*—For instance, "red Camaro" maps to node labeled *Car* with properties such as `Color` and `Model`.
- *Relationships*—The query implies relationships like "*Person* owns *Car*" and "*Car* captured by *ANPRCamera*."
- *Constraints*—These are the specific conditions that refine the traversal, such as the color being red, the model being Camaro, and the ANPR camera being located in a specified area.

This results in *constrained traversals*, which address questions like, "Among all these entities (cars, people, cameras), connected in this specific way (e.g., `OWNS_CAR`, `CAR_CAPTURED_BY_ANPR`), which ones possess the characteristics I'm interested in?"

Constrained traversals are the fundamental building blocks for constructing formal queries of any complexity. These traversals can be composed in various ways to build sophisticated queries that navigate intricate data relationships.

For example, we might start with an initial constrained traversal—possibly with aggregations—to identify specific nodes or subgraphs, which can then serve as starting points for further exploration in subsequent stages. This compositional approach allows us to address complex questions that require multiple layers of exploration and refinement. Ultimately, constrained traversals enable the translation of natural language intent into structured queries that a graph database can execute, effectively bridging the gap between human language and machine-readable data.

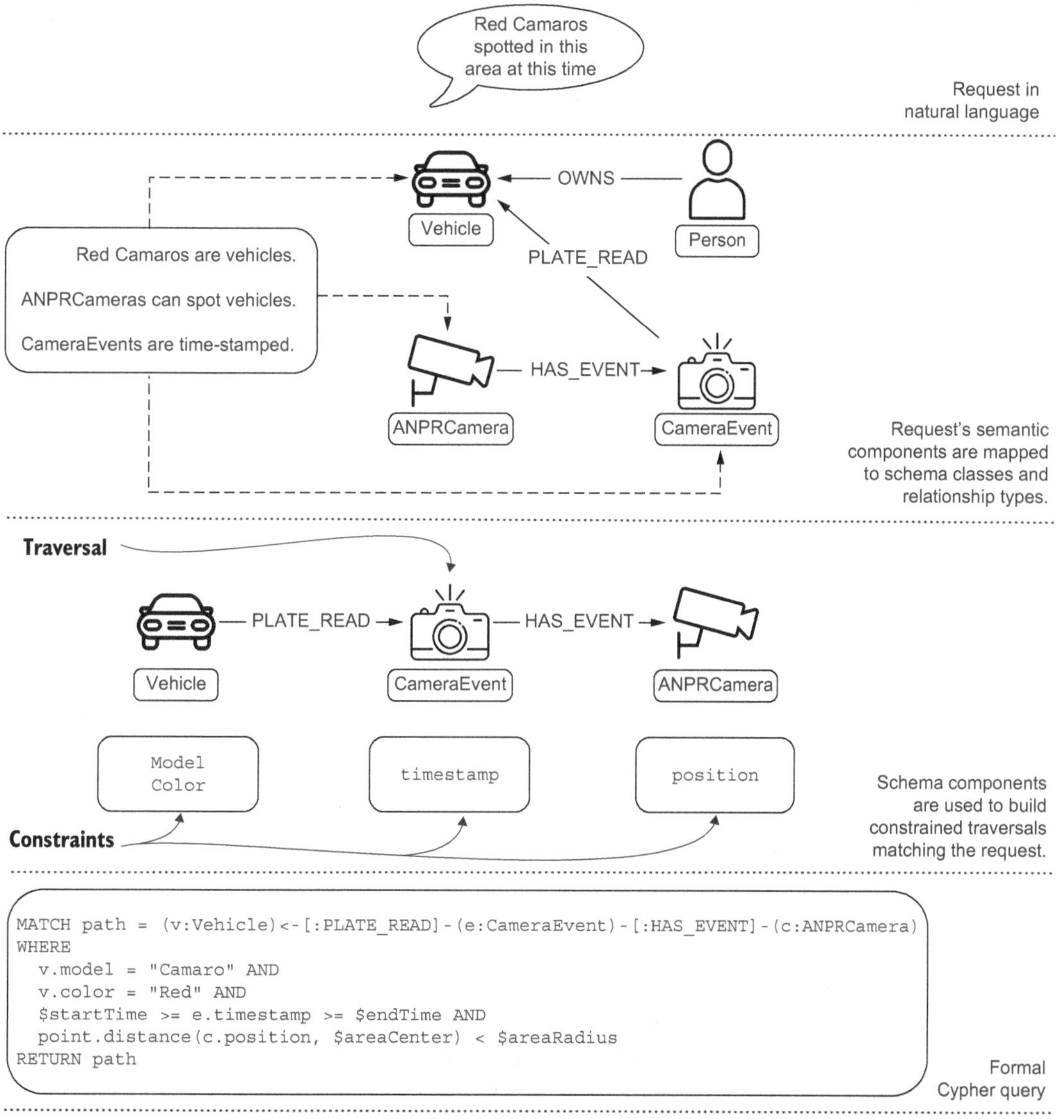

Figure 14.2 Translating a natural-language query ("Red Camaro spotted in this area at this time") into a formal Cypher query. The translation occurs in three stages: (1) parsing the natural-language request into semantic components, (2) mapping these components to schema elements (`Vehicle`, `CameraEvent`, and `ANPRCamera` nodes with their relationships), and (3) constructing a formal Cypher query with the appropriate traversal patterns and constraints. Domain concepts are systematically transformed into graph database operations, demonstrating the bridge between user intent and executable queries.

14.4 Think like an expert: Using metadata for enhanced querying

In the previous section, we explored how experts approach querying a KG by using their understanding of the schema to construct precise, context-aware queries. This process, grounded in constrained traversals, serves as a blueprint for extracting specific insights from complex data structures. However, this expert-based approach is not only the domain of human experts. With the advancements in LLMs, it is possible to translate this expert reasoning into a set of tasks that an LLM can perform, effectively allowing the model to think like an expert.

Expert reasoning, as we have outlined, involves a systematic approach to understanding and navigating the schema of a KG. LLMs, which are trained on massive amounts of text data, can recognize patterns and make inferences that closely resemble expert reasoning. They can parse and interpret the schema, understand how different entities and relationships interconnect, and use this understanding to inform their reasoning process. This combination of reasoning and schema comprehension allows LLMs to generate more accurate and contextually appropriate queries, mirroring the expert's ability to navigate the graph's structure.

In the following sections, we'll examine the core steps involved in answering questions using KGs:

- First we'll explore how to understand the intent behind the question (section 14.5). This step is vital because it helps route the request to specialized pipelines, if necessary, ensuring that the most appropriate method is used to answer the query.
- Next, we'll discuss how to extract and use metadata—essentially, an enriched or annotated schema—that provides the LLM with a deeper understanding of the graph (section 14.6). This metadata acts as a guide, enabling the model to navigate the KG more effectively.
- We'll also examine techniques to mimic expert reasoning in the LLM (section 14.7). Although there are intrinsic limitations in an LLM's reasoning capabilities, we'll explore strategies to overcome some of these challenges, bringing the model's performance closer to that of a human expert.
- Additionally, we'll explain how to integrate a summarization step to highlight the most important parts of the answer (section 14.8). This process not only helps in distilling the key information but also enables the inclusion of valuable insights.

Figure 14.3 gives an overview of our system's architecture and the interaction between its core components. We'll use this diagram as our roadmap to understand how the elements work together to process and transform user questions into meaningful results.

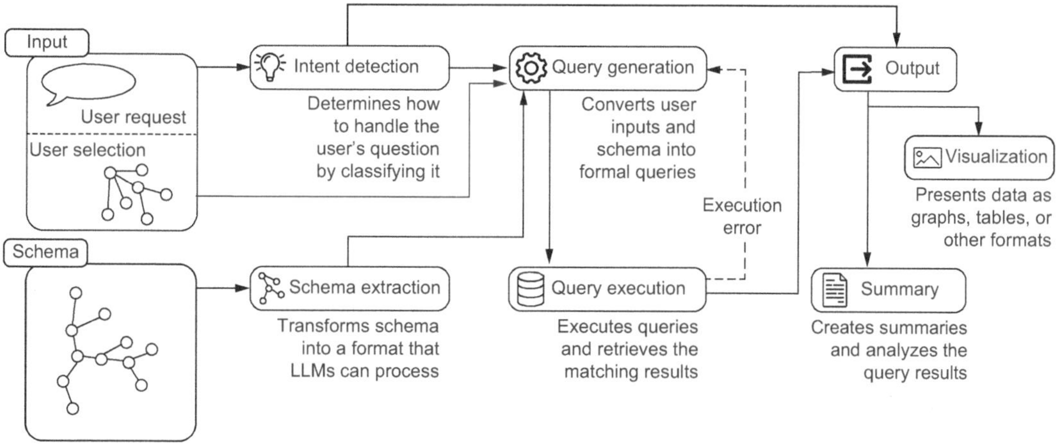

Figure 14.3 Overview of the system, highlighting the main components: Intent detection, Schema extraction, Query generation, Query execution, Visualization, and Summary generation. The system processes user questions and selection inputs while supporting error feedback during query execution.

Before we move on, it's important to recognize a significant paradigm shift in how we approach question-answering systems: shifting the focus from *generating an answer* to *asking the right question*. In traditional RAG systems, the process involves building a context around a question so that a grounded answer can be generated from the combination of the question and the context. The emphasis is on how to craft an answer that is both relevant and accurate based on the provided context.

However, in the approach we're exploring, the focus shifts toward converting questions into formal queries. Here, the challenge is not just answering the question but properly formulating the question so that it can be directly used to extract factual data from the KG. Although both questions and queries aim to uncover information, queries are essentially formalized questions designed to interact with the structure of the KG, ensuring precise and factual retrieval of data.

14.5 Intent detection: Understanding user expectations

Let's dive into our system architecture by exploring the first component: the Intent detection module (see figure 14.4). Why do we need to understand the intent to properly answer a question, and why should we do this at the beginning?

To answer the first question, we can revisit our "red Camaros" example. How should the answer be presented to the user? One option is to create an investigation board similar to those seen in crime movies, where we can add nodes and relationships. In this case, we would include not only nodes representing cars but also connections to the ANPR cameras that detected each vehicle. Alternatively, we could use a table representation that returns a list of cars with the plate number, camera location, and time of capture. Another option might be to draw a map, which would require the locations of the camera nodes. Each of these presentation methods has advantages, depending on the user's needs and preferences. We need to understand the user's intent so that we can identify the appropriate type of presentation and the right pipeline or chain to choose.

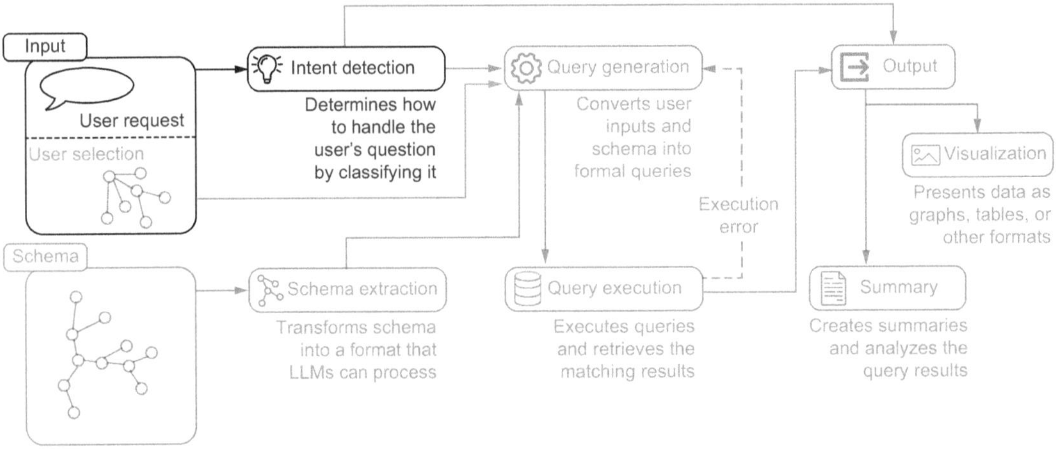

Figure 14.4 The Intent detection component analyzes user inputs to determine how to appropriately handle and classify the user's question.

We perform this step at the beginning for a couple of reasons. First, we aim to mimic expert reasoning, and understanding the intent behind a question is a fundamental first step that all experts take to provide satisfactory answers to their users. Second, this classification step relies on semantic understanding, a task that LLMs excel at. Because it is a relatively straightforward task, it is easy to follow and debug, providing a solid foundation for our question-answering system.

14.5.1 Classifying by visualization type

To build a classifier for intent, we must decide on the set of classes any question should fall into. This set is not written in stone; we can revisit it by adding or merging classes as we develop the system and as the system evolves in production.

Suppose our question-answering system is feeding a front-end layer capable of presenting the following:

- Graphs as interactive canvases with nodes and relationships laid out
- Tables with basic sort and search functions
- Charts or plots
- Interactive maps in a geographic information system (GIS)-like environment

As shown in figure 14.5, this creates a clear mapping between user intent and our system's visualization capabilities, forming the foundation for our intent detection approach.

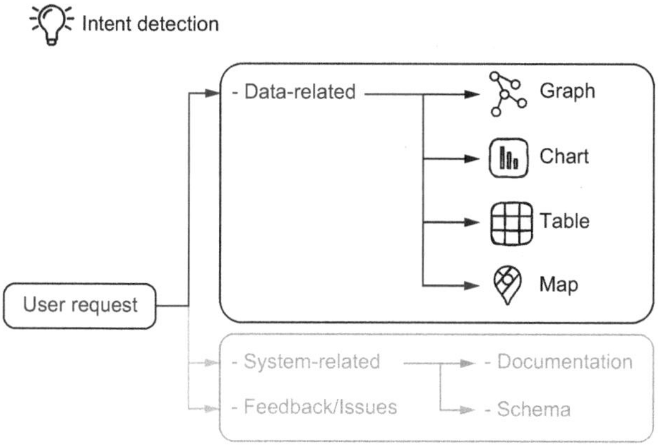

Figure 14.5 Intent detection system architecture for data visualization requests, showing how user requests are mapped to appropriate visualization formats (graph, chart, table, or map)

In this case, we can start by using a prompt to infer the type of representation the user wants to receive; this will be our intent detection, or at least the first version of it. A good classification prompt should have these characteristics:

- *Clear instructions*—The task is explicitly stated at the beginning, explaining what needs to be done.
- *Defined categories*—The categories are clearly defined so the model knows how to differentiate between them.
- *Examples*—By showing the model a few examples, it gets a clear idea of how the classification should work.
- *Boundary cases*—The prompt includes examples that sit near the boundaries between categories to help the model understand the nuances. This is especially important in classification, where similar inputs may belong to different categories.
- *Expected output format*—This guides the model on how to present the answers, ensuring consistency.
- *Fallback options*—If applicable, include a special category as a fallback, and instruct the model on when to use it. This can prevent forced or incorrect classifications.

The following example prompt implements such a classification task:

AN Given a Text delimited by triple backticks representing a user question, identify the best output of the presentation.

Select one of the possible outputs in the following list:

"graph", "table", "chart", "map".

The first step is to understand if the user explicitly asks for a specific output type to show the results.

For example, if the user asks for graph elements such as paths or nodes or relationships, then the output must be a graph in any case.

If the output type is not explicit it is usually "graph":

- "table", only when the user asks about aggregation, ordering, and statistics;
- "chart", if the user asks for plotting distributions;
- "map", if the user asks for showing locations, places or other entities with a strong location property;

If you do not understand the output from previous cases the output should be "graph".

Here you can find some examples:

Example: Location of last 10 narcotics related crimes

Output: {"type": "map", "reason": "type is map because it involves showing locations"}

Example: Distribution of crimes over time

Output: {"type": "chart", "reason": "type is chart because a distribution can be plotted"}

Example: "Maximum, minimum, and average number of crimes per district"

Output: {"type": "table", "reason": "type is table because aggregations are requested}

Example: "People involved in or related to crimes investigated by Inspector Morse"

Output: {"type": "graph","reason": "type is graph because entities and relationships are implied"}

The output must be in JSON format. Do not explain the result.

###Text:```{{question}}```

###Output:

The classification prompt is divided into three sections:

- *Task definition*—The first sentence defines the task generically, and other details are added in subsequent sentences. We introduce a clear bias toward the graph representation, and then we describe the expectation for each class.
- *Few-shots section*—We provide a set of examples, including the expected responses. The format of the response is also defined because the output structure is simple and it is easier to show than to explain. The examples are in the context of the law enforcement domain, and the response includes a reasoning step in addition to the answer.
- *The actual question*—Finally, we insert the question, following the format we provided in the few-shots section above.

The following are some examples of questions and classification results obtained using the previous prompt:

AN What is the location of the latest shooting?

{"type": "map", "reason": "type is map because it involves showing locations"}

AN How many crimes were committed per month in 2020 compared to 2019?

{"type": "chart", "reason": "type is chart because a distribution can be plotted"}

AN Who are the main suspects in the recent string of burglaries?

{"type": "graph", "reason": "type is graph because entities and relationships are implied"}

AN How many traffic fatalities occurred last year compared to the previous year?

{"type": "table", "reason": "type is table because aggregations are requested"}

We've done a decent job—our prompt meets most of the criteria we listed earlier. We are now able to label each question with an intent that matches the type of output we can present.

> **NOTE** You may wonder about the purpose of the `reason` field. The upcoming sections discuss how generating extra tokens affects the overall response of the LLM and how to exploit this knowledge to improve the quality of the results. For now, we are not planning to use the `reason` field in any downstream processing, but we will use it for debugging.

Next, let's take it up a notch by focusing on boundary cases and fallback options. The easiest way to obtain high-quality samples on the boundary is to observe misclassification during normal use. Consider this example: "What are the most common types of organized crime involved in human trafficking?" This question may be classified as a "graph" type because "entities and relationships are implied," even if it requires some aggregation and summarization.

On the one hand, the question is related to law enforcement, which often implies a need for visual representations of entities and relationships (e.g., networks of organized crime groups). On the other hand, the question asks for "common types" of organized crime, which suggests that some aggregation and summarization are required.

In this case, when we used our prompt, the system classified the question as a "graph" because the relationship between the different types of organized crime and human trafficking was more important than simply listing the common types, but it is not a clear-cut classification. There is no single correct and undebatable answer—but these are the types of questions we want in the few-shot section, as they will help shape the nuanced behavior of our system.

We took some liberties regarding fallback options criteria and included a significant bias toward the "graph" type, which effectively serves as a "catch-all" class. This is a reasonable choice; we are querying a graph database, after all.

14.5.2 Is it data, documentation, or just complaining?

To empower nontechnical domain experts to use the power of the KG, our solution must consider the broader spectrum of questions users may ask. Although the intent detection approach we've discussed so far is well-suited for handling data-driven queries, we also need to address more generic, open-ended inquiries that may not have a straightforward mapping to the graph database.

Consider, for example, the following questions:

- "Is it possible to export data from the system into a CSV file?"
- "How do I use the system to assess the risk level associated with a suspect?"
- "The system is too slow and keeps freezing. What can be done about it?"
- "It would be great if the system had [feature XYZ]. Can this be added?"

These questions are as legitimate as they are unexpected. They may not directly involve querying the KG, but they reflect real user needs and expectations.

Users interacting with a system like this are not limited to data-driven queries; they may also seek help with system functionalities, request explanations, or even provide feedback. It's reasonable to expect a variety of question types, which can generally be grouped into three categories:

- *Data-related questions*—These are the questions we have addressed so far, involving querying specific information from the KG.
- *System-related questions*—These are about how the system operates or its capabilities, such as exporting data or assessing risk.
- *Feedback and complaints*—Users may express frustration or make requests for improvements.

Among system-related questions, we can further distinguish between two important subcategories:

- *Documentation-related questions*—These questions can be resolved by consulting the user documentation, the user manual, or help.
- *Schema-related questions*—These are technical questions related to how the KG is structured and the decisions made during data modeling.

We can broaden the scope of the intent detection to encompass a full range of possible intents, as shown in figure 14.6.

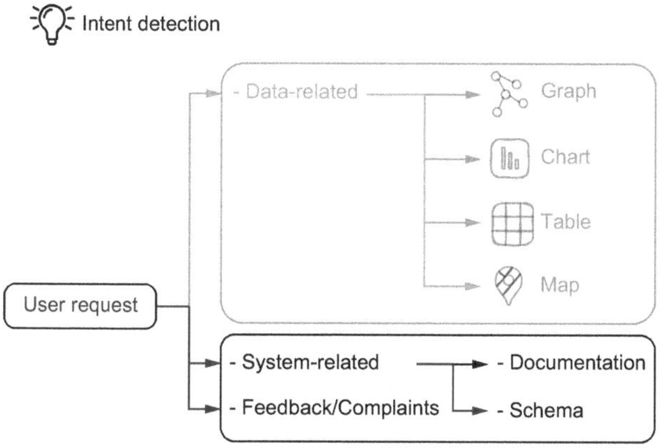

Figure 14.6 Classification of system-related questions in the intent detection system, showing how requests are routed either to documentation (for system functionality and feature questions) or to the schema (for KG structure queries). The system also identifies feedback and issues as a separate category for user complaints or enhancement requests.

With the range of potential user intents identified, the next critical step is crafting effective prompts for the LLM to handle this classification task. A well-structured prompt can guide the model in detecting the type of question and routing it to the appropriate pipeline—whether it's a data-related request, a system-related question, or user feedback. The following prompt shows how this broader intent detection can be implemented:

AN You are an AI assistant tasked with categorizing questions related to a law enforcement knowledge management system. Your job is to classify each question into one of three main categories:

```
1. **Data-Related:** Questions that require direct access to or
knowledge of the data within the system in order to be answered. These
questions focus on the content and structure of the data itself.
2. **System-Related:** Questions related to the system's functionality,
features, architecture, or design choices - information that would be
found in documentation, not necessarily in the data itself.
3. **Feedback/Complaints:** Questions that are either not answerable by
the system or are user feedback/complaints.

**If the question is classified as "System-Related,"** you will further
classify it into one of the following subcategories:
- **Documentation-Related:** Questions that can be answered by referring
to system documentation, user manuals, or help sections.
- **Schema-Related:** Questions related to the structure of the
knowledge graph or graph data schema.

**Task:** For each question below, first classify it into one of the
three main categories. If you classify it as "System-Related," then
further classify it into either "Documentation-Related" or "Schema-
Related."
```

```
**Example Questions and Expected Output:**

1. **Question:** "Is it possible to export data from the system into a
CSV file?"

   **Answer:**
   {
      "question": "Is it possible to export data from the system into a
       CSV file?",
      "category": "System-Related",
      "subcategory": "Documentation-Related",
      "reason": "The question asks about the capability of the system
       regarding data
      export, which falls under system functionality."
    }


2. **Question:** "How do I use the system to assess the risk level
associated with a suspect or location?"

    **Answer:**
    {
      "question": "How do I use the system to assess the risk level
       associated with a suspect or location?",
      "category": "System-Related",
      "subcategory": "Schema-Related",
      "reason": "The question involves assessing risk, which requires
       understanding the graph schema and structure of the data related
       to suspects and locations."
    }


3. **Question:** "What permissions do I need to access restricted data?"

   **Answer:**
   {
      "question": "What permissions do I need to access restricted
       data?",
      "category": "System-Related",
      "subcategory": "Documentation-Related",
      "reason": "The inquiry is about user permissions, indicating a
       question about system features and access controls."
    }


4. **Question:** "Why isn't the system responding to my queries?"

   **Answer:**
   {
      "question": "Why isn't the system responding to my queries?",
      "category": "Feedback/Complaints",
      "reason": "This question expresses a complaint about system
       performance, rather than asking for specific data or features."
    }
```

```
5. **Question:** "What types of data visualizations can the system
generate?"

   **Answer:**
   {
      "question": "What types of data visualizations can the system
       generate?",
      "category": "System-Related",
      "subcategory": "Documentation-Related",
      "reason": "The question seeks information on available features
       related to data visualizations, which pertains to system
       documentation."
    }


**Begin classification:**
{{question}}
```

This classification prompt is divided into three sections: the *task definition*, a *few-shot section*, and the *actual question*. Additionally, the expected output format includes a `reason` field, which is important for identifying potential misclassifications and understanding the model's reasoning.

Let's look at a misclassification example. Suppose we ask "How often is the knowledge graph updated to reflect the latest information?" A smaller or quantized LLM responded this way:

```
"question": "How often is the knowledge graph updated to reflect the
     latest information?",
"category": "Data-Related",
"reason": "The question concerns the frequency of updates within the
     data itself."
```

But a full-scale LLM gave this response:

```
"question": "How often is the knowledge graph updated to reflect the
     latest information?",
"category": "System-Related",
"subcategory": "Documentation-Related",
"reason": "The question is asking about the update frequency of the
     knowledge graph, which is a system-related feature that would be
     documented."
```

In this example, the question is related to how frequently the KG is updated. Although it's possible to infer this information by analyzing data, such as the creation or update timestamps of nodes, this approach would not be appropriate for a law enforcement knowledge management system. Attempting to determine the update frequency by analyzing the data may not provide an accurate conclusion, as the data could reflect how the information happens to be entered rather than how the updates are scheduled.

Larger models can detect that this question pertains to system functionality and refer to the documentation, labeling it as "System-Related" under "Documentation

-Related." Smaller or quantized models, however, may misinterpret the question as concerning the data itself and incorrectly classify it as "Data-Related."

The content of the `reason` field in both cases provides valuable insight. It suggests that the smaller model lacks context. This signals that we should enhance the task definition section by including relevant background information, helping guide the model to the correct classification.

To assess how well our prompt performs, we can evaluate it based on the criteria we established in the previous section and see if it includes clear instructions, defined categories, boundary cases, examples, and expected output format.

Design considerations for classification prompts

As we consider the design of our prompt for intent detection, it's essential to weigh the trade-offs between using a single broader prompt and implementing a multistage classification approach. This consideration applies to classification tasks in general.

Opting for a *single broad prompt* can be beneficial if simplicity and reduced management overhead are priorities. This method streamlines the classification process and can be effective when the model's accuracy is acceptable even for more complex tasks. It allows for quicker implementation and easier maintenance, particularly in environments where rapid deployment is necessary.

On the other hand, a *multistage approach* may be suitable if accuracy and flexibility in classification are more critical or if you anticipate frequent adjustments to how questions are categorized. This method provides more granular control over the classification process, enhancing the handling of complex questions and edge cases. By breaking the classification into stages, you can refine each step according to specific requirements, ultimately leading to more robust and reliable results.

Starting with a single broader prompt maintains simplicity while letting us evaluate the prompt's effectiveness in practice. As the complexity of requests increases or new requirements emerge, transitioning to a multistage classification system can be considered.

Postponing the decision to split the prompt into multiple stages also provides the opportunity to gather real-world examples. These cases can be invaluable in refining the classification process, ensuring that the eventual multistage approach is tailored to meet the specific needs of our application.

14.6 From schema to LLM-ready context

As shown in figure 14.7, we're focusing on the schema extraction phase of our pipeline. This critical step forms the foundation for transforming raw schema information into formats that LLMs can effectively process and understand.

Now we will build on this foundation by exploring how metadata, an enriched layer of schema information, can empower LLMs to replicate this expert reasoning, ultimately enabling nontechnical users to query KGs effectively. Here, the enrichments are those that would be beneficial to experts, as anything that makes the schema more understandable or actionable for an expert can be exploited by our LLMs.

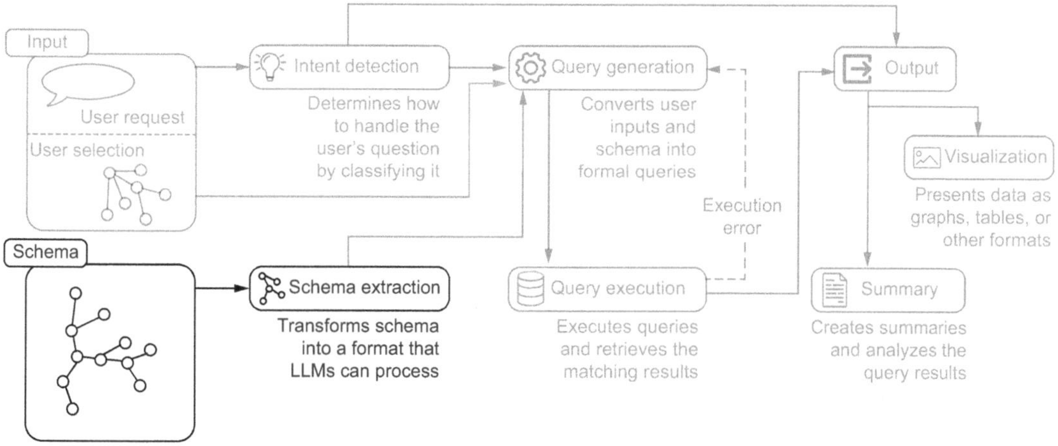

Figure 14.7 Schema processing pipeline, highlighting the transformation of the database schema into LLM-compatible formats. The diagram illustrates how raw schema structures are processed through schema extraction to create representations that LLMs can effectively process.

14.6.1 Schema extraction and representation

The challenge we face is extracting the schema from the KG and converting it into a form that can be processed by a language model. We can then use that schema information to help the language model better understand the question and produce a proper Cypher query.

At first glance, we could solve the first problem by invoking the `apoc.meta.schema` [1] function, which computes the schema based on the graph's current structure.

Listing 14.2 Response format for `apoc.meta.schema`

```
[
  {
    "label": "[LabelName]",
    "properties": {
      "[PropertyName1]": {
        "type": "[PropertyType1]",
        "mandatory": [true|false],
        "unique": [true|false]
      },
      "[PropertyName2]": {
        "type": "[PropertyType2]",
        "mandatory": [true|false],
        "unique": [true|false]
      },
      ...
    },
    "relationships": [
      {
        "type": "[RelationshipType]",
        "target": "[TargetLabelName]",
        "properties": {
```

```
            "[RelationshipPropertyName]": {
              "type": "[RelationshipPropertyType]",
              "mandatory": [true|false],
              "unique": [true|false]
            }
          }
        },
        ...
      ]
    },
    ...
]
```

However, a closer look reveals that the schema provided by this method is a *technical database schema*. It includes many details irrelevant to our needs, such as helper or administrative nodes, technical metadata properties, unnecessary or redundant type labels, unused relationships, and unused properties. These extraneous details clutter the schema with elements that are useful for database management but do not contribute to the core understanding of the domain. To address this, we need a *conceptual KG schema*: a distilled, meaningful structure that focuses only on the entities and relationships which convey the essential model of the domain.

The *conceptual schema* serves as a simplified, domain-relevant subset of the technical schema, stripping away technical complexities and irrelevant metadata. By removing auxiliary elements, the conceptual schema prioritizes clarity and usability, capturing the logical relationships and characteristics that experts rely on when reasoning about the graph.

This simplification is important for several reasons:

- *Alignment with human reasoning*—The conceptual schema reflects how domain experts understand the KG, using only the relevant entities, relationships, and properties to answer domain-specific questions. This aligns the schema more closely with the natural language model's approach to reasoning, making it easier to map questions accurately to graph elements.
- *Reduced cognitive load for LLMs*—Language models, particularly LLMs, are more efficient when given focused, relevant data rather than the full, complex structure of a technical database schema. By providing a streamlined conceptual schema, we allow the model to concentrate on meaningful information, increasing its ability to generate accurate and relevant Cypher queries without being distracted by extraneous details.
- *Minimized risk of query errors*—Technical schemas often contain implementation-specific elements, redundant labels, or metadata that could confuse the model, potentially leading to errors in query generation. The conceptual schema eliminates this noise, reducing the likelihood of misinterpretations that could result in incorrect queries.
- *Enhanced model interpretability*—A conceptual schema presents the KG in a more human-readable form, aligning it with how LLMs are trained to interpret text. By

focusing on the essential model of the domain, the conceptual schema captures the structure that LLMs can most effectively use to infer intentions and mappings.

To transition from the raw output of `apoc.meta.schema` to a conceptual schema, some human intervention is necessary. One approach is to describe the conceptual model manually, effectively "curating" the schema; alternatively, we can define a skip list to filter out unneeded elements from the APOC results, thereby distilling the technical schema to its conceptual core.

To make the conceptual schema interpretable for a language model, we must represent each node class and relationship in a clean, structured format that focuses on the essentials. This approach ensures that the LLM has a clear understanding of core classes and connections, as well as their properties and types, without the distractions of technical details. Figure 14.8 illustrates the key steps in transforming a technical Neo4j schema into an LLM-friendly conceptual representation.

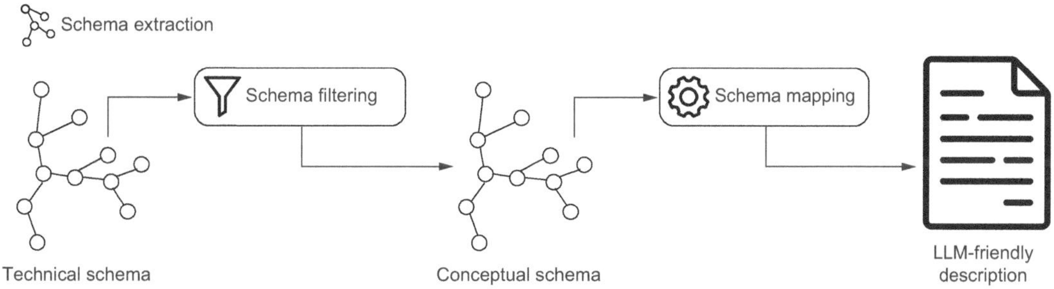

Figure 14.8 The technical schema obtained through the APOC call is filtered so it is reduced to the conceptual graph schema representation. The conceptual schema is then mapped into a textual format that can be effectively understood by LLMs.

In a *narrative schema representation*, nodes and relationships are described in greater detail and natural language, including rich context and examples (listing 14.3). Although this format is useful for human readers who need a thorough understanding, it can be more challenging for a language model to process when the goal is efficient query generation.

Listing 14.3 Narrative schema representation

```
**Nodes:**

1. **Vehicle**:
   - **Properties**: `color`, `make`, `model`, `style`, `plate_number`
   - Node example:
      - (:Vehicle
           {make: "Toyota", model: "Camry",
            style: "Sedan", plate_number: "XYZ123"})`
```

```
**Relationships:**

1. **OWNED_BY**: Represents the relationship of ownership between a vehicle
     and a person.
   - Example:
       - (:Vehicle {plate_number: "XYZ123"})
           -[:OWNED_BY]->
         (:Person {name: "Alice"})
```

As the schema grows, this approach can be verbose and less systematic. For a language model, this kind of representation may introduce challenges in parsing and understanding, particularly when the schema becomes large and complex.

In contrast, a more LLM-friendly format distills the schema into a concise, consistent structure that focuses on key entities and relationships, stripping away extra verbiage while retaining the essential details.

Listing 14.4 LLM-friendly schema representation format

```
Nodes:
(:Vehicle {
    color: STRING,
    make: STRING,
    model: STRING,
    style: STRING,
    plate_number: STRING
})

Relationships:
(:Vehicle)-[:OWNED_BY {since: DATE}]->(:Person)
```

This structured representation includes just the essential components—entity names, properties, and relationships—without extraneous descriptions or complex formatting. It is easy for the LLM to process because it uses a standardized syntax that aligns well both with the entity types and their attributes. The relationships are described clearly with property types and minimal but necessary contextual information.

14.6.2 Enriching schemas with descriptive annotations

In the previous section, we introduced schema descriptions as a way to bridge the gap between the KG's structure and the LLM's ability to generate accurate, meaningful queries. However, relying on the schema structure alone can hinder this process.

Suppose, for instance, that the user asks to "find all black vehicles involved in a crime." The LLM might naively translate this to `Vehicle.color == "black"`, assuming "black" is stored in a readable string format. However, if the database uses abbreviations like `BLK` for "black," this query will miss all relevant records, giving the impression that no black cars were involved in any crimes.

Another similar issue may arise with relationship ambiguity. Suppose the KG includes both the `COMMITTED` and `CO_OFFENDS_WITH` relationships. If the user asks to "list all suspects who have been in multiple crimes with another person," the LLM has no clear basis for determining which relationship to use. Is the question about those directly involved (COMMITTED) or individuals with co-offending histories (CO_OFFENDS_WITH)? Lacking a clear distinction, the LLM may choose incorrectly, amplifying the inherent ambiguity of natural language and leaving the user feeling as if they're communicating with a system that doesn't fully grasp their request.

To tackle these issues, we can mimic the actions an expert would take in similar situations. When faced with unfamiliar data, an expert begins by familiarizing themselves with the KG's structure, consulting any available documentation and data dictionaries. This careful review helps them understand the correct paths to take through the data and allows them to set constraints with precision, avoiding the pitfalls of ambiguous or misinterpreted terms.

As part of this familiarization process, experts may create a kind of "cheat sheet" to capture key insights—such as terminology, abbreviations, and relationship meanings—that aid in accurately constructing queries. For example, they might note that "BLK" is used instead of "black" in the vehicle color property, or that specific relationship types like COMMITTED and CO_OFFENDS_WITH capture involvement in criminal activities from different angles. By capturing this information, experts avoid mistakes and ensure that their queries align with the KG structure and semantics.

We can replicate this process of building a cheat sheet by systematically annotating the KG's schema, documenting node classes, relationship types, and properties with descriptions that capture these nuances. This annotated schema becomes a guide for the LLM, allowing it to make more informed and contextually accurate query translations. An example of such an annotated schema representation is shown in the next listing.

Listing 14.5 Annotated schema representation format

```
Nodes:
/* Represents a vehicle involved in various incidents or owned by individuals
    */
(:Vehicle {
    color: STRING, /* Color of vehicle, BLK, GRY, SIL, WHI, etc*/
    make: STRING,  /* Manufacturer: BMW, BUIC, CADI, CHEV, etc */
    model: STRING, /* Model of the vehicle: IMP, ALT, SON, SEB, CIV, etc */
    style: STRING, /* Body style: SUV, SEDAN, etc */
    plate_number: STRING /* Vehicle license plate */
})

Relationships:
/* Ownership relationship from vehicle to person, with start date of
    ownership */
(:Vehicle)-
[:OWNED_BY {since: DATE /* Date ownership began, ISO format */}]
->(:Person)
```

With these annotations as inline comments, the LLM has access to detailed descriptions that guide it in accurately interpreting the schema, leading to more precise queries which reflect the true data structure.

14.6.3 A practical approach to schema representation

Building on the previous discussions, we now propose a practical approach to streamline the process of refining and annotating the KG schema. This approach uses a YAML configuration file to manage the output of `apoc.meta.schema`, distill it by skipping irrelevant elements, and add rich descriptions to help LLMs understand the schema more effectively.

The YAML file serves as a central configuration point where users can specify which parts of the schema to exclude from processing, as well as provide detailed descriptions for key entities, relationships, and properties. The file includes two main sections: `skip` and `descriptions`.

SKIP LIST

The `skip` section allows users to filter out certain classes, relationships, or properties that are deemed not to be part of the core *conceptual KG schema* as we described it.

Listing 14.6 Schema config: `skip` section

```
schema:
    skip:
        classes: []            <- Classes to skip
        relationships: []      <- Relationships to skip
        properties: []         <- Properties to skip
```

DESCRIPTIONS

The `descriptions` section is where detailed annotations are added for various schema elements. Here, users can describe the purpose and semantics of classes, relationships, and properties, helping the LLM interpret the graph more effectively. These descriptions can be as granular as needed, ensuring that both the LLM and any human users interacting with the schema have a clear understanding of its structure.

Listing 14.7 Schema config: `descriptions` section

```
descriptions:
    classes:
        Class1: "Description of class 1"
    relationships:
        Rel1: "Description for relationship type 1"
    properties:
        Class1:
            property1: "Description for Class1.property1"
            property2: "Description for Class1.property2"
            [...]
        Rel1:
            property1: "Description for relationship property
  Rel1.property1"
```

The benefits of this approach include the following:

- *Customization*—Users can easily adjust the schema representation by editing the YAML file to include only the necessary components and tailor the descriptions to their needs.
- *Maintainability*—The YAML file serves as a centralized, human-readable configuration that can be easily updated as the schema evolves, ensuring that the schema remains aligned with the needs of the domain and the LLM.
- *Scalability*—As the KG grows, this approach allows for a manageable and scalable way to handle schema modifications, ensuring that the LLM can keep up with new data and relationships without becoming overwhelmed by unnecessary complexity.

An example of the output from this schema configuration approach is shown next.

Listing 14.8 Schema description: output example

```
### Graph Schema Overview

#### Node Types
(:Vehicle /* Represents a vehicle involved [...] */ {
    color: STRING, /* Color of vehicle, BLK, GRY, SIL, WHI, etc*/
    make: STRING,  /* Manufacturer: BMW, BUIC, CADI, CHEV, etc */
    model: STRING, /* Model of the vehicle: IMP, ALT, SON, SEB, CIV, etc */
    style: STRING, /* Body style: SUV, SEDAN, etc */
    plate_number: STRING /* Vehicle license plate */
})

#### Relationships
(:Vehicle)-[:OWNED_BY /*<description>*/ {since: DATE /* <description> */}]-
    >(:Person)
```

14.7 It's time to think: Understanding LLM reasoning

Now that we have a structured understanding of user intent and an LLM-friendly graph schema, we're almost ready to tackle one of the most challenging steps: translating text into Cypher queries. Figure 14.9 illustrates how query generation acts as a convergence point, combining processed user intent and schema data, while also using execution error feedback to refine and improve query formulation through an iterative process.

Just as we'll learn how important it is to guide LLMs to "take their time" with reasoning, we shouldn't rush through prompt design. LLMs are designed to understand context and generate responses that seem remarkably human by using the immense amounts of text data they were trained on. However, when presented with complex or nuanced questions, LLMs may "rush" to a conclusion, relying on shortcuts in the data patterns they've observed rather than fully reasoning through the problem. To tackle this tendency, researchers have explored techniques like the following:

- *Chain-of-thought prompting* [2] introduces intermediate steps into the model's response generation. By structuring prompts that require the model to articulate

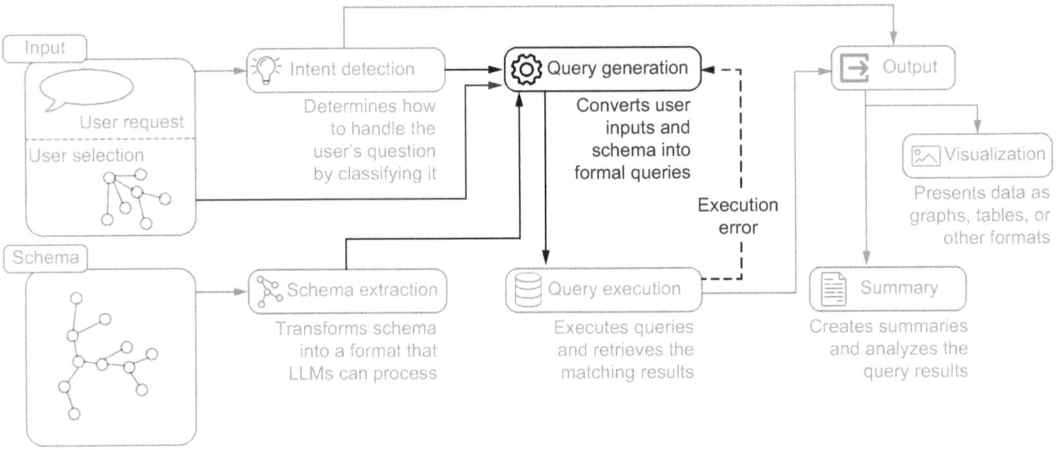

Figure 14.9 The query generation stage of the system architecture, highlighting its central role in converting user inputs and schema information into formal database queries

its reasoning step by step, this technique uses an LLM's pattern-based capabilities, encouraging it to take a more calculated approach rather than jumping to conclusions.

- *Scratchpad techniques* [3] embed intermediate "workings" in the LLM's output, where the model produces tokens that represent various steps or computations needed for reasoning through complex questions.

Both approaches give the model "time to think" by encouraging it to spend more computational resources on the problem-solving process before generating a final output. By modifying the prompt to "force" token-by-token generation before producing the final answer, these methods help allocate more computational capacity to each layer, effectively scaling the thought process in response to question complexity.

14.7.1 The order matters: Answer first vs. reasoning first

If an LLM is instructed to first provide the answer, followed by the reasoning behind it, the model may stick with the initial answer it generated. This is because LLMs typically produce one word (or, more precisely, one token) at a time, effectively committing to their previous choices as the generation progresses. This can lead to the model generating reasoning that is tailored to support the predetermined response, rather than reflecting an impartial, step-by-step thought process.

This consistency-driven tendency has been studied in recent research, which introduced the concept of *semantic consistency* [4]. The text corpora that these models are trained on typically exhibit a degree of logical coherence and internal consistency: what is said earlier is often used to support what is said later, and radical departures or contradictions are relatively rare. This consistency acts as a guardrail, preventing the models from engaging in what we would perceive as rambling speech.

However, this consistency can also become a constraint, due to the following problems:

- *Cumulative context*—Because the model generates tokens sequentially, the reasoning and context build cumulatively. This means the model's commitment to a particular answer can be influenced by the tokens it has already generated, reinforcing the idea of output consistency.
- *Error propagation*—If an error occurs early in the token generation process, it can propagate through subsequent tokens, as each new token is generated based on the previous ones. This highlights the importance of careful reasoning and validation at each step.

Figure 14.10 shows an example of how simply inverting the order of reason and answer generation can lead to significant differences in output.

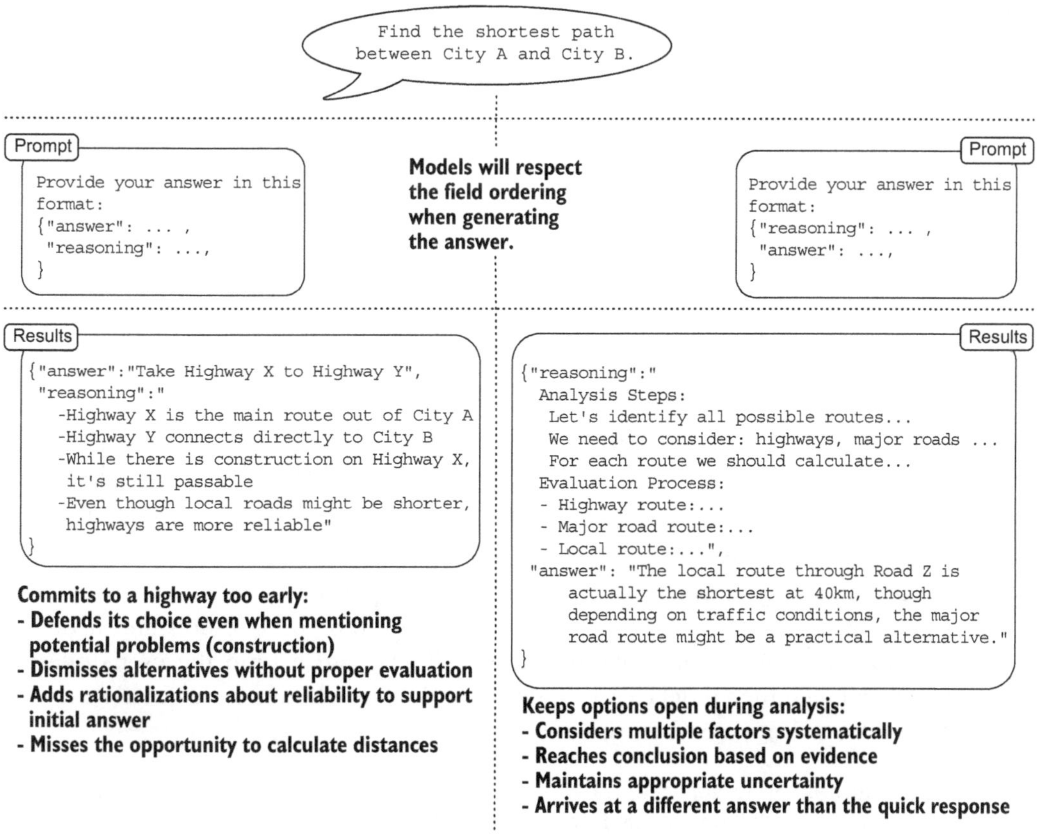

Figure 14.10 Comparison of two prompt structures for the same path-finding task. Left: The answer-first approach encourages quick, potentially biased responses with post hoc justification. Right: The reasoning-first approach promotes systematic analysis before reaching a conclusion. Note how the JSON structure in each prompt guides the LLM's thinking process.

To encourage transparent and reliable reasoning from LLMs, it's important to prompt the model to first provide its step-by-step reasoning, followed by the final answer. This structure forces the model to engage in a more thoughtful, deliberative process, as it must justify its conclusion through a balanced exploration of the problem, rather than simply rationalizing a predetermined response.

Postponing the reasoning step until after the answer can make sense in classification tasks. In these cases, we are more interested in understanding how the system justifies its choices, especially when it misclassifies. By using the reasoning provided by the model, we can gain insights into why the classification was incorrect and use that information to provide good examples that help clarify the classification boundaries, as we did in section 14.5.

14.7.2 Thinking in queries: From text to Cypher

Now that we've given both the model and ourselves plenty of time to think, it's time to put that thinking into action. Let's dive into crafting the prompt that will guide our LLM in generating the Cypher queries we need, using what we have built so far.

The prompt is structured as follows:

- A brief task description and question
- A schema definition with annotations
- Intent-dependent requirements
- Examples
- Optional user selection
- KG-specific annotations
- A reminder of the question
- A reminder of the requirements
- Output format specification

This structured approach forms a complete pipeline for transforming natural language questions into Cypher queries, as illustrated in figure 14.11. As we will see, the prompt includes elements we introduced in previous sections as well as new components.

BRIEF TASK DESCRIPTION AND QUESTION

We begin by introducing the task of translating a question in natural language into a Cypher query, anticipating that we will provide both the question and a detailed description of the schema. We use an HTML-like tag to wrap the user's question, which will help the model clearly understand the boundaries of the question and separate it from the rest of the instructions.

AN Your task is to generate a Cypher query for a Neo4j graph database, based on the schema definition provided, that answers the user Question.

The question we need to answer is:

<QUESTION>

{{ question }}

</QUESTION>
[...]

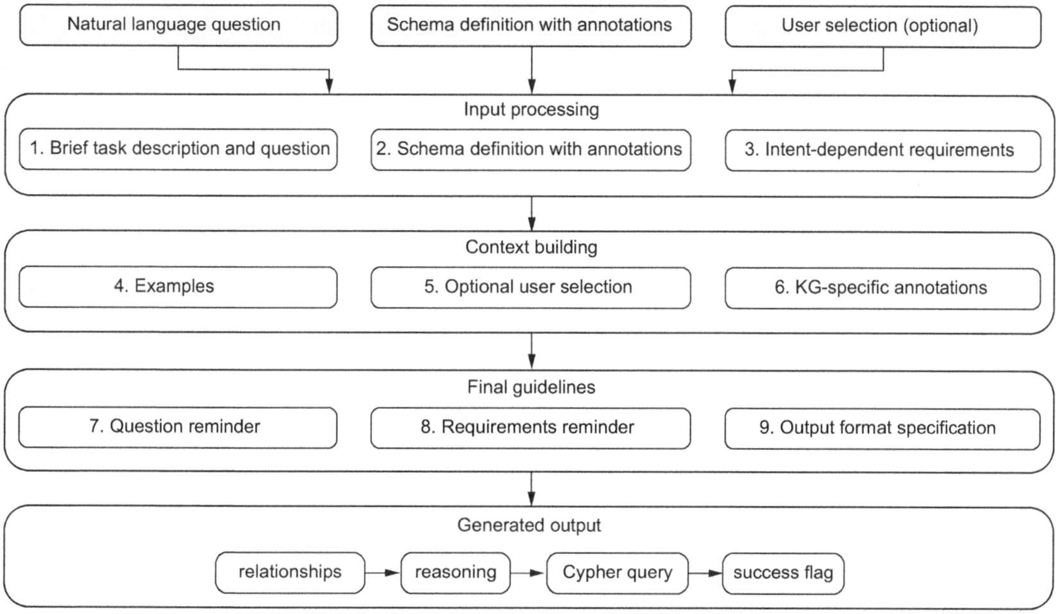

Figure 14.11 The complete flow of transforming a natural language question into a Cypher query, showing how three inputs are processed through structured prompt components. The process is organized into three stages (Input processing, Context building, and Final guidelines) that culminate in structured JSON output.

SCHEMA DEFINITION WITH ANNOTATIONS

In this section, we use what we developed during the schema extraction phase. The LLM-friendly format we introduced will seamlessly integrate with another HTML-like tag for this purpose. Using markdown such as `### Graph Schema Overview` or `#### Node Types` for headings will help the LLM create a clear structure for representing the schema. The `/* comments */` we added to annotate classes, relationships, and properties integrate the schema naturally.

AN [...]

The knowledge graph has the following schema, which the Cypher query must follow:
<SCHEMA>
{{ schema }}
</SCHEMA>
consider the comments as annotations
[...]

INTENT-DEPENDENT REQUIREMENTS

We use the output of intent detection to incorporate requirements that depend on the identified intent. In the case of a graph or map, we specify how the query should be structured. Specifically, we aim to retrieve not only the nodes that answer the question but also the relationships involved. For example, suppose we ask about red Camaros spotted by cameras in a certain area. We want to obtain information about the vehicles, the cameras, and the relationships that connect these elements. In case of a "table" response, we clarify that a tabular format is expected, so the model should select specific properties to display in columns rather than returning complete nodes or relationships.

AN [...]

{%if output_type == "graph" or output_type == "map" -%}

The result must be a graph so make sure to follow the schema and the following requirements:

- Return all the nodes and relationships matched, do not use anonymous relationships (such has (node0)-[:RELATIONSHIP]->(node1) instead use (node0)-[rel0:RELATIONSHIP]->(node1)

- Aggregate multiple traversals in a single MATCH pattern if possible: `MATCH path=(p:Person)-[acted:ACTED_IN]->(m:Movie)<-[directed:DIRECTED]-(d:Director) RETURN path` instead of `MATCH path=(p:Person)-[acted:ACTED_IN]->(m:Movie), (d:Director)-[directed:DIRECTED]->(m)`

{%-endif%}

{%if output_type == "table" -%}

The result must be a table, i.e. you must select nodes and relationship properties and rename them to be presented in a table

{%-endif-%}

[...]

EXAMPLES

This is a new component, although we introduced the few-shots technique previously. The idea is to assist the system in answering foundational questions that can serve as building blocks for more complex queries, while also demonstrating the expected format in a single instance. Examples are a powerful and relatively inexpensive way to enhance the quality of responses in many situations.

AN [...]

Use only the provided labels, relationships, and properties; do not use anything else that is not specified.

If you cannot generate a Cypher statement based on the provided schema, explain the reason to the user.

{{examples}}

You must respect relationship types and directions.

[...]

Optional user selection

This is another new component. If the system can represent nodes and relationships, it will probably also let users select nodes. Incorporating the current selection into the prompt enables users to refer to it in their questions. Users may choose to refer to the selected node as a whole or its properties, as in "Give me the older siblings of the selected person." The selected nodes are represented as a list of items, each containing the node label and its properties. If the user references a selection that is empty, the model highlights the issue.

AN [...]

{%if selection -%}

Current selection:

{% for node in selection%}

- {{node.label}} node with this properties {{node.properties}}

{% endfor %}

{%-else-%}

The selection is currently EMPTY. If there are references to selected nodes in the question, it is almost

certainly an error and therefore it is not possible to generate a response.

In this case, 'success' should be false.

{%-endif-%}

{{annotations.notes if annotations.notes}}

Do not include any explanations or apologies in your responses.

[...]

KG-specific annotations

In this section, users can include clarification notes that are relevant to the specific KG. These annotations provide context and enhance understanding, helping the model interpret the schema more effectively. By not integrating these notes directly into the prompt, we ensure that the prompt can be reused across different KGs. This flexibility allows for a more adaptable approach to query generation, as the annotations can be tailored to the specific nuances of each KG without altering the core prompt structure.

AN [...]

{{annotations.notes if annotations.notes}}

Do not include any explanations or apologies in your responses.

[...]

REMINDER OF THE QUESTION

We repeat the question near the end of the instruction prompt to reinforce the context and intent, which can lead to a more focused response. The schema definition section can be quite long, so the question may be located many tokens from the end of the instructions and the start of the response.

AN [...]

The question we like to answer may have some information that is relevant for the Cypher query:

<QUESTION>

{{ question }} {{ information }}

</QUESTION>

{%if output_type == "graph" or output_type == "map" -%}

Remember the requirements:

- Return all the nodes and relationships matched, never use anonymous relationships(ie [:RELATIONSHIP]), always use named ones (ie [rel1:RELATIONSHIP]).
- Aggregate multiple traversals in a single MATCH pattern if possible

{%-endif%}

[...]

Although language models, particularly those based on transformer architectures, do not inherently prioritize local context over global context—meaning they can theoretically focus on both local and distant tokens—these models can learn to give more weight to nearby tokens if they are more relevant for a particular task.

At this stage, we also provide an optional `information` field that can be relevant for generating the query. This field can be used, for example, to report a previous failure of the generated query, including the error message returned by the database. This allows the model to review its previous decisions and generate an error-free query in subsequent attempts.

Output format specification

Finally, we specify the format of the response, which must be a valid JSON object so that we can easily process it programmatically. We define each field we expect, provide hints for the expected value types for these fields, and include comments about the type of content we expect the model to fill in for these fields.

AN [...]

Use the "reasoning" field to explain your plan for the cypher query

Answer only in valid JSON in the following JSON format, nothing else (no <ANSWER> tags or anything like that):

{
  "relationships": [...], list of relationships to traverse, empty if not traversal is needed
  "reasoning": "...", this is the scratch pad for your reasoning
  "query": "<Cypher query>", must be a string and a valid Cypher query.
  "success": <true/false>, where true means that a Cypher query (following the schema) was returned.
}

14.7.3 Structuring output for reliable query generation

Let's dive deeper into the format of the output and the reason to select each field in a specific order. We start by asking the model to list the relationships it believes it should traverse. We do this because LLMs may hallucinate relationships that we didn't mention in the schema description; asking it to list the relationships it intends to traverse "out loud" significantly reduces the chance of this type of hallucination. Depending on the type of model, we may have to do some tuning. For example, if the model doesn't hallucinate relationships, we can safely remove this part. On the other hand, if the model commits too early to the relationships to traverse, we can soften the requirement for these fields by asking the model to list the relationships it will "potentially traverse," for example.

We then ask the model to generate the `reasoning` field. This gives the model time to think through the answer by breaking down the problem, defining a plan, and so on before committing to an answer. If you want to drive the reasoning process more precisely for specific use cases, you can add extra details under the "`Use the "reasoning" field to explain your plan for the cypher query`" section of the prompt, as well as through the examples.

We finally ask the model to produce the Cypher query to answer the question. Because we ask the model to generate this field after the `relationships` and the `reasoning` field, it will try to be coherent and not use nonexistent relationships. By guiding the model through the step-by-step process of identifying relationships, reasoning through the problem, and then formulating the final query, we ensure that the output is well-grounded and aligned with how a human expert would tackle the task. This helps us get results that are more reliable and trustworthy compared to simply asking for the Cypher query directly.

ENSURING EXAMPLE CONSISTENCY

To ensure that examples don't undermine this structured approach, they must conform to our response format to avoid introducing ambiguity during response generation:

```
{%for example in examples%}
Example:
<QUESTION>{{example.question}}</QUESTION>
{
  ...
  "query": "{{example.answer}}"
  {{ '"reasoning":"'+example.reasoning+'"' if example.reasoning else "..."}}
}
{%endfor %}
```

We use the "..." notation in the examples as a placeholder, indicating fields where we want to give the model the freedom to generate content autonomously. If we want to include important information in the reasoning step without significantly influencing the model's reasoning, we can run a prompt that asks the question in the example without including the `reasoning` field. This gives us the chance to check how the model would tackle the reasoning step without that guidance, and then we can modify the prompt to add the critical reasoning content we want to include without radically changing the overall response.

14.8 Response summarization: From results to insights

Having established a robust system that transforms natural language questions into actionable Cypher queries, our focus now shifts to ensuring that the results are as accessible and insightful as the queries themselves. Visualizing data as graphs provides a powerful way to explore relationships and structures, but it can sometimes leave users seeking clarity or deeper context. This is where summarization comes into play (see figure 14.12).

The summarization step holds a unique position in our pipeline as the first and only component that has access to the actual data the user is seeking. Whereas the previous steps focus on understanding the question and formulating the right query, summarization bridges the gap between raw data and user understanding.

Graph visualization excels at showing relationships and structures, but valuable information often lies in node properties or in the broader context of the results. A well-crafted summary can highlight these findings that may not be immediately visible in the visual representation. It provides users with a quick overview before they dive into a detailed exploration of the graph itself.

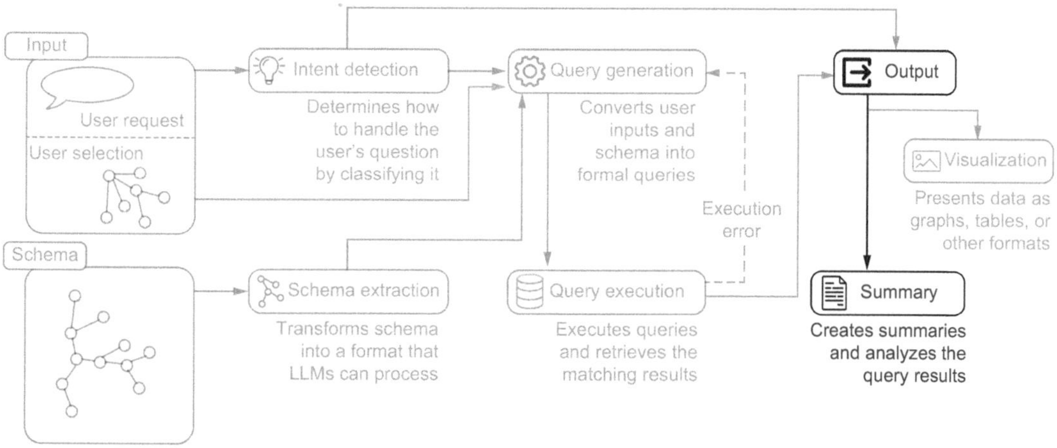

Figure 14.12 Output generation pipeline, highlighting the system's final stages of data presentation and analysis. Processed query results are transformed into visual presentations and analytical summaries, demonstrating the dual-output approach of visualization and summarization of query results.

Beyond its basic role of presenting results clearly, the summarization step can potentially be extended through post-processing to provide additional context and insights. This positions it as not just a final formatting step but rather a vital component for enhancing the overall user experience. Here is the prompt structure we'll use for summarization to achieve these goals:

AN Our user asked this question:
<QUESTION>
{{ question }}
</QUESTION>

To answer the question, we decided to execute this cypher query:
<QUERY>
{{ query }}
</QUERY>

The query returned a graph containing this data:
<RESULTS>
{{ records }}
<RESULTS>

{%if selection -%}

```
Current selection:
{% for node in selection%}
 - {{node.label}} node with this properties {{node.properties}}
{% endfor %}
{%-endif-%}

Your task is to summarize the results we sent to the user with the information just provided. Consider that the user will see the results in a graph format within a graphical user interface, but we also want to provide a textual summary along with the canvas.

Please keep in mind that much of the resulting data is actually irrelevant considering the question, but is returned anyway for completeness. Your job is to filter out this data so the summary contains only factual information that is relevant considering the question.

Does the question request analysis of the returned data? If so, include a few sentences to extract the requested analysis/insight.

This is the question again
<QUESTION>
{{ question }}
</QUESTION>

Answer only in valid JSON in the following JSON format, nothing else (no <ANSWER> tags or code blocks and so on):

{
  "results_analysis": true|false, Check if the question contains an implicit or explicit request for analysis of the returned raw data
  "reasoning": "...", Scratch pad for your reasoning. include reasoning about the summary and reasoning about the result analysis if needed
  "summary": "..." must be a string and a meaningful and factual summary (use \n and basic markdown tags to highlight the important bits).
}
```

Let's break down how this prompt is structured to achieve our summarization goals while maintaining flexibility for future enhancements. It begins by reconstructing the complete context chain, from initial question through query execution to results. Each element is carefully wrapped in HTML-like tags, creating clear boundaries that help the LLM understand the role of each component:

- The original question provides the user's intent.
- The executed Cypher query shows how we interpreted that intent.
- The query results represent our raw data.
- The current selection (if any) maintains user context.

The task description explicitly acknowledges the dual nature of our results presentation: users will see both a visual graph representation and our textual summary. This is vital because it guides the LLM to focus on complementing rather than merely repeating what's visible in the graph interface.

We explicitly instruct the LLM to filter out irrelevant data; this is a critical step, given that graph queries often return complete paths for visualization purposes. This filtering ensures that our summaries remain focused and meaningful to the user's original question.

The prompt introduces result analysis capabilities through a simple question: "Does the question request analysis?" This approach keeps the analysis tied to user intent rather than generating unrequested insights, and provides a foundation for future expansion of analytical capabilities while maintaining a clear separation between summary and analysis functions.

Before specifying the output format, we include a reminder of the original question. This repetition, like our approach in previous prompts, ensures that the model maintains focus despite potentially lengthy results sections.

The JSON output format follows our established pattern of progressive generation. First we generate a flag to identify whether the results analysis is required by the user, even if only implicitly. This flag is useful for monitoring purposes, as it compels the model to make an explicit decision about whether to perform the analysis. Additionally, when the flag is `true`, it significantly influences the subsequent reasoning step.

Next, the reasoning step must align with both the prompt and the analysis decision, incorporating any relevant analysis-related reasoning. Finally, we request the generation of the actual summary, including indications for typographic formatting to highlight the content when necessary.

This structured approach ensures that our summaries are consistent, relevant, and adaptable to future enhancements. The clear separation of concerns from decision-making through reasoning to final output makes the component both maintainable and extensible.

The summarization step completes our pipeline by transforming raw data into accessible insights while maintaining the flexibility to grow with evolving user needs. Its position as the final touchpoint with our users makes it a critical component for ensuring that the system answers questions accurately and also presents those answers in the most useful way possible.

Summary

- Expert emulation provides a systematic framework for building, improving, and extending KG systems. When facing any challenge, we can find solutions by asking "What would an expert do?" and breaking down their approach into implementable steps.
- A well-structured intent detection system requires two layers of classification. The first layer handles broader query categories (data-related, system-related, feedback), and the second identifies visualization needs.

- Converting technical database schemas into LLM-friendly formats requires filtering out unnecessary elements, adding contextual annotations, and structuring information in ways that align with how LLMs process and understand data.
- Prompt engineering for LLMs requires giving them "time to think." This means structuring prompts to encourage reasoning before answering and using techniques like chain-of-thought prompting to improve response quality and reliability.
- To work effectively, query-generation prompts need comprehensive schema context, the current user selection state, intent-specific requirements, and carefully chosen examples that demonstrate desired patterns.
- Result summarization works best as a complement to visualization. Rather than repeating what's visible in the graph, effective summaries highlight insights and patterns that might not be immediately apparent visually.

15 Building a QA agent with LangGraph

This chapter covers

- Implementing the expert-emulating approach
- Implementing investigation through question answering
- Adapting and improving the system

In this chapter, we'll create a practical application for querying knowledge graphs using LLMs. Drawing together the concepts and techniques explored in chapter 14—illustrated in the mental model in figure 15.1—we'll demonstrate how to build an integrated solution. Using LangGraph as our orchestration framework, we'll show how each stage can be combined into a seamless pipeline. To make this system accessible and user-friendly, we will use Streamlit as a frontend interface. The book's code repository contains the complete implementation and configuration files, so you can easily follow along and reference the code as we progress through the concepts.

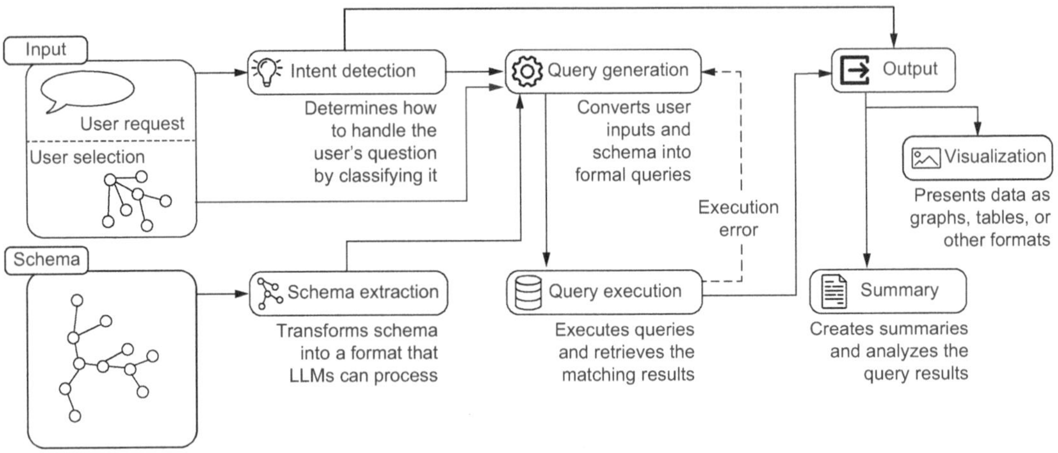

Figure 15.1 Overview of the system architecture introduced in chapter 14. We'll implement it using Streamlit to handle user input (questions and user selection) and output (visualization and summaries), and LangGraph will orchestrate the core pipeline.

15.1 Building the LangGraph pipeline

LangGraph is an innovative library designed for building stateful, multi-actor applications powered by LLMs. This framework is particularly suited for orchestrating workflows that involve complex reasoning and decision-making processes, which are central to our KG querying pipeline.

To better understand how LangGraph implements these concepts in practice, let's start with a familiar example: a basic retrieval-augmented generation (RAG) system that retrieves relevant documents and generates an answer to a question. Although simpler than our expert-emulating architecture, this example demonstrates the core principles we'll build on.

As shown in figure 15.2, the workflow consists of two main operations: document retrieval and answer generation. What makes LangGraph distinctive is its approach to component communication: rather than passing data directly between components, each one interacts with a shared state, similar to a whiteboard where each agent can read previous work and add their results.

The state begins with the user's question. The first agent, responsible for document retrieval, reads the question from the state and adds the relevant documents it finds. The second agent can then access both the original question and the retrieved documents to generate an appropriate answer, which is in turn added to the state.

At its architectural core, LangGraph implements these workflows as directed graphs, where each node represents a distinct agent function. These agent functions carry out their responsibilities by interacting with the global state—reading the relevant data and updating it with their results after execution. The edges in the graph

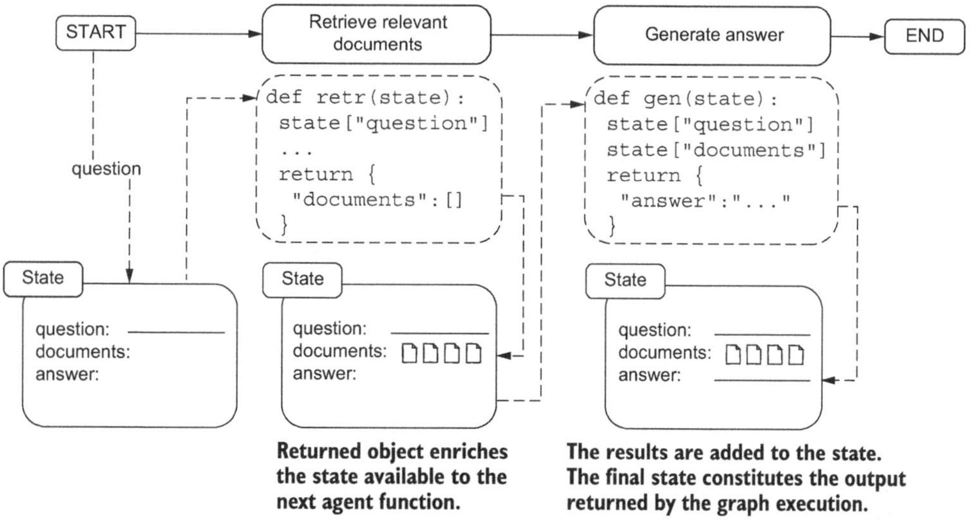

Figure 15.2 State-based communication between agent functions in LangGraph. Agents remain decoupled while communicating through an evolving `state` object. Each agent function receives and updates the global state independently.

determine the execution flow, specifying which node should be executed next. Importantly, LangGraph supports dynamic edge resolution, enabling workflows to branch based on arbitrarily complex logic. For instance, the next node to execute can be chosen based on the output of a preceding agent, ensuring flexibility and adaptability in designing workflows.

This approach ensures that the system maintains a coherent state throughout the workflow while enabling AI system designers to create a spectrum of applications, from router systems where LLMs are just one component among many, to fully autonomous systems where LLMs can determine and shape their execution paths. This flexibility in flow control makes LangGraph ideal for implementing our expert-emulating architecture, where we need to coordinate multiple specialized phases such as intent detection, schema extraction, and query generation.

15.1.1 System architecture overview

With LangGraph's capabilities clear, let's examine how the expert-emulating approach translates into an executable workflow. Figure 15.3 shows the core components of our KG querying system, from initial user input processing through intent detection, query generation, and result presentation, with each node representing a discrete agent function. Notably, this component structure maps naturally to LangGraph's agent/state architecture, where each processing step can be implemented as an agent function that receives and updates the workflow state.

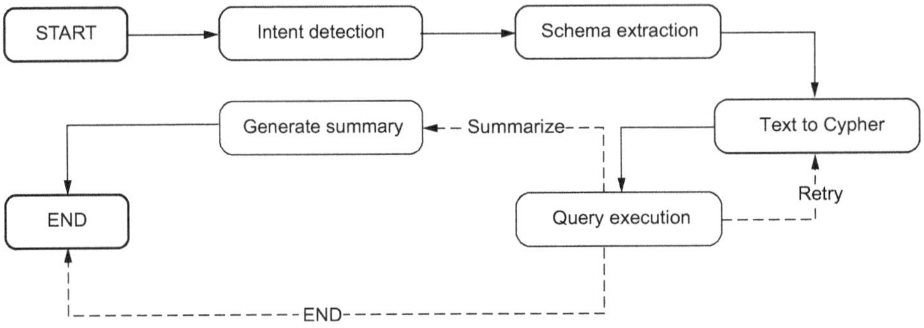

Figure 15.3 LangGraph implementation of the KG querying pipeline. The solid arrows show the main flow from intent detection through schema extraction and query execution, and dashed arrows indicate conditional paths based on query execution outcomes. This directed graph structure directly maps each component of our expert-emulating approach to a LangGraph agent function.

The LangGraph workflow, although central to our backend system, integrates with several supporting components and interfaces with frontend applications; figure 15.4 shows a broader architectural view. At the core of the backend sits our LangGraph workflow, consuming prompts and configuration from the configuration provider while dynamically accessing graph schema information through the schema provider. These supporting components handle critical setup tasks: the configuration provider manages prompt templates and system settings, and the schema provider extracts and formats database schema for LLM consumption.

The question processing interface acts as a bridge between the core pipeline and frontend applications. It exposes the LangGraph workflow as an event stream, allowing frontends to track pipeline progress in real time. This interface processes incoming questions, feeds them through the workflow, and streams state updates and final responses back to the user interface.

This architecture cleanly separates concerns while maintaining the flexibility needed for a conversational AI system. Each component has a clear responsibility: LangGraph handles the core question-answering logic, providers manage configuration and schema access, and the processing interface handles frontend communication.

In the following sections, we'll examine each of these architectural elements, starting with the supporting components that provide configuration management and schema translation services. We'll then explore the state management design that enables effective communication between pipeline stages, followed by the implementation of individual pipeline agents which form the core of our question-answering system. Finally, we'll look at how the pipeline integration layer brings these elements together into a cohesive system that can interact with frontend applications.

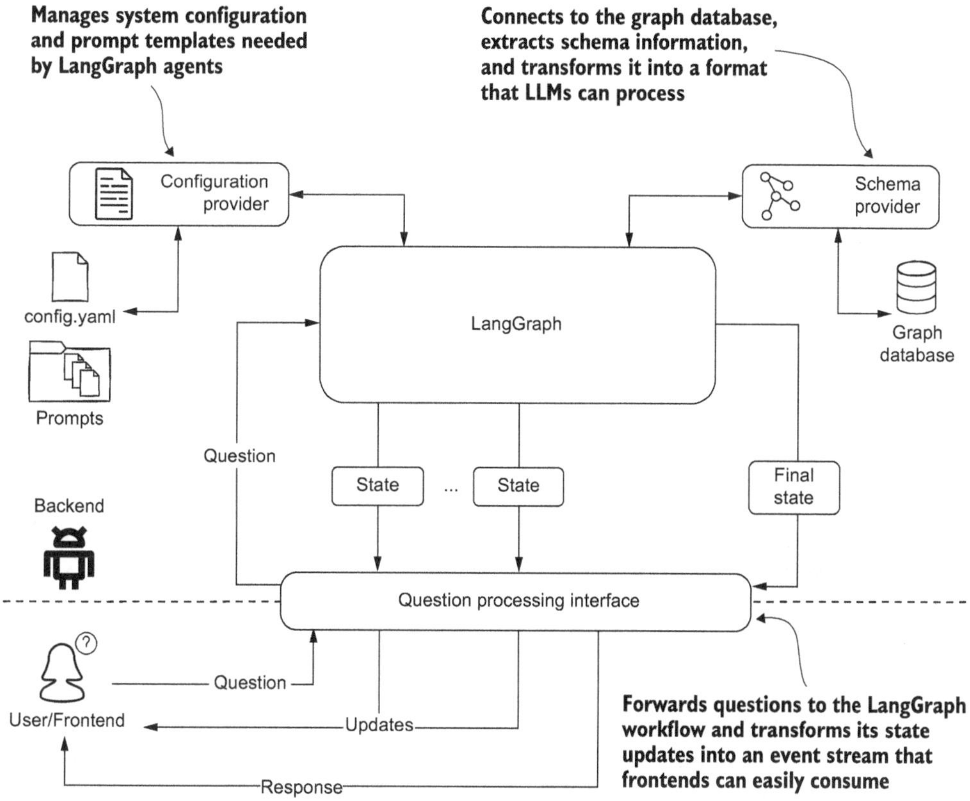

Figure 15.4 Backend architecture showing how the LangGraph pipeline integrates with supporting components. The configuration provider manages prompts and settings, and the schema provider handles database schema access. The question-processing interface bridges the core pipeline with frontend applications through an event-based API.

15.1.2 Configuring pipeline components

Before diving into the configuration details, let's examine how the configuration component fits into our system architecture (see figure 15.5). The configuration component serves as a centralized repository for storing textual elements that our question-answering system relies on, primarily prompt templates and KG annotations. This separation of concerns helps maintain clean and maintainable code by preventing these often lengthy text elements from cluttering the main implementation.

Our templates use the Jinja2 templating language, allowing for dynamic content generation at runtime. By isolating template definitions in the configuration, we create a clear boundary between template authoring and template rendering. The main code can then interact with these templates through a clean interface, remaining unaware of the underlying template composition process.

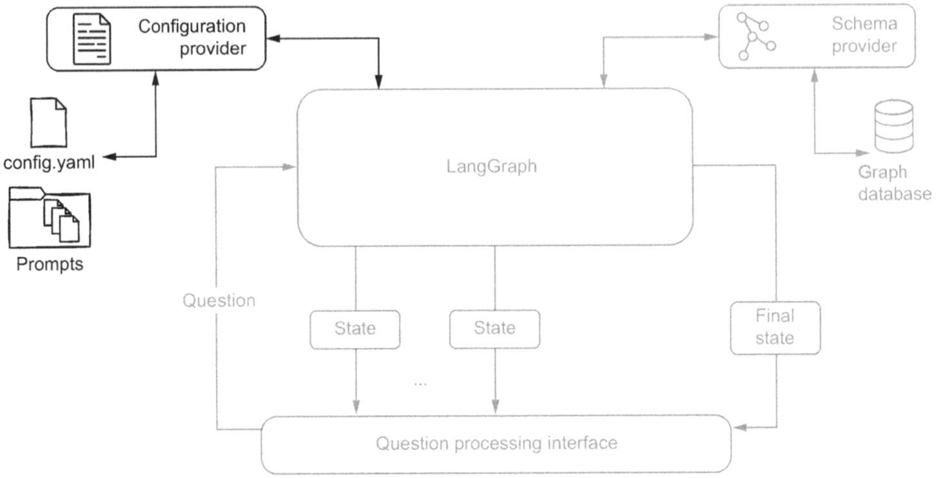

Figure 15.5 System architecture diagram highlighting the configuration provider component. The provider manages system configuration and prompt templates needed by LangGraph agents to process user questions.

This approach offers several advantages. First, it simplifies the tuning of KG descriptions and prompt templates, as all adjustments can be made in a single location without touching the core logic. Second, it provides a structured foundation for future extensions: adding new processing steps or modifying existing ones becomes more straightforward when all text-based resources are organized in one place. Finally, having a dedicated configuration component makes it easier to manage different versions of prompts and annotations, which is particularly valuable during the development and refinement of the system. The following listing shows an example of our configuration structure.

Listing 15.1 Configuration file example

```
notes: >
    - all POINTS properties are Neo4j Points (`point.distance()`
      and similar functions work for them)
    - do not expand ANPRCameraEvent unless you need
      to connect it to both Vehicle and ANPRCamera
    - a previous offender or known offender is defined by the fact that
      the node is connected to crimes
examples:
    - question: Crimes that occurred on March 14th, 2025
      answer: MATCH (c:Crime) WHERE c.date starts with "2025-03-14"
      reasoning: >-
          To find the crimes that occurred on that date, we leverage
          the <b>date</b> property of the crime node.
          Since it is formatted as an ISO string, we can use the
          prefix "2025-03-14" to get all crimes that occurred on that day.
          Since there is no traversal, no paths are returned
```

```
    [...]
    - question: Return one male known offender aged 20 to 22
      answer: >-
          MATCH path = (person:Person)
                        -[committed:COMMITTED]->(crime:Crime)
          WHERE (person.sex CONTAINS 'MALE' AND
                 person.age >= 20 AND person.age <= 22)
          RETURN path LIMIT 1
prompts:
    text_to_cypher:
        system: >-
            Your task is to generate a Cypher query for a Neo4j graph
            database, based on the schema definition provided,
            that answers the user question.
        template: templates/text_to_cypher.template
    intent_detection:
        template: templates/intent_detection.template
    generate_summary:
        template: templates/summary.template
```

The configuration combines three key elements: operational notes that guide query generation, examples that demonstrate proper query construction, and prompt template references. The notes capture essential domain knowledge and best practices for working with the graph database, and the examples provide question–answer pairs with detailed reasoning that help the LLM understand the expected query patterns. This combination of declarative knowledge and practical examples creates a rich context that guides the LLM in generating accurate queries.

The prompts section references external templates for different pipeline stages (intent detection, query generation, and summary generation), keeping the actual prompt templates separate from their configuration. This separation allows for easier maintenance and version control of both the configuration structure and the prompt content.

Each template can be modified independently without affecting the overall configuration, making it easier to experiment with different prompt variations during development. The next listing shows how the configuration component manages template loading and dynamic content generation.

Listing 15.2 Configuration component

```
class ChainConfiguration:
    def __init__(self):
        self.base = Path(__file__).parent
        self.config = self.load()

    def load(self):
        config_file = self.base / "chain_config.yaml"
        return yaml.load(config_file.open(), Loader=yaml.FullLoader)

    def get_prompt(self, name, **kwargs):
        system = self.config["prompts"][name].get("system")
```

```
        template_file = (
            self.base / self.config["prompts"][name]["template"])

        template = template_file.read_text()
        prompt = jinja2_formatter(template, **kwargs)

        return system, prompt

    def getAnnotations(self, reload=True):
        if reload:
            self.config = self.load()
        return {
           "notes": self.config["notes"],
           "examples": self.config["examples"]}
```

The `ChainConfiguration` class provides a clean interface for accessing our configuration elements. It offers two main methods: `get_prompt` for retrieving and formatting prompt templates, and `getAnnotations` for accessing the notes and examples. This implementation ensures that all configuration elements are easily accessible while maintaining a clear separation between configuration storage and use.

15.1.3 Schema translation service

Next, let's examine the Schema provider component and its interaction with the graph database in our system architecture (see figure 15.6). The schema provider is a vital component in our expert-emulating question-answering system. Although our goal is to automate schema extraction, we face a fundamental challenge that we explored in chapter 14: we need access to the conceptual schema, but we can only programmatically access the technical schema.

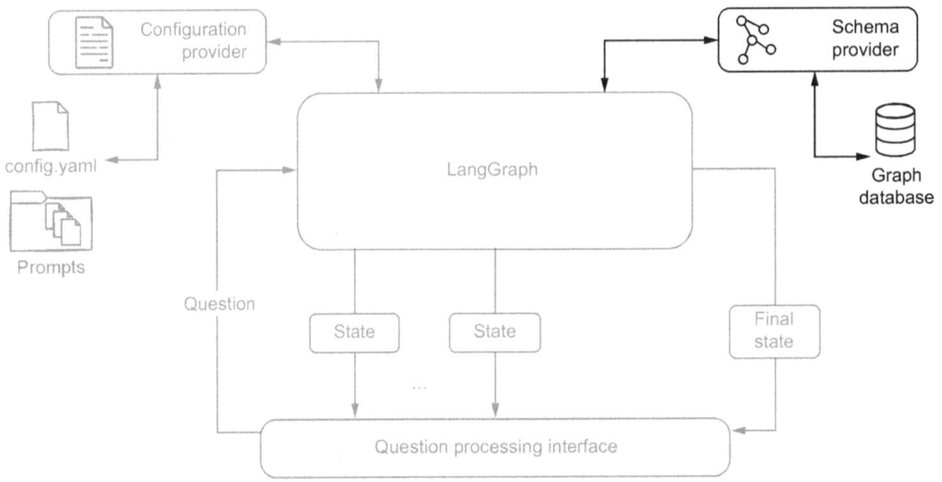

Figure 15.6 System architecture diagram emphasizing the schema provider component, which connects to the graph database to extract and transform technical schema information into LLM-friendly formats

To solve this, we've developed a configuration-based transformation approach that consists of two key components. The first component is a skip list that identifies which elements should be excluded from the conceptual model. These elements include technical nodes and relationships that don't represent business concepts, implementation-specific properties such as internal IDs and timestamps, and elements that would add unnecessary complexity to LLM prompts. The second component is a description section that enriches the filtered schema by adding business-level descriptions for nodes and relationships, contextual information about properties, and domain-specific terminology and constraints.

We store this configuration in YAML format, making it easy to maintain and update as the data model evolves. The schema provider follows a three-step process to transform the raw technical schema into an LLM-friendly format: it extracts the technical schema using Neo4j's `apoc.meta.schema`, filters out technical elements using the skip list, and enriches the remaining elements with business descriptions.

Let's examine how this is implemented in practice. First we need a data model that can represent both technical and enriched schema information, as in the following listing.

Listing 15.3 Schema provider: data model

```
@dataclass
class Property:
    """Represents a node or relationship property with an optional
       description"""
    name: str
    type: str
    description: str = None

    def __str__(self):
        """Represents the property as string in the format:
           property_name:TYPE /* optional description */ """
        ret = f"{self.name}: {self.type}"
        if self.description is not None:
            ret += f" /* {self.description} */"
        return ret


@dataclass
class Node:
    """Represents a node type."""
    items = {}
    name: str
    properties: list[Property]
    description: str = None

    @classmethod
    def mk_node(cls, name, value):
        """Creates a new node with the given name and properties
           from a dictionary.

           Args:
               name (str): The name of the node.
```

Dataclass representing a node or relationship property

Dataclass representing a node type

Keeps track of all nodes at a global level

Instantiates nodes using the node description from apoc.meta.schema

```
            value (dict): the node description as
                          returned by `apoc.meta.schema`
    """
    properties = [Property(name=k, type=v["type"])
                  for k, v in value["properties"].items()]
    properties = sorted(properties, key=lambda x: x.name)

    node = Node(name=name,
                properties=properties)

    for rel_name, rel_value in value["relationships"].items():
        Relationship.mk_rels(source=name, name=rel_name,
                             value=rel_value)

    cls.items[node.name] = node        ◁ Stores the newly created node instance in the Node.items dictionary

def drop_properties(self, skipProperties):
    """Drops specified properties from the node.

       Args:
           skipProperties (list): A list of property names
                                  to be dropped.
    """
    self.properties = [prop for prop in self.properties
                       if prop.name not in skipProperties]   ◁ Recomputes node properties by filtering out properties in the skip list

def __str__(self):        ◁ Assembles node components to form the desired node description format
    """Represents the node as string in the format:
       (:NodeType /* node class description */ {
          property_one:TYPE /* property one description */,
          property_two:TYPE /* property two description */,
          ...
       })
    """
    descr = ("" if self.description is None
             else f"/* {self.description} */ ")

    return (
            f"(:{self.name} {descr}{{\n    " +
            ",\n    ".join(str(prop) for prop in self.properties) +
            "\n})\n"
    )
```

This data model provides the foundation for our schema transformation process. The `Property` class handles individual attributes with their descriptions, and the `Node` class manages the overall structure and filtering capabilities. Building on this data model, the following listing shows how the `Neo4jSchema` class implements our core schema management functionality.

Listing 15.4 Schema provider main class

```
class Neo4jSchema:
    [...]

    def get_schema(self):        ◁ Initializes the schema using a technical schema from apoc.meta.schema
        with self.driver.session() as session:
```

```
        result = list(session.run(
            "CALL apoc.meta.schema({sample:-1})"
        ))[0]["value"]

        [Node.mk_node(k, v) for k, v in result.items()
         if v["type"] == "node"]

    @staticmethod
    def apply_configuration(config: dict = None):
        if config is None:
            config_file = Path(__file__).parent / "schema_config.yaml"
            config = yaml.load(config_file.open(),
                               Loader=yaml.FullLoader)["schema"]

        items = {node.name: node for node in Node.items.values()
                 if node.name not in config["skip"]["classes"]}
        Node.items = items

        for node in Node.items.values():
            node.drop_properties(config["skip"]["properties"])

        for node in Node.items.values():
            node.description = (config["descriptions"]["classes"]
                                .get(node.name))
            for prop in node.properties:
                property_description =(config["descriptions"]["properties"]
                                       .get(node.name, {})
                                       .get(prop.name))
                prop.description = property_description

        skip = config["skip"]
        relationships = {rel_name: rel
                         for rel_name, rel in Relationship.items.items()
                         if rel.source not in skip["classes"]
                         if rel.dest not in skip["classes"]
                         if rel.name not in skip["relationships"]
                         }
        for rel in Relationship.items.values():
            rel.drop_properties(config["skip"]["properties"])

        Relationship.items = relationships

    def __str__(self):
        ret = ["### Graph Schema Overview\n",
               "#### Node Types"]
        ret += [str(node) for node in Node.items.values()]
        ret.append("#### Relationships\n")
        ret += [str(rel) for rel in Relationship.items.values()]
        return "\n".join(ret)
```

Calls apoc.meta.schema on the full database without sampling

Parses apoc.meta.schema results using list comprehension

Converts the technical schema to conceptual by applying filters and descriptions

Uses schema_config.yaml from the package directory if no configuration is provided

Recomputes the node types, filtering out skip-list nodes

Removes properties in the skip list from Node objects

Uses the description from descriptions.classes.<class_name> if exists

Looks for descriptions.properties.<class_name>.<property_name>

Filters out relationships with the source node in the skip list

Filters out relationships with the destination node in the skip list

Filters out relationships in the skip list

Removes properties in the skip list from Relationship objects

Creates a Markdown representation of the schema with node types and relationships

The `get_schema` method retrieves the technical schema, and `apply_configuration` handles the transformation process according to our configuration. This implementation ensures that LLMs receive a clean, conceptual view of our data model while maintaining all necessary information for query generation.

In practice, this transformed schema serves several important purposes for our LLM components. It enables them to understand the domain model at a conceptual level, generate queries using proper entity and relationship names, and consider business rules and constraints during query construction. This approach creates an effective balance between maintaining technical accuracy and providing LLMs with an accessible, business-oriented view of our data model.

15.1.4 State management design

The cornerstone of agent communication in LangGraph is the `state` object, which serves as a shared memory space that agents can read from and write to. Each agent is responsible for populating specific portions of this state, creating a clear chain of responsibility throughout the pipeline. Let's examine the structure of this `state` object.

Listing 15.5 Pipeline agent's state

```
class AgentState(TypedDict):
    question: str
    output_type: str
    output_type_reason: str
    schema: str
    query: str
    query_reasoning: str
    query_message: str
    results_error: list
    summary: str
    summary_reason: str
    summary_analysis: bool
    information: str
    retries: int
```

This state structure can be broken down into logical sections:

- *Question input* (`question`)—Stores the original user request
- *Intent detection results* (`output_type`, `output_type_reason`)—Captures the detected visualization intent and the reasoning behind it
- *Schema information* (`schema`)—Contains the graph schema in LLM-friendly format
- *Query generation* (`query`, `query_reasoning`, `query_message`)—Holds the generated Cypher query and associated metadata
- *Error handling* (`results_error`)—Tracks any errors encountered during query execution
- *Summary generation* (`summary`, `summary_reason`, `summary_analysis`)—Contains the generated summary and analysis flags
- *Queries retry mechanism* (`information`, `retries`)—Manages the retry logic for failed queries

Each field tells a story about the pipeline's progress. The state not only carries data between agents but also maintains the context necessary for making routing decisions and handling errors gracefully.

15.1.5 Pipeline agent implementation

As we discussed earlier, our expert-emulating approach maps naturally to a LangGraph pipeline, where each step in our question-answering process is implemented as a specialized agent. Figure 15.7 shows this pipeline structure again, highlighting how agents are connected and how the flow of information progresses from the initial question to the final answer. In this section, we will look at how these agents are made and how they interact with the LangGraph `state` object.

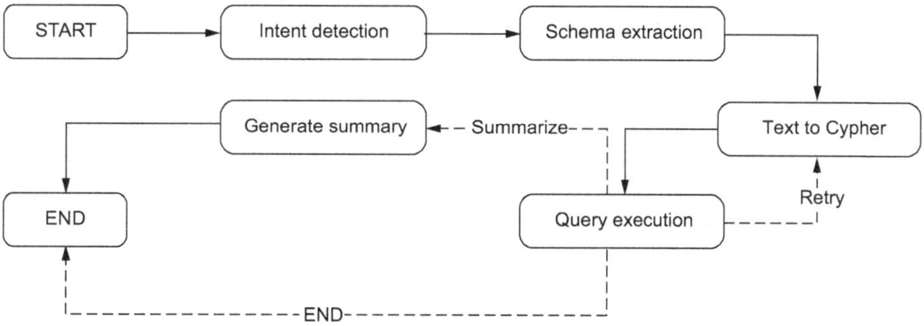

Figure 15.7 LangGraph implementation of the knowledge expert-emulating graph-querying pipeline

INTENT DETECTION AGENT

The intent detection agent serves as the entry point of our pipeline: it determines how the user's question should be visualized. It operates solely on the user's input question and enriches the state with visualization intent information.

This agent uses the intent detection prompt we discussed in chapter 14 to analyze the question and determine the most appropriate visualization type. The agent updates two key fields in the state:

- `output_type`—The determined visualization format (table, graph, or map)
- `output_reason`—The reasoning behind the selected visualization type

Let's examine the implementation in listing 15.6.

Listing 15.6 Intent detection agent implementation

```
def run_prompt(self, prompt, system=""):
    messages = [HumanMessage(content=prompt)]
    if self.system or system:
        system = self.system if not system else system
        messages = [SystemMessage(content=system)] + messages

    message = self.model.invoke(messages)
```

Handles prompt execution and response processing (annotates `def run_prompt(self, prompt, system=""):`)

Prepends a system message to the prompt if provided (annotates `messages = [SystemMessage(content=system)] + messages`)

```
    logger.debug(f" got {message.content}")
    payload = message.content
    payload = re.sub(r'^\s*```json\s*|\s*```\s*$', '',
                     payload, flags=re.DOTALL)
    return json5.loads(payload)

def intent_detection(self, state: AgentState):
    system, prompt = self.config.get_prompt(
                     "intent_detection", question=state["question"])
    results = self.run_prompt(prompt, system)
    return {
      "output_type": results["type"],
      "output_reason": results["reason"]}
```

Removes JSON code block markers from the response if present

Parses the response as JSON using the more lenient JSON5

Retrieves and renders the intent detection prompt template from configuration

Maps the response fields to their corresponding state properties

The agent retrieves the intent detection prompt template from the configuration, executes it with the user's question, and processes the LLM's response. The response is expected in a JSON format containing the visualization type and the reasoning, which are then mapped to the corresponding state fields.

SCHEMA EXTRACTION AGENT

The schema extraction agent serves as a bridge between our KG and the LLM components by using the Neo4jSchema object we introduced in section 15.1.3. Its primary responsibility is to convert the KG schema into an LLM-friendly format that subsequent agents can use for query generation and reasoning. The next listing shows how the agent handles prompt execution and response processing, with particular attention to JSON parsing and error handling.

Listing 15.7 Schema extraction agent

```
def schema_extraction(self, state: AgentState):
    assert self.neo4j_schema is not None, \
           "you need to provide a neo4j schema"

    self.neo4j_schema.get_schema()
    self.neo4j_schema.apply_configuration()
    return {"schema": str(self.neo4j_schema),
            "retries": 0}
```

Retrieves the full technical schema

Filters unnecessary schema components and adds descriptions as per the configuration

Updates the state properties with the LLM-friendly version of the schema and resets the retries counter

The heavy lifting is performed by the Neo4jSchema instance. The agent first ensures that a `neo4j_schema` object has been provided and then retrieves the current schema and applies any configuration settings we've defined. The resulting schema is converted to a string format that LLMs can effectively process. Additionally, the agent initializes the retry counter to zero, preparing the state for potential query retries later in the pipeline.

Text-to-Cypher agent

The text-to-Cypher agent transforms the user's natural language question into a Cypher query, considering both the graph's schema and any currently selected elements in the visualization. This contextual awareness allows users to reference selected nodes or relationships without explicitly describing them, making queries more natural and concise, as we discussed in section 14.7.2. As shown in the following listing, the agent adds two pieces of information to the state before executing the prompt: annotations from the configuration provider that help guide query generation, and the current selection state from the visualization interface.

Listing 15.8 Text-to-Cypher agent

```
def text_to_cypher(self, state: AgentState):
    extra = {
        "annotations": self.config.getAnnotations(),
        "selection": self.selection
    }
    params = dict(state) | extra

    system, prompt = self.config.get_prompt("text_to_cypher", **params)
    logger.debug(f"prompt: {prompt}")

    results = self.run_prompt(prompt, system)

    return {"query": results["query"],
            "query_reasoning": results["reasoning"],
            "query_message": json.dumps(results)}
```

The agent merges the current state with the additional context (`extra`), retrieves and populates the appropriate prompt template, and then processes it through the LLM. The results include the generated Cypher query, the reasoning behind its construction, and the complete LLM response for debugging purposes. These are stored in the state's `query`, `query_reasoning`, and `query_message` fields, respectively.

Query execution agent

The query execution agent, shown next, provides robust error handling and dynamic result formatting based on visualization needs.

Listing 15.9 Query execution agent

```
def query_execution(self, state: AgentState):
    try:
        results = self.neo4j_schema.run(state["query"])
        if state["output_type"] in {"graph", "map"}:
            self.results = list(results)
        else:
            self.results = results.to_df()
        results_error = None
        information = ""
    except neo4j.exceptions.ClientError as e:
```

```
        self.results = None
        results_error = str(e)
        logger.info(f"got error: {e}")
        information = f"""We tried:
                           {state['query']}
                           and we got:
                           ```
                           {str(e)}
                           ```"""
    retries = state.get("retries", 0) + 1
    return {"results_error": results_error,
            "retries": retries,
            "information": information}
```

The agent's logic is straightforward. It attempts to execute the query stored in the state and processes the results based on the detected intent. When dealing with graph or map visualizations, it preserves the results in their native format as a list of records. However, for tabular output, it converts the results into a pandas `DataFrame` using Neo4j's built-in conversion functionality.

Error handling is a vital aspect of this agent. If the query execution fails (typically due to syntax errors or schema mismatches), the agent performs several operations: it captures the error details, logs the failure for debugging purposes, constructs an error message that includes both the attempted query and the error description, and increments the retry counter to keep track of attempts.

The agent updates the state with three pieces of information. The `results_error` field contains the error message if execution failed, remaining `None` otherwise. The `retries` field tracks the number of execution attempts, and the `information` field provides detailed context about the error for potential retry attempts. This error information is important for the post-execution routing logic, which we'll examine next.

POST-QUERY EXECUTION

Figure 15.8 illustrates the routing logic implemented by this component, highlighted in the context of the overall pipeline. Unlike other components we've discussed, the

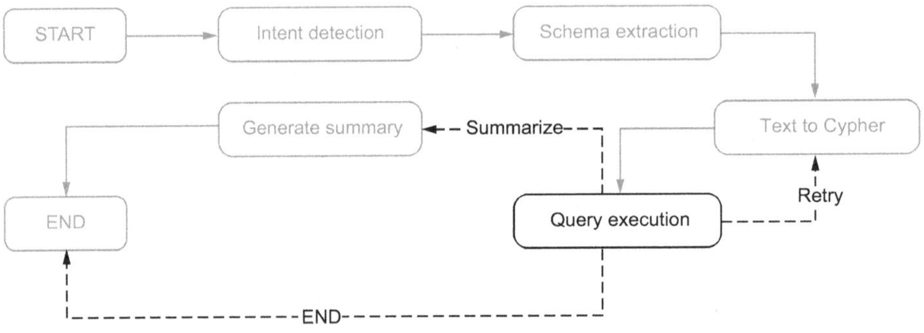

Figure 15.8 Post-query execution routing logic in the QA pipeline, showing decision paths for retry, summarization, and direct completion

post-query execution is not an agent but rather implements the routing logic as a dynamic edge in our LangGraph pipeline (see the following listing).

Listing 15.10 Post-query execution dynamic edge

```
def post_query_execution(self, state: AgentState):

    if state["results_error"] is not None:
        if state["retries"] < 3:
            logger.info(f"{state['retries']} runs, we retry")
            return "retry"
        else:
            logger.info(f"{state['retries']} runs are enough")
            return "END"


    if state["output_type"] in ("map", "graph"):
        logger.info("summarizing..")
        return "summarize"
    else:
        logger.info("no summarization is needed")
        return "END"
```

Handles query execution failures with retry logic up to three attempts

Routes to summarization for map/graph outputs; otherwise, completes

The routing logic follows two decision paths. First, it handles query execution failures by checking the `results_error` field in the state. If an error occurred, the component implements a retry mechanism that allows up to three attempts to execute the query. This gives our system resilience against temporary failures or cases where the LLM may need multiple attempts to generate a correct query.

Second, for successful queries, the routing decision depends on the visualization intent captured in `output_type`. When dealing with map or graph visualizations, the component routes the flow to the summarization step, as these visualization types benefit from additional context and explanation. However, for tabular results, which are typically self-explanatory, the pipeline can conclude directly.

This dynamic routing capability is a key feature of LangGraph, allowing us to implement complex flow control based on both execution results and user intent. The component's simplicity belies its importance in orchestrating the overall pipeline behavior.

GENERATE-SUMMARY AGENT

The final agent in our pipeline generates summaries for graph and map visualizations (see listing 15.11). It combines the query results and the schema selection to create a comprehensive context for the summary generation. It merges these elements with the existing state to populate the parameters for the summary prompt template. The configuration provider supplies the appropriate prompt template, which is then executed through the LLM.

Listing 15.11 Generate-summary agent

```
def generate_summary(self, state: AgentState):
    extra = {
        "records": self.results,
        "selection": self.selection
    }
    params = dict(state) | extra
    system, prompt = self.config.get_prompt(
                                 "generate_summary", **params)
    logger.debug(prompt)

    results = self.run_prompt(prompt, system)
    return {"summary": results["summary"],
            "summary_reason": results["reasoning"],
            "summary_analisys": results["results_analysis"]}
```

The agent's output enriches the state with three components: the actual summary text, the reasoning behind the summary, and a flag indicating whether additional analysis was performed. This completes our pipeline, transforming the original user question into a meaningful summary of the retrieved information.

PIPELINE ASSEMBLY

The implementation of our expert-emulating pipeline culminates in the construction of the LangGraph workflow. The next listing connects our agents into a cohesive graph structure.

Listing 15.12 Building the LangGraph pipeline graph

```
class Agent:
    def __init__(self, model):
        self.neo4j_schema: Neo4jSchema = None
        self.selection = []
        self.results = None
        self.config = ChainConfiguration()
        graph = StateGraph(AgentState)
        graph.add_node("intent_detection", self.intent_detection)
        graph.add_edge("intent_detection", "schema_extraction")
        graph.add_node("schema_extraction", self.schema_extraction)
        graph.add_edge("schema_extraction", "text_to_cypher")
        graph.add_node("text_to_cypher", self.text_to_cypher)
        graph.add_edge("text_to_cypher", "query_execution")
        graph.add_node("query_execution", self.query_execution)
        graph.add_conditional_edges("query_execution",
                                    self.post_query_execution,
                                    {"retry": "text_to_cypher",
                                     "summarize": "generate_summary",
                                     "END": END})
        graph.add_node("generate_summary", self.generate_summary)
        graph.add_edge("generate_summary", END)
        graph.set_entry_point("intent_detection")
        self.graph = graph.compile(checkpointer=self.memory)
        self.model = model
```

The graph construction follows a clear sequential pattern that mirrors our question-answering workflow. The `StateGraph` class from LangGraph provides the foundation, initialized with our `AgentState` type to ensure type safety throughout the pipeline.

Each agent is added as a node in the graph, with edges defining the standard flow between them. This graph structure implements our expert-emulating approach and provides the flexibility to handle errors and different visualization requirements seamlessly in a single unified pipeline.

15.1.6 Pipeline integration layer

Although LangGraph provides powerful capabilities for building complex workflows, we need to consider how applications will interact with these pipelines in practice. The simplest approach would be to use LangGraph's invoke mode, where we provide an initial state and receive the final result once the pipeline completes. However, this would lead to a less-than-ideal user experience: users might wait for extended periods without any feedback about what's happening behind the scenes. Figure 15.9 illustrates the integration architecture that enables real-time interaction between the LangGraph pipeline and frontend applications.

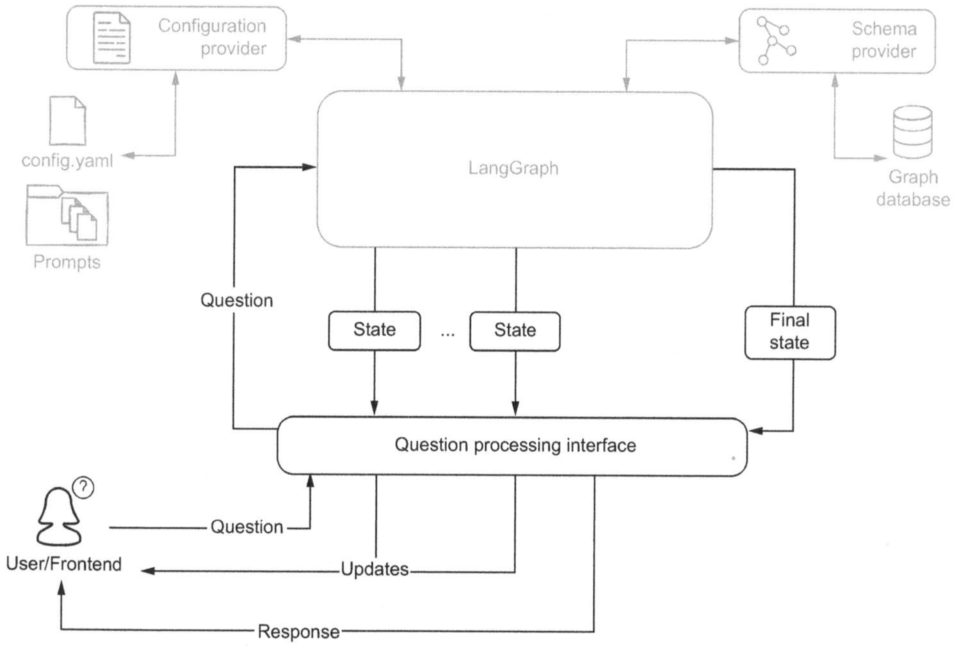

Figure 15.9 Pipeline integration architecture showing the question processing interface mediating between LangGraph state updates and frontend interactions

LangGraph offers a stream execution mode that provides visibility into intermediate steps, but managing these updates directly can complicate the application logic. To balance the benefits of streaming with ease of use, we've developed an interface layer that transforms the pipeline execution into a series of well-defined events that frontends can easily consume.

The core of this interface is a *generator function* that processes questions and yields a sequence of events. Generator functions are well-suited for this task because they let us maintain a simple, linear code flow while producing intermediate results. The pipeline execution transforms into a clean event stream featuring strong event typing and comprehensive state tracking, as shown in the following listing.

Listing 15.13 Question-processing interface function

```
def processQuestion(question, selection=None):
    config = { "configurable": {"thread_id": uuid.uuid4().hex}}
    if selection is not None:
        pipeline.selection = [{"labels": list(node.labels)[0],
                               "properties": dict(node)}
                                  for node in selection]
    else:
        pipeline.selection = []
    input = {"question": question}
    results = pipeline.graph.stream(input,
                                    config=config,
                                    stream_mode="updates")
    yield "update", "*detecting intent...*", input
    for result in results:
        node, value = list(result.items())[0]
        logger.info(f"got results: {node}, keys: {list(value.keys())}")
        current_state = pipeline.graph.get_state(config).values
        match node:
            case "intent_detection":
                yield "update", "*extracting schema...*", current_state
            case "schema_extraction":
                yield "update", "*generating query...*", current_state
            case "text_to_cypher":
                yield "update", "*executing the query...*", current_state
                yield "result", ("Reasoning", value["query_reasoning"]),
                                  current_state
            case "query_execution":
                if value["results_error"]:  #J
                    yield "result", ("ERROR", value["results_error"]),
                                      current_state
                else:
                    output_type = current_state["output_type"]
                    yield output_type, pipeline.results, current_state
                    if output_type in {"graph", "map"}:
                        yield "update", "*summary generation...*",
                                        current_state
```

Annotations:

- Configures the pipeline execution with a unique ID
- Sets up the internal selection list of dictionaries when a non-empty selection is provided
- Invokes the pipeline in stream mode, where each update contains only the changed portion of the state
- Processes each pipeline event in this loop until completion
- First update: tells the user that the pipeline is running the first step
- Extracts the agent's name and state updates from the LangGraph result format
- Extracts the current full state
- In case of intent detection or schema extraction, notifies the user of the next step
- Surfaces the text-to-Cypher reasoning as an intermediate result
- In case of an error in the execution of the query, surfaces the error message as an intermediate result
- Otherwise, emits a graph/table/map event with the results as payload

```
            case "generate_summary":
                yield "result", ("Summary", value["summary"]),
                                    current_state
    logger.info("no more results  sendin END")
    current_state = pipeline.graph.get_state(config).values
    yield "END", current_state, current_state
```

Surfaces the summary as an intermediate result

When the pipeline completes, fetches the final agent state

Emits an END event containing the final agent state

The function begins by setting up the initial configuration and state, and then it yields its first update event to inform users that intent detection has started. As the pipeline processes through each node, the generator yields appropriate events to keep the frontend informed. Each case in the pattern-matching structure corresponds to a specific pipeline stage, producing events that align with the current operation.

Each event produced by the generator follows a consistent structure: a triplet containing the response type, the response payload, and the current state of the pipeline. The response types fall into three categories:

- *Update events* inform users about the pipeline's progress. These events carry simple status messages like "detecting intent" or "generating query," helping users understand which step is currently executing.
- *Result events* deliver textual outputs such as reasoning steps, potential errors, or generated summaries. These provide deeper insight into the pipeline's decision-making process and help users understand how the system arrived at its conclusions.
- Visualization events represent structured outputs like graphs, maps, charts, or tables. These events carry the data needed to create visual representations of the query results, allowing frontends to present information in the most appropriate format.

By including the current pipeline state with each event, we provide frontends with complete context without making assumptions about how they may use this information. This approach maintains a clean separation of concerns: the interface layer focuses on transforming pipeline execution into a stream of well-defined events while leaving presentation decisions to the frontend.

The result is an interface that keeps users informed and engaged throughout the question-answering process while maintaining clean architectural boundaries. By transforming complex pipeline execution into a simple stream of events, we've created a foundation that supports rich interactive experiences without sacrificing maintainability or flexibility.

15.2 Streamlit application

Having built our LangGraph pipeline for expert-emulating question answering, we need an interface that allows users to effectively interact with and validate the system's capabilities. This interface must support several requirements that emerge from our expert-emulating approach.

The interface needs to support interactive graph visualization, allowing users to explore and select nodes and relationships. It must provide real-time feedback as the pipeline processes questions through its various stages. A chat-like interface is essential for natural language interaction; and the system needs to maintain complex state information about selected graph elements and processing context.

Streamlit's features align well with these requirements. Its native support for chat interfaces provides the foundation for implementing our question-answering interactions, complete with user messages and system responses. The framework's built-in data visualization capabilities, combined with its extensibility through custom components, enable us to create effective graph representations. Most importantly, Streamlit's Python-first approach ensures seamless integration with our LangGraph pipeline: there's no need to build complex APIs or handle cross-language serialization, as both frontend and backend operate in the same Python environment.

As our pipeline processes questions, it generates updates about its progress and intermediate results. Streamlit's session state system, combined with its automatic UI updating, lets us reflect these changes in real time without building event-handling mechanisms. Users can see exactly how the expert-emulating system processes their questions.

These characteristics make Streamlit particularly suitable for prototyping and testing our system. The rapid iteration cycle means we can quickly validate how different types of questions are processed and how various visualization options perform. The framework's low implementation overhead lets us focus on testing and refining the core expert-emulating functionality rather than dealing with frontend complexity. Although a production deployment may warrant a more specialized interface, Streamlit provides exactly what we need for developing and demonstrating our system's capabilities.

15.2.1 Application overview

Our next step is designing a functional interface that fully supports expert-emulating graph exploration. The interface must transform abstract requirements like "natural interaction" and "real-time feedback" into components that work together seamlessly. Figure 15.10 shows the main interface layout of our application.

The interface components map directly to the capabilities of our expert-emulating pipeline. Each element is designed to support specific aspects of the system.

At the heart of the application is the graph canvas, which visualizes the KG's nodes and relationships. This central view is complemented by different interaction areas that support natural exploration and questioning workflows.

The Selection column makes questions more natural and context-aware. Users can select specific nodes from the graph and then refer to these selections in their questions using natural language. For example, with certain nodes selected, a user may ask "What are the companies related to these assets?" rather than having to specify each asset explicitly. This selection mechanism is important for testing our system's context-awareness and verifying how well the pipeline understands and incorporates visual context into its query generation process.

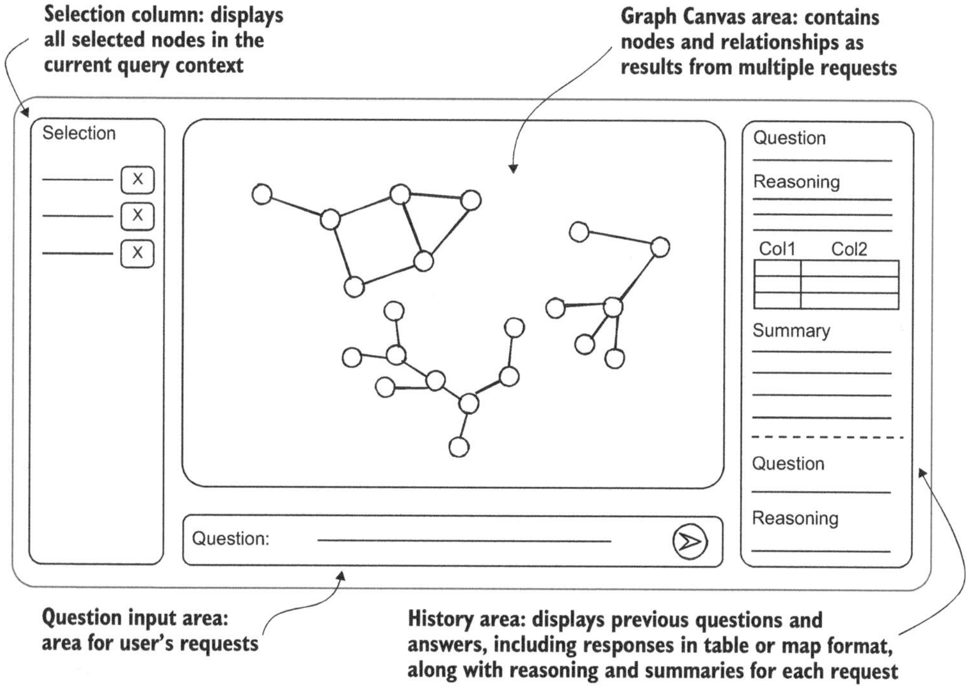

Figure 15.10 Application interface layout demonstrating a question-answering system with selection capabilities, interactive graph visualization, and real-time response tracking

The question input area at the bottom enables users to pose their questions in natural language. These questions can range from simple fact-finding to complex relationship analysis, all while maintaining a natural conversation-like interaction style.

The history area on the right provides a comprehensive view of the question-answering process. Our expert-emulating approach can generate different types of responses, so this area adapts to display various formats. When answers include geographic information, they are presented as interactive maps. When the system determines that tabular data will be most informative, it displays well-formatted tables. Importantly, this area updates in real time as the system processes each question, showing intermediate steps and final results as they become available through our pipeline.

The history area's real-time updates serve a dual purpose: they keep users informed of progress while also making the expert-emulating pipeline's reasoning process visible. This transparency helps users understand how their questions are being processed and why particular visualizations or response formats were chosen.

This design creates a fluid experience where users can explore the KG, ask questions about what they see, and receive rich, multiformat responses that suit the information being conveyed. Although each question stands as an independent interaction, the continuous updates and preserved history create a seamless exploration experience.

15.2.2 LangGraph integration

The integration between Streamlit and our LangGraph pipeline creates a real-time, interactive experience for users. Let's explore how these systems work together.

The integration follows an event-driven pattern. As soon as the user clicks the Send button, the question travels through the question processing interface to the LangGraph pipeline. Rather than waiting for the final result, our system provides immediate feedback as each agent in the pipeline processes the question. This real-time visibility helps users understand how their questions are being analyzed and answered.

As shown in the following listing, to manage this flow of information we implement a `MessageHistory` object that serves two purposes. First, it maintains the complete history of interactions, allowing users to review past questions and answers. Second, it stores the current state of the pipeline, tracking which agent is actively processing the question and what intermediate results have been produced.

Listing 15.14 Message history implementation

```
class MessageHistory:
    def __init__(self):
        self.messages = [{}]

    def update(self, message, finalize=False):
        self.messages[-1].update(message)
        if finalize:
            self.messages.append({})

    @staticmethod
    def display_message(msg):
        with st.chat_message("user"):
            st.markdown(msg["question"])
        with st.chat_message("assistant"):
            if "query_reasoning" in msg:
                st.markdown(f"##### Reasoning\n\n**output type**:\
                            `{msg['output_type']}`\n\n\
                             {msg['query_reasoning']}")
            if "table" in msg:
                st.table(msg["table"])
            if "map" in msg:
                map_ = folium.Map()
                nodes_to_map(msg["map"], map_)
                st_folium(map_)
            if "query" in msg:
                with st.expander("Query...", expanded=False):
                    st.markdown(f"```cypher\n\n{msg['query']}\n```")
                    st.json(msg["query_message"])
            if "summary" in msg:
                st.markdown(f"##### Summary\n\n{msg['summary']}")
                with st.expander("extra...", expanded=False):
                    st.json({
                        "summary_reason": msg["summary_reason"],
                        "summary_analisys": msg["summary_analisys"]
```

- `self.messages = [{}]`: Messages are stored as a list of dictionaries; the last one always represents the current message.
- `self.messages[-1].update(message)`: The dictionary representing the current message is updated with the new data.
- `if finalize:`: When the message is complete, a new empty dictionary is added to store the next message.
- `def display_message(msg):`: Defines how a single message is displayed in the interface
- `with st.chat_message("assistant"):`: The display adapts based on keys in the dictionary that signal which sections need to be rendered.
- `nodes_to_map(msg["map"], map_)`: Converts graph data stored in the "map" key into a format compatible with the map visualization library
- `if "query" in msg:`: Shows the generated Cypher query in a collapsible section along with text-to-Cypher process details
- `st.json({`: Adds summary generation details in a collapsible section for debugging purposes

```
            })
            st.json(msg, expanded=False)      <-- Includes the complete
                                                  message state for debugging
def display_messages(self):        <-- Displays
    for message in self.messages:      messages
        if not message:                sequentially
            continue
        self.display_message(message)
```

The `MessageHistory` class maintains a list of message dictionaries, with each message potentially containing different types of content—from simple text to complex visualizations. The `update` method allows for progressive building of messages, reflecting the step-by-step nature of our pipeline's processing. The `display_message` method renders different content types using Streamlit's components: Markdown for text, tables for structured data, and the Python's folium library for maps. The implementation organizes the information hierarchy, using expandable sections for detailed information like queries and summary reasoning.

The integration between user input and the LangGraph pipeline uses a reactive pattern that manages both temporary and permanent state updates. When processing a question, the system needs to show immediate feedback while also maintaining a permanent conversation history. This is achieved through two complementary mechanisms:

- Event handling with temporary placeholders shows real-time updates as the pipeline processes the question. These updates give immediate feedback but are transient, using Streamlit placeholders to display the current pipeline state.
- `MessageHistory` accumulates the permanent state of the conversation. Rather than showing updates directly, it collects the complete state for each message until it receives an `END` event. Then the page re-renders using `MessageHistory`'s display logic, replacing the temporary updates with the final, persistent version of the conversation.

This approach, implemented in the following listing, ensures that users see both immediate feedback and a permanent record of their interaction history.

Listing 15.15 User input handler

```
[...]
if question := st.chat_input("What is up?"):
    with chat:
        with st.chat_message("user"):          <-- Displays the user's question in the
            st.markdown(question)                  chat history under the "user" role
        with st.chat_message("assistant"):     <-- Creates a placeholder in the
            placeholder = st.empty()               "assistant" section for
                                                   displaying real-time updates
        selection = [state.canvas["byId"][int(item)]
                     for item in state.selection]   <-- Extracts selected
                                                        nodes from the canvas
                                                        state using their IDs
```

```
for response_type, response, current_state in \
    chain.processQuestion(question=str(question),
                          selection=selection):
    state.messages.update(current_state)
    match response_type:
        case "update":
            placeholder.markdown(response)

        case "graph" | "map":
            placeholder.markdown("*updating canvas...*")
            store_to_canvas(response)
            if response_type == "map":
                state.messages.update(
                    {"map":state.canvas["nodes"]})

        case "table" | "chart":
            state.messages.update({"table": response})
            placeholder.table(response)
            with st.chat_message("assistant"):
                placeholder = st.empty()

        case "result":
            title, content = response
            response = f"##### {title}\n\n{content}"
            placeholder.write(response)
            with st.chat_message("assistant"):
                placeholder = st.empty()

        case "END":
            state.messages.update(current_state, finalize=True)
            st.rerun()
```

Annotations:

- Sends the question and selection to the pipeline and begins processing
- Updates MessageHistory with the current pipeline state
- Routes event handling based on the response type
- For "update" events, displays the Markdown-formatted response in the placeholder
- For "graph" or "map" events, updates the canvas visualization with the graph data
- For map-type responses, stores node data for map visualization
- Stores tabular data in MessageHistory for table or chart responses
- Renders the pandas DataFrame as a Streamlit table
- Creates a new placeholder to preserve the table display
- Formats and displays result events with title and content
- Creates a new placeholder to preserve the result display
- Stores the final state in MessageHistory and marks the message as complete
- Triggers an interface redraw to show the complete response

When a user submits a question, the system creates placeholder elements in the chat interface that are progressively updated as the pipeline processes the question. The `match` statement handles different types of responses: updates to the chat interface for text responses, graph and map visualizations that are rendered in the canvas, tabular data that is displayed using Streamlit's table component, formatted results with titles and content, and an `END` event that triggers a rerun to ensure that all UI elements are properly updated. The combination of `MessageHistory` and this event-handling system creates a responsive and interactive experience for users.

15.3 Expert-emulating investigation

To demonstrate how our expert-emulating system works in practice, let's follow a realistic investigation workflow. We'll see how an investigator can use natural language queries to explore connections between crimes, surveillance cameras, and vehicles while using the system's ability to understand context and provide meaningful insights.

Our investigation will work with a subset of the KG focused on criminal incidents. As shown in figure 15.11, the schema connects *Crime* nodes (containing properties like `location`, `description`, and `date-time`) to *ANPRCamera* nodes (automatic number plate recognition cameras) through spatial relationships. The cameras generate *CameraEvents* when they detect vehicles, recording both the timestamp and location of each sighting. These events link to *Vehicle* nodes, which store properties such as `model`, `color`, and `plate number`. Vehicles in turn connect to *Person* nodes representing their owners, who may have links to *Crime* incidents through `COMMITTED` relationships.

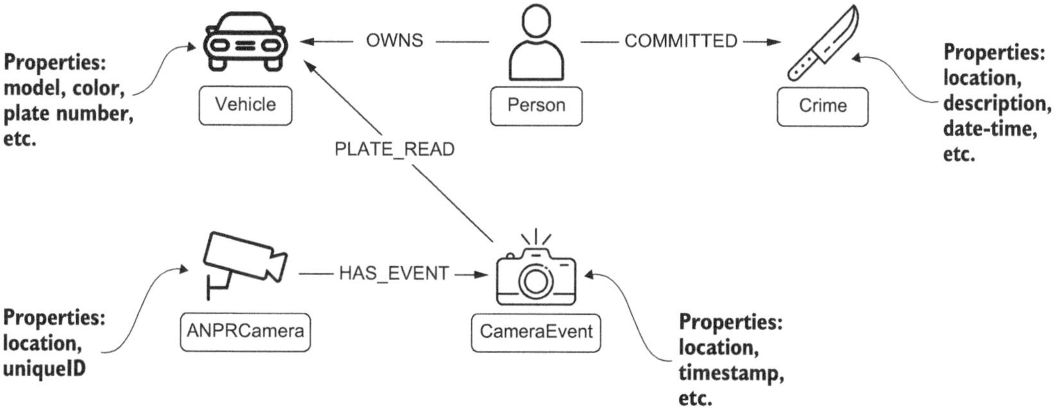

Figure 15.11 Focused schema visualization showing how *Crime*, *ANPRCamera*, *CameraEvent*, *Vehicle*, and *Person* nodes interconnect for investigative queries

This seemingly simple structure allows for sophisticated queries that combine spatial analysis, temporal patterns, and relationship exploration. Let's see how an investigator can use our system to identify vehicles of interest related to a criminal trespass incident.

15.3.1 Identifying the initial case

Our investigation begins by asking the system to identify a crime currently under investigation. This demonstrates the ability to understand and translate natural language queries that combine both explicit constraints ("currently under investigation") and implicit expectations (returning a meaningful crime for analysis). The system processes this request through our expert-emulating pipeline, first detecting that a graph visualization will be most appropriate for displaying a single node with its properties. The query generation component understands that we're looking for an active investigation and includes relevant constraints in the generated Cypher query.

Let's pose our first question to the system: "Return one crime node currently under investigation". Figure 15.12 shows the system's response, displaying a crime node representing a criminal trespass incident.

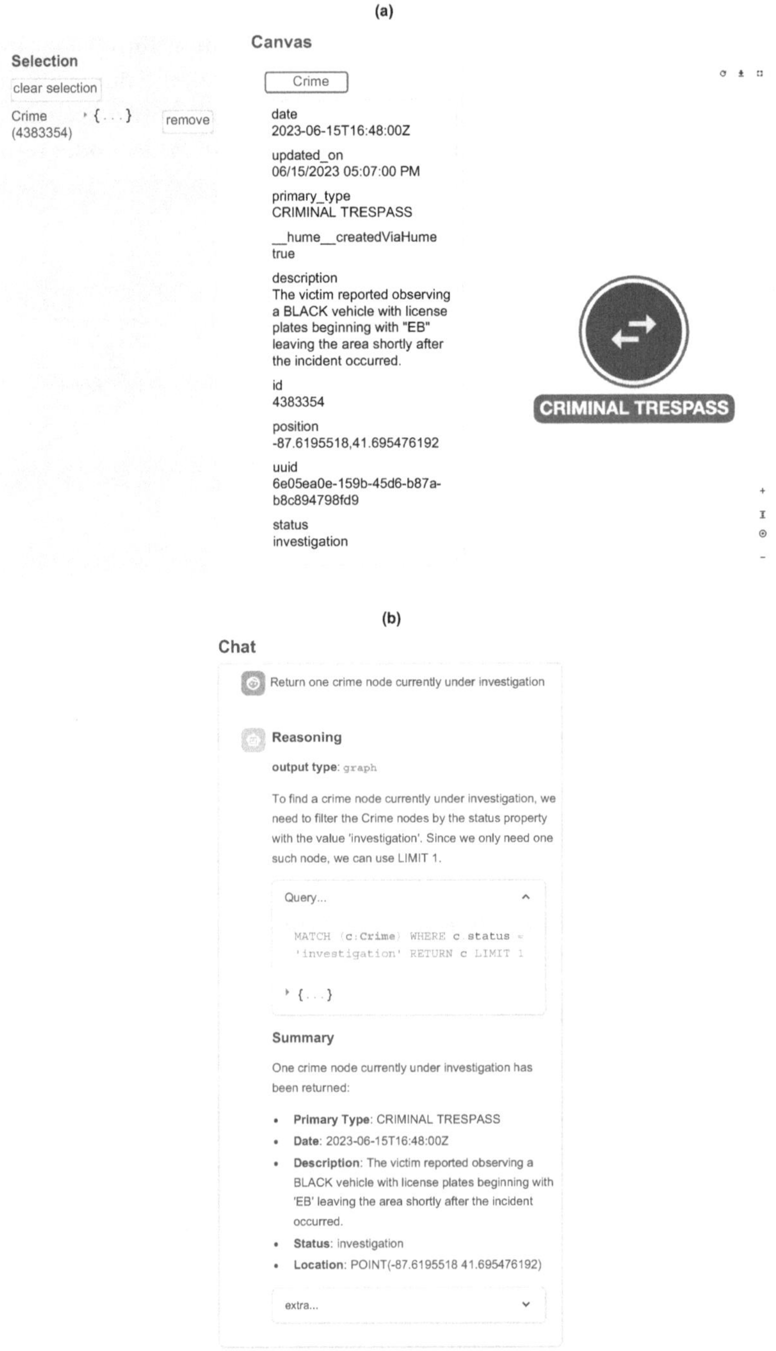

Figure 15.12 Initial query response showing a crime node currently under investigation. The interface shows (a) the Selection panel (populated by double-clicking the crime node) and the Canvas with an information panel displaying details about the current node in the center; and (b) the chat interface with query processing details.

When the crime node is clicked, detailed information about the incident appears in the canvas area, including a narrative that mentions a black vehicle with a partial license plate number starting with "EB". This information will become valuable as our investigation progresses.

In the chat interface, we can see the system's reasoning process, explaining why it chose this crime and how it structured the query to ensure that we received an active investigation. This transparency helps users understand how their natural language questions are being interpreted and executed.

The summary generated by our system highlights key aspects of the crime, including its classification as criminal trespass and the presence of vehicle information in the narrative. This demonstrates how our summary generation component can extract and emphasize relevant details that may be buried in property fields.

This initial interaction demonstrates several capabilities of our system: natural language understanding, appropriate visualization selection, and intelligent summarization of node properties. But more importantly, it sets the stage for increasingly complex queries that will use this context as we proceed with our investigation.

15.3.2 Spatial analysis of surveillance coverage

With our crime node identified, the next logical step is to check for surveillance coverage in the area. Our system's spatial reasoning capabilities allow us to ask about nearby ANPR cameras without needing to specify exact coordinates or distance calculations.

We double-click the crime node to add it to our selection and then enter this prompt: "Return any ANPR camera node located within 1 km from the selected crime." Note how we can refer to "the selected crime" directly; the system understands this context from our current selection. Figure 15.13 captures this interaction, showing how the system responds with both a graph visualization and an interactive map.

The canvas now includes the crime node, along with a newly discovered ANPR camera node in yellow. What makes this response particularly powerful is the system's decision to provide a map visualization alongside the graph view. The map displays two markers—one for the incident location and another for the camera—using colors that match their respective nodes in the graph.

The camera's position appears strategically valuable: it's located near an intersection that could be an entry or exit point for the area where the trespass occurred. This spatial insight, made immediately apparent through the dual visualization, suggests that this camera's data could provide useful leads for our investigation.

This step demonstrates several sophisticated capabilities of our system: spatial query processing, selection-aware natural language understanding, and intelligent visualization selection. The adaptive response, choosing the most appropriate visualization for the data at hand, is a key feature of our expert-emulating approach.

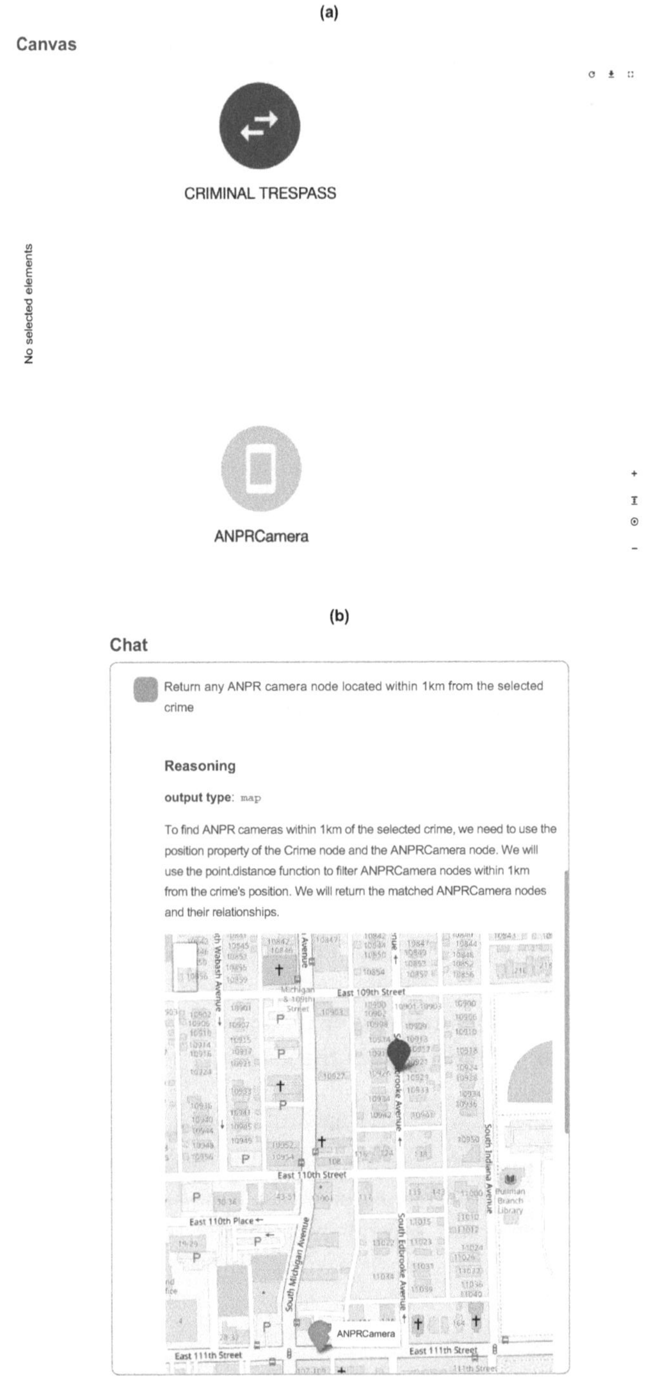

Figure 15.13 Spatial query response showing an ANPR camera near the crime location (a). The system automatically chose a map visualization (b) to display the spatial relationship between the crime and the nearby ANPR camera.

15.3.3 Vehicle pattern detection

We can now search for vehicles that match the description from the incident report. We include the ANPR camera by double-clicking its node, adding it to our current selection alongside the crime node.

Our next prompt uses this selection while adding specific vehicle criteria: "Return the vehicles detected by the selected camera on June 15, 2023. The vehicle is black and its license plate must start with EB." Note how we can combine references to selected elements ("selected camera") with explicit constraints about the vehicle's appearance and license plate. Figure 15.14 shows how the system expands our visualization to include matching vehicles and their detection events.

The graph now displays multiple vehicle nodes connected to our ANPR camera through detection events, with the query's reasoning visible in the chat interface. The system has understood the temporal constraint ("June 15, 2023"), the vehicle's physical description ("black"), and the partial plate number ("EB"), incorporating all these elements into a single coherent query.

The summary highlights each matching vehicle, providing an overview of potential suspects. This demonstrates our system's ability to handle multifaceted queries that combine node selection, temporal constraints, and property matching.

(a)

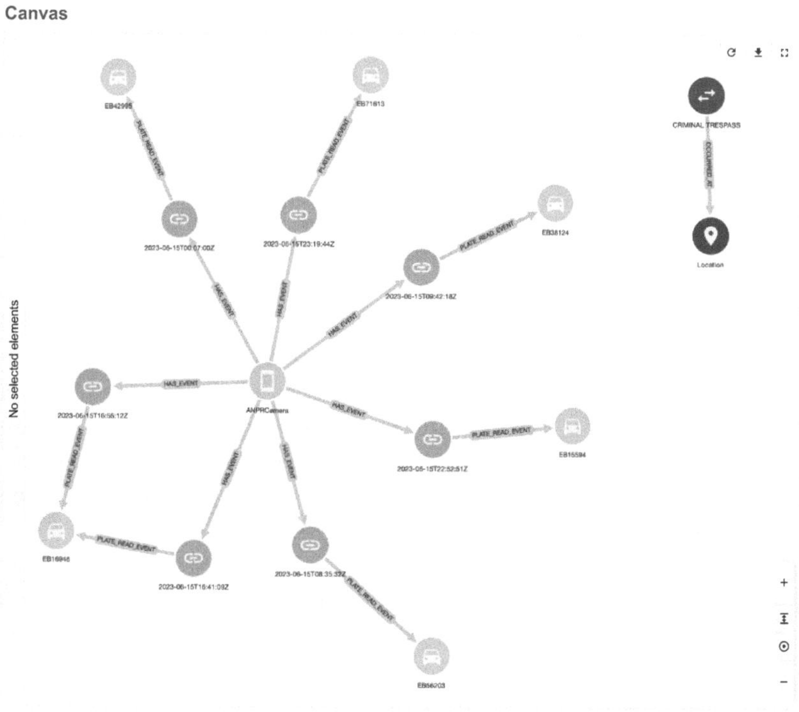

(b)

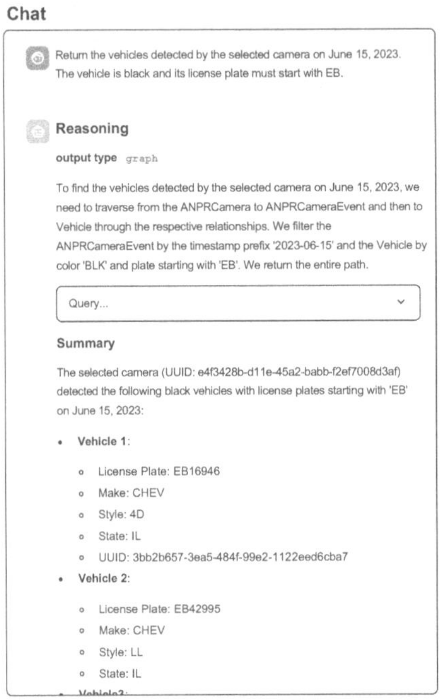

Figure 15.14 Vehicle query results showing matching vehicles and their detection events. Each path represents a complete vehicle detection record, with timestamps visible on the event nodes. The system's response includes both (a) the graph visualization and (b) a detailed summary of each vehicle's properties.

This step marks a significant advancement in our investigation, transforming isolated data points about a crime and a camera location into a set of vehicles that could be connected to our incident. But can we get more insight by providing additional context about our investigative goals? Let's explore this in our next prompt.

15.3.4 Context-aware request refinement

Let's refine our approach by using our expert-emulating system's ability to extract information from selected nodes and perform context-aware summarization. Instead of explicitly stating the vehicle description and date constraints, we can rely on the system to extract these details from our selected crime node. Moreover, by providing context about our role and investigative intent, we can guide the system toward generating more analytical insights.

We rephrase our prompt to reflect this investigative context: "I'm an investigator and I'm working on the selected crime. I need all the vehicle nodes that are compatible with the description and were detected by the selected camera the day of the incident. Are there any that seem significantly more likely to be involved in the incident?" The response, shown in figure 15.15, demonstrates how additional context transforms the system's analysis.

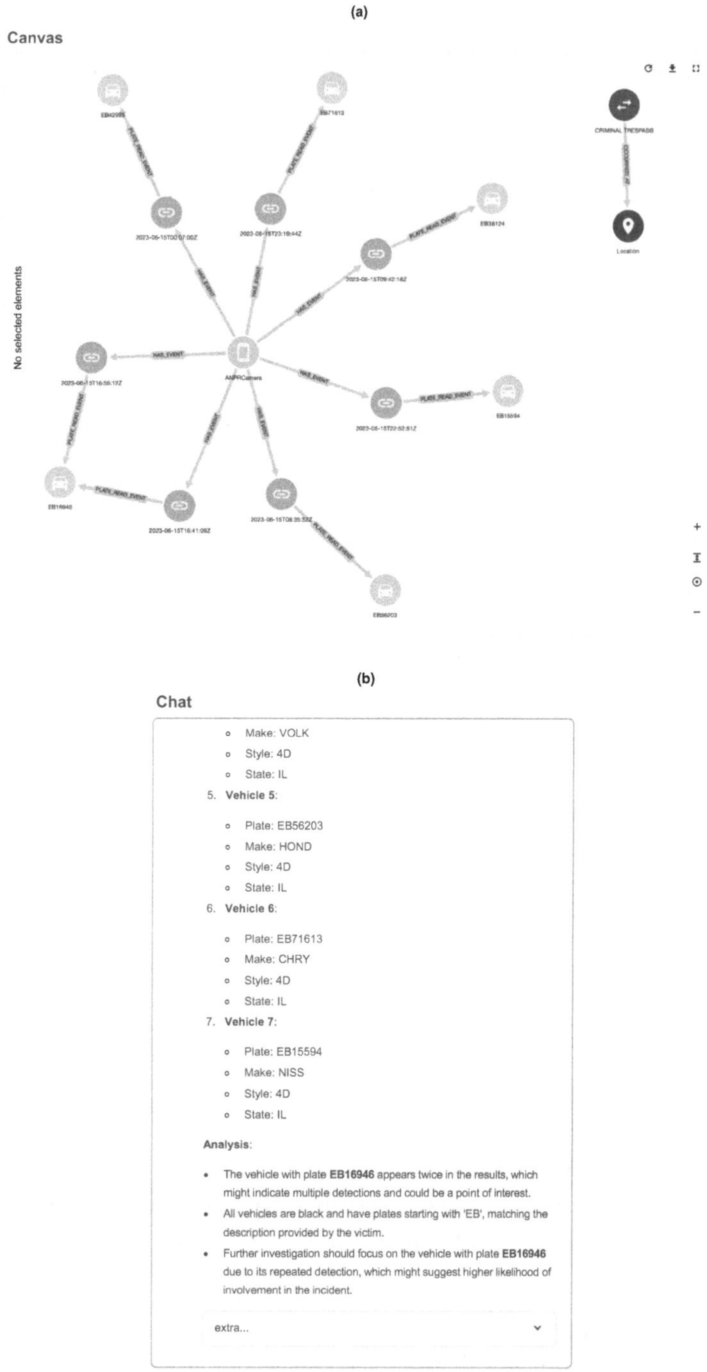

Figure 15.15 Enhanced analysis showing the same vehicle data with investigative context (a). The system augments its response in (b) with an Analysis section that identifies patterns of interest, demonstrating how additional context leads to more insightful summarization of the same underlying data.

Although the query returns the same vehicles as before, the summarization now includes a deeper analysis of the results. The system identifies an interesting pattern: one of the matching vehicles was detected twice around the time of the incident, suggesting a potential circuit of the area that warrants further investigation.

This enhanced response demonstrates how the system can autonomously extract and apply constraints from node properties, eliminating the need for explicit restatement. It also illustrates how providing investigative context—in this case, identifying ourselves as investigators seeking suspicious patterns—enables the system to generate more relevant and insightful summaries.

The system has moved beyond simply matching criteria to actively analyzing temporal patterns that may indicate suspicious behavior. This sets the stage for our final investigative step: examining whether any of these vehicles have connections to known offenders.

15.3.5 Historical record analysis

Building on our discovery of a vehicle with suspicious movement patterns, we can further enrich our investigation by considering the criminal history of vehicle owners. This type of background check is a standard investigative practice that our system can integrate naturally into its analysis.

We modify our prompt slightly: "I'm an investigator and I'm working on the selected crime. I need all the vehicle nodes that are compatible with the description and were detected by the selected camera on the day of the incident. Some of these vehicles may be owned by previous offenders. What vehicles are the most likely to be involved in the incident?"

Figure 15.16 reveals a significant breakthrough in our investigation. The system expands its analysis to include ownership relationships and criminal records, discovering that the vehicle previously flagged for suspicious movements is owned by an individual with a relevant criminal history.

Most notably, this person's record includes a previous conviction for criminal trespass—the same type of offense we're currently investigating. The summary agent recognizes the heightened significance of this connection, highlighting it in both the general summary and the analysis section.

This final step shows how the system can do all of the following:

- Maintain contextual awareness across multiple query refinements
- Integrate various types of evidence (spatial, temporal, and historical)
- Identify meaningful patterns and connections
- Present findings in a way that directly supports investigative decision-making

Through this investigation, we've seen how natural language interaction, intelligent summarization, and context-aware analysis come together to support real-world investigative workflows.

(a)

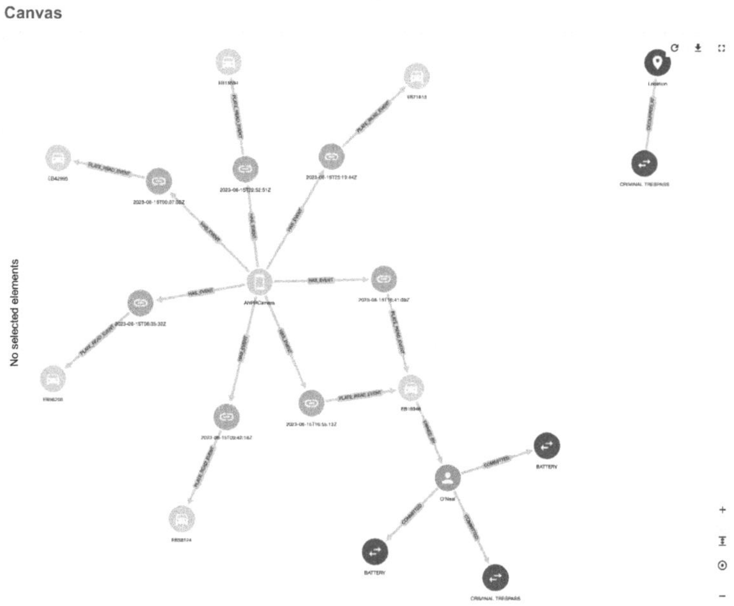

(b)

Chat

- **Primary Type**: CRIMINAL TRESPASS
- **Description**: The victim reported observing a BLACK vehicle with license plates beginning with 'EB' leaving the area shortly after the incident occurred.
- **Location**: POINT(-87.6195518 41.695476192)

The **ANPRCamera** node detected a vehicle with the following properties:

- **Color**: BLK
- **Plate**: EB16946
- **Make**: CHEV
- **Style**: 4D
- **State**: IL

This vehicle is linked to multiple past crimes:

1. **Crime**: BATTERY
   - **Date**: 2016-06-01T19:44:00Z
   - **Description**: AGG PO HANDS NO/MIN INJURY
   - **Arrest**: true
2. **Crime**: CRIMINAL TRESPASS
   - **Date**: 2016-02-22T11:37:00Z
   - **Description**: TO LAND
   - **Arrest**: true
3. **Crime**: BATTERY
   - **Date**: 2016-03-13T14:20:00Z
   - **Description**: SIMPLE
   - **Arrest**: false

Analysis: The vehicle detected by the camera matches the description provided by the victim and has a history of being involved in multiple crimes, including battery and criminal trespass. Given this history and the fact that it was detected near the crime scene on the day of the incident, this vehicle seems significantly more likely to be involved in the current incident.

Figure 15.16 Final investigative insight revealing criminal history. (a) The graph expands to show that a vehicle owner has connections to multiple prior crimes, including a previous criminal trespass. (b) The summary provides a detailed breakdown of the prior offenses, demonstrating the system's ability to integrate temporal, spatial, and historical evidence into a cohesive investigative narrative.

15.4 Future directions and enhancements

Throughout chapters 14 and 15, we've explored the development of a question-answering system for KGs. Rather than treating it as purely a language modeling problem, we've built a system that emulates how human experts work with graph databases: understanding schema context and constructing queries through reasoned steps. Our implementation shows how this expert-emulating approach can be realized through a pipeline of specialized agents, each handling distinct aspects of the process.

However, this implementation should be viewed as a foundation rather than as a turnkey solution. Its value lies not just in what it does but also in how it's built. The foundation's strength comes from its underlying architecture, particularly in how it approaches observability and expert emulation.

The system's transparency isn't merely for debugging; it creates natural points for collecting feedback and identifying improvements. Each component's decision-making process is visible, making it possible to understand what the system does and also why it does it.

Equally important is the expert-emulation pattern that underlies the design. When faced with new challenges or opportunities for improvement, teams can begin with a simple but powerful question: "What would an expert do in this situation?" This human-centric approach to system design makes improvements feel natural rather than forced; they emerge from understanding and modeling expert behavior.

In the following sections, we'll explore several paths for building on this foundation. These are examples of how the system's observable, expert-emulating nature enables specific types of improvements.

15.4.1 Learning from use

A natural starting point for system evolution uses one of our core design principles: comprehensive observability. Every query processed by the system generates rich information about user intentions, query patterns, and outcome effectiveness. This observable data creates opportunities for systematic improvement at multiple levels.

The most direct application of this observability lies in collecting and categorizing "complaint-like" questions: prompts in which users indicate that the system's response didn't meet their needs. Rather than treating these as failures, our observable pipeline lets us extract meaningful patterns from these instances. By categorizing these patterns using LLM-based analysis, we can surface common user challenges in a dynamic dashboard of pain points that will become a strategic tool for guiding development priorities and resource allocation.

Equally valuable will be the collection of successful interactions. When the system generates queries that users find especially helpful, the chain of reasoning can be preserved. These success patterns can then be systematically analyzed to identify what makes them effective, creating a foundation for enhancing our example database.

By analyzing patterns in user questions, we can also identify clusters of similar queries that may benefit from specialized handling. This understanding can be used to optimize downstream processes: for example, by selecting only the most relevant portions of the schema or by providing more focused examples for specific types of questions.

This learning from use demonstrates how our foundational architecture enables the system to evolve based on actual use patterns rather than predetermined rules. Improvements emerge naturally while remaining grounded in understandable, expert-like behavior.

15.4.2 Enhancing core capabilities

By consistently asking "What would an expert do?" we can identify and implement improvements that align with human expertise patterns while using our observable pipeline architecture. A key area for enhancement is schema handling, where we can emulate how human experts build their understanding of a KG's structure. Experts often run preliminary queries to understand how the data is structured and used, going beyond the basic schema definition. We can model this behavior by implementing schema enrichment agents that analyze data patterns and augment the base schema with additional context. This enriched schema information can then flow downstream to improve query generation and result interpretation.

For large-scale KGs, experts typically work with mental models at different levels of abstraction. A multilayer schema management approach could mirror this mental process. For instance, in our investigative KG, the bottom layer would contain all detailed nodes and relationships (crimes, vehicles, camera events, people), and higher layers would organize these into domain-focused views like vehicle monitoring or criminal justice records. The system could use these higher-level views for broad understanding (e.g., which domains to query) while preserving detailed descriptions for specific query generation. This layered approach manages complexity without sacrificing precision, much as human experts zoom in and out of different levels of detail as needed.

15.4.3 Advanced evolution paths

More ambitious evolution paths can significantly enhance the system's capabilities. These advanced approaches maintain our core principles while incorporating emerging techniques in language model applications.

A particularly promising direction involves moving beyond pure in-context learning for schema understanding and query generation. Our current approach of embedding schema information and examples in prompts is effective, but it faces scalability challenges with larger KGs. Fine-tuning approaches offer an alternative path. By using the schema itself as training data, we can develop KG-aware agents that have a deeper, more efficient understanding of the graph structure and relationships.

Studies have shown that in-context learning, although flexible, consistently underperforms compared to task-specific adaptation approaches [1], [2]. This performance gap persists even when both approaches have access to the same example sets. These findings suggest that moving toward fine-tuned components could significantly improve our system's performance while potentially reducing its computational overhead.

The transition to fine-tuned components wouldn't require abandoning our expert-emulating architecture. Instead, we could selectively replace or augment in-context learning components with fine-tuned alternatives while maintaining our observable pipeline structure.

This evolution path also opens possibilities for more sophisticated query planning. Fine-tuned agents could develop a more nuanced understanding of query patterns and their relationships with different graph structures, potentially leading to more efficient and effective query generation. The system could maintain its step-by-step reasoning approach while building on a stronger foundation of graph knowledge.

Summary

- An expert-emulating approach mimics how human experts interact with graph databases.
- LangGraph's state-based design enables creation of modular, observable AI pipelines where each component maintains independent reasoning.
- Pipeline integration architecture enables real-time streaming of processing updates to interactive user interfaces.
- Context-aware query generation combines schema knowledge, user selections, and conversational history for natural interactions.
- Multistep analytical workflows can integrate spatial, temporal, and historical analysis in a single coherent process.
- Message history management enables stateful conversations and real-time progress updates.

index

A

B

C

D

E

F

G

L

O

P

Q

R

S

T

U

V

W

Z